RELIGIOUS
AUTOBIOGRAPHIES

RELIGIOUS AUTOBIOGRAPHIES

GARY L. COMSTOCK

Iowa State University

Wadsworth Publishing Company
Belmont, California
A Division of Wadsworth, Inc.

Religion Editor: Tammy Goldfeld

Senior Editorial Assistant: Kelly Zavislak

Project Manager: Gary Palmatier

Designer: Gary Palmatier

Print Buyer: Barbara Britton

Copy Editor: Kim Saccio

Cover: Gary Palmatier

Compositor: Ideas to Images

Printer: Arcata Graphics / Fairfield

 This book is printed on acid-free recycled paper.

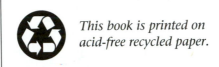

International Thomson Publishing

The trademark ITP is used under license.

Printed in the United States of America

2 3 4 5 6 7 8 9 10 — 99 98 97 96 95

Library of Congress Cataloging-in-Publication Data

Religious Autobiographies / [compiled by] Gary Comstock
    p. cm.
  ISBN 0-534-18780-3
    1. Religous biography. 2. Autobiography —Religious aspects.
3. Religion—Study and teaching. 4. Religions —Study and teaching.
I. Comstock, Gary, 1954–   .
BL72.R45 1994
200'.92'2—dc20
  [B]   94-20555
                                           CIP

Contents

Unit II — Religious Autobiographies   45

To my students,

and particularly to those in the 1991 seminar: Heather Carver, Loren Christensen, Paul Doerrfeld, Susan Schonberg Evans, Michael Marty, Michael Matthews, Fritz Naylor, Amy Rothell, Kevin Smith, Holly Hunt Strayer, Chris Sutch, and Joel Swanson.

Preface

IT **was a heady experience** to begin teaching Religious Studies after spending six years studying it in graduate school. I could hardly contain my enthusiasm about moving to the other side of the desk and having a captive audience for my ideas about hermeneutic phenomenology and reception aesthetics; reformed epistemology and philosophy of religion; reductionistic strategies in the psychological interpretation of religious beliefs; and the contributions of scholars such as Mircea Eliade, Wilfrid Cantwell Smith, and Alvin Plantinga. Unfortunately, the students in my Introduction to Religious Studies course were not nearly as enthusiastic, and I gradually realized that they were positively befuddled by arguments and thinkers I had studied for years. The fellow in the headphones bopping disinterestedly in the back row never looked up once at the name Paul Ricoeur, and the couple passing notes on the side seemed unmoved by methodological problems inherent in the attempt to define religion. Everything seemed to be going over their heads.

Something else hit me. After studying the curriculum requirements at my institution, I realized many of these same students might never take another course in the humanities. Business, Engineering, Agriculture, and Design majors, among others, had precious few opportunities to learn to think critically. I began to rechart the course from bottom up. In trying out different ideas, I happened to invite some speakers who, it turned out, fascinated the students. First there was the Fundamentalist minister from the local Great Commission Church; then the Jewish student rabbi who flew in from Cincinnati once a month; and finally the evangelical Christian woman turned Goddess-worshipping witch. To my surprise, I looked up one day and the back-row fellow had taken off his headphones and moved right up front. The couple on the side now stayed after class, asking probing questions and subjecting the guests' answers to critical scrutiny.

I threw away all my lectures on methodology and Great Figures in the Study of Religion. I decided to allow my students to do what they obviously wanted to do: study religious people. Later, I asked them to try to write their own religious autobiographies, and they responded energetically. We were having fun; I was learning to meet them "where they were" without compromising my academic expectations, and they were discovering the pleasures of thinking empathically and critically about "the Other." The result was that students actually *enjoyed* their reading and writing assignments, a brand-new experience for many of them. I still insisted they learn the main divisions of Religious Studies and some of our methods, arguments, and operating principles, but I found a way to accomplish this rigorous goal without denying them the inherent pleasures of true intellectual activity. My main goal in the class now is to help students acquire the ability to think empathically and critically, two basic skills all college graduates should possess.

In one semester students can be taught to think critically while being exposed to a diverse and multicultural cross-section of religions, but you must have good readings. I looked for a text that would present a range of powerful voices similar to those that captivated my students. I found none that gave women equal time with men. Without a text to fit my criteria, I began to assemble my own readings, composed of my favorite religious autobiographies. I chose autobiographies because they are a close substitute for guest speakers and they work. College students with little prior experience in studying religion often find it difficult to understand the religious perspectives of others, and there is no better way to help initiate such understanding than by presenting students with the hopes, fears, memories, and aspirations of others. When students hear the voices of contemporary wayfarers they identify with their struggles and ideals. Without access to actual Hindu, Muslim, and African-American men and women guest speakers, students find something in the first-person voice of these autobiographical texts that grabs them. Something in the narrative unfolding of character makes readers receptive to foreign religious experiences; something about the personal mood of autobiography makes them want to join the give and take of discussing the stories' meaning and significance.

The book in your hands is the result of my experiment. I have two goals for it. The first goal is to stimulate vibrant classroom discussions. Passionate and articulate argumentation in class begins with good texts, and there are no better texts than first-person narratives when it comes to introducing religion. This book contains some of the most provocative religious stories you will find anywhere, all of them lively and accessible to entry-level college students.

My second goal is to help students learn to think empathically and critically. Students can learn something important in one semester of Religious Studies: they can learn how to think empathically about the Other; they can learn to compare and contrast two narrative views of a single religious tradition; they can learn to make up their minds about the meaning and significance of the texts they read. Religion is the single most intriguing subject on earth, and I use it as subject matter to pursue the primary aim of an education in the humanities, the development of critical thinking.

The book contains fourteen paired autobiographies. Each autobiography is chosen because it shares a large number of themes with its accompanying story. Discussion questions at the end of each story encourage students to dig into the texts and may be used to challenge students to figure out what the two stories have in common. There are significant commonalities between each of the paired stories, but there are also significant differences. No religion is monolithic, and no single Catholic story can possibly represent all Catholics' stories. If students have but a single Catholic autobiography to read, they are tempted to think Catholicism lacks diversity and pluralism. Having two stories helps them defeat the natural inclination to take any one story as The Master Story of the tradition.

Each chapter consists of a brief introduction, the two narratives, and a set of discussion questions after each narrative. The introductions are not meant as general surveys of the religion; for that, students should be directed to a good introductory survey of world religions such as Ninian Smart's *Religious Experience*.[1] My introductions to the chapters prepare students to deal with the foreign beliefs, rituals, values, and institutions described in the readings. If students familiarize

---

1. Ninian Smart, *The Religious Experience of Mankind* (New York, N.Y.: Charles Scribner's Sons, 1984).

themselves with the introductions they should have little difficulty with the stories.

The narratives were selected on the basis of three criteria. All of the autobiographies chosen are:

1. written by "believers," adherents of the religion who present reasonably sympathetic portrayals of the tradition;

2. accessible to introductory-level undergraduate students; and,

3. substantive introductions to at least one dimension (rituals, beliefs, values, institutions, and so on) of one religion.

I also tried to arrange readings so that at least one of the two texts was written by an insider, someone who grew up in the culture and geographical space of the religion, whereas the accompanying autobiography came from someone closer to my students, a North American or European who begins the journey in Christianity or Judaism and moves toward the heart of the other religion. Finally, I tried to find at least one story for each chapter stressing the inward or mystical nature of the tradition, and another stressing its outward or political dimension.

General discussion about how to interpret these texts is found in chapter 3, "How Should I Respond to Religious Autobiography?" Empathic understanding is a central part of the academic study of religion because you cannot effectively criticize a position without first understanding it; but achieving this kind of understanding is not easy, and students need all the help instructors can give them. Discussion questions at the end of each autobiography should help to generate sophisticated classroom discussion. For example, the first narrative in the chapter on Hinduism consists of selections from Swami Agehananda Bharati's autobiography. Bharati's love for the sacred Hindu rituals overlaps with a theme found in the second narrative by Shudha Mazumdar. Mazumdar also loves the Hindu rituals, and one of the discussion questions suggests this parallel while inviting the reader to find others. As students identify commonalities between the stories they will begin to piece together for themselves the family of traits characterizing the pluriform traditions we call "Hinduism," "Islam," and "Judaism." This way of proceeding is important because it supports an inductive method of discovery in which students learn how difficult and yet how rewarding it is to find a genuine "characteristic," a trait common to most if not all of the subtraditions within a given religion.

Empathic reading is not the sum total of the academic study of religion, however, and students should have the opportunity to think critically about the claims each storyteller makes. In each paired set of readings, one of the stories presents at least one idea in tension with an idea expressed in the other story. For example, the selections from Mazumdar's autobiography suggest she has little time for abstract contemplation about the nature of the Divine. The selections from Bharati's autobiography, on the other hand, indicate he is quite taken with arcane theological speculation on *advaita* (monism). This is an important difference between Mazumdar's *bhakti* (devotional) religion and Bharati's *advaita* philosophy, and a discussion question invites students to reflect on its significance.

Finding points of tension among stories is a matter I have decided to leave up to individual instructors. After students have had a common experience reading and discussing each story with others, they will want to discover areas of potential disagreement, between authors and among themselves. To articulate various mythic models, rituals, values, and narratives will take them deep into the heart of these religious traditions. Probing, inquiring, suggesting new lines of interpretation, comparing these stories with others, raising critical questions, suggesting ways of reading that negotiate conflicts or resolve contradictions—all of these activities will place them squarely in the middle of Religious Studies and allow them to discover for themselves the complexity of religion. By focusing on one characteristic of religion (cultus, creed, code, community, etc.) in each chapter, my scheme introduces the major categories and methods of Religious Studies and provides fertile occasions for instructors to introduce their own discussions of favorite theories and theoreticians in ritual studies, myth, history, psychology, or sociology of religion, even hermeneutic phenomenology and Paul Ricoeur! But most important, the readings and questions help students to learn the skills of empathic and critical thought, skills they will find useful long after they have passed their humanities courses.

ACKNOWLEDGMENTS

This book began at the suggestion of my colleague in the Philosophy Department at Iowa State University, El Klemke. It took various shapes between 1986 and 1990 as I responded to comments and criticisms from fellow professors in the Religious Studies Program at ISU: Paul Hollenbach, Mary Sawyer, Ted Solomon, and, at the University of Northern Iowa, Martha Reineke. Whenever my interest began to wane, Sheryl Fullerton, previously the religion editor at Wadsworth, was there to comfort, encourage, and prod me. Tammy Goldfeld filled Sheryl's shoes admirably when Sheryl was promoted to executive editor. Toward the end, my daughter Krista used her fourth-grade editing skills and a red pencil to correct punctuation of part of one of the drafts, and by December of 1990 I had a final outline in place: a book of readings with two parts—autobiographies, on the one hand and, on the other, philosophical discussions of methodological issues raised in the stories. I did not envision the book going through yet another round of transmutation, but the manuscript fell into the hands of the students in our senior seminar and was never the same.

In the spring of 1991, I led a seminar on the theme of religious autobiography with a dozen undergraduate Religious Studies majors. Together we read many stories, including early versions of some of the texts collected here. Secretly I hoped the students would simply confirm the selections I had in mind and help me write discussion questions. Instead of validating my prior judgments, however, the seminar-ians responded the way ideal students do, with enthusiastic criticism, and soon my desk was piled with dozens of new autobiographies and philosophical articles suitable for introducing undergraduates to Religious Studies. The students had hunted down readings in libraries, recalled them from other patrons, borrowed them through interlibrary loan, and, in one case, traveled to Omaha, Nebraska, to photocopy them. As a result of their collaborative research and discussion, I was convinced to drop the half containing philosophical selections and beef up the half containing the autobiographies. Heather Carver suggested we include two stories from each tradition, and the group convinced me to include my story as an introductory example. I dedicate the book to these twelve bright students, fine representatives of the religion and philosophy students at Iowa State who have shaped the text and me.

As the book entered its final stage, I received helpful suggestions from a number of other professors of Religious Studies, including John Donaghy and Joan Rottler of Iowa State; Betty DeBerg of Valparaiso University; Marlin Adrian of Wheaton College in Illinois; Sallie B. King and Diana Edelman of James Madison University; Lawrence E. Carter of Morehouse College; Geraldine H. Forbes of the State University of New York, Oswego; Barbara Reed of Saint Olaf College; Charles Headington of the University of North Carolina, Greensboro; June O'Connor of the University of California, Riverside; Matthew Glass of South Dakota State University; Joel P. Brereton of the University of Missouri, Columbia; and James B. Robinson of the University of Northern Iowa. Gary Palmatier changed my ideas into images, Kim Saccio copyedited the whole thing, and Marge Langloss read some of the galleys. Thank you.

Finally, I thank Richard Noland for his criticisms, his friendship, and his love.

Introduction

Religious Studies Program
Iowa State University
Ames, Iowa 50011
23 February 1994

DEAR Reader:

Years ago, Victorian novelists opened their books the way I have opened this one, with a salutation to "Dear Reader." They began their works in this fashion to try to close the gap between themselves and their audience, as if a direct address would bring strangers nearer. Texts are odd things. Since we typically read by ourselves, texts have the effect of separating us from each other even though they are intended as messages to bring us together. Somehow books always manage to do two conflicting things at once: make bridges that bring people closer to each other while at the same time blocking the sender from the receiver. Textbooks are often the worst offenders on the blocking score because they are usually written in a third-person voice, just the kind of disembodied "objective" voice that is most difficult to place, most difficult to figure out from whence it is coming, and which therefore erects the most formidable barriers.

Since this is a book about religion, a subjective and often emotion-laden part of our lives, I did not want to write it in the usual way. Since this is a book about autobiography, a personal style of writing, I did not want to begin it without placing myself. I am a professor at Iowa State University and have taught courses in Religious Studies and Philosophy for ten years. I grew up in the Chicago suburbs in a tradition familiar to many of you, evangelical Protestantism. You may know that evangelicals are Christians like Jimmy Carter and Billy Graham who claim that salvation comes through Jesus Christ; that you must accept Christ as your personal Savior; and that your behavior should be guided by admonitions laid down in the Bible. The evangelical world has many institutions of higher learning, and I did my undergraduate work at one of them, Wheaton College, in Wheaton, Illinois, my hometown.

I tell you all of this not to try to evangelize you, but to let you know something about my past. My family has lived in Wheaton since 1961, when my mother and father moved there so that Dad, who was an ordained minister in the Christian and Missionary Alliance denomination, could work on a master's degree in New Testament. I met my wife, Karen Werner, at Fischer Hall, Wheaton's then all-freshmen dorm, during Orientation Week in 1972, and we married in August, 1976, after she graduated with a major in Christian Education and I graduated with majors in Religious Studies and English Literature. Obviously, my upbringing was deeply religious.

And what about you, "dear reader"? Some of you may have stories similar to mine. Perhaps you were raised in an independent Bible Church, or in one of the hundreds of Baptist churches, or in a Free Methodist, Nazarene, or Pentecostal tradition, and understand a great deal about how I was raised. Others will have backgrounds equally as religious but differing in significant details. Many of you will be Catholics, and many will be Methodists, Lutherans, and Presbyterians. Some may have only a casual acquaintance with a tradition and many may share the memory of having been dropped off as children at Sunday School by parents who went home to watch football. If you were raised in a mainline Protestant church, such as the Methodist, Presbyterian, or Lutheran churches, your religious upbringing may have been more liberal than mine. If you are in this group, you may feel that your religious story is not as well defined or dramatic as the ones you have heard from Christian Fundamentalists, the "born-again" wing of evangelicalism. Then again many of you will be Jewish, Muslim, Buddhist, Hindu, or Sikh. Many will be agnostic, believing there is no way of determining whether there is a God, and many will be atheists, quite sure there is not a God. If my experience in the classroom is representative, many of you will have a strong and unnerving feeling that you do not really know what you believe, no matter how strong your church or synagogue background may be.

That is where we start, each of us with our own religious stories and varying degrees of certainty about our religious, or irreligious, or antireligious convictions. If you come from a conservative tradition such as the one I come from, you may initially find the study of religion threatening, because the study of other cultures and belief systems sometimes calls our own into question. For example, when I left the safe evangelical confines of Wheaton College for the secular graduate breezes of the University of Chicago, the mother of one of my undergraduate professors told me that if I went to that den of iniquity I would surely lose my faith. Alas, she was right. The study of religions and philosophy in a secular atmosphere damaged my conservative beliefs and I found myself doubting what I had been taught about Christ. If your religious beliefs are of a certain type, the secular study of religion may be challenging, even painful.

But many challenges involve pain—and some challenges, like mountain climbing and horseback riding, are potentially life-threatening. Should we run from such challenges or meet them head-on? To embrace life, to affirm and develop our humanity, is to examine ourselves and others. Like climbing mountains, education has its risks but it also has its rewards. The ancient Greek philosopher Socrates said that the process of philosophical education, of learning to think critically, is like the process of giving birth. Rigorous reflection on intellectual matters is a process in which we give birth to something very important: ourselves. That is the aim of humanistic education in religious studies: to come to understand our present beliefs better and so build a basis from which to affirm, deny, or modify our beliefs. In the process, we are building, affirming, and modifying ourselves.

After years of study I came to reaffirm many of the central beliefs of my parents' tradition, but with a critical difference. I now have an intellectual foundation of my own from which to decide which beliefs to affirm and which to reject. A liberal arts education in Religious Studies is not aimed at undermining or shoring up students' current beliefs. It is aimed at giving students the foundations and skills necessary to assess for themselves beliefs they may have inherited.

The second reason for writing this letter is to call attention to the fact that we have different forms of language available to communicate with each other. This book uses a specific literary form, or *genre,* in order to introduce religion. An autobiography is a narrative written by and about its author. A narrative is a story, a form of language containing plot and character. Another ancient Greek philosopher, Aristotle, observed that narratives always tell of things that change through time: stories trace events along a temporal axis, from the beginning, through the middle, to the end. The temporal changes constitute the story's plot; in autobiographies, the plot focuses on events in the author's life. The events of your life story, for example, began roughly on the day you were born and will end roughly on the day you die. Right now, as you read this book, you are in the in-between times, *in medias res,* and you have decisions to make that will affect how the rest of your story goes. In addition to plots, there are characters in your life story; they include your friends and antagonists, your supporting cast. If you were to write your autobiography, which friends would make it into your text? Which friends would be peripheral? Would you consciously exclude any acquaintances?

Narratives are a specific kind of literary form, the form that uses plot and character. *Stories* is simply another word for *narratives,* and I will use the two terms interchangeably. Stories differ from other forms of language such as the letter form I am presently using, and from lyric poems, recipes, bibliographies, and encyclopedias. Pause a moment to think about these other forms. How does the form of the *letter* you are now reading differ from the form of the *stories* that you find in the rest of this volume? How do the letters and stories differ in turn from the entries in your library's *Encyclopedia Britannica?*

Stories, unlike most letters, poems, and encyclopedias, present a single plot, or a handful of interrelated plots. They do not begin "Dear Reader" nor end "Sincerely yours." They are not serial entries that describe unrelated topics, as in an encyclopedia. They do not give instructions for making tabouli salad, the way a recipe in the vegetarian *Horn of the Moon Cookbook* does.[1] And stories are not usually attempts to create a single vivid image or impression, as is the case with poems like Japanese haikus. Stories embody characters presented with choices and challenges, and they tell about decisions and actions that may take on mythic significance for the author. You will learn more about stories simply by reading this anthology of autobiographies.

Just as narratives are one, but only one, of many different kinds of language usage, religious experiences are one, but only one, of many different kinds of human experience. This is a book of religious autobiographies written by men and women from different religious traditions. Reading their autobiographies will enable you to listen to the stories of adherents of some of the world's religions, and challenge you to bridge the gap between your relatively familiar North American world and their initially strange world. There are two stories in each chapter because no religion is monolithic; for example, no one Jewish story can represent all Jews' stories. If you had only one autobiography

---

1. Ginny Callan, *Horn of the Moon Cookbook* (New York, N.Y.: Harper and Row, 1987).

by a Jew to read, you might be tempted to think all Jews' experiences were like the author's. Having two stories to read will help you fight the temptation to take any one story as The Master Story of the tradition.

In addition, you will also find in each chapter one autobiography by a man and one by a woman. Men and women often see the world very differently, so reading two autobiographies will help you gain a more accurate picture of the world as seen through the eyes of tradition and gender.

An initial warning, which I will repeat: Do not let the scheme I have adopted for presenting these autobiographies confuse you. I have chosen in each chapter to focus on only one of seven different characteristics of religion. In studying Native American religions we focus on ritual; in studying Hinduism, we focus on creed; in studying Zen Buddhism, we focus on the uncanny; and so on. I have chosen this method in order to simplify study and to introduce the categories and methods of Religious Studies. Do not think that the scheme implies either that:

a. ritual is the most important part of Lakota Sioux religion, or,

b. ritual is not important in other religions, like Hinduism or Zen Buddhism.

Neither (a) nor (b) is true. I think it fair to say that all seven of religion's dimensions are important in all religious traditions. So the fact that we emphasize character in studying Islam does not mean that character is more central than code or creed in Islam, and the fact that we focus on code in studying Honduran Catholicism does not mean that we could not just as easily have focused on Honduran Catholic history or character. Use the emphasis in each chapter only if it is useful; if you find it gets in the way, ignore it. The stories are the important thing.

Best wishes with your reading. If you have time to let me know what you think about studying religion by reading autobiographies, drop me a line at the Religious Studies Program, ISU, Ames, IA, 50011. And if you are so inclined, send me a copy of your religious autobiography. Maybe we'll see it in the next edition!

Sincerely,

Gary Comstock

Unit 1

About Religious Autobiography

Chapter 1

What Is Autobiography?

AN **autobiography** is the story of someone's life, or of some part of that life, as the author remembers, selectively constructs, and then tells or writes it. Autobiographies differ from other forms of language usage because they contain plots and characters. That is, an autobiography begins at some point in time, rehearses events affecting the author, explains the author's relationship to other characters, and ends at another point in time. Usually autobiographies involve some kind of complication or conflict which is resolved, to one degree or another, by the end of the tale.

Memory is central in religious autobiography because the stories look backward in time. Authors may anticipate future events, such as impending retirement or a new approach to their profession, but the bulk of their autobiographies will be taken up with things that have happened in the past: their religious instruction as a child; their confirmation in the tradition as a youth; their rebellion against faith as a young adult; and so on. Since the events related in the autobiography are told only from the author's perspective, readers should be alert to the possibility of other interpretations of the events. As the historian Carl Becker writes, "The history of any event is never precisely the same to two different persons, and it is well known that every generation writes the same history in a new way, and puts upon it a new construction."[1] The history of events in an author's life may not look

---

1. Carl Becker, "What Are Historical Facts?" in Hans Meyerhoff, ed., *The Philosophy of History in Our Time* (New York, N.Y.: Doubleday, 1959), p. 132.

the same to everyone, even to people very close to the author, such as the author's husband or mother. The history of events may also change for authors themselves as they mature and change over time. For example, your picture of your father may be vastly different today from what it was five years ago. Mark Twain reportedly remarked that "When I was eighteen I could not believe how ignorant my father was, but at twenty-one I was astonished at how much he had learned in three years," a saying that underscores the relativity of our judgments about characters we think we know well.

In writing their own stories, authors naturally seem to want to tell the story "straight," as close to historical fact as possible. But the fact that memories can change makes this a difficult task, as does another factor: the demands of the story form itself. Since stories must begin and end somewhere, authors are under a certain amount of pressure to bring closure to all of the problems they introduce. For example, if someone begins writing about his or her relationship with his or her intended spouse and then gets caught up in a long account of a struggle with an employer, the reader's expectations will constrain the author to come back to the intended spouse before the end of the story and tell the reader how that episode ended. Therefore, if there is not room for the author to tell how things worked out, the author will have a powerful motive not to introduce the episode of the intended spouse in the first place. For two reasons, then, there is a substantial amount of contingency and serendipity in the writing process. First, our memories are selective and not always reliable and, second, the literary form of autobiography itself exerts pressure to exclude episodes that do not fit the particular focus of the story.

There are many famous autobiographies in the field of Religious Studies, with few being older or more familiar than Saint Augustine's *Confessions*. In this work, Saint Augustine tells of his early attraction to pagan religion and physical pleasure, moving on to explain his conversion to Christianity. Studying ancient autobiographies produced by different religions is an excellent way to learn about the history of various traditions; but the autobiographies I have selected are more con-temporary than Augustine's. All of these stories come from individuals in the twentieth century.

The best way to come to understand any subject matter is to have representative cases to examine. I offer an episode from my own religious autobiography as our first test case.

A Night in Buena Vista, Colorado

Gary Comstock

It was an unusually dark night in Buena Vista, Colorado. It was chilly, as August evenings in the Rockies tend to be, and I had squashed my green Bandera down on my head after snapping shut the cuffs on my jean jacket. I could see very few stars overhead as I shivered in the hayfield, and could feel little more than the tips of my fingers. There was the occasional perfume of an invisible alfalfa plant, but my senses seemed in general as confused as the night. I remember only one sensation clearly: the sound of running water.

The hayfield was five miles north of Bueney, and it was the summer of 1972, just after I'd graduated from high school and not yet started college. I had gotten a job as a wrangler at Deer Valley Ranch, a Christian guest ranch, and there I was, living out my dream in cowboy shirts and boots, riding John Woolmington's horse, Sundance, and leading trail rides up the ridge, down through the pines, around Dead Horse Lake, and back to the corral.

Toward the end of June I was standing outside the lodge when the owner's niece and John's cousin, Lynn Smith, came walking down the steps before dinner. She had just flown in for the summer from her home in Florida. I resolved to sit next to her at lunch the next day, and to my surprise she picked me as her partner for birdie-on-the-perch during the Western Party on Thursday night. The next week I asked her to go on a Jeep ride, and she said she would ask her Aunt Sue. Aunt Sue consented, John lent us a jeep, and we drove up to the Alpine Tunnel together. I picked some wildflowers and gave them to Lynn; the next day I found a pink ribbon tied around my saddle horn.

There was a petite blonde at the ranch, Annie from Peoria, and I'd been interested in her until Lynn arrived. One night a big group of us had gone to a neighboring ranch and were returning to Deer Valley in the back of the hay truck. In the darkness, Lynn and I sat quietly, bouncing as one through the dip in the road where flash storms washed gravel down from the Chalk Cliffs into the creek. Lynn was serious. She turned to me and said, "If there's someone else, let me know now. I can handle it now if you want to see her. But just don't tell me later."

Not a day passed in July without Lynn and I spending several hours together. On my days off we drove to Vail or Aspen or jeeped up the valley past Saint Elmo, and every Monday morning we saddled up Sundance and Question Mark at 5:30 A.M. and rode side by side in front of thirty guests to the wranglers' breakfast. Afterward, we'd sneak kisses behind the tack-room door while the horses munched molasses oats from feed bags and the Dave Clark Five spun on the record player. Once, against Aunt Sue's better judgment I think, I borrowed Jim Amelsburg's red Volkswagen bug, and Lynn and I went to see Dustin Hoffman in *The Graduate* at the drive-in. Annie? Annie who? I spent every evening with Lynn, studying her hands and whispering secrets as the sun set between Mount Princeton and Mount Antero.

There were plenty of stars that August, except for the night I found myself lying in the hayfield. That was the night I spoke in tongues. Now, the evangelical tradition in which I was raised, the Christian and Missionary Alliance denomination, is an offshoot of the Methodists. The C&MA stresses evangelism and holy living. I was a good pastor's boy and was "saved," meaning I gave my life to Jesus Christ, before I was in first grade. (Like many other kids raised in evangelical homes, I would be saved another five or six times before I turned ten.) The other wranglers and crew girls and guests at Deer Valley were evangelicals like the Woolmingtons, but evangelicals do not, as a rule, speak in tongues, and I was not expecting to meet Christians who did.

One afternoon a young couple showed up at the ranch and the three of us spent several hours talking about spiritual matters. Rob and Patty invited me to dinner at their cabin and I went, in part because I was attracted to their mature and comfortable way of talking about

their Christian experiences, in part because I knew Lynn had gone to town for dinner with the crew girls.

After the three of us finished eating, we began to talk about a subject all of us enjoyed: what God was doing in our lives. I was brimming with the indescribable passion of young love, and I could not stop exclaiming how wonderful God had been to me by bringing Lynn into my life. Rob and Patty were clearly happy for me, but eventually Rob asked if maybe I wasn't confusing my love for Lynn with my love for God.

"What will you do with your life in return?" Patty asked.

"Are you totally yielded to God?" her husband wondered. "Do you love Him as much as you love her?"

I was confused. "Of course, I do. I mean, I think I do. Why? What are you getting at? I don't know what you mean," I replied.

"Are you living completely in God's will? Do you manifest the gifts of the Holy Spirit?"

"Oh. You mean the fruits of the Spirit, such as love, joy, kindness, and peace?" I said.

"Yes. Those. But there are more. Christians who are really in tune with God's Spirit, and not only with their own affection for other people, will have spiritual gifts exhibited in their lives."

I began to get nervous. "Do you mean gifts like speaking in tongues?"

"Yes, I do," he said with a gentle smile.

"Ah. But supernatural gifts like that were given at a specific time by God to serve a specific purpose. God does not want us to speak in tongues any longer, and we don't need to," I said. I remembered my father suggesting this view in a conversation about biblical interpretation. He had a master's degree from Wheaton College in New Testament, I had no reason to question his opinion, and it was handy at the moment. But my resistance to the tongues thing weakened as the couple talked.

"We speak in tongues. God gave us the gift, and he will give it to anyone who is completely open to Him. He will give it to you, too. We know this because the Bible says that when the Spirit comes, he will come 'with tongues of fire and with the sound of rushing water.' But you must let Him."

After half an hour of listening to myself protest, I began to wonder if my friends were not right, if I was not deluding myself by thinking my devotion to God was above and beyond my devotion to Lynn. If Lynn were to drop me tomorrow, would I still be as thankful and submissive to God? If I was really "yielded" to God, should I not be open to whatever gift He might have for me?

I told my friends I would like them to pray over me. They asked me to kneel, and then took a plastic Crisco bottle from the kitchen cupboard. Pouring a few drops into their hands, they prayed over it, asking for God's special blessing. They rubbed the oil on my forehead and placed their hands on my hair.

I do not remember the exact words of their prayer, but it went something like this:

O lovely Jesus and righteous Father, we honor and bless thy name. You can do anything. You have told us so, and we believe you. You will not give us a stone if we ask for bread. As a father cares for his little ones, you will care for us. Scripture tells us you will give us any good thing we ask for, if we ask in your name. We ask you, now, in Jesus' name, to drive the forces of evil out of this person. We renounce the Devil, in Jesus' name. We deny the power of the Evil One, O Lord. Cleanse this soul, O Lord, with the blood of Jesus, O Lord. The blood of Jesus, O Lord. We declare, in Jesus' name, that this man here is now a vessel of your righteous and holy Spirit, O Lord. He is clean and righteous, O Lord. He is righteous and clean, O Lord. Yes, Lord. O Lord. We pray it. Yessss, Lord. Yesssss, Lord. In Jesus' name, we declare it, Lord. We renounce Satan. We drive him away. Come into our room, Lord. Yes, Lord. Come to us, now, Lord.

The man pushed my head backward. I felt dizzy, and a bit disoriented, but I wanted to believe in what was going on; I wanted to open myself to the powers they invoked. I tried to concentrate on their words.

Descend now here, O Lord. Visit Gary with the wings of doves and the waters of Pentecost, O Lord. As you have given others the tongues of fire, O Lord, so give them now to this dear one, O Lord.

Then, the couple broke out of their rhythmic, semichanting, prayer, and began to make clicking noises with their mouths. They were speaking in a language, if it was a language, that I did not know. I was tremendously excited, if a bit frightened, when I first realized what they were doing. They were speaking in tongues. I wanted to, too. I did not then hear waters rushing over me or see flames arising around us and, try as I might, I could not get anything to come out of my mouth except good old English. After five minutes of trying, we all stopped and looked at one another. I told them, sheepishly, that I feared it was not going to work.

They told me I had to cooperate, that God did not miraculously make my mouth move, that I had to open my mouth and make the sounds. God would do everything else, but not that.

Somewhat embarrassed, I opened my mouth and began to imitate the clicking noises I had heard them make. This seemed to break the ice, and they immediately broke into their tongues again. Soon I was chanting rhythmically, something, if I remember correctly, that sounded like "Ticka-tocka-ticka-tocka, ogalliga-ogallaga-ogalliga-ogallaga." I was at once embarrassed and thrilled, not knowing whether I was speaking gibberish they could see through, or whether I was genuinely speaking in tongues. I remember vacillating between rapture and guilt. I felt guilt when I opened my eyes, saw the Crisco bottle and red-and-white checked curtains still in place, and realized that I was pretending to do something God ought to be doing for me. I felt rapture when I closed my eyes and concentrated on God's love and overwhelming power. Rapture felt better. I repeated the ticks and tocks and ogalligas over and over again, trying to keep my mind off myself, the Crisco bottle, and the ticks and tocks. If memory serves, I occasionally moaned something like: "Ohhhhhh-muhnee-manawa, ohhhhhhhh-manawa-munuma," moans of ecstasy, not self-consciousness. When I would come to myself, hold on, I would blush, look away, hope I had not been caught in the act. So I tried hard to let go, giving myself to that wonderful floating feeling, joining my friends, our spirits converging in worship on the rhythms of our ecstatic praises.

My moments of embarrassment and doubt apparently did not show through, and my two mentors and I continued in our prayer language for several minutes. Then they slowed down, I peeked, saw them opening their eyes, and we all smiled. God was with us; I felt he had touched me, even been in me, supporting me and urging me on during those centered floating moments. I had spoken in tongues, and I was exuberant. My lingering guilt and doubts faded, even though I was not sure I was doing it right. My friends assured me that the experience was genuine, that the Spirit was speaking through me, and that with practice I would get better at the skill of praising God in a voice and with a power not mine. I believed them but I was still surprised that God would give me this gift in addition to all his other blessings that summer.

After basking in that rare communal silence endurable only in worship or conversation with an intimate friend, I wanted to be alone. I walked out the cabin door, across the yard, and into the hayfield. There I confronted the darkness with my five senses, senses that seemed overloaded from the experiences of the last few hours. As I drifted away from the cabin I felt an urge to lie down in the alfalfa. I am not sure why I wanted to do this; it was cloudy, the moon was not out,

and it was cold. But I found myself on my back looking into space, taking deep breaths. I felt a strange peace, a kind of sacred ease with myself, my past, my family, my friends. I had left my prior summer job at Honey Rock Camp without Coach Chrouser's blessing; suddenly I felt relieved of my lingering concern over this matter. I knew I had verbally abused my sister, but now I felt mystically reunited with her. I had struggled with my parents, but somehow I felt their forgiveness too. My friends had told me that my guilt and sin would be "washed away" by "the blood of Jesus" and I began to experience the truth of their claim; I had the feeling I was at one with the hayfield, the stars, my sister, my parents, and the Lord. I did not then hear God's voice, or see, as my grandmother had once seen at the foot of her bed, an angel. But I heard something uncanny: water, running past my head loud and splattering.

It sounded as if I was at the base of a waterfall but I knew I was not. Having no idea where the sound was coming from, I sat up, looked around, cleaned out my ear with my little finger, shook my head. The sound did not go away. I squinted into the darkness. There were no creeks or streams or pipes in the vicinity, much less a waterfall. I started to get up, eager to look around, but another instinct intervened. I felt like someone was saying to me, "No, lay back down, I am here. Be quiet and know that I am here." I gave into this urge, a power that seemed to still my soul and enlarge my capacity to care about the things around me.

The moment in the hayfield was more strange and inexplicable than the one in the cabin. I had been an active participant as I worked to speak in tongues, but in the hayfield I felt more like a helpless patient, a passive observer overtaken by feelings of peace, forgiveness, and joy. The second experience was out of my control in a way the first experience was not. I could not make the sound go away. Still, as uncanny as it was, the second experience seemed ordinary, natural, even familiar.

As I lay in the grass my own everyday consciousness began to return and as it did, something extraordinary happened. My eyes and nose and fingertips must have warmed, because I had the feeling of regaining consciousness. Back in control of my senses, I thought, that sound will stop. I listened, certain that it had been part of a dream. But unmistakably, there it was. Then it hit me: Whether I "let go" or not, whether my senses were sharp or dull, the sound of running water was not an illusion. I had no explanation for it. Nervously, I rolled my eyes to myself, thinking that if I made light of the sound it would not frighten me so. Then I remembered the Scripture verse my friends had shared with me. When the Spirit comes, he will come "with tongues of fire and with *the sound of rushing water.*" It was only then, half an hour after speaking in tongues, that I began to believe in the supernatural validity of *glossolalia.*

Back at the ranch, I shared my experience only with Lynn who reacted in a skeptical but not hostile way. She did what she could to encourage me in my spiritual growth even though it had taken this unexpected turn, but she did not seek it for herself nor did anyone else with whom I had contact. For reasons that still are not clear to me, I saw very little of Rob and Patty the rest of the summer.

When I returned home to Wheaton, I did not talk much about what had happened. I knew that most evangelicals believed that the historical period in which tongues were valid had passed, so I tried going to a "charismatic" church. It did not feel the same as the night I shared with my friends. I began going, alternately, to the Bible Church I had attended in high school, and to an Episcopalian church attended by a small group of Wheaton College faculty and students. The fall quarter was difficult. At first, Lynn sent me regular letters and pictures and I would spend entire afternoons analyzing her words and memorizing her photos. In one letter she sent me a newspaper article called "Two Love in One," written by someone identified only as "Padget." It read:

Sometimes one feels that he or she has at last found that choice someone with whom to share the rest of their life.... In a relationship, our first love should be God then one another, in that order of responsibility. Secondly, our mind and heart must love our partner's soul along with their outward appearance.... God has an appointed time and place in which He will call a uniting together of two of His children. Until that appointed time, God wants to prepare us and teach us how to love that certain person He has promised us.

Lynn had taken a straightedge and underlined in black ink several of the phrases, including "love our partner's soul along with their outward appearance," and "love is a feeling to be learned." I still believe her love was genuine and our talk about marriage authentic, but she was home in Florida, I was in Illinois, and long-distance relationships are notoriously not easy.

Lynn was home every time I called in September. In October, I called at one of our regular times and her mother said she was out. By November I was talking as much to her mother as to her. During one conversation, however, Lynn's mother told me she did not know where Lynn was or when she would return my call. When we next talked, Lynn told me she was thinking about not coming up at Christmas as she had planned. Plane tickets were expensive, and she had just started a new job at a bank. She couldn't very well start a new job and then quit a month later. I spent hours walking around town that night in my tan trench coat, ending up in the Wheaton Bible Church on my knees. In spite of all of our long visits about what Padget meant by phrases like, "Two love in One and He enables them to Love One Another," all that Lynn and I had shared seemed to be slipping away. I went back to the text she had sent me and underlined a few phrases of my own, "Love is *patient;... not jealous;* love *never fails,*" but I feared her eyes would never linger over my favorite passages the way mine had lingered over hers. Would she never strain to imagine what I was thinking as I underscored this passage or that the way I had strained to imagine her thoughts?

Meanwhile, my speaking in tongues seemed to be in trouble, too. After I entered Wheaton College, I took a course from an English professor who spent part of the quarter talking about the ministry of the Holy Spirit. In his syllabus he wrote about the biblical passages that discuss Jesus' disciples receiving the Holy Spirit, and commented on the claim that everyone who receives the Spirit *must* speak in tongues:

> Of all the groups who received the Spirit in the book of Acts, only three are said to have spoken in tongues (Acts 2: 1–4, 10: 44–46, 19: 1–6). Speaking in tongues is not the normal experience for believers in the book of Acts, but it is the exceptional event that God uses in the lives of *some* to glorify himself and bring unbelievers to faith.
>
> If a second spiritual experience [that is, speaking in tongues after being saved] were something all believers need, the doctrinal parts of the New Testament would surely make it clear; in fact, they are silent about such an experience. Christians who have experienced a second or exceptional spiritual experience should not try to make themselves the norm for all other believers, and they should guard against the impulse to instill discontent or feelings of guilt in other believers who have not had the same experience.

Under such teaching I did not feel much like sharing my experience with my instructors or roommates, nor did I feel that my community was much interested in my "second or exceptional spiritual experience." Although my friend Cannon Dear and a small group did our best to initiate a charismatic Bible study on campus, it did not work, and my speaking in tongues became increasingly rare. My views about the contemporary validity of tongues ran increasingly in the direction of my esteemed professors as my own interest in the ritual withered.

The fall quarter at college was the most difficult of my life. I was cut from the freshman basketball team, thus ending what I thought would surely have been an NBA career. Just as traumatic, Lynn's letters came less and less frequently, and eventually stopped before the end of November. I would not hear from her again until late January, and on February 8, 1973, she would write a letter that begins as follows:

> Dear Gary,
>
> The time has arrived to be absolutely truthful and to accept what God is showing you and me. This is the last letter I'll ever write for you, this is the last time I'll ever show how much I really care.
>
> If you haven't seen it in me, I am born out of time and I am meant for another...
> I am refuting any previous vows to you...

Have you ever felt your closest friend pulling away from you? Then you will understand the kind of winter I had.

Because of what happened over the next year, my memories of the summer of 1972 became bittersweet. But some remain wholly unaffected and innocent. I will never forget the absolute joy of standing on the bridge over Chalk Creek, trying to rest my cheek as lightly as possible on Lynn's hair as we listened to the water behind us and imagined the future before us. I will never forget the strangeness of that Crisco bottle at my friends' place, or the wonder of the forgiven floating feeling I had on that dark night near Buena Vista. And though I can no longer find that faded pink ribbon, I still hurt a little when I remember her tears as Lynn turned to wave one last time from the ramp at Stapleton International Airport, headed for Florida and we knew not what.

Well, that is my religious autobiography, or an important part of it. Notice several things about it.

CHARACTERISTICS OF AUTOBIOGRAPHY

Plot

First, it has a plot. Plots are the watchspring of narratives, the tension that drives the story forward. Plots answer the question, What happened next? and they move us through characters' problems, from an initial setting, through some important decision, to a final resolution. In my case, the initial setting was a ranch in Colorado during the summer following high school. One of the decisions I made was to stick it out when my friends started speaking in tongues in their cabin instead of getting out of there as fast as I could. Part of the resolution of my story was the withering away of my speaking in tongues and the end of my relationship with Lynn.

In thinking about an autobiography's plot, ask yourself where the story begins and where it ends. What changes occur in the middle? What point, if any, is the author trying to make with the plot? Is there a lesson the author has learned from retelling the story? Is there a lesson the author wants to teach you? Ask yourself, too, whether some parts of the story go faster than others. For example, did you find yourself reading more quickly when I narrated the conversation in the cabin? If so, what is it about the "dramatic" parts of a story that make time seem as if it is going faster? Did you slow down when I came to the part where I heard running water in the hayfield? Perhaps the variability in the way we read mirrors the variability of our lives. Have there been times in your life when time seemed to speed by, and others where it seemed tomorrow would never come? If you were to write your own autobiography, what techniques could you use to make time go faster or slower for your reader?

Character

The second feature of autobiography is character, or the people whose thoughts and actions move the plot along. The main character of any autobiography is the person telling the story. My story is not about my father, although I mention him, and not really about Lynn Smith, although she plays a major role. My story is about me, and autobiographies are primarily about the people telling them.

Nonetheless, we often learn about the storyteller through learning about their acquaintances. Who are the main characters in my autobiography? How have I revealed them to you through the choices I made in constructing the narrative? In almost every tale you will find characters you would like to get to know better, and characters you would just as soon forget. Try to figure out what it is about the author or the author's friends and enemies that you find attractive or repulsive.

Mood

In addition to plot and character, there are at least two other dimensions of autobiography. Mood is the emotional element conveyed by the attitudes and predicaments of the characters. The mood of my autobiography is bittersweet personal reminiscence, the kind of reflective wistfulness you might expect from a thirty-nine-year-old man trying to recapture the sweet memory of his first love. Other autobiographies may be less emotional and more straightforward historical accounts while still others will be more socially and politically minded. Ask yourself as you read whether the author's focus is more inward, on himself or herself, or more outward, on the community.

Style

A fourth dimension of autobiography is style. As you will see, authors have varying degrees of skill in choosing the phrases and plots to express their memories. What rhetorical devices do they use to reveal different parts of themselves? In addressing the question, pay particular attention to the first paragraph of each story. My story begins on a chilly August evening in Colorado, but it easily could have begun with my birth, or with my first horseback ride as an eight-year-old, or with my waving good-bye to Lynn at the airport. Why do you think I began the story on the August night? Was there a reason? What effect did my choice of starting points have on you as a reader? What emotions did you feel as you followed the story?

Asking yourselves these questions will help you gain a better understanding of my story, but you should not stop with empathic understanding. Go on to ask critical questions. What events might have happened to me that I have chosen, consciously or subconsciously, not to include? What explanations of my tongues experience suggest themselves to you? Do any of your explanations undermine the explanation I seem to suggest, that the experience was caused either by the otherworldly workings of the Holy Spirit or by my own entirely this-worldly actions? I suggest that my experience with *glossolalia* has something to do with Lynn, and clearly I want to lead my readers in that direction. But, you might ask, isn't it possible that the episode in the cabin was wholly unrelated to your relationship with Lynn? Is it necessarily the case that our religious experiences and our personal relationships are connected? More generally: What motivated me to write the story, and what motivated me to write it *in the way* I wrote it?

To encourage you on this track, I have a confession. When I first wrote the story several years ago, I focused exclusively on the *glossolalia* episode, with the ranch mentioned only as background setting for the story. In that first version, there was no mention of Lynn. As I continued to revise, however, it occurred to me that the single most powerful memory of all of my experiences in Colorado concerned Lynn. I wondered what the story would look like if I wove her into one of the drafts, so I tried adding the dialogue in which "Rob asked if maybe I wasn't confusing my love for Lynn with my love for God." It seemed to work, and even though I hadn't initially remembered that subject coming up in that conversation, it did not seem far-fetched to imagine that it could have come up. As the story grew from a few pages to more than ten, Lynn came to play a larger and larger role, and the story seemed more and more true to life, more and more true to my overall experience that summer. Finally I produced a draft in which Lynn's story was completely integrated with the tongues story, and the result was the version you have just read. I had successfully folded the two stories into one, and the final product seemed more representative of myself than either story by itself. And yet the final product was composed of two memories I had not previously associated.

As long as I am confessing I must admit I still am not convinced that the two stories actually went together *in history.* As I remember the time, what went on with Lynn seemed, then, completely removed from what went on at my friends' cabin. What's more, after not having spoken to Lynn for nearly twenty years, I picked up the phone as this book was going to press and heard someone say, "Hi. This is Lynn Smith." We talked about many things, and I asked her whether she remembered my unusual religious experience. She said she did not recall my discussing it with her. So, even though I am relatively certain that I spoke in tongues the same summer Lynn came to the ranch, I am not sure the two stories belong together in the seamless way I have presented them here. Have I misrepresented my past, then? Perhaps. But perhaps not. Having studied religion for many years and seen how often religious experiences are causally related to other important events in our emotional lives, I do not find it surprising that the two stories go so well together. So even if I did not connect the tongues episode to my memories of Lynn for two decades, who is to say that my present perspective is not the right one? Perhaps Comstock the religion scholar understands his youthful summer better now, twenty years later, than he did before he had studied religion professionally.

I made this confession about the two stories in order to show that autobiographies are made objects, artifacts that authors selectively construct and reconstruct. As writers revise drafts they often take ideas apart, examine the pieces, bring in some new elements, and recombine everything into a new form; I dare say I have rewritten my autobiography fifty or sixty times. Autobiographies, then, are not dust-free mirrors of the past that unproblematically tell us how things happened. They are to various degrees imaginative constructions of authors who are trying to make a single story out of many disparate pieces.

By asking critical questions about autobiographies, you will demonstrate that you have read the texts carefully and are prepared not simply to "receive" the texts but to interrogate them, meet them head-on and appropriate them in a critical fashion. By asking these kinds of questions you will be building your own intellectual foundation, your own base from which to examine not only the beliefs and rituals of others, but your own beliefs and rituals as well.

Chapter 2

What Is Religion?

SCHOLARS of religion have debated the meaning of the word *religion* for some time and they continue to disagree about its precise definition. One of the central issues in the debate concerns whether or not the transcendent is necessarily part of every religion. What, exactly, is *the transcendent?* The question is difficult to answer because *the transcendent* means different things to different people. When many people think of the transcendent, they think of an all-powerful being such as God. Others think not so much of a being, but of a place such as Heaven. Still others think of extraordinary events, such as speaking in tongues, receiving tablets on Mount Sinai, or being cured of lameness by drinking holy water in Lourdes, France.

We can include all of these ideas in our use of the phrase. For our purposes, *the transcendent* means anything above and beyond the ordinary world, anything supernatural, divine, or miraculous, anything to which people refer when they use terms such as:

God	*Creator*	*Heaven*
Krisna	*afterlife*	*nirvana*
Yahweh	*the All*	*Hell*
Allah	*miracles*	*Salvation*

Many religion scholars think the transcendent is not a necessary feature of religion. One reason is that there are traditions, ordinarily thought of as religions, in which people do not believe in the transcendent. For example, adherents of Confucianism in China, and adherents of certain forms of Buddhism in China and India, explicitly deny the existence of a supernatural realm, as do many liberal Christians and Jews. To make transcendence a necessary feature of religion, then, would be to exclude these traditions as religions. But do we want a definition of religion that excludes Confucianism? Many do not. A second reason to exclude the transcendent as a necessary aspect of religion is that some scholars believe every person's life has a religious dimension to it whether or not they believe in the supernatural. According to these scholars, even atheists who explicitly and thoughtfully insist that they "do not have a religious bone in their body" *are*, nonetheless, religious. These scholars argue that everyone is ultimately concerned with something, be it justice or compassion or sexual pleasure or fame or bowling-and-beer weekends. So even people who are certain there is nothing more to the world than what we can discover with our five senses have, nevertheless, an underlying "faith" in something—if only their five senses. According to this broad definition of religion, whatever you have faith in, or whatever you are ultimately concerned about, is your religion. Consequently, every person is religious, like it or not. Consequently, a definition of religion must include everyone as religious, or else the definition will exclude from view this basic "religious dimension" of all human life. This is a second reason not to make the transcendent a necessary part of our definition of religion.

Not everyone finds these two reasons compelling, however. It would take us too far afield to settle the debate here, and we must not lose sight of our main task—the study of religion through the use of autobiographies. However, there is no getting around the fact that we must decide whether to use a narrower or broader definition, because if we do not decide we will be left in confusion about exactly what we *mean* by "religious" autobiography. I propose that we adopt the narrower definition of religion simply because it is useful. To distinguish things religious from things not religious, there is hardly a more obvious criterion than the otherworldly mystery, transcendence.

There are consequences of this choice, including the consequence that Confucianism, some forms of Buddhism, and some forms of liberal Christianity and liberal Judaism do not qualify as religions. But how much is lost by having to consider these movements secular cultural *traditions* rather than *religions?* It is a good thing to have linguistic categories available that allow us to make careful distinctions, and the distinction between secular and religious cultural traditions will be lost if we necessarily must consider every cultural tradition as religious. On the narrow definition not everybody is intrinsically or fundamentally religious. But perhaps not much is lost by allowing that some people simply lack a religious dimension, and much may in fact be gained by being able to allow that people who claim to have no religious dimension may in fact *have* no religious dimension.

A NARROW DEFINITION

It is not part of the view I am recommending to consider the transcendent to be an important part of every religious person's life, or the central feature of every religious tradition, nor even a necessary part of any particular religious belief or ritual. The transcendent might play a minor role in Christian denominations such as the United Church of Christ, and it probably plays no role at all in a synagogue's decision to hire ServiceMaster to clean its carpets. Aspects of religion other than transcendence may well be the most important aspects of a religion, and transcendence may play no role at all in many areas of religious life. Nor is it part of the view I recommend to think that the supernatural must be equally important to all believers within a tradition. This Reform Jew may believe that God literally handed Moses the Ten Commandments on Mount Sinai while that Reform Jew may wonder whether God exists at all. It is part of the view I recommend to exclude from consideration as *religious* autobiography any autobiography that makes no mention whatsoever of transcendence. Somewhere in every tradition or story deserving of the modifier *religious* there must be some element of belief in, or orientation toward, something divine or supernatural, even if that belief or orientation is not the most conspicuous part of the tradition or story.

One reason I adopt this view is because definitions are not much help if they exclude nothing. Definitions that include everything, or definitions easily stretched to include everything, are not much use. If everyone is religious, then what do we add to a description of someone by calling that person a "religious" person? If everyone has fundamental beliefs and ultimate concerns that are religious, then do we learn anything new about someone by hearing that they have "religious" beliefs and concerns? Broad definitions of religion fail us by failing to exclude anything. Narrower definitions of religion allow us to use the term in an informative way, so that by calling Satomi Myodo religious, we indicate that Myodo has some beliefs or practices that cannot be explained without reference to the transcendent. By calling Myodo's autobiography a "religious" autobiography, we are specifying that her story includes beliefs or rituals that make reference to the transcendent.

Are the consequences of the narrow definition bad? I do not think so. I take it to be one of the definition's virtues, not defects, that people who have thought about the matter and decided that they are not religious are, in fact, *not* religious by this definition. We should be wary of definitions that presume to tell people that they are *x* when the people deny that they are *x*. And I take it to be one of the definition's virtues that not all cultural traditions must necessarily be called religious. Only some cultural traditions are religious; others are secular.

The narrow definition of religion is useful, but I must remind you that many scholars of Religious Studies think it is too narrow, and others think it is misleading. Some will point out that the definition is overly influenced by Western religious beliefs, the Western religions being Judaism, Christianity, and Islam. Indeed, the supernatural plays a bigger role in Western religions than it does in some Eastern religions, so we must guard against the temptation to interpret those religions through a Western lens. Other scholars will point out that the narrow definition of religion is influenced by our own Western experiences with religion, just as all definitions are influenced by the experiences of their definers. Indeed, my preference for the narrow definition fits well not only with my study of religions, but also with my personal religious background. Nonetheless, the fact that whatever definition we choose will have been influenced by our backgrounds cannot constitute an argument against any particular definition. If it did, then we could never settle on any definition whatsoever. There are valid criticisms of the narrow definition, but they are not so powerful as to undercut it, and I will proceed with it in hand. Nevertheless, you are well advised to take the narrow definition with a grain of salt, and develop a certain degree of skepticism about all definitions of religion. If you find this theoretical matter interesting, you may return to it later in your study of religion by consulting sources your instructor recommends.

SEVEN CHARACTERISTICS OF RELIGION

What is religion? I have given pragmatic reasons to think it is in part a concern with transcendence, but what else is it? It is much more, as the following definition suggests:

> Religion is that part of some peoples's lives which involves rituals, beliefs, organizations, ethical values, historical traditions, and personal habits and choices, some of which refer to the transcendent.

Different theorists of religion divide the subject differently, as a casual perusal of contemporary textbooks will suggest. For example, in their book, *Ways to the Center*, Denise Carmody and John Carmody refer to W. Richard Comstock's five methodological perspectives on religion: the psychological, the sociological, the historical, the phenomenological, and the hermeneutical.[1] In his book *Worldviews*, Ninian Smart identifies six dimensions of religion: the experiential, the mythic, the doctrinal, the ethical, the ritual, and the social.[2] But in Robert S. Ellwood, Jr.'s *Introducing Religion*, we find yet another schema: the self, history, psychology, symbol and rite, sociology, and truth and conceptual expression.[3] Obviously, it would be impossible to try to squeeze all of these authors' ideas into a single framework, and very difficult to get them all to agree on a single set of categories. Nonetheless, there is continuity in the way religion scholars think about religion, and I believe there are seven features of religion recognized in one way or another by most theorists. It is easiest for me to keep them in mind by remembering words beginning with the letter *c:* cultus, creed, uncanny, community, code, course, and character.

Cultus, or Ritual

Religious rituals are rites, activities that religious people perform in accordance with formal or informal rules or customs. Like the Lord's

---

1. Denise L. Carmody and John T. Carmody, *Ways to the Center: An Introduction to World Religions,* 2nd ed. (Belmont, Calif.: Wadsworth Publishing Company, 1984), pp. 8–10; citing W. Richard Comstock, *The Study of Religion and Primitive Religions* (New York, N.Y.: Harper & Row, 1971), pp. 13–17.

2. Ninian Smart, *Worldviews: Crosscultural Explorations of Human Beliefs* (New York, N.Y.: Charles Scribner's Sons, 1983).

3. Robert S. Ellwood, Jr., *Introducing Religion: From Inside and Outside* (Englewood Cliffs, N.J.: Prentice-Hall, Inc., 1978).

Supper or eucharist, speaking in tongues is an activity performed in many ways, but always in accordance with the rules of some religious group. In my case, the Christian group in Buena Vista was very small: Rob, Patty, and me. But the group can be very large, such as the Catholic Church with its network of churches stretching around the world. Catholic rituals such as baptism and last rites are fairly standardized, and you can go into a Catholic church in Rome and see rituals performed there in exactly the same way they are performed in Salem, Oregon.

Rituals may be the most visible of religion's seven characteristics because the activities involved often take religious participants into, or at least through, public places. In my tradition, individuals and families get dressed up in their best clothes and go to church every Sunday morning. The ritual invariably takes us along city streets and sidewalks, to a place of worship made conspicuous by its steeple and corner bulletin board. The rituals of other traditions are surrounded by equally observable behavior. The *bar mitzvah* is a Jewish ritual performed when a boy is thirteen, old enough to assume religious responsibilities in the community. In the Hasidic community in New York, conservative Jewish boys may be seen every day of the week dressed in their black coats and black hats going back and forth between home and Hebrew school, their long forelocks hanging on either side of their faces.

Rituals are both *temporal* and *spatial* events. They are temporal because they happen regularly in time: every Sunday at 8:45 A.M. or so conservative Christian children head for Sunday School. Every Friday evening at sundown, Orthodox Jewish families light candles and invoke the spirit of the *Shekinah*, or holy shining presence. Rituals divide time into segments.

Rituals are also spatial because they occur at predictable places in our towns and buildings. Five times a day a *mu'azzin* climbs into a tower in the local mosque and chants, calling Muslims to prayer. Every weekday afternoon, conservative Jewish children carry their books from public school to Hebrew school. You may remember ritual by thinking of the word *cultus*, a word used by early historians of religion to describe the activities of prayer, animal sacrifice, and worship observed regularly in the ancient Israelite temple. But do not confuse cultus with *cult*, a term often used to refer to new religious movements. Cultus has a wider meaning, and does not have the negative connotation associated with the shorter word.

Our first two readings emphasize ritual. John Fire Lame Deer tells about the Lakota Sioux ritual in which he comes of age by having a vision in a hut on a hillside, and Mary Crow Dog tells of her participation in the traditionally male Sun Dance ritual. In both stories, the importance of particular place and time is stressed, as both authors insist that Native American rituals must be performed on Native land. Both of them also discuss the centrality of nature in their belief systems, and the ritual importance of their belief that nature is sacred. This leads us to the second characteristic of religion.

Creed, or Belief

Religious beliefs are ideas that adherents of a tradition hold to be true. Beliefs are formulated in propositions, or sentences, such as my friend's claim that "As a father cares for his little ones, you (God) will care for us," or the Lakota Sioux's claim that "Nature is sacred." To say that an adherent of the religion holds an idea to be true simply means that the adherent assumes an attitude of assent to the proposition. When asked if nature is sacred, a Lakota Sioux would assent—say *yes*—whereas a Fundamentalist Christian might dissent—say *no.* Religious beliefs, then, are "propositional attitudes," propositions toward which adherents have assenting attitudes.

Religious beliefs are rarely found by themselves. More often, they are embedded in stories, as when the Lakota Sioux's reverence for nature is expressed in a myth about the Buffalo Woman creating the world. In some traditions, beliefs are systematized and refined. Creeds are systematic statements of the central beliefs of a tradition and consequently are often repeated during worship services. I learned the Apostles' Creed by listening to the adults repeat it in church every other Sunday morning:

> I believe in God the Father Almighty, Maker of Heaven and Earth, and in Jesus Christ, His only Son our Lord who was conceived by the Holy Ghost, born of the virgin Mary, suffered under Pontius Pilate, was crucified, dead, and buried. On the third day he arose from the dead...

One of the first phrases Muslim children learn is the monotheistic creedal affirmation of Islam: *Allah u Akbar*—God is great.

Beliefs differ from rituals in the same way that math differs from basketball; the first is done in your head whereas the second is done with your whole body. Therefore, religious beliefs have more to do with what we think, and rituals have more to do with what we do. But while the two are distinct from each other, they are not entirely separable. Just as math can affect what you do with your hands when you see a blank piece of paper, and basketball can affect what you think about after the NCAA Final Four is decided, so religious beliefs can affect how you behave, and religious rituals can affect what you think about. What we think is affected by what we do, and what we do is directed by what we think. "God is great" is a proposition to which Muslims assent, but that propositional truth is regularly reinforced by the ritualistic repetition of bowing toward Mecca and praying to Allah. Bowing and praying are physical activities, things the Muslim does. Assenting to propositions are mental activities, things the Muslim thinks. The Muslim's thoughts direct his or her physical activities, and physical activities reinforce beliefs.

I have selected two readings from Hinduism in order to introduce the characteristic of religion we call creed, or belief. Shudha Mazumdar tells about the religious education she received from her mother, who believed that Shiva was the ideal man, a husband-god who cared so deeply for his wife that he rattled the heavens with his grief at the death of his wife-goddess, Durga. Like her mother, Mazumdar assumes an attitude of assent to the proposition, "The god Shiva is the ideal man," and this belief directs her to practice *puja*, a ritualistic worship of the small statue of Shiva. In turn, Mazumdar's *puja* activity brings her into closer contact with Shiva and reinforces her propositional attitudes about him.

Mazumdar's religious beliefs are an important part of her Hinduism, but she takes little interest in systematizing them or examining them for inconsistencies. She is more interested in the way her inherited beliefs keep her family together and support a communal network within which she can find her identity. Mazumdar accepts traditional Shaivite religious propositions but does not pay them much critical attention. Swami Agehananda Bharati, on the other hand, gives religious propositions a great deal of critical attention, and his autobiography is replete with accounts of philosophical lectures he has given on the meaning of religious terms. Bharati's religious beliefs are an important part of his Hinduism, but in a way that is different from Mazumdar. He spends a great deal of time reflecting on theological ideas, and winds up rejecting many propositions Mazumdar might accept. Bharati, for example, does not believe we should think of the divine in human terms, or even as something that "exists." In a curious way, Bharati's religious beliefs are antitheological in the sense that he denies the existence of God. However, he is not an atheist, because he also denies that God does *not* exist. In Mazumdar and Bharati we see two different sets of Hindu religious ideas and two different attitudes toward those ideas.

All of the seven characteristics of religion are intimately related, and creed is intimately related to cultus. Both Mazumdar and Bharati act out their creeds in cultic contexts, Mazumdar in *puja* and Bharati in his capacity as an ochre robe–wearing monk. Creed and character, creed and community, creed and course, creed and cultus: all seven characteristics of religion are deeply interconnected, and each of the characteristics is distinct from the others without being separable from them. When we study religious belief, therefore, we cannot ignore the development of those beliefs in the history of the tradition, or the ritualistic contexts in which they are acted out, or the personal affects they have on the character of the believer.

What distinguishes a religious belief from a nonreligious belief? There are many things I currently believe that I would not call religious beliefs: that my computer screen has a blue background, that today is Friday, that gays should be allowed to serve in the military. What makes a belief "religious"? Our narrow definition of religion holds the key: Religious beliefs are beliefs about the transcendent.

The unCanny, or Transcendence

Not all rituals and beliefs are religious. I see nonreligious rituals everywhere, such as at the annual pancake supper at Roosevelt School at which members of my neighborhood stand in line to get pancakes and syrup and then file to various tables to eat and visit. I see nonreligious beliefs in many places, such as in the remnant of an old hippie commune in the Willamette Valley of Oregon, where residents believe in the healing powers of marijuana. What distinguishes religious rituals and beliefs from nonreligious rituals and beliefs? According to our definition, religious rituals and beliefs are those that make some reference to transcendence. And what is transcendence? It is the extraworldly dimension of some peoples' lives: the holy, the divine, the supernatural, the extramundane, the world of gods and goddesses, living ancestors, ghosts, demons, and angels. The uncanny is the power that works miracles, such as causing someone to walk on water, to prophesy about future events, or to hear running water when there is no water in the vicinity.

On college and university campuses it is in the Department of Anthropology that careful study of religious ritual tends to occur, and it is in the Department of Philosophy that careful study of religious belief tends to occur. But study of the mysterious and otherworldly character of transcendence, particularly if such study depends on the acceptance of special truths revealed by a deity, may not be exhaustively explained by the methods of the social sciences or philosophy. Insofar as what we know about the uncanny must be revealed to us rather than attained by us, the uncanny cannot be known using the traditional scientific or analytical methods. Therefore, this dimension of religion is best studied in a Department of Theology, a department not found on every campus and, where it is found, a department that usually has strong historical ties to a particular religious tradition's way of understanding the transcendent.

The uncanny designates a part of religion unlike the other six dimensions. Social scientists often take a reductionistic approach to rituals, beliefs, histories, and institutions of religious individuals and communities. A reductionistic approach is one that denies the explanatory power of "otherworldly" forces and seeks to explain religious phenomena in terms of scientific laws and regularities. Each of the religious dimensions other than the uncanny may be approached in this way, and there are scholarly disciplines appropriate to each one. Anthropologists may study religious rituals, philosophers religious beliefs, sociologists religious communities, political scientists religious codes, historians religious histories, and psychologists religious character. Each of the other six religious dimensions yields itself to study in a secular context because it can be seen as a "this-worldly" dimension, a dimension with parallels in the nonreligious world. For example, nonreligious institutions have rituals, beliefs, histories, and institutions. Think, for example, of the U.S. Congress, or the National Organization of Women, or the Silverton, Oregon, Lions' Club, each a this-worldly group. The rituals, beliefs, and character of Congress or the Lions' Club can be studied using anthropological, philosophical, and psychological techniques and methods.

The transcendent dimension of religion, however, is unlike the other six because it does not yield itself to these methods. In order for the transcendent to be studied on its own terms, students must do something not required in other investigations: they must approach the subject matter with a certain naivete, a disposition to accept the validity of the transcendent, and they must not assume immediately that there is a scientific, this-worldly explanation for everything that happens. In writing about poetry Samuel Taylor Coleridge pointed out the necessity of "suspending disbelief." In following a poem, or movie for that matter, we grant the poet or filmmaker a certain leeway, allowing them the freedom of supposing that humans can fly like birds or dive like whales. We suspend our disbelief that things contrary to our accustomed laws can happen, and we open the door to the imaginative world the author creates.

To suspend our twentieth-century skepticism about things supernatural is necessary in order to study the transcendent on its own terms. The reason is that if we do not suspend our disbelief, we will from the start be committed to interpreting the uncanny reductively in terms of something else. We might be committed, for example, to reducing the transcendent to an aspect of someone's psychological state and might thereby always want to attribute a person's belief in the transcendent to "infantile longing," "superstition," or "psychological imbalance." Or we might be committed to reducing the transcendent to an aspect of a community's sociological mechanisms and might thereby always want to attribute a culture's experiences with the uncanny to the effect of "social forces of repression" or "unscientific ideology." Now, these explanations may, in the end, be true explanations or they may in the end not be true. But to start out our study of the uncanny already committed to them will not help us to understand someone's alleged encounter with the transcendent empathically because these explanations foreclose the possibility of taking a nonreductionistic approach to the uncanny. The person who encounters the uncanny, however, often takes a nonreductionistic approach to it; so students of religion who are unable to suspend their disbelief in the transcendent will be unable to probe very deeply into the religious person's inner world.

The transcendent characteristic of religion seems to be in a category of its own and for this reason I consciously depart from my standard in choosing *c* words to represent the various features of religion. In this case I use an "un-*c*" word, the *uncanny,* analogous perhaps to "the un-cola," the cola which is not a cola. By thinking of the transcendent as "the *un*canny," I remind myself that this feature of religion is a feature of religion unlike the others. Sigmund Freud used the word *uncanny* to designate the part of the world that impinges powerfully and mysteriously on us and cannot be controlled. The uncanny is that part of religion we think of when we hear words like *nirvana, Allah,* and *Messiah,* and when we hear stories about people speaking miraculously in languages they have not studied.

I have chosen Zen Buddhism as the context for discussing the uncanny because the autobiographies of Janwillem van de Wetering and Satomi Myodo exemplify an individual's experience with the transcendent. Janwillem van de Wetering is a Dutchman who has lived in a monastery in Kyoto, Japan. Preoccupied with the illusion of everyday existence, he studies Zen and comes to experience the uncanny as emptiness. Emptiness, he writes, is "the core of Buddhism. Emptiness, the great goal which is to be reached by losing everything there is to lose. Emptiness, the great danger…the final goal is to have nothing more to do, to be nameless."[4] What is it to be "nameless"? The question defies any answer. Why? Because "being nameless" is uncanny: to be nameless is to attain a state defying description.

Satomi Myodo has a different experience. She is driven to the study of Zen by difficult personal matters. Only at the end of decades of searching and wandering does she find the spiritual guidance she needs to discover *satori.* Satori is enlightenment, in which Myodo sees *Mu. Mu* defies definition, but it is something like awaking from a dream to find yourself immersed in the concrete realities of the spiritual unity of all things.

On the narrow definition, the uncanny takes a central place in religion because the uncanny and the transcendent are the same. However, we must remember at this point the dangers of the narrow definition. It is misleading to think that religion is only about the transcendent, or that the transcendent is the most important part of every tradition. Indeed, the uncanny features of religion always appear in mundane circumstances, as when my tongues experience was surrounded by very ordinary curtains, a bottle of Crisco oil, and my friends' supportive murmurs. The support and rules and expectations of other religious people calls to mind the next dimension of religion.

---

4. Janwillem van de Wetering, *A Glimpse of Nothingness* (New York, N.Y.: Houghton Mifflin), p. 132.

Community, or Society

Religions are composed of individuals believing this and doing that, building this temple and tearing down that one. Individuals rarely practice their religion by themselves. Even when solitary monks pray in the quiet of their cloister, their prayers are inspired by the language and vision of their particular society. Every religion has a communal or social dimension, a dimension clearly seen in large religious gatherings such as the Pope's annual Christmas sermon in Rome, when thousands of Christians gather in Saint Peter's square. But it is also seen in smaller gatherings, such as the tiny prayer meeting I had with my two friends in their Colorado cabin. The communal aspects of religion are studied in the discipline known as *sociology*, and sociologists of religion are interested in understanding and explaining the role of institutions and groups in religion.

Religions can help to form communities, as when the pieties of Muslims cause them to go on a *hajj,* or pilgrimage, to the holy city of Mecca. The second reading of chapter 7 tells of a community of Orthodox Jews whom Samuel Heilman encounters on a sabbatical in Jerusalem. This particular community consists of a *chavruse,* or Talmudic study group, in which are found the likes of Rav Moses, an authority on Talmud and unofficial teacher of the group; Reb Zanvil, who occasionally nods off during study; Eliahu, who offers interpretations inconsistent with the majority opinions; and Reb Yechiel Michl, who argues against Eliahu, pointing out that his interpretation agrees with that of Rashi, one of the greatest of commentators. In this loosely knit circle of Jewish men studying holy books in Israel, Heilman finds religion helping to create and support community, even though he has difficulty feeling totally at home in the community himself.

Religion is often a force for good, bringing lonely individuals together where they can find themselves in the rhythms of a group. But religion, it seems, is just as often a force for evil, unleashing the powers of hatred and contempt that lie beneath the surface of our collective psyche. Our first author in chapter 7, Judith Magyar Isaacson, tells of her struggle to keep her family together through the Holocaust. The Holocaust was genocide, an attempt to destroy all Jews, and religion played a role in it as the anger of German Christians helped the Nazis rise to power in Germany during the 1930s. For example, some German soldiers wore belt buckles reading "Für Gott und Führer," or "For God and the Fuhrer," and many Germans rationalized the death camps in the name of Christianity, telling themselves that Jews, after all, were the killers of Christ. Isaacson's story tells of the successive breakdown of Jewish social structures under the onslaught of the Nazi attack. Jews are physically displaced from their neighborhoods, family units are broken down, and finally the communal basis of Jewish familial piety, the relationship of children to parents, is threatened. Isaacson's autobiography raises chilling questions for central religious beliefs— beliefs, for example, in God's ultimate goodness and tender concern for children. Her story underscores the fact that religions are not always instruments of peace and goodwill: Religions can be used to serve evil, twisted ends. Whether religions are forces for good or evil raises the question of the moral values that religions pursue.

Code, or Morality

What sort of morality did the Nazis follow? Many Nazis were Christians and thought they were doing God's will by stamping out "deviant" people like Jews and homosexuals. When we ask questions about the relationship between God's will and people's moral values, we are asking questions about the code or rules that govern people's behavior. In Christianity, the Bible often serves as a source of moral values, and values found in the Bible include charity, justice, and liberation of the poor and oppressed. Given the message of the Bible, it is difficult to see how German Christians could rationalize the action of systematically exterminating millions of people simply because those people were not Christians. In the readings in chapter 8 we will find two Christians who live out moral codes very different from the Nazis.

Father Guadalupe Carney lives by a system of values that motivates him to go to one of the poorest countries in the Americas and work on behalf of peasants. His exposure to rural Honduran Catholics eventually leads him to call into question the assumptions under which he was raised: that the United States is always the friend of the poor; that U.S. policy in Central America is formulated with the good of Central Americans foremost in mind; and that the Catholic Church is working to alleviate poverty and hunger. Carney decides that the established Church is not preaching the message of salvation and liberation found in the Bible, and he devotes his life to a theology of liberation in which the needs of the poor and hungry come first.

Elvia Alvarado also learns a hard truth. She sees that women are not always valued as they should be in Latin American Catholicism, and she devotes her life to a code that calls into question the *machismo* of many Latino males. Like Carney, her system of morality is shaped by her experience in the Church and with Christ. It is a very different system of morality than the one found in Nazi Germany.

Course, or History

Religions exist in time and develop through history. Like stories, they have a beginning and a middle and, sometimes, an end. Like our lives, they follow a course, a trajectory or path through history from one point to another. The phenomenon of speaking in tongues has a history beginning, in this country, in the emotional upheaval of revivalistic Christianity. Reconstructionist Judaism has a history beginning in twentieth-century America.

The course of a religion has at least two dimensions, the first being the historical development of the tradition from earliest times. In his autobiography in chapter 9, Benjamin Mays briefly reviews the course of African-American history and the influence of religion. Mays retells this history because he believes it has been ignored or repressed in the history books, and he devotes his life to educating both blacks and whites about it.

If the first dimension of a religion's course is communal and sociological, the second dimension is more individual and psychological. Bessie Jones's autobiography explains that she grew up on the coast of South Carolina, where she inherited a tradition of singing and oral storytelling. From her parents and grandparents she learned the history of her tradition in the form of folk songs and rhymes handed down from generation to generation. In the discipline we call History of Religions, scholars try to trace the multitude of factors influencing a tradition from past to present. This task is easier if there are artifacts available to study: religious texts, objects, paintings, hieroglyphics. But many of the world's religions lack texts and are called *traditional* or *oral* cultures.

Unlike most of the other autobiographies in this volume, Bessie Jones's autobiography was not composed initially as a text but rather was written down by someone who interviewed her. As such, Jones's autobiography is interesting because it represents the oral tradition within African-American Protestantism. Her autobiography, like most of those in this book, highlights the course religion takes in the lives of individuals.

Character, or Personal Identity

The last characteristic is closely related to the personal course of religion, and has to do with the development of a person's character, both in the literary and the moral sense. The literary sense of character refers to the things that happen to us, the events that shape our lives and give us our "characteristics." The moral sense of character refers to the things we do, the actions we take to shape ourselves in the image we desire. In my case, meeting Lynn had a powerful effect on my emotions and desires, an effect that has persisted for twenty years. In my case, speaking in tongues had a less persistent, but equally powerful short-term effect on my religious beliefs and practices. Events like these shape our personal identity and present occasions for us to take control of our own destinies, making ourselves into the kind of people we wish to become. Religion shapes our personal identity, helps to make us into pious or irreverent or saintly or vicious or unremarkable characters.

The two readings selected to examine religious character are by Muslims. Jalal Al-e Ahmad is an Iranian and a critic of the established Iranian political and religious order. He writes about his experience on his *hajj* to Mecca, and his reflections show him to be a thoroughly modern man who is skeptical about many traditional Muslim beliefs. Al-e Ahmad knows that Islam shares central beliefs and values with Christianity and Judaism, beliefs such as monotheism and values such as the sanctity of every individual. But he is concerned about the influence of the Western consumeristic mentality on Islamic culture, and he devotes his life to writing imaginative stories and essays to hone the critical skills of his Muslim readers. In order to do this, he must answer the central question of religious personal identity, "Who am I?" a question he asks in the very first paragraph of his story. As a way of answering this question, Al-e Ahmad not only goes on his pilgrimage, but he writes about his experiences as a way to observe and find himself.

Zaynab al-Ghazali al-Jabili is an Egyptian Muslim whose character develops very differently from Al-e Ahmad's. Early in her life, al-Ghazali becomes active in a movement called the Muslim Brotherhood. The movement is aimed at suffusing all of Egyptian life with the principles and teaching of the prophet Muhammad. As Valerie Hoffman explains, al-Ghazali is

> editor of the section of *Al-da'wa* magazine entitled "Toward a Muslim Home"...[The section includes] a feature entitled "Know the Enemies of Your Religion" that encourages children to hate and fear Zionists, imperialists, and evangelicals, who are accused of working to undermine Islamic religion and society.[5]

In the popular press of the United States, stories sometimes appear about the oppression and mistreatment of women in Islam. Al-Ghazali's story shows that many Islamic religious organizations are now open to women, and that women have played an important role in Islamic society. Al-Ghazali's personal identity grows as she is able to press her case that Egypt should be a Muslim state in wider and wider arenas. In her story we see the effects on a woman's character of one of the world's most influential religions.

We have discussed the elements of autobiography and offered a working definition of religion. Although a narrow definition of religion, like every definition of religion, is contentious, I have given reasons for thinking that it is a fruitful approach. It is time to summarize our discussion, and to offer a definition of religious autobiography.

Religious autobiography is the story of someone's life, or the story of some part of someone's life, as that person remembers, selectively reconstructs, and writes it insofar as it involves cultus, creed, community, code, course, and character, some of which the author explains by reference to the uncanny.

---

5. Valerie J. Hoffman, "An Islamic Activist: Zaynab al-Ghazali," in Elizabeth Warnock Fernea, ed. *Women and the Family in the Middle East*: *New Voices of Change* (Austin, Tex.: University of Texas Press, 1985), p. 233.

Chapter 3

How Should I Respond to Religious Autobiography?

IN the first chapter I introduced the ideas of empathic and critical readings. In interpreting religious autobiographies we should try to respond first by attempting to understand the author's experience as the author understands it and, second, by raising questions of our own about the narrative. To read a text in the first way is to adopt a receptive stance, an attitude of mind in which we are open to instruction. In trying to understand another person's religious experience *empathically*, we display the virtues of empathy: an affinity for the Other, an inclination to harmonize our thoughts with theirs, to interpret the world through their conceptual categories, and to enter sympathetically into their feelings, emotions, and desires. In empathic understanding, we "stand under" the Other, as if the Other were our teacher, and we avoid making hasty judgments about another's words or deeds.

Empathic understanding is possible because humans are introspective creatures with an interest in knowing themselves. We learn that knowing ourselves comes through learning about others, and we learn that others are like us in basic ways: we all, for example, have experiences; we all want things; we all know what it is to be loyal to and betrayed by someone, and to be puzzled by someone's motives. Because we have interests, dispositions, and desires, we can understand that others' actions stem from interests, dispositions, and desires similar to ours. Therefore, trying to understand others in ways that are genuine and full of fellow-feeling is to engage in an activity that declares our solidarity, our common humanity with others.

The most important step in empathic understanding is to interpret the other's experience in *their* terms. In the end, of course, we must use our own categories to understand authors because understanding is ultimately possible only in terms with which we are familiar. But nonetheless, our own terms can be expanded, and we can acquire horizons and categories we did not previously possess. Before we allow ourselves to think that we "know" an author, we ought to "walk a mile in their moccasins" and, as we walk that mile, we ought to stretch ourselves, trying to interpret what we see in terms of the author's categories.

Each of us has a storehouse of concepts, memories, hopes, fears, and dreams we use to make sense of new surroundings, and empathic understanding enlists this past fund of experience to make sense out of new, foreign experiences. In empathic understanding of a text, aim at being able to give so careful an account of what you are reading that the authors, should they hear your interpretation, will be inclined to say, "Yes, that's what we experienced; that's what we meant: You understand us." The best way to elicit this sort of response, however, is not simply to repeat what the author writes, but to recall experiences of your own similar to the authors', drawing on them to highlight similarities and differences between your experiences and theirs.

EMPATHIC QUESTIONS

In reading a religious autobiography empathically, watch for the seven characteristics of religion. Here are some questions you might use as guides.

On Cultus

What ritualistic events in the story bind people together or tear them apart? For example, in my autobiography, what kind of religious action did my friends in the cabin want me to perform, and what was its function in our little community?

On Creed

What propositional beliefs does the author hold about the uncanny? For example, what worldview did my friends reveal in their prayer? Did they see the world as a giant peaceful sphere, or as a battlefield between good and evil?

On the unCanny

What is the nature of the transcendent in the author's experience? For example, did my experience with what Rudolph Otto calls the *mysterium tremendum* frighten me or reassure me? Did God appear in an ordinary and mundane way, or in a supernatural and miraculous way?

On Community

In what ways do the institutions and larger groupings of a tradition impinge on the author's experience? For example, were there groups of religious people in my experience that served to inhibit me from speaking in tongues? Were there groups that exerted communal peer pressure and encouraged me to do it?

On Code

What actions are regarded as evil by the author's community, and which ones are regarded as morally good? For example, the couple in my story was married, and believed that the Bible provides the moral norms for the Christian community. What do you think they would have said about the rightness or wrongness of premarital sex?

On Course

What are the religious histories of the individual authors? What are the longer religious histories of the traditions in which they are raised? For example, I referred to the Christian and Missionary Alliance denomination. How did that group originate, and how did its particular rituals and beliefs affect my identity? You probably know very little about the history of the C&MA. How would you proceed in trying to research this topic?

On Character

What sort of personality traits does the author exhibit? For example, I wrote that I wanted to get up and look around for the source of the running water, and yet I yielded to another impulse to relax and stay where I was. What does this decision tell you about my tendencies in the areas of being inquisitive, obedient, and predisposed to listen to authority rather than skeptically to question it?

Asking yourself questions such as these will help you to discover the religious elements of the autobiographies.

QUESTIONS ON LITERARY FORM

You should also be ready to ask yourself questions about the form of the materials. I have mentioned four characteristics of stories: plot, character, style, and mood. Here are some questions you might use to explore the *literary* constructions we call autobiographies.

On Plot

What is the plot of the autobiography? What is:

- the initial setting?

- the challenge the author must address, and the changes the author must make as a result of the problem?

- the final resolution of the problem or conflict?

On Character

Who is the author? What is the author's religious background? What sort of person is he or she when the story opens, and how does that change through the course of the narrative? Describe the author's likes and dislikes. Do you find the author interesting or offensive? Do you think you could be friends? Why or why not? How is the author's character revealed through:

- acquaintances?

- feelings, hopes, dreams?

- decisions about important matters in the story?

- decisions about how to present the author's self in the story?

On Style

Is the author self-conscious about writing a literary piece? Does the text read more like the author is sitting in your room talking to you, or more like the author has written, edited, and revised the manuscript fifty times? First sentences and paragraphs are important. Do the first words of the autobiography reveal the author's central religious concerns? Last words are also important. What is the last paragraph about, and how does it summarize the author's journey?

On Mood

What emotional tone does the author set? Is this a work of inward reminiscence like "A Night in Buena Vista," or does it have a more outward political focus? How does the story make you feel as a reader? Are any of the author's experiences similar to yours? Are there any experiences in the story you would definitely like to have, or definitely *not* like to have? Which experiences seem most strange to you? Which ones seem most familiar? Does the story make you want to learn more about the author's religious tradition, hopes, fears, beliefs, values, or practices?

Our first response to a religious autobiography should be an empathic one in which we try to get inside the author's mind by examining the scope and breadth of his or her religious experience and the literary construction of the text. But empathy is not the end of the matter, and we should guard against the temptation to think that everything we need to know about an author is right on the surface of the tale. As the example of my religious autobiography shows, there are powerful forces underneath the narrative surface working their illusions on readers and authors alike. Like authors, readers must work to unearth and identify the forces, and this is where critical thinking comes in. It is a tempting but untrue belief that autobiographies only *reveal* their authors. Authors give us highly selective versions of their histories, versions that paint the authors in the colors they prefer. Try to figure out why authors choose these colors rather than those. For example, why did I choose to tell about my experience with Lynn, and not about my experience with Kathy, the girl I dated as a senior in high school, or Karen, the woman to whom I am married? Why did I tell about a strange religious ritual I no longer practice rather than telling about a more mundane one I still observe? Why did I describe my father but not Lynn's? Authors have the ability to select the impression of themselves they want to leave on readers, and you should be attentive to the dimensions of each autobiography that *conceal* the authors. A proper response to autobiography requires critical thought about the illusions of autobiography.

CRITICAL UNDERSTANDING

What is *critical* understanding? Critical understanding is a more aggressive frame of mind in which we dispose ourselves toward questioning others. In trying to understand another person's religious experience critically, we display the virtues of constructive criticism: a desire for others to improve themselves by hearing thoughts that differ from, and perhaps conflict with, their thoughts; an inclination to disagree politely on matters of importance; an aspiration to render valid and discerning judgments; an attitude of analytical examination that identifies merits and weaknesses and culminates in decision. In critical understanding, we "stand over" the Other, assume the attitude of questioner, and refuse to believe naively authors' interpretations of their words and deeds just because they are *their* interpretations. We try to find interpretations that cohere with our own web of beliefs and expectations.

Perhaps the most important step in critical understanding is to try to anticipate dangers or weaknesses in the Other's experience, dangers or weaknesses that the Other may not see. "Walk a mile in their moccasins" is good advice, but when we are done we should see if we cannot imagine a better route, or a better way to build these moccasins. Here, we use our own storehouse of scientific beliefs, religious myths, and communal knowledge to raise questions about the "spin" the authors put on their memories. We want our critical questions to be constructive, not mean-spirited, and our questions should be the kind of questions that will challenge authors, not humiliate them. They should be the kind of questions authors will find helpful should they decide to rewrite their autobiography, and questions authors will find fruitful as they continue to think about their religious convictions. Others are not likely to be made better by our criticisms unless we have first convinced them we know what they have experienced. In sum, we are not likely to make constructive criticisms of others unless our criticisms are charitable and emerge from empathic understanding. But once we have understood others in this way, we have earned the right to "overstand" them to some degree, to interpret their experience *to* them.

One way to respond critically is to ask ourselves what the author has left out. Think about my autobiography. You may be thinking that it is plenty long and that I have not left out anything. It is true; I have included quite a bit of my life in the story. But notice, there is a great deal I have written nothing about. I wrote nothing about my experiences from birth until age eighteen, nothing about my other friends at Deer Valley, nothing about what happened to me after my freshman year in college. Nor did I analyze the validity of the biblical interpretations of *glossolalia* to which I allude in my story. I did not give you any information about how the world was perceived by other wranglers or crew girls at the ranch and I did not say anything about my parents' reaction to my experience. Authors cannot tell us *everything* about themselves (thank goodness!) and part of the pleasure of learning to read texts critically is learning how to read between the lines, how to figure out what the authors are *not* telling us.

A good strategy to discover what is missing is to read against the grain. Imagine yourself face to face with the authors. If they explicitly invited you to second-guess them, to question their judgments, how would you respond? What, for example, would you ask me about the selective construction I have used in writing my story?

Perhaps you would want to ask me one of the following kinds of questions:

- Given what happened to your tongues speaking after Lynn broke up with you, don't you think your charismatic friends were right, that your spiritual enthusiasm was really just misplaced love for your girlfriend?

- Perhaps your uncanny experience was not so uncanny at all: Given the fact that Colorado hayfields must be irrigated, could not the strange sound of running water have been coming from an irrigation ditch you simply could not see that dark night?

- Why did you let your tongues-speaking skill die? No religious experience miraculously continues by itself. Might you not still be talking in tongues if you had apprenticed yourself to a tongues-speaking spiritual master and worshiped in a Pentecostal church?

There are many other questions of a critical sort you could ask about my story, and I suggest the questions above only as examples.

CRITICAL QUESTIONS

Here are some general questions to keep in mind as questions you might ask any of the authors collected in this book.

1. What does the author not tell us that we would like to know?

2. How does the plot of the autobiography conceal important dimensions of the author's character? That is:

   • What experiences does the author seem unmindful of, or unreceptive toward?

   • What problems does the author ignore?

   • Does the author's way of resolving problems create any new problems?

3. Does the author have any failings? Does the author seem to underestimate the importance of:

   • his or her acquaintances?

   • his or her decisions about important matters?

   • the feelings, hopes, and dreams of others?

4. What don't you like about the author?

Authors might hide things consciously, as when I chose not to reveal details about the physical relationship Lynn and I shared. But they might also hide things unconsciously, as when I failed to tell you that I returned to my friends' ranch years later and discovered an irrigation ditch running right by the cabin. Things are not always the way our autobiographies make them seem, and because autobiographies conceal as they reveal, you must learn to read critically as well as empathically.

WRITE YOUR OWN

We have defined religion and autobiography, and read one religious autobiography. At this point your instructor may want you to try your hand at writing your own religious autobiography. In one way, this assignment will be an easy one, because the hardest part of writing a paper is usually deciding on a topic. In this case, the topic is straightforward—your life story—and your research is almost finished because you are already the world's expert on your topic! The majority of your research for this assignment will come *as* you compose the autobiography, because as you write you will start asking yourself questions, questions about your life and questions about your textual reconstruction of it:

- What events are most important in my life?

- Should I begin my story in conventional fashion with the date of my birth and the names of my parents?

- Or will my autobiography be more revealing if I begin it with the phone call in which I learned of my best friend's death in a car accident?

- Who am I?

- How do I communicate who I am?

As you research your life, select from it those events that have played a central role in forming your identity: accumulate facts, marshall your feelings, articulate your views, and then narrate a story based on the memories you consciously select.

Since writing a regular autobiography can be difficult, do not be surprised if you find the assignment of writing your *religious* autobiography particularly challenging. There will be difficult questions to answer. Which part of your life, if any, is the most religious part? Religious feelings are often very personal. Is the most religious part of your life something you even want to share with others? I must admit I had second thoughts about publishing my story after seeing it on the typed page and thinking about all of the people who might read it: Karen, John Woolmington, my colleagues in the Philosophy Department, my parents, Lynn. And having my memory of Lynn at the airport appear in black and white seemed somehow to make it less powerful. To have offered this once-private image to others had the curious effect of making it less vivid to me; I do not see Lynn's face as clearly as I once did. To decide on the precise focus of your autobiography, therefore, you must decide whether you want to share at all, and whether you can live with the possibility that writing down your memories may change them.

Once you have answered that question, you must decide whether to try to tell a little bit about your entire life or a lot about one aspect. In making this decision, ask whether you have had a particular experience, positive or negative or both, with religion. Perhaps you have had a dramatic conversion experience, or a specific episode with loving parents or an irritating rabbi, that affected you. If so, your autobiography may look something like mine in that its time framework will be limited to a definite period, perhaps a single month.

Then again, perhaps nothing miraculous or even unusual has ever happened to you. You may consider yourself an atheist, not a religious person at all. Can you write a "religious autobiography"? Probably not, if the narrow definition is used. But you can write an autobiography that explains why your autobiography is *not* religious. Use the assignment to figure out whether you have witnessed events or entertained ideas that moved you to become an atheist in this, one of the most religious of cultures.

Then again, perhaps nothing extraordinary has ever happened to you, but you believe in God for your own reasons. You may want to describe your experience in catechism class, or talk about some books that have helped shape your spirituality. Perhaps you have recently begun to think about life and death because someone close to you has died. Death has a way of leading all of us to ponder the mysteries of bodies, corpses, and souls, and it often causes old and young alike to doubt whether God loves us, or even whether God is there. Any one of these ideas could be your theme. In choosing your topic, remember that there is no right or wrong subject matter. You are writing about yourself, so whatever story you decide to tell *will be* the right story for you. Remember that writing your autobiography should help you express your experiences by giving voice to some of your deepest feelings in an idiom very different from most theological, philosophical, and scientific ways of speaking. But if you find the assignment a tough one, remember that it is also an important one. In some ways, it may be the college assignment that has the longest lasting significance for you, because this assignment gives you the opportunity to articulate the temporal drama of your life and to craft your many experiences into a single paper. Because the story form enables you to connect past events with present events and to make a changing temporal kaleidoscope of occurrences into one story, the result of this assignment may be a paper from college you want to preserve for your grandchildren.

Steps to Writing Your Autobiography

Here are some steps you may find useful in writing your religious autobiography:

1. Decide whether you want to write about a single event, about several related events, or about your life as a whole.

2. Identify the element or elements that, in your mind, qualifies the event or events as *religious*.

3. Is this religious element primarily a manifestation of cultus, community, code, character, course, creed, or the uncanny? Chances are that your experience(s) may have several of these characteristics, but try to identify the elements of religion that are most prominent.

4. Begin writing by telling your name, where you're from, who your parents are, and so on, just as if you were introducing yourself to a stranger.

5. Then get right into the story. Start at the beginning. Tell where you were, who you were with, and, most important, how you felt when the experience started.

6. Move through the middle of the story, telling us how the scene changed, how the characters in the story may have changed, and, most important, how your emotions changed.

7. Conclude by telling how the experience ended and what conclusions you took from it. Is it completely over? If not, how does it continue to affect you? If it is not over, are you happy or sad that it is not over?

Remember the overall purpose of this assignment and the potential personal significance it may have for you. The assignment presents you with the opportunity to reflect on the meaning of your life. Seize the opportunity and pursue it with empathic and critical understanding.

A LAST WARNING

I want to reemphasize a point made in the Introduction. The scheme adopted to present the following autobiographies should not confuse you. I chose to focus on only one of the seven characteristics of religion for each tradition, but this does not mean that each religion is especially connected with that characteristic. In studying Native American religions we focus on ritual; in studying Hinduism we focus on creed; in studying Zen Buddhism we focus on the uncanny; and so on. I chose the method in order to simplify study, but do not think that the scheme implies either (a) that ritual is the most important part of Lakota Sioux religion or (b) that ritual is not important in Hinduism or Zen Buddhism. It is fair to say that all of religion's seven dimensions are important in all traditions.

Unit II

Religious Autobiographies

Chapter 4

Lakota Sioux

C U L T U S

HEN I was a young child, my family drove west along Interstate 90 through the Black Hills of South Dakota. Along the way, we saw tourist stops selling "Indian" goods of one sort or another: eagle feathers, headbands with red and white beads, wooden pipes, plastic bows and arrows. I instantly wanted a pair of leather mocassins and a ticket to the "authentic Indian rain dance" held Saturday night. I was intrigued by Native American life, it seemed so exotic and different from mine. Later in life I learned the real history of the relations between what Mary Crow Dog here calls the *wasicun,* or "white man," and the "breeds," or Native Americans. Later in life I gained a different perspective on the value of the tourist stops for my culture and for Native American culture. In the two readings of this chapter, you will listen to parts of the life stories of two members of the Lakota Sioux tribe of South Dakota: John Fire Lame Deer and Mary Crow Dog. From these stories you will gain a more complete and accurate account of the "exotic" life of some Native Americans, and the tourist's view of "Indian" life will begin to fade as you learn about the real lives of two Lakota Sioux. Parts of their lives may still seem very different from yours, but other parts may be more familiar than you expect.

You will also be introduced to the dimension of religion that is probably the most visible of religion's seven characteristics: ritual. Rituals are activities that provide a temporal rhythm and coherence to the religious life of a community, activities performed at regular or irregular intervals. They are more or less formal observances and are sometimes serious, solemn, almost trancelike, as in a funeral. At other times religious rituals are less formal, and are sometimes merry, joyful, even humorous, as in some weddings. Going to Sunday School and church once a week on Sunday morning is a ritual observance, as is going to synagogue to study Torah on Saturday morning or facing Mecca five times a day to pray to Allah. Think of the function of a ritual in the way you think of the functioning of a grandfather clock. By regularly tolling the time, the clock lends structure to the afternoon and divides it into manageable fifteen-minute segments. When the chimes sound, we are alerted that one period has just ended and another is about to begin. By regularly marking different segments of our lives, religious rituals alert us that one period is ending and another beginning. When we go weekly to church, synagogue, or mosque, our lives are divided into segments, giving us the opportunity to reflect on memories of the seven days just passed and to prepare for events in the period to come.

The c word I have suggested we use to remember ritual is *cultus*. Cultus derives from a term used by early historians of religion to refer to the ceremonies observed in the ancient Israelite temple. There are several rituals that are central to Lakota Sioux life, and the selections that follow do not, of course, introduce you to all of them. But they introduce four rituals central to this way of life: the vision quest, performed individually by young people and marking a symbolic transformation out of childhood and into the adult community; the sweat bath; the peyote-induced visions of the Native American Church; and the Sun Dance. John Fire Lame Deer begins his story on a hill in his home country, the Badlands, or Black Hills of South Dakota. He is sixteen and on his vision quest, an occasion for adolescents to meditate on the past and ask for dreams by which to direct their future. Later in his story, Lame Deer describes the Sun Dance, in which participants memorialize the past and draw courage and strength from nature. The ritual introduces an element of human experience found in many but not all religious traditions: self-inflicted pain. Think carefully about the justifications Lame Deer and Mary Crow Dog offer for the voluntary suffering of the dancers. Ask yourself whether you find any parallel to rituals in your tradition or other traditions.

You may know that the tradition from which our two authors come is very old, and their communities have practiced similar rituals in North America for thousands of years. Before Columbus "discovered" this country, various civilizations comprising more than 100 million people stretched completely across the continents we know as North America, Central America, and South America. In the continental United States alone there were no fewer than five major language groups, with languages as different as English, German, and Italian: the Algonkian, the Iroquois, the Uto-Aztecan, the Athabascan, and the Penutian. What you may not know is that after Columbus made his trips from Spain, the European explorers arrived in such numbers, and with such overpowering weapons, that the native populations were decimated. In less than five hundred years, more than 90 percent of the indigenous people had been wiped out, either intentionally by explorers wielding guns or unintentionally by explorers unwittingly carrying exotic diseases from Europe.

Both Lame Deer and Crow Dog are Lakota Sioux, and in both autobiographies we learn that their communities have not escaped oppression and indignity at the hands of the *wasicun*. Lame Deer's grandfather fought at Wounded Knee, a Native American uprising in 1890 provoked by the failure of the U.S. government to keep promises made in legally ratified treaties. At that first incident at Wounded Knee, men, women, and children were massacred by U.S. troops. A second incident occurred at Wounded Knee in 1972. Crow Dog's story opens with the birth of her child as bullets fly during that episode, and she remarks early on that it is not easy to be a Lakota Sioux woman. What other examples of hardship does she give?

Mary Crow Dog married Leonard Crow Dog, a holy man in the American Indian Movement (AIM). In 1968 members of the Ojibway tribe in Saint Paul, Minnesota, began to organize themselves in an effort to address the poverty of inner-city Native Americans. They championed the wearing of traditional dress, and especially black hats with feathers in the headband. In 1972 AIM adherents occupied the area at Wounded Knee after being frustrated by their inability to focus the U.S. government's attention on their demands, and the seige climaxed in a gunfight with police. Mary Crow Dog's autobiography gives us one woman's perspective on her rising political consciousness, her love for her family, and her growing appreciation for the value of her religious tradition and its rituals. From her text we are able to gain an insider's perspective on what it is like to be a Native American woman. Ask yourself why Crow Dog wants to engage in the piercing of skin that has traditionally been reserved for Sioux men. Compare the way that her culture treats her first menstrual period with the way such an event is treated in white culture. And try to figure out what she thinks about the treatment of Lakota Sioux women by their own men.

Notice, finally, the importance of geography and place to the rituals described by Lame Deer and Crow Dog. Crow Dog writes that the area around Grass Mountain "is at the core of our existence." Why is that? Why would land be so important to Sioux identity, and such an important part of rituals like the Sun Dance? Is your place, your "land," at the core of your existence in a similar way?

John Fire Lame Deer

From John Fire/Lame Deer and Richard Erdoes,
Lame Deer: Seeker of Visions
(New York: Simon and Schuster, 1972).
Reprinted by permission of Richard Erdoes.

I was all alone on the hilltop. I sat there in the vision pit, a hole dug into the hill, my arms hugging my knees as I watched old man Chest, the medicine man who had brought me there, disappear far down in the valley. He was just a moving black dot among the pines, and soon he was gone altogether.

Now I was all by myself, left on the hilltop for four days and nights without food or water until he came back for me. You know, we Indians are not like some white folks—a man and a wife, two children, and one baby-sitter who watches the TV set while the parents are out visiting somewhere.

Indian children are never alone. They are always surrounded by grandparents, uncles, cousins, relatives of all kinds, who fondle the kids, sing to them, tell them stories. If the parents go someplace, the kids go along.

But here I was, crouched in my vision pit, left alone by myself for the first time in my life. I was sixteen then, still had my boy's name and, let me tell you, I was scared. I was shivering and not only from the cold. The nearest human being was many miles away, and four days and nights is a long, long time. Of course, when it was all over, I would no longer be a boy, but a man. I would have had my vision. I would be given a man's name.

Sioux men are not afraid to endure hunger, thirst, and loneliness, and I was only ninety-six hours away from being a man. The thought was comforting. Comforting, too, was the warmth of the star blanket that old man Chest had wrapped around me to cover my nakedness. My grandmother had made it especially for this, my first *hanblechia*, my first vision-seeking. It was a beautifully designed quilt, white with a large morning star made of many pieces of brightly colored cloth. That star was so big it covered most of the blanket. If Wakan Tanka, the Great Spirit, would give me the vision and the power, I would become a medicine man and perform many ceremonies wrapped in that quilt. I am an old man now and many times a grandfather, but I still have that star blanket my grandmother made for me. I treasure it; someday I shall be buried in it.

The medicine man had also left a peace pipe with me, together with a bag of *kinnickinnick*—our kind of tobacco made of red willow bark. This pipe was even more of a friend to me than my star blanket. To us the pipe is like an open Bible. White people need a church house, a preacher, and a pipe organ to get into a praying mood. There are so many things to distract you: who else is in the church, whether the other people notice that you have come, the pictures on the wall, the sermon, how much money you should give and did you bring it with you. We think you can't have a vision that way.

For us Indians there is just the pipe, the earth we sit on, and the open sky. The spirit is everywhere. Sometimes it shows itself through an animal, a bird, or some trees and hills. Sometimes it speaks from the Badlands, a stone, or even from the water. That smoke from the peace pipe, it goes straight up to the spirit world. But this is a two-way thing. Power flows down to us through that smoke, through the pipe stem. You feel that power as you hold your pipe; it moves from the pipe right into your body. It makes your hair stand up. That pipe is not just a thing; it is alive. Smoking this pipe would make me feel good and help me to get rid of my fears.

As I ran my fingers along its bowl of smooth red pipestone, red like the blood of my people, I no longer felt scared. That pipe had belonged to my father and to his father before him. It would someday pass to my son and, through him, to my grandchildren. As long as we had the pipe there would be a Sioux nation. As I fingered the pipe, touched it, felt its smoothness that came from long use, I sensed that my forefathers who had once smoked this pipe were with me on the hill, right in the vision pit. I was no longer alone.

Besides the pipe the medicine man had also given me a gourd. In it were forty small squares of flesh that my grandmother had cut from her arm with a razor blade. I had seen her do it. Blood had been streaming down from her shoulder to her elbow as she carefully put down each piece of skin on a handkerchief, anxious not to lose a single one. It would have made those anthropologists mad. Imagine, performing such an ancient ceremony with a razor blade instead of a flint knife! To me it did not matter. Someone dear to me had undergone pain, given me something of herself, part of her body, to help me pray and make me stronghearted. How could I be afraid with so many people—living and dead—helping me?

One thing still worried me. I wanted to become a medicine man, a *yuwipi,* a healer carrying on the ancient ways of the Sioux nation. But you cannot learn to be a medicine man like a white man going to medical school. An old holy man can teach you about herbs and the right ways to perform a ceremony where everything must be in its proper place, where every move, every word has its own, special meaning. These things you can learn—like spelling, like training a horse. But by themselves these things mean nothing. Without the vision and the power this learning will do no good. It would not make me a medicine man.

What if I failed, if I had no vision? Or if I dreamed of the Thunder Beings, or lightning struck the hill? That would make me at once into a *heyoka,* a contrarywise, an upside-down man, a clown. "You'll know it, if you get the power," my Uncle Chest had told me. "If you are not given it, you won't lie about it, you won't pretend. That would kill you, or kill somebody close to you, somebody you love."

Night was coming on. I was still lightheaded and dizzy from my first sweat bath in which I had purified myself before going up the hill. I had never been in a sweat lodge before. I had sat in the little beehive-shaped hut made of bent willow branches and covered with blankets to keep the heat in. Old Chest and three other medicine men had been in the lodge with me. I had my back against the wall, edging as far away as I could from the red-hot stones glowing in the center. As Chest poured water over the rocks, hissing white steam enveloped me and filled my lungs. I thought the heat would kill me, burn the eyelids off my face! But right in the middle of all this swirling steam I heard Chest singing. So it couldn't be all that bad. I did not cry out "All my relatives!"—which would have made him open the flap of the sweat lodge to let in some cool air—and I was proud of this. I heard him praying for me: "Oh, holy rocks, we receive your white breath, the steam. It is the breath of life. Let this young boy inhale it. Make him strong."

The sweat bath had prepared me for my vision-seeking. Even now, an hour later, my skin still tingled. But it seemed to have made my brains empty. Maybe that was good, plenty of room for new insights.

Darkness had fallen upon the hill. I knew that *hanhepi-wi* had risen, the night sun, which is what we call the moon. Huddled in my narrow cave, I did not see it. Blackness was wrapped around me like a velvet cloth. It seemed to cut me off from the outside world, even from my own body. It made me listen to the voices within me. I thought of my forefathers who had crouched on this hill before me, because the medicine men in my family had chosen this spot for a place of meditation and vision-seeking ever since the day they had crossed the Missouri to hunt for buffalo in the White River country some two hundred years ago. I thought that I could sense their presence right through the earth I was leaning against. I could feel them entering my body, feel them stirring in my mind and heart.

Sounds came to me through the darkness: the cries of the wind, the whisper of the trees, the voices of nature, animal sounds, the hooting of an owl. Suddenly I felt an overwhelming presence. Down there with me in my cramped hole was a big bird. The pit was only as wide as myself, and I was a skinny boy, but that huge bird was flying around me as if he had the whole sky to himself. I could hear his cries, sometimes near and sometimes far, far away. I felt feathers or a wing touching my back and head. This feeling was so overwhelming that it was just too much for me. I trembled and my bones turned to ice. I grasped the rattle with the forty pieces of my grandmother's flesh. It also had many little stones in it, tiny fossils picked up from an ant heap. Ants collect them. Nobody knows why. These little stones are supposed to have a power in them. I shook the rattle and it made a soothing sound, like rain falling on rock. It was talking to me, but it did not calm my fears. I took the sacred pipe in my other hand and began to sing and pray: "Tunkashila, grandfather spirit, help me." But this did not help. I don't know what got into me, but I was no longer myself. I started to cry. Crying, even my voice was different. I sounded like an older man, I couldn't even recognize this strange voice. I used long-ago words in my prayer, words no longer used nowadays. I tried to wipe away my tears, but they wouldn't stop. In the end I just pulled that quilt over me, rolled myself up in it. Still I felt the bird wings touching me.

Slowly I perceived that a voice was trying to tell me something. It was a bird cry, but I tell you, I began to understand some of it. That happens sometimes. I know a lady who had a butterfly sitting on her shoulder. That butterfly told her things. This made her become a great medicine woman.

I heard a human voice too, strange and high-pitched, a voice that could not come from an ordinary, living being. All at once I was way up there with the birds. The hill with the vision pit was way above everything. I could look down even on the stars, and the moon was close to my left side. It seemed as though the earth and the stars were moving below me. A voice said, "You are sacrificing yourself here to be a medicine man. In time you will be one. You will teach other medicine men. We are the fowl people, the winged ones, the eagles and the owls. We are a nation and you shall be our brother. You will never kill or harm any one of us. You are going to understand us whenever you come to seek a vision here on this hill. You will learn about herbs and roots, and you will heal people. You will ask them for nothing in return. A man's life is short. Make yours a worthy one."

I felt that these voices were good; and slowly my fear left me. I had lost all sense of time. I did not know whether it was day or night. I was asleep, yet wide awake. Then I saw a shape before me. It rose from the darkness and the swirling fog that penetrated my earth hole. I saw that this was my great-grandfather, Tahca Ushte, Lame Deer, old man chief of the Minneconjou. I could see the blood dripping from my great-grandfather's chest where a white soldier had shot him. I understood that my great-grandfather wished me to take his name. This made me glad beyond words.

We Sioux believe that there is something within us that controls us, something like a second person almost. We call it *nagi,* what other people might call soul, spirit, or essence. One can't see it, feel it, or taste it, but that time on the hill—and only that once—I knew it was there inside of me. Then I felt the power surge through me like a flood. I cannot describe it, but it filled all of me. Now I knew for sure that I would become a *wicasa wakan,* a medicine man. Again I wept, this time with happiness.

I didn't know how long I had been up there on that hill—one minute or a lifetime. I felt a hand on my shoulder gently shaking me. It was old man Chest, who had come for me. He told me that I had been in the vision pit four days and four nights and that it was time to come down. He would give me some-thing to eat and water to drink and then I was to tell him everything that had happened to

me during my *hanblechia.* He would interpret my visions for me. He told me that the vision pit had changed me in a way that I would not be able to understand at that time. He told me also that I was no longer a boy, that I was a man now. I was Lame Deer.

In the Museum of the American Indian in New York are two glass cases. A sign over them reads: "Famous Guns of Famous Indian Chiefs." They have five or six guns there, Sitting Bull's among them. A note next to one of these old breechloaders says that it belonged to the famous Chief Lame Deer, killed in a battle with General Miles, who generously donated this gun to the New York museum. I don't know what right old Bear Coat Miles had to be that free with other people's property. That gun didn't belong to him. It belongs to me. I am the only Lame Deer left.

I am a medicine man and I want to talk about visions, spirits, and sacred things. But you must know something about the man Lame Deer before you can understand the medicine man Lame Deer. So I will start with the man, the boy, and we'll get to the medicine part later.

Tahca Ushte—the first Lame Deer—was my great-grandfather on my father's side. He was killed by mistake. You could say he was murdered. A year before this so-called battle with General Miles, Lame Deer had made his final peace with the white man. He had made an agreement with the U.S. Government. By this treaty they measured off four square miles west of what is now Rapid City, South Dakota. This was to be a reservation for the chief and his people, and it was to be called Lame Deer after him. This land was to be ours forever— "as long as the sun shines and the grass grows." These days smog is hiding the sun and there's little grass left in Rapid City now. Maybe the white people had a gift of foreseeing this when they took our land before the ink on that treaty was dry.

Lame Deer said that he would sign this treaty if he and his people could go out on one last hunt and live for just one more summer in the good old way—going after the buffalo. After that they would all settle down on their new reservation and "walk the white man's road." The Government people said that this was all right and gave him permission for his last hunt. They shook hands on it.

The U.S. Government is a strange monster with many heads. One head doesn't know what the others are up to. The Army had given Lame Deer its word that he could hunt in peace. At the same time it told old Bear Coat Miles that any Indians found hunting off the reservations were to be attacked as "hostiles." Lame Deer had gone north in the spring of 1877 to his favorite buffalo range between the Rosebud and Bighorn rivers. He had camped in the Wolf Mountains along Fat Horse Creek.

The old people have told me that the prairie had never been more beautiful than it was that spring. The grass was high and green. The slopes were covered with flowers, and the air was full of good smells and the song of birds. If the Indians had only one more hunt left, this was how they wished it to be. Lame Deer knew that there were soldiers around, but this did not worry him. He had a right to be where he was. Besides, any fool could see that he was not about to make war on anybody. He had all the women and children with him. His fifty lodges were full of meat and hides. His people had come as to a feast. They were dressed in their finery and beaded goods. They were enjoying their last vacation from the white man.

General Miles was stupid not to grasp this, but I think that he acted in good faith. Nobody had told him about the treaty. He had six companies of walking soldiers and several troops of cavalry, more men than all the Indians together, including the women and children. The blue coats came tearing into the camp, shooting and yelling, stampeding the horses

and riding down the people. At the same time one of them carried a white flag of truce.

Seeing the peaceful camp from up close, Bear Coat Miles, I believe, changed his mind and regretted what was happening. He began waving his arms, trying to stop the killing, shouting over and over again, *"Kola, kola—* friend, friend." His Indian scouts took up the cry. They too started shouting, "We are friends!" It sure was a strange way for friends to drop in, but my great-grandfather pretended to believe them. He didn't want his people to be killed. He dropped his gun as a sign of peace.

General Miles rushed up to him, grabbed his hand and started shaking it. He kept shouting, *"Kola, kola."* But peace was not what his soldiers wanted. They wanted Indian scalps and souvenirs. Probably they also wanted to get at the women and girls. One trooper came riding up and fired his carbine at Lame Deer. Miles hung onto my great-grandfather's arm with both hands, but the chief tore himself loose and picked up his gun, shooting the man who had fired on him. Then all the soldiers opened up with everything they had, killing Lame Deer, his second chief, Iron Star, and about a dozen more of the warriors. Then they plundered the tipis, taking what they wanted and destroying the rest. Even General Miles was not too proud to take a few things for himself, and that is why my ancestor's gun is in a New York museum instead of hanging on my wall.

About those four square miles along the Rapid River: When the treaty was signed Lame Deer said, "If I ever die, or the school closes, this land shall go to my first son and, if he dies, to his son, and so on down the line." I tried to sue the Government for this land, and they said, "No personal Indian claims allowed." Maybe it was a good thing that they would not let us Indians keep that land. Think of what would have been missed: the motels with their neon signs, the pawn shops, the Rock Hunter's Paradise, the Horned Trophies Taxidermist

Studio, the giftie shoppies, the Genuine Indian Crafts Center with its beadwork from Taiwan and Hong Kong, the Sitting Bull Cave—electrically lighted for your convenience—the Shrine of Democracy Souvenir Shop, the Fun House—the talk of your trip for years to come—the Bucket of Blood Saloon, the life-size dinosaur made of green concrete, the go-go gals and cat houses, the Reptile Gardens, where they don't feed the snakes because that would be too much trouble. When they die you get yourself some new rattlers for free. Just think: If that land belonged to us there would be nothing here, only trees, grass, and some animals running free. All that *real estate* would be going to waste!

My great-grandfather Lame Deer was a chief of the Mni Owoju—the Planters by the Water—one of the seven western tribes of the Sioux nation. He had three wives. His first wife had three sons: Did Not Butcher, Flying By, and my own grandfather, Cante Witko, which means Crazy Heart. The second wife had one daughter. The third wife had no children. My other grandfather was named Good Fox....

Lame Deer explains that he, like many other Indian boys and girls, was raised primarily by his grandfather, Good Fox, and grandmother, Plenty White Buffalo.

Always, after working at a white man's job or a time of hellraising, I would go back to the old men of my tribe and spend many days learning about medicine and the ancient ways. Visions, a world beyond the frog-skin world,[1] have always been very important to us. You could almost say that a man with no vision can't be a real Indian. Out in the plains we get our visions the hard way, by fasting and by staying in the vision pit for four days and nights, crying for a dream. Other tribes have the same quest for visions but search for them in a different way. Eighty years

ago the Ghost Dance religion came to us from the south, from a Paiute holy man. People danced themselves into a trance until they saw their dead relatives. The Ghost Dancers were massacred at Wounded Knee and their dream wiped out with Gatling guns. Dreams are dangerous to the frog-skin world, which tries to keep them away with cannons.

I was about twenty-one years old when some men told me, "There's a new, powerful medicine. It's going to whirl you around. It will make you see God." As with the ghost dance, the men who brought us this new medicine were not from our own tribe. One was an Arapaho and the other a Black Foot, a man called Lone Bear.

I wanted to experience this and I went to their first meeting in a lonely shack. Six men were sitting on the floor of an empty room. They had a half-gallon can full of cut-up peyote. The Arapaho and the Black Foot were talking in their language. I couldn't make it out, but I understood what they were trying to say: "Eat this and you will see a new light!" I felt strange taking this new medicine and took only a few tablespoons at first. The peyote was powerful. The drum got into me. The gourd got into me. There were voices coming to me out of that rattle. I was closing my eyes, looking inward, into myself, hunkered down on my haunches, my back against the wall feeling my bones through my skin. I liked the peyote because it whirled me around. By midnight I was having visions. First I saw a square turning into a circle, into a half moon, into a beaded belt—green and blue—that was spinning around me. I could see myself as if looking down from a high mountain, sitting with the other six men, seeing myself crouching in the corner of that log house.

Suddenly I was back within myself. My eyes were on the logs, which seemed very close by, like looking through a magnifying glass. I saw something crawling out between the chinks. It was a big ant, maybe ten feet high,

---

1. The white man's world, which is concerned primarily with getting "frog-skins," that is, greenbacks, dollars.

the biggest ant there ever was, all horns, shiny like a lobster. As the ant grew bigger, the room expanded with it. I saw insects starting to eat me. I got scared and tried to get away but couldn't move. The leader, the road man, could tell that I was seeing something. He knew how I felt. He whirled his gourd around, shook his fan of feathers at me. I came back to life, back from someplace outside the log house, it seemed to me.

I was confused. I tried to think about somebody I loved, my grandmother, my uncle—but it didn't work. My thoughts were getting away from me like a stampeding herd. I tried to think about white men, about the frog-skin world—and that didn't work. I tried to think about animals but was unable to concentrate. The men had told me, "Eat this and you will see God." I did not see God. I couldn't think in complete words, only in syllables, one syllable at a time.

I made a prayer to the Great Spirit to help me, show me. A sweet smell came up not in my nostrils but in my mind. It wasn't a perfume or a scent from nature. Only I could smell it. I saw a book turn into a rock, the rock turn into a cave. I didn't know what to make of it, but there was something *wakan,* something sacred there. I knew it was good, but it scared me at the same time.

The leader handed me the staff and the gourd. It was my turn to sing, but I didn't know how and they had to pass me by. When the sun finally came up I was exhausted and light-headed. I was shook up. Something had happened that I could not explain. It would take a long time to think about it.

I became a peyoter for a number of years and went regularly to their meetings, but I did not give myself up wholly to it. I also got myself deeper into our old Sioux beliefs, the spirit world; listened to preachers, herb men, and the *yuwipi.* I was slowly forming an idea of where I wanted to go. I could dimly see my place, but I could also see a number of different roads

leading up to it and I did not yet know which one to take. So I tried them all, coming to many dead ends.

The police tried to stamp out this new peyote cult, as they had stamped out the Ghost Dance, not because peyote was a drug—drugs weren't on our mind then—but because it was Indian, a competition to the missionaries. The police didn't like me very much anyhow, aside from the peyote. I had a place in Pine Ridge and another one in Rosebud. At Pine Ridge I kept a girl. We weren't married according to the white man's view. The missionaries called it a common-law arrangement. They didn't allow this at the time and threw you in jail for it. They said, "You can't stay together with a girl unless you are properly married—our way."

I had gone to a peyote meeting and the police came and raided it. They came at twilight. I guess they must have smelled it or somebody had tipped them off. They broke the door open looking for the peyote but they couldn't find any. It was kept two miles away from the house and hadn't been brought in yet for the meeting. As they turned the kerosene lamp up, they saw me. At once they forgot about the peyote and took after me. I was a badman in their eyes, a bad example to all the little sheep on the reservation.

The cabin was only a thousand feet away from the border line between the reservations. The Pine Ridge *and* the Rosebud police were in on the raid, but each had to stay on his own side of the line. They were not supposed to cross it. I ran along the boundary, the Rosebud patrol car on one side, the Pine Ridge wagon on the other. They were taking pot shots at me to make me stop, but I knew they weren't trying to hit me; they didn't dare. If the Rosebud police came too close, I jumped across into Pine Ridge territory and the other way around, hopping back and forth across that line like some oversized grasshopper. Just when I was all tuckered out, my heart pounding like mad, I got into the pine hills where their cars couldn't follow me. They got out with their guns drawn, trying to keep up with me, but I lost them in the dark. They arrested my girl friend, but when I completely disappeared they turned her loose. They watched her, put her out as bait. But I wasn't that easy to catch. I lit out for Standing Rock for a while to let things cool down. I had a beautiful nest out there on the prairie for my girl.

I was a peyoter for six years. After that I quit it. I found out that it was not my way. It was a dead end, a box canyon, and I had to find my way out of it. I don't want to talk down this peyote cult. In many Indian tribes they have people believing in this medicine. Grandfather Peyote brings many people together, not only as members of this religion but as Indians, and that is good. Some tribes have had peyote for so long that it has become their main and only religion. Many people have forgotten their old beliefs, which the missionaries stamped out, and only the peyote is left; it is the only Indian belief they know. But for us Sioux it is something fairly new, different from our belief in the Great Spirit and the sacred pipe. Slowly I came to realize that I should not mix up these two beliefs, confuse them with each other. I felt that the time had come for me to choose—the pipe or the peyote. I chose the pipe.

At the time I quit peyote I had found out what a real Sioux vision was like. If you dream, that's no vision. Anybody can dream. And if you take an herb—well, even the butcher boy at his meat counter will have a vision after eating peyote. The real vision has to come out of your own juices. It is not a dream; it is very real. It hits you sharp and clear like an electric shock. You are wide awake and, suddenly, there is a person standing next to you who you know can't be there at all. Or somebody is sitting close by, and all at once you see him also up on a hill half a mile away. Yet you are not dreaming; your eyes are open. You have to work for this, empty your mind for it.

Peyote is for the poor people. It helps to get them out of their despair, gives them something to grab hold of, but I couldn't stop there, I had to go further. Once you have experienced the real thing you will never be satisfied with anything else. It will be all or nothing for you then....

Lame Deer is telling his story to a white man, Richard Erdoes, who has befriended him. Occasionally, the author addresses Erdoes directly.

Let's sit down here, all of us, on the open prairie, where we can't see a highway or a fence. Let's have no blankets to sit on, but feel the ground with our bodies, the earth, the yielding shrubs. Let's have the grass for a mattress, experiencing its sharpness and its softness. Let us become like stones, plants, and trees. Let us be animals, think and feel like animals.

Listen to the air. You can hear it, feel it, smell it, taste it. *Woniya wakan*—the holy air— which renews all by its breath. *Woniya, woniya wakan*—spirit, life, breath, renewal—it means all that. *Woniya*—we sit together, don't touch, but something is there; we feel it between us, as a presence. A good way to start thinking about nature, talk about it. Rather talk to it, talk to the rivers, to the lakes, to the winds as to our relatives.

You have made it hard for us to experience nature in the good way by being part of it. Even here we are conscious that somewhere out in those hills there are missile silos and radar stations. White men always pick the few unspoiled, beautiful, awesome spots for the sites of these abominations. You have raped and violated these lands, always saying, "Gimme, gimme, gimme," and never giving anything back. You have taken 200,000 acres of our Pine Ridge reservation and made them into a bombing range. This land is so beautiful and strange that now some of you want to make it into a national park. The only use you have made of this land since you took it from us was to blow it up. You have not only despoiled the earth, the rocks, the minerals, all of which you call "dead" but which are very much alive; you have even changed the animals, which are part of us, part of the Great Spirit, changed them in a horrible way, so no one can recognize them. There is power in a buffalo—spiritual, magic power—but there is no power in an Angus, in a Hereford.

There is power in an antelope, but not in a goat or in a sheep, which holds still while you butcher it, which will eat your newspaper if you let it. There was great power in a wolf, even in a coyote. You have made him into a freak—a toy poodle, a Pekinese, a lap dog. You can't do much with a cat, which is like an Indian, unchangeable. So you fix it, alter it, declaw it, even cut its vocal cords so you can experiment on it in a laboratory without being disturbed by its cries.

A partridge, a grouse, a quail, a pheasant, you have made them into chickens, creatures that can't fly, that wear a kind of sunglasses so that they won't peck each other's eyes out, "birds" with a "pecking order." There are some farms where they breed chickens for breast meat. Those birds are kept in low cages, forced to be hunched over all the time, which makes the breast muscles very big. Soothing sounds, Muzak, are piped into these chicken hutches. One loud noise and the chickens go haywire, killing themselves by flying against the mesh of their cages. Having to spend all their lives stooped over makes an unnatural, crazy, no-good bird. It also makes unnatural, no-good human beings.

That's where you fooled yourselves. You have not only altered, declawed, and mal-formed your winged and four-legged cousins; you have done it to yourselves. You have changed men into chairmen of boards, into office workers, into time-clock punchers. You have changed women into housewives, truly fearful creatures. I was once invited into the home of such a one. "Watch the ashes, don't smoke, you stain the curtains. Watch the goldfish bowl, don't breath on the parakeet, don't lean your head against the wallpaper; your hair may be greasy. Don't spill liquor on that table; it has a delicate finish. You should have wiped your boots; the floor was just varnished. Don't, don't, don't…" That is crazy. We weren't made to endure this. You live in

At the time I quit peyote I had found out what a real Sioux vision was like. If you dream, that's no vision. Anybody can dream. And if you take an herb—well, even the butcher boy at his meat counter will have a vision after eating peyote.

prisons which you have built for yourselves, calling them "homes," offices, factories. We have a new joke on the reservation: "What is cultural deprivation?" Answer: "Being an upper-middle-class white kid living in a split-level suburban home with a color TV."

Sometimes I think that even our pitiful tar-paper shacks are better than your luxury homes. Walking a hundred feet to the outhouse on a clear wintry night, through mud or snow, that's one small link with nature. Or in the summer, in the back country, leaving the door of the privy open, taking your time, listening to the humming of the insects, the sun warming your bones through the thin planks of wood; you don't even have that pleasure anymore.

Americans want to have everything sani-tized. No smells! Not even the good, natural man and woman smell. Take away the smell from under the armpits, from your skin. Rub it out, and then spray or dab some non-human odor on yourself, stuff you can spend a lot of money on, ten dollars an ounce, so you know this has to smell good. "B.O.," bad breath, "Intimate Female Odor Spray"—I see it all on TV. Soon you'll breed people without body openings.

I think white people are so afraid of the world they created that they don't want to see, feel, smell, or hear it. The feeling of rain and snow on your face, being numbed by an icy wind and thawing out before a smoking fire, coming out of a hot sweat bath and plunging into a cold stream, these things make you feel alive, but you don't want them anymore. Living in boxes which shut out the heat of summer and the chill of winter, living inside a body that no longer has a scent, hearing the noise from the hi-fi instead of listening to the sounds of nature, watching some actor on TV having a make-believe experience when you no longer experience anything for yourself, eating food without taste—that's your way. It's no good.

The food you eat, you treat it like your bodies, take out all the nature part, the taste, the smell, the roughness, then put the artificial color, the artificial flavor in. Raw liver, raw kidney—that's what we old-fashioned fullbloods like to get our teeth into. In the old days we used to eat the guts of the buffalo, making a contest of it, two fellows getting hold of a long piece of intestines from opposite ends, starting chewing toward the middle, seeing who can get there first; that's eating. Those buffalo guts, full of half-fermented, half-digested grass and herbs, you didn't need any pills and vitamins when you swallowed those. Use the bitterness of gall for flavoring, not refined salt or sugar. *Wasna*—meat, kidney, fat, and berries all pounded together—a lump of that sweet *wasna* kept a man going for a whole day. That was food, that had the power. Not the stuff you give us today: powdered milk, dehydrated eggs, pasteurized butter, chickens that are all drumsticks or all breast; there's no bird left there.

You don't want the bird. You don't have the courage to kill honestly—cut off the chicken's head, pluck it, and gut it—no, you don't want this anymore. So it all comes in a neat plastic bag, all cut up, ready to eat, with no taste and no guilt. Your mink and seal coats, you don't want to know about the blood and pain that went into making them. Your idea of war—sit in an airplane, way above the clouds, press a button, drop the bombs, and never look below the clouds—that's the odorless, guiltless, sanitized way.

When we killed a buffalo, we knew what we were doing. We apologized to his spirit, tried to make him understand why we did it, honoring with a prayer the bones of those who gave their flesh to keep us alive, praying for their return, praying for the life of our brothers, the buffalo nation, as well as for our own people. You wouldn't understand this and that's why we had the Washita Massacre, the Sand Creek Massacre, the dead women and babies at Wounded Knee. That's why we have Song My and My Lai now.

To us life, all life, is sacred. The state of South Dakota has pest-control officers. They go up in a plane and shoot coyotes from the air. They keep track of their kills, put them all down in their little books. The stockmen and sheep-owners pay them. Coyotes eat mostly rodents, field mice and such. Only once in a while will they go after a stray lamb. They are our natural garbage men cleaning up the rotten and stinking things. They make good pets if you give them a chance. But their living could lose some man a few cents, and so the coyotes are killed from the air. They were here before the sheep, but they are in the way; you can't make a profit out of them. More and more animals are dying out. The animals that the Great Spirit put here, they must go. The manmade animals are allowed to stay—at least until they are shipped out to be butchered. That terrible arrogance of the white man, making himself something more than God, more than nature, saying, "I will let this animal live, because it makes money"; saying, "This animal must go, it brings no income, the space it occupies can be used in a better way. The only good coyote is a dead coyote." They are treating coyotes almost as badly as they used to treat Indians....

We Sioux have a close relationship to the buffalo. He is our brother. We have many legends of buffalo changing themselves into men. And the Indians are built like buffalo, too—big shoulders, narrow hips. According to our belief, the Buffalo Woman who brought us the peace pipe, which is at the center of our religion, was a beautiful maiden, and after she had taught our tribes how to worship with the pipe, she changed herself into a white buffalo calf. So the buffalo is very sacred to us. You can't understand about nature, about the feeling we have toward it, unless you understand how close we were to the buffalo. That animal was almost like a part of ourselves, part of our souls.

The buffalo gave us everything we needed. Without him we were nothing. Our tipis were made of his skin. His hide was our bed, our blanket, our winter coat. It was our drum, throbbing through the night, alive, holy. Out of his skin we made our water bags. His flesh strengthened us, became flesh of our flesh. Not the smallest part of it was wasted. His stomach, a red-hot stone dropped into it, became our soup kettle. His horns were our spoons, the bones our knives, our women's awls and needles. Out of his sinews we made our bowstrings and thread. His ribs were fashioned into sleds for our children, his hoofs became rattles. His mighty skull, with the pipe leaning against it, was our sacred altar. The name of the greatest of all Sioux was Tatanka Iyotake—Sitting Bull. When you killed off the buffalo, you also killed the Indian—the real, natural, "wild" Indian.

The buffalo has wisdom, but man-bred cattle—that's just a factory-made thing. They have no sense. Those Mexican fighting bulls get fooled by the cape every time. They are brave, yes, but not very smart. Imagine those bullfighters taking on a buffalo. They'd all get killed. The man-bred bull, he keeps looking at the cape. But a buffalo wouldn't be horn-swoggled by a red piece of cloth. He'd be looking for the man behind the cape, and his horns would find him. Buffalo are smart. They also have a sense of humor. Remember when we were together last in the Black Hills? When it suddenly snowed after a very hot day? Those six big black bulls we saw near Blue Bell, just like six large pick-up trucks. They were so happy over that snow. Gamboling, racing around, playing like kittens. And afterward we came across the tame cattle, hunched over, miserable, pitiful. "Moo, moo, moo—I'm cold." The real, natural animals don't mind the cold; they are happy with the kind of fur coat and galoshes the Great Spirit gave them. White hunters used to call the buffalo stupid because they were easy to shoot, weren't afraid of a gun. But the buffalo was not designed to cope with modern weapons. He was designed to deal with an Indian's arrows....

As for myself, the birds have something to tell me. The eagle, the owl. In an eagle there is all the wisdom of the world; that's why we have an eagle feather at the top of the pole during a *yuwipi* ceremony. If you are planning to kill an eagle, the minute you think of that he knows it, knows what you are planning. The black-tailed deer has this wisdom, too. That's why its tail is tied farther down at the *yuwipi* pole. This deer, if you shoot at him, you won't hit him. He just stands right there and the bullet comes right back and hits you. It is like somebody saying bad things about you and they come back at him.

In one of my great visions I was talking to the birds, the winged creatures. I was saddened by the death of my mother. She had held my hand and said just one word: "pitiful." I don't think she grieved for herself: she was sorry for me, a poor Indian she would leave in a white man's world. I cried up on that vision hill, cried for help, stretched out my hands toward the sky and then put the blanket over myself— that's all I had, the blanket and the pipe, and a little tobacco for an offering. I didn't know what to expect. I wanted to touch the power, feel it. I had the thought to give myself up, even if it would kill me. So I just gave myself to the winds, to nature, not giving a damn about what could happen to me.

All of a sudden I hear a big bird crying, and then quickly he hit me on the back, touched me with his spread wings. I heard the cry of an eagle, loud above the voices of many other birds. It seemed to say, "We have been waiting for you. We knew you would come. Now you are here. Your trail leads from here. Let our

And again I heard the voice amid the bird sounds, the clicking of beaks, the squeaking and chirping. "You have love for all that has been placed on this earth, not like the love of a mother for her son, or of a son for his mother, but a bigger love that encompasses the whole earth. You are just a human being, afraid, weeping under that blanket, but there is a great space within you to be filled with that love. All of nature can fit in there." I was shivering, pulling the blanket tighter around myself, but the voices repeated themselves over and over again, calling me "Brother, brother, brother." So this is how it is with me. Sometimes I feel like the first being in one of our Indian legends. This was a giant made of earth, water, the moon, and the winds. He had timber instead of hair, a whole forest of trees. He had a huge lake in his stomach and a waterfall in his crotch. I feel like

The Sun Dance is the most misunderstood of all our rites. Many white men think of it as an initiation into manhood, or a way to prove one's courage.

But this is wrong.

The Sun Dance is a prayer and a sacrifice.

voices guide you. We are your friends, the feathered people, the two-legged, the four-legged, we are your friends, the creatures, little tiny ones, eight legs, twelve legs—all those who crawl on the earth. All the little creatures that fly, all those under water. The powers of each one of us we will share with you and you will have a ghost with you always—another self."

That's me, I thought, no other thing than myself, different, but me all the same, unseen, yet very real. I was frightened. I didn't understand it then. It took me a lifetime to find out.

this giant. All of nature is in me, and a bit of myself is in all of nature....

Staring open-eyed at the blazing sun, the blinding rays burning deep into your skull, filling it with unbearable brightness...

Blowing on an eagle-bone whistle clenched between your teeth until its shrill sound becomes the only sound in the world...

Dancing, dancing, dancing from morning to night without food or water until you are close to dropping in a dead faint...

Pulling, pulling away at a rawhide thong that is fastened to a skewer embedded deeply in your flesh, until your skin stretches and rips apart as you finally break free with blood streaming down your chest…This is what some of us must endure during the Sun Dance.

Many people do not understand why we do this. They call the Sun Dance barbarous, savage, a bloody superstition. The way I look at it, our body is the only thing that truly belongs to us. When we Indians give of our flesh, our bodies, we are giving of the only thing that is ours alone.

If we offer Wakan Tanka a horse, bags of tobacco, food for the poor, we'd be making him a present of something he already owns. Everything in nature has been created by the Great Spirit, is part of Him. It is only our own flesh that is a real sacrifice—a real giving of ourselves. How can we give anything less?

For fifty long years they jailed us if we danced the Sun Dance, calling it a crime, an "Indian Offense." Freedom of religion doesn't always include us Indians.

The Sun Dance is our oldest and most solemn ceremony, the "granddaddy of them all," as my father used to say. It is so old that its beginnings are hidden as in a mist. It goes back to an age when our people had neither guns, horses, nor steel—when there was just us and the animals, the earth, the grass, and the sky.

Nowadays clever people study sun spots through giant telescopes, and your man-made little stars zoom around the earth as if they were late on a job. You have even landed on the moon and left a few plastic bags of urine there and a few chewing-gum wrappers. But I think the Indians knew the sun and the moon much better in those long-forgotten days, were much closer to them.

Huddling in their poor shelters in the darkness of winter, freezing and hungry, hibernating almost like animals, how joyfully, thankfully they must have greeted the life-giving sun, let it warm their frozen bones as spring returned. I can imagine one of them on a sudden impulse getting up to dance for the sun, using his body like a prayer, and all the others joining him one by one.

So they made this dance, and slowly, generation after generation, added more meaning to it, added to its awesomeness. My father taught me, as he had been taught by his father, the learning and teaching going back to the beginning of time.

Wi wanyang wacipi—the Sun Dance—is our greatest feast that brings all the people together. I told you of *hanblechia,* the vision quest, one man, alone by himself on an isolated hilltop, communicating with the mystery power. Well, the Sun Dance is *all* the people communicating with *all* the mystery powers. It is the *hanblechia* of the whole Sioux nation.

The Sun Dance is the most misunderstood of all our rites. Many white men think of it as an initiation into manhood, or a way to prove one's courage. But this is wrong. The Sun Dance is a prayer and a sacrifice. One does not take part in it voluntarily but as the result of a dream, or a vision.

The Sun Dance you are about to witness is sponsored by someone who dreamed that he must undergo this ordeal to bring his son back from Vietnam, to bring peace to the people of this world so that they can understand one another. We will dance for this.

The dance is not so severe now as it once was, but even today it asks much of a man. Even today a man may faint for lack of food and water. He may become so thirsty blowing on his eagle-bone whistle that his throat will be parched like a cracked, dry riverbed. He may be blind for a time from staring at the sun so that his eyes see only glowing spirals of glaring whiteness. The pain in his flesh, where the eagle's claw is fastened in his breast, may become so great that a moment arrives when he will no longer feel it. It is at such moments, when he loses consciousness, when the sun burns itself into his mind, when his strength is gone and his legs buckle under him, that the visions occur—visions of becoming a medicine man, visions of the future.

Insights gained at such a price are even greater than those that come to a man on a hilltop during his vision quest; they are truly *wakan*—sacred.

One thing makes me sad. Here in the town of Winner live hundreds of Indian families eager to keep the old ways, but we are surrounded on all sides by white cattle ranchers. The only place we can hold our Sun Dance now is on the old fairgrounds where the local cowboys used to have their rodeos. It's not good enough for them anymore, they've built a new one and we have kind of taken this one over. The old grandstands are peeling and full of splinters, but they are still safe enough to sit on. You can still see the fading signs: "Drink Pepsi-Cola," "See Your Local Ford Dealer." Pretend not to see them.

Some communities are luckier, not so fenced in. They can still hold their ceremonies out on the open prairie, on whatever is left of it, but we will have a good Sun Dance here all the same. We will do it right, in the sacred manner of our forefathers, as our elders have taught us—at least as far as is possible at this time in this place.

We want you to understand and to watch, but not with your eyes only. This is a good hour to relate to you how we celebrated the Sun Dance in days long past, to make you see it in your mind in all its ancient awesomeness.

Just telling about it makes me a little uneasy. Formerly, we didn't talk much about it even among ourselves, and then only on solemn occasions, when twelve old and wise men were present to make sure that what was told was right, with nothing added and nothing left out.

I have said much about the pain of the Sun Dance, little about its joys. We Sioux are not a simple people; we are very complicated. We are forever looking at things from different angles. For us there is pain in joy and joy in pain, just as to us a clown is a funny man and a tragic figure at one and the same time. It is all part of the same thing—nature, which is neither sad nor glad; it just is.

Thus in the old days the Sun Dance was not all sacrifice but also a happy time when the choke cherries were ripe, the grass was up, and the game plentiful—a happy time for meeting old friends.

We were spread out then in small hunting parties from Nebraska to Montana, like pebbles flung in the sagebrush. But nobody would miss the Sun Dance, even if he had to travel hundreds of miles. At the Sun Dance you came across relatives whom you had not seen for a year and swapped stories with them of all the bad and good things that had happened to you in the meantime. Here boys met girls they could court and make love to. We Sioux have such a fear of inbreeding, with so many rules that forbid you to marry within your clan, that I think the Sun Dance was for many a young man his only chance to find the right girl.

Every family put up their tipi in the place that was proper for them, with the herald riding around the camp circle telling everybody what to do. These were days of visiting back and forth between tents, of good food, good talk, good company. This was a time for begging songs, the singers going from tipi to tipi collecting gifts and food for the poor. It was also a good time for girls to look for a special kind of herb with four buds that acted as a love charm—an herb that would make their lovers faithful. There aren't too many of these herbs around now, the women tell me. The Sun Dance lasted for twelve days: four days for preparing the campsite, four days for the medicine men teaching the participants the many things they had to know, four days for the dance itself.

The Sun Dance really began with the choosing of the *can-wakan*—the sacred pole.

It was always a cottonwood, our sacred tree. If you cut off the top branches, make a clean cut with your knife, you will find a design resembling a star at the core of each branch. In making their choice men were not looking for just the first, good-sized cottonwood they might come across. The most perfect of all trees was just good enough. To find it the tribe sent out four scouts, brave men of blameless character. It was a great honor to be selected for this task. The scouts rode off as if going on the warpath—painted and armed. They were looking for an "enemy" to capture—a wooden enemy, a forked cottonwood. When the scouts had found a worthy tree they returned at a dead run and made their report to the medicine men.

On the morning after, the camp was filled with excitement. The drums throbbed. Everybody sang brave-heart songs, black-facepaint songs. You know, a warrior who had distinguished himself in battle had the right

Some white men shudder when I tell them these things.

Yet the idea of enduring pain so that others may live should not strike you as strange.

Do you not in your churches pray to one who is "pierced," nailed to a cross for the sake of his people?

to paint half of his face black upon returning to the camp....

When the tree finally arrived in the camp circle a great shout of joy rose from all the people. Buffalo fat had been placed inside the pit that was waiting to receive the sun-dance pole. The fat was an offering to the Buffalo nation asking their help to feed the tribe in the coming year. A crossbar was fastened to the fork of the tree. To this were tied the rawhide thongs, one for each man who had made the vow to undergo the ordeal of "piercing." The top of the pole was decorated with strips of colored cloth, one each for the four corners of the earth. To the crossbar was also tied the sponsor's offering—a large bag beautifully decorated with bead and quill work around which branches of the choke cherry had been wound so that the bundle blended in with the leaves at the top of the tree. Inside the bundle was a choice hunk of buffalo meat with an arrow stuck through it. This ensured good hunting. The tree was also painted a different color on each side.

All this time the medicine man in charge was talking and praying to the tree and the pit in so low a voice that nobody could make out the words. At last the pole was raised. This was done in four stages. I guess by now you have caught on to this: that four is our sacred number, that we do everything by fours. While the tree was being raised the people were silent and not a sound was to be heard, but once it stood upright everybody raised a great cheer and the men fired their guns in the air.

For a short while there was some horseplay as men and women shouted jokingly at Iya and Gnaske—the two little figures with the big male parts. This banter had all to do with sex; it was what you might call "talking dirty." Ordinarily women would have been ashamed to speak this way, coarsely, with all the people to hear them, but at this one time it was all part of a rite and therefore good.

Now that the tree was up it was supposed to "speak" to the people. These words were sung in its name:

> I am standing
> In a sacred way
> At the earth's center
> Beheld by the people,
> Seeing the tribe
> Gathered around me.

Around the pole the sun-dance lodge was erected. Also called the "shade house," it was a circle of poles holding up a roof of pine boughs. From here the people could watch the dance. A little way west of the pole they made a square of earth—*owanka wakan,* the sacred place. It contained a measure of power given by the Great Spirit to be used for the people. Two lines traced within the square, small ditches, really, were filled with tobacco, covered with vermilion powder, silvery mica dust, and downy eagle feathers. The cross symbolized the four directions of the wind. Nobody was allowed to step between the pole and the *owanka wakan.*

A tipi was then set up for the dancers, and a sweat lodge was prepared for them. Now everything was ready for the actual Sun Dance, which lasted for four long days. There was no merrymaking, no visiting back and forth on the night before it. The medicine men prayed as the people stayed quietly in their lodges. For the first three days the men danced from dawn to sunset, blowing on their eagle-bone whistles, their bodies moving as one until they were faint with weariness. And then came the fourth, the most solemn day.

Before dawn on the last day the medicine men would go up a hill to catch the first rays of the rising sun, to welcome it, to ask for good weather and strength for the dancers. Those who had made the vow purified themselves in the sweat lodge and were painted, each in a different way according to his vow. They wore wreaths on their heads and wrists and long kilts of red cloth from their waist down. They all had their medicine bundles hanging from their necks. Women did not pierce like the men, but they, too, could make a sacrifice by having many tiny squares of flesh cut from their arms.

Led by the medicine men, the dancers made a solemn march from the sun-dance tipi to the dance circle. The medicine man who acted as intermediary to the Great Spirit walked ahead along a marked trail carrying a painted buffalo skull. This was placed upon the altar facing the sacred pole together with a loaded peace pipe. Before the men underwent their ordeal it was the babies' turn to have their ears pierced. A space had been covered with sage, and here the mothers sat with their little ones calling to this or that brave and wise man to perform this task. While the men pierced the tiny earlobes with an awl they told of their brave deeds and reminded the parents to bring up the children in the right way—the Sioux way. This was supposed to influence the minds of the children, but not right away, I think, because there was much crying and squealing among the little ones.

At last it was the men's turn, and that was no child's play, believe me. Nobody had been forced or talked into this, but once he had made a vow, he had to go through with it. You can't break your word to Wakan Tanka.

The piercing could be done in four different ways. For the "Gazing at the Buffalo" way the flesh on the dancer's back was pierced with skewers. From these were hung up to eight buffalo skulls. Their weight pulled the skewers through the flesh after a few hours.

The second way was "Gazing at the Sun Leaning." This was the one most used. The flesh on the dancer's breast was pierced about a hand's width above each nipple and a wooden stick or eagle's claw stuck right through the muscle. At the end of the dance each man had to tear himself loose.

The third way was "Standing Enduring." The dancer was placed between four poles. Thongs were fastened in his flesh—two in his chest and two in his back underneath each shoulder blade. The loose ends were tied to the poles and the dancer had to struggle bravely to free himself.

The last way was "Gazing at the Sun Suspended." In this case ropes were tied to skewers in a man's chest and back and he was pulled up into the air with his feet above the ground. This was the most severe test of all, as the dancer could do little to hasten the end of his ordeal by pulling or jerking but had to wait until his own weight finally ripped his flesh open. Some just kept hanging there until friends or relatives pulled them down.

Usually a man had his friends by his side, encouraging him, cleaning his wounds, and wiping away the cold sweat with a bundle of soft sage leaves. Plants used in this way made a powerful love charm prized by women. The skewers of sagewood, too, are sought after. The dancers present them to their friends, who use them to tamp down the tobacco in their peace pipes. A girl might also quench her lover's thirst by bringing him a little water to drink if thirst threatened to overcome him.

Some white men shudder when I tell them these things. Yet the idea of enduring pain so that others may live should not strike you as strange. Do you not in your churches pray to one who is "pierced," nailed to a cross for the sake of his people? No Indian ever called a white man uncivilized for his beliefs or forbade him to worship as he pleased.

The difference between the white man and us is this: You believe in the redeeming powers of suffering, if this suffering was done by somebody else, far away, two thousand years ago. We believe that it is up to every one of us to help each other, even through the pain of our bodies. Pain to us is not "abstract," but very real. We do not lay this burden onto our god, nor do we want to miss being face to face with the spirit power. It is when we are fasting on the hilltop, or tearing our flesh at the Sun Dance, that we experience the sudden insight, come closest to the mind of the Great Spirit. Insight does not come cheaply, and we want no angel or saint to gain it for us and give it to us secondhand....

I know of a man who was cured underneath the center pole. This guy had a bad case of arthritis. He could hardly walk or bend over anymore. And when he was stretched out underneath the cottonwood he had a vision. He saw a rider coming on at a dead run between the white flags wearing a single feather in his hair. He was gliding in from the west between the white flags, skimming in over the sun shade, astride a gray horse whose hooves never touched ground. That sick man was stiff with terror seeing this horseman come at him full speed. And he could feel the rider touching him with his lance and disappear. And that man got up and he could walk. His sickness was gone. There is a great power near the altar and the sacred pole during a Sun Dance.

The people are lining up to thank the dancers and shake their hands. They are bringing the large root from the foot of the pole, a root as big as a child, shaped like a human being, with arms and legs. They are chopping it up. It is a powerful medicine, and Pete and Bill will give a piece of it to each person. Come and join the line-up. You too have taken part in the Sun Dance, watching, listening, learning. You too must thank the medicine men, get a hunk of that root. It's good against rheumatism.

The sun-dance pole, the gift offerings, the tobacco bundles we shall leave to be blown over by the winds, the rains, and the snows, leaving them to nature, to the sky, to the earth from which they came. Here, take an extra piece of medicine to take home with you. And now, as we Sioux always say after a ceremony—even the most solemn, sacred rite—*wa uyun tinkte,* let's go and eat! I haven't had a bite since yesterday.

Discussion Questions: **John Fire Lame Deer**

1. What difference does Lame Deer notice between the way Native American and white children are raised? What significance does he attach to this difference?

2. What ritual precedes the vision pit? Have you ever experienced anything similar to the sweat lodge?

3. Describe the relationship Lame Deer sees between the sacred pipe and the earth. What happens to his body during his vision-seeking?

4. Explain the incident involving General Bear Coat Miles and Lame Deer's great-grandfather. What happened to the treaty that gave Lame Deer's ancestors four square miles west of Rapid City, South Dakota? What is Lame Deer's view of the development that took place there?

5. In the peyote ritual, Lame Deer feels as if he leaves his body, just as he did during his vision-seeking. Something feels different, however, and he concludes that peyote is not for him. Why do you think he reaches this conclusion?

6. Describe Lame Deer's relationship to nature. Have you ever felt a similar kinship with plants or animals? Why does Lame Deer say that white men have made it hard to experience nature "in the good way by being part of it"? Describe how Lame Deer thinks white people relate to the earth.

7. Lame Deer distinguishes between different kinds of animals. What is the difference, in his mind, between antelope, buffalo, and pheasants, and, on the other hand, sheep, cows, and chickens? What does Lame Deer think of today's sheep ranchers and the white man's meat market? What does he say about white people who have never killed one of the animals they consume? Describe how Native Americans view the buffalo and eagle.

8. The Sun Dance is a very sacred ritual for Lame Deer. How does he defend the practice of piercing? What spiritual work does piercing accomplish? What analogy to Christian tradition does he draw?

Mary Crow Dog

From *Lakota Woman* by Mary Crow Dog with Richard Erdoes. © 1990 by Mary Crow Dog and Richard Erdoes. Used with permission of Grove/Atlantic Monthly Press. Paperback available from HarperCollins, 10 East 53rd Street, New York, NY 10019.

A nation is not conquered until
the hearts of its women
are on the ground.

Then it is done, no matter
how brave its warriors
nor how strong their weapons.

—*Cheyenne proverb*

I am Mary Brave Bird. After I had my baby during the siege of Wounded Knee they gave me a special name—Ohitika Win, Brave Woman, and fastened an eagle plume in my hair, singing brave-heart songs for me. I am a woman of the Red Nation, a Sioux woman. That is not easy.

I had my first baby during a firefight, with the bullets crashing through one wall and coming out through the other. When my newborn son was only a day old and the marshals really opened up upon us, I wrapped him up in a blanket and ran for it. We had to hit the dirt a couple of times, I shielded the baby with my body, praying, "It's all right if I die, but please let him live."

When I came out of Wounded Knee I was not even healed up, but they put me in jail at Pine Ridge and took my baby away. I could not nurse. My breasts swelled up and grew hard as rocks, hurting badly. In 1975 the feds put the muzzles of their M-16s against my head, threatening to blow me away. It's hard being an Indian woman.

My best friend was Annie Mae Aquash, a young, stronghearted woman from the Micmac Tribe with beautiful children. It is not always wise for an Indian woman to come on too strong. Annie Mae was found dead in the snow at the bottom of a ravine on the Pine Ridge Reservation. The police said that she had died of exposure, but there was a .38 caliber slug in her head. The FBI cut off her hands and sent them to Washington for fingerprint identification, hands that had helped my baby come into the world.

My sister-in-law, Delphine, a good woman who had lived a hard life, was also found dead in the snow, the tears frozen on her face. A drunken man had beaten her, breaking one of her arms and legs, leaving her helpless in a blizzard to die.

My sister Barbara went to the government hospital in Rosebud to have her baby and when she came out of anesthesia found that she had been sterilized against her will. The baby lived only for two hours, and she had wanted so much to have children. No, it isn't easy.

When I was a small girl at the Saint Francis Boarding School, the Catholic sisters would take a buggy whip to us for what they called "disobedience." At age ten I could drink and hold a pint of whiskey. At age twelve the nuns beat me for "being too free with my body." All I had been doing was holding hands with a boy. At age fifteen I was raped. If you plan to be born, make sure you are born white and male.

It is not the big, dramatic things so much that get us down, but just being Indian, trying to hang on to our way of life, language, and values while being surrounded by an alien, more powerful culture. It is being an *iyeska*, a half-blood, being looked down upon by whites and full-bloods alike. It is being a backwoods girl living in a city, having to rip off stores in order to survive. Most of all it is being a woman. Among Plains tribes, some men think that all a woman is good for is to crawl into the sack with them and mind the children. It compensates for what white society has done to them. They were famous warriors and hunters once, but the buffalo is gone and there is not much rep in putting a can of spam or an occasional rabbit on the table.

As for being warriors, the only way some men can count coup nowadays is knocking out another skin's teeth during a barroom fight. In the old days a man made a name for himself by being generous and wise, but now he has nothing to be generous with, no jobs, no money; and as far as our traditional wisdom is concerned, our men are being told by the white missionaries, teachers, and employers that it is merely savage superstition they should get rid of if they want to make it in this world. Men are forced to live away from their children, so that the family can get ADC—Aid to Dependent Children. So some warriors come home drunk and beat up their old ladies in order to work off their frustration. I know where they are coming from. I feel sorry for them, but I feel even sorrier for their women.

To start from the beginning, I am a Sioux from the Rosebud Reservation in South Dakota. I belong to the "Burned Thigh," the Brule Tribe, the Sicangu in our language. Long ago, so the legend goes, a small band of Sioux was surrounded by enemies who set fire to their tipis and the grass around them. They fought their way out of the trap but got their legs burned and in this way acquired their name. The Brules are part of the Seven Sacred Campfires, the seven tribes of the Western Sioux known collectively as Lakota. The Eastern Sioux are called Dakota. The difference between them is their language. It is the same except that where we Lakota pronounce an *L*, the Dakota pronounce a *D*. They cannot pronounce an *L* at all. In our tribe we have this joke: "What is a flat tire in Dakota?" Answer: "A b*d*owout."

The Brule, like all Sioux, were a horse people, fierce riders and raiders, great warriors. Between 1870 and 1880 all Sioux were driven into reservations, fenced in and forced to give up everything that had given meaning to their life—their horses, their hunting, their arms, everything. But under the long snows of despair the little spark of our ancient beliefs and pride kept glowing, just barely sometimes, waiting for a warm wind to blow that spark into a flame again.

My family was settled on the reservation in a small place called He-Dog, after a famous chief. There are still some He-Dogs living. One, an old lady I knew, lived to be over a hundred years old. Nobody knew when she had been born. She herself had no idea, except that when she came into the world there was no census yet, and Indians had not yet been given Christian first names. Her name was just He-Dog, nothing else. She always told me, "You should have seen me eighty years ago when I was pretty." I have never forgotten her face—nothing but deep cracks and gullies, but beautiful in its own way. At any rate very impressive.

On the Indian side my family was related to the Brave Birds and Fool Bulls. Old Grandpa Fool Bull was the last man to make flutes and play them, the old-style flutes in the shape of a bird's head that had the elk power, the power to lure a young girl into a man's blanket. Fool Bull lived a whole long century, dying in 1976, whittling his flutes almost until his last day. He took me to my first peyote meeting while I was still a kid.

He still remembered the first Wounded Knee, the massacre. He was a young boy at that time, traveling with his father, a well-known medicine man. They had gone to a place near Wounded Knee to take part in a Ghost Dance. They had on their painted ghost shirts that were supposed to make them bulletproof. When they got near Pine Ridge they were stopped by white soldiers, some of them from the Seventh Cavalry, George Custer's old regiment, who were hoping to kill themselves some Indians. The Fool Bull band had to give up their few old muzzle-loaders, bows, arrows, and even knives. They had to put up their tipis in a tight circle, all bunched up, with the wagons on the outside and the soldiers surrounding their camp, watching them closely. It was cold, so cold that the trees were crackling with a loud noise as the frost was splitting their trunks. The people made a fire the following morning to warm themselves and make some coffee and then they noticed a sound beyond the crackling of the trees: rifle fire, salvos making a noise like the ripping apart of a giant blanket; the boom of cannon and the rattling

of quick-firing Hotchkiss guns. Fool Bull remembered the grown-ups bursting into tears, the women keening: "They are killing our people, they are butchering them!" It was only two miles or so from where Grandfather Fool Bull stood that almost three hundred Sioux men, women, and children were slaughtered. Later grandpa saw the bodies of the slain, all frozen in ghostly attitudes, thrown into a ditch like dogs. And he saw a tiny baby sucking at his dead mother's breast.

I wish I could tell about the big deeds of some ancestors of mine who fought at the Little Big Horn, or the Rosebud, counting coup during the Grattan or Fetterman battle, but little is known of my family's history before 1880. I hope some of my great-grandfathers counted coup on Custer's men, I like to imagine it, but I just do not know. Our Rosebud people did not play a big part in the battles against generals Crook or Custer. This was due to the policy of Spotted Tail, the all-powerful chief at the time. Spotted Tail had earned his eagle feathers as a warrior, but had been taken East as a prisoner and put in jail. Coming back years later, he said that he had seen the cities of the whites and that a single one of them contained more people than could be found in all the Plains tribes put together, and that every one of the *wasicuns'* factories could turn out more rifles and bullets in one day than were owned by all the Indians in the country. It was useless, he said, to try to resist the *wasicuns*. During the critical year of 1876 he had his Indian police keep most of the young men on the reservation, preventing them from joining Sitting Bull, Gall, and Crazy Horse. Some of the young bucks, a few Brave Birds among them, managed to sneak out trying to get to Montana, but nothing much is known. After having been forced into reservations, it was not thought wise to recall such things. It might mean no rations, or worse. For the same reason many in my family turned Christian, letting themselves be "whiteman-ized." It took many years to reverse this process.

My sister Barbara, who is four years older than me, says she remembers the day when I was born. It was late at night and raining hard amid thunder and lightning. We had no electricity then, just the old-style kerosene lamps with the big reflectors. No bathroom, no tap water, no car. Only a few white teachers had cars. There was one phone in He-Dog, at the trading post. This was not so very long ago, come to think of it. Like most Sioux at that time my mother was supposed to give birth at home, I think, but something went wrong, I was pointing the wrong way, feet first or stuck sideways. My mother was in great pain, laboring for hours, until finally somebody ran to the trading post and called the ambulance. They took her—us—to Rosebud, but the hospital there was not yet equipped to handle a complicated birth. I don't think they had surgery then, so they had to drive mother all the way to Pine Ridge, some ninety miles distant, because there the tribal hospital was bigger. So it happened that I was born among Crazy Horse's people. After my sister Sandra was born the doctors there performed a hysterectomy on my mother, in fact sterilizing her without her permission, which was common at the time, and up to just a few years ago, so that it is hardly worth mentioning. In the opinion of some people, the fewer Indians there are, the better. As Colonel Chivington said to his soldiers: "Kill 'em all, big and small, nits make lice!"

I don't know whether I am a louse under the white man's skin. I hope I am. At any rate I survived the long hours of my mother's labor, the stormy drive to Pine Ridge, and the neglect of the doctors. I am an *iyeska*, a breed, that's what the white kids used to call me. When I grew bigger they stopped calling me that, because it would get them a bloody nose. I am a small woman, not much over five feet tall, but I can hold my own in a fight, and in a free-for-all with honkies I can become rather ornery and do real damage. I have white blood in me. Often I have wished to be able to purge it out of me.

As a young girl I used to look at myself in the mirror, trying to find a clue as to who and what I was. My face is very Indian, and so are my eyes and my hair, but my skin is very light. Always I waited for the summer, for the prairie sun, the Badlands sun, to tan me and make me into a real skin.

The Crow Dogs, the members of my husband's family, have no such problems of identity. They don't need the sun to tan them,

> # I don't know whether I am a louse under the white man's skin. I hope I am.

they are full-bloods—the Sioux of the Sioux. Some Crow Dog men have faces that make the portrait on the buffalo Indian nickel look like a washed-out white man. They have no shortage of legends. Every Crow Dog seems to be a legend in himself, including the women. They became outcasts in their stronghold at Grass Mountain rather than being whitemanized. They could not be tamed, made to wear a necktie or go to a Christian church. All during the long years when practicing Indian beliefs was forbidden and could be punished with jail, they went right on having their ceremonies, their sweat baths and sacred dances. Whenever a Crow Dog got together with some relatives, such as those equally untamed, unregenerated Iron Shells, Good Lances, Two Strikes, Picket Pins, or Hollow Horn Bears, then you could hear the sound of the *can-gleska*, the drum, telling all the world that a Sioux ceremony was in the making. It took courage and suffering to keep the flame alive, the little spark under the snow.

The first Crow Dog was a well-known chief. On his shield was the design of two circles and two arrowheads for wounds received in battle— two white man's bullets and two Pawnee arrow points. When this first Crow Dog was lying wounded in the snow, a coyote came to warm him and a crow flew ahead of him to show him the way home. His name should be Crow Coyote, but the white interpreter misunderstood it and so they became Crow Dogs. This Crow Dog of old became famous for killing a rival chief, the result of a feud over tribal politics, then driving voluntarily over a hundred miles to get himself hanged at Deadwood, his wife sitting beside him in his buggy; famous also for finding on his arrival that the Supreme Court had ordered him to be freed because the federal government had no jurisdiction over Indian reservations and also because it was no crime for one Indian to kill another. Later, Crow Dog became a leader of the Ghost Dancers, holding out for months in the frozen caves and ravines of the Badlands. So, if my own family lacks history, that of my husband more than makes up for it.

Our land itself is a legend, especially the area around Grass Mountain where I am living now. The fight for our land is at the core of our existence, as it has been for the last two hundred years. Once the land is gone, then we are gone too. The Sioux used to keep winter counts, picture writings on buffalo skin, that told our people's story from year to year. Well, the whole country is one vast winter count. You can't walk a mile without coming to some family's sacred vision hill, to an ancient Sun Dance circle, an old battleground, a place where something worth remembering happened. Mostly a death, a proud death or a drunken death. We are a great people for dying. "It's a good day to die!" that's our old battle cry. But the land with its tar paper shacks and outdoor privies, not one of them straight, but all leaning this way or that way, is also a land to live on, a land for good times and telling jokes and talking of great

deeds done in the past. But you can't live forever off the deeds of Sitting Bull or Crazy Horse. You can't wear their eagle feathers, freeload off their legends. You have to make your own legends now. It isn't easy....

Crow Dog recounts her childhood years and explains her rebellious adolescence. She has run-ins with the police, is arrested several times, and gets involved in riots in Custer, South Dakota. She learns firsthand how the dominant culture treats "breeds," or "skins."

Most of the arrests occurred not for what we did, but for what we were and represented— for being skins. For instance once, near Martin, South Dakota, we had a flat tire and pulled off the road to fix it. It was late at night, dark, and very cold. While the boys were attending to the car, we girls built a good-sized fire to warm our backsides and make some coffee, coffee—*pejuta sapa*—being what keeps a roaming skin going. A fire truck went by. We did not pay any attention to it. A little while later the truck came back followed by two police cars. The police stared at us but kept on going, but pretty soon they made a U-turn and came back.

Across the road stood a farmhouse. The owner had called the police saying that Indians were about to burn his house down. All we were doing was fixing the tire and making coffee. The farmer had us arrested on a charge of attempted arson, trespassing, disturbing the peace, and destroying private property—the latter because in building our fire we had used one of his rotten fence posts. We spent two days in jail and then were found not guilty.

Little by little, those days in jail began adding up. We took such things in stride because they happened all the time, but subconsciously, I think, they had an effect upon us. During the years I am describing, in some western states, the mere fact of being Indian and dressing in a certain way provoked the attention of the police. It resulted in having one's car stopped for no particular reason, in being pulled off the street on the flimsiest excuse, in being constantly shadowed and harassed. It works subtly on your mind until you start to think that if they keep on arresting you anyway you should at least give them a good reason for it.

I kept on moving, letting the stream carry me. It got to a point where I always looked forward to my next joint, my next bottle of gin. Even when the friends around me seemed to cool down I could not stop. Once I got hold of fifty white cross tablets—speed—and started taking them. The people I saw in the streets were doing it, why shouldn't I do it also? It gave me a bad case of the shakes and made me conclude that roving was not that much fun anymore. But I knew of no other way to exist.

Sexually our roaming bands, even after we had been politically sensitized and joined AIM, were free, very free and wild. If some boy saw you and liked you, then right away that was it. "If you don't come to bed with me, wincincala, I got somebody else who's willing to." The boys had that kind of attitude and it caused a lot of trouble for Barb and myself, because we were not that free. If we got involved we always took it seriously. Possibly our grandparents' and mother's staunch Christianity and their acceptance of the missionaries' moral code had something to do with it. They certainly tried hard to implant it in us, and though we furiously rejected it, a little residue remained.

There is a curious contradiction in Sioux society. The men pay great lip service to the status women hold in the tribe. Their rhetoric on the subject is beautiful. They speak of Grandmother Earth and how they honor her. Our greatest culture hero—or rather heroine—is the White Buffalo Woman, sent to us by the Buffalo nation, who brought us the sacred pipe and taught us how to use it. According to the legend, two young hunters were the first humans to meet her. One of them desired her physically and tried to make love to her, for

which he was immediately punished by lightning reducing him to a heap of bones and ashes.

We had warrior women in our history. Formerly, when a young girl had her first period, it was announced to the whole village by the herald, and her family gave her a big feast in honor of the event, giving away valuable presents and horses to celebrate her having become a woman. Just as men competed for war honors, so women had quilling and beading contests. The woman who made the most beautiful fully beaded cradleboard won honors equivalent to a warrior's coup. The men kept telling us, "See how we are honoring you…" Honoring us for what? For being good beaders, quillers, tanners, moccasin makers, and child-bearers. That is fine, but… In the governor's office at Pierre hangs a big poster put up by Indians. It reads:

> WHEN THE WHITE MAN
> DISCOVERED THIS COUNTRY
> INDIANS WERE RUNNING IT —
> NO TAXES OR TELEPHONES.
> *WOMEN DID ALL THE WORK* —
> THE WHITE MAN THOUGHT
> HE COULD IMPROVE UPON
> A SYSTEM LIKE THAT.

If you talk to a young Sioux about it he might explain: "Our tradition comes from being warriors. We always had to have our bow arms free so that we could protect you. That was our job. Every moment a Pawnee, or Crow, or white soldier could appear to attack you. Even on the daily hunt a man might be killed, ripped up by a bear or gored by a buffalo. We had to keep our hands free for that. That is our tradition."

"So, go already," I tell them. "Be traditional. Get me a buffalo!"

They are still traditional enough to want no menstruating women around. But the big honoring feast at a girl's first period they dispense with. For that they are too modern. I did not know about menstruating until my first time. When it happened I ran to my grandmother crying, telling her, "Something is wrong. I'm bleeding!" She told me not to cry, nothing was wrong. And that was all the explanation I got. They did not comfort me, or give horses away in my honor, or throw the red ball, or carry me from the menstruation hut to the tipi on a blanket in a new white buckskin outfit. The whole subject was distasteful to them. The feast is gone, only the distaste has remained.

It is not that a woman during her "moontime" is considered unclean, but she is looked upon as being "too powerful." According to our old traditions a woman during her period possesses a strange force that could render a healing ceremony ineffective. For this reason it is expected that we stay away from all rituals while menstruating. One old man once told me, "Woman on her moon is so strong that if she spits on a rattlesnake, that snake dies." To tell the truth I never felt particularly powerful while being "on my moon."

I was forcefully raped when I was fourteen or fifteen. A good-looking young man said, "Come over here, kid, let me buy you a soda"—and I fell for it. He was about twice my weight and a foot taller than I am. He just threw me on the ground and pinned me down. I do not want to remember the details. I kicked and scratched and bit but he came on like a steamroller. Ripped my clothes apart, ripped me apart. I was too embarrassed and ashamed to tell anyone what had happened to me. I think I worked off my rage by slashing a man's tires.

Rapes on the reservations are a big scandal. The victims are mostly full-blood girls, too shy and afraid to complain. A few years back the favorite sport of white state troopers and cops was to arrest young Indian girls on a drunk-and-disorderly, even if the girls were sober, take them to the drunk tanks in their jails, and there rape them. Sometimes they took the girls in their squad cars out into the prairie to "show you what a white man can do. I'm really doin' you a favor, kid." After they had done with them, they often kicked the girls out of their cars and drove off. Then the girl who had been raped had to walk five or ten miles home on top of everything else. Indian girls accusing white cops are seldom taken seriously in South Dakota. "You know how they are," the courts are told, "they're always asking for it." Thus there were few complaints for rapes or, as a matter of fact, for forced sterilizations. Luckily this is changing as our women are less reluctant to bring these things into the open....

In 1971, when she is about twenty years old, the author is introduced simultaneously to Leonard Crow Dog, her future husband, and to the American Indian Movement (AIM). AIM is dedicated to the fight for Indian rights, and Leonard is part of it. Mary joins the movement, convinced that the white world will not graciously grant her justice before she asks for it. She, like all the other Native Americans she knows, must demand basic liberties, even fundamental freedoms legally owed to her.

The next section begins with a quote from her husband about reality and peyote, the drug used in the Native American ritual described by Lame Deer.

The white man's reality are his streets
with their banks, shops, neon lights,
and traffic, streets full of policemen,
whores, and sad-faced people in a hurry
to punch a time clock.

But this is unreal. The real reality is
underneath all this. Grandfather Peyote
helps you find it.

—Crow Dog

You should know that the movement for Indian rights was first of all a spiritual movement and that our ancient religion was at the heart of it. Up to the time of Franklin D. Roosevelt, Indian religion was forbidden. Children were punished for praying Indian, men were jailed for taking a sweat bath. Our sacred pipes were broken, our medicine bundles burned or given to museums. Christianizing us was one way of making us white, that is, of making us forget that we were Indians. Holding on to our old religion was one way of resisting this kind of slow death. As long as people prayed with the pipe or beat the little water drum, Indians would not vanish, would continue to exist as Indians. For this reason our struggles for Indian rights over the past hundred years came out of our ancient beliefs. And so, under the impact of AIM and other movements, more and more native people abandoned the missionaries and went back to the medicine men and peyote road men.

I went that way, too. Hand in hand with my radicalization went my going back to Indian traditions. To white people this may seem contradictory, but for me and for my friends it was the most natural thing in the world. This process had already begun when I was still a child. I felt that the kind of Christianity the priests and nuns of Saint Francis dished out was not good for my digestion. Jesus would have been all right except that I felt he had been coopted by white American society to serve its purpose. The men who had brought us whiskey and the smallpox had come with the cross in one hand and the gun in the other. In the name of all-merciful Jesus they had used that gun on us. Our sacred pipe and Grandfather Peyote had not been coopted and so I was instinctively drawn to them. Not that I could have put it in these words at the time.

To be an Indian I had to go to the full-bloods. My mother and grandmother were Indians, but I am a half-breed and I could not accept this. The half-breeds, the *iyeskas*, I thought, never really cared for anybody but themselves, having learned that "wholesome selfishness" alone brought the blessings of civilization. The full-bloods have a heart. They are humble. They are willing to share whatever happiness they have. They sit on their land, which has a sacred meaning for them, even if it brings them no income. The *iyeskas* have no land because they sold theirs long ago. Whenever some white businessmen come to the res trying to make a deal to dig for coal or uranium, the *iyeskas* always say, "Let's do it. Let's get that money. Buy a new car and a color TV." The full-bloods say nothing. They just sit on their little patches of land and don't budge. It is because of them that there are still some Indians left. I felt drawn to my stubborn old full-blood relatives, men like my Uncle Fool Bull who always spoke of a sacred herb, a holy medicine that was the Creator's special gift to the Indian people. He told me the legend of an old woman and her granddaughter who were lost in the desert and on the point of dying when they heard a little voice calling to them, a voice coming out of a tiny herb that saved their lives, and how the women brought this sacred medicine to their tribe and to all the native people of this hemisphere. I listened to these stories and one day I told my mother, "I'm gonna grow up to be an Indian!"

She did not like it. She was upset because she was a Catholic and was having me brought up in her faith. She even had me confirmed. I sometimes try to imagine how I must have looked in my white outfit, with veil and candle, and it always makes me smile. I was then white outside and red inside, just the opposite of an apple. It was old Grandpa Dick Fool Bull who took me to my first peyote meeting....

I sat close by him the whole night. Even though I was a young girl I took a lot of medicine. I saw a lot of good things, and I suddenly understood. I understood the reality contained in this medicine, understood that this herb was our heritage, our tradition, that it spoke our language. I became part of the earth because peyote comes from the earth, even tastes like earth sometimes. And so the earth was in me and I in it, Indian earth making me more Indian. And to me peyote was people, was alive, was a remembrance of things long forgotten.

The medicine was brought to me four times during the night by a man I did not know. It came to me before it came to Grandpa Fool Bull because I was sitting on his right. The man said something to me in Indian, very fast. I could not speak Sioux at the time, but it seemed to me that I could understand what he said, take in the meaning of his words. I was in the power. I heard my long-dead relatives talking to me. It was a feeling, a message coming to me with the voice of the drum, coming down the staff, speaking in the whirr of the feathers, breathing in the smoke of the fire, the smell of the burning cedar. I felt the drumbeat in my heart. My heart became the drum, beating and beating and beating. I heard things. I did not know whether to believe what

"Well, it's up to you. I can't tell you what to do!" But she also added something that I liked: "Remember, whatever, the Indian is closest to God." I understood what she meant.

Two weeks later I was staying at my grandmother's and a dream came to me. It was in the nighttime, toward morning. I tried to wake up but could not. I was awake and not awake. I could not move. I was crying. I opened my eyes once and saw my grandmother sitting by my bed. She was asking whether I was all right, but I could not answer her. In my dream I had been going back into another life. I saw tipis and Indians camping, huddling around a fire, smiling and cooking buffalo meat, and then, suddenly, I saw white soldiers riding into camp, killing women and children, raping, cutting throats. It was so real, much more real than a movie—sights and sounds and smells: sights I did not want to see, but had to see against my will; the screaming of children that

> **Dreams and visions are very important to us, maybe more important than any other aspect of Indian religion. I have met Indians from South and Central America, from Mexico and from the Arctic Circle. They all pray for visions, they are all "crying for a dream," as the Sioux call it.**

the voice told me, what Grandfather Peyote told me. Even now I cannot explain it.

When the sun rose, after we had eaten our morning food and drunk the ice-cold water from the stream, I felt as I had never felt before. I felt so happy, so good. When I got home I blurted out to my mother that I had been to a Native American Church meeting. Mom was hurt. In the end she shrugged her shoulders:

I did not want to hear, but had to all the same. And the only thing I could do was cry. There was an old woman in my dream. She had a pack on her back—I could see that it was heavy. She was singing an ancient song. It sounded so sad, it seemed to have another dimension to it, beautiful but not of this earth, and she was moaning while she was singing it. And the soldiers came up and killed her. Her blood was soaked up by the grass, which was turning red. All the Indians lay dead on the ground and the soldiers left. I could hear the wind and the hoofbeats of the soldiers' horses, and the voices of the spirits of the dead trying to tell me something. I must have dreamed for hours. I do not know why I dreamed this but I think that the knowledge will come to me someday. I truly believe that this dream came to me through the spiritual power of peyote.

For a long time after that dream I felt depressed, as if all life had been drained from me. I was still going to school, too young to bear such dreams. And I grieved because we had to live a life that we were not put on this earth for. I asked myself why things were so bad for us, why Indians suffered as they did. I could find no answer.

Crow Dog always says: "Grandfather Peyote, he has no mouth, but he speaks; no eyes, but he sees; no ears, but he hears and he makes you listen." Leonard does not read or write. He tells me: "Grandfather Peyote, he is my teacher, my educator." When he was in jail for having been at Wounded Knee, the prison psychiatrist visited him in his "house"—that's what they call their tiny cells. Crow Dog told him: "I don't need you. Peyote, he is my psychiatrist. With the power of this holy herb I could analyze you." The shrink did not know what to make of it. To a judge, Leonard said: "Peyote is my lawyer."

Crow Dog is a peyote road man. He is showing the people the road of life. Only after I married Crow Dog did I really come to understand this medicine. Leonard has the peyote, which we call *peyuta* or *unkcela*, and he has his sacred pipe. He is a peyote priest, but also a traditional Lakota medicine man, a *yuwipi*, and a Sun Dancer. Some people criticize him, or rather all of us who take part in Crow Dog's ceremonies. They say we should be one or the other, believe in the peyote or in the pipe, not in both. But Leonard cannot put his beliefs into separate little cubbyholes. He looks

upon all ancient Indian religions as different aspects of one great overall power, part of the same creative force. Grandfather Peyote is just one of the many forms Wakan Tanka, Tunkashila, the Great Spirit, takes. The peyote button, the pipe, a deer, a bird, a butterfly, a pebble—they are all part of the Spirit. He is in them, and they are in him.

Dreams and visions are very important to us, maybe more important than any other aspect of Indian religion. I have met Indians from South and Central America, from Mexico and from the Arctic Circle. They all pray for visions, they are all "crying for a dream," as the Sioux call it. Some get their visions from fasting for four days and nights in a vision pit on a lonely hilltop. Others get their visions fasting and suffering during the long days of the Sun Dance, gazing at the blinding light in the sky. The Ghost Dancers went around and around in a circle, chanting until they fell down in a swoon, leaving their own bodies, leaving the earth, wandering along the Milky Way and among the stars. When they woke up they related what they had seen. Some found "star flesh" in their clenched fists, and moon rocks, so it is said. Still others receive their dreams out of the flash of lightning and the roar of thunder. Some tribes get their visions with the help of sacred mushrooms or jimsonweed. Not a few experience insight in the searing steam of the sweat lodge. Crow Dog receives what for lack of a better term I call sudden flashes of revelation during a vision quest as well as during a peyote meeting.

The Aztec word for the sacred herb was *peyotl*, meaning caterpillar, because this cactus is fuzzy like the hairs on a caterpillar. Our Sioux word for medicine is *pejuta*. Peyote, *pejuta*, that sounds very close. Maybe it is just a coincidence. It is certain that peyote came to us out of Mexico. In the 1870s the Kiowas and Comanches prayed with this medicine and established what they called the Native American Church. By now the peyote religion is common among most tribes all the way up to Alaska. Since peyote does not grow farther north than the Rio Grande, we must get our medicine from the border region. It is in the Southwest that we have our "peyote garden."

Peyote came to the Plains Indians just when they needed it most, at a time when the last of the buffalo were being killed and the tribes driven into fenced-in reservations, literally starving and dying of the white man's diseases, deprived of everything that had given meaning to their lives. The Native American Church became the religion of the poorest of the poor, the conquered, the despoiled. Peyote made them understand what was happening and made them endure. It was the only thing that gave them strength in those, our darkest days. Our only fear is that the whites will take this from us, too, as they have taken everything else....

Peyote makes me understand myself and the world around me. It lets me see the royalness of my people, the royalness of peyote, how good it can be. It is so good, and yet it can be dangerous if a person misuses it. You have to be in the right mind, approach it in the right way. If people have the wrong thoughts about it, it could hurt them. But peyote has never hurt me; it has always treated me well. It helped me when nothing else could. Grandfather Peyote knows you; you can't hide from him. He makes the unborn baby dance inside its mother's womb. He has that power. When you partake of this medicine in the right way, you feel strength surging through you, you "get into the power," otherworld power given specially to you and no one else. This also is common to all Indians whether or not they use peyote, this concept of power.

Peyote is a unifier, that is one of its chief blessings. This unifying force brought tribes together in friendship who had been enemies before, and it helped us in our struggle. I took the peyote road because I took the AIM road.

For me they became one path. I have visited many tribes. They have different cultures and speak different languages. They may even have different rituals when partaking of this medicine. They may be jealous of each other, saying, "We are the better tribe. Our men used to fight better than yours. We do things better." But once they meet inside the peyote tipi, all differences are forgotten. Then they are no longer Navajos, or Poncas, Apaches, or Sioux, but just Indians. They learn each others' songs and find out that they are really the same. Peyote is making many tribes into just one tribe. And it is the same with the Sun Dance, which also serves to unite the different Indian nations....

Crow Dog's husband Leonard was imprisoned in New York on charges Crow Dog considered unjust. She visited him in jail, but the family—Mary, Leonard, and their three sons, Richard, Quanah, and Pedro—needed to get reacquainted when he was finally released.

The long months of Leonard's incarceration had changed us both. Mostly the change was good, but we had to get used to the fact that we had become different persons. At times it seemed to me as if I had never left Grass Mountain; at other times, I felt as if I had been absent for an eternity. I had spent almost one year in New York with little Pedro. There I had enjoyed my private room with a private bath, with all the amenities of a big modern city. People had made a big fuss over me, treating me like a celebrity. Now it was back to outdoor privies, to getting water from the river and doing the laundry in a tub with the help of an old-fashioned washboard.

Most of the New York women who had supported us had been feminists. On some points I had disagreed with them. To me, women's lib was mainly a white, upper-middle-class affair of little use to a reservation Indian woman. With all their good intentions some had patronized me, even used me as an exotic conversation piece at their fancy parties. I disagreed with them on their notions of abortion and contraception. Like many other Native American women, particularly those who had been in AIM, I had an urge to procreate, as if driven by a feeling that I, personally, had to make up for the genocide suffered by our people in the past. But my white women friends had also taught me a lot that had influenced me in many ways. I was no longer the shy Sioux maiden walking with downcast eyes in the footsteps of some man. I was no longer an uncritical admirer of our warriors, heroes when facing death at Wounded Knee, but often six-foot-tall babies at home. Facing death or jail they had been supermen, but facing life many of them were weak. Many of them could not take responsibility for their actions. A lot of women got hurt and were left raising children without a father. Once it had been the traditional role of an Indian man to take care of and protect his family as well as old widows and young orphans. Now they said to our women, "Let's you and me make a little warrior," after which they got lost, making little warriors somewhere else. That was the reason Crow Dog was always stuck with caring for so many outsiders, young and old.

Before New York I had taken certain things for granted, almost as a normal part of daily life. But after I had been away for almost a year it no longer seemed quite so normal to me that so many Sioux men habitually beat their wives. My sister Barb came to cry on my shoulder. She was living with a boy at Porcupine. "When that boy is sober," she told me, "he's good, a right guy, but when he's drunk he becomes a monster. He beat me up. He was off drinking last weekend. He came home and vomited all over me. I told him I was going for some clean clothes for myself. He said, 'No, you're not going anywhere.' I said I could not stay like this with puke all over me, and started to leave. He ripped off a two-by-four from the fence and used it on me. He started beating me with this

chunk of wood and messed up a couple of my ribs. So I left him for good."

I grinned and told Barb, "For a little thing like that, most Sioux women wouldn't leave their men."

My sister said, "Indian women are stronger than the men because they have to put up with all that shit, but I've had it."

I answered her: "Barb, we've been away for too long. We don't see things the way we used to."

Leonard was going through a similar phase of readjustment. He was feeling a lot of bitterness for what prison had done to him, and had to work it out of his system. His trials had made him famous among many Indians and whites alike. We both had to deal with innumerable letters, demands for help, money, spiritual comfort, and the performance of all kinds of ceremonies. Indian prisoners wanted him to visit them with his pipe and set up sweat lodges in their prison yards. Even white and black inmates asked for his assistance. He felt so strongly for everybody doing time that he turned them down only rarely. Wherever Indians tangled with the law, Leonard would travel there to help and I would travel with him. On top of it all he was still on five years' parole. As he put it: "They can put me back in jail just for spitting on the sidewalk." It was a great strain on both of us.

I noticed soon that Leonard was becoming more tolerant as far as women were concerned. He exhibited fewer of his old Sioux macho habits toward me and showed great understanding for my struggle to once again fit myself into reservation life, especially his life. I knew that it would take time before he could shake off his prison hangups. You cannot tell a person who has been fucked over for so many years just to shrug it off with a smile. We quarreled less than before. Leonard can be self-righteous, playing the holy man toward me. So I told him at the beginning of that new life of ours, "Hey, as soon as you get over your righteousness I'll get over mine. If you get mad at me, just calm down and I'll calm down too. I won't take my troubles out on you and you won't take yours out on me." He laughed and said that was all right.

I asked him, "What do you expect of me?"

He said, "You are a medicine man's wife. You are the water, you are the corn. You are the growing generation that you carry in your womb. I have a role and so have you. At the next Sun Dance you will stand there with the pipe representing Ptesan Win, the White Buffalo Woman."

Leonard tried to make me feel good by telling me about the role women play in Lakota legends and religion. Unlike in the Christian Bible where Eve is made from Adam's rib, in one of our ancient tales woman came first. As Leonard told it in his medicine talk, this First Woman was given power by the Spirit. She was floating down to the world in a womb bag and, as Leonard put it, she was four-dimensional—all the Creation rolled into one human being. She came into the world with a knowledge and with a back-carrier and in it she had all our people's herbs and healing roots.

First Woman had a dream and in her vision the Grandfather Spirit advised her: "On your left side, where your hand is, there is a stone." And when she awoke she found a piece of worked flint in her hand, the first tool ever. And then she had another vision in which a voice told her: "To the right there are some bushes. Go there! You shall bring up the generation!" She did not know what it meant but she did as she was told. First Woman went into her moon time and as she was walking a drop of her moon blood fell to the earth. Rabbit saw it. He started to play with this tiny blood clot, kicking it around with his foot, and through the power of Tkuskanskan, the quickening, moving spirit, the blood clot firmed up and turned into We-Ota-Wichasha—Blood Clot Boy—the First Man.

First Woman was given the power to create the things necessary for survival, the knowledge to plant corn, the knowledge to make fire with a flint and keep it going with the help of seven sacred sticks. She was given seven rocks to heat up in the fire to a red glow. She was given a buffalo paunch to use as her first soup kettle by filling it with water and dropping the red-hot rocks into it together with meat and some herbs. First Woman was the center of the earth and her symbol was the morning star. "Maybe she came from a star," Leonard finished his story.

Many times he also told us the story of the White Buffalo Woman who brought to our people the most sacred of all things, the *ptehincala-huhu-chanunpa*, the sacred pipe around which our faith revolves. This woman taught our people how to use the pipe and how to live in a sacred manner. After she had fulfilled her mission she bade farewell to the tribe, and as she wandered off the people saw her turning herself into a white buffalo calf. Then they knew that she had been sent to us by our relatives, the Buffalo Nation.

The Buffalo Calf Pipe still exists. It has been kept for many generations by the Elk Head family who passed it on to the Looking Horses who take care of it now. They live at Eagle Butte on the Cheyenne River Sioux Reservation. The pipe's stem is made of a buffalo legbone. It is so old that it can no longer be used for smoking. It is kept in a medicine bundle together with another ancient pipe whose bowl is made of red pipestone. The bundle is unwrapped very rarely on very solemn occasions. Leonard was privileged to pray with it on several occasions.

The way he told it to me, he was strangely scared at its unwrapping. All through the ceremony there were dark clouds drifting overhead amid thunder and lightning. This made Leonard look up and say, "Grandfather, we hear you!" All present made tobacco and cloth offerings to the pipe. Old Henry Crow Dog made a fire and burned sweetgrass and cedar for incense, fanning the bundle with these herbs' fragrance. Leonard made an altar.

He said that he was trembling doing this. They slowly unwrapped the bundle, layer by layer, until they beheld the holy pipe. As Leonard touched it he felt something like an electric shock, and when he took hold of it to pray he felt a great flow of power in his arms and veins filling his whole being. He wept. There were twelve men at that particular unwrapping and they all had a similar experience.

Leonard also told me that among many tribes the peyote people have a legend that the holy herb was found by an old woman and her granddaughter. They had become lost while gathering wild berries and nuts hundreds of years ago and could not find the way back to their village. Then they heard a voice saying: "Come over here!" Following it, they came upon a green round plant with a star design on it. This was Grandfather Peyote. He told them: "Eat me!" As they partook of this sacred food their minds cleared so that they found their way home. They brought the knowledge of how to use peyote to their tribe and to all the native people of this continent.

While Leonard stressed the importance of women in Indian religion, he was careful never to blur the role of men and women in traditional Indian life. When a number of AIM women formed an organization called Women of All the Red Nations, the first native feminist movement ever, he welcomed it. But when these women put on their own Sun Dance, excluding men from participating, he was angry. He said that our religion was all-inclusive. Neither men nor women should be prevented from taking part or going off by themselves. The only exception was that menstruating women should not take part in ceremonies because a woman's period is considered so powerful that it wipes out any other power and renders rituals ineffective. When, recently, a small group of women wanted to put on a lesbian Sun Dance, Leonard just freaked out. That was too much for him. Leonard has always protected the role of women in our

> **They slowly unwrapped the bundle, layer by layer, until they beheld the holy pipe.**
>
> **As Leonard touched it he felt something like an electric shock, and when he took hold of it to pray he felt a great flow of power in his arms and veins filling his whole being.**
>
> **He wept.**

rituals, but he has also been opposed to women doing things that can traditionally be performed only by a man. A lot of changes in thinking had occurred during his absence and he had to deal with that.

As always when facing a new turn in his life, Leonard went on a vision quest called "Crying for a Dream" in Lakota. The Crow Dogs' vision pit is situated on a high hill from which one can see for many miles in all directions. Surrounded by pines and sagebrush, it is a lonely but beautiful place where eagles nest and coyotes howl at the moon. The vision pit has been up there for many generations. It is an L-shaped hole leading into total darkness. Somehow it always reminded me of a grave. In a way the vision seeker is dead while crying for a dream, the more so because the Crow Dogs, once somebody is praying in the pit, cover the hole with a tarp strewn with sage, seemingly burying the vision seeker alive.

A vision quest lasts for four days and nights. Inside the pit you lose all sensations of having a body. Going into the earth womb, you are light-headed from the sweat bath to start with. You feel nothing but the damp earth at your back and the bed of sage under your sitting bones, and after a day or two, you feel not even that. You feel nothing, see nothing, hear nothing, taste nothing, because during a *hanblechia* you do not eat or drink. It is scary to cry for a dream, to be entirely thrown upon yourself, not knowing whether you are awake or asleep, or even alive. As a woman I go on a vision quest for a day and a night or, at most, two days. I don't think I could stand it for longer, imagining the earth walls closing in on me.

Leonard told me about his first vision-seeking. He was just a boy then, in his early teens. A spirit had told him to *hanblechia*. Old Man Henry and an uncle helped him. They put up a sweat lodge for him and purified him in it. His oldest sister had made a flesh offering, having someone cut little pieces of skin from her arms and putting them into a gourd rattle that he took with him into the pit. It comforted him that she had made this sacrifice. They put him in there for two days and nights, not an easy thing for a young kid to undergo. He received a great vision. He told me that he heard someone walking around above him, that he heard a voice. It was telling him: "We are taking you to a place where you will be taught."

Suddenly he was not in the pit anymore. He was standing in front of a sweat lodge and all around him were tipis and horses, as in the old days. He saw flowers, deer, herds of buffalo. He had been transported into a beautiful ghost world. A man in a buckskin outfit was talking to him. He told Leonard that whatever he was experiencing his elders would interpret for him. He was not to add anything to his vision but should also not leave anything out. The strange man then gave Leonard a small medicine bundle. When Leonard finally came out of his vision, he found an oddly shaped pebble in his clenched fist. He carries it in his medicine bag. When he went on his first *hanblechia* after getting his freedom he also received a vision, but a smaller one.

Some people crying for a dream for four days and nights do not receive a vision. It does or does not happen. Also not all vision seekers use a pit. Uncle Bill Eagle Feathers used to pray for a dream by just hunkering down on top of a hill. The spot he had chosen must have been used for this purpose for a long, long time because the whole hilltop was covered with ancient sacred things—animal skulls, rattles, medicine bags, disintegrating tobacco bundles, cloth offerings. It was a place of mystery and whenever I was up there I felt unseen presences. There was always a sharp wind blowing on that place and I wondered how Uncle Bill could have stood it, fasting and praying on that exposed, stormswept spot.

One thing that impressed me, living at Grass Mountain, was that for the people among whom I lived, every part of daily life had a religious meaning. Eating, drinking, the sight or cry of an animal, the weather, a beaded or quilled design, the finding of certain plants or certain rocks, had spiritual significance. I watched, listened, and learned. The process was odd. On the one hand I was still the same footloose half-breed girl who once had ripped off stores in many big cities; on the other, I was becoming a traditional Sioux woman steeped in the ancient beliefs of her people. I was developing a split personality. But so were all the modern Sioux around me, I think.

It touched me deeply to see medicine men and elders include even small children in their ceremonies, to watch the love and patience with which they were taught to participate. I remember little Pedro sitting in on his first *yuwipi* ceremony. He was still so small and the spirits whirled him around and he was yelling to me out of the darkness that they had shown him a glowing, many-colored bird....

At last came the time for me to sun-dance. One pledges at the end of one Sun Dance to take part in the following one. Standing right by the sacred tree I made my vow: "Next summer I shall sun-dance. I will do it so that Indian prisoners dear to me should go free." A year had gone by and I had to fulfill my promise.

Uncle Bill Eagle Feathers, who died a few years ago, was the intercessor, the living bridge between the people and the Spirit. As he called it, the Sun Dance was the granddaddy of all Indian ceremonies. He was right. *Wi wanyang wacipi*, the Sun Dance, is the most awe-inspiring of our rituals, occuring every year at the height of summer. In 1883 the government and the missionaries outlawed the dance for being "barbaric, superstitious, and preventing the Indians from becoming civilized." The hostility of the Christian churches to the Sun Dance was not very logical. After all, they worship Christ because he suffered for the people, and a similar religious concept lies behind the Sun Dance, where the participants pierce their flesh with skewers to help someone dear to them. The main difference, as Lame Deer used to say, is that Christians are content to let Jesus do all the suffering for them whereas Indians give of their own flesh, year after year, to help others. The missionaries never saw this side of the picture, or maybe they saw it only too well and fought the Sun Dance because it competed with their own Sun Dance pole—the Cross. At any rate, for half a century Indians could go to jail for sun-dancing or for participating in any kind of tribal ceremony.

For this reason, white historians think that there was no sun-dancing among the Sioux between 1883 and the 1930s, but they are wrong. The dance simply went underground. During all that time, every year some Sioux, somewhere, performed the ceremony. Henry and other old men still bear the deep scars on their chests from Sun Dances performed illegally in out-of-the-way places during the 1920s. All through our valley along the Little White River you can find traces of old, well-hidden dance circles. For half a century a handful of medicine men and elders kept the dance alive, passing on the songs that go with it and the knowledge of how to perform this ceremony, down to the smallest detail. Nothing was lost.

Leonard's chest is a battleground of scars from more than a dozen piercings. Since 1971 he has put on the ritual every summer on our own land. This happened in the following way: Many traditional people had become disgusted with the commercialization of the Sun Dance at Pine Ridge, with entrance fees and payments for picture taking, hot dog stands and ferris wheels, which made this sacred ceremony into a tourist attraction. So in 1971 a few medicine men, among them Leonard and Uncle Bill, Wallace Black Elk, and John Lame Deer, decided to perform the Sun Dance in the good old way instead of in a circus atmosphere. For their site they chose Wounded Knee where so many of our ancestors had been massacred by the army in 1890. They put up the arbor and the sweat lodge and after the preparation they began to dance. Then everything went wrong. A car drove up full of tribal police. Their chief told Uncle Bill and Leonard that they were forbidden to dance at Wounded Knee because "it was inflammatory and might draw people away" from their commercial Pine Ridge Sun Dance.

Leonard told the police boss, "Don't you know about freedom of religion? You're an Indian. How can you interfere with a sacred ceremony while it is going on?" The dancers, meanwhile, ignoring the police, continued dancing and blowing on their eagle-bone whistles. The police boss did not like the job he was sent to do. He was embarrassed and drove off.

On the second day the dancers were making flesh offerings when the sound of police sirens again drowned out their songs. This time the tribal police came in force with three squad cars. Their chief said, "I hate to do this but I'm ordered to arrest you." Bill Eagle Feathers wept. "I am the bad luck guy. Great Spirit, what did I do wrong?"

Leonard had a hard time keeping the dancers in line because it was a near-killing situation. Among the dancers was a group of young people calling themselves "Indians of All Tribes." They came from San Francisco where they had taken part in the occupation of Alcatraz Island. They wanted to fight the police. It took a great effort by Leonard and Uncle Bill to prevent bloodshed. Everybody was hauled off to court and fined. After a few hours the dancers were released but police occupied the dance ground to make sure that the ceremony could not be continued.

The dancers asked Leonard, "What are we going to do now?" One could not leave a Sun Dance half done. Not finishing it to the point of piercing was unthinkable. Leonard said, "We have made a vow to the Great Spirit and we must keep it." Somebody suggested continuing the dance at Rosebud, on Crow Dog's private land, where nobody could interfere with it, and all agreed that this was a good idea. But there was the problem of the tree. The sacred Sun Dance pole standing at the center of the Sun Dance circle is always a two-forked cottonwood tree. Men are sent out to scout for the most perfect tree they can find. They count coup upon it as in battle. A young maiden who has never been with a man makes the first symbolic cut with the axe. The tree must not touch the

ground when falling but must be caught by the men who will carry it to the dance ground.

Leonard was disturbed. The Crow Dog place was over eighty miles distant. How could men carry the heavy tree that far? The tree is sacred. At the height of the dance sick persons lie beneath the tree to be cured. Looking at it, some dancers had already received visions. How could it be transported?

Just about that time a large truck with long-haired young white people arrived. They had come all the way from the East Coast to learn about Indian ways. One of them told Leonard, "We overheard what you said. We'll put your tree on our truck and drive it all the way to your place."

Leonard objected. The tree had to be carried on foot in a sacred manner. To put it on a truck would be very bad. But then Bill Eagle Feathers, twice as old as Leonard and a sun-dancer many times over, stepped in. He thanked all those, Indian and white, who were present. He pointed to the young, long-haired people. "Great Spirit, look at them. They are poor like us. Look at their clothes. Look at their shoes. They call me a lousy Indian. They call them lousy hippies. We travel the same road. Grandfather, Tunkashila will understand. The Sacred Tree will under-stand. What we are doing is good."

He smoked up the young hippies with cedar and sweetgrass. And then the Sun Dance pole was loaded on top of the truck with all the offerings still attached to it, the four direction flags streaming from it in the wind. The truck was followed by a whole caravan of decrepit Indian cars. For a few miles it was escorted by a tribal police car and in it the unhappy police chief was standing up, praying to the sacred tree with his pipe.

After arriving at Crow Dog's place the dancers planted the tree in a hole filled with buffalo fat. Henry made two figures of buffalo hide, one figure of a man and the other of a buffalo bull. They stood for the renewal of all life, human and animal, because that, too, is an aspect of the Sun Dance. In the old days these figures always had huge male organs symbolizing what the dance was about—more people and more buffalo to feed them.

Everybody pitched in to smooth down the dance circle, put up the shade cover of pine boughs, and make everything holy. It took them the whole day to get everything ready to continue the dance. The next morning, at sunrise, Bill Eagle Feathers raised his pipe and blew on his eagle-bone whistle, praying for an

ritual, but I felt it deeply. I understood it with my heart even though not yet with my mind. I saw the tree, the people sitting under the shade, the dancers with their wreaths of sage, their red kilts, medicine bundles dangling on their chests. I heard the many eagle-bone whistles making the sound of a thousand birds. It made me feel good because I sensed the strong feeling between the different people and tribes. I looked at the men with their long, flowing black hair and at the women in their white, beaded buckskin dresses. It was so beautiful that it

> **I looked at the men with their long, flowing black hair and at the women in their white, beaded buckskin dresses.**
>
> **It was so beautiful that it brought tears to my eyes.**
>
> **I wanted to be part of this, I wanted to feel it, spiritually and in my flesh.**

eagle to come in as a sign that the dance was blessed. Within minutes, an eagle flew in low over the hills from the east, circled slowly over the dance ground, then disappeared in the west. They then finished the dance among the grass and pines, without loudspeakers or electric floodlights, in the old, traditional way. At this dance Leonard for the first time revived the old custom of dragging buffalo skulls embedded in the flesh of his back. He told me, "I took five steps with those skulls and it felt as if my heart was being torn out through my back." From that day on, every summer there has always been a Sun Dance at Crow Dog's place, and always the person acting as intercessor prays for an eagle to come in to bless the dancers and always the eagle appears. I was only a teenager when that took place.

I have sun-danced myself. I did not pierce until the second year after I began living with Leonard. At first I did not understand the whole

brought tears to my eyes. I wanted to be part of this, I wanted to feel it, spiritually and in my flesh. It was real compared to what I had known, not a hand-me-down belief but a personal reawakening that stirred a remembrance deep inside me. So I made a vow to sun-dance for four years, and the first time I found it hard to fulfill my commitment.

I began my dance by making a flesh offering. Leonard told me, "I'll cut the skin from your arm. That's a sacrifice. Your prayers go out for those suffering in jail, for friends who are sick. I will put the pieces from your arm into a square of red cloth, make a little bundle of it, and tie it to the sacred pipe. That way you'll remember this always." I made my flesh offering thinking of all the brothers and sisters who had died, who, I felt, had somehow died for me.

When the Sun Dance came out into the open again in the 1930s and '40s, and until recently when Leonard started the dance on our land, the piercing was comparatively tame. Just a small piece of flesh on the chest, over the heart, was pierced with a short skewer or eagle claw. To this was fastened a rawhide thong hanging from the top of the sacred pole, and the dancer then tore himself loose with comparatively little trouble. But under the influence of Leonard and the medicine men Pete Catches, Fools Crow, and Eagle Feathers, the self-inflicted pain has become more and more severe until now it is just like in the old Catlin and Bodmer paintings depicting the ritual of a hundred and fifty years ago. This has spread from Crow Dog's place to other dance sites and other Sioux reservations.

At a recent Sun Dance a friend of ours, Jerry Roy, an Ojibway Indian, underwent a different kind of self-torture on every one of the four days of the ritual. On the first day he pierced in two places on his chest and broke loose. On the second day he made flesh offerings from both of his arms. On the third, he dragged twelve buffalo skulls behind him. And on the last day he again pierced in two places on his chest and had himself hoisted to the top of the tree. He hung there from his breast muscles for a long time until finally some men grabbed his ankles and pulled him free.

At the same dance, Leonard "danced" with the tree. Instead of just tearing himself loose, he only pulled back until the flesh on his chest stretched out about six inches and then made the heavy cottonwood tree sway to his motion, which must have hurt him badly. He told me later, "I danced with the tree. It talked to me. Along and up those rawhide thongs I made a collect call to the Great Spirit. My body wasn't believing it. My mind wasn't believing it. But spiritually I believed." At another Sun Dance, Leonard had himself pierced in four places, two in front and two in back. Thongs were fastened in his flesh and tied to four horses, which were then driven off into the four directions.

I watched a young man dancing. He was a *winkte*—he was gay. He was as graceful as a young girl. He was standing between four upright poles. Rawhide ropes fastened in his flesh in front and in back had been tied to the poles. The young man had little room to move. His way of piercing had always been considered the most painful because he could not tear himself free by a sudden run or jump backward, but had to work himself free agonizingly slowly, bit by bit. He was swaying back and forth languidly, almost like a ballet dancer, his eyes closed, his face expressionless with just a trace of a smile, swaying back and forth, back and forth, the blood streaming from his wounds....

I pierced too, together with many other women. One of Leonard's sisters pierced from two spots above her collarbone. Leonard and Rod Skenandore pierced me with two pins through my arms. I did not feel any pain because I was in the power. I was looking into the clouds, into the sun. Brightness filled my mind. The sun seemed to speak: "I am the Eye of Life. I am the Soul of the Eye. I am the Life Giver!" In the almost unbearable brightness, in the clouds, I saw people. I could see those who had died. I could see Pedro Bissonette standing by the arbor and, above me, the face of Buddy Lamont, killed at Wounded Knee, looking at me with ghostly eyes. I saw the face of my friend Annie Mae Aquash, smiling at me. I could hear the spirits speaking to me through the eagle-bone whistles. I heard no sound but the shrill cry of the eagle bones. I felt nothing and, at the same time, everything. It was at that moment that I, a white-educated half-blood, became wholly Indian. I experienced a great rush of happiness. I heard a cry coming from my lips:

> Ho Uway Tinkte.
> A Voice I will send.
> Throughout the Universe,
> Maka Sitomniye,
> My Voice you shall hear:
> I will live!

Discussion Questions: **Mary Crow Dog**

1. In her first paragraph, Mary Crow Dog writes that it is not easy to be a Sioux woman. What examples does she give of the mistreatment of Native American women?

2. Geography and place are very important to Native Americans. Notice that in the several rituals Crow Dog describes, all of them are tied to the land. Indeed, she writes that the area around Grass Mountain "is at the core of our existence." Why do you think this is? Why do Sioux rituals such as the Sun Dance make the land so significant?

3. How did traditional Sioux culture treat a girl's first menstrual period? How does this compare with the way white culture treats the same event?

4. How have Native Americans been treated by the dominant white culture? What does AIM do for the self-esteem of these people? How did Crow Dog's in-laws react to attempts by Christians to evangelize them?

5. What does Mary Crow Dog think about men and their power? Does she think the way Sioux men treat Sioux women makes up for the women's poor treatment at the hands of white men? Why does she not blame Sioux men for the way they treat Sioux women?

6. Rituals demarcate and reinforce the boundaries of the community. Explain why Mary Crow Dog wants to pierce.

7. In her review of Mary Crow Dog, M. Annette Jaimes writes that Mary Crow Dog:

   > shows a profound insight into [AIM's defects], locating the source of the problem in a colonial system that has always found it imperative to overtly negate indigenous men (a symbol of power to the colonizer) far more extensively than native women (a symbol of submission within colonialism's distorted lexicon). After more than a century of colonial domination, much of Native America has internalized some portion of the symbolic and psychological matrices of imperialism, with its attendant male chauvinism ("A Review of Mary Ellen Crow Dog's *Lakota Woman*," *Indigenous Thought* ([October, 1991], p. 19).

   Explain what Jaimes means. In your explanation, refer to Mary Crow Dog's autobiography.

8. Here is another quote from Jaimes's review. Mary Crow Dog understands that:

> the extent to which an American Indian man displays sexist attitudes is the degree to which he continues to suffer under the yoke of colonialism's mental maiming. This in turn places her in a position to feel, express, and act upon a genuine sympathy towards the men who have abused and oppressed her, even while consciously refuting and resisting their thinking and conduct.

Do you agree with Jaimes's analysis? Give examples from Crow Dog's text to support your answer. Comment on Crow Dog's rejection of feminism as "mainly a white, upper-middle-class affair of little use to a reservation Indian woman."

9. How does Mary Crow Dog regard the white man's blood in her veins? Does her view about this change at all through the story?

10. Crow Dog notes that some people have criticized the ritual acts of piercing and flesh offering. She writes that some anthropologists think the dance is only a display of "the macho side of Sioux culture." Crow Dog admits that some of the young men may see it as a manhood test, but she defends the ritual and declares her interest in participating in it herself. Suppose you came to know Mary Crow Dog well. Would you try to convince her to stop piercing?

Chapter 5

Hinduism

CREED

HEN we study the creed or beliefs of a religion we are studying the propositions, the sentences, that adherents take to be true. There are many propositions Hindus take to be true, including the proposition that there are many gods. Some say there are as many as 330 million gods and goddesses in the Hindu pantheon. Because most deities have birthdays, Hindus have every reason to celebrate; on any given day there might be a million divine birthdays to observe. While Hindus believe in many gods, however, many Hindus also believe that the many gods are only different manifestations of a single impersonal principle, *Brahman*, and for this reason it is probably inaccurate to call the creed of Hinduism a polytheistic one. A better term is suggested by Ninian Smart: *kathenotheists,* people who worship different gods, but only one at a time.[1] Hinduism, then, is very much like Native American religions and Judaism in one important respect: there is a wide diversity of beliefs in the "family" of religions called Hinduism. Hinduism is not a single tradition but is composed of many traditions, traditions as different from each other as the Lakota Sioux religion in South Dakota is different from the Inuit's religion in Alaska.

The modern period of Indian religion began with the coming of British rule around 1800 C.E. (*C.E.* means "common era" and is an alternative way of referring to the period you may have learned to call A.D. *B.C.E.* means "before the common era," and replaces B.C.) Prior to this period, from roughly 1200 to 1700 C.E. during the Mogul empire,

---

1. Smart, *Religious Experience,*op. cit., p. 81.

Muslims dominated Indian politics as Islam joined Hinduism as a major religion of the Indian subcontinent. Hinduism was strong when Great Britain moved into the political vacuum left by the decline of the Muslims in the latter half of the eighteenth century. About the time this chapter's first author, Swami Agehananda Bharati, was born, a strong desire to expel the British was growing on the subcontinent, but it would be a lengthy struggle to restore the independence of India. The Indian best known in the United States is probably Mahatma Gandhi, whose honorary title *Mahatma* means "Great Soul." Gandhi pursued the struggle for freedom through nonviolent means. Both Bharati and our second author, Shudha Mazumdar, refer to him.

We focus in this chapter on religious belief. Some forms of Hinduism encourage belief in a warm and personal god, often Krishna or Rama. In the second story of this chapter, Shudha Mazumdar tells about the room her mother has reserved in their house for the worship of the god Shiva. Shiva is the ideal man, a god who is deeply devoted to his wife, Durga, and who shakes the heavens with his sobs when Durga dies. In the worship room, Mazumdar's mother practices *puja,* or devotion to a god. *Puja* worship is a ritual activity in which an image of the god or goddess is greeted, bathed, fed, and washed. *Puja* consists in part of vowed observances, rituals called *bratas,* in which fresh flowers and grasses are picked from the garden and are placed with rice and peeled banana before a small statue of Shiva. Mazumdar believes what her mother tells her, that if she performs her *bratas* regularly for four years, she will be blessed with a husband as full of love as Shiva.

Mazumdar does not believe in only one god, however. She acknowledges the validity of many gods, including Krishna and Rama, and so displays the pluralistic and tolerant attitude of many Hindus. Emotional devotion to a god is known as *bhakti,* and is practiced by Shaivites, who worship Shiva, and Vaishnavas, like Mahatma Gandhi, who worship forms of Vishnu. *Bhakti* religions, which are very practical, differ dramatically from Advaita Vedanta religion, which is intellectual and abstract. *Advaita* means nondualistic, and Vedantists of this school strive to overcome *maya,* the illusion that the external world of change and suffering is real. This sort of Hinduism also stems from the period of classical Hinduism, and is based on the writings of the medieval mystic and scholar named Shankara. In our first reading, Swami Agehananda Bharati expresses his belief in this more ascetic (that is, less emotional and more abstract) form of Hinduism.

Unlike traditional forms of Christianity, Indian religious beliefs often are not aimed at denying oneself in this world in order to achieve salvation in the next. Even though Bharati's beliefs do not fit this profile, many Hindus see the purpose of religion as convincing the gods and goddesses to bestow material prosperity and happiness in *this* life. Our second author sees things this way. Shudha Mazumdar writes that the "ultimate aim" of religious observance in most forms of Hinduism is "worldly bliss" and "fulfillment." For these Hindus, the purpose of worshiping a god or goddess is not necessarily to secure a place of righteousness in another world, but to secure a life of ease and plenty in this one. Mazumdar recites a verse to this effect, a verse promising you possessions if you say your *bratas* faithfully. The verse promises cows in the cowshed, corn in the storehouse, and "every year a son." Even Bharati, the intellectual monk, does not hide his love for plenty of spicy food. So Mazumdar and Bharati agree on at least one belief: that the ascetic or monastic ideal is not essential even though, as Bharati notes, many Indians seek to achieve the ascetic realization that ultimate reality, Brahman, and one's own self, *Atman*, are identical.

Here we reach the most puzzling aspect of Hindu belief. In the West, theologians occasionally embrace apparent contradictions among their beliefs, such as between the Christian belief that God is immaterial and invisible and that God was visible in the material body of Jesus Christ. Apparent contradictions such as these are relatively rare, however, and many theologians take pains to explain even these inconsistencies away, denying that the two beliefs are contradictory. In many forms of Hindu belief, however, thinkers seem to revel in contradictions. Bharati tells of a speaker who begins his address with a standard opening phrase: "My own self, in the form of you sisters and brothers…" What is the speaker saying? He is saying something like "I am you and you are me," a statement that would induce confusion among most Westerners, but appears not to concern the Indian audience. In studying Hindu beliefs, you must be prepared to encounter ideas unlike those now familiar to you.

Bharati's beliefs about the existence of God are worth noting. At one of his lectures he is asked whether he teaches "that it is not important to believe in a Being, a Supreme God." He replies he "certainly did preach that at times," adding that the sacred Indian texts allow Hindus variously to believe in a Supreme Being, to disbelieve, or to suspend judgment. The South Indian monk to whom he is speaking asks him whether he knows about the rule of *adhikarabheda*, that teachers "must not divulge things too subtle to the unsubtle, lest [the unsubtle] should be confused." Bharati answers he thinks "it is wrong to pamper the 'unsubtle,'" meaning that difficult religious teachings should be shared equally with the naive and the learned.

The disciplines in which we study religious belief are philosophy of religion and theology. As I noted in the Introduction, the study of theology differs from other disciplines in that those who study it must be willing to grant a certain amount of validity to the transcendent. If we are wholly skeptical about superior beings and supernatural powers, we are more likely to be interested in historical or psychological explanations of religious belief than in theological explanations. As you read the selections in this chapter, try to remain open to the validity of the transcendent and discover the particular nuances of religious beliefs on the Indian subcontinent.

As an object of academic study, religious beliefs can be studied from within a tradition, or from outside. Most of you will be studying Hindu beliefs from outside that tradition. As you seek to understand these beliefs in an empathic and critical way, think in terms of three stages:

1. **Discovery:** What are the specific propositions toward which adherents hold an assenting attitude? How do believers arrive at these specific propositions? What do the beliefs actually mean to the believers?

2. **Interpretation:** What is the order of importance of the beliefs? Which beliefs are most basic to the tradition or individual? Which beliefs are secondary and may be jettisoned if found to conflict with more basic beliefs? Whose interpretations of beliefs are authoritative?

3. **Justification:** Do the basic beliefs cohere with each other? Do believers give reasons for assenting to the basic propositions? Are the reasons persuasive?

When examining the beliefs of our own traditions we must first discover what our beliefs are before we can offer interpretations or justifications of them. The same is true when examining the beliefs of other traditions; but in looking at traditions not our own, the process of discovery is even more critical because we are apt not to understand the beliefs when we encounter them. In his first sentence, Bharati complains that many books about India present it as a place of odd wonders and mysteries. But to present Hindu culture this way is to mystify it, make it unreal. Instead we should aim simply to understand it. Most of us are "foreigners" when it comes to Hinduism, so we must go through the initial steps of discovery and interpretation judiciously and methodically. And we should feel entitled to assess the truth of foreign religious propositions only when we can articulate those propositions in ways that believers will recognize as their own. We cannot earn the right to say whether a foreign religious proposition is false—or true—until we have at least stated it in such a way that an adherent of the religion will say, "Yes, that's it; that is what I believe." When we have achieved this level of empathic understanding then, and only then, have we earned the right to try to judge whether some foreign religious belief is justified. If we decide it is justified, the next step may be to ask whether it is a belief we want to accept.

Swami Agehananda Bharati

From Swami Agehananda Bharati,
The Ochre Robe: An Autobiography
(Santa Barbara, CA: Ross-Erikson, 1980).
Reprinted by permission of Ross-Erikson.

Popularizing books [about India and Asia] have something in common that is very deleterious and should be scotched: the awed presentation of wonders, either real or pretended, and a constant high-pitched amazement at everything connected with the East. Because their readers suppose India to be a land of wonderful mysteries, the authors of the popularizing works play up that angle for all they are worth.

My aim in the present [autobiography] is exactly the opposite. I want to play down this element of the wonderful [because it]…tends to hamper any real knowledge and understanding of India…. I feel myself competent to do this, not only because I have obtained my own knowledge in the ordinary way by solid study, but also because I have experienced it—and still experience it—as a deeply involved participant. For myself as a monk, as a *sannyasi*, I am still a student, but for the Hindu I am an *acarya,* a teacher whose word with regard to the interpretation of Hinduist religious teachings must be accepted without cavil [argument], a man who may be criticized only in monastic didactic disputations [formal debates] or by pandits [teachers, learned people] in the company of pandits.

In this respect my case—to the best of my knowledge at any rate—is unique: I am a European by birth and appearance but the Hindu listens to me as a teacher of his own doctrines, though they were never before taught pastorally by non-Indians. There are, of course, quite a number of Europeans who have become Indian monks: the various Hindu Orders [religious groups] number about a dozen in their ranks, whilst the Buddhist Orders number at least a hundred. I know of three even amongst the Jainas [a nonviolent Indian religion]. But as the Hindus do not speak English, these non-Indian monks have *a priori* no full contact, and they live for themselves according to the teachings. They are often highly venerated by the Hindus amongst whom they live, but they are neither heard nor understood, because the learning of Indian spoken languages has its own difficulties. Some non-Indians speak Hindi, or some other Indian language, but always with an accent; and that is more damaging than one can imagine in the West, where people are not so phonetically sensitive as the Indians are. I speak without a foreign accent and I teach without an accent—as witness the congregations of 70,000 Hindus in Delhi and Allahabad and elsewhere, to which I have preached....

I am well aware of the risks I am running in writing this autobiography. First of all, you cannot please everyone, and in my case I am already well aware that I shall please very few—my experiences in three continents have already taught me enough for that. For the orthodox Hindu I am too Western; far too much interested in Beethoven, Tristan, Russell, semantics [figures and subjects of Western culture] and social intercourse with my fellow men. And for the still bigoted non-Indian I am not sufficiently like a monk; for, of course, he has a cut and dried idea of what a "monk" ought to be....

One of the points this autobiography will seek to demonstrate is that although my way of life is monastic this involves no contradiction with humanism, but rather a peculiar fulfillment. What interests me is a way of monastic life that is free of all oppressiveness, all repressions and all dogmas (which Indian monasticism is not, despite all the popularizers say about the tolerance of Hinduism); in short, a monastic humanism. I must again warn the occidental reader urgently against the arid severity of Indian monasticism. I do not want any vague mystical sentimentalism or any mystical urge "eastwards" to bar the way to a real understanding. Once the barren harshness and pedantic aridity of monastic neophytism is overcome then a new and splendid vista opens up: but as far as I am concerned it leads back to the individual—it is the way back after a great purification. And all the other things tradition

promises—participation in divine omniscience, union with the absolute, freedom from birth, death and reincarnation—these are subsidiary gifts. Not that I deny reincarnation of life after death of the body: let eschatology [doctrines about the end of time] stay put—in the Indopalingenetic teachings or in the Christian-Mohammedan [*Mohammedan* is an old term for Islam] doctrine of a Last Judgment. You choose your own eschatology by virtue of that doctrinary differentiation we must all make, taking what emotionally suits us, though 99 percent of us leave the decision to the last moment, when we are on our death-beds. For my part though, I think it is better and wiser to make the decision as soon as one has learned to think. But whether a man chooses a religion with God, a religion without a God, a philosophy with an afterlife, or a philosophy without an afterlife, does not matter much; it depends entirely on the constitution of the individual thinking human being. The only important thing is that he should choose in good time which way he wants to go; or, better, that he should choose through which form of meditation, through which way of thought, he desires to become a full human being....

Bharati was not always a Hindu, and was not always named Bharati. His given name was Leopold Fischer. He was raised as a Catholic in Vienna, Austria.

When I was nine years old I became a choirboy in the Karlskirche [Catholic Church]. I know perfectly well what attracted me: it was the ritual. Otherwise I just went to church like all the other children did. My parents rarely went, and they were, in the truest sense of the word, irreligious. They were Catholics because it was the thing to be in Vienna, otherwise they were not in the least interested in the Catholic Church, though they saw to it—for the same reason—that Hans and I went to church with Frau Blümel. I had made my first communion, and I enjoyed it, on account of the long candles, the sentimental pictures of Jesus, and all the to-do, particularly the group photograph afterward in Schwarzenberg Park. Incidentally, I never got as far as confirmation; by that time I was practically a pagan.

I went to the Academic Gymnasium; a sort of grammar school and nothing to do with gymnastics, except perhaps where the involvements of Latin syntax were concerned, and these were taught with almost medieval severity. But apart from this the school existed to hammer a particularly aggressive form of Catholicism into its pupils (though about half of them were Jews) and this made my schooldays into one of the decisive stages in my subsequent apostasy. It is not easy, and often quite impossible, in looking back on such an important phase to make any one person or persons "responsible" for it, but at least there was one master (a priest) who unconsciously did his best to make the practice of Catholicism obnoxious to me. He took us for religious instruction, and he was quite generally unpopular because of his pedantry, his frequent fits of anger and his violence. Religious instruction was the only subject that seemed to require hard blows and knocks. Our catechists were more irritable and showed less self-control in their behavior towards us than any of the other masters, and they shouted at us even more loudly than the notorious Latin master Professor Backenlacher, whose bawling could be heard out in the street when some unfortunate boy did not know an irregular perfect. Perhaps on its own all this would not have had quite such an effect, for you get over disagreeable experiences in school, but suddenly my specific relationship with this master worsened.

At the age of about thirteen I joined the Indian Club in Vienna—I was already keen on India and everything Indian, and I sought every opportunity of talking with Indian students, both male and female (most of them were studying medicine) about my proud attempts at Sanskrit and Hindi, languages my fellow pupils

had never even heard of before I mentioned them, but which then caused them to regard me with awed respect. Naturally I was also much impressed by the gods and goddesses and the pious wise men of India. My religious mentor got to hear of this, but instead of summoning me and discussing it reasonably he reacted by doing his best to make my life a misery; and during religious instruction he would thunder angrily against the "sinful, foolish, wicked heathen," and praise to the skies the splendid work being done, at great risk and sacrifice, by the Catholic missionaries in India. At the same time he would exhort the boys to pray for the poor Indian heathen children and collect silver paper for them. We all wondered what they wanted silver paper for, but no one dared ask.

One day I decided to take the bull by the horns so I went direct to the sacristy where this particular cleric could usually be found in the breaks. I was not yet fourteen, and with me I took a Latin missal that I had been given as a present, in the hope of using it as some sort of bridge to what I wanted to say and did not know how to. And now something happened that made a deep impression on me, so deep that I have never forgotten it. He looked at me with the expressionless eyes of a salamander and at the same time he began to scratch his back voluptuously, and at every movement his cassock moved ludicrously up and down his back. He probably did not realize that he was doing it; he did it so often that it had become a habit. At the same time he said slowly, and again and again without pausing, as though it were a litany: "Yes, yes, Fischer. Work hard. Work hard."

That was all, but it had a distinct traumatic effect on me. It was perhaps at that moment that my aesthetic sensibility in religious matters was awakened. From that time on it was no longer easy for me to avoid the feeling that Christian saintliness was concomitant with not taking a bath. Much later on when I became acquainted with medieval religious literature and found saintly writers recommending dirt as holy and condemning taking baths as a trap set by Satan for the downfall of Christian souls, my own feelings were corroborated. I had already heard vaguely that in some of the boarding schools run by nuns, girls were not allowed to take a bath....

Christian theologians regard the abandonment of physical ritual as progressive, as against the Jews; so did Protestant reform movements in the Middle Ages. I have never been able to share this view, regarding it as a form of aggressive primitivism whose psychological roots lie much deeper than in a mere aversion to empty ritual. For Hinduism bathing is a part of religious devotion, and belongs to religious ritual; and every Hindu holy place has or is a bathing place. It is utterly out of the question for any Hindu, no matter what his social status, to perform his religious devotions, or to enter a temple, without having bathed immediately beforehand. In this book I shall frequently have occasion to stress the great importance of the aesthetic factor in all things relating to meditation and religious practice, and to indicate to what an amazing extent aesthetic feeling is central in the emergent phenomena.

I think I am right in saying that if my stern religious mentor in Vienna had been merely religiously intolerant and fanatical, and had not at the same time been an offense to the eye and the nose, I might never have fallen away from the one true source of all Grace, the Catholic Church. At the very least it would have happened much later. I would have clashed with him, put up with some of his heaviest clouts, and perhaps revenged myself like any other good Catholic boy by putting a stink bomb in his desk. But that might have been all. Instead of that I remained resentfully silent and gradually drifted away.

In fact, this trivial and somewhat morbid episode is of importance, because at that time it could not be said that my apostasy and my

Hinduism had any, or at least any exclusively, rational and intellectual basis. I am reporting this development chronologically, and therefore I must record that what strikes me today as the argument against Christian teaching was not in my mind then. I also regard it as important to show the effect of compulsory catechism and enforced religious observances on a sensitive child. Just one last word about this religious mentor. It was at a time when Mahatma Gandhi was my hero, and his picture hung over my bed where formerly the crucifix had been. A trifle provocatively I asked the good Father where he thought the soul of the Mahatma would go after his death, and he replied: "Straight to Hell, of course. Where else?"

How did it happen that I went to India? It is a question I have been asked again and again by Indians and by Westerners, by priests, monks, and laymen—with a variety of motives, but always with concern. What caused the development that led the son of a well-to-do Vienna family to throw overboard the traditions of his own world, to abandon the shores of the blue Danube for the shores of the greyish Ganges, and to wander along the dusty roads of India as a mendicant monk? I can report very little about the beginnings of the process, and I do not propose to suggest anything mystical, since I can remember nothing of the sort in my childhood. Others may have seen it, but the people in my environment were not particularly observant. However, my Uncle Harry did tell me much later that once when I had measles I started up in bed and announced in a clear voice to my mother: "You see, mother; you come and you go; you come and you go; you come again and you go again—and one day it's all over." My mother could not remember anything about it, and, in any case, you can interpret the alleged words as you like: as a disconnected fever fantasy, as an indication of some metempsychotic experience, as an eruption of some slumbering knowledge, or as sheer nonsense. Whatever interpretation you choose will make no difference, nor will it be of any help. A Hindu would, of course, regard the words as a formulation of the doctrine of reincarnation, but I had the measles long before I had even heard of India.

When Fischer was eleven years old he read a novel by the Hindu poet Rabindranath Tagore and attended a concert and dance performed by the Indian troupe of Uday Shankar. He was so enchanted by things Indian that he became, at thirteen, the youngest member of the Indian Club in Vienna. As a teenager, he learned four Indian languages: classical Sanskrit, Hindi, Urdu, and Bengali. Here he writes about some of the Indians he met in Vienna.

Two episodes are deeply ingrained in my memory, and in the memory of those who witnessed them, which I know since I met a number of them afterwards in India. Dr. Chaudhuri was a very capable Indian doctor from Benares, and for a number of years he was President of the All-India Medical Association. He had come to Vienna for an operation, which at that time was performed only there, by one of Vienna's leading surgeons. He was in the Auersperg sanatorium and I went to visit him every day. In the same room with him was a highly educated Mohammedan from Northern India. On one occasion, to the great delight of Chaudhuri, I praised the tolerance of Hinduism and compared it favorably with the intolerance of the religion in which I had been brought up. However, the Mohammedan interrupted me and defended Christianity against my attacks.

Now the chief charge of Mohammedanism against Hinduism is that it has many gods and idols, whereas the Mohammedan does not regard the Christian as *kafir,* as a heathen, even though the doctrine of the Trinity strikes him as suspect. But for Mohammedans, particularly if they are Indian, the Hindus are the quintessence of the heathenism condemned by the Prophet. The truth is, of course, that Hinduism is no

more polytheistic [believing in many gods] than Islam, and the charge of ignorant Moslems and Christians is just baseless. The many idols, gods, and other heavenly creatures that populate the Hindu pantheon fulfill a function, though infinitely richer and wider, similar to that fulfilled by the saints of the Catholic Church. The fanatical Mohammedan is therefore often inclined to regard Catholicism, and in particular Catholicism in the Latin countries, as idolatrous, a prejudice he shares with a good many Protestant Christians.

The truth about Hinduism is that every Hindu, whether he belongs to a monist, a pluralist, a scholastic-absolutist or a theistic-emotional school of Hinduism, believes in the last resort in one, absolute, neutral, impersonal God, the *Brahman,* as the highest principle. This knowledge of God is a gnostic act, and "love of God" is not really the right expression to describe this devotion to, meditation on, or impersonal veneration of this highest, neutral principle. In order to make use of the emotional-human side of religious observance the Hindu postulates a multiplicity of divine manifestations that are intentionally anthropomorphic [human-like], and the worship of these manifestations, which are amenable to human longing and supplication, constitutes what one might call "the love of God." Each Hindu chooses the particular manifestation of the impersonal, absolute *Brahman* that accords with his own psychological and emotional makeup. For example, one Hindu may chose the flute-playing shepherd-god Krishna as his *ishta,* as his "chosen, beloved and divine ideal." Another may choose the dark goddess Kali. A third may prefer the ascetic god Shiva.

In short, the one impersonal God presents Himself in many manifestations and many functions. Just as one man plays the role of father to his sons, husband to his wife, friend to his friends, and master to his servants, so God is father to the one, lord and master to the other, a friend to the third, and so on. And as this supreme God is first of all a neutral omnipresent principle, it can manifest itself in either a male or a female form. It can manifest itself as the lover or the beloved, or as a much loved and cosseted child. Now both the Mohammedan and the Christian, who know no better, and who, unfortunately, often do not want to know any better, regard this multiplicity of forms and expressions as representing so many different gods. But a man is not five men because he is at one and the same time a father, a son, an uncle, a master and, say, a poet. On the other hand, the weightiest objection of the Hindu and the Buddhist to the Mediterranean religions, Judaism, Christianity and Islam, is psychological: no two men are the same in all things, and it is therefore impossible for all men to venerate God in one form or one function alone; for example, solely as a father, or solely as a just judge. Since then, what would those men do who desire neither fatherhood nor judgeship?

But our Mohammedan patient in the sanatorium Auersperg defended that philosophically weak but—for Mohammedans—emotionally very powerful principle that "there can be only one truth." I replied, on the basis of what I know now as I knew then, that, first of all, we cannot know whether there is only one truth or not, unless indeed, we let a particular faith simply state the matter for us; and secondly, even if there is only one truth there are many ways that lead to it. This is laid down very clearly in the canonical literature of Hinduism, and the Upanishad [Hindu sacred book] declares: *ekam sadvipra bahudha vadanti*—"There is only one truth, but wise men call it by many names." I quoted this passage to my two Indian friends who lay in the same sickroom but thought so differently in these fundamental matters. The Mohammedan fell silent, and from the expression on Dr. Chaudhuri's face I could see that he thought I had won a victory for Hinduism.

The second episode, which took place in the same period, was the birthday celebration for Mahatma Gandhi on 2 October 1937. A number of prominent people had been invited, including the Rector of Vienna University, and many famous doctors, since the Indians in Vienna were particularly associated with the medical profession. Dr. Kesarbani, who taught me Sanskrit [ancient Indian holy language], was unavoidably absent in Rome, and before leaving he had delegated to me the honor of reading the second chapter of the *Bhagavad Gita* [the sixth book of the *Mahabharata,* an ancient Hindu scriptural book that tells the story of Lord Krishna and his friend Arjuna] in Sanskrit, because there was no one amongst the Indian students who was sufficiently sure of his Sanskrit to undertake it. So I stood on a dais in the Hotel de France and read out the old text in clear Sanskrit before 350 invited guests from the Viennese *haute volée.* And it went off very well. Unknown to me, my Latin and Greek professor at the Academic Gymnasium was in the audience, and the next day the school was full of it and there were even notices in the *Neue Freie Presse* and the *Tagblatt,* the leading newspapers in Vienna. That was the moment when I decided to become an Indologist. I was fourteen years old at the time....

The divinity in its thousand radiant forms as taught in India, and in Asia under Indian influence, as both manly strength and female beauty, as philosophically neutral, as an abstraction, as nonexistent—this divinity is my ultimate interest. But not in the sense that I believe that it exists, in the way that I am quite certain of the reality of the moon or of the human digestive system; because, in fact, I do not know whether it exists or not, even though I may have experienced something that I will call divinity. My individual experience proves nothing; mystical experience does not confer the status of objective existence on what has been experienced. I, myself, postulate this divinity, or Godhead, and it interests me beyond all humanism or aestheticism. And if

> **The Godhead does not intervene except when It is identified with some part of the conscious or unconscious; it is a matter of indifference whether It exists or not.**
>
> **Its existence or nonexistence makes not the slightest difference to my meditation or my ritual.**

Kant were alive to ask me whether this is a moral postulate like his moral law, I should say no. If this postulate is to be qualified (and I hesitate to do so) then I would sooner call it an aesthetic postulate—even though theologians keep telling me that aesthetics is far inferior to religion.

It does not in the least follow that I therefore believe in the objective existence of this Godhead or divinity; in fact this existence is totally unimportant. As everything must be attained in person, and as the concept of mercy does not appeal to me, and repels me, just as does the ethically harmful concept of vicarious atonement; in short, as the Godhead does not intervene except when It is identified with some part of the conscious or unconscious, it is a matter of indifference whether It exists or not. Its existence or nonexistence makes not the slightest difference to my meditation or my ritual.

The same applies to more concrete ideas and actions. There is no such thing as Mother India; no ancestral or hero-spirits; there is also no nation and no people apart from the very few individuals we can meet in a land in a lifetime. Nevertheless, we can choose a ritual as though there were a Mother India, or as if there were a nation....

I became a Legionary [a voluntary association dedicated to a free India] because I chose a certain ritual—except that then I believed that "freedom," "heroism," "Mother India" and so on, were real things; whereas now I know that they are names. All those who have been brought up to mistake names for things—and that means all of us, because we were all taught that the "People," the "Motherland" (or "Fatherland" as the case may be), "Freedom" were real things, like gold, or Gandhi, only much greater; and we were also taught about a loving Father in Heaven; and as though they were things—things in the most general sense, as anything which can be said to *exist.* All of us who were brought up in this old and dangerous confusion find matters very difficult when we begin to abandon it, since only clear thinking can help us, and a recognition that much about which we thought as real things, and which gave us courage and confidence, was only names all the time. That is a bitter awakening, a deflation worse than any other we can experience.

There is, decidedly, no People, no Nation, no Motherland; all that really exists is "people." It is a collective name for a set of indescribable, fully satisfying experiences that resolves *all* problems. As the Upanishad puts it:

The knots of the heart are untwined;
All doubts have disappeared;
Mortal man becomes immortal;
Since he has seen the Highest.

Fischer moved to India from Austria and gradually acquired a following as a swami, *or holy man. He took a new name, Swami Agehananda Bharati, and entered a Hindu monastic order founded by the famous Samkaracarya (c. 750 C.E.). Bharati donned the ochre robe of the mendicant order and, later, began to preach his own hybrid religion of monastic Hinduism and Vedanta philosophy. In the passage that follows, he describes a lesson he gives in Ambala, India, where he is surrounded by Indian students of philosophy.*

I had been planning to give this audience some general bread and butter advice, but somehow, I drifted into Vedantic [nondualist philosophy] monistic jargon and spoke on the rather technical level of monistic dialectic for over an hour. There was silence and close attention and more questions from the audience after that than after more general sermons. Thereafter, I did not exclude Hindu metaphysical doctrine [doctrines about ultimate reality] from my range of themes for such occasions. Brahmin philosophy can be "brought to the masses" without losing its value in the process of popularization, in a way that is denied to Western philosophy. All Indian philosophy is finally intuitive and touches human, nonscholastic interests in spite of its scholastic jargon (which is indeed a formidable barrier to the simple Hindu). I am no longer impressed by the fact that most occidental teachers of philosophy deny the label "philosophy" to Indian thought for this very reason. Until quite recently I myself criticized Dr. Radhakrishnan [an Indian philosopher] for styling Indian thought "philosophy," but I have now practically abandoned the view that Indian thought is no philosophy just because it is not ultimately interested in discursive reasoning, in truth-functions and truth-tables, and I begin to sympathize more than I did then with the late R. G. Collingwood [a British philosopher]. He defined metaphysics as statements of *what* the axiomatic sentences in a particular philosophy were, not *how* those axioms came about or

whether they were correct or false. Thus I no longer deny that "I am the Brahman," the great dictum of the Upanishad, is a philosophical statement. It is metaphysical, and if Collingwood meant—although he did not say so—that metaphysics is the historical discipline in philosophy, filing the history of philosophy in the files of History rather than of Philosophy, then "I am the Brahman" is a metaphysical or an historical statement, but in any case a philosophical one.

This is to readmit Indian thought into "philosophy" in my own terminological tool-box; it is not to accept Indian thought as philosophy *par excellence,* in the sense in which I had accepted it before I became Agehananda. For then I accepted the Indian and debarred contemporary Western philosophy from the appellation, partly because I knew little about the latter, but mainly because my critical faculties were suspended in a phase of conversion and enthusiasm—a sacrifice of the factual and scientific at the altar of aesthetics and religious exultation. It was not that Russell and Wittgenstein and Moore [famous Western philosophers of the twentieth century] came to me first and were superseded by the Upanishad and its prolix adjuncts in East and West: no, the Upanishad came first (via the Hindusthan Academical Association of Vienna, via Vivekananda, and Subhas Bose and others). Then came Wittgenstein and Analysis [Linguistic Analysis, a popular school of modern philosophy]—and about this time the Upanishads, the Buddhist Dharma, and Analysis began to form a pattern in my mind to which I give the name "philosophy," regardless of the possibility of estranging both logicians and aesthetes. The only charge I really fear is that of eclecticism and it may appear as though my present attitude were eclectic. But this is not so, for an eclectic uses the pieces obtained from here and there either to build a system or to fit them into a preconceived system. I am not doing this, because I abhor systems of thought.

I do not think *eclecticism* denotes method; but if it did, I would not object to my *method* being called eclectic, or better, syncretistic. Many people and dictionaries use *eclecticism* and *syncretism* as synonyms, and there has been no ruling on whether this is permissible. I will suggest a terminological barrier: *eclecticism* is patchwork for a system; *syncretism* is methodology deriving from various sources. It is not possible to explain this to the Hindu pundit, because semantics has not yet entered his mind. (Although the Buddhist heretic developed rudimentary semantics as early as in the fourth century A.D.; heretics can be freer in their pursuit of philosophy of any kind.)

Until that sermon at Ambala, I had been embarrassed by my very special dilemma. I knew the logical shortcomings of Vedanta; I appreciated the analysts' work in dealing with religious propositions, but I also admired the Brahmin thinker of all schools who knew how dangerous logic might be to his ontology or theory of the essence of things, who nevertheless studied it with the same intensity as the logician aiming to attack ontology, but who rejected logic with a shrug when it arrogated to itself more than the right to arbitrate between various schools of ontology, for the Brahmin philosopher reserved for himself the final judgment as to what was more important in a total, albeit intellectual worldview. Here, the Brahmin is right, and the logician—Aristotelian or Indian or modern—is wrong: if the human being and its welfare is at stake (which means its spiritual welfare), then paradoxical, illogical, Vedantic or other nondiscursive speculation and meditation are more important than the syllogism or the truth-table. Until this meeting, I had also pitied the *satsang*-audiences, and this intellectual pity, which you are free to call snobbery, added to my embarrassment and restricted my topics to naive moralizing and edifying sermon. On that day, however, I realized that the *satsang*-audience is as interested, and perhaps more attentive, when

Vedanta and other Hindu "philosophy" is brought to it by the *sadhu* or the pandit, if only the latter can avoid scholastic jargon....

In explaining the absoluteness of the Brahman and the relativity of the world, the phenomenality of objects, the analogy of the snake and the rope, plus two equally simple analogies, have been used without modification from the Upanishad down to the present day. A man sees what he thinks is a snake, and he acts accordingly—he hits it, or he gets afraid, he may even die with terror; but if a clever person directs a light towards the object and makes the man realize that it was only a piece of rope, this particular illusion disappears, and questions like "When and where did the snake originate?" are no longer asked, or asked in a facetious manner. The "snake" is the phenomenal world, the "rope" the absolute Brahman....

We could not leave the dais before midnight, as many other speakers were yet to address the hall, and it would have been bad manners to leave. But just after midnight, after the *arati* [the act of waving a ritual lamp around a saintly person], my American friend and I were taken to the kitchen and fed sumptuously. The succulent vegetarian food given to *sadhus* [monks, or ascetic holy persons] in the houses where they speak draws on the resources of the Indian cuisine: it is drenched in *ghee* [clarified butter], exasperatingly tasty, completely fried and starchy and very unwholesome when taken late at night. But gluttony is no sin for the *sadhu*, provided it is vegetarian; in fact a *sadhu* who cannot eat a thorough meal of this sort is viewed with some suspicion. There is a lot of joking about the *sadhus'* and the Brahmins' delight in large quantities of rich, especially sweet food. This is the only field in which monks and pandits may poke fun at themselves and this for several reasons. To the pious Hindu the holy man is healthy through his holiness, therefore he must have good food, can digest it, and deserves it. He is a great person, hence his appetite for this permissible pleasure is also

Hinduism is nonhistorical;
it does not seek,
nor possess,
any historical founders.

The Christian missionary
has been standing in the
middle of the road, crying,
"You who are going to
worship Shiva and Vishnu
and the Goddess,
you will go to Hell!"

The Hindu cannot answer,
"You who worship the
triune God will go to hell,"
because Hinduism teaches
the very opposite.

It teaches that he who
worships God in any form,
as the triune Father-Son-
Paraclete, or as Shiva,
or as Vishnu, or Allah, will
be the better for it.

great. The explanation offered by common sense is that pure food, given in love and respect, is morally pure, and its enjoyment should be conceded to the ascetic [one who lives a holy life without physical luxuries] who has forgone all other ordinary pleasures. To this the psychologist's explanation adds: the *sadhu* has subdued the erotic element in his personality and this permits a smiling approval of gustatory enjoyment….

In my travels in the south [of India], I was often confronted with the problem of Christian conversion, and with Hindu reactions to it. With the Syrian Christians, or with any of the old Christians in India I have no quarrel. Nor for that matter with the converts, but I was distressed to realize that the majority of the Indian Christian clergy and many of the more primitive Western missionaries ascribe their success in proselytizing [making Christian converts] to the intrinsically greater spiritual merit of Christianity. This is disturbing because Hinduism has no weapon to counter this arrogance: Hinduism does not and cannot proselytize; it is not a world religion; one cannot become a Hindu as one can become a Christian or a Muslim, or even a Buddhist. I am myself not fully accepted as Hindu by very many learned, orthodox Hindus—I cannot be a Hindu by orthodox definition for a Hindu is one who is born into a Hindu caste, high or low. Hindu doctrine does not claim that its teachings are in any way superior to those of other religions, in fact it never addresses people of other faiths in whom it has no interest. But the Christian missionary has the Preceptor's [the teacher's, that is, Jesus'] own injunction to back him: "Go ye into all lands." When the Christian missionary goes to the Hindu and tells him, "What I bring you is the truth, because Christ said so," the Hindu has no call to counter the Christian by a similar device, because no one ever told him to go into the world and preach. Hinduism is nonhistorical; it does not seek, nor possess, any historical founders. The Christian missionary has been standing in the middle of the road, crying, "You who are going to worship Shiva and Vishnu and the Goddess, you will go to Hell!" The Hindu cannot answer, "You who worship the triune God will go to hell," because Hinduism teaches the very opposite. It teaches that he who worships God in any form, as the triune Father-Son-Paraclete [Spirit], or as Shiva, or as Vishnu, or Allah, will be the better for it.

There is a band of devoted Hindus in the extreme south, laymen most of them and intelligent men, who feel deeply humiliated at the way in which Christian missionaries have penetrated into their villages. Sri Velayudhan Pillay, proprietor of a small, fairly affluent bank, was their moving spirit. He was no great Sanskrit scholar, but he had none of the childish "We are spiritual in India, you are materialistic in the West, hence accept our guidance unless you want to perish," which lies behind the more vociferous of the spiritual children of Vivekananda and his compeers. Velayudhan just deplored what seemed to him the unchecked intrusion of a foreign tradition. "See what happens, Swamiji," he complained with tears in his voice, "the Christians have much of the money of Travancore. Had it not been for the valiant skill of some of our Hindu politicians in the last fifty years, Christians would have taken over and converted our shrines into churches." I tried to suggest that he might be exaggerating. "No, no, Swamiji, see for yourself. They will buy a little bit of land, perhaps an acre, in the midst of a Hindu village. That is cheap, and they offer more than Hindu buyers. Then they will erect a large cross in the center. Then they will build a little wooden church around it. Then there will be a big church one day, and our simple village Hindus will nod and say: 'God is with the powerful, perhaps the padres are right and we should cease worshipping our gods.' What shall we do, Swamiji, to counter these tricks?" I had an idea,

and I think I was not being facetious when I suggested to him: "Can you buy a bit of land in a predominantly Christian village?" "That is possible, but why?" "Well," I said, "buy an acre, and build a huge, beautiful *linga* (Shiva's phallic symbol) on it, of stone or wood. The *linga*, you know, is an abomination to all good Christians, and you will not even have to build a temple around it to scare them away." But Velayudhan shook his head sadly; such a thing could not be thought of—because it was not good to give offense to people, not even to Christians.

However, just at that time a call reached Velayudhan from a place nearby. In a little locality quite close to Nagercoil, there was a huge church—the place was called "little Rome" by the local people on account of the influence it wielded over the Christian communities around. Now it seems that the people of Vadakangulam had for some reason fallen out with the clergy and had made up their minds to revert to Hinduism, which until a generation ago would have been impossible for converts to Christianity or to Islam. There are several Hindu sects of medieval origin in the south that observe little or no caste-restrictions. A zealous preacher from one of them—it was a Shaivite group—had taken it upon himself to see those Nadas back into their ancestral fold. He was anxious to convince them that the caste Hindus around them would not resent their forebears' apostasy, although they had been Christians, of sorts, for about three generations. Aramugan Shastriar, the preacher, approached Velayudhan, and when he saw me he asked my host who I was. His eyes lit up when he was told; he turned to me and said: "You are sent by God, Swamiji. Why don't you come and give my Nadas the necessary *samskaras* [teachings] to make them Hindus again?" I was rather moved, but I refused. I tried to explain that I did not believe in any sort of proselytization, and that I opposed Hindus trying to make converts, or even reconverts, as I felt that such action was counter to the spirit of their tradition. Aramugan listened with rapt attention, but then he insisted that I should at least accompany him and Velayudhan and address the Nadas. To this I consented.

When we reached Vadakangulam, late in the evening, there was a crowd of at least 5,000, including some monks who were intoning Hindu *bhajans* [verses] in Tamil. Aramugan had made me up for the occasion: he had me remove my upper garment, so as to be sartorially thoroughly orthodox, and then he painted me with sandal and other fragrant ingredients, the *tripundram* (the parallel white stripes) being applied on my forehead, arms, and chest, indicating the worship of Shiva. If I am permitted a plagiarism, I looked like a leopard all over (Vivekananda used this description for this sort of orthodox paint). I had also had an all-over shave that morning, for the *sannyasi* either shaves his whole head or he does not shave at all—there is no such thing as partial shaving. He then led me on to the little dais that had been erected for us and introduced me to the expectant crowd in a fiery harangue. A pure *brahmacari,* he said, the very manifestation of the Vedic splendor, a man, who, learned in all sciences, having traveled all over the universe, has renounced the teachings that he thought unfitting, to become a Hindu. He then gave me a sign, and I spoke—in English, as I could not lecture in Tamil [one of the main languages in southern India] and neither Velayudhan nor Aramugan could speak in Hindi or Sanskrit. I spoke, and Aramugan translated. Or at least I hope he did. It is quite possible that what he said was something entirely different, because it seemed to me that there were many local references in his translation, and names were mentioned by him that I had never heard before.

The gist of my own lecture was simple enough: "The point is this, sisters and brothers. No one wants to impose anything on you; you are aware that there are social strictures in Hinduism which are not present in Christianity.

(Not so much the caste system, for South Indian Christendom has a caste-system of its own, an almost exact replica of the Hindu system. There are Brahmin Christian churches and there are non-Brahmin assemblies.) As for the teachings of Christianity, they are good, no doubt, but I for one think they do not blend with genuine Indian traditions. Christianity makes claim to universality; it claims 'we alone are right, all others are wrong.' Hinduism does not. Whether the Hindu or the Christian concept of the Supreme is to be chosen depends solely on the kind of individual the chooser is, but my plea for Hinduism is one of greater beauty—the Savior on the cross conflicts with the whole gamut of beauty that the Hindu teachers have proclaimed as steps toward the divine. The Christian teacher declares body and soul separate from each other: he regards God as separate from man; and when he speaks of the 'oneness' of God and the soul, it is oneness through an act of faith, of faith in the words of a personal teacher. He claims that there is but one son of God but the Hindu masters teach that each of you is Christ, each of you is the son of God, is God, you must only remember it. Worst of all, the Christian harps on sin, on the smallness of man; his God is so good and great, his man so wicked and small. There is no such teaching in Hinduism—the human being is not belittled in order to exalt God. God's greatness cannot be bought at the expense of the human being—at least in the Hindu view. If you make the step and revert to the *dharma* [Hindu stories and customs] of your ancestors, it will be a step of great courage, for as I said, there are immense social strictures in Hinduism, more than in Christianity. But there is freedom of the spirit, freedom of the intellect in Hinduism, which Christianity cannot give. It is up to you. You must choose. I am neither encouraging nor dissuading you."

Velayudhan whisked me off, back to Nagercoil, before I could see the reaction. But I learnt a short while after that the Hinduization of the Nada community at Vadakangulam maintained its progress. Now it may seem to some of my less perspicacious readers that the above episode was an act of conversion. That is not so. In the first place, it does not seem likely that my single appearance could in about 5,000 souls have changed a way of life established for about three generations. At the most, it is conceivable that my going to Vadakangulam gave some impetus to the endeavors of local Hindu leaders who believed, like Velayudhan and Aramugan, that the Hindu *dharma* should have the respect it deserves among its own people. I do not condone conversion of any kind and my purpose in accepting that invitation—it was the only one of its kind during my pastoral career—was simply to see how much truth lay in the claim of the Indian Christian clergy that Christianity could convert Hindus owing to its intrinsic merit, and how much justification lay in their somewhat brazen assumption that Hindus did not convert Christians because of the intrinsic inferiority of the Hindu doctrine. It is perhaps a good thing that scholastic Hinduism does not have to make a pretext of humility. Christian proselytism has often been in an almost pitiable predicament: even when it was in a position to use the stake and the rack [instruments of torture used to punish infidels], it had to use them with a humble mien. Hinduism never used any such means for the greater glory of God, because it did not really care for his greater glory....

Bharati preached to an unusual gathering in 1954.

Once in twelve years, all the monks, many Brahmins, and all the actively devout among the Hindus converge on Allahabad [a major Indian city] for their great congress, the *Kumbhamela*. It is mentioned in ancient scriptures, the Buddha knew about it. There is little organization and hardly any systematic exchange of views between the learned Hindus, lay and monastic, for Hinduism defies organization. Its means of communication are not

ecclesiastical. But during the six days of the great *Kumbhamela,* the yogic and scholastic labor of twelve years is brought to a forum: day and night, the monks and the pandits sit together in a profound contemplation and discussion; they address the masses of the pious, and the monks take part in the most gigantic procession of the thousands of processions that are part of the Indian scene.

The great *Kumbhamela* of 1954 occurred during my last year at B.H.U. [Benaras Hindu University]. The roads to Allahabad were jammed with streams of pilgrims; rickshaw pullers from as far as Patna—about 160 miles from Allahabad—had loaded their families onto their vehicles, pedaling them all the way. The more affluent rode in cars; there were special air services—all the motley means of transport, animal or mechanical, that India has at her disposal filled the thoroughfares in casteless unison. Friends from the German Embassy at New Delhi had come to see Benaras and they drove me to the *Kumbhamela.* As our somewhat incongruous new Opel rolled along the highway, past the pilgrims and the ox carts, we sang a few *Lieder* [Austrian songs] in four parts for a change (the wives were in the car, too), and we soon sighted the Phaphamau Bridge leading into Allahabad. In India there is no such thing as too large a crowd, yet what I saw here filled me with some fear. The municipality of Allahabad had ruled that all participants were to be inoculated against typhoid and cholera. Had this order been upheld, about one-third of the pilgrims would have stayed at home, for the hypodermic needle is a considerable deterrent to many a good villager. But just four days before the commencement, the order was rescinded—I never found out why and I myself had already taken the inoculations, which I loathe.

I was put in the tent of the Abbot [or head] of the Dashanami Monastery at Bile Parla in Bombay, one of India's most revered monks and scholars. A man of about fifty, husky, strong, fair-complexioned, spectacled, impressive, he spoke with a loud, clear, and yet rather soft voice. There was no trace of sanctimoniousness in his speech, and we recognized each other, for we had met in the lovely shrine of Kanya Kumari. "You will ride in the car with me and Swami Brahmanandaji," he ruled. I had actually been looking forward to marching in the two-mile long procession and taking the holy dip from a running start, as it were, but Maheshvarananda was firm. The proceedings began at 4:30 the next morning, with the sun still a mere streak of red on the eastern horizon. The procession emerged from the mile-long expanse of tents while the spectators—pilgrims, men, women and children, all ages, all castes— filled the dry and half-dry space along the processional route, looking like a beehive not yet on the move. The slogans and chants began—the monks called their exhortations in Sanskrit, the crowd lustily repeated them, adding its less-learned chorus to the controlled bedlam. The Naga monks, whom we had already met at Delhi, marched in front, clad only in the four directions [Nagas are clothed only in the winds, meaning they are naked], smeared with sacred ashes, with matted hair, huge beads covering their chests. Aged between eleven and ninety, they presented an impressive array in 1954 C.E. as in the days of antiquity. Our own group followed; then the Udasins, another highly respected ascetic order, more recent in origin, but of a similar type; then the Nirmalis, the only Sikh [another major Indian religion] monastic group (the founders of the Sikh religion were against monasticism, and this order is considered unorthodox by the most orthodox Sikhs, for whom family life is a *sine qua non*); then some Vaishnava groups, and then a host of other monastic and semimonastic groups. The monks in procession totalled about 20,000, the lay spectators half a million; the space around the sacred confluence was sufficient for about 150,000 all told.

Our car crept forward. There were some heavily bedizened elephants in front of us and more than 300 Nagas and *sannyasis* around us, marching slowly, step for step, chanting their hymns and stanzas. We approached the confluence and alighted from the cars. His Holiness the Shamkaracarya of Govardhana Matha, Puri, entered the river first; then followed our group. I must have been among the first two dozen to step into the water and the brief immersion was wild, unmitigated rapture.

Almost immediately thereafter, so it seems, some of the less considerate monks began pushing their way through the crowd and it was reported that some actually used their tridents. Exactly what happened was never clear, in spite of official inquiry, but some people—probably children and older women in the front rows— slipped into the water, and as others kept pressing forward from behind, there was an immediate stampede. Within twenty minutes death took a heavy toll on what should have been so auspicious an occasion: some 300 people were killed—trampled upon, or perhaps drowned—and about 900 injured. By that time the senior monks and I were already back in our cars, returning by a circular route to the camp. Everything came to a stop, but it was about half an hour before we became aware of what had happened, for although the site was only about 200 yards behind us, hundreds of thousands of people blocked our view. A young monk came up to me and screamed: "Maharaj, I have lost my nerve!" (a statement unthinkable from a Hindu monk save under excessive strain). He clung to the running board of our open car and began to tear at my *cadar*, crying like a child. "What can I do brother, what do you want me to do?" I shouted at him. "Do something, protect me, protect these wretched people, Maharaj. You have the power to do it!" As he said it, I had the power and I jumped out of the car, making my way back to the site of terror. How I did it I do not know, for there did not appear to be space enough for a mouse to pass through the stagnant, petrified throng, yet somehow, a path opened up before me, and I stood on the spot. The young monk had followed me, screaming, "He is the leader, he must save, he must bless!" I had never before realized so intensively how accidental a growth charisma is: once a person is placed at the focus of eminence, is physically present where leadership is expected, he acquires all the strength that is needed to fulfill the expectation, momentary though this may be—and in this phenomenon I see the main clue to the miraculous, for if miracles are ever performed, this is surely the explanation.

There was madness in the air around me, screams of anguish and agonized frenzy, yet under the influence of the situation my instructions sounded as calm as though I were a referee at a football match. Simple, commonsense instructions: "Be quiet, calm down, sit still where you are, sit down until the stretchers are brought, don't scream, nothing has happened, stop behaving like madmen." All these things must already have been said dozens of times, shouted at the victims and their loved ones, but the secular voices of help had remained unheeded. The moment I spoke, there was hushed silence. Those within earshot sat down, amidst the corpses, amidst their kin writhing in pain. Then, as soon as there was order, kind hands could begin to help.... Monks and lay volunteers worked together the whole day and half the night, cremating the dead, or what remained of them. There was not a hundredth part of the fuel needed to cremate the corpses, for no one had thought of such a calamity, but we struck upon some ingenious, if rather unpalatable devices to complete the obsequies. Nevertheless dead matter continued to float down the river, clogging the area around the Naini Bridge, for about two months after the *Kumbhamela*.

At one public lecture the speaker before me, a young monk, began his address: "My own self, in the form of you sisters and

> **There was madness in the air around me, screams of anguish and agonized frenzy, yet under the influence of the situation my instructions sounded as calm as though I were a referee at a football match.**

brothers" (a monastic opening phrase much favored by the Hindu Renaissance, threadbare, but doubtless new each time to quite a few persons in an audience of twenty thousand), "and you by my side, Forest of Ascetics (a traditional address), what do we mean by the fame of purity? By it, we mean adherence to the traditions of India. When Vijayalakshmi Pandit, our beloved Prime Minister's sister, was Ambassador in Moscow, Stalin did not receive her. When our Vice-President became Ambassador to the great country of Russia after her, Sri Stalin immediately received him with great honor. And why? Because, so the great Stalin said: 'I will not speak to women who do not cover their heads with the sari.'" The sermon lasted for well over an hour, but my wrath did not subside. When my turn came, I did not make a long preamble, but went *in medias res*. "Do you know, sisters and brothers, and Forest of Ascetics, what we mean by imbecility? By that we mean broadcasting things which are manifestly stupid in themselves. What my good fellow-*sadhu* told you was well-meant, but utterly false. Please listen, and listen carefully: Sri Stalin, in the first place, does not know that women in some parts of India cover their heads, with their sari or with anything else; had he known it, in the second place, he would rather have received a woman who did not cover her head, because she was about to break a bourgeois tradition by uncovering it (this required a longish paraphrase—but that was no longer a problem for me by that time); in the third place, women in most parts of the world do not cover their heads. Even in India, only North Indian women do so, and that is perhaps due to the influence of Islam, which made the Hindus alert or which contaminated their customs with slavery, for in ancient India women did not cover their heads. And in India today, South Indian Hindu ladies never cover their heads, not from Madras down to Kanya Kumari, and not again from Kanya Kumari up to Hyderabad. Only prostitutes cover their heads in some regions in the South...."

In another public lecture on the day after the procession I tried to show—in mild and popular terms—that the Hindu tradition did not envisage asceticism as the only way to achieve [spiritual] liberation; that many great seers and many schools of religious discipline had taught that killing the senses was but one of the ways, and that harnessing them, using all their strength toward the supreme goal was another alternative. The audience looked calm to me, but there was some commotion on the platform. As soon as I had finished, a bearded Vaishnava monk, clad in the yellow garment of his order, jumped to his feet (an unusual procedure, as monks generally address a meeting sitting cross-legged, even when using a microphone) and cried: "Swami Agehananda teaches that there is no need of sense-control, that one must indulge in sensual pleasures in order to achieve *mukti* [liberation], that the ascetic life is misconceived" and so on. I was distressed by this gross misrepresentation, particularly as the procedure on these occasions gives an earlier speaker no opportunity of speaking again—in fact the last speaker can with

impunity contradict, criticize, refute and distort almost everything that has gone before.

That same evening, a young monk came to my tent and asked me to present myself at the camp of His Holiness the Jagadguru Shamkaracarya Bharati Krishna Tirtha of Govardhanapitha, who had expressed his desire to see me. I was worried, as I felt sure this was a summons in connection with that morning's incident. As I entered the Supreme Patriarch's camp with considerable apprehension, I noticed that some of the most senior abbots were already assembled in a room behind which His Holiness had his private quarters during the festival. They nodded to me in a cordial way and began a conversation on general, mildly scholastic matters, as is the etiquette of monastic conversation. Very soon a curtain parted and His Holiness the Shamkaracarya entered. I stood up and prostrated myself before him doing the "obeisance with the eight limbs" (which means touching the floor with the forehead, the nose, the palms of the hands, the knees, and the toes), completing the salutation with the "rod-like obeisance" into which the earlier one merges when a monk greets the supreme master of his Order....

The other senior monks had evidently arrived earlier, as they did not repeat any obeisance. His Holiness sat down and joined in the talk, without so much as a hint of any forthcoming censure. After a while, however, the conversation became more technical, and I could see that I was being tested by a most elegant method: I was made to state my views in commenting on the scriptural themes under discussion. His Holiness, assisted by a second monk of his own advanced age, built up the questions unobtrusively, and when they finally asked, "Do you consider asceticism essential to achieve *mukti* and *jnanam* [supreme wisdom through nondiscursive intuition]?" the transition had been so gradual that the question caused no surprise.

I began to explain my viewpoint, and as none of the monks nor His Holiness himself interrupted me, I elaborated. I paused to see their reaction, but there were only encouraging, friendly faces around me—and I may even have noticed an approving smile now and then. The Shamkaracarya himself was serious, though not unfriendly. He did not smile once during the next three hours—the three hours in which I gave testimony of my beliefs to the supreme ones of my Order—but he looked at me with a deep, probing, interested gaze, not devoid of intellectual excitement. He had been a professor of mathematics many decades earlier, before he became a monk and before his spiritual and scholastic excellence carried him to the summit of the most revered hierarchy of the Indian realm.

I said that I did think asceticism was essential for the achievement of *mukti* and *jnanam,* but that there were different types of aspirants. Some have to sustain the ascetic life up to their last moment in the living body; others have to train themselves in ascetic disciplines, but once they have reached the poise that asceticism yields they must desist from further asceticism, because instead of advancing them, it harms them; it harms them because it creates such passions as it is thought to eschew—sloth, misanthropism, moodiness, frustration; and all these are passions, even if they are not shown in the doctrinary lists of human passions. Yet, abandoning practices does not imply changing from a monastic to a mundane way of life; rather, it means pursuing those activities and thinking those thoughts for which the thus-trained individual is best equipped—if he was a scholar, he must be a scholar again; if he was an artist, he must resume the practice of art.

"How then, Agehananda, can one distinguish a monk from an ordinary scholar, or artist, or from any good man in the world—certainly not just because he wears the ochre robe?" There is no sign, nor any combination of signs, by which a monk can be recognized by anyone, I averred. "Not even by his guru!" That I did not know. In fact, I added, "Looking like a true monk or 'appearing' or 'acting' like a true monk implies not *being* one, for such appearance panders to the criteria of the mundane." "That is true, Agehananda. There are many scriptural passages corroborating your view. Sages act like ordinary people, sometimes like madmen, sometimes like kings and ministers—no one can know their ways." "I have often been asked, venerable sirs," I continued, "why, if such is my view, I do not disrobe and dress in white, in ordinary clothes, as an ordinary citizen of the world, yet remain a *sannyasi* within myself. Why do I make a show of the ochre robe, why do I surround myself in that ochre smokescreen? It makes people suspicious; it makes lay scholars think I am a scholastic fraud, trying to buttress my inadequate knowledge of Hindu doctrine by the robe symbolizing that doctrine." "Don't they read what you write and publish, don't they hear what you speak, don't they challenge your knowledge?" "No, venerable sirs, colleagues never read what one writes; they seldom attend one's classes because their students would then think that they also went to learn from one. And as for challenging one's knowledge, they are too polite. Furthermore," I said, "policemen, from the betel-chewing police-sergeant to the Tennyson-quoting official in the Home Ministry, all think I wear the smokescreen of ochre hue in order to disguise sinister motives and interests in vicious things." "What things, Agehananda?" "Politics, fornication, disruption of young minds, and deliberate denigration of the Hindu lore."

"You do antagonize monks and laymen, Agehananda," said the South Indian monk after a short silence. "I do say, and say repeatedly, what I hold to be both important and excellent in our tradition." "Do you preach that it is not important to believe in a Being, a Supreme God?" "I certainly did preach that at times, for, as I understand the texts, we are free to see a

Supreme Being in them, or to deny it, or to suspend judgment, according to our interpretation of the Scriptures. When the Scriptures speak of the Brahman, of various Divine Manifestations, gods and *avatars,* of the Witness and of the Prompter, I regard all these statements as being in the category of yogic experience. Is that wrong?" "It is not wrong, Maharaj, it is compatible with Scriptures. Jaimini did not attach any importance to a Supreme Being;

of some extinct Indian schools—I did believe there was much good in that. "We do not necessarily agree with that view, but we cannot say that you are wrong. Try it out, by all means, but be prepared for dangerous risks."

"I believe in the merit of the ochre robe," I then said. "It is a uniform that sets us apart from the rest of society—it warns people not to take us lightly. It warns them also not to tempt us, or not to tempt us too severely. With the

> With the ochre robe draped over my body, I feel I can face temptation, just as a man, skilled in arms, feels readier for the fight when he puts on a military uniform.
>
> Psychological, no doubt, self-suggestion; but what is not?
>
> To me the ochre garment gives a strange quasi-canonical confidence.

Kapila's Samkhya philosophy is often said to be *nirishvara,* without God. But you do know that there is the rule of *adhikarabheda,* that you must not divulge things too subtle to the unsubtle, lest they should be confused?" I did know that. But as a man with pedagogic experience, I think it is wrong to pamper the "unsubtle," especially when they come for instruction. Shock-therapy, much in the manner of the Chan Buddhists of China, or the Zen Buddhists of Japan, and even

ochre robe draped over my body, I feel I can face temptation, just as a man, skilled in arms, feels readier for the fight when he puts on a military uniform. Psychological, no doubt, self-suggestion; but what is not? To me the ochre garment gives a strange quasi-canonical confidence. Its cool, austere, rough contact with my skin makes me alert, and more susceptible to things and persons around me. Perhaps this is because it helps me to identify myself with the culture I have chosen for my own? Would the Venerable Sirs object to this idea about the ochre robe, in my particular case?"

"There is no objection, because your case is unprecedented. None of the others who have worn the ochre robe had to *choose* this culture, as they were born into it. But we do not see why it should not prove an additional asset in your case, in the manner you have indicated. As for your 'canonical confidence,' Agehananda, that may well be so; we, who have worn the garment twice as long as you have lived, cannot pronounce upon this, for we do not remember how it feels to don any other. But, don't you think that this very garment marks you out as one who must preach in the tradition? And as this tradition has in the main postulated a Supreme Being—regardless of the fact that the Hindu *dharma* permits, or even at times suggests, in some of its teachers, nonacceptance of a personal God, or agnosticism—regardless of that fact, does not this robe enjoin on you a more literal pursuit of the homiletic [preaching] conventions?"

"Indeed it does," I mused. "But should we not try to exhibit the profoundness of this tradition by teaching without, or with less compromise? This is my point, and it is very close to my heart, and I welcome this opportunity of putting it to you, venerable sirs. Whether God is or is not—this has to be experienced, else it has no meaning. But suppose I experience God? Suppose I am completely convinced, through my own experience, that the Being of the Upanishads, the Brahman, is, and that I am It in essence? Nothing, venerable sirs, follows from my experience either for the existence of such a Being, or against it."

"But don't you think, Agehananda, that this view of yours is more Buddhist than Hindu? Is it not saying as much as 'all things are only perceived and have no existence outside perception'?" I did not think it was more Buddhist than Hindu, nor even idealistic in the sense of occidental philosophy—suspending my judgment on such epistemological [having to do with knowledge] distinctions as "idealism" and "realism," because I am not really interested in epistemology. "No, venerable sirs, my attitude about the 'existence' of God as compared with my attitude about the 'existence' of things is more commited, and I think it is closer to Hindu than to Buddhist thought, though some very late schools of Buddhism propounded somewhat similar ideas. My thoughts and feelings about the existence of God are private commitments; my attitude about *things* and their existence is a public commitment. I am unwilling to share with anyone my feelings and thoughts about the existence or nonexistence of God, because I am deeply convinced that teaching a way to conceive the 'existence of God' is fraught with disaster—it creates prophets, it creates fanatics. Prophets are fanatics; seers and mystics remain silent. Both in Greek and Sanskrit, venerable sirs, the word *mystic* means 'one who keeps silent,' silent about his experiences. The prophet is convinced that what he sees, what he feels, what he experiences is true in the same sense that the existence of his garment or his staff is true and he preaches it as truth; and that is a fallacy, for he cannot infer any such truth from his own, private experience. And (here I spoke in English, as this specific formulation cannot be unequivocally given in Sanskrit without an elaborate paraphrase, which would have deflected my main exposition) *private experience of an object of the religious sort does not confer existential status on the object* or more simply (here I resumed in Sanskrit) from the fact that a saint sees God, or the Goddess, or Krishna, or Rama or identifies himself with the Brahman, the existence of God or the Goddess, of Krishna, or Rama, or the Brahman *does not follow*."

"*Vakyamidam navinayuktih,* this proposition entails a novel reasoning," one of the monks, hitherto silent, exclaimed in genuine surprise, focusing me intensely with what I thought was a condoning frown. "Novel, but not inadmissible for, Agehananda Svamin, there have been thinkers in the Brahmin tradition who propounded views that do not clash with yours. There was Shriharsa, who said 'every proposition can be shown to be absurd, I have no proposition to make myself, because that could also be refuted. My own knowledge about that Brahman and the Universe and myself I do have, but I cannot formulate them because they are no one's concern.' This teacher in our own tradition, Agehananda, was similar to the Buddhist teachers, except that he accepted Brahman by implication. I take it you do the same. But don't affirm or negate it. Say nothing."

I did not, and would not have, even if the swami had not enjoined silence....

Years later, Bharati moved to North America, where spiritual seekers asked his advice on many matters. In North America he wrote his autobiography, which ends with the following words:

I put forward this claim, opening myself to all the criticism—cultural criticism I hope—that it will no doubt evoke, as the very special message of this book. I contend that cultural criticism is not only wholesome, but that it is the only possible intercultural contribution that can be made on the communicatory, discursive level. Panegyrics [praises] are easy, for they require no knowledge of the other's culture. If I praise Gandhi's teachings, I will have many friends in India and no Indian will oppose me even if my eulogy rests on a concatenation of vague notions, scant knowledge of the philosophical background and purely subjective enthusiasm—even though I may be saying the right things for the wrong reasons. On the other hand, if I criticize, I have to arm myself with detailed knowledge, for the spirit is weak though the flesh may be strong: human beings however civilized, connive at pleasant things said about them or about their kin, even when they know them to be untrue.

I will then submit this advice, that instead of ignoring doctrinal or ethical discrepancies and differences with a benign smile, let us instead point them out. Let us not persist in the imbecile idea—common to most of the well-meaning international organizations of our day—that the world's peoples will get together because "we have so much teaching in common"; for this implies that if, after all, it should transpire that we do not have so many beliefs in common, we should have to fight each other. Negatively, it would also imply that people who share the same doctrines never fight each other, which is blatant nonsense. The Theravada Buddhist Burmese invaded the Theravada Buddhist Siamese and burnt up Ayuthia, the former Siamese capital, breaking up some of the Buddha images to see if there was any gold hidden in them; nor did European Christian countries always live in amity with one another. No, our getting together, or at least our not shooting at each other must rest not on similar religious views, not on the fictitious "essential unity" of all religions and "good" ideologies, but on the simple fact that it is infinitely more pleasant and expedient not to shoot at each other.

Discussion Questions: Swami Agehananda Bharati

1. What are the basic beliefs in Bharati's creed?

2. The first paragraph of an autobiography often holds several keys about the meaning of the story. Read the first paragraph, which is really the beginning of Bharati's self-reflections. On the basis of the emphases you find there, which of Bharati's beliefs would you say is most basic?

3. What are the sources of Bharati's beliefs about God?

4. What would Bharati say about a female God?

5. Is Bharati's creed devoted more to attaining worldly happiness and bliss, or more toward renouncing this world? Explain your response.

6. What was Bharati's first impression of Christianity? Did his view of Christianity change throughout his lifetime?

7. Does Bharati think that Hindus should try to evangelize, or make converts of, people in other traditions?

8. Explain what you think Bharati means by these two sayings:

    a. "My thoughts and feelings about the existence of God are private commitments; my attitude about *things* and their existence is a public commitment."

    b. "...private experience of an object of the religious sort does not confer existential status on the object."

9. Do you think Bharati would assent to the proposition "God exists"? Why or why not?

Shudha Mazumdar

Photo credit: From the collection of
Professor Geraldine Forbes.

From Shudha Mazumdar,
Memoirs of an Indian Woman,
edited by Geraldine Forbes
(M. E. Sharpe, Inc., Armonk, NY 10504).
Reprinted by permission of M. E. Sharpe, Inc.

*Shudha Mazumdar was born in 1899 in Calcutta
and grew up in the region of India known as Bengal.
As she explains early on, she inherited traditional Bengali
religious customs from her mother, just as her mother
had in turn inherited the beliefs and rituals from
Mazumdar's grandmother.*

Mother faithfully maintained the various
rituals, functions, and social customs that had
been handed down to her by Grandmother.
In spite of my father's liberal ideas and
Western way of life, in faith he was essentially
a Hindu, and it was here that he and my
mother were one; both were religious and
pious without cant.

Many of my Mother's beliefs, to Father's
rational mind, were mere superstitions, but he
never seriously interfered or forbade anything
she chose to do within our home. He had at one
time tried his best to persuade her to eschew our
age-old customs and to adopt Western ones, but
she had been adamant in her refusal.

"At a very early age I was brought to this
house by your mother to keep the traditions. So
as long as I am here I must be true to the things
into which I have been initiated. Should you
leave this ancestral home of yours and live
elsewhere, then only in the new surroundings
and in altered circumstances can I think and act
according to your desires. Here I am not only
your wife, but the daughter-in-law of the
house…" she told him. And it was ever thus.
She kept her faith and lived up to her beliefs,
and rigidly adhered to the family traditions she
felt it her duty to uphold. We, the children,
knew in some measure how difficult was life for
her and how easy it could have been had she
agreed to follow Father's wishes. But no, she had
her own ideas of duty and those were of
paramount importance to her. The legacy left by
her mother-in-law lay heavily on her but she
bore all with equanimity. "A man may do
whatever he chooses, but that home is doomed
where a woman follows her own desires," was
one of her favorite sayings. Generous to a fault,

endowed with a priceless sense of humor, always self-restrained and fearless, she bravely stood up for what she considered to be true.

She had her own personal establishment including her kitchen, presided over by a Brahmin [the highest Hindu caste] cook, and a retinue of servants for the daily work. She also had a private kitchen where she made her own tea and every day some dishes for us, no matter how many had been prepared by her Brahmin cook and Father's Muslim one. Pir Mohammad had a detached cottage in our compound. Here he cooked his *belati khana* [English food] for Father's table and cared for the hens that fluttered about and squawked and laid their eggs in a specially built coop.

Although Mother never sat at Father's table, she never failed to be present when he sat for his meals in lonely splendor. It was nearly always long past midday before she had her own lunch and then only after her duties and her daily ritual of prayers and worship were complete. At night, the cook departed after having served us, leaving Mother's food in *dekachis* [pans] over the dying fires. Whether this kept it warm or not we never knew, for we were fast asleep before she had her frugal dinner, after her evening bath and prayers and after everyone else had dined.

We had our food from the hands of her Brahmin cook, but were occasionally allowed to taste the Western dishes from Father's table. However, the pleasure was brief. Immediately after having eaten this food, I had to undergo a thorough wash and change every item of my clothing before I was permitted to touch anything in Mother's apartment. Unorthodox food was considered unclean, and therefore I was unclean until I had been thoroughly washed.

I remember that the youngest of my brothers was very much against my partaking of this unclean food. When I expressed my surprise as to why I should abstain when he and all my brothers ate it, I was loftily told that they were men, and it ill-befitted me, one of the inferior species, to even dream of acting like

them. "Does Mother or Didi [elder sister][1] ever eat here, you stupid? You are a girl, so it's a positive sin for you to eat fowl or their eggs." I grew anxious and implored his advice as to how I could avoid commiting this terrible sin. "I will tell you what," he suggested sagely after much deliberation, "when Father calls you at dinner time, make a wry face—like this," and he painfully twisted his face, "and say you have a tummy ache." Now I was particularly fond of the tasty dishes prepared by Pir Mohammad, but what could I do? Even for their sake I dared not displease this despotic brother who could make life unbearable for me with his gibes and threats if I did not blindly obey him.

So the following day I repressed my unholy appetite and feigned an acute pain. Since Father was concerned, he did not press me much and thus I purchased the goodwill of my playmate by abstaining from custard pudding. But the plan failed to work for long. "Come now," coaxed Father, offering me a piece of chicken cutlet on his fork one day, "have this wee bit, I am sure this will not hurt you." The fragrance of the forbidden meat made me forget my vows. Docilely I accepted the offer while my brother looked daggers at me....

The vocation of every girl was to be a wife and mother, and the ideal held up to her for her future life was *seva,* service to others. The blessings of the elders of the husband's home were considered to be necessary ingredients for her happiness and prosperity, and these were to be earned by services, however small, given in loving respect. It was the pride and privilege of a bride to serve, but if she failed, her parents were blamed for her shortcomings, and the mother bore the slur of having failed in her duty towards her daughter.

----

1. Siblings are referred to by kinship terms rather than their given names. Thus, Didi is elder sister; Dada, the eldest of brothers; Mejda, the second-eldest of brothers; and Chorda, the youngest of the elder brothers.

> The existence of *Atman*, the Godhead or divinity within men and women, is accepted as a fact by all those who are of the Hindu faith, and that the highest good is the realization and the expression of that divinity.

Since much would be required of the girl when she attained womanhood, a system of education began to prepare her for her future life from her earliest days. As nearly all things in India hinge on religion, this training was also centered in religious thoughts and practices.

It aimed at imparting an elementary knowledge of the basic ideas that were considered by a Bengali family to be good and true; it was accomplished through the medium of little rituals and prayers and fasts. These rituals had some connection with objects that were familiar to the child such as plant and animal life. By this system of training, the child was taught to be disciplined and dutiful and responsible. She who undertakes a lesson of this kind is said to have undertaken a *brata*. The literal meaning of *brata* is "vow." So the child takes a vow to do a certain thing that must be performed.

Many are the *bratas* performed by Hindu women regularly during certain times of the year, but there are also *bratas* that are only for the young unmarried girl. The child is left to do everything in her own way. Unlike the usual Sanskrit prayers that need a priest to prompt them, the *mantras* [sacred formulas] used in performing these *bratas* are generally in simple Bengali verse that the child learns by heart and recites unaided.

The *tulsi brata* teaches the child how to care for the bush of sweet basil that is so dearly cherished in every Hindu home. The cow *brata* makes her familiar with the four-footed friend whose milk not only sustained her in infancy but is still an important item of her daily food.

There is another delightful *brata* called *punyi-pukur*, or the lake of merit, in which the child digs a diminutive lake and, seating herself before it, prays to Mother Earth for the gift of tolerance and for the fortitude to endure all things lightly, as does Mother Earth herself.

The prayers are quaint and the requests are remarkable for their naivete. Worldly bliss is sought in many forms. For instance, in one *brata*, the little devotee desires:

> Cows in the cowshed, and
> Corn in the storehouse
> Vermilion between the parting of my hair
> Every year a son, and
> May not a single one die, and
> Never may a teardrop fall from my eye.

Each *brata* has a tale that accompanies it. At the conclusion of her *brata,* the girl must sit with her group of friends and listen to the legend that has been woven round it.

Even though my Positivist [a European school of philosophy] grandfather was no more, his wife was to live to a good old age and took a lively interest in family affairs. She looked with disapproval on my bare knees and frocks, foretelling sorrow for my mother, through me, if she persisted in allowing Father's Western ideas to permeate our household. So whenever "young grandmother" (for that is what we called her) came for a visit I was careful to stay away from her.

But one day she caught sight of me and said to my mother, "Well *bau* [daughter-in-law], your daughter is growing up. Are you making her take an interest in any *brata niyamas?* She is old enough to make a beginning, or does her father desire to make her a *pucca memsahib* [genuine foreign woman]?" Mother looked at me thoughtfully and nodded, "Yes, she has just stepped into her eighth year...."

The existence of *Atman,* the Godhead or divinity within men and women, is accepted as a fact by all those who are of the Hindu faith, and it is believed that the highest good is the realization and the expression of that divinity. To achieve this, various spiritual disciplines and techniques were recommended by the sages and seers of ancient times.

As realization is attained through the mind, attempts are made to train the restless mind from one's earliest years. The training is done according to certain rules that demand regular practice and form the basis of the concept of *yoga.* The daily routine of the vast majority of Hindus (women in particular) is governed by rules that are in fact connected with those rules of discipline preliminary to yoga. First, there is the visit to the toilet followed by a bath. Then, dressed in clean clothes, comes prayers or meditation, and only after this is it possible to eat. This became my morning routine at the age of eight and I have not deviated from it.

One of the most popular *bratas* in Bengal for the unmarried girls is Shiva *puja* [worship]. The great Shiva is the ideal male, and a maiden is blessed with the words: "May you be granted a husband like Shiva." He is well known for his deep devotion to his beloved wife, Durga, and for the havoc he wrought throughout heaven and earth in his wild paroxysm of grief when he lost her. As old as the hills, the beautiful legend has still the power to thrill many a girl of the Hindu faith and make her long for a husband, not as resplendent as Indra, King of the Gods, but as great as Shiva. For the great yogi [a person who practices yoga] cared nothing for earthly riches and dearly loved his wife. Mothers initiated their daughters in this *brata,* for it

was believed that the benediction of Shiva could bring the devotee a husband as greathearted and loving as he.

Bysakh, the first month of the Bengali year, is considered to be an auspicious time to commence any *brata niyama.* So, on 14 April (New Year's Day in Bengal), Mother made me undertake my first *brata,* the Shiva *puja.* I was then eight years old and learned to perform the little ritual every morning before I went to school. For this, the first *niyama* was observed; that is, I had to a have good bath and wear a crimson silk *cheli* sari, the correct dress for the occasion, and not allow a single morsel of food or drink of any kind to touch my lips before the conclusion of the ceremony.

Rising early in the morning, I first bathed and changed, and then I ran to the garden to pick some flowers and fresh young blades of *durva* grass with which to perform the *puja.* The ritual had to be finished before I could have breakfast, dress, and run, in frock and pigtails, to be ready at the gate where I waited breathlessly for a school bus that arrived unfailingly at 8:30 A.M.

On the ground floor of Mother's establishment was our *puja* room. No one was allowed to enter this sacred room with unclean clothes, and leather footwear had to be left outside the doors. On its faded saffron walls were pictures by Ravi Varma, color prints of various gods and goddesses with gilt frames tarnished by time.

On a large lotus inlaid in black and white marble on the marble floor reposed the beautifully wrought white marble throne of Lakshmi, the goddess of fortune. On this was the *pali* of Lakshmi—the token of prosperity. The *pali* was a wickerwork basket, not unlike a Grecian urn in shape, filled with recently harvested golden paddy and some *cowries,* seashells, used as currency in very ancient times and considered now to be symbols of wealth and good fortune.

Crowning this *pali* was another basket containing toilet articles of the goddess. In shape it was a miniature *pali,* usually made of wicker embroidered with seashells and trimmed around the edges with some red material. This is the emblem of happy wifehood that the young bride carries when she leaves her father's home for her father-in-law's. Besides the comb and mirror are lengths of gaily colored ribbon for her hair, a pair of conch shell bangles, a *kajallata* [collyrium pot] with which to darken her eyes, and the little vermilion box with its crimson powder that is cherished so dearly by every married girl in Bengal. From the moment she becomes a bride, vermilion begins to play an important part in her life.

After the marriage ceremony, her bride-groom dips the edge of a silver comb in the bright powder and marks the center parting of her hair. After that day, every morning and evening for the rest of her life, she renews the ruby red mark with the edge of her comb. Only when death takes her husband away from her does she rub off the mark and put away her beloved vermilion box forever. Water from the Ganges [the main Indian river, sacred to many Indians] was stored in a huge brass jar. The great river Ganga [Ganges] that rushes from the snowy Himalayan regions, cascading down to the plains below, flows through Bengal on her way to the sea, making the land green and fertile. Loved and revered throughout India, the Ganga is spoken of as a goddess in Indian epics and her waters are considered very holy.

Facing the *puja* room was a small open courtyard, the floor of which was paved with cement, except for a square in the center in which the earth was left bare. This was the place of sacrifice. Into this soft earth was fixed a very old, worn, forked piece of wood that is called the *hari-katha.* Here, once a year in October (on the night of the full moon), during the Kojagori Lakshmi *puja,* a pure white goat was beheaded by the man who by vocation was entitled to perform this sacrifice. He was called the *karma* and, as his forefathers before him, did this work

for a small fee. This was the only sacrifice that was performed at our home....

In the *puja* room, Mother taught me how to make the necessary arrangements for the ritual with a set of small copper utensils I had been given. In the little water vessel I poured out some Ganges water and first washed the flowers, the *durva* grass, the leaves from the *bael* tree so loved by Shiva, and *aconda,* which was difficult to obtain in town, but was sometimes supplied by our *mali* [gardener]. Daily he brought a fresh sprig from our *bael* tree, and from this I would select the unblemished tender young three-leaved shoots. The *durva* grass had to have three blades, too. The grass and the fresh flowers I picked from our garden were separately placed on a little copper flower plate. Crimson and cream sandalwood would then be separately rubbed with water on a stone slab and the paste thus formed scraped up into tiny little bowls. Finally, a handful of uncooked rice was carefully washed and heaped on another plate, and on this I placed a peeled banana. This was the *naibedya,* food offering.

In an earthen pot in a corner of the *puja* room was kept some soft mud from the Ganges, and with a fistful of this substance I would mold my symbol of Shiva. I never could make this in a proper manner and was often in despair, for my Shiva would insist on being a crooked one, which boded no good for me. In a flat dish, I put my Shiva on a sprig of *bael,* then lit a little lamp and placed the food offering and the flower plate on either side, sitting on a small carpet to perform my ritual.

First I gave my Shiva a bath by gently sprinkling a little Ganges water from the tiny copper shell-shaped vessel over him three times. Every time I did so I murmured, "I salute thee Shiva." Then, dipping a few flowers and leaves in the sandalwood paste and holding them in my joined palms, I said a little prayer before making my offering. Briefly, some of the

attributes of Shiva were mentioned, and it
ended something like this:

> Lord I am so small a maid
> That hymns of praise I know not
> Aconda flower, leaves of bael and water from
>   the Ganga
> Be content with these my offerings,
> O Bhola Maheshwara.

Bhola is the name of Shiva meaning
"oblivious one," for unlike other gods he is said
to be oblivious to formal ritual and is content
with a wild flower or a leaf if it is offered with
love and devotion. Maheshwara is another
name of Shiva, and it means "great god."

This offering too was made three times.
Generally I closed my eyes, trying to visualize
Shiva with the patch of deep blue on his fair
throat, the third eye of wisdom on his forehead, and matted locks piled high on his head.
There was such a picture of Shiva on the wall,
with a slim crescent moon shining from above
and a sweet little face peeping out from behind
the moon. "Who is that peeping out behind
Shiva?" I had once asked. "Oh that is Mother
Ganga," was my Mother's casual reply. "But
why is she there?" I persisted. "Because
Bhagiratha begged her to come down to earth.
She was pleased with his penance and prayers
and consented to do so if he could make Shiva
agree to receive her, for otherwise the earth
could not bear her weight. So Shiva, who is
ever ready to help his devotees, bore the first
impact of her mighty waters on his head.
This made it possible for Bhagiratha to obtain
salvation for the soul of his ancestors."

"Tell me more..." I begged breathlessly. "I
have no time, it's all in the *Ramayana* [the great
Sanskrit epic that tells the story of Rama, his
wife Sita, and brother Lakshmana]; you must
read it for yourself." "But that is all about Rama,
Lakshmana, and Sita," I protested, remembering
that she had read aloud the "Banishment of

Sita." "Bhagiratha was an ancestor of Rama,"
was her short reply as she hurried away.

Every year for four years I regularly performed my Shiva *puja* throughout the month of
Bysakh. I had been told that I must not think of
anything else while I performed my *puja,* but
this was a difficult order to follow. Once, I had
devoutly closed my eyes as usual when offering
flowers and, on opening them, found to my
surprise and awe that a full blown flower had
covered my Shiva like a cap. I ran to inform
Mother and dragged her in to see the miracle;
she smiled and said perhaps I had said my
prayer with "one mind" and that was the sign
that the great god was pleased with me.

Many were the *bratas* that Mother performed. Amongst them, the *Savitri brata* was
very important. This fell on a dark, moonless
night in June. For three scorching days, when
the sun was merciless, the rites of this *brata*
enjoined fasting and prayer. It required great
patience and fortitude. Few dare to undertake
this *brata,* which is considered the most difficult of all *bratas.* But she who can successfully
perform this every year for fourteen years,
without a break, is blessed by Savitri and will
never know the dread pangs of widowhood.
A common benediction for married women is
"May you be like Savitri." The immortal story
of Savitri, who was able to persuade Yama, the
God of death, to return her husband to her, is
known to every girl. And it is the prayer of every
wife that she may be blessed with her husband
till the end of her days....

In the years following my marriage, I came to
learn many new things about politics and
religion, although I still enjoyed the games of
my childhood. My introduction to politics was
in 1905 when I was seven years old and Mother
served us with a *phal-ahar* [fruit meal] when it
was neither a fast day nor a *puja* day. It was not
a holiday nor did I hear of any holy purpose, so
I was somewhat puzzled to notice the unusual

silence in the kitchen and find that no fires were burning at all. On inquiry I learnt it was associated with the *Swadeshi* movement.

When the Viceroy, Lord Curzon, decided to partition Bengal in 1905, a great wave of national consciousness swept over the country. It had started first in Bengal where, as a sign of mourning, kitchen fires were not lit on 16 October 1905. People at this time took an oath to boycott foreign goods and pledged themselves to wear only *swadeshi* [of our own land] items of clothing.

It was also at this time that the *rakhi bandhan* ceremony was revived by the writer of many patriotic songs, Rabindranath Tagore. On the full moon day of Sravana, a *rakhi* [strands of saffron homespun yarn] was tied by the girl on her brother's wrist. Even if the male was not her brother, with this bracelet on he was honorbound to protect her. It was a pledge taken by the courageous to shield the poor and the weak.

With the passing of time, the small skein of yellow silk or cotton gained wider significance and became the symbol of unity. Thus it was that, under the impact of the emotion roused by the partition of Bengal, men embraced and bound themselves to each other using the *rakhi* as the symbol of unity and fraternity. Led by Tagore, high and low participated in it and used it to signify the unity of Bengal—nothing could tear them asunder; they were unaffected by the partition of Bengal and would defend each other till death. To this day, even in the altered circumstances of modern times, this charming festival is observed all over India. The full moon, *purnima,* in August is still known as *rakhi purnima* for it is at this time every year that the tying of *rakhis* takes place, followed by feasting in an atmosphere of goodwill, fraternity, and unity.

I became aware of other aspects of the movement three years later, but this time it was through a young cousin of mine. He was a tall and lanky youth who usually teased me, but that evening when he visited us he was unusually quiet. Mother had entertained him with freshly fried *loochis*—*loochis* seemed to be always ready to be served with a curry of seasonable vegetables, together with a sweetmeat, to anyone who happened to visit us in those days.

After partaking of these snacks he came to the veranda to wash his hands and rinse out his mouth. Drying his hands on the towel that I held out for him he looked at me gravely and said, "Do you know what I have got with me?" patting his pocket. I shook my head. He held up a little paper pellet. "The ashes of Khudiram!" he said.

I started. "Yes," he added with a smile, "his body was cremated last evening." "Who was he?" I ventured. "What! You do not know Khudiram? You seem to know nothing!" was his contemptuous reply. "He worked for the *Swadeshi* movement and he gave his life for our country. He was hanged by the British at dawn." And saying this, my cousin dramatically departed. This was on 21 July 1908. Twenty-year old Khudiram was one of the earliest revolutionaries, and after his death, this song was on the lips of all young people:

O Mother for a while
Bid farewell to me,
I'll wear with a smile
The hangman's noose
For all the world to see!

An elder brother is *dada* in Bengali, and this is what I called my eldest brother. He was religious-minded and inclined to be orthodox, but he became an ardent follower of Swami Vivekananda [a teacher of meditation who traveled to Europe and the U.S. and introduced Hinduism to the West], who molded the minds of many of that generation. After graduating, Dada passed his law examination. He was enrolled at the High Court, but he never practiced, for to practice would mean twisting the truth to suit the case and the client, and he was very much averse to this. Or perhaps he did practice and I never knew anything about it, for my knowledge of him was limited to his interest in the Ramakrishna Mission [a modern ascetic Hindu Order]. Once, soon after his marriage, he had a disagreement with Father and disappeared. Eventually he was found at the Belur Monastery, where he had gone with the intention of renouncing the world and taking holy orders. Before this was carried out he was discovered by my uncle and persuaded to return home. Truthful to the extent of rudeness, forthright and quick tempered, he gave me my first lessons in the teachings of Sri Ramakrishna. But I was very young then and I did not know that they came from the great saint.

One evening, when we were at dinner and Mother was serving us with appetizing *loochis,* I asked him, "Dada, how many gods are there and which is the true one?" Reading the Christian scriptures had raised doubts within my mind. "Why, I thought you knew there was but one God," was the reply. "Yes, but at school...." "Oh, is that what is troubling you?" laughed Dada. "Look, it's just like this," he said, and here he raised his tumbler. "We call this *jal,* Muslims call it *pani,* the French *l'eau,* and the English *water.* All these many names mean just one thing. It is the same with God. He has many names, but He is but one."

Once I was assailed with doubts about the Almighty. "How are we to know that He *is?* We do not see *Him,*" I asked Dada, with much trepidation, for he was more than fifteen years older than myself and was usually stern and aloof. But I always went to him instead of my other brothers, for he looked with understanding and affection on my questioning mind. "I will tell you of a disciple who asked the same question of his teacher," Dada replied with a smile. "Oh did he?" I broke in breathlessly. "Well, you must let me tell you the story, but I will spare you what the teacher did to his disciple." "What did he do?" I interrupted

> "Look, it's just like this," he said, and here he raised his tumbler. "We call this *jal,* Muslims call it *pani,* the French *l'eau,* and the English *water.* All these many names mean just one thing. It is the same with God. He has many names, but He is but one."

excitedly. "He thrashed him soundly till the disciple yelled for mercy." I gasped. "The teacher then asked the disciple what was the matter," continued Dada. "Matter!" shouted the disciple in tears, "why you have beaten me and hurt me, and I am in such pain." "Hurt you? Pain? What is pain? I can't see the pain you mention," said the teacher. "It's here," moaned the disciple, pointing to his back. "Where?" the teacher asked, bending over him. "I can't see anything." "I can't show it to you," wept the disciple, "but it is very real, I feel it!" "Ah," said the teacher, "that is just it! Now you understand—God, too, cannot be seen with mortal eyes, He manifests Himself only through His works and is realized only by His devotees." And with this story I had to be content.

The convent teaching raised a fresh conflict in my young mind and I came to him again one day with another problem. "Which is the true religion?" I asked. "All religions are true," he replied. "They are but so many roads that lead to God. Some roads are broad and some narrow, some are long and some are shorter ways to the same destination, that is the only difference," was his reply. "Then it does not matter much, does it, which road we take?" I asked, surprised at my own boldness. "But it does matter," he retorted. "It all depends on how you look at it. You may reach your destination through a flower-filled garden, or through an unclean latrine, it is for you to choose which path you prefer."

Dada was pious, but his language was not always polite nor was he inclined to be patient. He was rather blunt in speech and prided himself upon his ability to call a spade a spade. I am indebted to this brother of mine for a good bit of my education. I am also indebted to him for arranging my marriage....

Orthodox Hindu weddings are performed according to the Vedic rites that have been maintained for countless years. From very ancient times the responsibility of the ceremony belonged to the father or the elder of the family, and was shared in varying measures by other relations and kinsmen, friends, and neighbors. Every attempt is made to assure the material and spiritual welfare of the girl and boy about to be married, and hence these many ceremonies are performed by the families of both the bride and the groom. A vital interest is taken in all the proceedings, and as there is no marriage document, family and friends are essential as witnesses to the marriage ceremony.

Abhuti is an abbreviation of the word *abhyudayika,* which means "that which brings prosperity." There are actually three rituals in the ceremony. It commences with the worship of the goddess Shasthi and the sage Markandeya. Shasthi is the deity who presides over children, whom she shields from all evil. In the *dhyana murti* [image to be meditated upon] she is holding a child in her arms. The elder entrusted with performing this ceremony (always someone from the paternal side) prays that the progeny of the bride, or of the groom as the case may be, might be blessed with health and long life, and by Shasthi's grace reach a high plane of mental, moral, and spiritual elevation. Markandeya was a great ascetic who by severe penance and austerity achieved immortality. His spirit is invoked and his grace sought in the same manner.

After the invocations of Shasthi and Markandeya, certain aspects of Shakti, the divine force of power and the cosmic feminine principle, are invoked. The different aspects of Shakti are referred to as the Sixteen Mothers. These include Gouri, the beautiful daughter of the Himalayas who gained Shiva by the force of her austerities; Padma, another name of the goddess of wealth and prosperity; Sachi, the consort of Indra and goddess of enjoyment; Savitri, the consort of Brahma and goddess of creation; Jaya, the goddess of victory; and Vijaya, the goddess of unvanquishable might and power. The other Mothers represent the power of peace, sustenance, contentment, memory, and many others. When all these beneficent forces have been invoked, they are symbolized in the "cords of good fortune" that are worn on the wrists of the bride and the bridegroom as a token of the benedictions of the Sixteen Mothers....

The evening is full of excitement. First, servants from the bride's home arrive bearing the wedding gifts and baskets of flowers for the *phul shajya* [bed of flowers]. There is also new raiment for both, as well as fragrant sandalwood paste and an entire set of floral ornaments for the bride. On the "auspicious night" she wears bracelets, armlets, neck chains, rings, and a crown, all skillfully created with bright flowers. The walls of the bridal chamber are festooned with flowers and the bed is strewn with them, and it is into this room that the bride is led to meet her bridegroom.

I well remember my first arrival at my father-in-law's house, for I almost died within the gilded palanquin that carried me to my husband's ancestral home. We were very much in *purdah* [seclusion of women from public spaces] in those days, and nice women were neither seen nor heard, especially new brides. I had all this explained to me by Jushi-di and others who were anxious that I do the right things among my new relations. Feeling rather sick and forlorn, I looked at Mother. She seemed to have a cold; she cleared her throat several times and then nodded and said in a low voice that I should always listen to Khokar-jhi. When my eyes fell on Father, I noticed he was blinking with a frown on his face. "They will miss the train if there is any more delay…" said someone, and I was led to the landau. In the midst of all these strangers I derived comfort from the thought that Khokar-jhi, formidable though she was, followed in a hired carriage. "Your Dada will come and see you soon and your Sripur uncle will come to fetch you when the 'ten days' are over," were Mother's parting words, and that was also another comfort.

My father-in-law had reserved the entire compartment for myself and my husband and my maids. The train started from Sealdah sometime after 2:00 P.M., and ambled along in a leisurely fashion till five hours later it reached the small town of Murshidabad. Khokar-jhi had rearranged my veil and given me a reminder to behave properly, but neither she nor I had noticed that my sari had rucked up a little in front, so both of us were adequately ashamed when someone pulled down my sari as I stood uncertainly at the open door. As I wondered how I would descend, someone held out a hand from below and helped me to alight. No sooner

had I done so, than the train gave a piercing whistle and started to move. Fervently I prayed that Khokar-jhi and Parvati were not borne away with it. From beneath my veil I recognized the person who had so kindly made me presentable and assisted me to dismount as my father-in-law. Aware of a large crowd and much commotion, I felt safe as I followed him to the gorgeous red and gold palanquin. Although I had never been in a palanquin before I was thankful for its shelter and to see Khokar-jhi.

It was a spacious palanquin made comfortable with silken quilts and velvet cushions. Khokar-jhi leaned back on a fat gold-embroidered bolster and beamed approval at the manner of my reception, but I felt suffocated as the sliding doors closed. We were hoisted onto many shoulders, and the bearers commenced a plaintive chant that kept time with their pace. No light filtered through the chinks as it had been draped with a piece of heavy gold brocade. I could hear a brass band playing selections of English music and the clamor of crowded streets, and I felt I could not breathe. Pushing aside my veil I gasped, "I'll die…oh Khokar-jhi, what shall I do now? I'll surely die!" "Hush child, this is only for a little while," was all she said and I felt I could weep aloud in my agony…. The moments passed like hours. I clenched my hands, my breath came short and fast…suddenly the bearers stopped, the palanquin rested on the ground…the doors opened and a whiff of God's blessed air cooled my face. I drew a long breath, Khokar-jhi quickly pulled down my veil, someone reached for my hand and helped me out.

Lights dazzled my eyes. Before me was a great gate flanked by the auspicious water jars crowned with green coconuts. I heard the high notes of the wedding oboes, the sonorous sound of the conch shell, and the traditional cries that women raised when they ceremoniously welcome the bride. As I entered the threshold I became aware that I was not alone. Beside me walked my husband and though I did not know him then and had hardly seen his face I found comfort in his presence.

Once again he took my hand, and the scent of his jasmine garland was borne to me by a passing breeze. The silver anklets tinkled on my feet as I walked with him to his home, but first we bowed low before the grave of an old fakir [Muslim mendicant] at the entrance where a little earthen lamp cast its flickering light. No one knew exactly when he lived and died and why he was buried here, but it was said that the blessings of this Muslim saint rested on the old house, and his spirit guarded it ever since it was acquired by Rai Udai Chand Mazumdar in 1825....

Mazumdar relates a memory about a dream from her teenage years.

Being left much to myself [after my marriage] I was blessed with leisure to read and reflect. I was then nineteen and had somehow turned towards serious literature and developed religious tendencies, not in consonance with my years. My acquaintance with the *Bhagavad Gita* had ripened into love and I found myself greatly drawn towards Sri Krishna and his wonderful teachings in the *Gita*.

There was a small spare room and this I converted into a retreat for meditation and prayer. I read a fixed number of verses each morning and mused long over the commentaries and tried my best to grasp their purport. I became painfully aware of my failings, yearned to improve myself, aspired to live a spiritual life, and ventilated my thoughts in a diary. I had read much but apparently digested little, for as I look back I find I was obsessed with a good deal of self-pity and was something of a prig. My discovery of the ephemeral quality of the things of the world tinged my thoughts, making me less interested in my home and surroundings. I prayed long, fasted

occasionally, and all this rather worried my husband, but he did not interfere.

I remember having strange dreams at this time about flying through space, and would awake unrefreshed and weary, as if I had actually flown over long distances. One dream is still deeply etched in my memory: I was flying with a feeling of great exhilaration towards the southwest, when all of a sudden clouds parted before me and I beheld Goddess Kali [Shiva's consort, the dark Goddess of All, venerated by Bengalis] representing time and death. The awesome towering figure rose from the earth to the skies and was so terrible to behold that I covered my face with both hands and turned aside. When I opened my eyes, the dread image was no more and the sky was bright and blue.... Then a rosy glow appeared, and again the clouds were rent asunder and from within appeared a most radiantly beautiful figure clad in crimson. She too seemed to have the earth for her footstool and her shining diadem touched the skies. She looked at me with benediction in her eyes and with a smile held out a rose-colored lotus. I stretched forth my hands...the flower fell on the earth and lay with its petals scattered around; its white heart with the golden center revealed the tips of the little seeds embedded within.... *"Tuley ney, Tuley ney!"*—"Pick it up, pick it up!" The indescribably sweet tones of the divine voice echoed in my ears as I awoke with the rays of the newly risen sun on my face. At the time this seemed no more than a beautiful dream, but many years after I realized the significance of this vision that was vouchsafed to me.

In April 1919, the shooting of unarmed citizens of Amritsar at Jallianwalla Bagh created a great stir. Strict censorship had at first prevented news of those outrageous events in the Punjab from leaking to other parts of India. But nevertheless, news of the atrocities spread, and a mighty wave of horror and indignation swept the country.

One morning in June I opened the *Statesman* and was thrilled to find the historic letter addressed to the [British] Viceroy Lord Chelmsford in which Sir Rabindranath Tagore renounced his knighthood. With breathless interest I read through it again and, like countless others, saluted his valiant spirit with reverence and love.

My heart beat rapidly as I read, "…the least that I can do for my country is to take all consequences upon myself by giving voice to the protests of millions of my countrymen surprised into a dumb anguish of terror. The time has come when badges of honor make our shame glaring in the incongruous context of humiliation, and I for my part wish to stand shorn of all special distinctions by the side of those of my countrymen who for their so-called insignificance are liable to suffer degradation not fit for human beings."

"Robi Babu," as we call Tagore in Bengal, was dear to me before, but now this glimpse of his flaming spirit and the beauty of his noble gesture completely captivated me and I longed to set my eyes on him. The opportunity came sometime in September that year when Santosh Babu, the Rector of the Santiniketan School, invited us for the *Sharodotsab* [autumn festival].

Santiniketan was but a few hours' journey by train from Suri. The song festival would commence at sundown, so dinner was served at an early hour. My husband dined with our host in a separate apartment, but as I never appeared before Santosh Babu, my food was sent to me in my room. Afterwards, when it was dark, I was escorted to the enclosure reserved for women and, from here, avidly enjoyed the feast of Tagore's melodious songs, so exquisitely rendered by the students of Santiniketan. Later I had the joy of seeing the poet himself on the stage. We returned to Suri at three o'clock in the morning, and although I had a splitting headache my heart overflowed with happiness at having beheld Tagore at last….

Mazumdar became interested in politics. In 1920, she resolved to attend the Congress in Calcutta at which leading Indians were expected to denounce the British rulers of India.

The new daughter-in-law of the family, Abola, clung to me and said I surely would not go without her! Mother was aghast at our doings. Whatever was the world coming to? Here was the *nutan bou* [new bride] with her husband away in England, wanting to attend a Congress meeting! She was much against all these newfangled ideas and held me to blame for them, but since Dada, noted for his sobriety and orthodox views, had sponsored our cause she eventually gave her reluctant permission.

On the day of the opening session we set out very early with Dada. As I clutched my ticket in one hand and held firmly onto Abola with the other, I remembered Mother's warning that the responsibility was mine and that I would have to account for any mishap that might occur to the *nutan bou*. Somehow, I managed to find two good seats in the small enclosed area reserved for ladies. Once seated, I looked around for known faces but alas could not find any and voiced my disappointment. "The Congress leaders have not come as yet," said the friendly girl by my side. I gazed at the vast sea of faces before me in wonder. "There they come!" she whispered excitedly. "Who—?" I asked humbly. "Why the Ali brothers of course!" and seeing their tall stalwart figures I felt ashamed not to have recognized them before.

One by one they came, the fighters for India's freedom, and I was shocked to the core when a man in front of me stood up and hissed "Spy!" when Annie Besant entered. "What does he say?" I whispered in great distress, for I could not understand how anyone could use that word to Mrs. Besant. "Oh, he is quite mad," was the reply. "Just you watch and wait, you'll find a few more like him." Then I heard the wonderful address of the President, Lala Lajpat Rai. In forceful language and impeccable English he dwelt on the wrongs done in the Punjab and charged Michael O'Dwyer with all the barbarous atrocities that had been inflicted on the poor people of the state.

Sir A. Choudhury gave a spirited speech in faultless English, and a rather plump upcountry lady, whose name I learnt was Mongola Devi, spoke in Hindusthani, and I thought it would have been better if she had not gesticulated so much. After her came a veiled lady who sang a Hindi song that condemned the Hunter Committee, Rowlatt Act, and Sir Michael O'Dwyer. She lifted up her hands and circled round within the rostrum like a dancer, and I closed my eyes and clenched my hands and wondered how she could make that exhibition of herself. Later, when I asked Dada the meaning of this little act, he laughed and said it was to satisfy the masses. I had indignantly replied that if they wanted entertainment of that sort they ought to have gone to a theater and not come to the Congress session. We accompanied Dada to the Congress another day and I was relieved to see that the seat next to mine was occupied by the same knowledgeable young woman.

I attempted to take an intelligent interest in the proceedings, but my eyes wandered and I found myself absorbed more in my surroundings and the people assembled than in what was said by the speakers. But I well remember the main resolution. Because the ladies' enclosure was on the left side of the rostrum and some distance away, I had only a partial glimpse of the insufficiently clad figure who came to move it.

He spoke clearly and seemed to be very sincere. After mentioning the wrongs done by the British government in the Punjab, he said there was only one way our people could redress their wrongs, prevent a repetition of the same, and vindicate national honor. That was to establish *swaraj* [Indian self-rule]. And until the wrongs were righted and *swaraj* achieved, the only course left open for the people of India was to adopt the policy of progressive nonviolent noncooperation. The people were advised to surrender their titles and honorary offices, resign from nominated seats in local councils, refuse to attend government levees and *durbars,* withdraw their children from schools and colleges owned, aided, or controlled by the government, boycott British goods and buy *swadeshi* [Indian-made] cloth to help the millions of weavers in the country, and revive the art of spinning and weaving in every home.

I breathlessly watched people speak for and against the resolution. The Ali brothers supported it, as did an elderly man on whom the years sat lightly. "Pundit Motilal Nehru," whispered my companion reverentially, and I could hardly tear my eyes away from that proud patrician face when I remembered that wonderful portion of his Presidential address from the previous year: "What is our ultimate goal? We want freedom of thought, freedom of action, freedom to fashion our own destiny and build up an India suited to the genius of her people.... We must aim at an India where all are free and have the fullest opportunities of development, where women have ceased to be in bondage and the rigors of the caste system have disappeared...."

There was a lengthy debate, and much excitement prevailed when C. R. Das, with other leaders of Bengal and leaders of Maharashtra, strongly opposed it. Suddenly, there was a great furor near the rostrum and loud shouts from the assembly. "What's happened?" I asked. "Why, the resolution is passed," my companion said gleefully, as she settled her sari more decorously on her head prior to departure. "Who was the man who moved it?" "Oh, that was Gandhi!..."

Pandit Nehru, presiding over the forty-fourth session of the Congress declared in an address that the time had come for India to march forward to win independence. Those who would come forward to free the country from foreign rule would be recompensed with suffering, imprisonment, and death, he warned. Following this the decision was taken that 26 January would be observed as Independence Day. On this day the Congress flag would be flown each year and the pledge of independence taken.

I do not recollect any great enthusiasm about this amongst the people I happened to meet. Those with vested interests flouted the idea and said the Congress was crazy. Gray heads were shaken in disapproval; it was felt to be a fantastic idea. Only the youthful hearts danced at this daring aim, and those who lacked the courage to openly espouse the cause did so in secret.

I was in Kidderpore in January of that year of 1930. We were gathered round the tea table that morning when loud voices in the street drew us to the veranda. It overlooked the large expanse of the "lotus pond" where at one time, so the legend runs, the flowers really blossomed. A long pole had been planted beside its placid waters, and many people were assembled

and the sergeant quietly intervened. Conforming to nonviolence, the youth did not resist, and we saw him calmly follow the sergeant to the lorry.

"Bande Mataram!" cried the crowd in one voice, and this was repeated again and again till he was out of sight. Another sergeant came to the pole, pulled it up, flung it into the "lotus pond," and carried away the flag. The people watched in silence. We were about to leave when a sudden ripple of amusement made us turn to see a tiny paper flag fluttering gaily in the morning breeze. The sergeant walked back in silence, plucked the flag, and thrust it into his pocket. The crowd tittered and began to disperse; a little urchin came capering along the road and shrieked to another who had just arrived: "Hah! You did not see the fun, they took away Gandhi!"

Anyone who came in conflict with the police over the Congress ideals was labeled "Gandhi" by the common people; in fact, the Civil Disobedience Movement itself was given this name. Sometime later at Basirhat, hearing

> ## Anyone who came in conflict with the police over the Congress ideals was labeled "Gandhi" by the common people; in fact, the Civil Disobedience Movement itself was given this name.

to witness the raising of the flag at the appointed hour.

A young man in white homespun seemed to be in charge of the function. Two motor lorries containing red-turbaned constables appeared on the scene. We could not hear what the European sergeant said, but the young man was seen to shake his head firmly in the negative. The police force waited, and so did the silent crowd. The clock struck eight. The *khadi*-clad youth moved to hoist the Congress flag

distant cries of "Bande Mataram," defiant yells, and voices raised in anger, I asked our little sweeper girl what was happening down the road. All she said was, "Only Gandhi," as she calmly continued to eat her guava with relish.

When the Viceroy made it clear that independence for India was out of the question, the Congress Working Committee authorized Mahatma Gandhi to start Civil Disobedience. But, before this was done, a moving letter was sent to Lord Irwin in which Gandhi explained how he desired to convert the British people by nonviolence. "It is my purpose to set in motion the force of nonviolence against the organized force of British Rule. This will be expressed through civil disobedience...." The Viceroy's answer was unsatisfactory and Gandhiji wrote, "On bended knees I asked for bread and received a stone instead. The English nation responds only to force, and I am not surprised by the Viceregal reply. India is a vast prison house, and I regard it as my sacred duty to break the monotony of peace that is choking the heart of the nation for want of free vent...."

Amongst the points that had been presented to the Viceroy were total prohibition, protective tariff on foreign cloth, and abolition of the salt tax. It was felt that salt, like air and water, was the property of the people. On 12 March, accompanied by his seventy-nine followers—and my heart pounded to find Sarojini Naidu was in this movement—Gandhiji began his historic march to take the salt depot at Darsana. He reached his destination on 5 April.

People pored over the daily papers and discussed the outcome of all this with mounting excitement; it was now realized that nonviolence was not a form of negation but a definite scheme of resistance. Civil disobedience came to be termed *satyagraha* [truth crusade]: to be prepared to endure imprisonment, sufferings, and penalties for the cause, to never ask for any monetary help, and to implicitly obey the leaders of the campaign. A large number of people became aware of the spirit of Gandhi's teachings, and were stirred to the depths. They cast aside worldly considerations and joined his crusade with faith and fervor.

"He has been arrested and taken to Yervada Jail," Chorda announced mournfully one morning. Then we came to know of the message he had left—that neither the people nor his colleagues should be daunted. He was not the conductor of the fight; that was God who dwelt in the hearts of all. Only faith was necessary; then God would lead them. Entire villages were to picket or manufacture salt, women were to picket liquor, opium, and foreign cloth shops, and young and old of every home were to daily ply the spinning wheel, twirl the *takli* [spindle] to produce plenty of yarn, and create bonfires made of foreign cloth....

In the next passage, Mazumdar recounts a near-death experience and her consequential beliefs about the relationship of body and spirit.

The broad river Asrumati flowed in front of our bungalow, and beyond the garden at the back was a spacious pool enclosed by high banks. Beyond this was a high school where Donny became a day scholar. He would walk home for lunch and was on the whole fairly happy here. Both he and I learned to swim in the pool, at first supporting ourselves on huge banana trunks used as floats. We hugged them and kicked our feet immoderately while Romu instructed us. He had learnt to swim at Manikgunge, but it was his father, an expert swimmer, who watched us on Sunday mornings to see how we were progressing.

He had warned us about places that were deep—two people had lost their lives in that tank—and he instructed us never to enter the waters alone. I broke my promise once and was very nearly drowned. The waters were high due to untimely rains, and I missed my footing on the slimy steps. I was being carried away when the man who was weeding the garden happened to look up, saw my plight, plunged in and rescued me. Gratefully giving him some remuneration I swore him to secrecy; he was not to tell the master. But eventually it was I who confessed and was soundly berated for my rash act.

I remember that for some days after I had a curious sense of detachment from my body. It was a singular feeling. As I applied the usual powder that evening, I seemed to see someone else in the mirror. I looked critically at the reflection and recollect saying aloud: "What are you trying to beautify? This face that would have been sodden in the waters of the pool and brought forth swollen and ugly—this husk that your loved ones would have turned away from in horror and made haste to dispose of in the funeral pyre before the dawn of another day? Body and spirit were separate you had heard, but now you know it. Confined in this cage of flesh that decomposes, you are but here to play the game of life for a little while till the call comes to leave it. Do not forget this glimpse of the ultimate truth."

I exalted in this knowledge and grew a little light-headed over the insight gained of my real self. But the glory faded as time passed and the mists enveloped my mind. Once more I fondly fancied the fleeting things of life, and the folds of *maya* [illusion] were firmly retied over my eyes. But the memory of that brief encounter with truth lingered, and I yearned to reexperience it.

In the silent afternoons the villagers would pass our house on some errand to town, and often their voices would be raised in song. They were songs with plaintive tunes, melodious and haunting, sung in rustic but subtle and sweet words, and my mind would turn them over trying to understand their inner meaning. Once a saffron-robed mendicant, plucking at his lyre with its single string, the *ektara,* sang a song that expressed thoughts common to our people. The lilt and beauty of the rhyming words with their puns and alliterations cannot be translated; I can but try to give the sense of the song. The devotee complains that his beloved Lord is indulging in a game of blindman's bluff with him in life and forever eluding him. And this is what he says in loving reproach:

> Oh Lord in this world's play, blindfolded has
> Thou placed me
> And striking at me sayeth, it's Thy Hand that
> struck me.

> Then I hear Thee say, "Catch me I am here!"
> Lord, it pleases Thee to play, but my heart is
> struck with fear.
> Stretching forth my hands to search,
> I wander and grow weary,
> Thou who art so near and dear, yet remain
> a stranger.
> The day is near its end,
> The play when will it end?
> Cease Thy game I beg of Thee
> I confess I am beaten. I have no strength or
> skill to catch Thee,
> From my eyes untie the folds, let me behold
> Thee I pray,
> And dear Lord in Thy Mercy, take my
> griefs away.

In the next passage, Mazumdar describes Hindu beliefs about the goddess known as Durga. The autobiography ends with Mazumdar befriending a lonely girl.

In childhood, the happy time spent in Saidpore had been too brief. On my first visit to a village I had been left free to wander at will; and my days there were a cherished memory. Mother had told us about the Durga *puja* celebrated at her paternal home with such a wealth of detail that we longed to see it. But during that festive season her duties at Kidderpore had never allowed her to leave during my unmarried days, so when my uncles invited us when we were at Basirhat, I rejoiced. My sisters-in-law and their children were with us, and we were all invited.

Every god had contributed towards Durga's unsurpassed beauty. It is told how Shiva's energy formed her lovely face, and Vishnu's her eight strong arms. Her beautiful breasts were from the moon, her slender waist from Indra, King of Swarga [Heaven]; her black silken tresses from Yama, the god of death; her shapely ears from Vaiyu, the wind god; and her dazzling eyes from Agni, the god of fire. One by one, each part of the body was created to complete the form of a perfect woman. The *devas* [gods] then armed her with celestial weapons, and in the invincible armor given her by Viswa Karma—the Divine Craftsman—she was both beautiful and terrible to behold. The king of all snakes gave her a neck chain of deadly serpents, each with a glittering jewel on its head. The sea clothed her in imperishable robes, crowned her with a dazzling diadem, adorned her with golden bracelets and armlets and a gem-set ring for each finger, and her beautiful feet with ornaments. The sea god's gifts were fragrant lotus and a garland of flowers that would never fade. And, since the *asuras* [demons] would use ruthless violence to work their will on the world, the fierce lion was given to serve her as her steed. The mighty goddess, resplendent with strength, beauty, and power thus arrayed, laughed aloud with flashing eyes as she placed her feet on the lion's back. "Victory to Simha Bahini!" cried the *devas* joyfully. "Victory to She who rides the lion!" And "Simha Bahini" became one of her names.

It is only in Bengal that with Durga, the symbol of invincible power, is seen lovely Lakshmi, the power of wealth, protected by the power of arms in the form of the elegant Kartick, the god of war. On her left stands the shimmering form of Saraswati, the power of culture, guided by Ganesha, the spirit of wisdom, and Demos, the lord of the common people. At the feet of this scintillating group full of beauty and grace lies brute force, ugly and evil, vanquished by the glorious goddess. Thousands stand before her with folded hands to cry "Bande Mataram!"—"I bow to Thee, Mother!"

She was the patriot's vision of an India victorious and free, with her wealth and culture restored; she was the pride of her people, released from the bondage at last. To others, she symbolized the yearnings of the spirit towards values that crowned life with fulfillment and bliss—the ultimate aim of human existence.

Durga *puja* in Bengal is celebrated with elaborate ceremony when the heavy rains and gusty winds have subsided and autumn has come. The days of mud and slush are gone, the earth is clothed in tender and bright flowers. The wild tawny rivers are tamed and flow calmly in their course now, reflecting the azure heavens. The sun shines from cloudless skies when the monsoons have passed; the days are golden, the bright moon and starlit nights stir the spirit, and people are heard to say with a reminiscent smile, "Why, already there is a scent of *puja* in the air!"

The wealthy, the needy, the worldly, the spiritually inclined, the happy-hearted, and the miserable, all look forward to this national festival. Though moved by different sentiments, the same shining thread will be found to enrich the texture of their lives and thoughts. It is a joyous occasion that helps to spread goodwill and maintain social obligations. It is a time of blissful reunions—children who had left home to seek their fortunes in distant places join their families during the *puja* vacation. It is a season for exchange of gifts, and the weavers who had stored best *dhotis* and saris raise their prices to make a little extra profit, since the traditional presents are clothing. The poor hope to obtain a new garment and perhaps a proper meal, for almsgiving is a special feature of the festival and the rich are reminded of their obligations. The elders make gifts of garments as a token of their blessing and, attired in these, the younger generations make their obeisance before the Mother and pray for her benediction. It is only here in Bengal that the spirit of the primordial energy is invoked in sculptured clay. Special craftsmen mold, tint, and adorn the image, accurately following the word pictures given by the *rishis* [sages] in our scriptures.

The Durga *puja* would be at its best in the village where the festival is celebrated with pomp and circumstance by the local *zamindar*. His tenants, both Hindu and Moslem, receive new clothes when they come to their landlord's mansion to join the many activities connected with the ritual worship of the Mother. They feast here for the four festive days, and special attention is given to the poor, for it is said that Daridra Narayana, the Lord Himself in the form of the poor, has come to partake of gifts and hospitality from the home that is blessed with the Mother's presence.

As we reached Saidpore, the tinkle of bells and sound of conch shells proclaimed that the ritual worship of Mother Durga had already commenced. The old house wore a festive look, the courtyard was teeming with people, and noisy children were romping about. A group had gathered round the drummers, demanding that drums should be beaten right now rather than later at *arati*, when the drum and gong usually go together.

There seemed to be a current of joy in the air when my uncles and aunts and cousins came forward to greet us. We went together to the temple, for it was nearly time for the *pushpanjali*, the flower offering ceremony, in which everyone participated.

We stood silently with hands folded before the great sculptured group including Mother Durga and her divine children. The snarling lion at her feet had his teeth on the bleeding monster, Mahisasura, around whose neck was coiled a serpent with outspread hood. This was of particular interest to the younger people, but we only had eyes for the serene face of the Mother. A mysterious smile played on her lips and her eyes were tender. Lights and incense and rich offerings of many kinds, including masses of flowers, were placed before her. There were bunches of bananas, large and luscious fruits, and rough clay plates piled high with sugar cakes and other sweets from village folk who had placed their humble gifts before the Mother in thanksgiving.

Soon, the *puja* was over…. "Anjali! Anjali!" the word went round and family members,

guests, and visitors assembled before the Mother. The priest began distributing flowers to those who had not brought any. Hearing a titter, I turned. A very young girl stood diffidently at a distance and some girls were looking at her in amusement. She wore a red-bordered sari, a broad streak of vermilion between the parting of her hair and a large crimson dot on her brow. Her face was sad and forlorn. With folded hands she was raptly gazing at the Mother. She did not come forward to join us in the floral rite, nor was she called for the function, which is common courtesy extended to all devotees at a time like this….

The girl is a widow of low status, unable to remarry because of cultural prejudices.

Her head was bent. I took her hand. "Would you like to come for *arati*, evening prayers?" She looked uncertainly at her mother. I hastened to add that I would be there with her. My cousin nodded approval. Together we watched the evening ritual being performed by the priest. The incense was fragrant, the flowers were colorful, the atmosphere was soothing, and the Mother of the Universe smiled with benign grace. The girl beside me had her hand in mine; her lips were moving in prayer and tears flowed from her eyes…. Looking on her, I remembered those beautiful lines of Tagore:

> Mother, I shall weave a chain of pearls for thy neck with my tears of sorrow.
>
> The stars have wrought their anklets of light to deck thy feet, but mine will hang upon thy breast
>
> Wealth and fame come from thee and it is for thee to give or withhold them.
>
> But this my sorrow is absolutely mine own, and when I bring it to thee as my offering, thou rewardest me with thy grace.

Discussion Questions: **Shudha Mazumdar**

1. What are the basic beliefs in Mazumdar's creed?

2. The first paragraph of an autobiography often holds several keys about the meaning of the story. Read the first paragraph. On the basis of the emphases you find there, which of Mazumdar's beliefs would you say is most basic?

3. What are the sources of Mazumdar's beliefs about God?

4. What would Mazumdar say about a female God?

5. Is Mazumdar's creed devoted more to attaining worldly happiness and bliss, or more toward renouncing this world?

6. Does Mazumdar believe that spiritual phenomena can cause physical phenomena?

7. Does Mazumdar believe that worship of Shiva should be emotional?

8. After she nearly drowns, Mazumdar sees someone in her mirror. What does the apparition tell her to believe about the relationship between body and spirit?

9. Mazumdar's *bhakti* religion does not seem to encourage the kind of arcane theological speculation we saw in Bharati's *advaita*. How would you explain this difference?

Chapter 6

Zen Buddhism

THE UNCANNY

IN defining religion I suggested that the characteristic that most marks an experience as *religious* is the uncanny. Unlike the code, creed, cultus, or course of religion, the uncanny cannot be explained. Most of the things that happened to me that night in Buena Vista can be explained. We can explain my seeing a bottle of Crisco by appealing to physical principles, such as the principle of light refracted off of a plastic surface onto a human retina, and to the existence of objects invoked in such principles, such as light bulbs, bottles, and human eyes. We can explain my friends' interpretation of the Bible by appealing to historical activities, such as people preserving old books generation after generation, and to contemporary activities, such as believers sharing a common language and knowing various strategies for interpreting sacred texts. We can even explain what I heard while lying in the field. I did not hear an eerie sound, as if there were UFOs and extraterrestrials circling my head. I heard a very ordinary sound, the sound of running water, a sound I could very easily explain (with some help from my colleagues in physics, engineering, and psychology) in terms of physical principles and objects, such as the movement of sound waves from water to human brains, and in terms of mental operations, such as my memory of what water sounds like when it falls onto a hard surface.

To explain something is to set it in a wider context, to render intelligible what might be unfamiliar and unintelligible. Explanations need not be "scientific" in any narrow sense because some things are best explained in more humanistic terms. For example, my fondness for the young ranch couple might be explained by telling a story that sets my affection for them in the context of my psychological development. Psychologists trying to explain what happened to me that night might note that I was far from home when I met Rob and Patty. They might further observe that the couple may have functioned for me as surrogate parents. Almost everything that happened to me that night, even the unusual things, can be rendered intelligible by being set in a wider context of physical, psychological, and sociological laws.

What defied explanation for me that night was the *source* of my speaking in tongues, and the *cause* of my hearing the running water. So long as I believed that *I* was the source of my tongues speaking, I had an explanation for the experience. *I* was hallucinating or in some other way "making it up." So long as I had an explanation, the experience was not inexplicable; it was embarrassing. When I thought the tongues were attributable to the Holy Spirit rather than to my own impulsive babbling, however, my embarrassment faded and the experience became inexplicable. At these times, the source of the sound of running water was inexplicable and remained a mystery to me. I had no scientific explanation for it and, when I went searching for one, I found nothing. Only much later, when I returned to the ranch and discovered a ditch near where I may have been lying, did a scientific explanation suggest itself to me. At the time, however, even though the sound itself was not mysterious, the source or cause of the sound was uncanny, and I chose to attribute the source of the sound to a supernatural being, the Holy Spirit.

In Zen Buddhism, many things can be explained. The history or course of Buddhism can be explained by alluding to Siddhartha Gautama, who experienced his great enlightenment in India in about 600 B.C.E. Buddhism spread from India and flourished throughout Asia, becoming the dominant religion of countries as diverse as China, Vietnam, and Japan. In Japan, Buddhist history is divided into eras, with the Meiji era beginning in 1867 C.E. when Emperor Meiji began his reign. Our second Buddhist author, Satomi Myodo, was born before the Meiji era ended in 1912.

The creed of Buddhism can also be explained. According to Buddhist teaching, the final end of human striving is the cessation of all striving, the ending not only of all our lust and greed but the ending of all our desires. In enlightenment, we no longer experience hate or envy, but we also no longer experience passion or selfish attachment. We overcome ourselves, break free of the bonds of our fleshly existence, and experience *nirvana*, ineffable bliss, freedom, and enlightenment. Buddhists believe in the Four Noble Truths. The first truth is that life intrinsically involves suffering *(dukkha)*. The second truth is that our suffering is caused by our striving, or wanting *(tanha)*. The third truth is that there is an answer to our dilemma, and the fourth truth is that the answer can be found by following the set of practices called the Buddhist Eightfold Path.

The rituals of Zen Buddhism, an outgrowth of the larger Buddhist tradition, can also be explained. According to tradition, Zen Buddhism began in China roughly in 500 C.E. when the first Zen patriarch developed a new form of Buddhist practice. Bodhidharma stressed the importance of attaining internal peace, selflessness, and strength through meditation. In Japan, the enlightenment at which Bodhidharma aimed is called *satori* or *kensho*, awakening to one's own true nature. You may attain *kensho* if you take a teacher and submit fully to the master's authority. The Zen student goes to the Zendo, or meditation hall, to attend *sesshin*, formal periods of concentration in which the master, or *roshi*, questions the student, posing *koans* or dilemmas insoluble by reason, e.g., What is the sound of one hand clapping? As our first author in this chapter, Janwillem van de Wetering, tells us, masters on occasion will strike students with sticks so as to sharpen the students' powers of concentration, like splashing cold water in the face. Van de Wetering struggles to attain the traditional lotus posture while sitting in *zazen*, a form of meditation in which the student sits with legs tucked underneath the thighs, and hands held together in the lap, palms up.

Many things in Zen Buddhism can be explained, but the central insight of Zen cannot. The central, uncanny, insight is satori. Satori is not a transcendental being like the Holy Spirit in Christianity, and yet satori occupies the same conceptual space in Zen Buddhism that the Holy Spirit occupies in Christianity. Satori is that for which there is no suitable explanation. Satori can only be experienced, not satisfactorily explained.

In our two autobiographies, Janwillem van de Wetering and Satomi Myodo explain many things. Van de Wetering describes the methodical art of pursuing satori by meditating on a koan. Myodo describes her painful journey through acceptance, rejection, motherhood, and temple meditation to eventual enlightenment. But neither author claims to be able to explain the uncanny dimension of their religious achievement. Neither one has scientific or psychological explanations for what they experience, and both reach the limits of their vocabularies and imaginations in describing their encounters with the transcendent.

Janwillem van de Wetering is a Dutchman who, ten years before his autobiography opens, had gone to a monastery in Kyoto, Japan, to find the meaning of life. He was gloomy and preoccupied with the illusion of everyday existence and resolved to study Zen. At the monastery he had met an American named Peter who helped him with his meditation and gave him a place to live while he studied with the old master. Ten years later, van de Wetering has returned to Amsterdam. Peter comes to visit him and, while they are talking, van de Wetering learns that Peter has finished his study of Zen and has several disciples studying with him. On the way to the airport, van de Wetering decides to study with Peter and asks if he will take him on as a disciple. Peter agrees, and our author soon flies to America to live on his new master's small farm. Some forty people live there in seven small houses, growing their own food communally and meditating every morning from 3:30 to 6:30 A.M. in the Zendo, a temple modeled on Japanese plans.

Van de Wetering finds his experience with Zen in America different from his experience in Japan. In Japan, his master was distant and he did not even know his name. By contrast, he knows Peter as an old friend. In Japan, he was disappointed to learn that Zen masters smoked, drank, and had sex. By contrast, Peter drinks very little and seems cerebral and calm. But many things are the same: the pain van de Wetering feels after sitting still for twenty-five minutes in the Zendo; the simple meals of stew; the attempt to empty himself of his ego.

Van de Wetering experiences the uncanny as emptiness. Emptiness, he writes, is "the core of Buddhism. Emptiness, the great goal that is to be reached by losing everything there is to lose. Emptiness, the great danger…the final goal is to have nothing more to do, to be nameless." He tries to understand this truth through meditating on it, but he seems unable to grasp it. He walks outside one day and encounters a fox, which he perceives as part of the emptiness of the world. He tells his friend Simon that devoting your life to getting money and property is "not intelligent," and his friend agrees, adding that "being guided by a master" is intelligent. But being guided to where? Janwillem asks. This is the question that cannot be answered.

Van de Wetering does not have a single dramatic enlightenment experience, but toward the end of his story he realizes that he has learned "real wisdom." What is the wisdom of liberation? "'Not to be expressed in words,' I said cleverly. 'Real wisdom can never be expressed in words,'" he writes. But then he realizes that he is being clever, and he tries again:

> I know that freedom exists...The turning wheel seems eternal. Life follows life, heaven follows heaven, hell follows hell.... Are you sure? I asked...You sit on a cloud, free from all influence of the wheel of life, and you watch the endeavor of the little people who are still rummaging about in the limited space of their egos?

Van de Wetering seems to experience the uncanny through Zen meditation, but he finds it very difficult to say exactly what the uncanny is. It is something like freedom, and something like emptiness. But then again, it is not freedom, not emptiness. Words cannot express it; one must experience it.

Satomi Myodo was a Japanese actress and mother. She was born around the same time as Shudha Mazumdar, just before the turn of the twentieth century. The daughter of poor farmers who lived in the mountains, she became pregnant as a teenager and felt she had been "unfilial," disloyal to her parents. She gave birth to a girl and married her daughter's father, then had difficulties caring for the child and making the marriage work. She experienced mental disorientation and hallucinations, and quickly moved from having mystical experiences to simply going insane. Eventually she left her husband and gave up the child to her mother-in-law. She became a *kageki* actress in the equivalent of a community theater, but she was very unhappy.

Eventually she quit her job, left everything, and sought satori. She began her study in Sapporo, Japan, under minimal supervision. After long periods of meditation, she had a vision of a monkey climbing into a tree and bumping its head against the sky. "Just then," she wrote, "I myself unmistakably became Amenominakanushi-no-Okami" (a god of the Japanese Shinto tradition), which means she became a transcendent creator god. There seems to be a tension and movement in Myodo's experience between a desire for ecstatic experiences like this one, characteristic of the Shinto tradition, and a desire for calm experiences, like the insight and inner peace characteristic of Zen. In any case, her ecstatic experience of enlightenment did not last, and she sought instruction from a well-known Zen master, Yasutani Roshi.

When Myodo finally attained her goal, she said to herself that the out-breath in meditation is "*Mu*...The in-breath too is *Mu!*" *Mu* is the realization of oneself, the coming into being of Truth, Dharma, Reality.

> Next breath, too: *Mu!* Next breath: *Mu, Mu!* "*Mu,* a whole sequence of *Mu!* Croak, croak; meow, meow—these too are *Mu!* The bedding, the wall, the column, the sliding door—these too are *Mu!* This, that and everything is *Mu!* Ha ha! Ha ha ha ha ha!"

For Myodo, *Mu* was the uncanny.

Whether emptiness or *Mu,* the uncanny is prominent in Zen Buddhism. As you read van de Wetering's and Myodo's autobiographies, ask yourself how their experience with the uncanny differs from the uncanny experiences of John Fire Lame Deer, Mary Crow Dog, Swami Bharati, and Shudha Mazumdar.

Janwillem van de Wetering

It was five to three in the morning and the snow crackled under my shoes. It was well below zero and the cold made the trees creak. Peter had given me a flashlight and I was using it anxiously, I had slipped already, on a patch of ice that I had mistaken for snow and my hand was bleeding, cut on a stone. The coffee, which I had drunk too quickly, was sloshing about in my empty stomach.

It could be worse, I thought. There must be concentration camps and jails where the prisoners aren't even given coffee in the morning.

We were on the way to the Zendo, the meditation hall built by American boys from Japanese plans. We were crossing a small bridge.

"From here onwards you are on holy ground," Peter said. "Now we are very close to the Zendo, and here on the left, near that large rock the old teacher's ashes are buried. We don't talk here and we don't smoke."

I switched my flashlight off. I could see my way by the lights coming from the Zendo's windows, and now, for the first time, I saw the wooden building with its strangely shaped roof. The architect had done well with the materials at hand. The temple was quiet and powerful. There was a veranda with shelves, already filled with shoes, neatly arranged. I took mine off and wanted to go in in my socks. Peter tapped me on the shoulder. No, I thought. I won't take off my socks. But Peter did and I followed suit and walked on the cold stone tiles, very carefully, on the sides of my bare feet. Back into the silent awesome discipline of a meditation temple. A place of fear, of pain, but also a place of adventure. I was older now, I should be more mature. I would suffer less, I was quite sure of that and I bowed almost cheerfully, greeting the Buddha statue at the end of the hall. When I had a chance to look at the statue I recognized it as an image of Manjusri, the bodhisattva holding a sword, and with the sword it cuts thoughts, imagination, ego. This particular statue was very beautiful, quiet and energetic, calm and ready for anything. A bowl filled with nuts served as an offering. Very practical; nuts don't rot very quickly and don't have to be replaced all the time. Incense smoldered and the heavy smoke vibrated through the hall.

Not a bad place to spend a week in, but there was a little thought bothering me. A meditation hall, the thought told me, is perhaps a sort of kindergarten. We go there because we have told each other that we will. We have promised to spend a week in the silence of the hall. We have made rules and we have promised to obey them. In turns we walk around and supervise each other's efforts. We even hit each other, nicely of course, in a way that doesn't really hurt. But perhaps we should do this on our own. In a cabin, in a small camp right back in the forest. And there we should face ourselves, or what we think this "self" is, and destroy it, and break free. Without any discipline from outside, without a teacher who eggs us on, with tricks, with a bell, with a short stick. Who encourages and ridicules us in turn. The Buddha did it on his own.

A real holy man does this on his own, I told myself.

But you are not a holy man, I said, and sighed, and bowed to my cushions and climbed on top of them and wrenched my legs into the half lotus, right foot turned upside down and resting on the left thigh. The left foot I tucked under the right thigh. I still couldn't manage the full lotus, the ideal position, the free seat from which you can roar into space. It would come. It took Peter a long time too. I promised myself that, one day, I would sit in the full lotus. I might have to break my leg like the Zen master who had a crippled leg that wouldn't do as it was told, and before the master died he broke the crippled leg and twisted it into the right position and died in it, a few hours later. All his life he had been a slave to his leg but he died a free man.

The meditation leader rang his bell. Four strokes and four times the full sound died slowly, with tremors, ebbing away. I straightened my spine, regulated my breathing, and concentrated, for the umpteenth time, on my koan. In an hour or so I would face a new Zen master and present my answer to this koan of mine, the most prized and the most frightening possession I had ever owned. I would meet Peter in the sanzen-room, exactly as I had met the old master hundreds and hundreds of times in the Kyoto monastery. I felt neither excited nor worried. The attempt at concentration had become a habit. The need to force an answer had gone, long ago. I no longer wanted enlightenment. I really didn't want anything at all. I just wanted to sit, quietly, for twenty-five minutes until the *jikki jitsu*, the meditation leader, rang his heavy bell again. And then I would go out and stretch my legs and do a few physical exercises and come back again, and sit for another twenty-five minutes. If there weren't to be any pain it might go on forever. I felt quite peaceful and repeated the koan and fought the sleep that hung on my eyelids and told me to close my eyes and relax and float off. I was prepared to do my best, it was all I could do anyway. The path I had been following seemed the right one, it didn't lead anywhere perhaps but the direction seemed right and I plodded along, as the proverbial Zen ox plods through the swamp; when his feet get sucked into the mud he applies a little more strength and goes on. He can't see where he is going for the horizon is invisible. It's foggy. The ox doesn't complain, he grunts a bit, the plaintive bellowing has changed into an occasional snort.

When the *jikki* rang his bell I looked at my neighbors, quickly, I didn't want them to know I was looking at them. My neighbor on the right was fat, dressed in a white jersey and an enormous walrus mustache decorated his round jolly face. He was sitting in the full lotus and blew heavily through his wide nostrils, making the hairs of his mustache wave. On my other side I saw a very slight girl, or young woman. I jumped off my seat, bowed to it (cushions are always bowed to in a Zendo, they are the future, or present, point of escape), bowed again at the door, and joined the small crowd on the veranda. In Japan the monks sneaked off into corners during the short breaks and puffed at cigarettes and talked but here a pure silence ruled. Some stared out into the night, others did exercises, and massaged their legs. A very serious crowd. These were the true volunteers; the Japanese monks had been forced into the temple life by their fathers, here everyone had come by his own desire, the desire, if Buddhist philosophy is right, to break desire.

But why? Hindu philosophy has an easy explanation. Microbes are born and die and are born again. Slowly their small souls develop and a lot of microbes become one bug, a lot of bugs, eventually, become one mouse, a lot of mice, one dog, two dogs become one stupid man, the stupid man lives many lives and becomes a little cleverer. Finally he realizes his soul is caught. He wants to become free. He knows his desire to be a man, a special man, an individual, holds him back. He feels the limitations of his ego as a wall. He has the feeling that he wants to break the wall. Each life makes the desire to break desire stronger. And one life becomes the last life. He breaks his desire and becomes…An angel? A god? A being on another planet? A bodhisattva? The Hindus may be right. Six hundred lives or so and a man is free. Any man. He can't help it. The longer he lives, in his chain of birth and rebirth, the more evolved he becomes. The soul, the *Atman*, becomes tired of the endless cycle. It gradually formulates the idea that liberty really exists. It feels caught. The undeveloped man doesn't feel caught. But the developed being looks for a guide, and finds a guide. Whatever you want will happen eventually. Give it time, be patient and go on want-ing, and one day the guide appears, if it was a guide you were wanting. And then the trip starts, the final trip. The disciple is fearful and nervous and unhappy. He finds a lot of faults in his guide. He may want to run away, and he may, in fact, give up. But the guide will show up again. And the disciple really wants to know the way out, even if he is fearful and nervous. He can't stay where he is, he can't go back, what else can he do but try to follow the guide? And he doesn't really know what he wants to achieve because the goal, freedom, is beyond his power of conception.

Not a bad theory I thought. But I hadn't come to the Zendo to think, I had come to sit still. And concentrate, of course, concentrate on the key word. The word made my koan, and the koan….

"Repeat that word till everything falls away," the old master had said. I tried and time fell away. The bell rang again, another twenty-five minutes gone. In Japan I had never wanted to believe the monks when they told me that there is no time in the Zendo. The old monks said it. The young monks knew all about time; it ticked away slowly on the *jikki*'s cheap alarm clock. In Japan [when van de Wetering had taken up Zen] I had counted the minutes if I wasn't asleep or sunk away in some dream or other. Time was torture. But now there had been no time. The endless bubbling thoughts had been strangely absent. Miracles, after all, did exist.

The third period had no miracle. My old friend, pain, was with me again. It started as a slight tremble in my left foot and quickly became a raging fire. I moved, the pain stopped for a minute and came back again, furiously, because I had frustrated it. I moved again. The *jikki* spoke to me on the veranda during the interval.

"Don't shift around. You bother the other people. If you do it again I'll have to ask you to leave."

"I was in pain," I said.

"I know. We all are at times. Pain is no reason to move."

The short speech annoyed me. It was abusive, I thought. I felt alone, unable to relate to this bunch of fanatics. The young monks in Japan had moved when they were in pain and I had been able to identify with them. Here I was opposed by storm troopers, all bent to get to whatever-or-wherever-it-was exactly according to their rules and to what the master told them.

Americans make good soldiers, I thought. They win wars. And I am a European. We are fumblers, we make a mess, but sometimes our lives are interesting. If ever I get anywhere I will have got there by mistake.

But I retracked this line of thought. Don't underestimate the Americans. They saved us. If they hadn't come to Europe with their tanks and chewing gum and indifferent courage, where would I be now? In a slave camp or dead. And they had allowed me to come to this place.

But still, the *jikki* had insulted me with his unfeeling message. The memory of one of the Japanese monks saved me in the end.

He was a conceited fellow but whenever the head monk admonished him he would smile pleasantly. I had asked him how he managed to be so patient. The other monks were easily frustrated, I had often seen them kick trees when the head monk had worked on them.

"Well," the conceited monk said, "who am I? I don't exist. I have no real identity. I am quite empty inside. A good Buddhist has to make an effort to remember his own name."

He surprised me and I couldn't think of anything to say. I knew him as a show-off. He was always telling us how clever he was at chopping wood, climbing trees, harvesting cucumbers. But then he explained it to me again.

"Who am I," the conceited monk said, "that I can be insulted?"

Sanzen came.

Guided by the *jikki*'s eternal bell we went outside and walked to the house nearby where Peter waited, Peter the Master. *Sanzen* is the direct contact between master and disciple in formal Zen training. When this type of Buddhist training first began, in ancient China, contact between master and disciple had been very free, there were no fixed times; *sanzen*, like lightning, could strike anywhere and anytime. The master would plant his koans when his disciples least expected it. They might be chopping wood together, or out on a walk, and suddenly the question was there and the disciple would try

> Repeat that word
> till everything
> falls away,"
>
> the old master
> had said.

> I tried
>
> and time fell away.

to formulate an answer and the master would laugh, shake his head and suggest that the student try again, later. But when the monasteries grew and the number of disciples increased, *sanzen* had to be caught in a discipline. People, whenever they live in groups, automatically make rules. Now the masters receive their disciples at set times. Peter, like the Japanese masters, continued the tradition. But his influence wasn't limited to *sanzen*-time. He might strike anytime of the day. And koans aren't solved in *sanzen*-rooms only.

My turn came. I didn't feel tense as I ran up the stairs. Quickly I remembered what I would have to do. Three full prostrations as a greeting to the master, bow when coming into the room, bow again when leaving the room. This extreme politeness has meaning. The disciple reminds himself that he is nothing, and knows nothing. He, from the jail of his individuality, his subjectivity, faces the ultimate, the insight of the master. Buddhism admits that the disciple, after all, is something. But whatever he is, he is no more than a forever-changing mass of properties and habits, temporarily caught in an ever-changing body of flesh. The master is very different, a being of another kind. The master also inhabits an ever-changing body of flesh but he is no longer human, for he has found the

The endless bubbling thoughts had been strangely absent.

Miracles, after all, did exist.

way to freedom and has discovered the final point of that way. The master can no longer be defined and his humanity is a mask. When the disciple prostrates his body on the floor of the *sanzen*-room he creates, for himself, a certain distance. Perhaps the daily contact with the master has led him to believe that the master is another human being, somebody he can talk and joke with. But *sanzen,* even when it is full of words and jokes, is no ordinary conversation. *Sanzen* connects the deepest part of both master and disciple, the part that is realized in the master and may be realized in the disciple. The disciple bows down in the dust, not only for the master but also for himself. *Sanzen* is, perhaps, a breakthrough. The protecting layers that cover and form the personality of the disciple are broken, peeled off, like an onion can be peeled off. And when the last layer goes and nothing remains, then....

The *sanzen*-room was no novelty to me. It copied the old master's room in the Kyoto monastery. When I faced the figure opposite I knew I had not changed masters. There was no difference. The human form facing me, quietly, in deep concentration, vibrating power and peace, didn't differ from the form of the old master. At that moment I could never have said, "Hello, Peter" [even though it *was* Peter].

I said my koan in Japanese, as I had been taught. When the master rang his bell I made my three farewell prostrations. Outside, on my way back to the Zendo, I realized that I had spent less than a minute in the *sanzen*-room. I had received the usual treatment. But *sanzen* doesn't consist of bows and bells. Anything can happen. In Japan I had lived through a *sanzen* that must have lasted close to half an hour. When two people meet each other in concentration the result can be staggering.

The morning session finished at 6:30. I walked back to the house. The *jikki,* now appearing as a pleasant young man, in his middle or late twenties, was chopping wood and smiled at me. He introduced himself as Rupert. There was no mention of his outburst in the Zendo. The temple's demon had changed into a nice fellow.

"Are you the disciple from Holland? Peter told us about you, we vaguely knew you existed. I am glad you could come."

I offered him a French cigarette and he sniffed at the tobacco and put it behind his ear.

"You are the first Dutchman I ever met."

I looked stupid and made my mustache tremble.

"We are a mad race."

"Yes," Rupert said, "but Americans aren't quite normal either. All earth is populated with madmen."

Which was true, and I went inside.

Peter was frying eggs in the kitchen and pointed at the table where a bowl of soup was waiting for me. In Amsterdam I never have much breakfast but here, with the biting cold and the unusual strain of sitting still for hours without being allowed to fall asleep, my stomach had managed to work up an appetite. I even ate the fat fried sausages Peter put on my plate.

He sat down and grinned. I didn't say anything and ate. I knew that this was the same man who had faced me, an hour ago, in the *sanzen*-room, but I could neither understand nor accept it.

"You are welcome to sleep here tonight," Peter said, "but after that it may be better for you to live with the others. Rupert has a cabin, quite close by. I asked him to put you up, you can be of use, there's a lot of wood out there that needs chopping and stacking and he may let you cook the meals. During the day he usually works at the farm here, or at the sawmill. You can do that as well, if you like. You can organize your own daily routine, you won't stay long enough to fit in but it doesn't matter. I'll invite you both for dinner now and then and there are some people you should meet. I may visit you from time to time. Work it out for yourself."

I went on chewing and nodded. I wasn't particularly worried, Rupert didn't scare me.

"We'll have some irregular meditation the next few days and a proper *sesshin,* an organized meditation week, starting next Monday. That will change your routine again, you people will be sitting some ten hours a day."

I nodded again. I had come for that week. The first week of December is Rohatsu. December the eighth is the day that the Buddha, 2,500 years ago in India, sitting under a tree in the full lotus, had found his ultimate enlightenment. All Buddhist sects celebrate the day. The Zen sect with its tough tradition has made the preceding week into an ordeal, a week of almost uninterrupted meditation. The *sesshin* [meditation period] is called *Rohatsu*, which simply means "Eighth Day."

The thought of Rohatsu made me feel uncomfortable but I wasn't really frightened. I had been through a Japanese Rohatsu, with almost sixteen hours of meditation a day. No matter how tiresome or painful this American week might be, it would never beat the Japanese torture. And anyway, I had no choice. Forces were pulling and pushing me, my own forces, and I couldn't fight them. There is no choice, I was quite sure. The important events of a man's life are unavoidable. A man may think he chooses, but he only does what he has to do and later he calls, whatever it was he did, his "choice." He says he wanted to do it, but he experienced what he had to go through. A theory that is hard to prove, or disprove. Why did I go to Japan? Why had Peter suddenly appeared in Amsterdam? Why does a man stare at his own face one morning while he is shaving and why does he suddenly know that he will change the direction of his life? Why did the Buddha sit down under a tree and decide that he would not get up again until his last question was answered? Why did Bodhidharma, the first Zen master, walk from India to China to sit in meditation in a cave for nine years before his first disciple found him to start a training that, eventually, would make him the first Chinese Zen patriarch?

I helped with the washing-up, chopped some wood in the garden, slept for an hour and lunched by myself in the kitchen. In the afternoon I went out for a walk. Peter's farm was close to the sea. The shore is twisted and there are many small bays and coves. Within a quarter of an hour I was walking on a rocky beach with no one around. The ice had taken strange shapes. I saw transparent bubbles, covering rocks gleaming in the sunlight. I walked on the ice and it broke under me. I admired the roots of fir trees embracing the boulders of the shore. A small squirrel abused me because I disturbed its peace. Blue birds, looking like the jays of the Dutch forests, circled around my head. They seemed tame and were probably used to being fed by Peter's disciples.

In between the rocks I found some crab shells. The crabs, I was told later, are horseshoe crabs. I picked up a shell and turned it over. Inside the legs were neatly folded and the claws still undamaged, the body itself had shrunk into a small brown ball. A long horned tail projected itself from the shell, beautifully shaped and tapering off into a sharp point.

> Why did Bodhidharma come to China?
> The monk points at a fir tree.
> "The fir tree over there."
> The master nods.
> The monk might have said "the shell of the horseshoe crab."
> The creation is perfect. Everything is the way it should be. There is nothing to ask, nothing to explain. There is no difference between the created and the uncreated. The mystery is with us all the time and it is no mystery.
> You understand a little, very little. And while you think you understand you begin to doubt again.

And you continue walking, on a field of stones, illuminated by the afternoon's sun, or in a street choked with petrol fumes, or on a battlefield where they are trying to kill or maim you, using the most ingenious weapons that can be invented. You are a riddle and you live in riddles.

And still the answer is very close, and you know you will find it.

The author continues to notice differences between his new American Zen community and his old Japanese monastery. There are twenty-four men and twelve women working and meditating alongside each other at Peter's farm. Van de Wetering remembers that women were never allowed in the Zendos in Japan, where women could meditate and even become masters, but were segregated away from the men during sanzen. In Japan, monks often begged for alms, and van de Wetering regrets that Peter does not allow it. To the author, begging is an art, almost a dance, between giver and receiver, and he misses it for the spiritual discipline it represents.

The winter continues.

I woke up. Rupert had gone and the alarm hadn't been set. It was close to 9 A.M., ridiculously late for life in the commarde. We were still in the holidays and I stretched luxuriously under the blankets. Coffee, breakfast, a cigarette, wash up and wander away. A day of emptiness.

There was a note on the table signed by Rupert. "Have gone for the day, enjoy yourself."

I would.

But within an hour I was at the farm, looking for Peter. I remembered the story the old teacher had told about a devil. A devil who has nothing to do, no routine or program, is liable to get himself and his master in dire trouble. I smiled at my own thought. Life at the commarde was pretty safe, I wouldn't be able to get into much trouble. But still, one never knows. I might as well watch it.

Emptiness, the core of Buddhism. Emptiness, the great goal that is to be reached by losing everything there is to lose. Emptiness, the great danger. If you have nothing to do, you run a lot of risks and the training frowns on you. Yet the final goal is to have nothing more to do, to be nameless, to be stripped of the last aggression, the last defense.

When Bodhidharma, the Indian Zen master who took Zen to China, was invited by the emperor, the meeting immediately became a display of vanity on the emperor's part. He told the master about the many monasteries and temples he, the Emperor of China, the son of heaven, had originated and financed. He told Bodhidharma about the great spreading of Buddhism, all over China, and all due to him, the emperor. He asked the master what this important display meant and Bodhidharma said, "It means nothing, a great emptiness."

And when the emperor, stupefied, asked the master who he, this messenger giving this weird reply, really was, Bodhidharma said, "Don't know," turned on his heels and left the court.

I looked for Peter but was told he had left for the day. The farm was very quiet. I found a girl in the cowstalls and asked if I could help her.

"No," she said, looked at me and asked, "who are you anyway?"

"Don't know," I said, turned on my heels and left the cowstalls.

I wandered into the forest thinking about Bodhidharma, the free spirit who knew exactly what he was doing and where he was doing it. A free spirit creates the situations he chooses to be in. Where would the old monk have gone to after leaving the heavenly court of Peking? What would he have had for dinner that night and where would he have found the money to pay for it? Or was he beyond all that, like the advanced yogis who can live on the wind?

Emptiness, the core of Buddhism.

Emptiness, the great goal that is to be reached by losing everything there is to lose.

Emptiness, the great danger.

The final goal is to have nothing more to do, to be nameless, to be stripped of the last aggression, the last defense.

And where was I going now?

I had lost my way. The paths on the estate all looked like each other. Everywhere around the bare trees faced me, creaking, sometimes even exploding in the frost. Eventually I managed to find Rupert's cabin and ate. I spent the afternoon meditating, timing myself with the alarm clock, which I set for periods lasting a little under one hour. I gave myself ten-minute breaks and did physical exercises to restore the bloodstream in my legs. I had often read about yogis sitting for six or more hours at a stretch but I had never seen anybody actually do it. I slept for an hour, read a bit and wandered out into the forest again. The sky was overcast filtering the moon and the snow reflected the vague mysterious glimmering light.

What was I doing in this world?

I didn't have to worry about making a living over here, there was nobody to care for. No daily work, no needs. No vacation either, no doctor had told me to relax for a while. I was suspended in my own existence, wandering in a world of bare trees. The trees were alive. I flashed my torch and could see the buds, waiting for spring.

I had lost my way again and I was quite alone. A free spirit creates the situations he chooses to be part of. The emptiness frightened me. Would I allow fear to creep close and jump me? Would I sit down on this dead log, smoke a cigarette and dream in circles? "No fear," I thought. I kept on walking. I moved one leg, then the other. The direction is probably right, in any case I know of no better direction. There is a koan to be solved. I have to blow my nose on it, clear my head, and then throw the koan away and blow my nose on a fresh koan. The master has an endless supply. They'll clear my head, all of them, and the final one may blow my head off.

No shortcuts and no simplicity. Only one part of the teaching is simple. The disciple has to meditate. For hours and hours. Every day. Insight is caused by long sitting. Early in the morning when the world isn't moving yet. Quietly, in a corner of the room. Or in a meditation hall, or outside, on a rock under a tree, or in the loft of an old gable-house in Amsterdam, or a proper temple with mats on the floor and special cushions and perhaps a Buddha statue on a shelf. The quiet vibrations of smoldering incense can be helpful. But meditation can be done anywhere. There are people who meditate under the bridge of Calcutta where the traffic grinds continuously. Meditation is the Zen master's recipe, the base of his teaching. And for the rest he forces you to do the impossible and make you jump through walls or off the precipice. Let go! Let go! Don't hold on to anything. And don't disregard your doubts. Let your doubts move you on. Don't think that you have found something because it's about time that you have found something. Go on, do the best you can. And know that there is no guarantee whatever that you will ever make it.

I was mumbling to myself as I walked. All very well, but here I was in the forest, alone, lost and not too sure about what I was trying to do. By allowing myself to wander about in emptiness I was taking a grave risk. The old teacher was right when he warned about living without a routine. I might have been better off if I had stayed in the cabin, meditating or reading near the fire. Here doubt attacked me with its full force.

I wanted to meet someone. But who?

A human being? Another lost soul? But what good would that do?

Not a human being.

What then? An angel, a bodhisattva? An illuminated being from a higher sphere?

No, no god. He would make me jealous.

The fox approaches you gracefully. His plumed tail points at the sky. He is a large fox, about twice as big as the little foxes you have seen in the Dutch zoos or the stuffed corpse you were shown in the room of the biology teacher at high school.

This is a very beautiful fox, with a gleaming reddish-brown back and a fluffy white belly. He is dancing on the snow, lifting his feet with no effort at all. He is coming straight at you.

Good God, you think, there are still miracles in the world. A being that has nothing to do with me, a human. An animal who lives in the forest, who knows every sound, every form, around here.

He is large and healthy and intelligent. He has enough to eat and all his meals are adventures.

The fox is still coming at you. You have stopped thinking, you are merely meeting a fox. You wouldn't even have been frightened if, on this narrow track lined with moonlit trees and protected by the night's silence, you had met a wolf, or a bear.

The fox doesn't slow down. He comes so close that you can look him in his large light-brown eyes. He is looking at you as well and he jumps, not at your throat, but aside, off the track, and there is no change in the rhythm of his movement.

You look back and he is on the path again, his plumed tail waving up and down. You keep looking at him till he disappears in a bend of the path.

Rupert was staring at me when I got back to the cabin. He probably felt responsible for my comings and goings but I didn't give him a chance to open his mouth.

"I have seen a fox, Rupert," and I indicated how big the fox had been. "With a plumed tail and light-brown eyes."

He allowed me to finish my description and poured hot water on the powdered coffee.

"A good omen," he said when I had finally finished. "I have never seen him but I have heard stories about him. He must be the same fox. There are so many of us living around here now that the wild animals have gone away but that fox keeps on showing himself. He isn't afraid of us."

I thought of the ghost stories of Japan, often dealing with foxes who may be witches or dead disciples of masters. These witches can take on the form of a fox at will while they leave their own human body in a safe place but the dead disciples take the fox's form as a kind of punishment. They have committed some sin, some error, and a fox's life is their fate.

I was sure that this fox was neither a witch nor a temporarily punished human soul. He was a fox in his own right and he enjoyed being a fox. And he had helped me considerably, appearing at exactly the right moment.

"I have news for you," Rupert said as he gave me my coffee. "Tonight we can only sleep for four hours. We'll have to get up at 2:30. Peter has canceled the rest of the holiday, tomorrow we have a new *sesshin* waiting for us. I have been driving around all evening to tell everyone."

"And what did they think about it?" I asked sleepily.

"Ah well," Rupert said, "they grumbled a bit but I don't think anybody really minded. We came here to do something, not to visit each other and drink ginger brandy."

I let it go. I saw the plumed tail of the fox and it swept me asleep. When the alarm's grinding woke me up I felt as if I had slept for at least eight hours and the fox had been with me right through the night.

The next *sesshin* had started and was slowly gliding away into the past. Peter had told us, when it began, that the *sesshin* was supposed to be a "little" one. I couldn't see anything "little" about it. Like any *sesshin* it would last seven days, and we were sitting some seven hours a day. We were working in the mornings, mostly chopping wood and stacking it, but there was a nice long break in the afternoon. That break had become my private adventure and I was, almost desperately, using the two hours of which it consisted.

I had discovered Simon's rock garden and, perhaps even more important, his private lavatory. The blue jays had taken me there. I saw them fussing about amongst the trees, talking to each other with their raucous voices and had taken some bread with me, trying to win their confidence. I meant to see if they would come and eat from my hand. But they kept flying away and, following them, I suddenly found myself in a very strange garden. The snow-covered bushes looked as if they had been planted and circled an area in which someone had placed a fairly large number of strangely shaped rocks. It was late in the afternoon when I found the garden and the rocks threw their shadows far across the thick snow. I didn't want to walk about too much as my tracks would spoil the almost austere geometrical designs of bushes, rocks and shadows. I sat on one of the rocks and merely gazed about me.

Now that I had stopped trying to make contact with the jays they no longer played their game of hide and seek and hopped around me until one, the female, landed on my arm with a soft thud and began to pick at the bread. She shoved the largest part of the sandwich off my hand and her mate picked it up and flew to another rock where he began to eat it slowly. The silence calmed him and eased his greed. I felt very peaceful and lit a cigarette. The place was all mine, or ours rather as the jays were now my friends, and I could do with it as I pleased.

I began to compare the garden to other gardens I had seen, Japanese temple gardens and gardens of the large mansions in Holland where the merchants of the Golden Age once lived. The dreamlike quality of the rocks and their shadows on the snow reminded me of some of the paintings of Dali and Delvaux but then I got shocked back into reality. I was doing it all wrong. Why compare? Why, for the sake of all holy men, wizards and fakirs, why compare?

I should look at it, I told myself, just look at it. Become one with it, as the old teacher had told me in Kyoto. To compare is the activity of the poor man, the man who will always be poor because he keeps poverty in his mind. He tries to grab new possessions and wants to evaluate them by comparing them with other things he has grabbed before. This garden was one of the manifestations of reality, the miraculous world to which we all belong. Why want to own it if it belongs to us anyway? And who is this "me" and this "us"? The garden is. And if it is destroyed, by a bulldozer or an earthquake, or because the universe pulls itself inside out, as it may very well do, any minute now, the reality will still *be*.

So I sat on the rock, and tried to *be* for a while.

Until I heard the sound of a door opening and closing, followed by the sound of someone clearing his throat and followed by the sound of someone creaking through the snow. I didn't see anything but I could determine the place of the sounds and I went to investigate. There was a cluster of trees nearby and right in the middle of this cluster, on a bulge of ground in the shelter of an immense pine tree, a small cabin with a sloping roof and an ornamental door. I approached the cabin with some reverence. It might be a meditation hut or contain a private altar with a Buddha statue. The roof looked Japanese but the door was very American, I had seen doors like that in some of the more elegant holiday houses around, oak doors, thick, with elaborately carved garlands of flowers and leaves.

I opened the door carefully, ready to bow to the unfathomable smile on the face of the Buddha statue but stepped back and laughed. This was no place of reverence, it was a privy, plain and simple. A low seat with a hole, nothing else. And very convenient. I took my trousers down and sat on the seat. The door closed.

This wasn't so good. It was dark in the cabin, the small window hadn't been washed for some time and the pine needles outside absorbed most of the light of the low sun. I pushed the door open with my foot and propped a broom, found in the privy, against it so that it wouldn't fall closed again. And then a real wave of happiness surged through me. This was it, undoubtedly. There was no temptation to compare this time. The open door gave me a view of a narrow path, winding through the trees and the heavy dark-yellow light colored the dead needles covering the track and the branches of the trees with their shining bark. Whoever had built this privy in this particular place was an artist, a master architect of land-scapes. Not even in Japan had I ever seen such blatant beauty. The sudden activity of my bowels coincided with the general explosion of awareness. "An enlightening shit," I thought and laughed and a voice hailed me.

"Is that you?" the voice questioned and I shouted back that it was me.

"Come and have tea when you are fin-ished," Simon shouted. I reluctantly pulled up my trousers and bowed to the privy.

In the Kyoto monastery the privy had a miniature altar, high on a shelf, to remind the monks that the Buddha nature is every-where and can be realized in the meanest actions. I hadn't been able to prove the thought at the time.

Simon was waiting for me at the end of the path and I apologized for having strayed into his garden and used his lavatory without his permission.

And then a real wave of happiness surged through me.

"That's all right," Simon said. "What's mine is yours. But the garden isn't mine and neither is the privy."

"But surely all this belongs to your grounds here?" I asked.

Simon smiled. "I suppose so," he said, "but I was only given this small piece of land right here by Peter. All the other ground is part of his estate."

"Did you design the rock garden and build the privy?"

"No," Simon said, "it was here when I came. A very odd man did all that. He was in Japan, I am told, for a number of years and spent all his time in wandering around Zen gardens."

"Didn't he study Zen as well?"

"Sure," Simon said, "he meditated and was a master's disciple, but the gardens were his life."

"And why did he leave here?"

Simon smiled again. "Why do people leave?"

I didn't insist. I knew why people left. I had left myself. You can leave on your own, and the master can tell you to go. "Will he come back?"

Simon looked in the direction of the rock garden. "I think so. That garden is perfect. Wherever he is now, he will think of it. He was here for quite a few years. I have been told that

This was it, undoubtedly.

Whoever had built this privy in this particular place was an artist, a master architect of landscapes.

he is wandering around the country now, in a small camping truck, with his dog. He takes odd jobs and stays for a while and then he starts his truck and he is off again. Eventually he'll show up. He hasn't finished here and he should be coming back until, one day, the master tells him that there is no more."

"Will we have to be *told* that there is no more?" I asked.

Simon patted me on the head; they all seemed to have learned that trick from Peter.

"Don't ask so much," Simon said, "don't you know that all the answers are in yourself?"

"I know nothing," I said peevishly.

We had tea in his luxurious living-room, with the fire spreading its crackling warmth. Simon was talking about karma and reincarnation.

"This reincarnation business was quite a comfort to me once," Simon said, "until I realized that reincarnation means the will to live. It is a power that drives us on, step by step, towards death, and death is a door. It says EXIT on one side, and you are forced through it and wander on and when you look back it says ENTRY, and when you go further, as you have to, there is no choice, there is another door coming near saying EXIT. It is the door of birth. And so it goes on. There is no end to it. And you are always between doors, and suffering continues."

"You can laugh at times," I said, remembering my recent merriment in the privy.

"Sure," Simon said, "I shouldn't complain. But the idea of having to go on and on bores me. It's no comfort to know that one life follows another and is itself the prelude to a new life. Life continues and with it fear. Fear of death, fear of birth. Real, definite death would be more of a comfort. It will be a true ending. No more to come."

"All this trouble for nothing?" I asked.

"*Nothing* is the key," Simon said.

I jumped up. "It's time, we have to go back to the Zendo. If we go now we won't have to rush."

"All right," Simon said, following my example, "I hate rushing too. There's nothing worse than having to run up to the Zendo worrying all the way about whether you are going to make it on time or not."

Outside he slipped and fell against the wall of his cabin. A nail scratched his hand which began to bleed. I bandaged the wound for him.

"Do you always carry bandages with you?" he asked.

"Of course," I said and showed him my collection. A many-purpose knife, a small pair of scissors, a torch, a screwdriver, sunglasses, notebook, ballpoint, cleaning gear for my glasses, etc.

"Very practical," Simon said.

"Aren't you practical?" I asked.

"About the same as you are," he said. "I carry a similar collection as yours, but no bandages. I'll buy some tomorrow. They will be handy. Sure I am practical. I work and try to earn enough to be able to live comfortably. In the meantime I try to learn. I believe in karma, I will have to be in a continuous position of being able to accept the consequences of my previous deeds. And I try to do the right thing when I can do it, which is about all the time."

"Yes," I said, "one has to be careful." The conversation frustrated me. "Certainly," I said, "we have to be practical. Only do what is necessary. Earning money is necessary for instance, but only up to a point. After that point money creates nothing but soap bubbles, power and property you can't use. My uncles own a lot of houses, yachts, stuff like that. The houses produce rent that they can't spend and the yachts rot in some harbor. To earn money that way is not very intelligent perhaps."

"Exactly," Simon said and patted me on the shoulder. He giggled. "It seems I am more intelligent than your uncles. To spend time here, here where earning money is almost impossible, is a pretty clever occupation. Like meditation and being guided by a master."

"Guided to where?" I asked.

Simon stopped and I stopped as well and looked back. He made a good picture with the pine trees framing him and the blue jays circling above his head. A squirrel had followed us and was watching us from a low branch, nervously holding on to a nut.

I walked back and asked again. "Guided where?"

"Look here," Simon said irritably, "how the hell would I know? Maybe you should know. Maybe you are an advanced disciple. I never even know who is advanced and who is not. But I do know that I have no real knowledge. Or are you trying to ask me one of these tricky questions to show how clever you are, or, why not, are you trying to help me on my way perhaps?"

It was my turn to giggle. It's the master's task to ask tricky questions. Disciples only stumble along and think they discover something or other every now and then.

"Don't worry, Simon," I said, "I am not trying to be clever. And I don't know where I am going. I suppose we should all be on our way to *nirvana* but it seems to me, lately, that it would be unacceptably arrogant to assume that *we,* of all people on the planet, will reach, thanks to this training, a sphere *outside the circle of reincarnation.* Why us, and not the others?"

Simon had started walking again. "Well," he said, "I don't know what the others are doing. I am concerned with the training, I am a master's disciple. My *karma* took me to this forest and all these funny little buildings and here I meditate and meet my master. Here I can change my karma. Karma is real, I suppose, for even Peter mentions it occasionally, although he evades all direct questions or answers them in such a way that you are still groping around for something you can put your hand on. You know the story about the boy who went to Mr. Singh?"

"No," I said.

"Listen to this," Simon said and put a heavy hand on my shoulder. "There was a boy here who only stayed for a few months. A real mystic with an enormous black beard for hiding his face behind. He had decorated his head with gold earrings and he wore an embroidered suit. The rear of his jacket was most impressive. He had embroidered a mountain on it that was being climbed by dragons, evil forces. And on the top of the mountain throned a magnificent rooster, the symbol of Good. A very strange fellow he was, but quite likeable. He meditated a lot, far more hours than we did, and it took a good deal of effort to get him to do some work. Whenever we had to chop wood or work in the gardens I would have to go and fetch him and I even had to pull him out of the Zendo where he was sitting by himself. All he wanted to do was sit still and concentrate."

"Not bad," I said jealously.

"Some show, eh?" Simon asked. "I don't mind meditation but I don't really enjoy it. It is only because of the discipline that I meditate a lot, if I wasn't forced I would sit for an hour a day, but that boy sneaked into the Zendo whenever he could. And still, he didn't seem to be getting anywhere, or so he said. He claimed that he would sit there, reasonably quiet, with his thoughts pushed away and his stomach or central nerve knot or whatever it is we have around there, glowing away like blazes but nothing really happened to him. He wasn't getting enlightened he said."

"What did he expect?" I asked. "Fireworks? Visions?"

"Hmm," Simon said, "what is it we expect? I also ask myself at times what I am sitting for, it seems that the only thing happening is the *jikki* hitting his crazy bell every twenty-five minutes."

"So he left, this embroidered boy of yours?"

"He left," Simon said, "he didn't run away. He announced his departure and said he wanted to visit a guru in India, a very special guru who claimed that he could enlighten his disciples by merely touching their heads in a certain way. The man was supposed to be called Singh and the boy had the address. *Singh* means lion and it is the surname of most Sikhs. There must be millions of Mr. Singhs in India, but the boy claimed he would find *his* Mr. Singh without any trouble at all and Peter let him go."

"He couldn't very well prevent him from going," I said. Simon nodded. "But Peter said something that interested me. He said that he wondered if Mr. Singh would be able to change that boy's karma."

I thought about it. Karma cannot be destroyed by Mr. Singh, that was pretty obvious.

It seemed as if Peter was telling us that karma was hindering us, our own karma, the relentless result of our previous actions. And we might assume that Peter believed in karma, or he wouldn't have mentioned the word. And if he did believe in karma he would also believe in reincarnation, for karma is the force that kills us and shoves us back into the world through our mothers' vaginas. Now bad karma, according to the rules, can be diminished, even broken, but only by our own effort. We can try to do the job in one life, and if life is too short, continue in the next. There's always a chance, there has to be an opportunity because life will have no purpose if there isn't. If jail is forever the will to escape is neurotic."

"Ah," I said, "so that's why your meditation is practical. You are trying to scrape bits off your karma. Evil karma disappears and good karma helps you on your way. Your way to where?"

Simon stopped again. "There you go again," he said. "I don't know where I want to go. I want to go *on*, I imagine."

One of the blue jays croaked and Simon pointed at it. "Over there," he said, "look at that blue jay. He is at the beginning of his career. He still has to become a human being. Now I *am* already a human being, but it is no more than another stage. I have to be practical and use my chances so that I can improve my fate. If I don't I may even glide back and become an animal or a bird."

I watched the jays.

Simon shook his head. "No. It can't be true. I don't think we can glide back. Even if we do everything wrong we will still learn. Life must, automatically I suppose, mean an improvement. Every life pushes you a little ahead. What do you think? Do you think you may be a rabbit in your next life?"

"I don't care," I said.

"Would you *want* to be a rabbit, or a squirrel, or a jay?" Simon asked surprised.

"Why not?" I asked.

Simon laughed. His laughter worried me because he wouldn't stop. The tears came into his eyes and he doubled up as if he was in pain.

When he could talk again the words came out slowly. "You are right," he said. "Why should I be worried about becoming a rabbit? Why should I think about karma? Of course Peter refuses to discuss it."

The grin on his face stayed there till we reached the Zendo. He looked very solemn when he made his bows.

You are eight years old. It is Sunday evening. You have been granted an extra hour before bed.

The family is playing Monopoly. You have been told that you are big enough to join them.

You lose. You are losing continuously. Your stomach cramps with fear. Nearly all your possessions are gone. The money pile in front of you is almost gone. Your brothers are snatching all the houses from your streets. The last street is being sold. You have to give in. You have lost. There is sweat on your forehead.

And suddenly you know that it is only a game. You jump up with joy and you knock the big lamp over. It falls on the floor and drags the teapot with it. The others are angry with you but you laugh when you go upstairs. You know you are nothing, and you know that you have nothing. And you know that not-to-be and not-to-have give an immeasurable freedom.

Later the feeling goes but you remember that you have had it. You know that once, when you were eight years old, you knew freedom.

One afternoon as van de Wetering is sleeping, an intruder awakens him by pulling off his blanket. His name is James, and he is a writer. Van de Wetering is fascinated by him, and invites him to go meditate. To our author's surprise, James agrees.

"That was very pleasant," James said, "very restful. I feel a lot better."

"What were you doing while you sat there?"

"Yes," James said. "What was I doing? I dreamt a little about my youth. I tried to breathe as slowly as possible. I thought about our conversation and during the last period I concentrated."

"On what?"

James grinned.

I could imagine what he must have looked like as a young man. The striped suit, the expensive gold watch, the wig, the disciplined good manners became transparent.

"I concentrated on the unimportant. All my life I have been interested in the eastern religions and methods although I have always remained a Christian. The emptiness of Buddhism and Taoism fascinates me. To be empty, to know that nothing matters. Do you know that? Do you know that nothing matters?"

I looked serious and said that I knew, but then I qualified my statement. I said that I *suspected* it.

"Yes, yes," James said as if he hadn't heard me. "It's the truth. Nothing matters. That Buddha of yours doesn't matter either. Neither does my Christ, or Mohammed or Ramakrishna. None of the prophets, the sons of God. *Nirvana* itself doesn't matter. And we matter least of all. Self is the absolute joke. It goes even further. Emptiness, the mysterious Tao, the Stone the alchemists looked for, the teaching of the witches...."

He interrupted himself. "Witches can really do tricks, do you know? They can fly and change themselves into objects and animals. This is indeed a strange life, full of possibilities."

"I don't know anything about witches," I said, "but I am quite prepared to believe that they can fly."

"Yes," James said, "but it is of no real importance. There is, I have thought that for a long time, longer than I can remember, maybe from the first moment I could think, nothing more fascinating than the idea that only the really indifferent can win."

I moved aside a little so that there was more distance between us. I studied the way he walked. Marabous walk like that, I thought. The birds of prey, tall and stately, which I had seen in the zoo and on film.

Not a bad comparison, I thought. He is the bird of prey, and I am the prey. He rips the flesh off my bones. I don't matter, and my idea of Buddhism doesn't matter either. *Nirvana* itself is of no importance. Whatever I do is empty, and even emptiness is neither the beginning, nor the end, nor the goal of our existence. Whatever I try to hold on to has no substance.

"You have to let go," James was saying now, "that's what reading about Buddhism has taught me. Whenever you try to hold on to something you are lost. You will be ripped to pieces and it hurts. But to let go is not easy. Perhaps it's the most difficult action for us who have to live in this world. To learn how to let go must be the supreme effort. I don't envy you your training."

I saw his car now, he hadn't parked it on Rupert's driveway but further along, in between some trees. It was indeed an exceptional car, an old Bentley, a status symbol par excellence.

"Ah," James said, "there's my car. It's time to thank you for your hospitality. You have been of great help to me. Here is my card. I am driving back to New York now. Perhaps you will look me up one day."

"Thank you," I said, "and what are you going to do now?"

"Continue living," James said, "or would you want me to give it all up and live here, in this commune?"

"I don't want anything," I said.

"You are trying not to want anything," James corrected. "But that's very commendable. You must do the very best you can. And then you will come to the place where you can let everything go."

"And then I have arrived," I said morosely.
"Exactly," James said.

I wished him a good journey. He allowed me to hold his dry cool hand again. The engine ignited and the Bentley drove off.

You meet someone.
The other.
You meet the other.
You are polite. The other is polite.
You eat each other a little.
After his departure you are slightly damaged.
And what do you do then?
Do you repair the damage and do you become again what you were?
Or do you go on as you are?
Damaged, but lighter.

It was 7:00 A.M. and I stood on the veranda of Rupert's cabin. I had just come back from the morning's meditation and didn't feel like going inside where the cold dank room was waiting for me. I would have to wash up and prepare breakfast, and sweep the floor and set the table, and, worst of all, persuade the stove to burn instead of smoke.

I had a few minutes. Rupert would be due in half an hour's time, he had gone to do some repairs on the antique truck's engine powering the sawmill. There was no need to go in straightaway, I could smoke and think a little.

But it was cold and I felt the need of a little movement. I stamped my feet and the boards of the veranda responded with a deep hollow sound. I tried again and the sound got even better. The stamping grew into a slow dance and I began to hum and clap my hands. I laughed, and stopped. A dancing dervish. Dancing can be very religious. The dervishes lost their ego while they twirled and howled. Buddhist monks are also known to dance. The Tibetans have their lama dances and the Zen priests go in for intricate ceremonial jigs, I had seen them do these in the court of the magnificent main temple of our sect in Kyoto. But dancing isn't the main occupation of Zen monks. They prefer to meditate. Long meditation gives deep insight. One of Peter's statements, one of his very few, coming from his own experience.

I tried to calculate how many hours I had meditated. Three thousand perhaps. Or four? Is that a lot?

And did I have this deep insight now?

Sure, sure, I told myself. Don't be too modest. You do have insight, dear boy. It won't be very much and there will be others who have more insight, a couple of billion times more, but that subtle point can be ignored. Insight is insight. You know why you are alive. No, I said, I don't know why I am alive. I have merely stopped asking myself, because I have stopped caring. The question has disappeared. But questions only disappear because they have been answered. So what was the answer?

Not to be expressed in words, I said cleverly. Real wisdom can never be expressed in words. Don't be clever, I told myself.

All right, I said. I have understood, or I have begun to understand that "I" do not exist. Which means that "my life" does not exist either. And you don't have to ask about the purpose of something that isn't there.

You are still being clever, I said. And I was right. But how should I handle this? How can the inexpressible be expressed? How are moments of insight described? How do you indicate that you are on the right path?

Buddhism is negative. It will tell you what it is not. When you insist that it must be something it merely allows for an open space, which you can fill in as you like. It is only specific about its method. It tells you to meditate, to be conscious of what you are doing, to do your best. It tells you to earn your daily food in a decent manner. It prescribes kind speech and thought. It suggests that you should create your own situations, rather than being pushed around by yourself and others. It warns that you should not avoid your own doubts. It recom-

mends trying things out for yourself. It abhors all dogma. It doesn't like you to impose your opinions on others. And it stresses that you should know yourself, your own laziness, pride and greed, which, together, constitute the power that turns the wheel of life.

One moment, I told myself. I do know something. I know that freedom exists. It seems to be the central point of Buddhism. The turning wheel seems eternal. Life follows life, heaven follows heaven, hell follows hell. The will to live creates new births and new deaths. But freedom can be reached at any given moment. The Buddha liberated himself, the Zen masters liberated themselves. Whatever they could do you can as well. You have to keep on trying.

Are you sure? I asked. Did you experience this freedom? And if you did, what is it? Is freedom symbolized by sitting on a cloud, as the Buddha did on the posters that you saw in Ceylon? You sit on a cloud, free from all influence of the wheel of life, and you watch the endeavor of the little people who are still rummaging about in the limited space of their egos? And where is that cloud anyway?

Well, the cloud is here. The cloud isn't outside your life. You shouldn't look too far. Freedom is right here, where it has always been. When you try to escape you make a silly mistake. But how do you know that this freedom exists?

Freedom exists, I said stubbornly.

Are you frightened now? I asked. Did I touch the sore spot in your faith? Do you want to stop this discussion? Are you losing your temper because I am kicking against the shelf that supports your importance? Do you think the shelf may break and that you will drop into the bottomless hole? Are you worried about losing something?

No. I wasn't frightened. Freedom exists and will go on forever. Freedom is not connected with the ego. Whether the ego believes in it or not, it will always be there. It's outside illusion.

Discussion Questions: **Janwillem van de Wetering**

1. How does van de Wetering come to experience the uncanny? How does he feel while seated on the privy? At the end of his story?

2. The last paragraph of an autobiography often holds several keys about the meaning of the story. Read the last paragraph, which is really the summation of van de Wetering's self-reflections. On the basis of the emphases you find there, do you think van de Wetering found the danger of his search frightening once he arrived where he was going?

3. Why do you think van de Wetering chooses to pursue satori (enlightenment)? Given his personality, do you think he could have chosen not to pursue it?

4. Do contemporary Americans have any sports that we approach as spiritual disciplines the way van de Wetering approaches meditation?

5. Does van de Wetering's Zen place much significance on the importance of worship?

6. What do you think James means when he tells van de Wetering that "Nothing matters…. Self is the absolute joke"? What do you think he means by saying "You have to let go"?

7. Van de Wetering titled the first part of this reading "The Horseshoe Crabs." Why do you think he did this?

8. The author remembers a dentist in Japan telling him that he once thought Zen was a shortcut. Van de Wetering asks, "Isn't it?" and the dentist replies "There are no shortcuts." What does this saying mean to you? Can you think of any analogous areas of your life in which this would apply?

Satomi Myodo

When I was young—until the age of twenty or so—I was no good at all. I was a real devil! Why was I like that? Of course this was the result of my karma, but what additionally spurred on that bad karma was, first and foremost, the contradiction between my elementary school's curriculum in ethics and the everyday life of the adults around me. During ethics period in school we were made to listen to all sorts of lectures in "moral education" and were prevailed upon to "be good" and "tell the truth," and so on. When I went home, however, I found lies and deception. One moment a guest would arrive and my parents would say sweet words to his face and play up to him, but when he left, instantly, like a hand turning over, they would bad-mouth and ridicule him. Such events were not unusual. I wondered if this went on only in my home; but no, whatever home, whatever adult—even my respected schoolteacher—all were the same. I didn't know what to make of it. "What is this all about?" I asked myself. "Oh, I get it! As a subject of study, the morality we learn in school is best just drummed into the head, like a recording. But life and morality are two absolutely different things. The reality of everyday life is built on lies." It got to the point where the question of truth and falsehood ceased to enter my mind. This was my elementary school period.

With these attitudes, I entered Girls' High School. I went to the Public Girls' School, which took as its motto "Good Wives and Wise Mothers."[1] Every Monday morning the principal would assemble all the students in the auditorium and give a talk. It was always bound

---

1. Satomi-san apparently entered Girls' High School about 1908. At this time, elementary schools were coeducational, but education was sex-segregated thereafter and girls went straight from elementary school to Girls' High School. In 1900, four years of education were universally compulsory; in 1907, this requirement was raised to six years. Few girls received an education beyond elementary school

to be scrupulous and exhaustive instruction for the benefit of the future good wives and wise mothers. At the conclusion of the talk he invariably added a word of advice: be careful with members of the opposite sex. According to this advice, the male of the species is nothing but a fearful wild beast with gnashing fangs that will swoop down upon any young girl he fancies. How could a girl concerned with her future prospects sacrifice herself to this beast? Don't be careless! Don't go near them! Don't look them in the face! Such were his stern words. He would then give some concrete examples. I was subjected to these lectures every week for four years until graduation. The aim of this grandmotherly kindness was to cultivate the flawless good wife and wise mother and to preserve her virginal innocence until marriage. In my case, however, things turned out just the opposite.

I absolutely couldn't stand men! A man to me was some kind of disgusting jet-black panther. What was marriage? What was a good wife and wise mother? Wasn't she the prey of that despicable panther? Was there ever such a contradiction? Was there ever a speech so degrading to us? Was he saying that right now men were like wild animals to us, but that later—when we married—they would become blessed, godlike beings on whom we should rely? How absurd! I felt very indignant toward the principal's speeches. At the same time, a fierce resentment blazed up in me toward "them"—those beasts who gobbled up the pure virgins. I was especially disgusted with charming men; I imagined that their charm would

---

in this era in Japan. For a poor country girl like Satomi-san to go on for further education was remarkable indeed, especially considering that she was an only child and her labor was needed at home. Moreover, the school she attended was an elite institution. Satomi-san was clearly both very bright and very much indulged by her parents. As for the school motto, this was the standard motto for female education at the time.

cause even greater injury to the virgins. I cursed those men as the bitterest enemy: "I put the evil eye on you! I wish you would drop dead!" My heart's desire was to directly approach this dreadful beast, twist him around my little finger, and toss him over my shoulder. I wanted to deliver a shattering blow.

At that time, my life revolved around the world of literature. After graduation from Girls' High School, I went to Tokyo, dreaming of becoming a writer. I stayed at my uncle's house and became the student of a certain novelist who was famous at the time. But my feelings toward men had not changed. I selected a target, devised a plan of attack, and steadily began to carry it out. My chances of victory were quite good, I thought. "He's bound to fall for it!" I told myself, thinking it would be easy for me to knock him speechless. I had faith in myself.

But what a mistake! At the critical moment, *bang!* the bottom fell through. The one whose luck gave out was not he but I: I got pregnant. At that time, unlike now, abortion was a terrible thing. I was afraid of being punished if I had one. My future prospects were pitch black. What could I do? I didn't want to hold on to him just to finish him off. Since things had turned out like this, I no longer cared about his state of mind. He was in love with me, but that was not at issue for me. It was unnecessary even to think of marriage.

My studies meant a lot to me. But I was pregnant. I returned to my parents' home, alone and without purpose. My parents were poor farmers in a mountain village in Hokkaido. I was an only child. My parents' sole desire was to make something of me, with their limited means. To do this, they had sent me to an exclusive girls' school and had even gone so far as to send me to Tokyo to advance their desire. But this parental love had never once gotten through to me and touched my heart.

Meanwhile, I just grew more and more fretful. But since in this case I certainly reaped what I had sowed, I couldn't complain. My parents seemed to have vague suspicions about my extraordinary bodily condition but deliberately avoided referring to it. I wanted to be severely scolded, condemned and thrown out, or told to go kill myself. But I was going to have to be the one to bring the subject up, somehow or other. I too kept silent.

Every day the three of us silently arose, and silently we went to work in the fields. As for me—with my body, which couldn't be more shameful, and my face, which one could hardly bear to look at—I just wanted to crawl into a hole and disappear. Looking like a barrel whose hoops were about to burst, and in a condition of utter despair, I was incapable even of dying. I could do nothing but sit back and watch my shame grow. I felt wretched, miserable, ashen— as if I were traveling alone at night through an endless wilderness, wearily dragging one foot after the other.

One day I went as usual to the fields, working and getting covered with dirt. From a distance, my father urgently called my name. I went to see what he wanted and found Father squatting at the edge of the field, gazing intently at something. A moment passed. I felt a little strange squatting quietly by my father's side. Absently, my eye caught his line of vision. There was nothing but a single weed growing there. Softly, Father began to speak.

"I've been watching this for some time…it's quite interesting…. Look! A winged ant is crawling up the weed. It climbs up, little by little…it seems to want to reach the top. Oh, it fell! There—it's climbing again! For some time now it's been doing this over and over again." Just as he said, a winged ant was climbing up the weed and falling, falling and climbing up again.

"Here! Climbing again! Look, it must be tired now. When it's tired, it stretches its legs and beats its little wings up and down like that. That's how it restores its energy. Then, when it's rested, it starts climbing again."

Father continued to speak without taking his eyes off the brave little insect. I too inadvertently became intrigued. I stared at it intently for quite a while. Suddenly, it hit me—I understood what my father was getting at! It was unbearable! I quickly got up and left his side. I ran to the shady side of the field where no one could see me and fell down wailing. I cried and cried in anguish.

"Oh, Father, I understand; I really understand! Do you love me so much? I'm so unfilial![2] Do you still cherish such hope for me, when I am so disgusted with myself? How unworthy I am! But how grateful! I'm sorry! Oh, Father, from now on I promise to be a filial daughter! I promise to make you happy!" I determined to repay my father's love, no matter what. Just then, an iron shackle was broken and at once a broad expanse of light burst upon the world.

I had never known such a wonderful world as the one I experienced in that moment. I saw the grass and trees, the hills, river, fields, and stones, the hoe and sickle, the birds and dogs, the roofs and windows—all shining brightly under the same sun. For me it was a wonderful breath of fresh air. Both the animate and the inanimate were vividly alive, familiarly addressing me and waving their hands. Struck by the unearthly exquisiteness of this world, I broke into tears and lifted up my face, weeping, in ecstasy. I saw right through myself and completely emptied my bag of emotional problems. All those words about morality that I had heard at elementary school, and that I had thought were just lectures to be forgotten, suddenly took on the form of living truth for me.

---

2.   Filial piety is a fundamental virtue in Japan. It involves not only respecting and obeying one's parents, but caring for their needs and serving them as well. Ideally, one should forget oneself and act to fulfill one's parents' wishes.

"So there is such a thing as sincerity after all. There is a world of truth. Now that Father's sincerity has touched me, I understand what it is. What a lucky person I am! I've found sincerity! I've found the lost jewel!" With warm tears flowing freely, I gained the sure and unshakable conviction that "at the bottom of all things is sincerity." I felt as if I had gained a million friends.

As I looked back at the mass of immorality I had been, I saw what a gloomy and anxious state of being it was. I couldn't help pitying those who had not yet awakened to sincerity. What a miserable way to live! Somehow or other, I felt, those people must be made to comprehend sincerity. Somehow or other, they must be drawn into its realm. Thus I immediately resolved, "From now on I will dive right into the midst of those people, maintaining sincerity to the end. I'll even die for their sake!"

I was prepared to meet rejection. Ridicule, misunderstanding, abuse, even physical attack—did any of it matter? My mind was made up. "Even into a blazing fire, brandishing the single word *sincerity*—onward!" I believed without a doubt that sincerity could raise the dead. I danced with joy! I felt like running around in circles, shouting, "There is such a thing as sincerity! Honestly there is! Please believe me! I beg you!" But could I get people to believe me?

Certainly there was such a thing as sincerity. I believed in it. "But what is sincerity? What is its true nature?" I asked myself. Though it was faint-hearted of me, I knew I couldn't give a definite answer to the question. "I'm no good at that kind of thing. For that you need someone who has mastered the Way and penetrated sincerity. Such a person can give a satisfactory answer to anyone," I thought. To clarify the true nature of sincerity would be the first step in my search for the Way.

I realized that until this time I had been impure and cold-hearted. I had never shed so much as one tear for truth. I had never

thought of others nor felt the need to do so. Self-centered and capricious, I had thought I could play with others in any way I wanted. I had thought "honest person" was another term for "great fool." I had cherished the superiority complex of an evil person. I was haughty, but in truth I was an insignificant nobody. The moment I was struck by my father's sincerity, though, I truly turned around 180 degrees.

I gave birth to my elder daughter in December of the year I returned home. The baby's father had come to my home about two months before. The son of a Hokkaido stationmaster, he had gone to Tokyo to study but quit school to come live with me. He was a handsome man, steadfast and pure-hearted. My parents immediately announced the wedding party and invited the people of the village.

My husband did all sorts of unfamiliar work—chopping wood, caring for horses, anything and everything. The next year I gave birth to my second daughter. But even though I was the mother of two children, I didn't feel like a wife to him, and the husband-wife love never developed. I did not want to get a divorce, though. Why? For the sake of the children. I couldn't burden the innocent children with the unhappiness brought on by my immorality. I felt there could be no excuse for making them orphans,[3] come what may. The atmosphere at home, however, began to move in the opposite direction of these intentions. A chasm was gradually opening up between my husband and my parents. I was in a predicament. If I spoke, I would make the bad feelings between the two sides worse. So I held my peace. Finally, one night, my father and my husband quarreled over an insignificant thing. In the end, my husband stormed out of the house in the middle of the night.

---

3. Satomi-san, in line with her culture, equates a fatherless child with an orphan.

I lived on with my parents in our Hokkaido mountain village, gathering firewood and cultivating the fields. Until now my mental energy had been dissipated in the delusory condition of the sixth consciousness.[4] But starting from the time my husband left and lasting for about two years, my mental condition was in a very strange spiritual stage. Was it some kind of bizarre mysticism? Was it lunacy? Often, while remaining in this same body, I leaped over the world of humanity and ascended to the distant world of beginningless eternity. There I was completely enfolded in the heart of God. I lost my form and became one with God, the solitary Light, which peacefully, truly peacefully, shone out all around. It was indescribable, blissful fulfillment. This condition progressed until I stumbled into the world of absolute nothingness and lapsed into unconsciousness. From this state I again advanced until hallucinations began to appear.

My first hallucination occurred right after the children's father left me. It was a day in late spring. I say "late spring," but this was the north country and, moreover, a village deep in the mountains. The cuckoo had finally begun to sing and the farmers breathed a sigh of relief, as that was the signal that the last frost had passed. It was planting season. I went, as usual, into the fields. I worked alone.

As I gazed out over the broad expanse of gently sloping mountain fields, brilliant flecks of sunlight sparkled like scattered gold dust. Heat waves shimmered from the surface of the freshly plowed mounds of earth. I had finished a section of the work and was rather tired, so I sat down on a pile of chaff between the fields. In an instant, before I knew what hit me, I fell into a trance.

I don't know how much time passed then, but suddenly, from out of nowhere, I heard a grave voice calling out my name, "Matsuno! Matsuno!"[5] I blinked my eyes open and again heard the voice, saying, "Look over there!" I peered over suspiciously, and...how strange! A moment ago a field of plain dirt had been there, but now the field was bursting with peas in full bloom. I looked more closely and...what?! The pea field was crawling with green caterpillars. The rustling sound they made as they devoured the leaves, stems, and flowers made me choke.

"The human world is decimated like this, too!" This was simultaneously the message of the voice and my own intuition.

Then *pop!* in an instant the pea field vanished and the place became a dense forest.

"Huh?" I wondered for an instant.

"The roots are already cut"—that voice again! I strained my ears.... "The roots of the rampant evil of this world are already cut in the invisible world. Matsuno, stand up and fight!" This was the stern command.[6]

"I will!" I vowed. "I'll just have to give a push and that'll finish it off!" I danced for joy with my sense of mission. In that moment, I returned to my usual self. The vision vanished;

---

4. Satomi-san means that her state of mind had been "normal" until the time her husband left. Buddhists, however, see this apparently normal state as a deeply deluded condition. This reference to the sixth consciousness, or *manovijnana* in Sanskrit, introduces us to a complex exposition on the nature of the mind and its functions according to Buddhist psychology.... Suffice it to say that the sixth consciousness is the principle of delusion, i.e., that aspect of the mind which discriminates between "me" and "not me" and hence gives rise to egotism, selfish desires, and self-centered behavior.

---

5. This is Satomi-san's given name until she takes on the Buddhist name "Myodo."

6. In other words, the roots of evil have been severed already in the spirit world, so Satomi-san is commanded simply to take care of the leaves and branches of evil—an easy job with the roots already cut.

"The roots of the rampant evil of this world are already cut in the invisible world. Matsuno, stand up and fight!"

This was the stern command.

the voice ceased. But the psychological effect continued vividly, guiding me forcibly and casting a definite hue over every aspect of my daily life.

My mind was abnormally strained. I felt a thrill of adventure in embracing this "sacred mystery," as if I were soaring to the peak of a distant, towering mountain. The "sacred mystery" was the "vow to the *kami*"[7] that I must not betray. I felt that if so much as one word of this leaked out, the demonic powers

would instantly profit, the vow would lose all efficacy, and I would plunge headlong into hell!

From then on, I kept seeing these visions and dreams, and at the same time I became so impatient to carry out my vow that I couldn't keep still. I burned with the feeling that I must soon go to Tokyo to proceed with my sworn objective. But I could not formulate a concrete plan to accomplish it.

I came to wonder whether I really needed such a plan. "Anything would be all right; the important thing is to get going. Strike out! Forward! Hup, two, three, four! That's the way! No need to worry about the next moment, just press ahead! Step by step, hurling myself against all obstacles!"

One day I stood before my father and mother and made a formal request. "Please send me to Tokyo again." This was three months after my husband had left home.

"What do you want to do in Tokyo?"

"Study."

"Studying is fine, but what on earth would you study?"

"I can't say."

"Why not?"

I kept silent. I couldn't tell anyone. The divine secret must not be revealed!

My mother burst out, "You probably want to go to your husband's place. Well, that's understandable—"

Father broke in, "Well, if you want to go, all right, but I—"

"No, it's not that," I cut him off. I knew what he was going to say. I appreciated his grandmotherly heart, but what was that to the new me?

I advanced one step: "Really, it's selfish, but I'd like to ask you to take care of the children for a little while."

Both parents stared at me in bewilderment for a moment, and then Father asked, "You want to leave both children with us?"

"Yes! Please, will you?"

---

7. *Kami* are spirits or deities that are traditionally believed to inhabit Japan. Mountains, islands, stones, fields, the sky—*kami* may be found anywhere the Japanese feel the presence of the numinous. Shrines to the *kami* are found throughout Japan.

"We can't do it. Take one along with you!" Father quickly replied.

I was defeated. "All right." There was nothing I could do about it, I thought. "Well, I have one more request." I rallied myself for my second approach.

"Go ahead."

"I need about a hundred yen." This took death-defying courage.

"What would you do with a hundred yen? Thirty yen is plenty. I'll give you that, all right?"

"All right." There was nothing I could do about that either.

Thus, with a nursing child on my back and thirty yen in my pocket, I left immediately for Tokyo. I say thirty yen, but the thirty yen of that day was worth more than ten thousand of today's yen.[8] Anyway, for less than five yen, I was able to go from Sapporo to Ueno Station, Tokyo.

Myodo travels to Tokyo and begins to study philosophy of religion at Toyo University. Her husband's aunt becomes distressed with Myodo because the aunt thinks Myodo is neglecting her baby in order to keep up with schoolwork. Myodo's father comes, assesses the situation, and agrees with the woman. Myodo's baby is taken from her, and Myodo is crushed: "Surely the child cried for my breast," she writes. She composes a poem that denigrates herself while expressing deep longing for her baby, Sumiko:

> This mother is worse than a demon.
> If I die of insanity
> Don't grieve, my Sumiko.

It was several months later, a snowy February night. As I lay on my bed between sleeping and waking, my mind drifted off to a garden with alpine flowers in bloom, the likes of which I had never seen. In a little while, a lacquer-black darkness seemed to fall like a curtain before my eyes. In the midst of this darkness, a huge, round, blood-red flower suddenly burst open. It looked like fireworks bursting in the sky. Just then my whole body was seized by a violent and uncontrollable trembling.

Suddenly, in my delirium, I saw a sword in the ceiling just above where I was lying. It was pointing down at me, piercing through the ceiling boards as if it would drop right onto my windpipe. I saw it as if I were looking through a pane of glass. "It's there to kill me," I thought. "It's the landlady. There's something evil about her. She thinks I suspect something and is afraid I'll expose her. She's scheming with her accomplice to do away with me! But the *kami* will stand by me! I have nothing to fear! I'll fix them—I'll get the jump on them!"

I got up quietly and slipped my coat on over my nightgown. Thus dressed, I escaped from the house through the second-floor window, running from roof to roof. I walked briskly away, letting my bare feet guide me. I was not cold nor was I even chilled. I finally reached a place that I thought was a beach. As I gazed out over the dark surface of the ocean, my thoughts ran like this: "I've got to cross the ocean and get to the Kegon Waterfall at Nikko. In the pool below the waterfall, someone is crying out, 'Life is incomprehensible!' It's the young philosopher Fujimura Misao![9] He has thrown himself into the water and he hasn't come up yet! I'll jump in and save him!" When, as I believed, I did so, he floated lightly

---

8.   This was written in 1956, so of course the thirty yen of that day would be worth a great deal more now.

9.   Fujimura Misao (1886–1903) was a student at an elite high school. He commited suicide by throwing himself into the Kegon Waterfall at Nikko, leaving behind a suicide note in which he asserted, "Life is incomprehensible." This suicide occurred at a time of rapid social and cultural change in Japan and was taken as indicative of the times, a symptom of the tremendous demands being made on the Japanese people. The suicide was a great shock to the people of the Meiji era.

to the surface, though he had been down there a long time.

Suddenly, a voice cried, "Halloooo!"

"Yah! It's the accomplice! The rat!" I was frightened and tried to run away, but that guy grabbed the sleeve of my coat. Spinning around, I slipped out of the coat, leaving it in his hand, and ran away. He chased after me again and grabbed my nightgown. Once more I spun around and left him holding it.[10] Wearing just my underpants, I dashed away as fast as I could. From here and there people came running and surrounded me. I looked and saw that they were all policemen. It was the dead of night. I spent that night in a detention cell and was carried forcibly the next morning in a rickshaw to a mental hospital. I had finally gone insane.

> When I speak
> My lips are cold.
> The autumn wind....[11]

One day the nurse came to summon me, saying I had a visitor. When I entered the reception room, I was surprised to see my father standing there alone. He had come all the way from Hokkaido to pick me up. For a moment I was startled and at a loss: must I leave this pleasant hospital and return to the world of corruption? The painful memories of the past that I had utterly forgotten came flooding back all at once. "What an evil woman I am. I abandon my children, separate from my

husband, and cause my parents such worry.... Was my first insight into sincerity wrong somehow? Was I deluded? What on earth is karma anyway?" Thinking such thoughts, I put my beloved hospital behind me and walked out with my father.

Father abruptly asked, "Well, what do you want to do now?" I had no idea. Unlike before, my mind was all foggy and indecisive. For now, at least, I had no desire to go to school. I suddenly remembered an uncle named Tetsumei on my father's side who was chief priest at a temple in Hakodate.

"Please send me to Tetsumei's."

"Nonsense." Father would not hear of it. He said, as if to himself, "It's no good taking her back to Hokkaido. Maybe I should talk it over with Goto-san." Goto-san was the landlady at the newspaper shop.

Goto-san spoke kindly. "I have an acquaintance who is a master of physiognomy. Go see him and you'll be able to settle on a good plan."

I was soon taken to the home of this so-called master by Goto-san. He gave this appraisal: "By nature, this woman is extremely imitative; therefore, if she were to be an actress, she would certainly succeed. Within that field, if she were to be a *kageki*[12] actress, her success would be all the greater."

Goto-san made up her mind quickly. "Any occupation would do; if you could even be a success, it would be wonderful. If you were successful, you'd make your father very happy. If you were to go to school or something, it would take a long time, and who knows whether or not you would succeed. Why not become an actress instead?"

---

10. The coat and nightgown are kimono-style.

11. This poem is quoted from the famous haiku poet Basho. According to T. P. Kasulis, Basho expresses in this haiku "the Zen qualms about putting things into words." Satomi-san's use seems to be less epistemological and more emotional. I take her meaning to be: "Whatever I say, it isn't right; I should keep silent." Cf. T. P. Kasulis, *Zen Action Zen Person* (Honolulu: University Press of Hawaii, 1981), p. 28.

12. *Kageki* is a kind of theater, much like an operetta or a musical revue. The plays have simple plots and depend heavily on music and staging for their popular appeal. The cast is all female, the actresses playing both male and female roles. It was most popular in the Taisho era (1912–26) but can still be seen today.

I felt that the priest's learned talks were truly jewels
taken from an infinite storehouse.

He was far superior to the
ordinary religious person.

I was deeply impressed by his sermons
and admired the personal character
that shone through his words.

Father, too, was inclined to go along with this. I was reluctant, but I couldn't help being moved by his ardent parental love and his desire to help me. For me to succeed according to his desire—even if only for a while—would make him happy, and this I wanted very much. "To be sincere is to forget myself and serve others, to abandon all of my own desires and fulfill my father's expectations." Thus I admonished myself....

Myodo becomes a kageki actress and meets with modest success in her profession. Unfortunately, her success does not satisfy her, and she begins to visit temples, seeking out religious teachers. Over the next twenty years, she investigates many different traditions and attends many spiritual meetings but here, as in her professional career, she does not find what she is looking for. Finally, she turns to Zen.

There is a Soto Zen temple in Sapporo called Chuoji Temple. Its chief priest was a renowned monk, proficient in both learning and virtue; soon he was to become abbot of the Soto headquarters temple. Every week at Chuoji, there was a meeting on Zen doctrine with lectures primarily on koans. I had joined this group some time ago. I felt that the priest's learned talks were truly jewels taken from an infinite storehouse. He was far superior to the ordinary religious person. I was deeply impressed by his sermons and admired the personal character that shone through his words. I occupied a seat at Chuoji for a long time, feeling that under this priest's influence, someday even my cloud of delusion would clear up. I heard talks on koans from the *Mumonkan,* the *Hekigan,* and the *Shoyoroku.*[13] But my mental condition was as usual, and I went around and around in the same old circles. "This won't do!" I thought. Thus, for the first time, I became seriously interested in doing *zazen.*

In the Maruyama district, not far from Sapporo Jinja, there is a Rinzai Zen temple called Zuiryuji. Joten Roshi, then of Zuiganji Temple in Matsushima, was a former resident at Zuiryuji who, I understand, had restored the temple and painted a picture of Bodhidharma.[14] In his day, they say, there were a considerable number of practicing monks

13. All famous collections of koans.

14. Bodhidharma is the traditional first patriarch of Zen and a favorite subject in Zen art.

there. Every year at the spring and fall equinoxes, Joten Roshi came to Zuiryuji and presided over a week-long *zazen sesshin.* I decided to attend. As I arrived, I saw a large stone signpost inscribed with "Hokkaido Dojo" standing next to the main temple gate. With the idea that this would be the final and decisive battle, I walked through those gates. It was about the time of the start of World War II.

In the room designated as the Zendo,[15] about thirty men and women who appeared to be laypersons were sitting in rows before a statue of the Buddha. All of us received the koan *Mu* from Joten Roshi. I felt that at any moment I could realize awakening and silently and earnestly repeated "*Mu, Mu*" at the bottom of my *hara.*[16] I thought I could surely awaken within the one week. Presently a bell was rung. The participants began to line up in front of the gong and, stiff as I was, I had to go too. So, imitating everyone else, I entered the room. I was completely ignorant of the proper behavior for the room, though. As I bowed to the Roshi, who was sitting inside, I screwed up all the courage in my body and suddenly, from twelve feet away, let out with, "The Mind is the Way!" This was an intuition I had had once when I was doing *misogi.* I thought that this kind of thing was satori.

"Such a theory is all wrong," replied Roshi.

"It's not a theory," I thought, though I was unable to reply.

Day after day, in this manner, I rushed on blindly. Then, in the last meditation period, I dimly realized how to fix the direction of my mind. With this boost to my self-confidence, I thought, "Great! I'll certainly realize satori by

the next spring equinox! Then I'll be sure to receive Roshi's endorsement! Satori isn't a very easy thing, though...."

In order to practice meditation, I quickly left my family ("severing all karmic bonds")[17] and moved into a hut attached to the back of that Kannon shrine by the waterfall where, until the previous year, an old charcoal maker had lived. I was accompanied by Chimpe-san, a little dog that the charcoal maker had left behind. Inside, the hut was gloomy. The coarse tatami mats were sooty and laid out loosely, unattached to anything. In a large, built-in hearth in a corner of the room, a jet-black, soot-covered pot hook dangled down. While living in this hut with Chimpe-san, I helped out with the charcoal making and found work in the fields. Living the most meager of lives, I continued with *zazen.*

At first I felt I would reach satori within a week. Then the spring equinox came and went, then the fall equinox, and the spring equinox repeated, until finally the fifth fall equinox approached. I had still not achieved satori! I didn't intend to meet Roshi personally until I achieved satori; I thought it would be useless. In truth, I thought I would easily attain satori and then meet him. But the more I practiced *zazen,* the less things turned out the way I expected.

"What is this all about?" I asked myself. "It must be because I've got some impurity left in a corner of my heart. The first thing I've got to do is find it and get rid of it." I had probably heard a talk at a temple once about the six perfections.[18] Knowing that one perfection completes

---

15. The room set aside for *zazen* practice.

16. The *hara* is the lower abdominal region. In *zazen* practice, one is often told to concentrate all of one's energies in the *hara* and to put one's mind in the *hara,* because it is believed to be a center of mental and physical energy.

17. In Buddhism, to leave home represents the severing of karmic bonds, i.e., the severing of attachment to delusion and self-interest. Shakyamuni Buddha established the model by leaving the comforts and pleasures of home to search for religious truth.

18. The six perfections are six kinds of practice in which Mahayana Buddhists engage. They are: giving, keeping the Buddhist precepts, endurance, effort, meditation, and wisdom.

the other five perfections, I had made a Hinayana-type giving vow.[19] I had tried to fulfill it, but I thought that at some time I must have fallen short and that that failure must be what was blocking my achievement of satori. Something occurred to me.

I had recently visited Mr. K———, who had returned not long ago from Manchuria and lived in the neighborhood. Mr. K——— and his wife were living in a worn-out charcoal kiln that looked like a mud hut. The inside was empty. There were hardly any household goods; of bedding, I could see nothing but two blankets. It was one room without a closet, just like my hut. In this place, and approaching the last month of pregnancy, Mrs. K——— was sleeping, covered with her blanket, when I visited.

"You must be cold."

"No, we've got a Korean stove," she replied.

The three futon quilts I was using popped into my mind then, and I thought of giving one of them to this woman who would soon be a mother. But when I returned to my hut I felt stingy. In spite of myself, I had hesitated up to that moment.

"This is terrible! I've got to knock out this impure nature once and for all!" I thought. So, quickly adding some old clothes to the futon, I returned with them secretly, late at night, to the K———s' place.

"Great! Now I'll realize satori! Surely by this equinox satori will open up and—though a little on the late side—I will have to meet Roshi!" I was enthusiastic and, rousing my spirits, I repeated "*Mu, Mu*" doggedly. Thus, at last, the anticipated fall equinox arrived.

But without satori.

And once again the equinox passed.

And yet, still no satori. Thus it became late fall, and even then I couldn't break through.

"Oh, I'm no good! I can't achieve satori no matter what I do! What deep crimes I must have committed! And what a dunce I am! Maybe I could wipe out my crimes with religious practice, but my stupidity...no matter what I do, it isn't going to improve! Why should a stupid creature like me expect to attain a wonderful thing like satori?" A flood of emotions forced their way into my heart. Tears fell from my eyes, and I cried out loud. A spray of rain suddenly hit the small window of my hut. The night deepened.

I can't die
With my heart full of longing.
The autumn rain.

I would have liked to die! But I thought thus: "Even if I die, this suffering won't end.[20] Besides, I'm not the only one; somewhere in this world there may be one or two other dull-witted people like me, suffering like me. Well, I'll keep on living! And, along with people I've never met, I'll probably keep on suffering. But I only hope that I am one of those who will awaken to satori at the end of this life. No, I emphatically do not say 'this life.' Even the next life, or the following one, would be fine. And, all right, it's fine even if I am eternally unable to achieve satori! This is my vow! Now that I have made it, it can never in the future be changed!" Thus I vowed firmly in my heart.

In that moment, my tenacious grasping onto satori was suddenly cut off.

As I thought this, I lost consciousness. I don't know how long I remained unconscious, but I awoke suddenly, as if from a dream. In that moment, strange things began to happen.

---

19. Hinayana Buddhism, the so-called Lesser Vehicle, and Mahayana Buddhism, the so-called Great Vehicle, are the two great traditions into which the Buddhist world is divided. By "Hinayana-type giving vow," Satomi-san means a vow to give things in a literal sense. Satomi-san hopes that by practicing the perfection of giving, the sixth perfection, wisdom or enlightenment (her goal), will also be achieved.

20. This is because she would be reborn with the same karma from which she wanted to escape.

First—and I admit it was hazy—what seemed like a life-soul made of a gaseous substance spontaneously came into being and swelled up and up until it became, in the next moment, some kind of strange and unknown animal-like creature. Like a monkey climbing up a branch, it ascended quickly and agilely. In a moment it reached the top and bumped its head on the sky. Just then, I myself unmistakably became Amenominakanushi-no-Okami.[21] This went a step beyond the spheres of *kami* possession or "oneness of *kami* and person" that I had hitherto known. In the next moment, the room shrank and the universe was transformed into its essence and appeared at my feet. "Ah! The beginning of the universe—right now!... Ah, there is no beginning!"

The next moment, the whole world became a deep blue, glowing and rippling, magnificent whole. "Ah! I gave birth to Buddha and Christ!... The unborn, first parent...that's me! I gave birth to me! I was what I am before my parents were born!"

These strange, intuitive worlds unfolded instantaneously one after another, as if boldly resolving great issues in huge strokes and with dazzling speed.

"Satori! It's satori! I've awakened! It must be satori!" I snatched Chimpe-san, who was sleeping nearby, up into my arms and walked around the room saying, "Thank you, Chimpe-san! Thank you, Chimpe-san!" I felt as if the whole world had all at once been turned upside down.

Dew drops, even dust—
Nothing is unclean.
The own-nature is pure, the own-nature is pure.[22]

Kami and Buddha—
I've searched for you everywhere.
But you are here, you are here!

The mental world had stagnated in me for a long time without the slightest stirring. Now it sprang abruptly into life. There is absolutely no comparison between so-called ESP, psychic powers, and so forth, and the special mental phenomena that occurs when one forgets about the world accessible to the senses. The latter is the vivid activity of the total self.

I spent many days dancing gratefully with the joy of one who has come upon a prolific and eternally inexhaustible spring. Still, I wondered if this was the real thing. I wanted to get explicit certification as soon as possible, but Joten Roshi wouldn't be coming until next spring. So I went to see him.

My unborn parent,
How dear, how beloved.
My parent is here!
My parent is me! Me!

I set out with this and the two *waka* poems[23] in my pocket. Fortunately, I

---

21. Amenominakanushi-no-Okami was one of the *kami* in the ancient Japanese pantheon as recorded in the Japanese classics. In the Restoration Shinto of Hirata Atsutane (1776–1843), this *kami* is elevated from a rather obscure position to become the creator god of the entire universe, all-powerful, all-knowing, and eternal. Understood in this way, this *kami* never became an object of widespread personal faith, presumably because of its philosophical, otherworldly character, which is quite alien to the native Japanese tradition.

22. Dew drops and dust are symbols for this world of evanescence and delusion. According to Zen philosophy, everyone possesses the innately pure Buddha nature, or "own-nature." This means that all have the potential to attain enlightenment. Once enlightened, one can see that this world, which appears contaminated with the dust of hatred, greed, ignorance, etc., is in fact pure and always has been.

23. The poems are given above ("Dew drops..." and "Kami and Buddha"). A *waka* is a poem composed of thirty-one Japanese syllables.

caught the Roshi at the entrance, just as he was going out.

"I met you five years ago at the fall equinox *zazen* meeting," I said, skipping the formalities.

"Is that so?" the Roshi replied, carefully scrutinizing my face. "You've become quite an old woman, haven't you?"[24]

"Yes. You've become quite old, too." The Roshi smiled and stroked the top of his head. I quickly took the sheet of poems out of my pocket and showed it to him.

After a moment, the Roshi said, "You've come to quite a good level, but…"

"But what haven't I reached yet? And how do I get there?" The Roshi closed his mouth and said nothing.

"I keep hearing that I must cut off all thoughts and become 'not-self,' but are all the things that come up in the mind evil thoughts that must be severed?" I asked.

"Not necessarily."

"But how can you tell the difference between the good and the evil ones?"

One after another, things I wanted to ask came flooding out. But this was just a standing chat with the Roshi, whom I had caught on his way out, and I had to restrain my overabundant questioning. I asked a question on the run: "What's the point of so strenuously repeating '*Mu, Mu*'?"

"Yes, that's just like putting a heavy stone on top of a pickle barrel."

"I get it! The moment you take off that heavy stone, the passions and delusions pop up from the bottom, yelling 'Nyaah!' just like a jack-in-the-box, eh?" I said half to myself.

With the parting words "Yes, that's right," the Roshi left hurriedly. He was quite noncommittal. So was my satori all right or not? Afterward, I went twice to pay a call, but both times I was turned away at the door. With

things having come to this pass, the vivid mental life of that time gradually faded; the turning wheels slowed. Simultaneously, my happiness and inspiration cooled and finally were completely extinguished.

I became rather sick and tired of working so hard for satori and wondered, "Isn't the suffering inherent in the three poisons[25] and the passions itself each individual's process of religious practice? Aren't the pain and pleasure of the ten worlds[26]—just as they are—one great state of religious practice? Self-realization or no self-realization, when one considers that all things are always treading the one path of religious practice, it's clear that there is nowhere outside this from which to intervene. It's fine, just as it is! It's precious, just like this! It's wonderful! Such a thing as the 'salvation of all sentient beings'[27] is a lot of uncalled-for meddling!" I felt dispirited and desolate, like still water gradually turning stagnant. "What a strange place you've fallen to!" I thought. "This can't be the right track!" But I did not have the means to get myself out of that place.

The following year, in early February, I went to Zuiganji Temple in Matsushima seeking Joten Roshi's guidance, as I couldn't wait for him to come to Hokkaido. But here, too, it ended in ambiguity because I couldn't express myself adequately and formulate the right questions.

It was the period before the end of the war when food was extremely difficult to get. In the waiting room at the station, below the seat,

---

24. In a culture, such as Japan's, which values age, this is a polite thing to say and not in the least rude or insulting.

25. The three poisons are greed, anger, and delusion.

26. The ten worlds are the ten states of existence of living beings: beings in hell, hungry ghosts, animals, fighting demons, human beings, and heavenly beings; *sravakas, pratyekabuddhas,* and bodhisattvas (three categories of Buddhist saints); and buddhas.

27. Serious practitioners of Mahayana Buddhism vow to save all sentient beings before they themselves attain final enlightenment or *nirvana.*

were the bodies of two people who had starved to death, stretched out and covered with mats. Starving people, half dead and half alive, were tottering about on both sides of the platform, looking as if they would collapse right then and there. Either they were resigned or their minds were gone, because their faces had carefree expressions as if nothing were wrong at all. "Ah! To collapse and die where you fall! How simple!" I envied those people.

Roshi did not come to Hokkaido for the March equinox. I was desolate. Before long, my wonderful experience sank into the deep shadows of my subconscious....

Late in life, Myodo develops a close spiritual ("Dharma") friend, Hayakawa-san. The two do not always see eye to eye but are unfailingly supportive of each other.

Fortunately Hayakawa-san and I were able to carry on our unparalleled friendship as usual and without incident. Whenever we met, the first thing we asked each other was, "Have you found a good teacher yet?" As it happened, during my time with Shibata Sensei, I had had a young Dharma friend named Minamikawa-san who once said to me, "Zen is no good as doctrine alone. You've really got to do *sanzen* [personal interview with a Roshi] or it's all a lie." My friend recommended the Zen Master of Chitose to me at that time, and I remembered him now. When I told Hayakawa-san about him, she became very enthusiastic. Saying she would try visiting him first, she made her preparations quickly and went out alone. She had such self-confidence in Buddhism, she probably had something in mind.

To get to Chitose took over two hours by train and streetcar. When she returned, she reported, "That priest is really sharp!" She clearly had been taken down a notch by him. She added, "I made an appointment to visit again at the end of the month—you included." This was May of the year after I lost Shibata Sensei.

The Zen master's name was Suga-sama. At first glance, his eyes made him seem unapproachable, but all the same, I felt I could open up to him completely. When he met me in the main temple room, the first thing he said was, "I hear you've studied Buddhist thought." I felt embarrassed. He went on, "But that kind of thing is worthless! You don't derive any real capability from it!" I could hold back on that subject no longer, and chattered on and on boldly, even about things I wasn't asked.

"Have you ever done *zazen?*" the Zen master asked.

"Yes, quite some time ago, at Zuiganji under Joten Roshi." "Did the Roshi say anything to you at that time?"

"Yes, he just said to sit with *Mu.*"

"Were there any experiences that you can think of?"

"Yes." I quickly told him about my experience. That was what I most wanted him to hear.

After a moment he said, "You should by all means go to Mitaka Convent in Tokyo. Please go there and practice for at least a year. I'll give you a letter of introduction." I made up my mind instantly to do so. He added, "Don't forget Joten Roshi's kindness."

As we withdrew to the living room, he said, "Because of your experience, there are as many as two cracks in the rice paper.[28] However shallow, satori is satori." I was totally overjoyed. I felt like a jewel that had long been hidden in the depths of a treasure chest had finally been brought out and seen in broad daylight. In fact, I had previously tried to talk about this experience with two monks, but one laughed and would have nothing to do with me, and the other put me off with, "That was just a momentary emotion." Thus I also thought it might be that kind of thing, and since then I had spoken of it to no one.

---

28. That is, there are as many as two cracks in the veil of illusion that prevents her true, enlightened nature from shining out.

"Practice in a convent is quite tough, but you're still equal to it. You should go soon, though, before your physical strength declines," said the Zen master.

"Where is the convent?" asked Hayakawa-san from beside me.

"In Tokyo."

"Oh? Chief Priest, her circumstances are such that I don't think she can possibly go off to Tokyo. Please, make her your disciple and look after her yourself."

"The meddling begins again," I thought.

The Zen master said, "I'm busy now; I can't take on any disciples."

"Then please put off her going until next year."

"No!" To me he said, "Go quickly before your enthusiasm cools!"

"I will!" I replied and thought, "There's no need to say anything else! This is clearly my last chance. I'm going, no matter what!"

"You'll be lonely, but you must endure it," the Zen master said to Hayakawa-san.

"Yes, very lonely," said my elder sister despondently.

I returned home and disposed of all my affairs at a single stroke. Going about making my farewell visits, I came at last to my parents' grave. The family had been angry when I told them of my plans, saying, "At your age, going off to Tokyo to practice Buddhism? Grandmother! What's the matter with you?" Their anger was justified. I was unfilial to my parents, undevoted to my children. Yet even I longed for the place where my parents were buried. I loved my family and felt compassion for them. "Oh, why can't my heart find peace like other people's? Will this turmoil never end?" I wondered. As I stood before my parents' grave, bitter tears unexpectedly fell from my eyes.

I had an old friend with psychic powers called the Predicting Sensei. He tried with all his might to stop me, saying, "If you leave here now, you will lose your life in no time at all!

Please put off this Tokyo trip for a while!" Two or three difficulties in addition to this arose, but I felt happy about the decision, and my heart was perfectly at peace. I thought to myself, "I still haven't obtained the Way. Time flies like an arrow! One moment is long enough here where there is no teacher; I mustn't linger! Facing my goal and taking this step, even if I were to die now, I would still be satisfied!" My whole body was flush with the joy of this moment of self-affirmation. Thus I set out wholeheartedly for Mitaka Convent. It was the second day of July.

When Myodo arrives at Mitaka Convent from Hokkaido she has another setback; the prioress will not admit her. Instead, Myodo visits the Roshi who lives with his wife in Taiheiji, near the convent.

"**Please do stay here.** The Roshi should be back soon," the Roshi's wife consented cheerfully.

"Thank goodness! Thank you so much!" I thought.

When the Roshi returned, he showed me to the public bath, where I relaxed and unwound. When I left the bath, the Roshi was waiting for me at the entrance. I was very grateful. "What a kind person!" I thought.

I expected to take my leave early the next morning, but Roshi asked, "Why not stay here until things are settled at the convent?" I was happy to hear him say that, but I couldn't help thinking it over. There was no reason to believe I would ever be able to repay this kindness, even partially, and that troubled me. I hesitated for some time, but in the end I accepted the offer.

Four days later word came from the convent, and I quickly went there.

The prioress was gentle and kind, yet she also possessed great mental power, unmarred by the tiniest flaw. Once the greetings were dispensed with, she said, "I have thought a great deal about you.... I think it would be best if you were to live in a believing layperson's home and travel from there back and forth to the convent for religious training. I'm looking for such a home for you now."

"Oh no!" I thought. "That's terrible! That might be all right for somebody else, but for me it's no good. I've got to be admitted!" I well understood that the prioress was concerned about me. But really, the dilemma of my double life had given me no end of trouble for many years. I had finally come to feel that I absolutely had to stop straddling the fence—I must be either laywoman or nun. If I couldn't practice Buddhism in the convent, so be it! But to practice like that, going back and forth, would be no practice at all!

I concentrated my resolve. "Don't underestimate the power of sincerity!" I thought. "As long as I have breath, even if 'like dew at the edge of a field, I vanish,' I will push straight ahead, despite mountains, despite rivers! If I fall down, I'll get up again! If I stumble, I'll right myself! Just advance! Just advance! To either life or death!"

"I want to practice *takuhatsu,* but it's not right to do so as a laywoman," I said as I had planned.

"Do you have any relative hereabouts, or someone who could guarantee you?"

"No." I guarantee myself! But I suppose that insofar as I am my own guarantee, there is no assurance.

"If you became ill, it would be a problem, wouldn't it?"

"Please don't concern yourself over that!" I thought there was no need to worry about such things before they happened.

"You shouldn't say that. In such a case, you become a problem to those around you."

"Yes, you're right...." I gave in.

After we had gone back and forth with several questions and answers, the prioress said, "We have an age limit at this convent; only women in their twenties or thirties may enter."

"Aha, the trump card! Did I fail the test? Well, I guess there's no point in further discussion," I thought. Nonetheless, I kept trying. I asked her, "Can't something be done about that?"

"No. We can't break the rules of the convent just for you."

"Of course. So here, too, I am defeated," I thought. I tried one last approach. "If you cannot consent to have me as a practitioner, can't you find some kind of use for me? Anything at all, I won't mind! I'll do anything, anything! But please just let me stay in some corner. I beg you!" Unexpectedly, a teardrop rolled off my face. I bowed down. There was nothing more to say. My ammunition was exhausted.

In the end, the convent doors would not open for me. Once again I had exhausted the bottommost depths of my heart. I had tried my

I spent many days dancing gratefully with the joy of one who has come upon a prolific and eternally inexhaustible spring.

Still, I wondered if this was the real thing.

best. There was nothing to be done about it! There was no karmic tie. Thus I was satisfied and felt no regrets.

I returned to Taiheiji to tell the Roshi of the poor outcome at the convent. "Well, what will you do?" he asked.

"Go back to Hokkaido, I suppose." I was thinking of going to see Zen master Suga.

"But you went to so much trouble to come here from Hokkaido to practice Buddhism."

"Yes," I said, feeling a sudden tightness in my chest.

Roshi said, "Maybe you could stay here...." After a pause he added, "Well, think it over carefully." I was pierced to the marrow by this compassion. However, since this was something I couldn't very well decide with my heart, I postponed the reply until the next morning. I had two problems. First, I considered, I would feel bad if I couldn't give Zen master Suga an account of the whole course of events. And second, I wondered if I could really presume upon the kindness of the Roshi and his wife like this. But, I thought, besides practicing Zen, I could help out the wife for a month or two and then return home. Thus I stayed on.

The Roshi took me to the Zen meetings at Soseiji Temple in Nakano. There for the first time I heard *teisho.*[29] It was brusque and plain yet had a wonderful power. I listened with intense concentration, holding my breath. But in fact, I didn't understand well. Again, the Roshi spoke to me in detail about *zazen*—the right way to do it, things to watch for, and so forth. This too was something I was happy to hear at last. I was deeply impressed by this meticulous guidance, which exhausted the limits of kindness. Finally, I made up my mind to engage in really thorough practice with Roshi.

Though I didn't neglect my other duties for my own individual practice, I felt I must first and foremost sit in *zazen.* Thus I rose early

---

29. A formal talk given by a Zen *roshi.*

every morning and meditated, facing a wall in the corner of the kitchen. While doing *zazen,* various important but previously overlooked questions frequently came to mind. At such times I always asked Roshi about them and received an explanation. In other cases too, whenever problems arose, I always received guidance. I tried never to let questions linger in my mind. Thus, after a month in Tokyo, I received permission to join a five-day *sesshin* at Shinkoji Temple.

At the first *dokusan,*[30] Roshi examined my mental state. Even there I couldn't help speaking of the baggage of past experiences that I lugged around.

Roshi said, "That is *makyo.*[31] Please try to start all over again."

"Really?" I thought. "All right, if that's the case, I will get a fresh start." Thus making up my mind, I sat enthusiastically with *Mu.* But all of a sudden—were the old experiences of sinking into *kami* possession working their mischief?—I slipped into a state of blankness, as though drunk. When I came to my senses, I thought, "This is no good!" and tried to have another go at it. But no matter how many times I started over, each time I was captivated before I knew it and drawn into the lair. Thus the *sesshin* came to an end in this indefinite state.

Again, Roshi took me to the Zen meetings at Tokorozawa's Raikoji Temple. There, once a month, there was *zazen* and *teisho.* This time the *teisho* was on the *Mumonkan*'s "Kasho and the Flagpole."[32] The tatami mats of the main hall

---

30. The private interview with the *roshi* in which the student presents his or her mind for examination.

31. An illusion produced by the intense mental effort of meditation.

32. The koan reads, "Ananda once said to Kasho, 'The World Honored One [the Buddha] transmitted to you the brocade robe. What else did he transmit to you?' Kasho called out, 'Ananda!' Ananda answered, 'Yes, sir.' Kasho said, 'Pull down the flagpole at the gate.'"

at Raikoji were worn at the edges and tattered. When I saw that, I found myself thinking, "When I worked as a *miko,* business really thrived; I could have easily had these mats fixed. Maybe I should become a *miko* again! Even that isn't altogether useless in the work of liberating the dead who have lost their way."

Just then—"Aha!"—I caught myself. "You fool! That's the flagpole! Yes—when the merest glance casts a reflection in your mind, that's the flagpole! Knock over that flagpole in your mind! One after another, knock them down!" This is how I took "Kasho and the Flagpole." Until now my *zazen* practice had been grasping at clouds. Now I had discovered a principle to guide my practice. I thought to myself that I must never lessen the tension in my *hara.*[33]

There was no August *sesshin* at Shinkoji Temple, so I'll go on to the September *sesshin.*

It was the second day of the *sesshin.* I was working very hard with my *hara,* saying, "*Mu, Mu,*" when all of a sudden—"Unh!"—it was as if three people had pulled me over backward. "Oh no!" I thought. I repulsed this with effort, straightened my posture, and resumed, "*Mu, Mu.*" Then again "Unh!"—I was dragged down.

"This is awful!" I thought. I kept trying to pull myself together, but no matter how many times I tried, it was no use. "What now?" I thought. "I wonder if I'm dozing off." When the walking meditation[34] was over, I thought to myself, "Okay, now!" and sat, hardening my *hara* all the more. As I did so, once again it started. "Very strange," I thought. "I know! It's a possessing spirit! The spirit of a dead person." (In possession by spirits of the dead, one is

thrown onto one's back, facing up; in the case of spirits of the living, one is pushed over onto one's face.) "I don't know if it's a good spirit or a bad spirit, but there's more than one of them, anyway!...Okay...."

"Hey! Everybody!" I said silently to the spirits. "Wait a minute, please! When I attain *kensho,* I will without fail perform a memorial service for you. Until then, please be patient and wait quietly on the spirit shelf."[35] With this statement to free me of their presence, I sat with all the more intense effort.

After that, I was not dragged over as badly as before, but if my effort slackened even a little, I was instantly pulled down. This continued all day.

I was dead tired. That evening when I tried to settle down to sleep, the instant I laid my head on the pillow, I saw: "Ah! This out-breath is *Mu!*" Then: "The in-breath too is *Mu!*" Next breath, too: *Mu!* Next breath: *Mu, Mu!* "*Mu,* a whole sequence of *Mu!* Croak, croak; meow, meow—these too are *Mu!* The bedding, the wall, the column, the sliding door—these too are *Mu!* This, that and everything is *Mu!* Ha ha! Ha ha ha ha ha! That Roshi is a rascal! He's always tricking people with his '*Mu, Mu, Mu*'!... Hmm. I wonder if, after this, I should rush to Roshi's room for *dokusan.* No, that would be childish...."

I felt as if a chronic disease of forty years had been cured in an instant. I slept soundly that night.

Very early the next morning was *dokusan.* Abruptly, I said, "Roshi, I saw *Mu.*" At least I was able to say that much clearly. Then Roshi examined me in a number of ways, and *kensho* was confirmed.

"You slept soundly last night, eh?" asked Roshi.

"Yes, I slept well," I answered truthfully. They say that the night after *kensho,* you can't

---

33. That is, she determined to maintain the concentration of psychophysical energy in her lower abdomen, which was to be used as energy for meditation.

34. In prolonged *zazen* sessions, a period of walking meditation is interspersed with rounds of seated meditation.

35. The spirits of deceased persons are enshrined on the "spirit shelf"; they are believed to inhabit that area.

sleep for joy, but that wasn't the case for me; my mood wasn't particularly affected. "For some reason, I feel quite calm," I thought. I felt as if I had finally gulped down some big thing that had been stuck in my throat a long time. And the fog in my mind had all at once lifted. I thought, "So this is *kensho,* eh? If even a dull person like me is able to see *Mu*—albeit ever so slightly—then in the whole world there isn't a single person who can't attain *kensho!* 'Seek and you will find. Look and you will see. Knock and it will be opened to you.'[36] That's right! That's true!"

"Visiting Zenkoji Temple, drawn by an ox."[37] I had been drawn by a mind that sought. It seemed as if I had been going around and around in circles, repeating the same mistakes over and over for forty years. But now that I have awakened from the dream and can see clearly, I know that the saying "You don't have the same experience twice" is really true. Not a single step is given to repeating the past or to useless efforts. I can see now that things which seemed redundant or insignificant at the time were all necessary conditions for what followed.

It is also clear to me that the return of this lost child to the original home for which she has longed is a gift. I have returned home thanks to the compassion and skill of the buddhas and bodhisattvas. "Amida's five eons of practice was for me, Shinran, alone."[38] Ah, thank you! Thank you! All things in the universe have together nurtured small and insignificant me. They have given their very lifeblood for my sake.

> Ah, hardship—more and more it
>   accumulates.
> I have my limits, but I will try
>   with all my might.
> Pressure makes you into a jewel.

These verses [written by my teacher] have been with me constantly since beginning Buddhist practice. They always spur me on and arouse feelings of aspiration and gratitude. They are the words of an enlightened person—my beloved teacher. Today, let me return them to him[39] to express my gratitude for his kindness:

> To exist is to accumulate hardship.[40]
> Only thus can my life continue to flow.
> *Gassho*

---

36. Cf. Matthew 7: 7.

37. This is a reference to a well-known legend. One day an old woman who was irreligious and greedy was hanging clothes out to air when a neighbor's ox ran by and caught the clothes on its horns. Chasing after the ox without realizing where it was leading her, she followed it into the nearby Zenkoji Temple. When she realized that she was in a spiritual place, she made a prayer for the next life. Moral: Even a chance event may in the end lead to good consequences.

38. Amida Buddha practiced Buddhism for eons in order to acquire the capacity to save humanity— not human heroes, but ordinary, confused people. Though this quotation from Shinran (and Satomi-san's subsequent statement) may appear egocentric, it is in fact the opposite. It is an expression of overwhelming gratitude for an utterly undeserved gift.

39. "The Master [Shinran] used to say, 'When I carefully consider the Vow which Amida brought forth after five kalpas' contemplation, I find that it was solely for me, Shinran, alone! So how gracious is the Original Vow of Amida, who resolved to save me, possessed of many karmic sins!'" (Ryukoku University Translation Center under the Direction of Ryosetsu Fujiwara, *The Tanni Sho: Notes Lamenting Differences* [Kyoto: Ryukoku University, 1962], p. 79).

40. The first five syllables of Satomi-san's poem are the same as the first five syllables of her teacher's poem.

Discussion Questions: **Satomi Myodo**

1. The first paragraph of an autobiography often holds keys to the meaning of the story. Read the first paragraph. On the basis of the emphases you find there, do you think Myodo approached Zen with the kind of curious detachment with which van de Wetering seemed to approach it? Or did she approach it out of a driving internal need?

2. Do you think contemporary Americans have psychological problems that drive them to seek spiritual comfort the way Myodo was driven to seek "the Way of Truth"?

3. Van de Wetering's experience of satori was characterized by insight and inner peace. Did Myodo's experience seem similar to van de Wetering's? Were there any differences? Was Myodo's experience, for example, more ecstatic, otherworldly, than van de Wetering's?

4. One definition of worship goes like this. In worship, the worshipper assumes that there is a gap between the sacred and the profane, between the holy world of the Spirit and the fallen world of this life. Worship is a ritualistic occasion on which the worshipper tries to assume a position in which the Spirit can graciously close the gap, and so allow the worshipper to become reconnected with the Spirit. The worshipper does not become one with the Holy, but rather recognizes his or her rightful place of subordination to the Holy, the Spirit. If you interpret worship in this way, does Myodo's Zen place much importance on worship?

5. Van de Wetering seemed to have little need for religious community beyond the tiny community of Zen seekers and their master. What would you say about the role of religious community in Satomi Myodo's Zen? Do you think van de Wetering's seemingly aimless, purposeless way of achieving self-realization would have worked for Myodo, who so needed direction? Why or why not?

6. Reread the following paragraph in which Myodo recounts her feelings after her father forgives and reassures her.

   > I had never known such a wonderful world as the one I experienced in that moment. I saw the grass and trees, the hills, river, fields, and stones, the hoe and sickle, the birds and dogs,

the roofs and windows—all shining brightly under the same sun. For me it was a wonderful breath of fresh air. Both the animate and the inanimate were vividly alive, familiarly addressing me and waving their hands. Struck by the unearthly exquisiteness of this world, I broke into tears and lifted up my face, weeping, in ecstasy. I saw right through myself and completely emptied my bag of emotional problems.

How do you think she felt? Has the world ever looked "wonderful" and "shining brightly" to you? Was your feeling connected to some relationship you have with a person?

7. What do you think the voice means in Myodo's vision when it tells her that "The roots of the rampant evil of this world are already cut in the invisible world"? Which part of Myodo's experience seems most uncanny to you? Why?

Chapter 7

Judaism

C O M M U N I T Y

 E **VEN though they are introspective individuals** who tend to keep to themselves, van de Wetering and Myodo are unable to achieve enlightenment all alone. They encounter the uncanny by apprenticing themselves to spiritual teachers, and they seem to find themselves only after they have experienced the presence of others on religious quests similar to theirs. Van de Wetering, for example, finds Zen satori by joining Peter's commune, whereas Myodo's journey brings her into contact with several different Zen communities. As these and other examples in this book suggest, the religious quest seems to be a joint one with others, even for those like van de Wetering and Myodo whose journey is relatively solitary. In similar fashion, we acquire a holistic view of religious traditions by learning not only about the uncanny character of individual religious experiences but by learning how these individual experiences bring seekers together. *Community* is a word that refers to this social or institutional dimension of religion.

Judaism is a thoroughly communal tradition. The oldest of the three Western religions (Judaism, Christianity, and Islam), Judaism traces its roots back to ancient Israelite history. Many of the views and practices of ancient Israelite religion form the basis for the teachings and traditions in the Hebrew Bible, the book Christians call the Old Testament. As heir to this earlier tradition, Judaism adopted its self-understanding as a community descended from Abraham, with whom a God named Yahweh entered into a voluntary agreement or covenant. Abraham was to become the father of the nation of Israel, which would inherit the land of Canaan and become the vehicle by which all nations of the earth would receive blessing. Judaism also adopted the earlier self-understanding that Israel's ancestors had made a covenant or pact to become the special people of Yahweh at Mount Sinai after Yahweh had freed them from slavery in Egypt. In exchange, they were to obey the laws revealed by God through Moses and recorded in the first five books of the Bible.

From its beginnings, Judaism has been a religion not of solitary individuals but of a people, a group gathered around the *Torah*. Until the mid-1800s it was incumbent on all Jews to observe the laws of the Torah. Some of its laws have been abandoned by many Jews today, especially those regulating diet, the observance of the sabbath as a day of rest, the ritual monthly cleansing of women, and the exclusion of women from active involvement in synagogue worship. However, religious practice remains more important than religious belief to Judaism and all Jews. Whereas Christianity stresses orthodoxy, or "right *beliefs*," Judaism stresses orthopraxy, or "right *behaviors*." Right behaviors are those commanded by God or derived through oral tradition from the Torah. To be a right-behaving Jew is to find oneself in a community with likeminded or, better, likepracticing, folk, and to live as part of God's chosen people.

Today there are at least five major subgroups within Judaism: Orthodox, Hasidic, Conservative, Reform, and Reconstructionist. Orthodox and Hasidic Jews worship and study in Hebrew, and teach full following of the Torah. Fully "observant" Jews are those who follow the letter of the Law, eating kosher diets and doing no work on the sabbath, for example. To keep kosher means to obey the dietary proscriptions found in the Torah which require, among other things, that meat products and milk products not be eaten from the same plate, so that a kosher kitchen contains two sets of dishes for different kinds of foods. Hasidic Jews typically are not Zionists, people who want to see Israel politically established as a Jewish state. Orthodox Jews may or may not be Zionists. Both the Orthodox and Hasids, however, generally expect the Messiah to return and establish Israel as the Promised Land.

Reconstructionist and Reform Jews are more secular and rationalistic, with roots in the nineteenth century's German Enlightenment and its typically skeptical attitude toward religious authority. In the United States, Reconstructionism is a twentieth-century Jewish movement stressing dynamic creativity in adjusting Judaism to modern times. Reform Jews worship in English and do not observe all of the laws regarding sabbath observance or kosher diets. Women play an active role in Reform synagogues and may be ordained as rabbis. Whereas Orthodox Jews are almost always devout monotheists, it is not unusual to find Reform Jews who do not believe in God. The Reform movement, begun in Germany in the middle of the nineteenth century, is most prominent today in America. It rejects the doctrinal authority of the Talmud, although its position on Zionism has changed over time. Whereas once Reform Judaism repudiated it, Zionism is now officially embraced, even though the Pittsburg platform did not initially endorse it.

Conservative Jews tend to be more pious and to put more stock in studying the Talmud than do Reform Jews, but Conservatives are more free than the Orthodox to adapt the Law to modern conditions. Conservatives keep the sabbath and observe dietary laws insofar as they think it is reasonable for them to do so, but they ordinarily do not devote their lives to *lernen,* or studying the intricacies of the thousands of Talmudic laws and narratives. Of the four groups, Conservatives are the most Zionistic, and American Conservative Jews typically are very supportive of Israel.

Jews learn right behavior by studying the Hebrew Bible and the traditions that have grown up around it. This is especially true among the Orthodox. A central ritual of Orthodox community life is the study of the Torah at the *yeshiva,* or Hebrew school, where pairs of men explore various interpretations of the text while surrounded by other pairs noisily doing likewise. Historically, Orthodox women have been excluded from extensive study of the Torah and were generally taught by other Jewish women the laws governing household affairs. There have been a few exceptions through history, however, and in Israel today there are more and more Orthodox women studying the full range of Torah laws in female pairs, like their male counterparts.

The Torah established the original laws of Jewish life, but it was written thousands of years ago. Obviously the authors could not anticipate all of the dilemmas Jews would encounter, nor could they lay down rules to govern every legal or moral situation that would arise. Therefore, a body of commentary arose in which the Torah was extended to new problems. The new body of literature is called the *Talmud,* a collection of writings begun in the period called Rabbinic Judaism during the first century after Christ. The Talmud consists of two parts, the older Mishnah, which comments directly on legal rulings found in the Torah, and the younger Gemara, which extends the Mishnaic teachings to situations not considered in the Torah or Mishnah. The Talmud is not closed, and the Orthodox *bet din* continues to generate Oral Torah.

This chapter's first author, Judith Magyar Isaacson, was raised in what she tells us is known as the Neologue tradition, the most prominent form of Judaism in her hometown of Kaposvár in southwestern Hungary. The Neologue tradition in eastern Europe is analogous to the Conservative Jewish tradition in the United States: not as observant of the old traditions as the Orthodox but not as liberal as the Reform. For example, Isaacson, who was born in 1925, remembers that the lid on her grandfather's casket was not nailed tightly, an Orthodox Jewish custom meant to remind observers that they must always be ready for the coming of the Messiah. Like Orthodox Jewish children, Isaacson learned Hebrew along with stories of the biblical patriarchs, the "father governors" or founders of early Hebraic religion: Abraham and his son, Isaac, Isaac's son, Jacob, and Jacob's son, Joseph. In one passage early in her text Isaacson finds herself thinking "Here am I!" a response that calls to mind an episode in the Hebrew scriptures in which the biblical character Samuel willingly answers God's call saying "Here am I!" The sociological backbone of the Jewish community structure is the relationship between parents and children and, given the dominant role men have played in the transmission of scripture and religious authority in Judaism, the relationship between father and son has particular significance. But it is regarding Abraham's wife, Sarah, that God makes one of the central promises of Judaism: that her offspring, her "seed," will be as many as the sands of the ocean, the stars of the sky. Isaacson draws on this biblical metaphor in the title of her autobiography, *Seed of Sarah: Memoirs of a Survivor*.

For all of its immersion in the tradition, however, Isaacson's family is not Orthodox, and she, for example, does not seem to believe strongly in the story of the imminent return of the Messiah. She begins her story when she is twelve years old and she is in *gimnazium*, the European term for what we in the United States call middle school and high school. She attends the Neologue synagogue with her family, a much larger and more ornate structure than the simple Orthodox prayer hall nearby.

Isaacson grew up during World War II, when Nazi Germany was trying to take over Europe in the 1940s. During this period the Germans exterminated millions of people in death camps, mostly Jews, but also gay men, lesbians, and gypsies, all of whom were deemed "socially unfit" or "deviant," and lacking the "Aryan look," the blond hair and blue eyes of the so-called master race. Our reading consists of powerful selections telling of the author's experience as a teenager in the concentration camps.

Isaacson's immediate religious community is her family, and we learn about her close relationship with her grandparents, parents, and siblings. However, Isaacson, who is known to her friends as "Jutka," loses touch with her father when all of the Jewish inhabitants of Kaposvár are shipped to the camps and, at the first separation of young healthy women from old and sick women at the Auschwitz camp in Poland, young Jutka watches as she is separated forever from her grandmother Nana Klein, her other grandmother Vago, and her Aunt Ica. Her mother survives only by running into the line of young healthy women where Jutka and her Aunt Magda have been directed.

As we saw in John Fire Lame Deer's autobiography, religion can function as a powerful cohesive force, knitting individuals together into communities. As Isaacson's story shows, however, it can also be a frightful, mad force, destroying individuals and communities. Many of the Nazis were Christians and, proud of their beliefs, some wore belt buckles reading "Für Gott und Führer"—For God and the Fuhrer. German Christians accused Jews of being the killers of Christ, and rationalized their actions in theological and Christological terms. Their debased form of Christianity served as the foundation for the living hell they created for their victims. You will enter this world in learning about Isaacson's personal and communal history.

Our second author is Samuel Heilman. Heilman's mother survived the Holocaust, and the author writes that according to his mother, "the Psalms" saved her. Heilman lives in two worlds. On the one hand he is a thoroughly modern American man, a professor of sociology at a leading university in New York City. On the other hand, he was raised an Orthodox Jew by pious parents who helped to instill in him a love of the

Torah and an appreciation for the study of the Talmud. When Professor Heilman becomes eligible for a sabbatical, he resolves to go to Jerusalem to see whether he can bring these two worlds together.

Many cities contain a variety of different religious communities, but Jerusalem seems particularly noteworthy on this score. As Heilman explains, a walk through its streets will bring you face to face with Eastern Orthodox Christian monks in black flowing robes, dark-skinned Yemenite Jews quietly reciting Psalms, and Muslim *mu'azzins* calling faithful followers of Muhammad to prayer five times a day. In this fascinating mixture of peoples and personalities, Heilman hunts for a *chavruse*, a group of men engaged in *lernen*, the spiritual study of the Hebrew Scriptures and the Talmud. He knows, of course, that the study of the Torah, the written tradition, and of the Talmud, the oral tradition of Torah-interpretation, replaced the rituals of the Temple as the central focus of Judaism after the Temple was destroyed in 70 C.E. As he describes the contemporary scene in Jerusalem,

> where once the sound of sheep going to the slaughter on the Temple Mount must have filled the air, the voices of Jews reviewing their sacred texts could now be heard through the windows of the *yeshivas* and houses of learning that dotted the Jewish Quarter of the city.

But he does not feel comfortable in the study groups he initially encounters, and he continues to look for the right *chavruse* throughout his stay.

Religious communities are not confined to the living. Heilman discovers that study of the Talmud connects him with groups of Jews who engaged in *lernen* centuries ago. His spiritual teachers caution him that he cannot successfully study the sacred writings by himself: "the words of the Torah cannot be sustained by the solitary individual." He finds a *chavruse* in the neighborhood called Shaarey Chesed that consists of people like Rav Moses, an authority on the Talmud and the unofficial teacher of the group; Reb Zanvil, who occasionally nods off during study; Eliahu, who often offers interpretations that are inconsistent with the majority opinions; and Reb Yechiel Michl, who argues against Eliahu, pointing out that his interpretation agrees with that of Rashi, one of the greatest of commentators.

When Heilman hears the group praying the words of the *Shma*, he is struck by the way their voices blend together and by the fact that these were the words of millions of Jewish victims in the Nazi death camps. He reflects on the fact that the Jewish community bridges the gap between the living and the dead:

> When they intoned these ageless words, in the same accents and cadences as the generations before them, they overwhelmed time and brought back memories that all of us in the room—no matter our age or origin—shared.

And then he explains how the singing of the prayer seems to subsume his individual identity and merge him with others into a corporate whole: "One's own voice necessarily becomes caught up in that of others, and the call of those sitting nearby extends it." Later, during the final silent prayer called the *Amida*, Heilman has an uncanny experience of the men's unity:

> Each man stood with feet together, unmoving, and recited the nineteen blessings that make up this devotion. And then the men who stood in this room seemed at once indistinguishable one from another, for all were one with the house of prayer and with one another, seeming to me like a single standing mass.

But religious communities do not always make you feel like an insider, and Heilman spends much time reflecting on the fact that he is not a Hasidic Jew like so many of these pious residents of Jerusalem. He speaks eloquently about the "barriers of biography," a phrase we might profitably apply to other texts in this volume. Heilman notes that communities have a habit of repelling outsiders, even those intent on getting inside. Thinking about his Shaarey Chesed *chavruse*, he notes that "there were barriers of biography that simply precluded my staying within this world. As if by some sort of biological rejection process, the strangeness in me was forcing me out."

As you read Heilman's autobiography, ask yourself how the study of sacred texts has helped to shape the Jewish community into a single community. Pay particular attention to Ben Bag-Bag's quotation at the opening of the story. How has Bag-Bag's opinion affected the shape of the Jewish community? In what way has it defined the institutional character of Judaism and the individual lives of Jews? But also ask yourself to what extent the particularity and unique interests of the Hasidic Jews Heilman meets keep others out, and to what extent all religious communities erect their own idiosyncratic "barriers of biography."

Judith Magyar Isaacson

From Judith Magyar Isaacson,
Seed of Sarah: Memoirs of a Survivor
(Urbana, Il: University of Illinois Press, 1990).
Reprinted by permission of University of Illinois Press.

Spring 1938

Kaposvár: a speck on some maps, a void on most. "Virágzó Kaposvár—Blooming Kaposvár" perches in the hills beyond the Danube, the dozing capital of Somogy county in southwest Hungary. Kaposvár was my home, my universe.

Mother, father, and I lived on Kontrássy Street, on the second floor of a two-story house, in four bright, spacious rooms. Our rented apartment spread above the *Somogy Journal,* and the daily rumble of the printing press would be the only thing to shake the tranquillity of our lives.

On school days, the bathroom was always mine from seven to a quarter past. Mother would wake me five minutes earlier, because I liked to spend the time lying under my *dunyha,* a puffy down quilt. On winter mornings, I needed those extra minutes just to gather courage to get up.

I would strip to the waist in the unheated bathroom to give myself a fast rubdown with icy water, watching steam rise from my shoulders. At thirteen, I liked to linger at the mirror that reflected a new me, with an elongated waist and two tiny jutting breasts. Then I would pull on winter underwear and my school uniform, a pleated navy skirt and a blouse styled like a hussar jacket. The Hungarian Ministry of Education had recently ordered all private schools to exchange their traditional sailor blouses for this national motif. Someone in government must have had a fit of patriotism—in defiance of Hitler, I hoped.

"You can have the bathroom now," I would call, and my father would come, humming a *csárdás*—a Hungarian dance tune. He would halt his morning singing only to shave. With the razor dancing on his cheeks, he would purse his lips and whistle instead....

His gleaming white skin and brisk stride made him seem much younger than his thirty-eight years. His face was lean with a short, straight nose, which I admired, fearing that my own might someday acquire the slight Vágó bent that came to my mother's family in late adolescence. A Jewish nose—what a curse that would be! More than ever before, everyone aped the "Aryan" look, however senseless Hitler's designation might be.

On snowy mornings I would join my mother at the family-room window to watch the snow. "Esik a hó, a dal ma megered—Snow flakes descending, stove's hearth throbbing"— mother liked to quote the well-known line from Babits, the twentieth-century poet, whenever we woke to a snowy morning. Babits and Ady—the Hungarian Verlaine and Baudelaire—were our favorites; we both knew scores of their poems by heart.

I would answer her with a line from Shelley—in the Hungarian translation, of course: "Késhet a tavasz, ha már itt a tél?—If winter comes, can spring be far behind?"

The room would be fragrant with burning wood and fresh-baked rolls, brought from my grandfather Vágó's bakery by his young apprentice, who delivered them daily in a wicker pack-basket, as he did to scores of customers. Mother would step lightly toward our massive tile stove—the color of burnished copper—and stretch her arms to the purring, tall, rectangular solid as if it were a living thing. I liked her best in her ankle-length robe of black corduroy, patterned with miniature yellow roses that set off her wavy, seal-black hair.

Breakfast was always a croissant and an emperor's brioche, with fresh butter and my mother's homemade jam. I always drank cocoa and my parents had café-au-lait.

Punctually at 7:45 I would leave for school, only three blocks away on Eszterházy promenade, Kaposvár's only asphalt-paved street. Along the icy sidewalks two strips of snow hid the canna beds, two long, dirty *dunyhas*. Bare trees stood guard, trembling in the wind.

I attended the third form in the girls' *gimnazium*—Somogy county's only preparatory school for the more-bookish daughters of the middle class, a nonsectarian school of eight forms, for ages ten to eighteen. Its three-story, grey stone structure was impressive, until one compared it to the boys' counterpart, which resembled a palace.

I always made it to school by five minutes to eight and would dash up to the second floor two steps at a time—my private game, a secret superstition, like dodging cracks in asphalt pavements.

One day, my race was suddenly interrupted by no less a personage than Dr. Ferenc Biczó (pronounced *Bitzo*), a professor of the upper forms, who was a colorful, controversial figure and a brilliant lecturer in Hungarian and Latin literature. He stood on the landing, a veritable statue of himself, one foot posed before the other, hands clasped behind his back in studied nonchalance. His open coat exposed a protruding vest bursting its buttons and the narrow slit of a pocket, which held a heavy gold watch and chain. He was a bachelor, whom several upper-form girls hoped to marry on graduation— despite his round paunch, bald pate, and forty-odd years.

Mesmerized by his august presence, I stopped, looked hesitantly, and for the first time saw at close range the ruddy cheeks, the gold-rimmed spectacles, and the fleshy nose with blue and crimson veins. A Mona Lisa smile, in a middle-aged, male edition, played furtively on his thin, purple lips. It was rumored in town that he liked his wine. The alcohol, it was said, gave him inspiration.

Dr. Biczó was something of a local legend in Kaposvár, a town given to culture almost as much as to gossip. My young aunt Magda Vágó, a great Biczó admirer, had prepared me to honor his exalted position long before I entered the *gimnazium*.

"Magyar," Dr. Biczó pronounced in a lordly cadence. He knew my name!

"Yes," I whispered. A biblical "Here am I!" would have better fitted my mood, for I felt as if I had been addressed by a divine presence.

"You are Magda Vágó's niece," he said. "Vágó, a young lady of talent." I barely nodded. My favorite aunt was eight years my senior; I was amazed that Biczó knew the connection.

"Please, Vágó—I mean Magyar—report to my office at ten o'clock recess." He continued his stately ascent without a word of explanation.

After this exalted command, I skipped the steps three at a time, my braids flying off at the sides. I paid only scant attention to the morning lectures, and, as soon as the bell rang for recess, I dashed to the third floor, the upper-form territory. But once there, I slowed down considerably, awed by the elongated torsos and round breasts parading up and down the corridor.

Biczó's study was off limits to all but his privileged. It took most of the courage I could muster to approach his inner sanctum. When I appeared at the open door, he glanced at me momentarily over his gold-rimmed spectacles, and then returned to his reading. His study was lined with books, arranged by subject, from floor to ceiling. A pale February sun washed the heavy oak desk and illuminated a small, exquisite oil painting on the far wall. Slowly, theatrically, he lifted his bald pate. "Hmm… Judit Magyar." I had the distinct impression that he enjoyed my amazement, and I gave a mute curtsy, just as mother had taught me: right tiptoe behind left foot, fingertips lifting the rim of the navy pleated skirt to the prescribed one centimeter.

Biczó leaned back in his chair, crossing his short arms over his stout chest. "Well, Magyar," he said, "I understand you recite poetry." He had heard! I nodded, feeling my face grow warm. Dr. Biczó closed the book ponderously as he added: "I understand that you won first prize in the lower-form competitions."

That gave me back my courage: "I did. With a poem by Ady."

"Ady, no less! Well, I've got something far less sophisticated for you." His thin lips dipped at the corners, then slowly eased into a smile.

"How would you like to be the sole representative of the lower forms at our March Fifteenth Festival?"

March Fifteenth was the anniversary of the 1848 Hungarian revolution, and the yearly festival was the only public performance offered by our *gimnazium*. Everybody of importance came, from the mayor to the shopkeepers. Within the world of the lower forms, a solo performance at the festival was like winning the Nobel Prize. There was nothing higher to strive for.

"At the March Fifteenth Festival?" I gasped, hardly believing.

"Yes, at the festival," he smiled, and handed me a book opened to a lengthy poem. I blushed deeply, and Dr. Biczó chuckled. "Recess is nearly over," he said, "you'd better get back downstairs, Magyar."

Returning to class, I was as concerned about a costume as I was about the poem. I would have to appear in a national dress, handmade for a small fortune. I did not want to tax my parents with such an unnecessary expense. My best friend, Ilona Pogány, soon offered me hers, but it proved too short. Next day, I rushed up to the second floor during recess. Overcoming my shyness, I called at the door of the sixth form: "Does anybody have an outgrown Hungarian costume?"

Marika Erdos jumped up: "You're Judit Magyar, aren't you?" I merely nodded. Everyone knew Marika; she was a celebrated upper-form scholar and performer. But I hardly expected her to know of me. "I hear you're to recite the lower-form poem at the festival," she said. "I did, three years ago, and I'm sure mother kept my costume. Let me see…" she sized me up with her eyes. "Oh, yes, it'll fit you fine!"

The next morning, Marika brought the dress to school. I was overjoyed. Costumes were generally paprika-red, sheet-white, and grass-green, resembling the Hungarian flags, but Marika's was unique. The vest and headdress were fashioned of crimson velvet, decorated with sparkling stones. Over the embroidered white silk skirt hung a miniature jade green apron—a work of art.

"I shall be wearing Marika Erdos's costume," I boasted to Dr. Biczó during our rehearsal, proud of the connection.

"Oh, Marika Erdos," Biczó beamed, "one of my top young scholars." Three years my senior, Marika was all I wanted to become: tall, sophisticated, dashing. The fact that she was not Jewish did not concern me, but the fact that she had fashionably full breasts did. I envied their soft bounce under her navy uniform. I expected to grow tall, and I strove to become dashing and sophisticated, but only God could bestow such breasts.

I learned my poem by heart and rehearsed it for hours each night. Unfortunately it was a patriotically contrived ode, trite and childish. "Don't exaggerate that awful rhythm," mother coached, "you're rocking me to sleep. Tone it down. And make your voice resonant: like silver bells in the wind." But camouflaging the rhymes and rhythm wasn't easy. Even while I practiced diligently, I couldn't help but laugh at the poem, so amateurish compared to an Ady or a Babits. I complained to my Aunt Magda. "It smacks of the principal," she jeered with the patronizing air of the recently graduated. "I'm sure Dr. Biczó didn't choose it." But as the weeks passed, the poem grew on me, and as I declaimed to mother, I waxed so emotional that tears collected on my lashes. Hadn't my great-grandfather Weiss volunteered in the revolution? Hadn't my father and my paternal uncles fought in the World War? Secretly, I prayed for another upheaval and the chance to risk my own life for my country.

A few days before the festival, Dr. Biczó listened to me recite the poem in its entirety. He nodded his bald head with satisfaction: "Just think what you could do with a great poet like Ady."

The next day, 13 March 1938, which turned out to be a day of historical significance, raced by like any other for me. School in the morning, our main meal at noon. After a dish of veal stew and several walnut-filled *palacsintas*—Hungarian crêpes—my parents lay down on the divan for their siesta, and I was off for a private lesson in French shared by Ilona. Afterwards, we played in her yard.

In the evening, I had supper, poem rehearsal, and homework.

By parental edict, bedtime came punctually. I slept on the studio couch in the family room, and had already crept under my *dunyha* when father turned on the forbidden voice of BBC from London, broadcasting in German. Our radio set was a novel gadget, its unnatural voice a shocking intrusion. But I knew how to block it out.

Mother was listening to the news while knitting by our copper-colored stove; her elegant, long fingers whirled, making me pleasantly drowsy. Father knelt in front of the radio, as if in prayer, on the elaborate little Persian rug mother had made for his birthday, last April. His fingers turned the dials: BBC was difficult to get. His back was to me, slim and supple under his herringbone coat, and his light brown hair was close-clipped where it met the neck—the short, powerful neck I loved. Secure and serene, I was drifting off to sleep when a male voice announced in German: "This is BBC...Hitler's armies occupied Austria today... At this very moment, Jewish women are on their hands and knees mopping up Vienna's major promenades..." I sat up, terrified. Hungary would be next on Hitler's route. And we were so near...Will my mother be mopping up Kaposvár's Fo Ucca[1] (Main Street)? I already saw her, slumped on her hands and knees, her lovely hands blue from the icy rags and her black wool coat dragging in horse dung.

---

1. Ucca is the spelling we used. It has since been changed to Utca.

As soon as father shut off the radio, I confronted him with "Will Hitler try to take over Hungary too, Papa?"

Father bit his lower lip. "I hope not..."

"What if he decides to gobble us up?" I anguished. "Would our army repel him?"

My father was a reserve officer, and I expected total reassurance. But he only muttered as if to himself, "They would, if they could." Seeing my fright, he embraced me. "Don't fret, Jutka (pronounced *Yutka*). We'll stop them before they cross that border! Go to sleep now; there is school tomorrow."

At breakfast, my parents spoke only of the Germans, of Hitler and Vienna. They turned on Radio Budapest, the government mouthpiece. Just the day before, its tone seemed almost impartial, but now it parroted Berlin: "the victorious German armies...the Jewish women in their ill-gotten jewelry..."

"My God, my God," mother frowned, "and Austria was occupied only yesterday! Will Horthy[2] sell out completely? I don't trust him, Jani. Do you?"

I was aghast. How could my mother speak of our Governor Horthy disrespectfully? Father shook his head and waved toward the closed door to whisper: "Watch out! What if Mari is listening?" We had a maid like most middle-class families, since wages were minimal and housework arduous, but our village maid, Mari, was hardly a Nazi spy. How nervous my parents must be, I thought, alarmed.

"What about Jutka's recital?" mother burst out. "A Jewish girl can't very well appear as a symbol of Hungarian womanhood now."

Father's blue-grey eyes grew dim behind the glasses, "I guess you'd better resign, Szivecském—my little heart—before they tell

_____

2. Miklos Horthy, whom we called *kormanyzo,* "governor," had headed the government since November 1920, when he was appointed "temporary" regent.

you to. Go and see Dr. Biczó about it first thing this morning."

At quarter to eight, I was in Dr. Biczó's study. He did not seem at all surprised to see me. Did he know I was Jewish? Yes, he did, but it did not matter; this was Hungary, not Austria. Shouldn't I resign my role just the same? Absolutely not, he said. "This is a private institution of classical learning, not some public school."

"Yes," I murmured, "but will the principal allow it?"

Biczó jumped from his chair to pace the room. "He'd better allow it, if he wants his festival," Dr. Biczó waved me off, kindly but firmly.

If Easter was for Christians and Passover for Jews, March Fifteenth was a holiday for all Hungarians. We children always wore spring coats and white knee socks for the first time, no matter how icy the weather. It was the only way to display the ribboned corsages, red, white, and green, like a bouquet of spring flowers. As I stepped onto Kontrássy Street, breathing the sunlit, purified air, I hummed one patriotic song after another. The scare I had suffered two days before had vanished. Vienna seemed far away, and Hitler's armies safely beyond the borders.

Kontrássy Street was celebrating with me: the two-storied houses were on parade, joyfully waving their tricolored flags. Corsaged and light-footed, I, too, was part of the holiday. But carefree as I might have seemed, my child's instincts feared doom; even as I skipped and hummed my way to school, my feet automatically leaped over each crack in the pavement.

Today, our classes were celebrations, and the whole day was spent with history, poetry, and song. In the evening I arrived at school in Marika's splendid costume, jumping with excitement. Among the participants, I was the only child. Our art instructor made up my face with the concentration of a true artist. She held me at arm's length: "You look lovely, Magyar:

> **"Dirty Jew!"**
>
> **"Away with the Kike!"**
>
> **Shrill, mocking whistles sprang up from all directions, hissing their hatred and spite.**
>
> **I shivered, terrified.**
>
> **Our friendly auditorium, where I had so often played and exercised, was transformed into an enemy den.**

the picture of a little *Hungarian* girl." She thinks I don't look Jewish, I figured, and skipped off, foolishly taking it for a compliment.

My poem was second in the program. All through the Bartók-Kodály choirs, I trembled behind the heavy, plush curtains, waiting for Dr. Biczó's cue. At the stroke of his plump finger, I parted the crimson drapes and stepped on stage. Mother had warned me of this terrifying moment: "Just pretend that all those heads are cabbages." But unfortunately there were no

heads for me to see. Only darkness, threatening darkness. Under the dazzling light, I stood isolated, vulnerable. I curtsied, lifting the embroidered silk skirt with two fingers, and heard my voice choke up as I announced the title and author. Breathlessly, childishly, I began:

> Magyar lányok, tudjátok-e
> Micsoda nap van ma?
> A magyar nép dicsoségét
> E nagy naptól kapta.

> Hungarian girls, say,
> What day is today?
> *Magyar* people's glory
> Stems from this day.

"Shut up, Jewess!" a belligerent voice thundered from the void. Coarse shouts startled me from terribly near: "Dirty Jew!" "Away with the Kike!" Shrill, mocking whistles sprang up from all directions, hissing their hatred and spite. I shivered, terrified. Our friendly auditorium, where I had so often played and exercised, was transformed into an enemy den. Unseeing, I faced a nightmare. My knees shook above the white knee socks and my teeth chattered audibly. All my instincts propelled me backstage. But I would not give in.

I took a deep breath and dug my nails deep into my palms. My eyes had become accustomed to the spotlights, and I forced them to stare into the void. I gave another curtsy, this time low, unhurried, formal—just as I had learned in folk dance. Proud of my newfound courage, I smiled involuntarily.

Applause sprang from the dark hall, first sporadically, then solidly from all directions. Here and there, a mocking whistle soared above the clapping, but no one shouted anymore.

I decided to recite my poem from the start:

> Hungarian girls, say
> What day is today?

My voice surprised me. It was fuller, stronger than before, almost adult. The large hall echoed it encouragingly, and there were no interruptions until the final din of applause. One more curtsy, and I backed offstage, exhausted but exhilarated.

"Well done," smiled Dr. Biczó, and I ran to change into my navy dress uniform with the tricolor corsage.

It was with some trepidation that I went to Dr. Biczó's study the next morning to return the book containing my poem. What would he say about the Nazi interference? Could he possibly understand how terrifying it had been?

He received me kindly, "Excellent performance! Your voice is well suited to a large auditorium." Not a word about the demonstrators.

"The whistles…" I mumbled.

"Oh, yes!" he interrupted. "Some lunatic fringe, no doubt. Do you know, Magyar, how many *Nyilasok*—Arrowcross[3]—there are in all of Kaposvár? No more than a hundred, surely. In a population of thirty-five thousand." He rapped his pencil against the desk for emphasis. "They pose no danger. I hope they did not frighten you."

"Oh, no…" I hung my head.

"Have you ever read Plato, Judit Magyar?"

I hardly knew who Plato was. "We haven't had him, professor, sir."

Dr. Biczó stepped to the nearest bookshelf and slowly, with great formality, extracted a thin, worn volume and handed it to me. "You may take it home, Magyar, but please, be careful. I don't make a habit of lending my books to students. Note the dialogue *Gorgias,* and remember, Magyar, what Socrates teaches us: 'It is better to suffer an injustice than to commit one.'"

I held the frayed book as if in prayer. "Thank you, professor, sir," I curtsied. Down in the courtyard, a willful March wind bent the shivering poplars. I watched through Dr. Biczó's window as one of the young trees bowed humbly to the ground and stood upright again.

The year 1939 passes as Judit Magyar continues to excel in Dr. Biczo's classes. Antisemitism in Hungary increases.

Next year, in 1940, the Jewish holidays were late. Yom Kippur was on 12 October. As usual, my uncle Dezso came home from Budapest, and talking animatedly, the Vágó tribe walked along Berzsenyi Street to the synagogue together.

Father was an officer at labor service again, and as usual Grandpa Vágó stayed at home, making some feeble excuse. Grandfather Klein had been the only pious member of our family, and soon after his death I lost the fervent faith I had. We Jews of Kaposvár, like the Jewry of western and central Hungary, were hardly a devout group, celebrating the high holidays only, and we used to be scolded by our rabbi for being "Yom Kippur Jews"—just as we are in Auburn, Maine, today.

At the main entrance to our Neologue[4] synagogue, mother, Grandmother Vágó, Magda and I embraced my uncles, then entered the women's more modest door and climbed the winding stairs to the balcony.

My eyes were soon drawn downstairs to the men. They did not all wear the traditional prayer shawls, but they all wore hats: white yarmulkas for the ancients, black bowler hats for the elderly, grey felt for young adults, school caps for adolescents. Of course, I looked for the school caps of the boys' *gimnazium* and blushed when the tallest tilted toward me. Anti had positioned himself on the opposite side to exchange glances over our prayer books. I smiled, then shook my head: no flirting on the Day of Atonement.

---

3. The Hungarian Nazis' emblem was an arrowed cross, in lieu of the swastika.

4. The small orthodox congregation of Kaposvár met in a hall next door to our large Neologue synagogue.

The women's balcony embraced the men's congregation on three sides. Here, too, I could distinguish the hats: matrons in solemn black, young women in bright felt with stylish veils, girls in berets. I wore a white beret pulled to the side Parisian fashion.

Once more my gaze was drawn downstairs, this time to the second row, right. Would father's and Grandfather Klein's former seats be taken? They were not. My eyes on their empty bench, I was transported to a past Yom Kippur.

I am seven or eight, still young enough to pray with the men. Mother has dressed me in a white sailor dress to go to synagogue with father and Grandfather Klein, who wears a prayer shawl over his dark suit and a festive black bowler hat. Father lifts me on the bench and shows me the temple all in white: the arc with its gold embroidered lions, the Bible scrolls in their festive garments, the cantor and Rabbi Hercog in their solemn robes. The stained-glass windows lend an unearthly light. Father is cheerful, but O'Papa and I are under the funeral spell. "*Oshamnu,*" we sob in God's own tongue, "we have sinned." I lean against O'Papa's black-suited arm—I am less shy when I stand on the bench—and I strike my chest with my right fist at each confession, boldly like the men: "We have sinned, we have acted falsely, we have been rebellious…"

I picture God as a white-haired ancient. He resembles Grandfather Vágó, but even taller and thinner, leaning on a dark cloud, just above our temple. Before him are two massive books, one in white, the other in black—the Book of Life and the Book of Death. A winged messenger reads off a long sheet of paper. "Judit Magyar has sinned," he frowns, using my formal name. "She has preferred her German to Hebrew. She has been vain. She has been disobedient. She hasn't given her pennies to beggars." I squeeze O'Papa's warm hand and chant with him in Hebrew: "*Selach lonu*—pardon us." His strong voice carries my plea to God. Hurriedly, I add a

silent vow: "Dear God, I'll give all my pennies to a beggar child tomorrow." Charity, I had learned in religious class, averts the evil decree. The Almighty reaches for his gold pen and inscribes me in the Book of Life.

The author's grandfather Klein, "the only pious member of our family," dies and her father suddenly begins to follow all of the orthodox Jewish customs, including the custom of not shaving for thirty days after the funeral. He is observant for a few weeks, and then discontinues his orthodoxy. He is inducted into the Hungarian army. Isaacson and her family hear rumors about Jews being dragged to death camps like Dachau, but they do not believe them. Hitler occupies Hungary in 1944 when Isaacson is nineteen. Jews are forced to wear a yellow Star of David on their clothing. Then, in the summer, all the Jews of Kaposvár are confined to a ghetto and, on 2 July, they are made captives in the town's stables awaiting deportation by train. Most of the men have already been removed to forced-labor camps although Jutka tells of her best friend, Ilona Pogany, having to listen as her father is tortured by the Nazis for information on where he has hidden his wealth. Ilona's father does not tell them.

The women waiting for the trains share their fears about being shipped on "girls' transports" to the Russian front to be enslaved as prostitutes for German soldiers.

5 July–8 July 1944

I don't remember much about the loading of the train: all I know is that Ilona's family and mine got separated. I recall the moment the engine pulled us out of the Kaposvár station with an intensity that still hurts.

Our cattle car was packed with seventy-five people. I was crouching on my pack, squeezed between mother and Nana Klein. An SS officer came and closed the door. I heard him bolt it—from the outside. It was dark. The engine gave a sudden tug. "We're leaving," Nana choked. "I can't believe this. We're really leaving."

Where to? I tensed. The train was moving east. Toward the Russian front? I leaned across

Nana's and Ica's laps, and they held me tight against the lurching of the wagon as I fitted an eye to a splintered crack. Kaposvár's two-story railroad station glided by. Quickly, I glanced at the upstairs windows. "No one came to see us off," I murmured. "No one."

The white station sign, KAPOSVÁR, glided into view with its familiar black lettering. I shut my eye against it. "Kaposvár," I murmured, recalling childhood journeys. I felt angry and rejected: my home let me go without a farewell. "Mama," I murmured, shocked at my own words, "I never want to see Kaposvár again."

"You can't mean it, Jutka," she sighed. "You can't mean it."

I rode for a long time with lids shut, blocking the tears. When at last I glanced around in the dim light, my eyes were met by a dark gaze, the bride Sári Holló's.

No one in the suffocating cattle car looked more forlorn than our honeymooners. They perched across the aisle—an inch-wide space—a pathetic pair, caged, stifled. Even with his unshaven cheeks, the young husband stayed miraculously debonaire, his beige slacks neatly pressed, his blond hair smoothly parted. Most everyone else soon looked like week-old vegetables; the groom resembled a fresh-plucked pear.

Not so the bride. With her black hair and peaked nose, she mirrored her name—Holló, raven. I was annoyed to find the honeymooners facing me in the wagon. Why couldn't I be with friends? Of course, I was lucky enough to stay with my family, perched between the Vágós and the Kleins. My sweaty arms were glued to mother on the left and to grandmother Klein on the right.

Two fifteen-year-old girls shared the wagon with us, identical twins, with white skin and red hair that blazed even in the dark. "I pity them," I said, but mother sighed: "I pity their mother more."

Two tin pails stood in the middle of the wagon; one for water, the other for a toilet. I

held my bladder until evening; Nana Klein held hers longer.

Dr. Gero and his young family were huddled near us. He was a dentist, his wife a piano teacher. They had two children: Tomi, age eight, and Marika, age six, who was known in Kaposvár as an exceptionally talented young pianist. During the journey, I often sat with Marika on my lap, her blond curls sticky, her childish mouth gaping for air. By the second day, she wanted no more stories or games. "Lack of oxygen and water," her father explained. Marika dozed on my lap, panting and sweating, until the mug came around. One gulp per person per day was our ration for those three and a half days. We had dry food in our rucksacks, but we couldn't move to reach it, and besides, we were too thirsty to eat.

Marika took her gulp of water and sighed with relief. "Take one more, Marika," I urged her in a whisper, "It's all right." Surely, I reasoned, there must be one extra gulp for our youngest.

Marika's blue eyes were filled with reproach. "But Jutka," she said, as if we were playing some game, "it wouldn't be fair." She passed the mug. I took a sip, a moment's ecstasy, and handed it to Grandmother Klein.

At night the roles reversed: Marika crept back to her parents, and Grandmother Klein pretended that I was a child again—night and day we wished to cradle or be cradled. "Sleep, my little one, sleep," grandmother would murmur, gently pulling my head way down to her shoulder.

As night changed into gloomy morning, our cattle train rumbled along. Old Mr. N., one of Grandfather Vágó's former card partners, died. "Lucky for him," sighed Grandmother Klein.

Dr. Gero suggested that we say Kaddish in the wagon. "There might be no funeral," he explained to sobbing Mrs. N. No more funerals, I thought, remembering the two I had attended: O'Papa Klein's formal obsequies in a snowstorm, and Grandpapa Vágó's lonely rites in summer heat. Remembering my dead grandfathers, I silently congratulated them.

Two neighbors tied the body of Mr. N. to his rucksack with a belt and suspenders, so he would take up no more room than before. I was relieved to be sitting at a distance. Sári Holló was enough of a burden every time the train lurched, our knees touched and she shrieked as if electrocuted.

As darkness fell, I tried to sleep bent sideways, my spine in agony. If only Nana weren't so short. In her sleep, she would beg: "A bit of soda water! Please, a bit of soda water." As soon as she dozed off, I sat straight, tipping my head forward to avoid the ceiling. When my back felt relieved, I agonized over my knees. I offered Fate a deal: if only I could unbend my knees again, I'd be content. Ambition? Ridiculous. The Sorbonne? Extravagance. Just let me unbend these knees and I'll be modest. Forever.

On my left, mother kept a silent vigil. Her poor arthritic knees, I thought. But only once or twice. The rest of my family vanished. I listened to the churning of the wheels and to the fevered pantings of our honeymooners. "If only this journey would end…" I prayed. But to a god I no longer trusted.

The third day dawned. In the half-light, I gaped at Sári. Surrounded by seventy-three people, she was obscenely stripped to a pair of lace pantaloons and a delicately embroidered bodice—the trousseau of a past generation. My young eyes could hardly believe it: under the sweat-soaked chemise, the forty-year-old bride revealed the breasts of a sculpted Aphrodite. But her face was haggard, her pupils dilated. "Hurry, darling," Laci whispered, struggling to pull on her dress. Shrieking, Sári resisted.

"Let her be," cautioned Dr. Gero, "Let her be. Madness can be catchy." During the day Sári vacillated between lucidity and insanity, but Dr. Gero assured us she would recover once the journey ended.

Our train sped through potato and rye fields and villages with Polish signs. I watched it through a crack. How far to the Russian front? I wished my geography were better.

As the third day faded into night, I tried to sleep to escape the nightmare. Wisps of images floated disconnected, then merged into a recurring dread.

Barefoot and naked, I felt myself shivering in a snowy clearing. Above me dark clouds, around me a black forest. The woods were quiet. Yet I knew death was crouching.

I stood on the edge of a fresh-dug ditch, my toes glued to its icy rim. To my left, a line of girls—all nude—with swollen breasts and pregnant bellies.

"I don't belong!" I gasped, wanting to fly away. My arms winged apart, but my toes held to the icy rim. The forest exuded a revolting stench. I was paralyzed by fear.

Suddenly, German troops emerged, their guns protruding. A giant soldier strode behind me, his foul breath odiously close. I ripped my toes from the frozen rim and dove into the pit. Midair, I shrieked, falling, falling.

I woke. Would I be raped? Buried alive? A girls' transport! How to escape it?

Suddenly, I heard an engine whistle, then the rumble of many trains. Electric lights filtered through the cracks, hitting gaunt faces and blinking eyes. The noise grew frantic as the engine slowed down: rattling, whistling, barking, shouting. It sounded like the East Station at Budapest. Mother smiled, squeezing my hand: "A city, I bet!"

I pushed my eye into a crack: a long cattle train passed us. What was inside those windowless wagons? People? I thought of the Italian Jews who rode through Kaposvár in bolted cattle cars only last year. We could not quite believe it then.

A white station sign glided into view with black gothic lettering. "Auschwitz," I read, turning to the others.

At last, the double doors that had been bolted at the Kaposvár station slid wide open.

I felt my lungs swell in ecstasy.

But the summer breezes brought a strange aroma.

Magda sniffed, leaning forward: "My God!" she whispered. "It smells like burning skin."

"Auschwitz?" said mother. "I've never heard of it."

The engine crept through the busy station, then chose a lone track ahead. Soon, a second sign crept into view. "Auschwitz-Birkenau," I reported.

Our train came to a jolting halt. The journey was over. We idled for a long time at the Birkenau station. Old Mr. S. had a heart attack, or something equally dreadful. Dr. Gero crawled over to examine him. "Lack of oxygen," he said.

At last, the double doors that had been bolted at the Kaposvár station slid wide open. I felt my lungs swell in ecstasy. But the summer breezes brought a strange aroma. Magda sniffed, leaning forward: "My God!" she whispered, gazing left. "It smells like burning skin. Like chickens singed of feathers."

I stretched my neck and gasped. Giant flames lapped at the night sky. "A forest fire perhaps?" I guessed.

Magda shook her head. "Gruesome," she muttered to herself.

Gently, Aunt Ica embraced Nana, pointing at the opposite direction. "Look, Mama. Street lights. How civilized!"

Two skinny male attendants jumped up into our wagon. They looked alike, in striped pajamas and matching caps. Aghast, Magda pointed at the string of digits over their chests: "Look, they're numbered!"

"Bokanovsky twins," I told her, trying to make her smile. "Sprung from a test tube in the *Brave New World*."

"Robots," she shuddered.

In broken German, the men instructed us to leave our packs behind. "How efficient," mother remarked, but to be on the safe side, I pulled out our toothpaste that hid the gold teeth, and stuck it into my pocket.

The two men grabbed people by the arm pits, and threw them pell-mell down by the tracks. The thin, mechanical arms worked fast.

In just a few minutes there was room enough to move about.

My knees in agony, I got up, my back bent by the low ceiling, only Grandmother Klein was short enough to stand up. "Don't get separated from us, Jutka," she fretted. "I'm scared for you." Had my prudish grandmother heard about mass rape at the Russian front?

People jumped off at the side as fast as they could; the attendants now unloaded only the old and the invalid. But instead of dropping them straight down as before, they heaved them toward the embankment with an immense effort. I watched, horrified, as they swung dying Mr. S., dead Mr. N., and live Mrs. N. all in the same direction. Sári let out an insane scream as she flew after them.

"Jump, everybody!" called Dr. Gero, and he leaped, catching his children.

"Magda, quick!" I called, sailing off at the side. "Hand me grandmama."

Too late. Grandmother Vágó hung like a rag doll in the robot's arms. From up high, she addressed him in polite German: "Please, help me down." The mechanical arms stopped in midair, and slowly, gently, the robot placed grandmother down by the tracks. "Danke schön" [Thank you], she said, as if a gentleman had helped her politely out of a carriage.

Magda tossed the others to me. Mother was thin, Nana Klein and Aunt Ica child-size: I caught them easily. Then Magda leaped, and our family was on solid ground.

"Goodbye, Jutka," Dr. Gero embraced me with his free arm. "Avoid a girls' transport. God bless you."

The crowd was streaming toward the railroad station. "Rest a minute," I told my family, "I'll be right back." The earth was heaving under my feet as I elbowed my way through the mob. Did they toss the insane with the dead? I must find out. It will give me a clue to this place, Auschwitz-Birkenau.

At the curbing, between two glaring lights, I found a hill of people, the living and the dead piled like a haystack. The flaming sky framed it all. A funeral pyre!

I searched, nauseated. Was Sári among the dead? Buttocks on faces, heads over jerking feet, necks falling off the edge. At last, I spotted her buckled shoe, still kicking at the bottom. I glanced from Sári's shoe to my sandals; they had been neighbors on the long journey.

I should leave at once, I thought, but the pile held me. I recognized a face: Dr. Margit Nemes, my former professor of French and German. She was buried several bodies deep, shrieking insanely, eyes dilated, mouth foaming. My skin went clammy, my eyes dimmed. I mustn't faint! Not here. Not now. An SS guard was approaching. What if he spots me and throws me on the pile? I backed away, swallowing hard. My family! How could I have forgotten them? Dizzy, I pushed my way through the crowd. So much happened in a few seconds, I was trying to sort it out. Dr. Nemes looked insane. Each wagon must have had its share of demented. But why did they pile the old and the insane with the dead? Poor Mrs. N., Sári, Dr. Nemes… I mustn't think about them. Was I cruel? I agonized. So be it. Better be cruel than mad. It's a new world, a different planet. I must adjust to it.

At last I spotted my family waving from the tracks. "Where have you been?" mother scolded. "I've been frantic."

"Nearby," I muttered.

"Stay together," she grabbed my hand. "Stay together." It was a command that was to guide us through the months ahead.

Nana Klein blinked her shortsighted eyes: "Where are we, Jutka?"

Aunt Ica took her by the arm. "Come with me, Mama."

Here and there SS soldiers stood guard with baggy breeches and stiff boots. Some held hounds on leash. I shuddered with the primordial fears of childhood.

Ahead of us, a tall SS officer was shouting commands: "To the showers! To the showers!" Families parted readily, men to the left, women to the right. Everybody expected to meet again after the showers.

We queued up, anxious to bathe and drink at last. "Showers," sighed grandmother Klein. "I would have preferred a tub."

"You'll like a shower, Nana," I coaxed her. "It's more hygienic."

Beyond the railroad tracks, once more the line branched in two. Why? What was going on? I slipped ahead to investigate. Under a bright light, an SS officer was conducting a selection. I did not see Ilona, or any of my friends, but I did recognize several women from our wagon. From a distance I watched the selection. Children and older women went to the left, the rest right. Perhaps we girls will be safe, I thought. But the next moment I saw youthful Mrs. Gero being shoved to the right, away from her children.

I was scared for them, especially for Marika, and I went ahead to listen as a stocky SS woman tried to calm everyone. To each frantic question, she gave a curt but reassuring reply: "Yes, mothers may visit their children. Please understand, women over forty and children under sixteen won't have to work, so they must be separated from the rest. Don't worry, they'll have comfortable quarters. Yes, you may visit each other tomorrow." It all sounded fairly reasonable. I returned to my place in line and naively relayed all that false information word for word.

"The cutoff is forty!" mother panicked. "What to do? What to do?"

"You won't have to work, Mama," I consoled her. "It'll be easier on your arthritis."

The small remnant of our family now reached the parting of the ways. Aunt Ica went first, with Nana Klein. Ica was mother's age. "Left!" signaled the SS officer. Ica did not protest. I watched them walk away arm in arm, my aunt and my grandmother, two diminutive ladies with diminutive steps.

Grandmother Vágó was next, with Magda. In an instant, the SS split them apart. Magda started after her mother, but the SS shoved her rudely to the right. "Stay with the young ones, Magda," said Grandmother Vágó. "I'll be all right." And she hobbled on alone, bent and stiff-legged.

Mother and I were next. The SS whisked us apart, but mother hung on, staring into the officers eyes, as if daring him to separate us. The officer threw her a surprised look. "Wie alt bist du?—How old are you?"

My first reaction was, he talks. And then, it's no use.

Mother lied without a moment's hesitation. "Acht-und-dreissig—thirty-eight." It worked. The SS flung us to the right.

In less than thirty seconds, our family had been cut in half. "Mama," I said, "how did you think to lie?"

"It just came to me."

"You're amazing, Rózsi," Magda allowed, scampering up. "But what about mother? She'll be alone."

"Why do you say alone? She'll be with Ica and Mama Klein." Magda walked on without replying. Mother persisted: "We'll see them tomorrow. After work."

A low cement building appeared ahead of us, all lit up. The flaming sky seemed nearer now, and the smell of burning flesh sharper, but I was too thirsty to pay much attention to it. For a moment I glanced at the stars, happy to recognize the Great Bear to my right. Childishly, I felt safe, walking between my mother and my aunt. But all the way to the showers, Magda kept repeating, "Poor mother. My poor little mother."

Jutka will never again see her two grandmothers or her Aunt Ica. She, her mother, her Aunt Magda, and all the Jewish women have their heads completely shaved by the Nazi guards. Afterward, Jutka does not recognize her own mother sitting right next to her. They are in the Birkenau death camp, part of Auschwitz.

July 1944, Auschwitz-Birkenau, Lager B III
Our barracks were unfinished, because there was no room for us elsewhere. Inmates of surrounding barracks named it "Mexico"—the poorest of the poor. We, its inmates, wore rags instead of striped prisoners' garb, sipped soup brewed of twigs and leaves, and suffered the blazing sun without drinking water. No one was meant to survive there for more than three weeks. And no one did.

Without bunks, each half-built barrack held five hundred. No room to lie down. At night, we slept on the dirt floor, sitting cross-legged or lying on someone else's buttocks. The weak dozed, standing up, pushed against the walls. (Decades later, I was to recognize similar conditions in a chicken coop.)

During the day, we lined up for *Zähl Appell*—head count—and stood in rows of fives for hours and hours. Those who collapsed were trucked away. Between head counts, we tried to sleep. Night and day, I had a recurring dream.

Sweating under my dunyha, I woke on Kontrássy Street. The faucet was dripping only a few yards away. "Water!"—I rejoiced and ran where the bathroom would be. Water trickled, then cascaded, cool and soothing. I bent to the sink and opened my mouth to it. I gulped, ecstatically.

On an especially hot day at noon, as I woke from this dream still gasping from thirst, I found myself outside on the bare ground. I couldn't see my mother anywhere in the crowd. "Magda!" I shook my aunt, my voice barely audible. "Where is Mama?" She pointed at the hunchbacked beggar sitting at my toes—his bald head was bouncing up and down, his white tongue hung loosely between cracked lips.

I pulled myself up to my knees and squinted into the haze. Thousands upon thousands of bald heads covered the flat terrain as far as the eye could see—mushrooms wilting on the parched soil. "Magda," I moaned, "Mama's gone." The hunched lump stirred at my feet and a familiar, graceful hand clasped mine. "It's I, Jutka. It's I."

I held the long fingers with the familiar nails—pink, rounded shells, elongated and pearly. "Sleep, Mama," I whispered. "Go back to sleep." And gently I cradled her bald head in my lap.

Isaacson finds her friend Ilona and together they contemplate committing suicide by throwing themselves on the electric fence.

Ilona did not come to the Puddle the next day, or the next. I thought she had changed her mind about the electric barbed wire fence. Magda warned me it would be a horrible death; she was for hanging ourselves, instead. "I'll make a rope out of my gypsy dress," she offered. "We'll take turns." But nothing came of it. We were too lethargic. By the end of our first week at Birkenau, we regained our senses. Often, we'd talk of home, of family and friends. "When shall we see the grandmothers and Ica?" I wondered.

"Never," Magda whispered.

"What d'you mean?"

"Nothing," she groaned. "I didn't mean it."

"Of course not," mother soothed. "We must be patient."

The Germans rarely visit Lager B III-b. The kapo, or head, of this part of the camp is a Polish female prisoner whom the Germans force to beat her compatriots. She picks Jutka for her assistant, but Jutka soon surrenders the post, unable to participate in the beatings. Upon resigning, she decides to investigate other parts of the camp.

Along the way, I met a novel sight: a pair of spectacles perched on an inmate. I approached the elflike creature dressed in a petticoat. With her small, shapely breasts and bald head, she looked part girl, part boy. "You kept your glasses!" I laughed. "That's amazing!"

"Not really," she flashed a leprechaun smile. "I wore them in the showers." She tore off her lenses and grinned at me, squinting. "See? I'm blind without them." With spectacles back on her tiny nose, she eyed me, gaily: "Where're you from?"

"From Kaposvár."

"I'm Éva Jámbor," she introduced herself. "From Zalalövo."

I reciprocated by giving my name—a rare exchange in Birkenau. We sat down on the dry clay and struck up a conversation, my first since I arrived here nearly three weeks ago. It turned out that we were nearly the same age, and both planning to study comparative literature after the war. "The mind reels!" laughed Éva, finger to her forehead. "We'll be in the same class at the University of Budapest."

"How about Paris? Have you thought of the Sorbonne?"

She leaped to her feet like a ballet dancer. "I'd love to discuss it some more, Jutka," she smiled. "But not now. I must run. My mother'll be worried."

"Mine too," I chuckled. "This is beginning to sound like at home. Will you visit me next? At Lager B III-b, by the Puddle."

"Listen, Jutka, I've got an idea!"

"You don't say," I grinned. *Idea* was not a word one heard at Birkenau.

"I'm serious. It's Friday, and there is a Mrs. Paskusz leading sabbath prayers by the Puddle."

"The mind reels," I mimicked her. "Sabbath prayers at Birkenau?"

"She's been in touch with the underground."

"I can't believe it! But I'll come. Why not? When does she start?"

"Sometime before last *Zähl Appell*."

"See you then."

"**Which of these creatures** would our famous Mrs. Paskusz be?" I asked Éva as we met late that afternoon.

She pointed at a mob forming within the mob: "That must be her circle." A short woman stood at its center, surrounded by a group of young girls. "I'm Lea Paskusz," she introduced herself as we edged near her. "This is my daughter, Kornélia." Mother and daughter resembled each other, both short, with olive skin and flashing black eyes—Kornélia's delicate beauty contrasting with her mother's leathery look. Mrs. Paskusz had a prayer book in her hand, and she pulled out two candle stubs from the folds of her blanket. "Sorry, no matches," she apologized as she placed the candles on her young daughter's outstretched palms—a living candelabra.

"Where did you get the prayer book and candles, Mrs. Paskusz?" Éva asked.

She smiled mysteriously: "I've got my sources."

Mrs. Paskusz's sabbath prayers started with "*L'ho Dowdi*," the introductory song familiar to me from childhood. Recalling Friday night services with O'Papa Klein, I wiped a tear. "Mustn't wax sentimental," I whispered to Éva.

After prayers, Mrs. Paskusz turned into war reporter, briefly recounting the latest Allied advances on both fronts.

"How d'you know all this, Mrs. Paskusz?" asked a pert voice.

"I've got my sources," she repeated. She bid us spread the news, then blessed us in Hebrew with hands extended: "The Lord bless thee, and keep thee. The Lord make his face to shine upon thee and be gracious unto thee. The Lord turn his face unto thee, and give thee peace."

"Amen," we murmured.

Jutka, her mother, and Aunt Magda are moved with the other prisoners to a camp at Hessisch Lichtenau, Germany. They work in factories in terrible conditions, but manage to keep their spirits up. Still, they narrowly escape being sent back to Auschwitz and the gas chambers. A Jewish woman named Manci becomes their kapo.

1944–1945

At Lichtenau, we held no prayer meetings, except during the High Holy Days. We fasted on Yom Kippur for the prescribed twenty-four hours, but fasting had become a way of life, so we hardly noticed it. "Whether I stay Jewish or not, I shall always fast on Yom Kippur," I told mother. "I must remind myself that people go without food day after day."

"A fine resolution, Jutka," she nodded. "But what do you mean, if you stay Jewish?"

"Nothing, really…" I shrugged it off, but I had been fantasizing about emigrating to Australia, where I would marry a gentile. Why inflict persecution on my descendants?

In October our daily rations increased and our nightly soup thickened, even yielding an occasional cube of meat. Before long, some of us got back our periods. The SS even issued cloth sanitary pads, and we laundered them in the unheated lavatory, feeling feminine.

As cold weather set in, we received much-needed clothes, and footwear too, to replace our ruined shoes. The guards handed to each of us two sets of flannel underwear, a used dress, a worn, light coat, and—to our intense relief—a pair of Dutch wooden shoes. It helped us celebrate the approaching holidays.

There were no candles for Chanukah, but we sang the traditional melodies and exchanged some fabulous recipes—commiting them to memory.

Late in winter, some Frenchmen informed us that the Americans had occupied nearby Kassel, and from then on we expected them in Lichtenau any day. The munitions factory ran out of chemicals, and the SS dragged a group of us high up into a black forest to build a new channel for a stream. Our train stopped at Helsa, a fairy-tale village nestled in an iceberg's lap, near Lichtenau. The houses were half-timbered, with gingerbread designs painted over their fronts.

"How idyllic," Éva marveled, "like an illustration for *Hansel and Gretel*."

"It might be the setting for an opera," breathed Meda Dános.

"Pfui!" Marcsa spat. "Shame on you, both. It's stinking German."

Our rows of fives climbed up a winding mountain pass, and I gasped at a wider and wider expanse of translucent sky and snow-capped ridges. "The Gothic gods chose a splendid habitat," I muttered. "It's heaven—for Germans."

Panting from the climb, mother spoke with effort: "Next year we'll visit the Tatras with Papa. That'll be heaven…"

By mid-morning we reached a sun-drenched plateau, blanketed with half-thawed pine needles and patches of snow. The SS distributed road-building implements with an important air, but the work was a sham to keep us occupied: the frozen ground did not yield to the pickax.

As the sun neared its summit, the SS women bid us collect dry branches to build a camp fire. Busily roasting their aromatic sausages, the guards paid only slight attention to us. We made our modest holiday: munching bread, warming our fingers by the flames, taking leaks in the nearby woods. Daringly, I stayed behind in a sunlit clearing, hoping the bloodhounds wouldn't sniff me out. The warmed, moist earth exhaled the pungent aroma of decay and rebirth. A small bird was chirping on a pine branch, reminding me of Lorincz Szabó's lilting poem, "Nyitnikék," about a tiny bird's endurance and faith: "Akinek tele rosszabb mint

az enyém / és aki mégis csupa remény—As
winter grows meaner and leaner / its song of
hope thrills clearer and keener."

"We'll make it until spring," I told my
feathered comrade.

Suddenly, Hyena, our homeliest overseer,
startled me with her rough voice: "You're
playing hooky, bitch!" she barked at me.
"Instead of pissing, you're loafing here. Thinking of men, no doubt. Ha ha!" Mutely, I shook
my head and started toward my comrades.

Hyena grabbed my arm and slapped me on
the cheeks: "Don't lie to me!" she roared. "I can
read your face. But dreaming is all that's left for
you, bitch. After the war, you'll be transported
to a desert island. No males—not even natives.
Much use'll be your fancy looks, with snakes for
company. Do you suppose the Americans will
win the war? That would be your death sentence. We'll shoot you Jewish bitches before the
Americans come—it's the Führer's decree. Your
fate is sealed either way: No men. No sex. No
seed of Sarah."

*Once again the women are loaded onto a cattle train.
They stop in Weimar, after having heard that the
American liberating forces are approaching. They have
barely enough food to last three days, but they are
locked in the car for a full week.*

Spring 1945

Our train had left Weimar just before the
Americans arrived and I did not expect to be
freed at our next stop either—much less to meet
my future husband there.

As we started our five-by-five march from
the Leipzig railroad station, accompanied by our
Lichtenau guards and dogs, I overheard the SS
laughing and cheering: "Have you heard the
latest? Our luck is changing!"

My pulse skipped a beat: what was happening?

The Kommandant and the Oberscharführer
Zorbach—who had once surprised me as I
washed myself naked in our Lichtenau barrack

—walked by me. Zorbach sounded jubilant:
"Roosevelt is dead, our Führer will win!"

"Oh, no!" I cried out in Hungarian.

"Shut up, you scum!" His stiff boot kicked
me in the crotch. The excruciating pain in
my most private flesh unnerved me completely.
"All is lost, the Germans will win," I thought,
desperately.

Éva Jámbor bent down to whisper: "Jutka,
listen. Do you know who will be the next
president? I've heard about him from my Dutch
friend. Vice-President Truman—true man. Get
it? He'll win the war, you'll see."

I got up, despite the pain, and let mother
and Magda drag me along before the Oberscharführer could kick me again.

Herded by guards and hounds, we crossed
a large section of Leipzig. As the pain subsided,
I gazed around me: the afternoon sun flashed
through a vast array of windowless arches,
obscenely displaying their gutted insides. This
was not the Leipzig I had read about, a city
famed for its fairs, where Bach played the organ
in Saint Thomas's Church. All around me,
the ruins of ancient Rome seemed multiplied
a thousand times.

"The Germans can't last," a comrade
muttered. "They must be living like rats in the
cellars."

I imagined a woman crawling on her knees,
cradling an infant in front of her. "Serves them
right!" I echoed—my voice a spiteful stranger's.
What have I become?—I shuddered, shocked at
my own words. Have I no pity left, not even for
the children?

Just before nightfall, we arrived at Lager
Tekla, a small Hungarian Jewish women's camp
that had been half bombed out by the Americans. We were assigned two to a cot. Magda
became separated from us because she still
counted as a Lager worker and was given a cot
in Manci's barrack. But at the first shriek of the
sirens, she sneaked out to crawl in with us. The
move probably saved her life: Manci's barrack
was among those bombed out.

The *kapo* escaped with only a burned hand, but her friend, Klára, who had been given my job as cleaning woman to the Kommandant's mistress, was among the dead. By the light of the flames, I gazed at her scorched corpse in dread: Klára had taken my place....

Three days later, as gunfire boomed in the west, the Kommandant called us for *Zähl Appell*. "We're moving east again," he barked, hoarsely, "this time on foot. Be prepared to run at a fast pace," he cautioned, "stragglers will be shot without mercy." Before dismissing us the Kommandant solemnly added: "The disabled may remain in the infirmary. But I wouldn't stay if I were you."

Perplexed, a group of us confronted the *kapo*: "What to do with the sick, Manci?"

"Don't let them stay in the infirmary if they can walk at all!" she cautioned, the twitch of her eye betraying her anxiety.

Worried about mother, I asked advice of a Frenchman across the fence. "The SS brought in a truckful of kerosene," he told me in a whisper. "They'll be setting the camp on fire, we figure."

I ran for Magda, and we discussed it in a hurry.

"Rózsi cannot survive a forced march," she warned. "Would you leave her dying by the wayside?"

"Of course not."

"You see, it's dangerous to stay, but suicide to go," Magda shuddered, and we agreed to stay.

Mother welcomed our decision with her usual optimism: "We'll be liberated within the week."

As we entered the spacious infirmary, we found only six occupants in it, all desperately ill—including Magda Braun, who had been shot in the stomach. The rest of our comrades had all chosen to march, despite their sorry state. I felt myself go rigid. Could we three be right and all those hundreds be wrong? But there was no time to hesitate. Our Italian doctor, Luciana Nissim, told mother to crawl into bed at once

and she let Magda and me sneak under her blanket. Quickly, mother pulled the covers over our heads. "You're so thin, you're hardly noticeable," Luciana assured us before she left.

Within minutes, the door opened, and I recognized Hyena's rasping laughter. "No malingerers today!" the SS guard jeered. "Don't you worry," she reassured mother in a falsely honeyed tone. "We'll get you by truck. You'll see your daughters tomorrow."

"I know I will," mother nudged us gently with her toes.

Early next morning, I awoke to two SS women appearing at the door. "Mach schnell!—Hurry up!" they called, and the nine of us escaped Lager Schönau before its destruction.

The SS led us through the gate, and guided us into a wide open field. Magda and I carried Magda Braun sitting on our interlaced hands, her spindly arms around our shoulders.

"Let's gang up on the SS and grab their pistols," I told Magda, as I surveyed the vast field surrounded by gaping ruins. "There isn't another German in sight."

"Forget it," Magda shook her head. "We don't even know how to pull the trigger."

The SS women herded us to a large garrison, situated by a single pair of railroad tracks. One of them pointed at a row of idling coaches stretching beyond the curve: "This afternoon, you'll be going east by passenger train! We trust that you'll repay us for saving your lives, when the time comes. Auf Wiedersehen."

We entered a large hall swarming with women. They were not concentration camp prisoners but forced laborers, a distinction immediately evident from their fleshier look and their colorful peasant outfits with wide skirts and flowered kerchiefs. I wished I could understand their Slavic chatter.

Suddenly, I noticed three stately, well-dressed blondes in animated conversation with an SS officer. As soon as the SS departed, I edged close to them. The women switched from German to Polish, then to French, so

I could understand every word they said:
the SS had allowed them to stay behind to
be liberated.

"Pardonnez moi" [Excuse me], I interrupted
them, "I overheard your plans. I'd like to stay
with you, together with my comrades. We're
only nine."

They were aghast, but it did not take me
long to strike a bargain: I promised to keep their
secret, and they agreed to hide us. The *kapo*
noticed our blue-and-white triangular emblem.
"The SS may return for you Jews," she warned,
as she led us to a windowless cubbyhole in the
basement. "If they do, I'll tell them that this
is a quarantine for contagious diseases. Take off
your clothes and hide them well, then wrap
yourselves into these blankets. Oh, yes, be sure
not to come anywhere near us. Do you hear!"

"Jawohl, Kapo," I nodded, feeling more of
an outcast than before. When I heard the passenger train leaving, I was once more overcome
by doubt. Had we made a fatal decision?

Late that night, some Polish women
dragged three men shrieking in pain thumping
down the stairs. I felt nauseated: the men were
burned to charcoal, their skin and clothes
hardly distinguishable. The women deposited
them into the nook next to ours. The former
kapo told us that they were Czech prisoners of
war who had barely escaped from a neighboring Lager—probably our former camp,
Schönau, we figured.

My worst fears were confirmed just before
dawn, as I awoke to a blinding light. The Polish
kapo held a flashlight, as an SS officer pointed
his pistol. "Are these wretches Jewish?" he
thundered.

"They're Polish," the *kapo* lied. "Watch out,
they're highly contagious."

"Let them kiss my boot then," snarled the
SS. "Say something in Polish, bitch!" he roared,
kicking us each in turn. "Talk, or I'll shoot you
in the head."

"They're too sick to talk," said the *kapo*, but
the officer continued to test us, his heavy boot
rolling us around like sacks.

I closed my eyes, holding my blanket
tightly around me. What if a feverish comrade
cries out in Hungarian?

"Let the swine rot in their own filth,"
roared the SS at last, and off he went, cursing.

The *kapo* returned, radiant: "Thank God,
we're free of him!"

We spent the next two-and-a-half days neither
as prisoners nor free. The Germans had fled,
but the Americans hadn't come yet. The *kapo* let
us go upstairs, where we found some fancy con-
serves in a small cupboard formerly reserved for
the SS: roast pork, goose liver pate, and sardines.
We thought it may be our last chance to eat
well, so we gorged ourselves on the rich fare.
No wonder we spent the whole night expelling
it from both ends.

Freedom came on the third day, not in
the shape of a victorious army—with drums
and generals as we had dreamt—but in the
person of a dusty American telephone opera-
tor. We rushed out as he appeared on the
road, a tiny uniformed form on a motorcycle.
The Polish girls pulled him off the seat and
hugged him from all sides, but we stood by,
trying to take it in.

"You girls just wait," he protested with a
flushed face. "Thousands more will pour in
tomorrow. Please excuse me; I must fix some
telephone wires." The next moment, he vanished like an apparition we had dreamt.

The following day, 20 April 1945, we were
officially freed, but were still too dazed to fully
appreciate it. The Americans moved us into a
second-rate hotel in one of Leipzig's half-
bombed-out districts. The nine of us Hungarian
Jews were given rooms along the same corridor,
Mother, Magda, and I sharing a triple. After a
nourishing meal, mother lay down, thankful for

a real bed, and so did our sick comrades. Only Magda and I decided to go out. "For heaven's sake, don't get lost!" mother fretted as we embraced her.

The German soldiers had fled, the civilians hid. The main thoroughfares were completely taken over by motorized American troops, tossing cigarettes and Hershey bars at the throngs of liberated slaves who shouted and sang in a cacophony of tongues. All of Europe seemed represented.

"It's a veritable tower of Babel!" Magda shook her head. "I can hardly believe this."

The truth was, I could hardly believe it either. I wished we could be with our Lichtenau comrades, or in Kaposvár, with family and friends, instead of with this wildly celebrating mob whose speech often seemed foreign to me.

I answered Magda with something like: "Don't you just love it though?" and I spun her around, until she laughed, helplessly: "Enough, enough! You make me dizzy."

"Look," I flapped my arms, feeling more relaxed and happy, "I think I could swim up into the air! We're free! Really free!" Magda soon caught the fever, and we sang and danced, blending into the ecstatic mob.

In May the three women move in with some Hungarian Jewish women in Markleeberg, five kilometers from Leipzig. There, Jutka meets the man she will soon marry, a Jewish American captain named Irving Isaacson. A graduate of Harvard Law School, he brings Jutka to his home in Maine, U.S.A., where she eventually becomes Dean of Students at Bates College.

In 1977 she returns to Kaposvár with her daughter, Ilona, named for her childhood friend. Together they find Dr. Biczó's grave in the Catholic cemetery.

Reading the inscription on the black iron cross, Ilona remarked: "Dr. Biczó died in 1945, I see. Another war victim?"

"In a way, yes." Placing a smooth, round pebble among the rest [of the stones on the grave], I straightened up with a sigh: "Let's get back to our hotel, Ilona. Enough cemeteries."

As we descended into the sunset, Ilona turned to me: "Tell me about Dr. Biczó. What happened to him?"

"A good man," I mused, "I used to think him one of the best. Do you know what Sári Móritz just told me? Dr. Biczó died of sorrow over his martyred students. Very melodramatic, isn't it? Unfortunately, there's another version. The night before last, a childhood acquaintance told me in Budapest that Dr. Biczó drank himself into the grave— haunted by a bad conscience."

"A bad conscience?"

"Apparently, soon after our transport left for Auschwitz, Dr. Biczó was called to military duty and placed in charge of a Jewish forced-labor unit. His men were eventually transported to a German concentration camp, but after the war, a single survivor returned to Kaposvár. He claimed that Dr. Biczó had been a harsh Kommandant, cruel when drunk and frequently drunk."

"Do you believe that? It's hearsay from a single witness."

"With a survival rate of 5 percent, how can there be many witnesses? Dr. Biczó liked his wine, that much I know, and being in charge of a forced-labor camp does harden a person."

"Suppose it's true about Dr. Biczó. Could you forgive him?"

"Had I stayed a *kapo*'s helper at Auschwitz, could I forgive myself? You know, of all the things I lost during the war, I wish I had Plato's *Gorgias* still. Dr. Biczó had underlined a quote by Socrates in black ink: 'It is better to suffer an injustice than to commit one.' Perhaps this prompted me to quit assisting the *kapo* at Auschwitz."

"Where did Dr. Biczó die? In Kaposvár?"

"Yes, that much is clear. And everyone agrees that he was despondent in the summer of 1945. Most of his Jewish students had been killed; he must have mourned them. Then came the report about Marika Erdos—his all-time favorite. When he heard it, Dr. Biczó collapsed of a heart attack. My classmates insist that he died on Eszterházy Street, in front of the girls' *gimnazium* of Kaposvár."

"Marika Erdos? The girl who lent you her Hungarian costume? What happened to her?"

"Raped and killed."

"Was she Jewish?"

"According to the Nazis, she was—although her parents had converted before Marika was born. But she escaped Auschwitz. In the spring of 1944, Marika was attending the University of Budapest…"

"Budapest Jews weren't all taken," Ilona remembered. "The Russian invasion interfered, didn't it?"

"Yes, but Jewish girls were still being transported—directly to the Russian front. Marika escaped that ordeal as well: university friends hid her in an attic."

"Like Anne Frank."

"In a way, yes, but Marika was never discovered. The day the Russians liberated Budapest, Marika was among the first to venture into the streets. The capital was in tumult, drunken troops everywhere, hardly any women in sight. Marika was raped and shot on the bank of the Danube."

"Oh, no!"

We were climbing toward the peak now, panting hard; upper Main Street seemed steeper than when I used to coax my two-wheeler up by its handlebars. On the crest, we stopped to rest. A brick-red sun perched on the horizon, illuminating Kaposvár's rooftops, just as I remembered them.

I was still projecting Marika Erdos's image with the flowing brown hair and the full breasts I had envied, when Ilona softly said: "Thousands of women were raped during the war, but no one hears about them."

"The Anne Franks who survived rape don't write their stories."

"Will you?"

"I've already finished one chapter, Ilona. After this trip, I know I'll go on. I seem to owe it to the dead."

"You owe it the living," Ilona suggested.

In July 1978, I revisited Auschwitz with my son, John Magyar Isaacson, and his wife. We spent a day inspecting the place, and I was able to get some specific information.

Most important, I found out why some of my own recollections differed from the accounts I had read. Our transport was among the last ones to come from Hungary on 8 July 1944, and due to the unusual number of arrivals, the SS were forced to change their customary procedures. The gas chambers and crematoria couldn't accommodate everyone judged unfit for work, so hundreds were piled along the railroad tracks to be immolated—just as I had feared.

It was due to this heartless haste that we were housed in half-finished barracks, clothed in rags, marked with a painted red cross instead of wearing prisoners' garb, and provided with hardly any food or water. It was also due to this haste that we escaped tattooing.

While visiting the Auschwitz museum, John asked our young Polish guide to tell us something about Birkenau, Lager B III-b. This prompted a memorized paragraph she uttered in a Polish lilt:

"Lager B III-b used to be called 'Mexico' by the other inmates. It was the poorest of the poor. No food, no water. No one survived there for more than three weeks."

John said softly, as he glanced at me: "This is my mother. In the summer of 1944, she spent three weeks in Lager B III-b."

Mutely, the young girl stared at me as if I were some ghost. At last she muttered, shaking her head: "I don't know right words. Pleased to meet you."

"Pleased to be alive," I nodded.

Discussion Questions: **Judith Magyar Isaacson**

1. Dr. Biczó gave Jutka a copy of Plato's *Gorgias*. What was her favorite line in it? What did the passage mean to her?

2. What happens to Jutka's bond with her mother as their hardships at the hands of the Nazis become too much to bear? Could your relationship with your mother survive what Isaacson, her mother, and her aunt survived?

3. How do you think the Germans rationalized their treatment of the Jews? Religion can be used as the basis of communal justice and peace, in the way Gandhi used Hinduism and Martin Luther King, Jr., used Christianity. How can religion also be used to tear down communities and perpetuate injustice and unthinkable horror?

4. Commentators have remarked on the alleged "passivity" of the Jews in the camps. What do you think they mean?

5. In Elie Wiesel's autobiographical account of the Holocaust titled *Night* (New York: Avon Books, 1969), Wiesel witnesses the death by hanging of a young child. When someone behind him whispers "Where is God?" Wiesel finds himself answering that God is there, in that child, dying. Do you think Isaacson would agree with Wiesel's answer? Why or why not?

6. Some have said that the Holocaust is a problem for Jewish theology, that no Jew ought to be able to believe in God after God failed to rescue his "chosen people." Do you think this is true? Do you think it is true only for Jews, or does the Holocaust affect every religious community that claims to believe in God? Is the Holocaust a problem for Christian theology?

7. Could religious community be possible even after giving up belief in an all-loving and all-powerful God? Is it possible for *anyone* to believe in God after God's apparent silence during the mass destructions of the 1940s?

Samuel Heilman

From *The Gate Behind the Wall* by Samuel Heilman. © 1984 by Samuel Heilman. Reprinted by permission of Georges Borchardt, Inc., for the author.

I hold that each man has a self, and enlarges his self by his experiences. That is, he learns from experience: from the experiences of others as well as his own, and from their inner experiences as well as their outer. But he can learn from their inner experience only by entering it, and that is not done merely by reading a written record of it. We must have the gift to identify ourselves with other men, to relive their experience.

—J. Bronowski

Study the Torah again and again, for everything is contained in it; constantly examine it, grow old and gray over it, and swerve not from it, for there is nothing more excellent than it.

—Ben Bag-Bag

Generation after generation, the Jewish people have repeated a story, recounting events that took place nearly two thousand years ago, when around the city of Jerusalem, in which the Holy Temple stood, Roman legions camped and laid a siege from which the Jews could not escape. Some Jews, the zealots, or *biryoni,* looked upon this siege as opportunity. They would not wait the months and years the full stores of food allowed and set about at once to prepare for a battle they fully believed they could win. They burned the stores, in hopes that by that act the spirits of their fellows would be fired to bring about the glorious war in which the pious few could triumph over the mighty infidel. The Holy Temple would never fall; Jerusalem would stand forever.

Within the city was a man—Rabbi Yochanan ben Zakkai—who did not share this vision. He looked upon the *biryoni* as too much attached to earth and stone. For him the Temple, holy as it was, had already fallen; the Jerusalem of this world was on the edge of ruin. For his people to ascend from it, another gateway had to be found. But first he had to find a way out of the earthly city. At every gate *biryoni* stood guard. They meant to keep everyone inside until the moment when fighting would erupt. Only the dead would be allowed to leave—for they had other places they could go.

"Take me out as a dead man," the rabbi said to his students. The word went out that the great sage had become ill, had grown worse, had died.

And when all Jerusalem thought the sage was gone, he called his students together and asked them to place him inside a casket. Eliezer, his greatest disciple, lifted his head while Yehoshua, another student, took his feet, and thus they carried him through the streets until at sunset they reached the gate behind the city wall.

"What is this?" asked Abba Sikra, leader of the zealots who barred the way.

"A dead man who is going to another world," the students answered. And then they added: "You know well the law that the dead may not be buried inside the city."

But the *biryoni* wanted to run their spears through the body to make certain the man was dead.

"Here lies the great sage Rabbi Yochanan ben Zakkai!" the students cried out. "Would you so dishonor the remains of such a man?"

So Abba Sikra relented and the gates were cracked open. Thus, Eliezer and Yehoshua carried the casket until they came near the camp of the Roman legion and its commander, Vespasian. There at last they opened the box. The rabbi arose and stood before the Roman.

"Hail and peace, O Emperor!" he greeted him. And as Vespasian watched the "dead" man come to life, the rabbi repeated his greeting: "Hail and peace, O Emperor!"

"I am not Emperor," Vespasian answered.

"But you shall be," the rabbi said, "for no one but a king could hope to conquer Jerusalem."

As they spoke, a messenger approached from Rome and told Vespasian their Emperor was dead and Rome decreed that he must lead the nation.

There is some dispute in Jewish tradition about what happened next, about who spoke and what was said. In every version of the tale, however, the conclusion is the same: Vespasian turned to the rabbi and said, "I leave from here and there shall come another who will take my place to lay this siege. But since you were the first who saw for me what I had not yet seen, I shall reward you with a single wish. What will it be?"

Again there is dispute about what next was said and what requested, what could be got and what could not. But in the end, as all agree, one plea was made and not rejected: "Give me Yavneh and its scholars."

Behind lay earth-and-stone Jerusalem, the one to which Abba Sikra and the *biryoni* had attached themselves. Its Temple could be burned, its holy vessels carried off, its inner sanctum desecrated. Not too far away in that same holy land sat Yavneh, a settlement in which dwelt men who plumbed the depths of scripture and of God's law, and here another temple was being built. But this was not a temple of the earthly regions; it was one in which the scholar was the priest, in which true service came through study, in which the Torah was the holy of holies. Here, the rabbi felt, the future Jerusalem lay.

The Temple fell, and earthly Jerusalem burned. The *biryoni* fought and lost. Some ran into the desert, to Masada, where once again the few would face the many and once again would lose. But the path Yochanan ben Zakkai had opened was still being traveled. Since his time, the road between the two Jerusalems had passed, for many Jews, through texts—between the lines of black on white, around the scriptures and their Talmudic interpretation. The Temple now was portable; the stones were words, the walls ideas—and nothing could destroy them.

Wherever groups of Jews gathered, they found their Yavneh and built their temple by forming a study circle—a *chavruse,* as it was called. And thus they reconstructed lost Jerusalem.

The great sage Rav said—and some say it was Rabbi Shmuel bar Marta: "Greater is the study of Torah than the building of the Holy Temple...."

I live in two worlds and have done so as long as I can remember. In one, I am attached to an eternal yesterday—a timeless faith and ritual, an ancient system of behavior. In that world, I am an Orthodox Jew. In my other world, there is little if any attachment to the enchantment of religion or sacred practice, and what is happening today or tomorrow matters far more than the verities embedded in the past. In that domain, I am a university professor of sociology.

To live in these opposing spheres I have often found it necessary to divide myself, placing different aspects of my character in different compartments. On Friday nights and sabbaths, during my daily prayers, in my home with my family, through the food that I eat and inside the synagogue, I have been attached to the Judaism of past generations, guiding my life by the strictest rules of behavior and belief. At other times and in other places, I have transformed myself into a modern man who tries to be a part of the contemporary society around him.

In order to carry on this double life, I find myself trying at times to forget one side of my identity while playing my other parts. Without this selective memory, this capacity to dim the lights in one room while I am in the other, I would have to teeter precariously on the edge of estrangement, never feeling quite at home in either of my two worlds.

I have thought at times of abandoning one of my two worlds in favor of the other, to be at last at one with myself. But each time I think of doing so, I recall the famous parable of the dove who, feeling the resistance of the wind in his feathers, dreamed he would fly better in a vacuum. And then I realize that for me there can be no such flight. Besides, I realize that each world has become more attractive to me by the possibility of life in the other.

Yet if for me compartmentalization is possible and sometimes even desirable, it is far from satisfying, for it forces upon me a kind of abiding denial of parts of my self, a walling up of experience and existence. So I, like many other modern Orthodox Jews, people who move between religious tradition and the secular present, have tried wherever possible to collapse the boundaries between these two worlds and find a way to make myself whole. This is the story of such an effort.

"Nu," as he looked at me, my local rabbi asked, "are you *lernen* at all? Do you ever pick up a *Gemara?"* He tapped the open volume of Talmud that he held in his hand as he spoke.

I shrugged my shoulders. For months since my move to his suburban New York community, he had been asking me this question at least every other week. Every time he reminded me of my Jewish obligation to *lern,* to ritually review the Talmud, I thought only of a book filled with archaic legalisms, implausible stories and arcane rabbinic debates that had never been able to capture my imagination.

Although we worshipped in the same place, the rabbi was not like me. However much he entered into contemporary life and values, he still could open up a holy book and spend his hours *lernen,* during which he turned away from present-day America and let himself pass into another time and place in which tradition was the master, in which the unrelenting past still reigned. Because he loved to wander in that tradition, he often sat beside the wall of the synagogue while waiting for his congregation to assemble for prayers and quietly read through a page of Talmud or some rabbinic commentary. And every now and then, if I was there early and waiting too, he'd call me over and try to take me with him through a piece of text. But while I sat with him and tried to follow along, more often than not I found the words blurring before my eyes and my mind wandering off to some other place and time.

For nearly a year I always answered his recurrent inquiry with a shrug. The rabbi knew that my world was the university, my special interest sociology, and that into this way of life the Talmud did not easily fit. Each time he asked his question, he'd look piercingly and unblinkingly into my eyes for just a moment, then finally shrug too and turn back to the book which, always open, lay there between us.

Throughout my years in the precincts of modern Orthodoxy, where people strive in principle to remain committed to the strictures of observant Judaism while remaining neither remote from nor untouched by contemporary society, I have been taught that however archaic various aspects of Jewish life and observance might seem, they can all be understood in ways that would make them sparkle in the light of contemporary life. There is nothing so old that it cannot be made part of the modern world, no tradition so ancient that it could not be made a living part of contemporary reality. The old can be made new. Not only that, but the modern world is not so radically new that one could not find its reflection in the past. The new can be made holy.

The task of reconciling the old and the new has not been easy. Few rabbis or religious leaders I found around me could or would help. The norm has seemed to me to be "Every man for himself"; and so I have slowly—not always successfully—been weaving my way between modernity and Orthodoxy, trying to find a way to make of my life a single tapestry. But in that fabric, an important Jewish thread, one that ran through thousands of years of my people's history, was for a long time still missing. I had not found a way to study Torah.

Of all that Judaism values, nothing is more highly treasured than the study of Torah, the great sacred literature whose core is the Bible and whose mantle is the Talmud.

Talmud. In Hebrew, the word means "study," the teachings that one acquires from his predecessors. But the Talmud is more: a multivolumed compilation of ancient rabbinic debate and commentary—the *Gemara*—about an oral tradition—the *Mishna*—which the faithful believe was first revealed at Sinai. Filled with narrative and legal disputation, it is a somewhat cryptic and not altogether systematic record of oral discussions that took place in the first-century academies of Jewish learning in Palestine and later, between the third and fifth centuries, in Babylonia, which, following the exile, became the new center of diaspora Jewish life. There, scholars reviewed the legal pathways of Jewish life—the *halacha*—while they explored custom, belief, folkways and history through homily and narrative—the *aggada*. And over the centuries since then, Jews have tried to repeat that process. At home, in the synagogue study hall—the *bes medresh*—in the academy of Jewish learning—the *yeshiva*—they would gather to recite and review the Talmud, the great repository of rabbinic and Jewish wisdom.

Since the Talmud contains not only rabbinic discussion but also citations of scripture, laws and legends, review of it can be said to subsume all of Jewish sacred literature. It rests upon and above all other holy books. And those scholars who have deciphered its logic and fathomed its wisdom likewise sit at the pinnacle of Jewish learning.

I was never one of those scholars. Unlike many Orthodox Jews, I could not luxuriate inside a page of Talmud or rabbinic commentary. Nor could I connect with its logic or see beyond its apparently parochial concerns. The arguments it put forth and the situations it described had always seemed too far away from the world I inhabited and the concerns in my life. To join with others in the review of a most sacred Jewish text, the great Oral Law, the Talmud was something unappealing. The text's concern with the minutiae of law, its tele-graphic style and tortured prose, the compli-cated and often unbelievable legends and endless reinterpretations of ancient biblical verses had never worked their magic on me. Scriptures were important—and I had long ago learned to appreciate at least their narrative portions and homilies—but throughout my years as a young boy in the *yeshiva,* I had found Talmud opaque at best and sometimes even boring. I simply could not understand its appeal for so many of my fellow Jews, both present and past.

Many of those Jews still inhabit parts of the Orthodox world in which I dwell. For them, what is often called in the Yiddish vernacular *"lernen"*—a term freighted with Jewish history and attachments to living sacred texts—has always appeared to me to be a gate whereby they enter the life of piety and awe. These are people who come to the holy books not so much to exercise their intellect as to express their devotion and attachment to a God whose revealed word they believe the books contain. These traditionalists have always seemed able—at least temporarily—to find ways of escaping the claims of modernity by involving them-selves in Talmud. For them the best questions are those the tradition has already asked and answered, and the most touching narratives are those everyone already knows. For them, the past is master.

Although I could not bring myself to join these people who plant themselves around a holy text, I knew—and was reminded by those around me who celebrate the traditional Orthodox Jewish way of life and *lernen*—the review of the holy words and ancient ideas is, after all, an activity associated with the heart

> **My earliest memories were of a Jewish world where prayer was a daily occurrence and where the Torah remained the single most important source of illumination.**
>
> **In the natural order of my Jewish life, a man was not complete— was not a man— if he abandoned his obligation to *lern.***

of my religion. My earliest memories were of a Jewish world where prayer was a daily occur-rence and where the Torah—the central organiz-ing element of our religion—and all it symbol-ized remained the single most important source of illumination. Throughout my life, therefore, I believed I had to wait until I would be ready to penetrate that experience.

In the meantime, however, I entered the university and found another way of life to embrace. Charmed by the cultural riches of Western civilization and its spirit of free inquiry, which as a boy I had seen only from an Orthodox Jewish distance, I began in college to find an intellectual home outside the Orthodox Jewish world. Secular learning, with its seemingly limitless reach, was much more appealing than the theologically limited scholarship of the *yeshiva* or ritual study of the synagogue study hall.

I became attracted to the social sciences, to anthropology and sociology. As my religious parents and grandparents had spent hours over holy books, I spent my time reading the classics of social science, trying to discover through them the meaning people gave to their lives and the ways they exhibited their character. Gradually, my Jewish library—the holy books I had been collecting since my *bar mitzvah* in hopes that I might someday penetrate them and discover their value for me—became pushed aside by the literature of my new discipline. Where volumes of Judaica had once sat, I now placed books by the giants in my field: Franz Boas, Emile Durkheim, Erving Goffman, Margaret Mead, and Max Weber. My shelves still contained holy books like *Ethics of the Fathers* and *The Code of Jewish Law,* the great moral and legal compass of Jewish tradition; but more often than not it was my teacher Erving Goffman's seminal studies *The Presentation of Self in Everyday Life* and *Behavior in Public Places* that I took in hand to study and peruse. While my way of life remained that of Orthodox Judaism, my career became sociology. Both background and career made their claims upon me, and thus I made my way between the particular demands of each. My heart and home were Jewish, but my mind and work became more and more caught up in the thicket of my academic discipline.

Culture embedded in the lives of people all around me, more than ancient sacred texts, was what I devotedly tried to read. The creations of humanity and the rules of social behavior rather than the machinations of God or religious law aroused my interest. The ancient sacred prov-inces of Judaism—the universe of the Talmud—seemed increasingly distant and limited. They described a world that hardly seemed real. Laws concerning ancient Temple sacrifices, disputations about whose ox gored whom or tales of humble scholars and brilliant rabbis were hardly of concern to a young intellectual—even an Orthodox one. It was sociology and anthropology I wanted and felt an obligation to study, not the venerable holy books of my people.

Quietly, I sometimes attempted to forget about trying to penetrate the world of the Talmud and *lernen.* I sought instead to sing the tune of the times and be in harmony with the contemporary world. The singsong of *Gemara lernen* was dissonant with that aim; it seemed to shift one inescapably into the past. Laboring through Talmud pages or sitting with men who reviewed them endlessly seemed to me a drag on my movement into the present and its surroundings.

But even after college I could not forget about *lernen.* The competing authorities of my social science were insufficient, their vision flawed by an almost obstinate flight from all truths. A capacity to observe all life from some neutral, objective distance and the celebration of cultural relativity, while perhaps useful for scientists, could not replace the Jewish world completely. It did not provide me with a spiritual anchor. One might live *on* sociology and anthropology, but to me it seemed impossible to live *for* them. A person needed more. Besides, I knew that in the natural order of my Jewish life, a man was not complete—was not a man—if he forever abandoned his obligation to *lern.* However modern I might be, I was still attached to that sacred duty. If I did not engage in *lernen* it was not because I summarily rejected its legitimacy. I just did not know how I could make that old way of study fit into my new frame of mind....

When early in my career I had chosen to investigate and document my own Orthodox synagogue life, I had done so believing that as

an insider I could supply, through both intro-
spection and a sense of the relevant questions
to ask, information about dimensions of inner
life not readily available to other researchers. I
argued in sociology journals and before academic audiences that by doing this I would be
able to give a fuller picture of the synagogue
than could any outsider, however well prepared
and trained he might be.

I did not plan to write about the synagogue
out of any religious sensibility—or so I led
myself to believe at the outset. I simply chose a
setting I knew best, one I could sociologically
exploit and expertly describe. But to accomplish
this, I spent more time in the synagogue than
ever before in my life and in the process
discovered more of its meaning for me than I
had ever imagined possible at the outset. And
when I had finished my book, I realized that the
double pattern of my life had repeated itself
in my work: I had found my way back into the
traditional synagogue from my new home in
the university via the tools of my social science.
At the same time that I had pursued my vocation, I had been able to bring together the two
worlds I inhabited. Participant-observation was,
at least in part, for me yet another expression of
my modern Orthodoxy.

But *lernen* still remained outside my reach
and beyond the capacities of my profession—
or so I thought until one Friday night when my
rabbi inquired, as usual, about my *lernen.*

I had come to the Friday-evening synagogue
service quite early, and no one else except the
rabbi was there. As always, he sat over an open
book. Seeing me walk in, he called me over to
sit beside him as he *lernt* a page of Talmud. The
long, thick columns, the boldface letters told a
tale he thought I knew.

"It bears *lernen,*" he explained, and he
proceeded to review the familiar history of
Yochanan ben Zakkai. For some reason—
perhaps it was the dramatic way the rabbi read
the text or the story he recounted—my mind

was held at attention that evening as I listened
to him and followed his finger down the page.

The narrative over, the rabbi looked up
from the text and, with the book still open,
began to recount the history of Jewish study. He
told me how for some, study became vocation—
rabbis, *yeshiva* students, scholars. Others, like
me, immersed in other pursuits, injected the
review of the sacred texts into the ebb and flow
of their lives. Evenings, in the morning after
praying, at the sabbath table, they would by
way of *lernen* enter, for a time, the holy regions.
The Book became the entrance to the temple,
the study of it worship. The rabbis and the sages
all agreed: "The study of Torah excels all." No
Jew could hope to find salvation except by
climbing out of the exile of ignorance and into
the redemptive light of *lernen.* Study was no
longer the practice just of scholars but was for
everyone a lifetime mission.

Said Rabbi Yochanan ben Zakkai: "If you
have *lernt* much Torah, do not claim credit for
yourself, because you were created for this
purpose."

"But the Torah," said the sages, echoing
scripture, "is not in heaven." And they added:
"Great is the study of Torah, for it gives to those
who do it life in this world and in the world
to come."

For the rabbis, scripture—the written word
of God—was just the beginning. The Talmud—
the great collection of rabbinic commentary
and scholarship, the written repository of the
oral tradition—was its completion, the source
of real wisdom, the Book that had preserved
and protected the Jewish people since the
destruction of the Holy Temple and the exile
that followed.

The move from scripture to Talmud is an
ascent to the higher regions of wisdom. This
journey could be made alone by those who had
skill and dedication. The rabbis of the Talmud,
however, had encouraged study in a group.
"The words of the Torah cannot be sustained by

the solitary individual," the sages asserted. Members of the *chavruse*—the study circle—could help one another reach the heights. Sitting down together over the long pages and working their way through narrative and debate, they open up a way that leads through tales and conversation to what once was and can still be the heavenly Jerusalem.

"*Nu?*" my rabbi ended, and held my eyes as tightly as he could.

I said nothing.

He took a deep breath. "Look, you told me many times that you're a sociologist whose method is participant-observation—you learn by watching while doing."

I nodded.

"*Nu,* so go do some participant-observation among those who *lern.* Find your way into a *chavruse.* Discover Yavneh and its scholars. Build a new Jerusalem."

For days I thought a lot about his story, about the centrality of Jewish study in Jewish life and about my own work. The rabbi had told me nothing new, but still there'd been something in his tone, his challenge to me to take my discipline and apply it to my Jewish world, that struck a sympathetic chord. Perhaps I could use my discipline to beat a path to *lernen.*

The idea of me, a modern Orthodox Jew and social anthropologist, observing and participating in *lernen,* a way of life at once foreign and familiar, began increasingly to capture my imagination. The dual character of the project was appealing; it fitted neatly into the pattern of my life and work. I'd do again what I had done already in the synagogue. I would enter an experience, identify with those who *lernt,* in hopes that this might finally reveal to me and others what so attracted those who did it but eluded me still. Besides, I felt a lingering Jewish obligation to try once more to reach the Torah's heights. This double motivation upon a dualistic man was just enough to move me forward into *lernen.*

I was due for a sabbatical; I had been seeking a research project to fill that time. Now I had one: to examine at first hand the study of Talmud and the people who engage in it....

For a time, I wandered into Talmud classes at a number of local synagogues. But as I tried to attend to turns of logic and Talmudic reasoning, I got hopelessly lost and frustrated. I could still not connect what I was hearing with what I already knew. So I focused my attention on matters of language and interaction. The approach was strictly sociological. Yet while this approach allowed me to analyze the way in which the Jews I observed studied their sacred texts, it did not allow me to enter into the experience, to participate fully, to share their states of being. I needed to go elsewhere.

"There are ten portions of wisdom in the world," said the sages, "nine in Jerusalem and one in the rest of the world."

No place seemed better for the effort than where it had all begun so long ago. Besides, I had never been to Israel and thought that as a Jew who sought to enter the heart of a Jewish experience I ought to go to the spiritual center of the Jewish people. Over the centuries, the spirit of Yavneh had found a home in the Holy Land. And so at last we went—my wife and sons and I—up to Jerusalem.

"The earthly Jerusalem that sits atop Zion," said the ancient Talmudic sage Rabbah in the name of his teacher Rabbi Yochanan, "is not like the heavenly Jerusalem. Into the Jerusalem of this world all who wish to ascend may ascend; but into the heavenly Jerusalem only the invited may ascend and enter."

While only invitations may get one through the gates of the heavenly Jerusalem, a walk along its earthly avenues and alleys allows at least a glimpse of that other reality. For weeks, I wandered through the city to get a feel for what it was. A stream of images washed over me, and even now those visions come back to me with all the freshness of a first impression.

Inside a sleek and streamlined bus that winds its way through the contemporary, western side of the city, a friar in sackcloth robe sits. Amid the sound and rhythm of the modern world, his quiet solitude seems somehow still unbroken. Along a downtown street awash in shoppers and tourists, a hooded, black-draped figure floats silently past: an Armenian monk with headdress shaped like his holy Mount Ararat is on his way back to his monastery. Behind a small and faceless door beside the city's outdoor market, a group of pious Jews with bearded faces and wiry earlocks reviews an ancient sacred text through which they glimpse another place, another time. Their voices rise and fall in special cadences; their dialogue puts life into immemorial words. In a corner of the busy central bus station, as people rush to make their connections, a dark-skinned Yemenite Jew sits and quietly recites the Psalms from a shredded little book he holds in hand, his body slowly swaying back and forth.

A walk or drive toward the east and there, inside it all, surrounded by its modern counterpart, the aged city sits, a vision of that other time and other place. Behind its ancient walls, where those who dwell in higher regions may easily feel at home, are other faces, other rooms. Some anchor one to here and now and some to the hereafter. Through one of seven gates inside its ageless golden walls, left and up neglected stairs, across the alley from the Arab souk filled with eager shoppers and shrewd or enterprising merchants who offer every earthly pleasure, one comes up onto the roof of the Church of the Holy Sepulcher. There, in eerie silence, appears a little village of Ethiopian monks who keep a vigil in this holy place. The one-room adobe huts in which they dwell are closed from view. In a small green wooden door, a tiny window through which the passerby may glance reveals a little cot and a cross upon the wall. And in the

courtyard stands a small black man. He leans against a green wrought-iron railing, his arms draped around the banister in what seems a loving embrace. He smiles and lets the visitor inside the tiny chapel he must guard. And there the other time and other place can once again be seen—this time more clearly than before—but still not entered uninvited.

The bells of nearby churches begin to toll, and suddenly cassocks appear; doors open and once again are closed. And through it all, the *mu'azzin* calls and lines of Moslems begin to form as people make their way five times each day to worship in the place from which Mohammed ascended into heaven. The one Jerusalem increasingly intrudes upon the other.

Around another corner is a door, and then an alley. Turn left and right, then turn once again and climb, and there another crossroads between the heaven and the earth. Here is a Jerusalem that is more than simply a place on the map. Here is the embodiment of an idea, a symbol of a glorious past and hopes for the future. El Aqsa and its silver dome sits atop the mountain from which Mohammed left for heaven, on which the Holy Temple of the Jews once stood and where, before it all, Abraham bound Isaac and prepared to send him to another place far different from the one he knew.

The Holy Temple is long gone. Destroyed at first by Babylonians and then rebuilt and burned again, this time by Romans, who left only the outer walls, half crumbling—against which now the Jews, returned, still whisper prayers and pause within their daily lives to get a glimpse of holiness. Between the cracks are notes with names and quoted lines of scripture that those on earth have sent to God in hopes that through this little act of piety they'll keep the gates of heaven slightly open and let their spirit rise on through. For those who press their faces against the ancient stones, the object of their prayers is a passage to the heavenly

Jerusalem whose gates mirror those of the earthly one.

A Jew once steeped in this tradition, I stood for many hours before this holy place. While staring at the sacred stones and those who seek an entry into heaven there, I could not but think of Jews who raise themselves by other means. For them neither prayers nor acts of special piety at venerable walls lead the way to higher regions, but rather meditation and review of hallowed books. That way, as I already knew, had begun with Yochanan ben Zakkai, who led his people from crumbling holy stones to sacred books and learning, a path that in some way I stood ready to follow.

Gazing out one morning at the Old City, with its impressive walls and imposing history, I realized that while its temporal gates were easy enough to find, it might be quite a bit harder to discover the gateways to *lernen* and gain entry into a *chavruse*. To follow in the steps of Yochanan ben Zakkai, who had made Torah study the great new edifice of Jewish life, I supposed I had to begin at the Temple Mount and then come away from its relic remains to the living temple that had been created in the world of Jewish study. Where once the sound of sheep going to the slaughter on the Temple Mount must have filled the air, the voices of Jews reviewing their sacred texts could now be heard through the windows of the *yeshivas* and houses of learning that dotted the Jewish Quarter of the city.

To reach that quarter, I walked from where I stood on a hill on the western side of the valley toward the ancient walls on the other side. Those walls were relics of generations past. Buried by centuries of debris, they had been uncovered by the Jews who had gained control over them in 1967. What archeologists had discovered was that each new ruler of the city had built his walls on or near the remains of the previous walls. There one could find two-

thousand-year-old Herodian stones mixed in with older Hasmonean blocks and next to Crusader bricks, all of which were used anew by Turks in the sixteenth century. In the ramparts of the Old City of Jerusalem, time had been shredded and history rewoven. Old walls made new through a process of uncovering seemed the right metaphor for my own quest.

I walked through the Jaffa Gate, the busiest and in many ways most imposing entrance, and turned southward, shuffling through the sea of cultures in the square inside. Behind me now were the Arab Christians whose homes spread out around the Via Dolorosa and the Church of the Holy Sepulcher. On the left I would pass the Armenians, who, living within the walls of a monastery that closed its gates at nine each evening, tended to keep very much to themselves. Between these two quarters was an eddy of tourists from the West and Moslems on their way in to the bazaars on David Street that served as a kind of spine down this backside of the city. And just beyond the Armenians and ending at the Western Wall, the last remaining structure of the Holy Temple that once had stood where a golden-domed Mosque now did, was the Jewish Quarter, where I hoped my entrance into the heavenly Jerusalem, the way of *lernen,* could be found.

Like all of the Old City, the Jewish Quarter is a maze of narrow streets and alleys, many of which have names that resonate scripture, Talmud and Jewish history. Inside, the combination of the foreignness of the surroundings and the familiarity of the names made me at once anxious about continuing and reluctant to turn around and leave. Perhaps it was all those years of repeating in my prayers that Jewish longing for Jerusalem, perhaps simply the lure of the new; maybe it was the sound of Hebrew that echoed from the windows of the quarter and the steady rise-fall cadences of Talmud study that I heard when I passed near the doorway of Yeshivat ha-Kotel. Whatever the source of my attraction, the result was an undeniable desire to move further and further into the heart of this Jewish part of the city.

Crossing a large square near Yeshivat ha-Kotel, the Talmudic academy set up almost in the shadow of the Temple Mount, I found myself walking along a street called simply "Rechov ha-Yehudim"—Street of the Jews. To my right was a small sign that marked the entrance to a "Chabad House," one of the outposts of the Lubavitch Hasidic movement. Lubavitch, with its rebbe, or charismatic leader, Rabbi Menachem Schneerson of Brooklyn, was one of the few groups of Hasidim that enthusiastically greeted Jewish seekers, one of whom—like it or not—I had in a way become. And "ChaBaD" was the acronym for *chachma* (wisdom), *bina* (understanding) and *da'at* (knowledge)—the three great rungs of Jewish study that Lubavitch had taken as its motto. I thought therefore that here was a place where I might find the way in—if not to *lernen* then perhaps to wisdom, understanding or knowledge.

Opening the door, I entered a small courtyard from which led other doors on all four sides. In a corner was a stone staircase leading to the sound of voices engaged in study. But these were the young voices of *yeshiva* boys reviewing their texts—not the sort of circle I was prepared to enter. So rather than ascending the stairs, I went instead toward the left and what appeared to be a rather large office.

It was late morning, and most of the place was empty. There were some pamphlets and holy books lying about, and I picked them up to get an idea of who visited this place. The booklets were in English and French and were filled with what could best be called advertisements for God—pitches pushing the observance of those commandments which the Rebbe had decided were the key to getting Jews back onto the proper religious path. For women there was a little booklet about the importance of lighting

the sabbath candles and for the men one on why and how to don *t'filin*—phylacteries.

The holy books were something else. These were for those who had already been persuaded of the value of a traditional life and wanted to plumb its spiritual depths. Here was a copy of the *Tanya*, a collection of the wisdom of the founder of ChaBaD, filled with homilies, moral teachings and epigrams about scripture and Jewish mystical texts. And then, of course, there were some volumes of Bible and Talmud.

Heilman is not interested in studying in the formal, institutional setting of the Lubavitch school, so the next day he goes to a synagogue in the Jerusalem neighborhood of Shaarey Chesed, where he finds "a group of people for whom Jewish study was as much a part of their lives as eating and sleeping." Walking through a corridor and by a study table, Heilman enters the bes medresh, *the room devoted to study and prayer. Other men, their heads covered with the traditional* yarmulke, *are seated at a table: Reb Tuvia, who wears a Stetson; Moishe, who talks to himself; Yaakov and Zeesel, who rarely say anything; and the teacher, who claps his hands to let everyone know that it is time for* ma'ariv, *or evening prayers.*

When it seemed that everyone was ready to pray, one last man would usually wander in. In his late sixties, shaped a bit like a down-filled pillow and wearing a beard that was streaked with gray, he walked languorously toward the front of the room and sat down along the eastern wall, the place reserved for the most honored among the worshipers. To the uninformed he might have seemed to be wearing a bathrobe and slippers. I had, however, long ago learned that this was the garb worn by the well-dressed traditional Jewish scholar. His "robe" was a brocaded gray caftan, or *kapote*, which indicated a certain noble character. His slippers were the shoes only a scholar who did not spend his day at manual labor or in the world outside the *bes medresh*

He could make the biblical Joseph

into a contemporary of everyone in the room

and then just as easily sweep

all of us gathered around him back into time

and into a narrative that dripped with

memories of a Jewish world that seemed to

have perished in the fires of Nazi Europe.

could wear. As he passed through the room, others stood or leaned forward, and when he reached his place, I saw the *gabbai* nod a signal to the man who would lead us in prayer to commence. And now everyone stood to bow—this time to the holy Ark and not to any mortal—as the *ma'ariv* began.

Later, I would learn that this man for whom we had apparently been waiting was "the Maggid," known throughout Jerusalem as one of the last who still kept up the tradition of true preaching. On sabbath afternoons he would hold court in this same room, which was then filled to the walls, and would review the portion of the week, weaving into it a variety of homilies and visions, stories and parables. He could, for example, make the biblical Joseph into a contemporary of everyone in the room and then just as easily sweep all of us gathered around him back into time and into a narrative that dripped with memories of a Jewish world that seemed to have perished in the fires of Nazi Europe. It did not matter whether or not one had actually seen that world for himself, for

under the spell of the Maggid one could see it with all the nostalgia of personal reminiscence.

He was a master storyteller, an actor who animated his stories with heart-cries of "Oy-yoy" that could make even the most hardened cosmopolitan into a parochial who yearned for the world of the *bes medresh* and a past that was part of the traditional Jewish consciousness he thought he had long ago abandoned.

The Maggid sat somewhere between his audience and his own imagination. Sometimes I could notice one eye closed and the other carefully watching for the reactions of those who waited on his every word. But this performance was not simply some cynical effort to dazzle those around him. It seemed, rather, a display of the division in the Maggid's being. On the one side—the one on which his eye was open—he was attached to the people he could see before him, trying to satisfy their craving for a spiritual and Jewish experience. But on the other—the side of his closed eye—he looked inward and from thence upward to heaven. Only here he seemed to find the source for what the outer world brought forth from his mouth. It was a complicated business, and often it set him to swaying back and forth or nodding his head up and down, as if he were being simultaneously buffeted and pulled by the concerns of this world and the other.

He did not just tell his stories: he literally sang them. Sometimes he would stop at some particular word that charmed him and repeat it in a variety of voices and melodies until everyone seemed as lost in and fascinated by it as he. It was always a masterly performance, and often I would walk out not quite sure precisely what he had said—but all the same deeply impressed by having heard him say it. In this I was clearly not alone.

"How beautifully he speaks," I once heard someone say. Clearly a part of this experience was aesthetic as much as anything else. Perhaps this was what was meant when people referred to him as a *"shayner Yid"*—a beautiful Jew.

Now, however, as I stood in the small synagogue surrounded by weekday worshipers, I did not yet know about the sabbath talks. Instead, I simply paid attention to what would happen next.

For a short while, everything seemed to proceed normally. The prayers were swiftly paced, as weekday services commonly are. But then we reached the *Kriyat Shma,* the recitation of the credo of faith that is perhaps the central article of Jewish prayer. It is composed of verses that appear throughout the Bible, and it is known by its electrifying opening line: "Hear O Israel, the Lord our God, the Lord is One." Recited originally, according to tradition, by Jacob's sons as they stood at his deathbed and promised him that they would follow in the faith of their father and his forebears Isaac and Abraham, it has become the single most memorable verse in the liturgy.

For this generation, it has perhaps additional resonances that emerge from a more recent deathbed. Millions died with these words on their lips as they stood before the Nazi killers

who sought to silence once and for all their cry and credo. Many of the men of Shaarey Chesed were survivors of the Nazi onslaught; others were their children and kin. When they intoned these ageless words, in the same accents and cadences as the generations before them, they overwhelmed time and brought back memories that all of us in the room—no matter our age or origin—shared.

Now, the custom of extending the intonation of this line is a long one. As one begins the words *"Shma Yisrael,"* one lifts a hand toward the eyes, which are covered, and calls aloud for all to hear that the Lord is one. One's own voice necessarily becomes caught up in that of others, and the call of those sitting nearby extends it.

I was used to this sort of devotional contagion. What I was unprepared for, however, was the intensity of the call that I heard tonight. Long minutes passed as each word of the *Shma* was cried out. And between each word—no, each syllable—and the next, there was a pause, as if the worshipers needed to rest and breathe and consider the philosophical possibilities of continuing.

Last among the voices I heard from behind my hand was a very deep one, a bass so profound it seemed less a product of the larynx than an echo of a sound deep within the chest cavity. It was the voice of the Maggid. When he paused, there was silence for a moment—as if everyone had to swallow hard before continuing; and then the congregation resumed the hum and murmur of their prayers as they completed the three paragraphs of the liturgy.

The prayer, which normally lasts less than five minutes, stretched out for closer to ten. Each man seemed intent on extending his time in the *Shma* beyond that of his neighbor, as if each were vying with the other for the attention of heaven. The sociologist in me suggested that the displays were for the benefit of partners in prayer, efforts to demonstrate a holier-than-thou commitment to liturgy. But the Jew in me wondered if perhaps these men were not in some way trying to shake their God into attentiveness. It was, after all, the slowest worshiper who could hold on to his Lord the longest.

I cannot say exactly which of these motives moved me. I do know that it was not long before I began to lose myself in prayer and recited these familiar words of the *Shma* with an attachment that I had not had since those days in grammar school when the first conscious motives of prayer invaded my adolescence. These feelings were now, however, more absorbing, for they arose, it seemed, out of the more secure consciousness of maturity. That I could still be so moved by old prayers was a surprise to me. To be sure, I had always told people that that was why I prayed. But now what had been simply a logical argument became a psychological reality. And the convergence of the two was startling and even unsettling.

Tonight, however, on my first night at Shaarey Chesed, my prayers were not yet ready for enthusiastic extension, and so I finished with plenty of time to spare. I looked around and listened to others. In the rush of my own prayers, it was something I did not often have a chance to do.

"Hishomru lochem..." Beware lest your heart be deceived, and then you turn and serve other gods and worship them; for then the Lord's anger will blaze against you, and he will shut up the skies so that there will be no rain.... These lines of prayer, at once familiar to me and yet somehow strange, seemed tonight to resonate with an authenticity I was not used to hearing. The men who spoke them inhabited a land that depended on rain, the land promised and described in what they recited. They could know when their prayers were or were not acceptable simply by looking out the window. Some did just that as they intoned that line.

But it was a different authenticity that struck me that night, for most of those I watched did not look for the rain or any other

sort of instant, divine quid pro quo. Instead, they seemed to dwell upon and within their prayers as if the very act of praying were sufficient fulfillment, even more important to them than any anticipated godly response.

It occurred to me then, as never before, that some people prayed not so much to their God as for themselves—for the transformative power of prayer itself. My own expectations of prayer seemed to have been caught at a very different stage. I still looked upon liturgy as a vehicle for requests from some divine Parent. And when I no longer believed that such requests were efficacious or even conceivable, I had ceased praying with devotion and continued mostly out of inertia and the hope that someday my prayers would once again become meaningful to me. But because I believed that forsaking the demands of tradition was far more dangerous than holding on to them—even if that meant that I carried out practices which were often opaque or even devoid of meaning for me— I had kept on praying....

Finally we reached the *Amida,* the silent prayer that is the climax of all Jewish liturgy. Each man stood with feet together, unmoving, and recited the nineteen blessings that make up this devotion. And then the men who stood in this room seemed at once indistinguishable one from another, for all were one with the house of prayer and with one another, seeming to me like a single standing mass. Then slowly, one by one, the murmured prayers ceased, and finally one solitary voice remained: the Maggid's. Then it too fell silent. And I shuddered; for at the moment when that prayer stopped, the spell was broken. A few men closed their books; a few began to chat with one another. Those whose faces had been moved in prayer became once again simple men. Although they still stood inside this little chapel, their faces once again had the profane and distracted look of men outside. And that subtle but unmistakable shift raised my involuntary shudder.

In a moment, the final *Kaddish* was recited and the men began to leave the room. A few stopped next to the Maggid and chatted. His erstwhile competitor, the self-effacing thin man, walked slowly to the bookcase and removed one of the largest books, opened it, seemed to read a brief passage and then replaced it on the shelf. Then he too quietly left the room.

I waited a few minutes, wondering if the room was ever completely abandoned. Now I noticed that the focus shifted from the pulpit in front toward a corner in the rear where a few of the men were moving some of the tables together to form an "L" shape. At the same time, a cherubic-looking little fat man walked toward these tables. I had not noticed him during the prayers, but now, as all those remaining greeted him, it became clear that if the Maggid and his congregation had been the heroes of the *ma'ariv* story, then this man, Rabbi Moses—as I later learned he was called— would be the center of a new drama that was about to begin in this room.

The *gabbai* also joined the group in the corner. Taking a moment to turn off all the lights in the room except for the two that illumined the corner, he next stepped to the bookcase in the back and took out seven volumes of the Talmudic tractate *Zevachim*. This was a text that dealt with the sacrifices that centuries earlier were brought by all believers who came to worship at the Holy Temple.

"Is there a *chavruse* here?" I asked him, although the answer was obvious.

"For the last sixty years, without exception," he answered. For that long had a group been gathering around these tables after the conclusion of *ma'ariv* to review the Talmud. No one of those present had been in the circle all that time, but each one could be linked to another who in turn was linked to someone else who ultimately was tied to one of the originators. Here was the great Jewish chain of being that begins with Moses at Sinai and runs through Joshua, the Elders, the Men of the Great Assembly and generations of others, finally reaching the countless little circles of Jews who continue to review a Torah they believe was once divinely revealed.

"May I join?"

"Please"—and with that I was motioned to sit next to the Rav, who asked me whence I came....

The nature of what we *lernt* was such that it denied continuing contact with the world outside the room as we knew it. Talking and reading about sacrifices no longer brought to a Holy Temple no longer standing was by no means easy for me at first; I had always been rather bored by those sections of the Bible in the book of Leviticus that described the order and detail of the priestly activities and sacrifice; so even had I been able to follow every nuance of the Yiddish with which my *chavruse* reviewed these matters, I would have been hard put to get it all straight. But for these men, all that was no problem. They threw themselves into the text and through it back into time. As we sat there in this little ground-floor chapel in Shaarey Chesed, we looked out not on the streets as they now were but on a world of a distant past now magically made present. It took a while for me to find my way around the Temple Mount through the medium of this class, but in time I learned exactly where I could and could not go.

I had to learn exactly what sacrifices could and could not be brought, who would have to bring them and precisely how they were to be handled. But all this was not to be a part of some lessons to be intellectually assimilated. Rather, the learning I did came in through the imagination. All this became apparent to me one evening as I sat down to review *Zevachim* with my *chavruse*.

It was a December evening. The last few days had gone through the Jerusalem weather pattern to which I was fast becoming accustomed. First came the wind carrying with it all the dust from the Judean desert in the east.

Next came the rain that washed all the dirt out of the air and spread it as a light layer of mud over everything and everybody. Then came a clear day in which the dampness of winter fairly clung to the cold. There was no place in the city to really warm up, since no one kept the heat on for more than a few hours each day—it was simply too expensive. So while the temperature rarely dropped below forty degrees Fahrenheit, it always seemed colder than a New England winter, since that forty degrees remained clattering around in one's body forever.

Sitting at the table in Shaarey Chesed, I could still feel the rain, wind, and cold of the last few days. It made me glad that Zanvil was wedged against me on the right and the Rav on my left.

Once we entered the world of the Talmud, however, it was rather easy to forget the cold and the present and become warmly wrapped in the heat of Talmudic disputation. In the liminality of the beginning, however, I found myself gone from the present but not yet having arrived at the past. I waited for a cue, an opening.

"Ehhh," the Rav intoned. It was one of those elongated oral pauses that allowed him to get his bearings in a complicated page. It helped us too, especially when the Rav's pace exceeded my own capacity to keep up. The discussion in the Talmud was about exactly how large the Sacrifice of Thanksgiving had to be, and what happened if that offering turned out to be blemished.

I really didn't care. I had never cared about such things, for to me they were archaic beyond imagining. But these men did care. As we reviewed each move the ancient priests would make in their ritual preparation of the sacrifices, I could begin to see all that rush of activity a bit more clearly. It was evident my partners around the table were walking into the page and onto the Temple Mount with all the assurance of old hands. When they came to a discussion of the sprinkling of blood on the altar and wondered

aloud whether or not the priest bent his wrist in that act, it took only a quick look back into their own memory to see precisely how the ritual was carried out.

But this memory was of course not theirs in origin; it was a memory acquired from the text. Their many years of review had allowed them to construct that ancient Temple and altar in their minds and people it with priests and worshipers. It only seemed to me—the outsider—that they were looking into their own memories.

When I had first come upon these men, I had seen them as hopelessly archaic, charming throwbacks to another age. Sitting now with them and watching them spiritedly chart their way into a past which I, as a Jew, shared with them, I began to look at myself as hopelessly

> **When I had first come upon these men, I had seen them as hopelessly archaic, charming throwbacks to another age.**
>
> **Sitting now with them and watching them spiritedly chart their way into a past which I, as a Jew, shared with them, I began to look at myself as hopelessly trapped in my own time.**

trapped in my own time. And so even though I cared little for sacrifices and all they implied, I found myself wanting to travel back with them by way of the texts.

All this does not mean that they went into the pages as one. In fact, they often argued about exactly where that text could take them. And that made it harder for me to tag along. It happened that night.

The text described a man who was about to eat a minimal quantity of his sacrifice, as mandated by the law. He took a mouthful from the lamb and an equal amount from the breads, both of which constituted his sacrifice. But what if one part of this sacrifice is ritually spoiled? It depends on when he eats it, the teacher explained.

Reb Eliahu, however, had found an alternative reading of the text. In his, this would be the case only under specific circumstances.

"If you want to say it that way you may; but I read it this way," Reb Yechiel Michl remarked, ratifying the Rav's interpretation of how things were done.

The Rav paused.

"Rashi," Yechiel Michl said finally, citing the authority of the great commentary on the page, "reads it as I do."

"But there's another version in the *Shita Mekubetses*," Eliahu argued.

"It can't be right!" Yechiel Michl cried, lifting the pen that he used as a pointer to keep his place. "It can't be right!"

"Look, why make it hard for yourself?" the Rav answered. "With that version, the whole argument has to be changed; and then nothing will hold together."

"All the g'dolim [great scholars] see it Rashi's way," Yechiel Michl noted. He stood on the shoulders of scholar forebears—and with whom did Eliahu stand?

"Look, it's not too hard to see it my way too, and the majority isn't always right."

Eliahu was talking about the majority of great scholars, but he could just as easily have been talking about himself and us. There was no real distinction between the arguments on the page and those in the class. Then was now, and now then. The Talmud had always found ways of shredding and collapsing time. "There is no earlier or later in the Torah" was, after all, one of the primary organizing principles of exegesis. I had always assumed that that principle affected only the written page; but now, as it had in America, it began to dawn on me that the students of the text could become swept up in this same turbulence of time.

"And I say," Rav Moses announced, cutting short the controversy with a tone of judgment, "that you can read it this way and that."

The judgment, I thought, did not change anything at all. That was exactly where we had begun—with two versions of the line. But then there was a change; I could feel it in the room and around the circle. What had changed? Why were the men satisfied with a judgment that returned us to the status quo ante?

I had been using a little tape recorder in order to capture as much as possible in each class. From the start I had explained to the men with whom I *lernt* that for me each word they spoke was important, as this was what I hoped to study as well as the texts themselves. No one seemed to object to the little machine that lay on the table and swallowed up their speech. In fact, everyone seemed intent—at least, at first— on getting himself into the record. For Reb Zanvil this was something to be done furtively. And often I would see my partner on the left watch the little green light that flashed as the recorder took in various sounds to see if it would catch even his coughs and snorts.

That little machine allowed me to take a second look at the world I entered whenever the books were opened and the men gathered around them. Tonight it would help me discover what had been so momentous about Rav Moses's judgment.

When I returned home, I rewound the tape to find the moment when the little exchange took place. Carefully I wrote down all the words of the discussion and began to review them as carefully as my *chavruse* had themselves reviewed the sacred texts. And then I saw it. I listened again to the tape to be sure that what I saw in this transcript was what I could have heard in the class. I closed my eyes as I listened and tried to place myself back inside the room and at the L-shaped table.

Everything had been spoken in the present tense. What had perhaps for others been an archaic controversy between two alternative versions of an ancient text was for these men a fresh argument. They were not just citing divergent texts; they were almost composing them afresh. So finally, when the Rav arrived at the same judgment that the redactors of the text had reached generations earlier, it was not simply an echo of that decision out of the past. Instead, it had all the freshness and novelty of the original decision. The laughter I heard in reaction to his decision was the delight that these men felt in being able to work out their different opinions along the same pathways, the tried and true pathways of their antecedents. Even their controversies did not distance them from the world of the Talmud but rather kept them immersed in it. Only if I allowed myself to see the old as if it were fresh and new could I too share in the delight, could I come to care about sacrifices at the Temple.

The idea, to be sure, was not altogether new to me. Orthodox Jews who try to live lives attached to the past yet embedded in the present often find themselves forced to overcome time in this way. For the most part, the effort is not made. Compartmentalization is rather the rule—where past is past and present present, and one simply learns to dim the lights in one room while passing into the other. Logic has nothing to do with it, and striving for consistency is avoided like sin.

But the Talmud class is something different. Here compartments collapse, and rooms open into one another. Anyone who does not accept

this reality runs the risk of becoming overwhelmed either by the irrelevance of his texts—as I often had been in the past—or by the importance of the present. I returned to class the next night prepared to let myself into the past wholeheartedly.

I began to attend the classes at Shaarey Chesed every evening. After several weeks I was accepted as a regular in the circle, and when once or twice I did not attend, I was greeted with special warmth upon my return.

"We kept your seat for you," I was told.

In time, I too was handed a pinch of snuff at the beginning of the class; and when that happened, I had the feeling that I had penetrated the life of the circle. But while each week I felt a closer tie to the men with whom I shared this special hour every evening, I never quite got over a sense of distance from the text. There was little in the order of the sacrifices that could fire my imagination, and try as I might, I could not quite visualize the scene at the Temple in the same way that my *chavruse* did. Whenever I thought about the rituals and procedures, my mind instead pictured a slaughterhouse with the lowing of calves and the bleating of goats all being killed and seared and smeared. The holy priest with his smudge of blood on his thumb and toe, with his white garments or gold garments, could not inspire me with awe as he seemed to be able to inspire my partners around the table....

At home, sometimes even as I lay in bed, I would turn on my tape recorder and listen to the gently rising and falling tones of the *lernen* and imagine that I was a young boy sitting outside my grandfather's study listening to him review the holy books and feeling a sense of security in the knowledge that all was right with the world. It was, to be sure, an adopted fantasy, for I had never known my grandfathers, nor had I ever gone to sleep to the sounds of *gemore-nign*. But it sustained me through the cold Jerusalem winter and gave me a sense of belonging that I seemed to need.

"What have you done all your life?" the rebbe asked.

"I have gone through the whole of the Talmud three times," the learned man answered.

"Yes," the rebbe replied, and then inquired, "but how much of the Talmud has gone through you?"

Maybe it was my habit of listening to the tapes in bed or perhaps it was the opacity of the texts, but more and more I found myself dropping off like Zanvil during the class. What had so caught my fancy during those first days now became more and more routine, and I was losing my grasp on the proceedings. To be sure, I had been changed by the Shaarey Chesed experience. My prayers were now slower-paced, and I stopped to think about the meaning of all the words I used. No longer could I rush through the liturgy as I had done on that first night. I knew all the characters in the room, knew who would stand for whom and who was widely respected as well as those who ran after respect but never seemed to catch up with it. And I learned what it meant to be part of a *chavruse.*

But I learned about the limitations of my experience as well. As much as my partners were willing to accept me and as open as the congregation was, there were barriers of biography that simply precluded my staying within this world. As if by some sort of biological rejection process, the strangeness in me was forcing me out. More and more I found excuses for skipping evenings at Shaarey Chesed.

In time I returned to the circle there, and whenever I did I found my seat waiting for me. The men had missed me, but no one was ever

certain how long I had been away. They, as I already knew, had a very different notion of time from mine. They dealt in eternities; I was stuck in the present. If I wanted to find a teacher and *chavruse* to fit my needs, I would have to search elsewhere....

Heilman meets a man named Yosef Moshe Reichler in Mea Shearim. Reichler tells Heilman to go see his son, Menachem Reichler, and Menachem recommends that Heilman join a Bratslav bes medresh, Hasidic study group, in the neighborhood of Katamonim. The author finds the experience spiritually compelling, but eventually decides he is not a Hasid and cannot accept all of the teachings of the Hasidim. He settles into another chavruse in Heichel Baruch which he finds conducive to learning Talmud. Before returning to America at the end of his sabbatical, he revisits the Reichlers in Mea Shearim, eager to show them that he has indeed learned the spiritual necessity and craft of lernen. Menachem Reichler asks cynically, "So, what have you been lernen?" and Heilman responds by assuming the role of maggid shiur, teacher, and expounding the role of Talmud as the "mantle" of Torah to Menachem and his father, Reb Yosef Moshe.

When I had finished, Reb Yosef Moshe spoke first.

"Do you remember what I told you about people who are possessed by their books?"

I nodded.

"I was afraid that you were much more interested in acquiring a library than in becoming possessed. And when I saw you today and you told me that you had bought more books, I worried that you were still afflicted with this acquisitive disease. I think Menachem was wondering too."

Menachem said nothing.

"But now that I have heard you, I am no longer worried."

He was right about one thing: I had become possessed. I told him how I had spent the day *lernen* and how the night before my mind had become caught up with what I had reviewed, as if all I had been through had suddenly and finally exploded into my consciousness.

"Rabbi Hannania ben Yaakov tells us," he said, laughing, "that if one is kept awake in the night by words of Torah, it is a good sign. Do not worry that you have become so possessed. It is a blessing, for the Torah is 'a tree of life to those who grasp it.'"

"But not without a mantle," I added. Reb Yosef Moshe laughed again, and I did too.

Hearing our laughter, Mrs. Reichler opened the door and entered.

"Finished?" she asked.

"A pause," her husband answered. "There's never a finish as long as we live and breathe—only a pause."

He was right again. I had embarked upon a path that had no end. There would be cross-roads when I moved from one *chavruse* to another, when I followed one line of study or another, when I returned to my life in the university. But there was no end in sight. I had the entire Talmud and Jewish tradition before me. I would not enter completely into it, but at least I now could stand at the gate.

Reb Yosef Moshe was getting tired, and I stood up to leave. Menachem was going too. We walked through the courtyard together, but soon I fell a few steps behind; I was still weighed down by my bundle of books. As the hemp began to cut into my hand again, I wondered silently if I hadn't taken on too much, if I would really continue to *lern* from all these volumes after this day. And while I thought about this possibility that my time in the *bes medresh* might be limited by who I was and where I might be going, Menachem led me out of the streets of his world as if he knew that I could not and would not stay there. He said nothing and looked straight ahead, but he walked slowly enough so that I could just about keep up with him. With Menachem in front, we crossed Mea Shearim Street and climbed a few steps that took us into a maze of alleys that in turn opened into a narrow and deserted passage that wound its way around the back of a row of houses. In all my visits to the Reichlers, I had not ever left this way. Turning a corner, we suddenly found ourselves near the end of the lane and just short of the center of town. Menachem stopped, as if he were approaching some invisible border. Instinctively, I stopped too.

For the first time since we had left his father's house he turned toward me. He looked into my eyes and spoke to me as if he had been reading my thoughts, and as though I knew he had. As he spoke, his voice solemnly quiet, I felt as if he were at once pleased by my progress and wary of it.

"A scholar once came to a great rebbe. The scholar was no longer young—he was close to thirty—but he had never before visited a rebbe. 'What have you done all your life?' the rebbe asked him. 'I have gone through the whole of the Talmud three times,' the learned man answered. 'Yes,' the rebbe replied, and then inquired, 'but how much of the Talmud has gone through you?'"

Menachem paused and then stretched out his hand to shake mine. He had never touched me before. "According to the effort is the reward," he said, and walked away.

Discussion Questions: **Samuel Heilman**

1. Heilman opens his autobiography with a quotation from J. Bronowski that reads, "each man has a self...; he learns from...the experiences of others as well as his own.... We must have the gift to identify ourselves with other men, to relive their experience." Why do you think Heilman begins with this passage? How does the quotation illuminate his own experience?

2. Heilman also quotes Ben Bag-Bag: "Study the Torah again and again, for everything is contained in it...grow old and gray over it." What is Heilman's attitude toward this idea at the beginning of his sabbatical? How does his attitude change over the time he is in Jerusalem?

3. Vanessa Ochs is a contemporary Conservative Jewish woman who resolves to study the Torah and, like Heilman, goes to Jerusalem to do so. But, as she points out in her autobiography, *Words on Fire: One Woman's Journey Into The Sacred* (San Diego: Harcourt Brace Jovanovich, 1990), the Jewish tradition has encouraged women to learn only the Torah they need to be observant. Ochs quotes the opinion of the twentieth-century Rabbi Baruch Epstein, that "girls do not have the intellectual stability" required for Torah study, and Ochs begins her autobiography with the words of Rabbi Eliezer ben Hyrcanus, an influential rabbi from the first century: "The words of Torah should be burnt rather than taught to women." How do you think a Jewish man like Heilman would react to a woman like Ochs who wants to study the Talmud?

4. Why do you think Rabbi Eliezer ben Hyrcanus wrote centuries ago that "The words of Torah should be burnt rather than taught to women"? What does Heilman think about the Jewish prohibition of women from studying the Talmud?

5. Heilman talks about the feeling of always being an outsider among his Jewish Jerusalem colleagues, even in the Shaarey Chesed *chavruse*. What do you think he means by the phrase "barriers of biography"? What particular features of his *chavruse* appear as barriers to him? Can you identify barriers of biography in the religious communities encountered by other authors in this volume?

Chapter 8

Honduran Catholicism

CODE

HE stories by **Isaacson and Heilman** witness to the power of religious values, their power to support religious communities and their power to destroy them. The high value placed on family relationships in Judaism enabled Isaacson to endure if not conquer the hell of the Holocaust, and the high value placed on maintaining the "purity" of the German race led the Nazis to try to exterminate everything not German and Christian. Moral codes played a central role in this episode in Jewish history, just as they played a central role in Native American and Hindu religious history.

The Nazis may have called themselves Lutherans or Catholics, but their actions toward the Jews were inconsistent with the message of the Bible and the official teachings of the Catholic Church. The Bible and Church authorities stress the virtues of charity, justice, freedom, and peace making, not violence, injustice, oppression, and murder. Nonetheless, Christians raised in different cultures have been taught varying interpretations of these core values, and children raised in Nazi Germany must have received a very different understanding of charity from parents involved in gassing people.

There are seven sacraments of the Catholic Church, rituals in which God's grace is manifested to the community. The sacraments are baptism, confirmation, the eucharist, penance, marriage, ordination, and anointing of the sick. Catholics believe that God chose to reveal the nature of the deity in God's son, Jesus Christ, who came to earth in human form, was born to Mary, was crucified, and raised from the dead. The first author in this chapter, Padre James Guadalupe Carney, comments that God was crucified "for seeking justice and the liberation of the poor," and that Christians who follow Christ by seeking justice and liberation should not expect honors and awards but rather "trials and sufferings." Through self-sacrifice Christians are "sanctified," made more holy and Christ-like. Here is a very different interpretation of Christian values than the Nazi interpretation.

The Catholic moral code stresses the sanctity of life. The Church is officially opposed to abortion, for example, holding that the fetus is a full human being from the moment of conception. Nor does the Church condone euthanasia, mercy killing of people in pain, and it insists on distinctions between the sexes. The Church does not ordain women, for example, holding that religious authority derives from Jesus Christ and Saint Peter, the man to whom Christ delegated authority on earth; therefore, only men can be priests. And Catholics believe sexual activity is sacred, to be reserved only for those who are married. These are just some examples of Catholic religious values intended to guide individual behavior. Our readings focus as much attention on different Catholic views of society, and of the proper political-economic structures needed to form a just society, as on the official Church teachings about the virtues needed by individual Catholics.

Padre ("Father") Carney was born in 1924 in Chicago and raised in the Midwest. He had six brothers and sisters, who settled in places like Saint Louis, Minneapolis, and Detroit. Their father, a veteran of World War I and a salesman for the Burroughs Adding Machine Company, fell in love with the woman who would become his wife when she was a headline singer in a Milwaukee opera company.

Carney went to mass every morning with his father when he was eight years old, learning to value equality, sharing things with others, service to one's community, and brotherhood with all. Unfortunately, he also learned that these values were not the only ones held by North American Catholics. His family moved to Saint Louis when he was seventeen, and he began attending Saint Louis University High School, where he quickly learned that those who compete for honors in sports and school are praised while "those who lose or lag behind are often looked down on." He came to believe that the educational system in the United States prepares Americans only for competing later on in the economic world of capitalism. It is a very deep and penetrating teaching of individualism and selfishness. It is also a subtle teaching of violence, to live according to the law of the strongest.

Carney played one year of football at Saint Louis University, but his career was ended by an injury to his left knee. When he was twenty-four he began studying for the priesthood, becoming a member of the novitiate, or entering class, in the Society of Jesus. Members of this religious community are called Jesuits and are known for their keen intellects and advanced education. After seminary, Carney spent three years as a missionary in Belize, a country north of Honduras. He alternated between the United States and Honduras, finally ending up back in Honduras in 1964 where he worked in a parish called Progreso in an area known as Yoro. He was struck by the poverty and exploitation of workers in the Yoro banana camps, and vowed to live his life for the liberation of the poor, a central value in the moral code of Latin-American liberation theology. After living in Central America, Carney adopted the Latino first name by which he was known to the campesinos, or peasants, Guadalupe.

Our second author's background could hardly be more different from Carney's. Elvia Alvarado was not from the United States, was not born into a middle-class family, and did not receive a high-quality education. Alvarado was born to a poor campesino family in Honduras, a country that is 95 percent Catholic. She was at work by the time she was seven, and a mother by fifteen. She had five more children with three other men. Her education was minimal, and she came to the Catholic faith indirectly when she began to teach and organize mothers in clubs sponsored by the Church.

As different as she was from Carney, however, Alvarado's Catholic values directed her toward the same ends. She wanted to free Honduran women, children, and families from the oppression of poverty, and she came to believe that praying to God is not enough for salvation, that good Catholics must help others in order to be saved. Her boyfriend at the time, Alberto, who was also father of some of her children, opposed her work, especially when Elvia was elected to travel from village to village to organize programs to help feed poor women. As her project became bigger and bigger, the Catholic Church withdrew its funding, and Alvarado and other women had to form a new organization, the Federation of Campesina Women. In spite of the obstacles, Alvarado forged ahead.

Alvarado here describes the problems facing Honduran campesinos: lack of food, loss of landownership, few medical facilities, and deteriorated infrastructures. Alvarado thinks these social and economic conditions are not unrelated to her faith. Indeed, she writes that she understands herself as one who is seeking to become like Jesus Christ, a man who organized others to struggle against injustice. "As long as the poor don't believe in each other," she writes, "they will continue to be poor."

Alvarado is also concerned about the machismo culture in which she lives. Many Honduran men, she claims, are alcoholics and beat their wives. She argues that Honduran men need farmland to own and work in order to overcome their own oppression and begin to correct their oppressive attitudes toward women. In 1962, Honduras passed an agrarian reform law enabling peasants to form cooperatives and take over land that large landowners no longer used. Alvarado believed that law should provide a basis for needed reforms in the Honduran countryside, but it was never fully implemented.

Alvarado is a determined woman, whose courage and conviction comes from her faith in Jesus Christ. However, she is honest about her doubts regarding the existence of God, and sometimes wonders whether Christ should be considered less as a divine figure to be worshiped and more as a political hero to be imitated.

As you read Carney's autobiography, ask yourself why Padre Guadalupe finds himself increasingly opposed to the established Catholic Church in Honduras. Why does he believe that the United States, along with other developed countries, "exploits, or more correctly, robs the riches of the 80 percent of the world that remains poor and underdeveloped"? Ask yourself to what extent you think religious people should get involved in politics, and whether they should get involved at all. If you think they should be politically active, are there any limits to their activity? Along these lines, why does Carney insist that his Catholicism is inextricable from his views about a just, or morally justifiable, sociopolitical order? Do you agree with him?

As you read Alvarado's autobiography, ask yourself about the religious values she espouses. Thirty years after the agrarian reform, Alvarado became a leader of the National Union of Rural Workers and spoke out against the Honduran Congress. In March 1992, for example, she was quoted in an international publication as opposing a new law she claimed would reverse the gains of the past by driving peasants off their land. What is it in her character that provides her with these rich leadership skills? And what are her views about the proper relationships between women and men in the traditional Latin-American culture of machismo? How do her Catholic values inform her political views?

Padre Carney

Selections from *To Be A Revolutionary* by
Padre J. Guadalupe Carney. © 1985 by
Padre J. Guadalupe Carney Fund, Communication
Center #1. Reprinted by permission of
HarperCollins Publishers, Inc.

After my First Holy Communion, when I was eight years old, I enjoyed walking to the parish church with my father every morning at 6:00 A.M. for mass and communion. Afterward we would eat breakfast, and then my father would leave for his office in his car. I was also a server at mass from the time I was eight years old.

I was a great sports fan. As soon as I could walk, I started to play baseball, basketball, and football. I had a lot of talent for sports and played on all the school teams. It seemed as though sports were the biggest interest of nearly all the boys, and every minute of my free time and every school vacation were spent practicing. I also learned to be pretty good at swimming, boxing, wrestling, tennis, golf, ping-pong, volleyball, and track.

Since my father was the oldest of thirteen children and from childhood had had to work to help his family, he knew a bit of everything, carpentry, plumbing, electrical work, and so on. Thus he taught his sons to enjoy doing all the jobs around the house, like cleaning, painting, and repairing the house and the car. I am grateful to him for the fine training he gave us. To this day I enjoy and prefer to do such things as wash my own clothes, fix things in the house, cut the grass with a machete knife the way Latin-American peasants do, and chop wood.

We never had a servant or any household help at home, though, after the end of the Great Depression of 1929, we enjoyed a middle-class standard of living. North Americans, in general, have this good quality of enjoying manual labor, even though they may be rich. Of course, the very rich do have servants to do all these tasks.

Along this same line, our father encouraged us to get jobs in order to earn a few dollars in the afternoons after school, on weekends, and during school vacations. At the age of nine I was a newspaper boy for the *Dayton Daily News,* which I distributed every afternoon to the houses in our neighborhood that had subscriptions. I had about forty regular customers who paid me on Saturdays.

For five years I had this paper route. With my earnings I bought my first bicycle, and also balls, gloves, and other sports equipment that I wanted, besides paying for all my own books and other school material and all my own clothes. Since my father played a lot of golf, he helped me get a job as a caddy at his golf club during school vacation in the summers. My sisters also got small jobs, like baby-sitting for the neighbors, to earn enough for their clothes.

Americans learn from their childhood how to be good, efficient, docile, obedient employees or workers. It becomes very natural for them to enter into the capitalist system of competition and of seeking personal gain, because in school and in sports children learn to compete with each other to see who wins the prize or the highest marks. Those who win are praised and honored, and those who lose or lag behind are often looked down on. This prepares them for competing later on in the economic world of capitalism. It is very deep and penetrating teaching of individualism and selfishness. It is also a subtle teaching of violence, to live according to the law of the strongest. Instead of teaching children to share things with others, to seek equality and brotherhood, to serve the community (which are Christian ideals), they are taught to seek their own advancement, their own development and betterment. Sad to say, Catholic grade schools, high schools, and universities participate in this type of education.

My inseparable friend during these years that we lived in Dayton was Jack Early, who was a year older than I. At this moment there comes to mind the memory of his teaching me how to fish in the Miami River, which passes through Dayton. You can imagine how very hard it was for me and for my brother and sisters to separate ourselves from our friends in Dayton when the Burroughs Adding Machine Company transferred my father to Toledo, Ohio, in 1937.

At the time of the move, I only needed one more year to graduate from grade school. It was especially hard for me to leave the sports teams, because this last year in grade school would have been my best year in sports. To go to a new school in a new town, to start from scratch making friends among the eighth-graders, who had already formed their close friendship ties with classmates of the last seven years, to try to win a place on the sports teams already formed—all this caused in me feelings of resentment against my parents.

But nothing could be done about it, and we all moved to Toledo, which in those days was slightly larger than Dayton, about 300,000 inhabitants. Within a few months I was quite happy with my new parish school (of the Cathedral in Toledo), with my new teachers (nuns), with my new friends. Right away I made the different teams of the interschool sports competition, got a job selling *The Toledo Blade,* bought a new bike, and, as I recall, even had my first crush—on a classmate named Dorothy.

After I graduated from grade school, my parents enrolled me at Central Catholic High School, where my older sister was studying. This was a marvelous new world for me. I remember that the nuns who ran this diocesan high school were very friendly and understood young people. Once, when I did something wrong (I do not remember what it was), my teacher instead of punishing me, began to cry (because I was her favorite), and I could not help crying also, even though I was very ashamed to do so in front of all my classmates. This was a coeducational school, with boys and girls together in all the classes except religion.

I used to ride to Central High every day on my bike, taking a big sack of sandwiches for lunch, and always stayed after school to practice with the different high school teams. From my second year, I was on the first team in football, basketball, baseball, track, and tennis. Our teams played in well-organized leagues with all the other high schools in town, and each high school had its stadium and gymnasium. Football was, and still is, the most important sport, with the most ferocious competition among the high schools and universities of the United States, and it has always been my favorite sport.

I remember Russell, the fellow who lived next door to us in Toledo and attended the biggest public high school in town. He was the star of their football team and, thus, a big hero, not only for me, but for all the people in the city. Well, it was he who taught me how to throw and catch the football correctly. Russell played with my brother and me for hundreds of hours in the street in front of our houses.

I have often thought about the advantages and disadvantages of these sports for young people, because in the new society that we want to form in Central America we want to take advantage of whatever is good in the old society and get rid of whatever is bad. Sports are really important for the development of both boys and girls, especially team sports. Besides being good recreation, they foster friendships, help in physical development, and teach coordinated and planned teamwork, subordinating the individual's desires to those of the team.

We have to figure out how to retain these advantages while eliminating the very bad tendencies that sports often instill: the spirit or mentality of violence, of domination, of conquest or winning over the other, the spirit of standing out, of seeking honors and glory, of pride, of selfishness, and the danger of making sports a god, a principal interest in life. Perhaps we Christian revolutionaries can contribute a bit to solving this problem in the new society.

All these disadvantages of sports that I mention had been manifested in me, especially the pride and the seeking of vainglory. I really think that sports were the false god that I most adored during my whole childhood and youth, even though, not only out of custom, but more and more from personal conviction, I continued with daily mass, communion, and family rosary, and served mass as an acolyte in the cathedral.

I was very sincere in trying to keep the sixth and ninth commandments with regard to sex and purity. During all this time in Toledo I had plenty of girlfriends and went to many dances and parties. In spite of having a lot of young friends from the sports teams who had as their false god the seeking of sexual pleasure, who adored this above all things, I could not be compromised in this area. Really palpable to me was the force for resisting temptations that daily prayer and the sacraments gave me. I had a great fear of sin, not so much out of fear of hell as fear of offending God, who so clearly loved me and helped me succeed in sports and in my studies.

Now, however, I recognize that this fear I had of offending God was out of fear of losing his help. I thought that God rewards those who carry out his commandments with success in this life, and punishes or denies his help to sinners. These are primitive ideas about God.

Now that I know better the only true God revealed in Jesus Christ, the God crucified for seeking justice and the liberation of the poor, I know that God rewards those closest to him with trials and sufferings in order to sanctify them. God is a loving Father who treats us as adult and free sons and daughters. God never punishes anyone; he does not send anyone to hell. We ourselves, with our sins, and the "situation of sin" (as it was called by the Latin-American bishops at Medellín) in which we live, are the cause of the punishments we suffer: from poverty, from corruption, from war, from the exploitation of one person by another. We cannot blame God for that. If I get sick or if there is an earthquake, God is not sending these things; it is just the nature of the world that God handed over to us to dominate and control. Little by little the spirit of truth is illuminating scientists on how to control different diseases, the flooding of the rivers, and other things. We are evolving little by little toward the humanization of this world, toward human control over the universe.

The idea of asking everything from God is very deeply ingrained in Catholics, and it is true that Christ taught us to ask our Heavenly Father, "Give us this day our daily bread." But it seems ridiculous and alienating to me to ask God to cure me when I have a cold, or a cut on my foot, or a headache, or to ask him to send rain for the crops, or give us nice weather for a picnic. I remember that the whole student body went to mass on the days of our big football games to ask God for a nice day without rain and for victory in the game. Immediately before starting a game, when we were out in the stadium, all the players would go into a huddle with the coaches to say Hail Marys, asking her to help us to win.

It was not until I was in the novitiate of the Society of Jesus that the Holy Spirit enlightened me to rebel against the custom in the novitiate of asking the Virgin Mary for a nice day without rain for our hike in the country. I thought, "The farmers are undoubtedly asking God for rain for their crops, and we Jesuits are begging him not to let it rain." I remember in high school playing against LaSalle High School; the Salesian Brothers who run it were praying three Hail Marys with all *their* players and students for a victory against *us*. Across the field, our faculty and students of Central Catholic were praying against them. And later, in 1969 in the short war between Honduras and El Salvador, there appeared in the newspapers a photo of a Salvadoran bishop blessing the pilots and their planes before they took off to bomb Honduran cities. At the same time all the people in Honduras were asking God to give them victory over the Salvadorans.

We all want God to intervene to solve our problems for us. That is what (in many cases) I call ridiculous: as if God had to choose between those he was going to favor, the Honduran Catholics or the Salvadoran Catholics, those of Central Catholic High or those of LaSalle, the farmers who need rain or the Jesuits who want to go to a picnic. That is what in every case I call alienating—expecting God to solve the problems that we ourselves should solve.

This kind of religion is what Marx called the "opium of the people." Opium is a tranquilizing drug that puts one to sleep. This "religion" teaches people that it is God who sends or takes away disease, rain, flood, war, and plagues that destroy crops, that it is the will of God for some people to be rich and others poor, for some to be owners and others their workers. This kind of religion is like opium; it tranquilizes the people, makes them conform themselves to the unjust systems of exploitation. Thus it is clear that the custom of many Catholics to ask God for everything, thinking that everything that happens comes from God or is God's will, prepares them to react to life passively, resigning themselves to unjust social class distinctions.

The Catholic Church has been, and in some of the teachings of many bishops, priests, and nuns still is, alienating—that is, it makes human beings less human, less free. Instead of helping people develop themselves, it impedes them. All kinds of slavery, ignorance, vice, and superstition are alienating. They take away from people the responsibility to "dominate the earth," to use science to solve problems of sickness, of floods, and so on, and to form a society of real brothers and sisters. For example, when Guatemala suffered the terrible earthquake about ten years ago that killed thousands of poor families and children, Cardinal Casariego of Guatemala told the people in his sermons that it was God punishing them for their sins. What kind of a God is this who kills little children?

These are all ideas taken from a literal, narrow understanding of the Old Testament of three thousand years ago. These people knew nothing of modern science and explained everything mysterious to them in nature—the coming of rain, for example—as direct acts of God. (God opens a few doors of the heavenly dome covered by water so that some water can fall on the earth.) Even in the time of Christ,

> The Spirit of God that all of us—Catholics, Buddhists, or even atheists—have in our souls, is continually trying to illuminate our minds and move our free decisions toward the Truth and toward love.
>
> That is the way the Spirit of Jesus is moving the evolution of the world and its history toward the formation of his Kingdom, the society of perfect brotherhood and sisterhood.

about two thousand years ago, everyone, including the Evangelists, called miracles or direct interventions of God whatever phenomenon they could not explain—the curing of a sick person, victory in a war, and so forth. For some examples, just read the psalms: King David is continually asking God to destroy the Egyptians, to punish his enemies—as if the Egyptians were not God's sons and daughters also! Today when Catholics ask God to cure sickness, to send rain for the crops, or to protect them against earthquakes, what they are really asking for is a miracle, an extraordinary intervention of God to change or suspend the regular course of the material nature of the world.

I do not believe that God works material miracles very often. He certainly could; and some of the events in the life of Jesus, like the Resurrection, without a doubt were miraculous suspensions of the laws of physical nature to show us that God indeed rules the universe. But *I do believe that God continually intervenes directly in history in human souls, spiritually, by means of what we call his actual grace.* The Spirit of God that all of us—Catholics, Buddhists, or even atheists—have in our souls, is continually trying to illuminate our minds and move our free decisions toward the Truth and toward love. That is the way the Spirit of Jesus is moving the evolution of the world and its history toward the formation of his Kingdom, the society of perfect brotherhood and sisterhood.

Well, then, instead of asking God for material miracles to solve our material problems, we should carry out this Spanish refrain: *"a Dios regando con el maza dando"* ("asking God for it, but with the hammer doing it"). Or we should follow the advice of Saint Ignatius of Loyola: "asking God as if everything depended on him but doing it myself as if everything depended on me." What we definitely should ask God for is his spiritual help to understand things and the courage to act as we should….

When Carney is a junior in high school, his father is transfered to the Burroughs office in Saint Louis. The family moves there in June 1941.

In June of 1942, I graduated from Saint Louis University High School (SLUH) with high grades on my report card. This "graduation thing" bothered me. There were big expenses; just in order to go along with the rest, you had to buy an expensive graduation ring and a new suit for the big "graduation ball," which lasted all night in one of the best hotels in the city.

There was much pressure to belong to "high society." Many of my classmates were showing off new cars that their parents had given them as graduation presents. For the dance we were supposed to buy a formal "tuxedo" to wear. I managed to rent one from a pawn shop; I knew that this would be the first and last time I would ever use one. I did not buy the graduation ring, either. I was already forming a little bit of class consciousness. I resisted the silly hollowness of "high society" and of some of my rich friends.

In my opinion, there was (and still is) a lot of pressure in U.S. high schools to learn the customs of the rich. Parents and even some Jesuits encourage these customs of the "high society" in the students. In my time I do not recall any campaign by the Jesuits to promote social consciousness in their students, to get them to know a poor neighborhood of the city, to at least visit some poor families at Christmas to give them a gift basket of food, as the Jesuits at SLUH do nowadays. Even now there remains a lot to be done in the area of social service. I was in the United States in 1979, after I was expelled from Honduras, and I again noted a tendency toward self-centeredness in many young Jesuits, in many of their students, and in young people in general in the United States. It seems as though they lack social consciousness. What is happening in the rest of the world does not seem of major interest to them.

I have the notion that the selfishness, or self-centeredness, in American youth today is worse than it was in my time, and that it is because the propaganda of the consumer society is worse today. Today much of education, propaganda, and stimulation in the capitalistic system is designed to form self-centered individualists who seek their own development and comfort rather than to form youth that will take as a goal in life the service of others.

What a difference there is between education in the United States and in Nicaragua, where I am writing this two years after the triumph of the Sandinista revolution! A big part of the youth of Nicaragua fought in the armed insurrection with the Sandinista Front for National Liberation, and thousands of them gave their lives for the liberation of their people from the long Somoza dictatorship, which was always supported by U.S. governments. In 1980 practically all the high school and university students, voluntarily and without pay, went out to remote mountain villages to live with poor campesino families during the five months of the great literacy crusade. In the towns and cities the young workers and housewives who knew how to read taught those who did not. Ninety thousand taught four hundred thousand how to read and write in five months!

The sixty thousand young students (including the sons and daughters of the rich) in this small country of 2.5 million shared the life of the poorest campesinos, enduring hunger and a complete lack of the comforts of modern life. The young students lived and worked where there are no roads, no electric lights, no piped-in water, no schools, no medical clinics, no bathrooms. They lived the way 60 percent of the Nicaraguans and more than 60 percent of all humanity live.

The majority of North Americans cannot even imagine how this two-thirds of humanity in the third world live. And at present, just about all the Nicaraguan students are voluntarily out working in the fields and mountains helping to pick cotton and coffee during their school vacations. The socialist system of education combines study and work. These kinds of experiences open the eyes of the middle- and upper-class youth and make them feel compassion for their poorer brothers and sisters. They forget themselves when they see that their brothers and sisters are lacking even the most essential food that is needed for good health. This is the educational system needed to form the new man and the new woman that Saint Paul talks about in his epistles. In a socialist society it is harder to be selfish. I do not mean to say that socialists are not selfish (this is the original sin that we all have), but the socialist society and socialist system of education try to form men and women who are not selfish, who sacrifice themselves for others, for the community.

Carney spends three years as a soldier in World War II, but decides he cannot kill the enemy, even the Nazi soldiers, because "we are all brothers." After he gets out, he spends a year roaming the country, and then a year working on the Ford car assembly line in Detroit. He falls in love with a woman named Colleen and they talk of marriage, wrestle with sexuality. He decides, however, that he does not want to marry; he wants "to wander through the world looking for God, helping the poor." In 1948 he decides to become a Jesuit and he goes to seminary. Two years later he takes the vows of poverty, chastity, and obedience. He resolves to become a missionary to Honduras and "to identify...with the poor, live with and like the poor."

In 1955 Carney goes to British Honduras, now known as Belize, and spends three years as a missionary. Then he returns to the States and spends four years studying theology in a Kansas seminary. He writes that he "endures" this time only because he dreams of returning to Honduras, which he visits in July and August 1961. He spends 1962 in Kansas, and 1963 in Colombia. He is delighted to learn that his next assignment is back in Honduras, where he wants to

work in the parish of Progreso, located in the area called Yoro. In October 1964 he arrives back in his adopted country, intending to live with the poor and work against the oppression they experience at the hands of wealthy agricultural landowners. He has heard about a famous preacher in Progreso named Ramón Alberdi, a Spaniard forced to leave his native country after criticizing the right-wing dictator, Franco. Alberdi is now preaching against injustice in Honduras.

On my return to Honduras, our superior, Fred Schuller, assigned Jim O'Brien to the parish of Negrito to help Father Bill Ulrich take care of the municipalities of Negrito, Morazan, and Santa Rita. I was assigned to the parish of Progreso to take the place of Father Jim McShane, who was sick and had to return to the States for an operation. Ramón Alberdi was the pastor and took care of the big city of about thirty thousand Catholics with the help of Miguel Renobales, who had just come to Honduras after many years of work in the Jesuit Landivar University in Guatemala.

Miguel wanted to work with the poor, and I admired how he, an aristocratic Spaniard, left the rectory every day on foot to visit and help the people in the poorest sector of Progreso, called Pénjamo. For one who had spent his whole life in the comfortable, rich universities of the Jesuits in Spain and Guatemala, this was a great sacrifice.

Ramón Alberdi was the best preacher I have ever heard. He had the gift of speaking in the language of the people with such vivid examples of the reality of injustice and exploitation that surrounded us and that he continually denounced, that he roused the consciences of a lot of people. At the same time some of the big landowners criticized him and denounced him to the military authorities who governed them. Nonetheless, Ramón was a great friend of most of the rich families of Progreso; he visited their homes, belonged to the Lion's Club, and went to the stadium every Sunday with them for the big professional soccer games.

More than for the rich, however, Ramón had great love and friendship for the poor, the labor leaders, the youth, indeed, every class of person, including the diocesan priests and the religious women of the whole country. All these groups invited him for talks and spiritual retreats, and the theme of his talks almost always was the Social Doctrine of the Church.

Ramón was a Basque, had left Spain after criticizing the dictator Franco and later Nicaragua after criticizing the dictator Somoza. After three years in Progreso, in 1964 he was the most famous priest in the country. The military authorities, the bishops, and our superior feared him, persecuted him, and warned him not to criticize the military government so much, not to be so "involved in politics." Besides his sermons at two of the Sunday masses, which attracted more and more people, especially the men and the youth, and his talks to different groups all over the country, he also spoke often over the radio and wrote articles for the newspapers. I learned a lot from Alberdi.

In those days in the parish rectory alongside the big church in Progreso lived Alberdi, Renobales, and myself; and in the Jesuit Instituto San José on the outskirts of Progreso lived other Jesuits, including Brother Jim O'Leary, Fred Schuller, Paul Van Fleet, who was the director of the high school, the teaching scholastics (Jesuit seminarians) Ray Pease, Steve Gross, Bill Barbieri, and my closest friend Tom Quiery, who was in charge of the Apostolic School. Father George Toruño had started this Apostolic School for boys who had finished grade school and aspired to be Jesuits. They boarded at the school for their high school studies and for some spiritual formation as future priests; it was like a minor seminary. But it never gave fruit. At one time they had up to twenty boarders, but they were mostly young fellows who were taking advantage of this opportunity for a free ride through high school. In the ten years it functioned, five boys went to the diocesan seminary and another five entered the Jesuit novitiate, but none of them persevered; not one reached the priesthood.

With Alberdi and Renobales taking care of the big city, I was left with the eighty villages and twenty banana camps that also belonged to the parish. Some of these communities were big, like Urraco Pueblo with its twenty-five hundred inhabitants, and Agua Blanca Sur, Quebrada Seca, Toyos, Finca Birichiche, and Finca Monterrey, each with more than a thousand; and some were small, like San Antonio, in the mountains, with some twenty houses, Arena Blanca with thirty houses, and others. The idea was to visit and form the Church in all of these hundred communities with approximately thirty-five thousand Catholics.

There were four Spanish sisters, Missionary Crusaders of the Church, who were still wearing their long habits and headgear. They had a sewing school in the big hall of the parish clinic that Father Murphy had started, and they helped us with the pastoral work in the city and at times in the villages, going out with me in our old International Scout jeep.

Progreso is in the Sula Valley on the banks of the Ulúa River; that is why it is called the Pearl of the Ulúa. This valley has probably the most fertile land in all of Central America. There used to be more swampland before the Yankee engineers of the United Fruit Company had them drained by a system of canals, which also serve for irrigating the banana farms with pumps. About half of this great valley was ceded to the Tela Railroad Company (subsidiary of the United Fruit Company) by the unpatriotic, bought-off presidents of Honduras at the beginning of this century. The rest of the best lands of the Sula Valley were in possession of the big cattlemen, principally of San Pedro Sula and Progreso.

The tens of thousands of campesinos in the valley, many of whom were former workers on the banana farms, had no land of their own. Year by year they rented small plots from the landowners or moved onto the marginal land that was not used for banana or cattle production. Just a very few campesinos had been able to buy small plots of their own for their corn and bean crops.

Practically all the villages of the parish in the valley could be reached by car, and there were only eight villages in the mountains that I had to visit on horseback. From Agua Blanca Sur to the south, near Santa Rita, out to Pavón at the northern extreme of the parish was about seventy miles. Every afternoon I used to leave Progreso for one of the communities for mass and baptisms and to notify other communities which day I would visit them. Just to go around like this to all of my communities to get to know them for the first time took me about four months. At the same time I was making a kind of written census of all of these communities so that I would be able to know them better and remember the facts about each one.

Even in this first visit I tried to promote the idea of forming the Legion of Mary in each community, as we had in Yoro. Up to then, the priests had visited the villages and camps only for the sacraments and to personally teach catechism to the children for their First Holy Communion. In many places, however, they had named "majordomos" to help them with the visits, and in some places they had organized the Apostleship of Prayer with its *Celadores* who distributed the monthly leaflet of the Apostleship. There was no other kind of church organization.

Jim O'Brien, who had the villages of the Negrito parish, Tom Quiery, who had the Apostolic School and helped O'Brien with his villages, and I used to meet frequently as good friends. We would reflect together about an apostolic plan for the evangelization of the villages, which were so many that we could visit them personally only a few times a year. We studied together an article in *Maryknoll* magazine that explained how the Maryknoll priests in the mountains of Peru formed men "catechists" for each village to get their community

together on Sunday for a kind of a Catholic Bible service. They had songs, prayer, and readings from the Bible with a dialogue explanation. Once a month the priest would meet with these catechists to prepare with them the Sunday gatherings of their communities for the following month....

For the apostolate in the city of Progreso I tried to interest Alberdi and Renobales in the *Cursillo de Cristiandad* (little workshop in Christianity) movement. Ever since I took the *cursillo* (workshop) in San Antonio, Texas, in 1962 on the way down to Honduras, I had wanted to promote them. But...it was the American secular priest, Vincent Prestera, who had started giving these *cursillos* in Tegucigalpa in 1964 with great success. They really caused a rejuvenation in the Church there, in the bourgeois sector at least. Very many men and women in the capital "were converted to Christ," lived *"De colores"* (song of the *Cursillo* movement), received Holy Communion even daily, and started to help give these *cursillos* in other cities. Miguel Renobales, Paul Van Vleet (director of our Instituto San José), and I went with twenty men from Progreso to take one of these *cursillos* in San Pedro Sula, and later Father Prestera came to give one in Progreso for fifty more men.

Since I had too much work with so many villages, Van Fleet became the spiritual director of these *cursillistas*. The movement in Progreso advanced and did a lot of good for many families. In general, though, it was a movement for the bourgeois class; a few poor workers entered but did not persevere.

Since I was not very revolutionary yet, I supported this movement in the Church and used to go to many of their *Ultreya* (follow-up) meetings. A few years later, when I understood more about the class struggle in the world and within the Church also, I realized that the *Cursillo* movement can be alienating if it is too individualistic. By putting the most emphasis on avoiding personal and matrimonial sins, one calms the conscience so there is no worry about the larger social or structural sins and injustices that are what most ruin this world. Not only does it often fail to instill a social, revolutionary conscience, but rather it is a substitute for this, and so it is counterrevolutionary.

The same thing happens with the charismatic or Pentecostal renewal movement within the Catholic Church. It is often alienating by putting too much emphasis on personal conversion, on the personal relationship with Jesus and his Holy Spirit, thereby keeping the people from getting involved in politics, in the struggle to change the sinful structures of society.

This whole trend of false spirituality says that to change the unjust structures of society you have to first change people. If individuals are just and loving, society will be just. They do not realize the great fact of reality: that a selfish, unjust society inevitably produces and forms selfish, exploiting, violent men and women. We must change at the same time the person and the society, with its structures for exploitation of the workers. We have to have a continual, double revolution: the economic-social-political revolution and the cultural-spiritual revolution. I have recently read several serious studies showing that a great deal of money comes from the United States, from the CIA and its front foundations and agencies, to foster the charismatic Protestant and Catholic religious movements in Latin America in order to challenge and counteract the movement of liberation theology. But in 1964 I did not understand all this....

I am not exaggerating when I say that I learned more real theology in the eight days with the parish team of San Miguelito than in four years in the theologate in Kansas. It was April of 1965 when Tom and I had the providential good luck of learning how the new Latin-American church is formed, "the

Church born from the people" in small basic Christian communities (BCCs) that later, in 1968, the bishops promoted in their documents of Medellín.

San Miguelito was a new suburb of poor workers that Panama City was developing on its outskirts. Bishop McGrath of Panama asked the diocese of Chicago to send a team of priests to start a new parish in this big new suburb. In 1963 Father Leo Mahon arrived with two other American secular priests and four Maryknoll sisters. Leo was a true genius in modern theoretical and pastoral theology. Every morning the parish team of priests and nuns got together to reflect about the gospel and to make a synthesis of theology that they would then teach to the people. They visited all the families in their homes and helped the people of the new suburb make their own school, get water and light, and so on.

Then each priest, with a sister, took a small zone in the parish to start inviting the youth and the adults, especially couples (whether they were married by the Church or not), to get together with them one night a week in one of their homes for a Bible reflection. Each study group had about ten couples and a few single persons. They had adapted for Panama the basic gospel initiation course they had used in Chicago with Spanish-speaking people there, called the Family of God course. There are fourteen themes for dialogue with people in small groups. This course is the most simple and beautiful synthesis of the gospel of Christ and of the plan of God for this world that I have ever seen.

The people discuss Bible texts to see how God wants this world to be a paradise, a society of brothers and sisters all united as one big family, the family of God, with everyone sharing their possessions with each other. Sin, or more clearly expressed, "injustice" and "selfishness," is what goes against this plan of God; living in the grace of God is living according to this plan. Christ came to teach us to live

This whole trend of false spirituality says that to change the unjust structures of society you have to first change people.

They do not realize that a selfish, unjust society inevitably produces and forms selfish, exploiting, violent men and women.

like that, and left a model community of the New Society that we want to form, the primitive Catholic Church, the first BCC, which indeed lived like the family of God. We are supposed to imitate Christ's model community by forming a BCC in every zone or neighborhood. This BCC will be "a light" for the rest of the people, a "ferment" or "leaven" in the mass of people to stimulate them to form the New Panama (and the New Honduras).

After fourteen weeks of meeting like this, the group has a sense of unity and friendship among themselves. To solidify this even more and for the personal conversion of each one of its members, the whole group lives together, as in a retreat, during two and a half days on a weekend for an adapted *Cursillo de Cristiandad*. This retreat uses the techniques of the *Cursillo* movement that promote repentance and conversion and union and joy among themselves, but it changes completely the theological content and the passive method of the traditional *cursillos* and uses instead the message and active methods of the Family of God course, repeated now at a more profound level.

After this *cursillo* almost everyone goes to confession and starts receiving communion

every Sunday, and those who lived together unmarried get married. The group continues to meet in one of their homes each week for a prepared Bible reflection and to plan actions for helping their neighborhood, but now they coordinate the dialogue themselves in rotation. On Sundays all the different groups in the parish, which are now basic Christian communities (BCCs) in formation, come together in the big parish church for mass. They sing the *"Misa Panamena,"* which one of the musicians of the parish in Panama wrote and which all Panama afterward was singing....

Tom Quiery and Jim O'Brien return to Honduras with ideas for starting BCCs there.

Meanwhile, I took advantage of the time that Renobales was still in the parish to visit my family in the United States. We were supposed to make these visits every three years for six weeks of vacation. I got free passage going and coming on the banana ships of the "Great White Fleet" of the United Fruit Company. The two-and-a-half-day voyage from Puerto Cortés to New Orleans was again very restful and a great opportunity to feel the grandeur of God in contemplating the immensity of the sea and of the heavens.

I spent my time in the States visiting a few days with my mother and sisters, Eileen and Maureen, in Saint Louis, and then going to visit my other sisters in their homes in Michigan, Ohio, and Massachusetts. At that time my brother, Pat, was living in Massachusetts with my sister and her family while he studied at Boston University after leaving the Jesuits. I returned to Saint Louis to make my annual eight days of the Spiritual Exercises before going to New Orleans and returning to Honduras.

My sisters always insisted on paying my trips to their homes so I could spend a few days with their families every three years. I always finished my visits to the States by giving thanks to God that I did not have to live there in that "rat race," that life in the "consumer society." I always returned to Honduras with renewed enthusiasm for sharing the life of the poor campesinos.

Carney continues to promote the Delegates of the Word program in all of the villages in his area. The program was started by Canadian priests in the south of Honduras who identified men in each village to lead a "Celebration of the Word of God" each Sunday. The men are called the Delegates of the Word of God.

Right from the start we had decided to accept only men as Delegates of the Word, and to incorporate the women in the apostolate as catechists for the children.

Tom and I always talked about having married priests and women priests in the Church some day, but because of the situation in our Honduran Church it would not be good to have women leading the Celebration of the Word. Our reason was that the Church in Honduras is a women's church. Very few men go to mass or even show up for the baptism of their children, and when they do go, they stay out by the door. Women lead the traditional popular religious ceremonies like the novenas,

the burial services, and the processions, while the men (if they go at all) stay outside without participating.

This tactic of ours of insisting from the beginning on finding men to celebrate the Word of God has changed the Catholic Church in Honduras. The other parishes, in general, have followed this same policy, and right now in Honduras there are around eight thousand men Delegates of the Word who feel responsible as leaders of the Church in their communities and who attract other men to participate in the Church. Other movements also tried to incorporate the men into the Church, like the *Caballeros de Cristo Rey*, the *Celadores* of the Apostleship of Prayer, and the *Cursillos de Cristiandad*. If we had allowed women to be Delegates of the Word, in many communities there would never have been any men participating in a Celebration of the Word.

Tom and I used the same tactic for the Legion of Mary. It, too, had always been a women's organization. Bill Brennan in Yoro encouraged the men to join, but the women always dominated it. In my villages in Progreso I insisted that the president and at least two of the five-person board of directors of a praesidium and of the curia of the Legion had to be men. When I explained to the women the reason for these rules, they were very much in agreement; we had to get the men involved in the Church. In our Progreso villages we also changed the apostolic line of the Legion by giving them as their principal apostolic work a visit to all the homes to get the people to attend the Celebration of the Word. Wherever we had the Legion, it was much easier to organize the Celebration of the Word and maintain a good attendance, always putting the emphasis on getting the men and the youth to participate.

Let me go back and explain how God's providence gave me, as a gift from heaven, a campesino apostle of Christ who would help me in all of this. He was José Ayala. It was in December of 1964, when I was making my first visit to Toyos, one of the bigger villages of the parish. When I went to announce the coming mass, the old woman majordomo of the church there told me that there were hardly any Catholics left in Toyos. Everyone had gone over to the Protestant Pentecostal sect that rented a house near our church for their daily services.

We had the mass, and a small group of people assisted with great devotion. It was more than a year since a priest had visited Toyos. After mass a campesino, José Ayala, introduced himself to ask me if he could start teaching catechism to the children. He had been a catechist in Guatemala, although he had been born in El Salvador. He told me he had been living in Toyos now for six months and it was a shame to see the Catholics go to the Protestant services just because there were no Catholic services for them. He hoped I would return very soon and promised to go from house to house to invite the people for the next mass. I told him that I would not be back very soon for mass, but that if he could get ten more men, he should send me word and I would return to organize the Legion of Mary in Toyos.

In a few days I received a letter from José telling me that he already had a good group of men ready. When I went to Toyos, there were twenty men with José waiting for me at the church. We organized the Legion just with men, with José as president and with the task of getting more men.

When I returned the following month, they had forty men. They eventually had a praesidium of sixty men in Toyos, and José organized another one just for women with about sixty women. He went around to the other nearby villages organizing the Legion of Mary, and afterward, when we started the Sunday Celebrations, he helped me organize them in many villages.

Later on I organized my first agricultural cooperative with these sixty Legionaries from Toyos as its base. It was wonderful for me to have these campesinos as my personal friends.

Quiery, O'Brien, and I gave them courses on the Bible, but they were the ones who actually taught us. These Christian campesinos opened the gospel for me. I did not really know the true Jesus Christ, the campesino of Nazareth, until these apostolic leaders commented on the verses of the gospel in our common meditations. I did not understand anything about the humble life of Mary, the campesino girl from Nazareth, until I contemplated the Honduran campesino women splitting wood and bringing it home on their heads to light the fire and cook. I fell in love with the Honduran campesino, and this love increases in me with each year of my life. I want to live and die with them and for them....

The other big event that the Holy Spirit provided for me in 1965, and the most important one for my metamorphosis as a revolutionary, was my meeting up with the ANACH, the National Association of Honduran Campesinos. Right from my first visits to the villages, when I returned from Third Probation at the end of 1964, I started to ask the campesinos where they worked, how they made their living, how much they earned, how many years of school they had, who the owners were of all this good farmland that surrounded their villages, where they were born, how long they had lived in the village, if they had land to farm, what they planted, why they were so poor...and so on. I would visit their homes, at least some of them, to speak to them in this way before and after mass in each village I visited.

The Sula Valley, where the parish of Progreso extends all along the right-hand bank of the biggest river in Honduras, the Ulúa, has the richest farmland in the country. Nevertheless, in its villages most of the people live in frightening, inhuman poverty. "Why?" I kept asking myself, and kept asking the people in each village. I was collecting a lot of facts, the answers to the questions I asked in each village—not to write them down, but for my own information, and as a way of making conversation with the campesinos. They were pleased to have someone show an interest in their way of living.

This is a summary of what I learned, written as approximations, not as scientific or exact data, about the inhabitants of the seventy villages of our parish in the valley in 1965. I am not including the twenty banana camps where the families of thousands of the permanent workers of the Tela Railroad Company lived or the eight villages in the mountains above Progreso where the people lived a little better because each family had a small plot of their own land. But this description is more or less valid for the rural population and the poor *barrios* (neighborhoods) of the cities throughout Honduras, which account for about 85 percent of the population of the country. The situation of most of these people has not bettered since 1965. In the opinion of many people, it has indeed worsened.

First of all, most of the houses were what are called *champas* (shacks) with dirt floor, roof of palm leaves, and walls either of sticks tied together by vines, or of mud plastered on a network of sticks tied together. These *champas* consist of only one room about six yards long and five yards wide. Generally there is a small kitchen shack apart, or if not, the mud stove for firewood has to go in one of the corners of the house. Fitted into the house might be two or three beds of heavy cord strung on a wooden frame and covered by a reed mat, or a canvas folding cot on which the whole family, maybe eight kids plus parents, have to sleep. An older boy might sleep in a hammock.

Their food consists of rice, red beans, corn tortillas, and coffee—three times a day. They eat a little meat, maybe in soup, about once a week, or a little bit of white cheese. The milk for the babies is from their mothers' breasts. Often this is the only food a baby gets until it is two years old. That is why so many of the children start out their lives physically debilitated, which

scientists say even affects the development of their brains. I do not know what the infant mortality rate was, but many families told me that they had, for example, fourteen children and that only seven were still alive.

The health of the people in the Progreso villages is just about the worst I have seen in the whole country, with the exception of the Jicaque Indians in the mountains of Yoro, who are in even poorer health. The reason, besides the lack of good food from childhood, is the lack of hygiene in the house and kitchen and the contaminated water that everyone drinks from the rivers or creeks close to the villages. In these rivers, the people all take their baths, the clothes are washed, and all the cows, pigs, and dogs wander. A big village like Toyos, which has more than a thousand inhabitants, still, in 1981, does not have a piped-in water system; everyone hauls water from the river, and almost no mother boils it, in spite of all the campaigns to teach them to do this to kill the germs.

The small children go around naked because of the tremendous heat around Progreso, crawling around and playing on the dirt floor of the house, the kitchen, and the yard, and sticking into their mouths any object that interests them. Some small children eat dirt, which naturally makes them sick. The doctors say that they eat it, not only because they are hungry, but also because the dirt contains some iron, which is what is most lacking in their diets. They are all anemic. Almost all the campesinos lack iron in their blood.

It is remarkable how a man, undernourished, anemic, and maybe with tuberculosis (which is quite common) can work all day long under the tropic sun, swinging a big machete (knife), cutting the weeds in the pastures of the rich cattlemen. I, who am strong, have tried it, and I cannot take eight hours like that. The campesinos and Indians of Latin America are not lazy, but they are sickly. Father Murphy started a parish medical clinic in Progreso, which the Notre Dame nurse, Sister Charles, now runs. But it must be very frustrating to cure a child of worms in its stomach and to see it two months later in the clinic full of worms again; or to give a pile of vitamin and iron pills to a child for profound anemia, knowing that it is food, good nourishing milk, meat, and vegetables that this little brother or sister of ours needs.

The diet that I have described is that of a campesino family that has a father who has a job. Maybe 10 percent of the families are without a man; he may have abandoned his woman and children and joined up with another woman. These abandoned women, and also the widows, wash clothes or sell tortillas, or oranges, or the lottery—or who knows what—to halfway feed their children. Another 30 or 40 percent of the families cannot afford even the ordinary diet because the man does not have a steady job, can only find work a few days a month. These are the campesinos who could not rent a piece of land, even only an acre, to plant their *milpa* (cornfield) or their beans. Another 30 or 40 percent of the campesinos of the parish do not own land, either; however, they do manage to rent some, maybe three or four acres, for one crop of corn planted by the same system used by the Maya Indians, namely, first burning the brush and weeds, and then throwing four or five seeds in a little hole made with a pointed stick.

Only about 10 percent of our campesinos have their own piece of land and, thus, some security. They can at least plant, even though floods or insects or plant diseases leave them little certainty of having a good harvest. Another 10 percent or so have more or less steady jobs as cowboys, grass cutters (with a machete), and milkers for the rich cattlemen who have almost all the good valley land that does not belong to the Tela Railroad Company (and also much of the land of the Tela, which they can permanently rent).

Why are the campesinos so poor who live in this rich valley? They are farmers who have neither land they can plant nor a steady job to earn a salary. If they do get a few days' work chopping the meadows or helping cultivate someone else's crops, they make very little. In 1965 they earned seventy-five cents for an eight-hour day's hard work. Since 1981 they earn the new minimum wage of two dollars (U.S.) a day, but because of inflation, with that two dollars they can buy just about what they bought with the seventy-five cents in 1965, that is, practically nothing.

The prices in Honduras (of food, clothing, medicine, etc.) are about the same as in the United States. Then how do those live who do not find a job, who earn nothing? The official statistics for 1980 put the average annual income of all the Hondurans (including the millionaires) at $450, but half the families (like our campesinos) earn only $90 a year. How do they subsist? Only God knows.

Those who have not lived with the campesinos in their villages, or with the campesinos who live in a poor, jobless barrio in the cities, do not believe these figures that I am giving. Well, here is another unbelievable fact: 6 percent of the human race, those that live in the United States of America, consume half of all the world's riches. Many Americans cannot believe this statistic; it is against their interest to believe that 80 percent of humanity is under-nourished. It also took me a long time to comprehend that the *rich, developed countries live well precisely because they exploit, or more correctly, rob the riches of the 80 percent of the world that remains poor and underdeveloped.*

Let us take Honduras as an example. (However the case is more or less the same for all the countries of the third world.) Bananas are among the principal riches that Honduras produces. The owners of practically all the banana plantations and the owners and controllers of all marketing for bananas are the two U.S. transnational companies, the Tela (United Brands Company) and the Standard (Castle and Cooke). The University of Honduras published a study to show that of every dollar of Chiquita (of the Tela) or Cabana (of the Standard) bananas that are sold in the supermarkets of the United States, only seventeen cents was spent in Honduras for everything: for production (including irrigation), for labor, for transportation inside Honduras, for taxes to the government of Honduras, and so on. The other eighty-three cents goes to the United States for transportation and other marketing expenses there, and for profit to the shareholders.

The study also showed something of the shameless robbery of hundreds of millions of dollars that these two companies have been perpetrating over the years by evading a big part of the moderate taxes that Honduras has established.... These two United States companies, backed up always by the U.S. State Department and embassy in Tegucigalpa, have... installed and...have taken out most of the "democratic" governments of Honduras.

Coffee production in the decade of the seventies rose to equal the value of that of bananas in Honduras. Most of the coffee plantations do belong to Hondurans, but since almost all the coffee goes to the United States, the greatest part of the profits from Honduran coffee goes there, too. The profit is not so much in the production but in the marketing of the product. It would be interesting to know how much the U.S. importers of coffee pay the Honduran exporters, and then, how much the consumer pays for this coffee in U.S. supermarkets.

Cattle (beef) is the next important rich product of Honduras, but five of the seven butchering and packing houses for exportation of this meat belong to U.S. companies, and again, almost all export is to the United States. Until the late seventies the Tela was the owner of the biggest herds of cattle in Honduras on the best farmland of the Sula Valley....

It is worth adding here that these two U.S. banana companies are also the major shareholders in almost all the main industries that exist in Honduras, like breweries, cigarette factories, polymer plastics plants, the cardboard box factory, meat packing and exporting houses, and so on. Who are the real owners of Honduras?

Even of the products produced by Hondurans, like coffee, cattle, wood, sugar, cotton, and African palm oil, the final owners and the ones who set the prices, who control the international markets, are always North Americans. As I have repeatedly said, the big profits are not in the production but in the marketing of these products. A small decrease in the price of coffee in the States, for instance, can mean a 30 percent lowering of the dollar reserves of Honduras. We are a country completely dependent on the United States. We are a colony of the United States—economically and politically. I have pointed out here only a few aspects of this sad reality; the financial dependence of Honduras on U.S. banks is still more profound.

The biggest business in the world is international banking. Lending money for interest is easy profit. The Latin-American bishops have said that for each dollar that the United States gives or lends to Latin America, at least two dollars return to the United States in interest and in the purchase of U.S. goods. All international bank loans are conditional: you have to spend a big part of this money in the United States, for technicians, machinery, and so on.

The external debt of the Honduran government in 1980 (according to IDB) was $918 million, owed to U.S. private banks and to international banks like IDB (Inter-American Development Bank) that are made up fundamentally of U.S. capital. Supposing that the rate of interest was 12 percent annually, Honduras would have to pay to these banks 12 percent of $918 million, which is $110 million each year, just in interest. In 1982 foreign debt was $400 per capita. Where do the riches of Honduras go? Why is the United States rich, and why does Honduras remain poor? Is Honduras a free, independent, sovereign state? Honduras is a perfect example of what the bishops in Medellín called "neocolonialism," and condemned as "a situation of sin."

The bishops used another example of the terrible exploitation under this neocolonialism. They explained that the primary materials, like wood and minerals, and the agricultural products, like bananas, coffee, sugar, and meat, that the poor countries export are continually decreasing in value compared with manufactured items that they have to buy from the industrialized countries. In this way, conclude the bishops, the rich, industrialized countries are always becoming richer, and the poor countries are always becoming poorer. As an example, in Honduras in 1970 you could buy a Ford truck imported from the United States with so many sacks of Honduran coffee; now, in 1981, this same truck will cost you four times as many sacks of Honduran coffee.

When someone becomes a revolutionary, it is because he or she understands that the basis for getting a poor country out of its underdevelopment is for it to liberate itself from the exploitation of the rich countries. The necessary prerequisite for the development of Latin America is for it to free itself from foreign imperialism. These countries are rich. Honduras has great riches, but most of these riches leave Honduras to make the United States richer. It is easy to understand why we Honduran revolutionaries are very anti-imperialist. We are not against the people of the United States, but against the imperialism of the United States. The liberation of the oppressed Hondurans, which Christ came to announce and to put into practice, starts with liberation from the effects of this great sin of neocolonialism. *Christians of the United States have the serious obligation to help get rid of this greatest of all U.S. sins.*

Imperialism means to have an empire, to have other countries under your control, as colonies, for the benefit and enrichment of your own country. England was imperialistic in the last century, Spain, in the sixteenth century. The Roman imperialists ruled supreme in the time of Christ, with Palestine and practically all the countries of the civilized world under their yoke. The Jews of Palestine had to pay huge taxes to the emperor Augustus Caesar in Rome, and a big part of the riches of Christ's country of Palestine went to Rome. Rome had its soldiers and its governor, Pontius Pilate, ruling the nation of Palestine.

Many Jews wanted to liberate themselves from this imperialism that despoiled them of their riches. There was a guerrilla movement of liberation, called the Zealots or the Canaanites (one of Christ's twelve apostles was Simon the Zealot, a member of the guerrillas). One of the principal bases of the Zealot guerrillas was in the mountains of Galilee, only five miles from Nazareth; that is why Jesus knew many of these people.

As a trap, the Jewish Pharisees asked Jesus if they should pay taxes to Caesar or not. When Jesus was captured and finally brought before Pilate, the Roman ruler of all Palestine, the Jewish authorities accused him, saying that he was "stirring up the people, saying that we should not pay the taxes to the Roman emperor, and he also alleges that he is the Christ, that is, a king" (Luke 23:2). They involved Jesus in the anti-imperialist politics of his day in order to assure his death. Nowadays in Central America they would accuse Jesus of being a communist in order to assure his death at the hands of the government security forces (the secret police), the death squads, or counter-insurgency military forces. But the financing, training, and "advisers" for the killing of Christ would, sad to say, most likely come from the

United States for the sake of preserving its Central American colonies....

We Christian revolutionaries believe that the construction of true socialism has not been fully completed anyplace in the world; not in the Soviet Union, not China, not Cuba. Thus, we Christian revolutionaries in Central America are not going to establish a Socialist government copying the Soviet model, nor any other model, but we will create a pure Central American model, and in Honduras, a pure Honduran model. These models will be completely impregnated with true Christianity that seeks the total liberation of men and women.

We Christian Revolutionaries of Central America believe that the basis of the new Christian Socialist system will be a spirit of equality and brotherhood, rather than seeking personal gain. This search for personal gain, inculcated continuously by propaganda, education, and structures of capitalism is a main cause of the injustices that we suffer at every level of life. The strongest, the most unscrupulous go ahead in the world. Meanwhile, the weakest and the workers are used by the owners as servants, or as a means of production. In the same way, the strongest countries, with the same selfish mentality, exploit the poor countries. The nations often act like animals, the strongest eat up the weakest.

Under the capitalist system in which we live today (including Russia, which has the same mentality, really), life is a struggle. My country is against other countries; my business is in competition with other businesses to see how much I can get. Even the worker has to be in competition with the other workers to see if he or she can get ahead. This is the so-called free enterprise system, free competition, free market, the consumer society. Well, this is what I call materialism. This system foments selfishness and injustices, hatred, and class warfare.

All this is contrary to what Christ taught us. Love your neighbor as yourself. If we are all

How can I accept that some have privileges and others none?

How can we follow a system that demands that its members live only for themselves?

brothers and sisters, men and women, white and black, professional people and illiterate people, Catholics and Communists, how can I accept that some have privileges and others none? How can we follow a system that demands that its members live only for themselves? Each one in opposition to others? Each one fighting to see what he or she can get?

We Christian Socialists want to help liberate people from this consuming drive for personal gain and to build a Christian Socialist society with structures that will not encourage self-seeking at the expense of the common good. The great means of production will belong to the entire community of people for the sake of all in order to redistribute the resources equally among the citizens. At the same time, there will always be private property for personal use, like family homes and family means of production without any exploitation of workers. Each one will work for the common good according to the individual's ability and receive an adequate wage for his or her work.

I could say that these two years in exile from Honduras have been for me like a long spiritual retreat, in which I am looking for the will of God for this revolutionary who has finished his metamorphosis.

Since "the task of every revolutionary is to make the revolution," the only question for me is: how? in what capacity? with which organization? I have the deep desire (which I am convinced comes from the Spirit of Jesus) to completely join the Honduran guerrillas. All of us Hondurans who are truly Christian should do so. Since I am now a Christian revolutionary, I now clearly understand that there is only one road that leads to the liberation of the oppressed in capitalist Honduras: the revolutionary war of the people. I am not less a Christian, nor less a priest, by also being a revolutionary. I am more Christian than ever; I can more truly love my neighbor, especially the poor. Now I can love them efficaciously, and really help in their liberation and salvation.

We Christian-Marxists who believe in God fight side by side in Central America with the Marxists who do not believe in God in order to form together the new socialist society of brothers and sisters, which will be pluralistic, not totalitarian, that is, which will respect the beliefs of everyone. A Marxist is never dogmatic, but is dialectical. A Christian does not dogmatically condemn anyone, but respects the beliefs of others. A dogmatic, anticommunist Christian is not a real Christian; and a dogmatic, anti-Christian Marxist is not a real Marxist.

I will have to give up being a Jesuit for a time, until the triumph, because the present laws of the Society of Jesus do not permit a Jesuit to be a guerrilla fighter. It pains me to have to do it, but I want to be honest and not hurt the Jesuits by joining the guerrillas as a disobedient fugitive from the Society, forcing them to expel me. My Catholic priesthood no one can take away from me; nor will I ever renounce it.

Ninety percent of the guerrilla fighters in Central America are Catholics and need the presence of a priest not only for the sacraments, but to help them reflect evangelically about what is going on. If the armies of the capitalist bourgeoisie can have their chaplains, with much more right the people's army of liberation should have its priest chaplains. At any rate, I have to be with my people in their struggle for liberation.

To finish my book, now that I have finished my metamorphosis, I invite all Christians who read this to get rid of any unfair and un-Christian prejudices you have against armed revolution, socialism, Marxism, and communism. I would hope that this book has helped you get rid of any mental blocks that you might have because of capitalist propaganda and a false, bourgeois version of Christianity that has been put into our heads since childhood. There is no contradiction whatsoever between being a Christian and a priest, and being a Marxist revolutionary.

Some Christian revolutionaries want to distinguish between "socialism," "Marxism," and "communism." Since there are so many types of socialism, a Christian can easily be a "socialist." Christians can also call themselves Marxists, while always explaining that though they accept and use this scientific analysis of society and method for transforming society, they do not accept the philosophical atheistic world vision of Marxism. Some want to reserve the use of the word *communism* to describe the totalitarian type of socialist society that has existed especially under the repressive regime of Stalin in Russia, which, of course, no Christian would want. But the regime of Stalin was neither socialist, nor Marxist-Leninist, nor communist.

We in the modern age will have to learn what real communism could be—a really Christian society, the Kingdom of God, which I have often described in this book. The socialism that we want is a necessary step toward this Christian communism. In the twentieth century there is no "third way" between being a Christian and being a revolutionary. To be a Christian is to be a revolutionary. If you are not a revolutionary, you are not a Christian!

Ad Majorem Dei Gloriam!—For the greater glory of God!

Discussion Questions: **Padre Carney**

1. Carney does not like "the capitalist system of competition." Why? Do you agree with him? Compare his views about the disadvantages of sports with his views about their advantages.

2. Marx called religion "alienating," an "opium of the people." How does Carney explain what Marx meant? Carney agrees that some kinds of religion are like a "tranquilizing drug" that "makes [people] conform themselves to the unjust systems of exploitation." What kinds of religion does he have in mind? To what "systems of exploitation" is he referring?

3. Are there any forms of religion that Carney thinks are *not* alienating? Describe one.

4. Describe the pattern of landownership in the fertile Sula Valley, some of "the most fertile land in all of Central America." What does Carney think about the United Fruit Company, the presidents of Honduras, and "the big cattlemen"?

5. Describe Carney's ideas about women in leadership roles in the Church. Does he think priests should be allowed to marry? Does he think women should be allowed to lead the Celebration of the Word in Honduras? Why? Does he hope that someday there will be women priests?

6. What does Carney think of the *Cursillo* movement? What do you think about Carney's claim that most Christians are phony and materialistic and care more about fitting in with the crowd than with following Christ?

7. Describe life in the rural areas of the Sula Valley and the poor barrios of Honduran cities. What does Carney say is the "serious obligation" of all Christians in the United States?

Elvia Alvarado

From Elvia Alvarado, *Don't be Afraid Gringo*
(San Fransisco, CA: Institute for Food
and Development Policy, 1987).
Reprinted by permission of the Institute
for Food and Development Policy.

My father was a campesino. He didn't have any land of his own, so he worked for the big landowners as a day worker. My mother raised chickens and pigs, and baked bread to sell at the market. They had seven children—five girls and two boys.

By the time I was six years old, I knew that my parents didn't get along. One of the problems was that there wasn't much work for my father. He'd go looking for work every day, but most of the time he didn't find anything. So he'd go out and get drunk instead. Then he'd come home and pick fights with my mother and hit her with his machete.

My mother would keep quiet when my father hit her. She knew that if she opened her mouth, if she dared to argue with him, he'd hit her more. But we kids would cry and scream and beg him to stop.

My mother finally decided that she couldn't take such abuse any longer, and she left him when I was seven.

After we left, my father moved to the coast. We never saw him again. Years later, after I had my first child, we got a telegram saying he had died. He was buried out there on the coast.

My mother worked like a mule to take care of us, and we all helped out. We'd get up at three in the morning, in the dark, to help bake bread, make tortillas, feed the pigs, and clean the house. All my brothers and sisters worked hard—the boys in the fields of the big landowners, the girls in our house. At the age of seven, we were all working.

My father never let my older sisters go to school. He couldn't see why girls needed an education, since they'd only go live with a man and have babies. But my mother wanted us to learn, and since I was still young enough she decided to send me to school.

I was in school from the time I was seven until I was twelve, but I only finished second grade. That's because the school in the town where I grew up only went to second grade. But I really wanted to learn, so I kept repeating second grade over and over again—five times— since there was nowhere else for me to go.

I can't say I had a happy childhood. We didn't have any toys; we didn't have time for games. We were too busy for that, since we were always working.

The only happy moments I recall were the dances on Saturdays, when my mother let me go dancing with my girlfriends. There'd be guitar players in the village square, and on special occasions they'd bring in a marimba band.

The other thing I liked was going to church. On Sundays we'd go to catechism class; we'd sing religious songs and learn the prayers. Sometimes the priest would make *piñatas* for us in the square. All the kids in the catechism class would get candy, bananas, and sodas. That was a big treat for us....

I never really had much of a childhood at all. By the time I was thirteen, I was already on my own. My mother went to live with a man in town. He didn't want to take care of her children, so she left us behind in the village. I wouldn't say she abandoned us; it's just one of those things that happens in life. She kept coming around to see how we were. To this day my mother always comes by my house to see how we're doing.

But it was hard when she first left us. I went to live with my older brother, who was married and had his own family.

My brother no longer talks to me because of the work I do. He works for one of the big landowners, and he calls me a communist because I try to organize the campesinos that don't have any land. But when I first went to live with his family, he treated me well.

After I'd been living with my brother for about two years, I started going out with a boy named Samuel. We were both fifteen years old and didn't know what we were doing. When we fooled around, I had no idea I'd get pregnant— but I did. In those days, no one ever taught us

the facts of life. The adults said that children weren't supposed to learn about such things. So we were left to figure it out on our own.

I remember that the first time I got my period I was terrified. I saw that my vagina was bleeding from the inside. I ran into the woods to take off my panties and look at the blood. I went back home, got a pail from the kitchen, and went to bathe myself. I thought that maybe taking a bath would stop the bleeding. But I just kept bleeding and bleeding.

I was so scared that I stuck some rags in my panties and laid down in the bed. I wrapped the blanket around me, covering myself from head to foot.

My mother came in and asked what was wrong, but I was too ashamed to tell her. I said I had a headache, but she knew I was lying. After I'd been in bed for a few hours, she finally said, "OK. You better tell me what's wrong, or else get out of bed and get back to work."

So I told her I was bleeding between my legs. "Don't be scared," she said. "All women get the same thing. It'll last about three days and then go away." When I got the same thing the next month, I wasn't so scared because at least I knew what it was.

Nowadays, the kids learn these things in school. But when I was young nobody told us anything.

Anyway, when my brother found out I was pregnant, he was furious. He said he was going to kill me. I hid in my older sister's house and he went there looking for me. When she told him I wasn't there, he said, "OK. Tell that little slut that I'll be back, and that I'm going to get her with the six bullets I have left in my gun. Because I don't like what she's done to me. I've taken care of her for two years, and look how she's repaid me."

My sister came back crying. She'd never seen my brother so mad. "You better get out of here quick," she said. "The best thing you can do is go to the capital where he won't be able to find you."

I didn't know what to do. I was only fifteen, and I'd never been to the capital before. I'd never even been to Comayagua, which is just a short bus ride away. What on earth would I do in the capital all by myself?

I wrapped my two dresses in a piece of cloth—that was my suitcase. I was barefoot because I didn't even own a pair of shoes at that time. My sister gave me the money for the bus fare, and I took off for the capital.

When I got off the bus, I didn't know where to go and I didn't have any money. I asked someone where the nearest park was, and I went and sat down on the park bench. I was three months pregnant, and my stomach was just beginning to show.

I sat on the bench for hours, crying and crying. I kept thinking, "What in the world will become of me? Where can I go? How am I going to eat? Where am I going to sleep?" It was getting dark. People kept walking by and staring at me.

At about 11:00 P.M., the caretaker of the park came and asked me why I was sitting there so long. I told him I was just relaxing, but he said, "You've been here for hours. I saw you when I came on at six o'clock and it's now eleven. What's wrong?" He looked at my bundle. "You're not from here, are you?"

I told him I was from Lejamani, and that I was sitting in the park because I'd never been to the city before and I didn't know where else to go. I said I was exhausted and asked if I could spend the night in the park.

He said, yes, I could sleep in the park, and that he would watch me and make sure nothing happened to me. I put my bundle under my head as a pillow and fell asleep.

Early in the morning I woke up to the sounds of the women setting up their stalls in the market nearby. They were lighting fires to warm up coffee and milk for breakfast. I sat on the bench watching them. I was starving but I didn't have a cent.

The caretaker saw me and came over. "You don't have any money, do you?" he said. "Here, take this and buy yourself some bread and a cup of coffee." He gave me fifty cents (one *lempira*).

When the caretaker's shift was over, he warned me, "Look, muchacha, another man will be coming on now. He's not like me, and he might not let you stay here."

So I left. I put my bundle under my arm and started ringing doorbells, asking for work. But I was dirty and dressed in rags, so no one wanted to give me work. I walked up and down the streets, day and night, but couldn't find anything.

In the evening I went back to the park after the same caretaker returned for the night shift. I slept in the park again and began knocking on doors the next day. At the end of the second day, I found work.

I was hired as a cook in someone's house. It was a husband and wife with two children. The woman hired me because she realized I was pregnant and felt sorry for me. She said she'd pay me ten dollars a month, and I could stay there until I had my baby. But after that I'd have to leave, because she didn't want a baby in the house.

I worked there for six months. The woman was good to me, and every month I'd save the ten dollars I earned so I'd have money to buy things for my baby.

Some women have all kinds of problems when they get pregnant—they get nauseous and lose their appetite, or they have headaches and get real tired. Not me. The only way I ever know I'm pregnant is because I don't get my period. Otherwise I have no other signs.

I worked right up to the last day. When I started getting bad pains, I told the woman I worked for and she took me to the hospital.

I didn't know anything, because it was my first child. But when I felt the labor pains, I just gritted my teeth and clenched my fists until it passed. I didn't cry or anything.

The nurse said, "When you get a really strong pain that doesn't go away fast, push so the baby comes out."

She showed me this cement board they strap you on with your legs wide open—with everything sticking out. She said I should use it when the baby was ready to come out.

I had these pains, and they'd come and go, come and go. Then they started coming faster and faster, until I got this big pain that wouldn't go away. I said to myself, "Ah-ha. This must be what the nurse was talking about."

So I ran over to the board, stuck my legs in the stirrups, and pushed hard. I felt something wet coming out first. And then I felt the baby zooming out, like water rushing out of a bottle when you take the top off. The baby started crying, and one of the other pregnant women ran to tell the nurse.

The nurse came running over, furious. "Why didn't you call me?" she yelled. "You're not supposed to do this on your own." She grabbed the baby, cut his cord, and stuck him in a tub of water.

I don't know why she was so mad. She never told me to call for help, so how was I supposed to know? I just did it by myself. The next day I left the hospital.

After I had my baby, I went back to Lejamani and lived with one of my sisters. Two years later I got pregnant again.

It's very recent that women have started taking pills and things to keep from getting pregnant. When I was young there was nothing like that. We just got pregnant and had our children.

We were taught that women should have as many children as they can. And we were also taught that when a woman gets pregnant it's her responsibility, not the man's, because she let him touch her. If the man didn't want to marry the woman or help support the child, there wasn't anything the woman could do about it.

When I got pregnant the second time, I didn't bother going to a hospital. I just had the baby at home. I suppose I'm lucky that all my births have been easy; I never had any problems. I've heard the doctors say that when you're pregnant it's good to get exercise so that the child doesn't stick to your stomach. I think that's true, because with all my children I worked and worked until the last minute—washing clothes, ironing, baking bread, grinding corn, making cheese. My stomach would be tremendous. But when it came time to give birth, one big push and whoosh—they'd come out.

The father of my second child didn't have a job, and he wasn't faithful to me either. On top of that he tried to boss me around. So I decided to raise the child by myself.

The father of my third child was no better. As soon as he found out I was pregnant, he left. So many men in Honduras are like that. They stay with a woman just long enough to have a child, then they disappear and don't do anything to help support the children. They usually don't even admit that the children are theirs.

After my third child, I went to work in the capital as a maid so I could support my children. They stayed behind with my mother. By that time my mother was living on her own, and she wanted the children to keep her company. I earned fifteen dollars a month and I sent all the money home.

This time the people I worked for didn't treat me very well. They were always yelling at me for something—that I didn't cook the food right, that I burned a pot, that I broke a dish. If I broke something, they'd take it out of my salary. I'd get so nervous whenever mealtime came around, because I knew they'd yell at me for one thing or another.

Part of my job was feeding their big dog. You should've seen the food that dog got! Sometimes he got the leftovers, but sometimes I'd make a special meal for him. My boss would give me meat, tomatoes, and oil and tell me to cook it up for the dog.

And every time I fed that dog, I'd think of my own children. My children never got to eat meat. The fifteen dollars a month I sent them was hardly enough to buy beans and corn. But that dog got meat almost every day.

I wasn't allowed to eat the same food the family ate. I'd get beans, tortillas, and rice. The family would eat in a beautiful, big dining room, and I'd eat in the kitchen with the dog. So sometimes I'd steal the dog's food. I knew he wasn't about to say anything, so I'd swap dishes with him. But I always wished I could wrap the food up and somehow get it to my children.

I only got time off to visit my children every three months. I'd leave early on Saturday and return Sunday night so I could be back at work on Monday. Aside from that one weekend every three months, the rest of the time I never had a fixed day off—only when they felt like giving it to me.

I stayed there for two years. Then I returned home to Lejamani.

It was there that I met Alberto and we started living together. I left my children with my mother because she wanted to keep them. But a few months after Alberto and I started living together, the children told me they wanted to come live with us.

I was delighted. But a few days after they arrived, Alberto started fighting with them. He wouldn't give them food. "Let them go back to your mother's house," he told me, "because I'm not about to feed another man's children." What could I do? I had to send them back.

Even while they were living with my mother, they'd come to see me during the day when Alberto wasn't around. I'd give them whatever I had—a tortilla, a piece of bread. I remember one day the oldest boy was sitting at the table eating a tortilla when he heard Alberto come in. He grabbed the tortilla, stuffed it in his shirt, and ran out of the house. I felt awful.

"Look what you've done," I yelled at Alberto. "I can't even give my own children a scrap of food. They're terrified of you. I work my ass off trying to make a few pennies to support my children, and you have no right to stop me from feeding them."

That was when I started having my doubts about living with Alberto. But I was pregnant again, and had nowhere to go.

Alberto and I had three children together. While he worked out in the fields, I stayed in the house taking care of the children, cleaning, making bread to sell, collecting milk from the landowners to make cheese—anything to earn a few pennies.

Part of the time we were happy together, but Alberto had the same problem my father did—he liked to drink. So while I scraped and saved to buy food for the children, he would spend his money on booze. But at least he didn't hit me like my father hit my mother, and he was good to his own children. That's why I stayed with him.

> # Every time I fed that dog, I'd think of my own children.
>
> # The fifteen dollars a month I sent them was hardly enough to buy beans and corn.
>
> # But that dog got meat almost every day.

After I'd been living with Alberto for fifteen years, I began to work with the mothers' clubs that the Catholic Church was organizing. At the meetings we'd talk about our problems and try to help each other out. We also did practical things like distribute food to malnourished children, grow gardens, and go to talks about food and nutrition. And we'd pray together, too.

At first Alberto didn't want me going to the meetings at the church, but I refused to listen. "I have every right to go out," told him. "I'm not doing anything bad like you're doing—going out to get drunk and spending the little money we have. I'm trying to do something good."

I loved going to the meetings. It became the high point of my week, because it was a chance to get together with other women and talk about the problems we had in common—like how to keep our children fed and our husbands sober. We learned that we had rights just like men did. We learned that we had to stop being so passive and start sticking up for our rights.

I became very active in the club and was elected president. About a year later, the Church invited me to a week-long course for social workers. They invited fifteen women, and at the end of the course they were going to choose five women who'd be paid by the Church to travel all around the area organizing more mothers' clubs.

Of course Alberto didn't want me to go to the course. I'd never been away from the house since we started living together. But I was determined to go, and I wasn't about to let him stop me. "I love you," I told him, "but I've changed. I know I have responsibilities as your wife, but I also have a responsibility to the Church and the mothers' clubs."

"Now that you have your meetings and your courses, you're not the same woman you used to be," he complained. It was true, I wasn't the same. Now when he came home drunk, I'd put up a stink. I was more independent, too,

since I had my own group of friends. And my work in the club made me feel important; it made me feel like I really had something to contribute to the community.

"That's right," I told Alberto. "I have changed. Before I was stupid; now I'm not the idiot I used to be. But that doesn't mean I don't want to be your wife anymore. I just want things to be different."

"Yeah," he said, "now you want to be running around all over the country instead of being home where you belong."

"I'm just going to Comayagua," I told him. "I'll be locked up in the church, taking a course. It's not like I'm going to be hanging out in the street like you do. And don't worry," I joked, "what I have is all yours. No one's going to take that away from you." But he wasn't very amused. He still didn't like the idea.

I got a friend to come and watch the children. The day the course started I said to Alberto, "OK, I'm going away for a week. If you want to stay and watch the kids, then stay. If you want to go away, then go. It's your choice." He decided to stay.

I was so happy when I got to the church. I'd never been to a course before, and I was eager to learn. They read the roster: so-and-so, present; so-and-so, present. And when they said "Elvia Alvarado" and I said "present," I was so proud. So were the other women. Everyone they invited had come—all fifteen of us. I'm sure they all had problems like I had, but we all made it.

We worked in groups—three groups of five each. We were all nervous, because we felt so stupid. Most of us didn't even know how to read and write. But the teachers tried to put us at ease. They said it didn't matter how much formal schooling we had, that we all had lots of practical knowledge and we all had something to offer. They said we were there to learn together, and that everyone should speak up and say what was on their mind.

Our first assignment was to look at the reality of Honduran campesinas—what we did in our homes, what problems we had. At first the women were scared to say anything. I was one of the bravest. "Elvia, Elvia," they said to me. "What should we say?"

"Don't be so shy," I said. "Don't you know what we do at home? Whatever we really do, that's what we say. And the one who writes the best will put it down on paper."

We worked hard all week, talking about our experiences as women and mothers. We talked about the most serious problems in our communities—the lack of good drinking water, no health clinic, no transportation, things like that. And we talked about how we could solve some of these problems.

It was something completely new for us. We never really discussed all these community problems, and we surely never felt that we could do anything about them. But just talking about it together made us feel like yes, maybe we could do something to make our lives a little easier.

At the end of the course, it was time to pick the five best students, the ones that would go on to organize women in other areas. I know it was hard for the teachers to pick just five of us. We'd all become good friends, and we were all full of enthusiasm. But we understood that the Church didn't have enough money to pay all of us.

When they were about to call the names of the best students, I suddenly got very nervous. I saw that it was my chance to do something different with my life, to do something good for myself and other women. The mothers' clubs had opened my eyes to another world, a world where people got together and tried to change things. I wanted to take what I had learned and share it with others.

I must have been lost in thought when they called the names out, because before I knew it everyone was congratulating me. I had been the first one picked.

They divided the five of us up by sector. I was to cover La Libertad, up in the mountains.

I was supposed to visit all these small communities—La Candelaria, Campo Dos, El Indio, Valle Sucio, Lajas, La Colmena. I'd never even heard of any of them before.

Our main job was to organize the women so we could distribute food to the most malnourished children. First we had to make a list of all the young children and their ages, whether or not they were breast-fed, and which women were pregnant. Then we were supposed to help them set up a feeding program.

The church organizers made a schedule for each of us—how many communities we were to visit, how many days in each place. Because you can't just go for one day and expect the women to say, "Here we are, all organized and waiting for you to tell us what to do." No, you have to spend at least three days in each community, convincing the women to get together. At that time there were no women's organizations. It was a completely new idea. Besides that, the region I was supposed to cover was far away, and the villages were hard to get to. We figured it would take me a month....

Well, you can imagine Alberto's reaction when I told him I had to leave the house for a month! He hit the roof. He said no, that I had to stay home and take care of the children. I insisted I had an obligation to the Church that I had to fulfill. But the fighting between me and Alberto about my work never stopped.

I left the children with Alberto and the same friend that looked after them the first time I was gone. The Church paid me seventy-five dollars a month. But out of that I had to pay my transportation and food, so I didn't have much left for the kids, and that was a problem.

I loved the work. I'd go from village to village organizing the women, setting up feeding programs. And we didn't stop there. We planted gardens; we even got construction materials and started building roads. You see the nice roads we have in this village? Some of them we built ourselves through the mothers' clubs. Together with the other women organizers, we set up a tremendous women's organization throughout Comayagua.

But every time I'd come home after being away from the house for a few days, Alberto would start fighting with me again. He would say that I wasn't really working, that I was out sleeping with all the campesinos. He'd tell me to wash myself before I got into bed with him.

I'd say, "Look, if you don't want to sleep with me, don't do me any favors. But don't accuse me of sleeping with other men, because you know that's not true."

On top of all that, I'd still have to put up with his drinking. I'd call him a drunk, and he'd call me a communist because I was organizing the women. The worst part was that he'd come home drunk and start throwing things around and try to hit me.

Finally I got fed up and said to him, "I'm sorry. I've been living with you for eighteen years, and I really don't want to lose you. I don't want my children to grow up without a father. But you're making life impossible for me. I'm not going to stop my work, because I'm convinced that we Hondurans must do something for this country. And if you can't accept that, then you'll just have to leave."

Well, he refused to leave. He was really attached to me, since he was used to having me do everything for him. So finally I said, "*Calabaza, calabaza, cada uno para su casa,*" which is our way of saying, "You go your way, and I'll go mine." I took the children and moved out of the house.

For years we moved from place to place, living with friends and relatives. It was very hard for the kids. But last year we finally got our own house. After so many years of floating around, it's like heaven to have a place of our own.

I can't say I enjoy being single. I must admit I get the desire to be with a man. "Elvia," my friends say to me, "it's not good for you to be without a man for so many years. It's not right to deny your body that pleasure." And I'm

no spring chicken. But when I get dressed up to go out, I still look pretty good. Good enough for the men to come after me.

But I've taken a hard look at my life; I've looked at the relationships I've had with men. And I realize that I could never again live with a man who didn't share my values, who didn't have the same Christian principles, who didn't have the same devotion to the campesino struggle. The struggle is my life, and I could only share my bed with a man who shared the other parts of my life as well.

Many of the men who are involved in the struggle still want their wives to stay at home. They don't want their women to be active. So I've got a tall order to fill—to find a man who's not only sensitive to the campesino struggle but to the women's struggle as well!

I still thank the Church for having opened my eyes. Working with the mothers' clubs, I learned how important we women are and how important it was for us to get organized.

Those of us who were the main organizers were being paid by the Catholic Church. We didn't get much money, but it was enough to keep us going. We managed to set up dozens of mothers' clubs. The women were well organized, and were taking on all sorts of activities.

Then all of a sudden the Church pulled the rug out from under us. It stopped the program and took away all the funds.

Why? They said there was no more money, but we don't think that's what happened. We think they were afraid of how far we'd gone.

It was the Church that first started organizing us women. I'd never done anything before getting involved in the mothers' clubs. The Church forged the path for us, but they wanted us to follow behind. And when we started to walk ahead of them, when we started to open new paths ourselves, they tried to stop us. They decided that maybe organizing the women wasn't such a good idea after all.

They wanted us to give food out to malnourished mothers and children, but they didn't want us to question why we were malnourished to begin with. They wanted us to grow vegetables on the tiny plots around our houses, but they didn't want us to question why we didn't have enough land to feed ourselves.

But once we started getting together and talking to each other, we started asking these questions.

We came to the conclusion that there were three classes in Honduras: the upper, the middle, and the lower class. The upper class are the rich people—the landowners, the factory owners, the politicians. They're the ones that have the power. The middle class are the workers in the city. They don't have as much money or power, but they're better off than we are. We're at the bottom of the ladder, especially the campesina women. Because not only are we exploited by the other classes, but by men as well.

So we started talking about the need for some changes. And then the very same Church that organized us, the same Church that opened our eyes, suddenly began to criticize us, calling us communists and Marxists. It was at this point that the Church abandoned us.

We didn't know what to do when the Church pulled out. We were well organized and had begun to see some gains from our efforts. We didn't want the work to fall apart.

So we gathered together the thirty-six leaders of all the women's groups to figure out what to do. We agreed that the work of organizing campesina women was too important to drop. We already had this functioning organization and we didn't want to see it fall apart. So each group reported how much money it had saved, and we decided to join all our savings and give the organization a new name—the Federation of Campesina Women, or FEHMUC. That was in 1977.

The leaders went back to their clubs to explain to the women that although the Church would no longer support the mothers' clubs, we Honduran women now had our own organization, run and directed by us.

I worked many years with FEHMUC, setting up cooperatives, trying to raise women's income. But I still kept coming up against what I thought was our biggest obstacle: the fact that we campesinos didn't have land to grow our food on. Most of us didn't have any land; some families had small plots but not big enough to feed themselves. I felt that without land we'd never get out of our poverty. I also knew some of the other campesino organizations, the ones the men were in, were trying to regain land for the poor. I decided to join the UNC (National Campesino Union) and later the CNTC (National Congress of Rural Workers) so I could participate in the struggle for land.

If you visit Honduras and just drive along the main highway, you might think Honduras is a rich country. The road is all smooth and paved, and the people who live alongside the highway look pretty well off. But most Hondurans are campesinos who live far removed from the highway. They live in what we call *asentamientos,* or settlements. These are villages that are not even connected to the highway by a road. Oftentimes the only way to get to these *asentamientos* is by horse or hiking on foot. So the real Honduras is hidden from view, but for most campesinos it's the only reality we know.

For the campesinos in the *asentamientos*, it's hard to make a living. If they have any land at all, it's usually the worst land—hilly with poor soils. Because the best land is the flat land the big landowners own.

The campesinos who have land of their own plant corn and beans for their families to eat. When harvest time comes, they put part of the crop aside and sell the rest. They need money to buy things like clothing, medicine, and any food they don't grow themselves.

Whenever there's a family crisis, they have to sell off part of their food to get cash. So they often run out of beans and corn to eat and have to go into town and buy them at the market-place—for double the price they sold them for. The campesinos are always selling cheap and buying dear. That's why they never get ahead.

The guys with the fat wallets, the middle-men, come into the village and buy the campe-sinos' crops for next to nothing. But the cam-pesinos need the money and have no choice. Who else can they sell to? How can they get their crops to market? There are no roads to their villages, no buses that stop there. The only transportation is their mules and their own backs.

Campesinos who don't have land are even worse off. They work as day laborers, either for a landowner or for another campesino who needs help. The daily wage in the countryside is $1.50 to $2.50 a day. But even with these low wages, they can't find enough work.

Many campesinos are forced to migrate in search of work. When it's time to harvest coffee, they go to the mountains where the coffee is. They stay for a few months. Sometimes they take their families along so everyone can help. Sometimes the men go alone. In the south there used to be temporary work in the cotton fields, but no one seems to grow cotton anymore.

There also used to be more work on the banana plantations, but they use so many machines nowadays that there's hardly any jobs for the campesinos anymore. Now they have planes to spray the fields with pesticides. I think they even have machines to cut the bananas from the trees. So not only do the banana companies take land from the campesinos to grow the bananas, but with all their fancy equipment they don't even give us jobs.

The campesinos in the *asentamientos* don't have houses. They have what we call *ranchos,* which are made of bamboo or sugar cane or corn stalks. The roof is made of leaves and sugar cane, sewn together tightly to keep the water out.

The *ranchos* are just one big room, with dirt floors. Some have wood doors, others don't

have any. At least they don't have to worry about locks or anything like that, because there's really nothing to steal.

The room is divided by pieces of cloth hung from the ceiling. One part is the kitchen, where the stove is. The other part is the bed for the parents, and then there's a separate section where the children sleep.

The campesinos either sleep in beds made of wood, covered with a thin mat, or they sleep in hammocks. Some sleep on a mat on the floor. They don't have sheets, just a blanket or a quilt made out of rags.

The only other furniture is a table and chairs. The campesinos make the tables them-selves. And if they can't afford chairs, they sit on tree stumps.

They don't have bathrooms or running water. The women fetch the water for cooking and cleaning. They bathe in the river or stream.

In the towns, life is completely different. There are schools and stores. The houses are better—they have cement floors and tiled roofs. Many have two or three rooms, with a separate kitchen. Some have electricity and running water. But in the *asentamientos* there's nothing like that.

The campesinos live on tortillas and beans—three times a day, every day. When we have the money, we buy other things like rice, sugar, coffee, and cooking oil. Sometimes eggs. Those of us who live in the valleys can't raise our own chickens, because there's a disease that kills them all off. Only women that live higher up can raise chickens.

We don't have money to buy milk or meat or anything expensive like that. We buy cheese sometimes, because you can buy it in small amounts—ten or twenty cents' worth. And once in a while we buy bread at two and a half cents a roll.

We know what a good diet is. We know that a good diet has all sorts of things in it— milk, eggs, meat, vegetables. But we poor people can't afford those things. A bottle of milk costs thirty or forty cents. With that money we could buy enough tortillas to feed the whole family....

We usually buy second-hand clothes at the market. I have no idea where the clothes come from. All I know is that they're cheaper than new ones. We used to buy material and take it to a seamstress. But the material has gotten so expensive, and the seamstresses charge an arm and a leg. A piece of material for a man's pants costs about ten dollars. And then another four or five dollars to have them made. It's cheaper to buy used clothes.

Sometimes we get donations of clothes from the United States, through groups like Catholic Relief Services. Last year I got two big packages of clothes from them and took them to the villages to divide them among the poorest campesinos. But with so many people in need, it doesn't go very far.

As the clothes get worn, the women sew them and sew them and sew them. You should see some of the clothing the campesinos wear. They look like a bunch of patches held together by threads.

I know campesinos that don't even have a change of clothing. When their clothes are dirty, the woman takes her children to the river to wash. They have to wait until the clothes are dry again so they can put them on and go back home....

For the campesinos who live in the *asentamientos* it's hard to see a doctor, because there are no clinics nearby. When they're very sick, they have to go to the hospital in town. But since there are often no roads to their communities, the neighbors have to carry the sick to the road by hammock. Then they have to wait for a bus to town. So by the time they get there, it may be too late.

They also have a hard time getting their children to the doctor. They have to get up at the crack of dawn to get to the clinic before 7:00 A.M. Then they stand in line till 8:00 A.M., when the nurses start making the list. At about eleven the doctor begins to see patients. The worst

thing is that you wait and wait, and you might not even get to see the doctor. It depends on how many people are there and what kind of mood the nurse is in. Sometimes you have to beg to be seen.

In one of the communities I visited last week, the woman left her house at 4:00 A.M. and carried her sick child for miles and miles. By the time she got to the clinic they told her all the appointments for the day were taken, and she should come back tomorrow! That's the kind of treatment the campesinos get. No wonder so many of our children die....

The worst diseases our children get are diarrhea, measles, chicken pox, fever, vomiting, and of course, malnutrition.

Measles are very dangerous. They appear in summer, when it's really hot out. If the bumps just stay on the outside, it's not as dangerous. But if they get inside the children, the children get fever and turn bright red. Lots of our children die from measles.

The children get diarrhea when they're teething, or they get it from drinking water that isn't boiled. When the diarrhea isn't too bad, we stop giving them milk—just rice water—and we buy some pills in the store. If that doesn't help, we take them to the doctor and they get antibiotics. But by the time they get rid of the diarrhea, they're usually all thin and sad looking.

Look at my granddaughter. She's a year old and has diarrhea right now. My daughter took her to the doctor, but the medicine they gave her only made the child sicker. Now they say she has second-degree malnutrition, and that we have to feed her healthier food—eggs and milk and things like that. But where are we supposed to get the money for those foods?

In the adults, there's a lot of tuberculosis and diabetes. The ones that get tuberculosis get all thin—pure bones—and they cough and cough. And the ones with diabetes get yellow and their stomachs bloat up.

We also have a lot of cancer. The doctors say that smoking gives cancer. But here the men smoke more than women, and women get more cancer. So I don't know how that can be.

The worst problem women have is anemia. Almost all the campesinas are anemic. I don't know if it's because we have so many children, or because we don't have a good diet, or what. But anemia makes women feel tired and weak.

The rich have it easier when they get sick, because as soon as they start feeling bad they run to the doctor. The doctor gets the tests right away, and poof—they get medicine and they're all better. But by the time the poor get treated they're already so sick that it's harder to cure them.

The rich can also go outside Honduras to get treated. They go to Costa Rica or to the United States. Like the former president, Suazo Córdova. They say he has diabetes and that every once in a while he goes to the United States to get his blood changed....

The world of the rich is completely different. You should see the mansions they live in! We don't even call them houses—we live in houses, they live in mansions. The only poor people you see are the maids who clean their houses and take care of their children.

When I have to go to the rich neighborhoods, I get terrified, because there are all these armed guards around and you get the impression they don't even want you walking on their sidewalks. You should see how these soldiers swarm around the U.S. embassy, their rifles ready for action.

One day I had to go into one of those fancy hotels in the capital, the Honduras Maya, to leave a message for a lawyer. I was terrified to go in. I was afraid they'd stop me at the door and say, "Sorry, but you're not allowed in. It's for rich people only."

I got up my courage and went in anyway. It was like being in a foreign country, because it's not the Honduras I know. I didn't see people like me, Indians—only gringos and other foreigners, or rich Hondurans. There were a lot of fat people with blond hair.

I found out that one night in that hotel costs eighty dollars. Eighty dollars just for sleeping! I couldn't believe it. Who the hell can pay that kind of money? That's what a campesino earns in two months! I was dying to see what one of those rooms looked like, so I could find out what kind of bed you get for eighty dollars.

I looked outside and saw this beautiful pool, with the gringo children laughing and splashing around in the water. It was hot out, but they were nice and cool. They were having a great

Why should there be rich people that have more than they need and poor who don't have anything?

God didn't plan it that way.

He planned for us to be equals.

That's why we have to build a society where everyone has the right to live a decent life.

time playing in the water. And I wondered, "When will our children ever have a chance to splash around in a pool like that?" It hurts to think that I can't even give my grandchildren a decent meal, while these blond children have everything.

I always look at the children of the rich. They have rooms full of toys, while our children play with old cans and sticks. And their children are so healthy, so full of life. They're so much more active than our children are. I say to myself, "Could it be that we Indians are idiots?" But no, I think their children are smarter because they're better fed and better educated, not because they were born that way.

I want my grandchildren to have the same chances that those children do. Why shouldn't our children have toys? Why shouldn't they be well fed? Why shouldn't they go to good schools and get smart?

We're fighting so that we, too, can share our nation's wealth. We're fighting so that we, too, can live well. We all want to have good houses—with cement floors instead of dirt, with running water to take a shower and clean water to drink. We all want electricity so we don't have to ruin our eyes with those gas lights we use. We all want real bathrooms, with toilets that flush and sinks that have running water. Of course we want those things. Aren't we human beings? Don't we have the same rights that rich people do?

Why should there be rich people that have more than they need and poor who don't have anything? God didn't plan it that way. He planned for us to be equals. That's why we have to build a society where everyone has the right to live a decent life.

I know I'm not going to see it in my lifetime, and I know it's too late already for my own children. But I'm fighting for my grandchildren. I'm fighting so that one day they, too, can enjoy all the wonderful things this world has to offer.

Maybe it sounds like I have my head in the clouds. But I've heard about these astronauts in the United States who've gone into outer space. And I figure, hell, if these astronauts can get to the moon, then why can't ordinary folks like us learn to share the earth?

I was brought up Catholic, and I go to mass every Sunday when I'm home. I like to listen to the sermons. And when they're celebrating mass in one of the communities I'm visiting, I always go in and listen. I even listen to the people preaching in the street, because they're speaking in the name of the Lord.

Here we baptize children when they're a few months old. When we can, we dress them up pretty in a white dress. Even the boys get dressed up that way, if the parents can afford it. I was baptized and so were all my children.

When a man and woman live together without getting married, in what we call a "free union," the Catholic Church says they live in sin. They can't go to confession because they can't receive the host if they're living in sin. And if you're not married and you want to baptize your child, the two parents can't go to the church together. Only one can go with the child.

I haven't taken confession in years, from the time I was a child. That's because I was living with a man and wasn't married. So I go to the mass, but I don't take confession. My children don't confess either. The people that confess are usually the youngest and the oldest—the ones that don't do so many bad things.

My mother is very religious. She's one of those old ladies that spends her life in the church. She just prays and prays, day and night. We have a very different idea of what religion is. She doesn't understand what my work is about, why I want to make changes in the way we live. She thinks we should be thankful for the little we have and leave well enough alone. I suppose she thinks that if she prays enough, God will come down from the sky with a plate of beans for her to eat.

But I don't think that God says, "Go to church and pray all day and everything will be fine." No. For me God says, "Go out and make the changes that need to be made, and I'll be there to help you."

For me, the story of Christ proves we can make changes if we fight hard enough and if we never lose faith in what we're fighting for. Remember when Christ was captured and put on the cross with two others? One was a thief, and I can't remember what the other one was. Maybe he was a thief, too.

When they were on the cross, one of the thieves said to Christ, "Hey, I thought you were so powerful. If you're really the King of Kings, why don't you save yourself? Why don't you save the both of us?" Christ kept his head down and didn't answer him.

Then the other one said, "Hey, Christ. When you're in paradise, remember me." He was saying that Christ should remember that they'd been captured together, that they'd been tortured together. And Christ answered this one. He said, "On this very day you will be with me in paradise."

That's the same as it is today. There are plenty of poor campesinos who don't believe in our struggle. They say, "Elvia? Hah! Why should I believe in Elvia? She's just a poor campesina, a nobody. No, I believe in so-and-so, because he's got bucks. He's got a car. He has a tractor. Maybe I can get him to plow my land. He can help me, that's why I listen to him. But Elvia. Hah! What could Elvia possibly do for me?"

There's a saying that goes, "As long as the poor don't believe in each other, they will continue to be poor." And that's the truth.

All this has a long history. It's just like the life of Christ. Just like there were people who refused to believe in Christ, so there are campesinos who don't have faith. Just like

they captured Christ and tortured him, so the soldiers capture and torture us. And just like Christ died for the poor, so we die for the poor. The day they kill me, I'll know that I died for a just struggle; I'll know I died like Christ did, fighting for the poor.

But not all priests read the Bible the same way. There are priests who've had it easy all their lives. They're from rich families. Their parents paid for their education. They spent lots of time in Miami, in El Salvador, in Costa Rica—living like kings while they were learning the word of God.

A lot of those priests don't give a hoot about the poor. They hardly even know that poor people exist. They are great, holy priests, and that's all that matters to them. With their booming voices, they celebrate mass and speak the great words of the Bible. But they don't even listen to what it says.

You see, the Bible talks about how Christ suffered for the poor. But these rich priests don't talk about that. They turn the Bible around; they preach just the opposite of what the Bible says. In the mass, they yell and scream about what a sin it is to touch what is not yours, and how you must have great respect for private property. And they go on and on about the Kingdom of God.

Instead of making things clear, they leave everyone in the clouds. They say the poor are poor because they were born poor. So that's their lot in life. Period. You must live your life as God gave it to you. You must live in your poor shacks, because that's what God gave you. And if you're content with what God gave you and you live your life humbly without causing trouble, you'll have your reward in heaven.

The worst of all are the politicians who use religion for their own benefit. Take our former president, Suazo Córdova. Suazo Córdova was supposedly a great Catholic. That's how he tricked the people. They thought he was like the Pope of Rome because in his speeches he talked about God, and the Lord, and the Virgin of such-and-such. And you should see the church he had built in La Paz, his hometown. What a church! It's built on top of a hill, with these smooth wide roads and lights leading up to it. But what did Suazo Córdova know about God—except the God of money? Suazo Córdova got rich in office, while the people got poorer. As the saying goes, the rich dress up as sheep.

The Catholics aren't the only ones who twist the Bible around. The Evangelicals are even worse. They're the ones that go around clapping their hands and singing. We call them believers. Excuse me if any of the people who read this book are "believers," but here in Honduras those Evangelical pastors are the worst hypocrites. They just live off the people. And they go around telling the campesinos that the only thing that matters is the Lord. They tell the campesinos they shouldn't take over the landowners' land; they say it's a sin to work with the campesino groups.

Some campesinos I know became believers and then decided to leave the campesino groups they were working with. When I asked them why, they said, "We can't do this anymore because now we're believers. The pastor says it's a sin to be involved in campesino groups. So we're going to devote ourselves to the Lord instead."

"Your pastor wants to talk about sin?" I asked them. "Does he tell you it's a sin to die of hunger? Does he tell you it's a sin that your children are malnourished? Does he say it's a sin that you can't give them a decent meal, decent clothes, a decent education? Does he say it's a sin for pastors to live as well as he does while his people go hungry?"

Anyway, the campesinos are free to do what they want. No one can force them to stay with the campesino groups once they become Evangelicals. But I think it's a shame what happens to these believers.

I've been talking about the priests who side with the rich. But there are also many

priests, mostly the ones lower down on the ladder, who are with the poor. Their sermons are different; they're beautiful. They make the Bible come to life. They say we must love our neighbors, that we must have solidarity with our neighbors, that we must serve our neighbors, that we must serve each other. They say we should follow the path of Christ, who gave his life for the oppressed.

There are priests who have died for their work with the poor. Ivan Betancour died in the Horcones massacre in 1975. One of the campesino groups that recovered land in Comayagua is named after him. And Father Rodimiro was killed at the same time. They both worked with the poor—that's why the military killed them.

We have good relations with the priests who are sympathetic to our cause. But ever since the two priests were killed at Los Horcones, the priests don't join us in the land recoveries anymore. They may support us, but they don't join in.

These priests that side with the poor have to be careful nowadays. They really can't say what they think anymore, because the other priests listen carefully to everything they say. The big bishops and that Pope in Rome, they don't let these priests say what they want. And the best priests are persecuted by the military. They're accused of being communists and Marxists.

Take the example of Father Tito. I don't even know what his real name is, because we've always called him Tito, ever since he was a boy. Father Tito comes from a poor family. His family didn't live in the city; they lived in a little village in the mountains. That's why Father Tito identifies with the poor.

About three years ago there was a big uproar in Father Tito's parish. The military arrested a bunch of *Celebradores de la Palabra*, Delegates of the Word. The Delegates of the Word aren't priests, but religious people who lead small groups in reading and studying the Bible. Since there aren't enough priests to get out into the remote villages, the priests train these delegates to go out and carry on the teachings of the Church. But since some of the delegates also get involved in organizing the poor, the military calls them communists and tries to get rid of them.

Well, after the soldiers arrested the delegates in Father Tito's parish, they went to the church looking for Father Tito. But he escaped and sent word to the Monsignor of Tegucigalpa that the military was after him. The Monsignor sent for him and kept him in the capital. I suppose the Church and the military came to some agreement, because Father Tito was later sent home.

Then about nine months ago, Father Tito was visiting some small villages along the coast. He was celebrating mass with some of the Delegates of the Word when the army captured him. For nothing, absolutely nothing. Only because he identifies with the poor and practices the true evangelism.

Somehow, the people in Father Tito's parish found out he'd been arrested. And they were furious, because they'd heard that the gringos from the nearby Palmerola Army Base were involved in capturing him. Rumor had it that he was picked up by Honduran soldiers in a U.S. military jeep.

The people from his parish went out into the streets. "Why did they arrest Father Tito?" they shouted. "Father Tito's no thief; he's not a murderer. He's a priest, and they have to respect him. He's not an old rag they can throw around as they please. No, he's a priest, and they must respect him."

The whole parish took to the streets. I was right there at the time, because I was working with one of the campesino groups in the area. Someone got the idea that we should all get out onto the highway. They said they'd probably take him to the base at Palmerola or to the capital. In either case they'd have to pass by.

So we ran to the highway, which is the national highway, and we put rocks across it so the cars couldn't pass. In a few minutes the highway was backed up with cars and buses and trucks.

And sure enough, soon we saw a string of army jeeps. They were sounding their sirens, wheeee, wheeee, trying to get through the traffic. And smack in the middle of the military patrol was Father Tito's car. We ran and surrounded the military cars, shouting, "Respect Father Tito. Respect Father Tito. Let Father Tito go."

The people were throwing orange peels and watermelon rinds at the military jeeps, shouting and screaming. "You'll have to kill us all first if you want to get through here with Father Tito," we shouted.

And the campesinos forced one of those big passenger buses to block the road so the soldiers couldn't pass.

When the military saw that things were getting hot, they called in on their radios to the Palmerola Base. We heard them talking to their chiefs at the base.

"OK," the soldiers told us. "Father Tito is not under arrest. He's just coming with us to answer a few questions. He's coming on his own free will, because he's not under arrest."

"No," we said. "If he isn't under arrest, then why does he have to answer any questions? What are you going to ask him, if he hasn't committed any crime?"

They insisted that they weren't going to do anything with him, and that he would be right back in his church.

So the group decided to compromise. "OK," we said. "We'll get out of the highway, but we want to go with the Father wherever you're taking him." So we got a few cars together, and a group of campesinos went along. Not all of us could go, because there weren't enough cars. So most of us stayed behind while the rest followed the Father.

We got out of the way to let them through—first Father Tito, then the military, and after them the group of campesinos shouting, "Free, free, free Father Tito. Free, free, free Father Tito."

They took him to the city and kept him there a few hours, then let him go. That's how the people saved Father Tito. But to this day they keep harassing him—watching where he goes, whom he talks to.

I don't know where in the Bible it says it's a sin to organize. What about the example of Christ, who called his neighbors together and formed the seven apostles?

Christ was a great organizer. When he saw that the people were oppressed by the Pharisees, he decided to organize them. And the people followed him—first a few, and then more and more of them.

Christ walked up and down the mountains, preaching. He didn't preach in churches. No, he preached outside, in the countryside, under a tree, anywhere. He said, "All those who listen to me, come to me. And whoever doesn't want to listen to me, don't come." He meant that those who listened to him would be saved. And the apostles followed him all around while he preached....

I feel like I know Christ because they talk about him so much in the Bible and every-where. He was a human being who lived on the earth thousands of years ago. But I don't feel like I know God. And I must admit that some-times I wonder if he even exists.

There's a man in the town where I live whose name is Pedro. He doesn't believe in God and he just comes right out and says it. He doesn't care what people think of him. In fact, I think he likes to piss them off.

One time we were going out hunting. He loves to hunt animals. And someone said, "It's a good day for hunting. Thank God it's not raining."

Pedro snapped back at him. "Don't be such an idiot," he said. "God doesn't exist, so don't bother thanking him for the good weather."

That made this other guy really upset. "But God does exist," he insisted. "And you shouldn't talk like that, because he hears everything you say."

"Oh yeah?" Pedro laughed. "Did God tell you that himself? When's the last time you saw him? Did he stop over at your house for a drink?"

Everyone in town talks about Pedro. They say, "Pedro doesn't believe in God. That man is worse than a communist. That man is"—what's that word? Oh yeah—"an atheist." And they say that atheists are worse than communists.

But Pedro just laughs at them. When they say he won't go to heaven he says, "Heaven? What heaven? There is no heaven. The only thing up in the sky is the clouds."

So who knows what the truth is? Sometimes I think that if God really does exist, then why hasn't he come around to spend some time with us so we can get to know him? Or why hasn't someone who's spent time with him recently come back to tell us what he's like?...

For me what exists is a spirit. What exists is faith and hope. If I'm walking along a mountain road and I'm thirsty but there's no water around, I say, "God grant me some water so I can quench my thirst." I have faith that I'll come across a stream or a spring along the way. And with this faith and hope, I keep walking and walking and walking. And after walking for miles, I finally come upon a stream. I thank God for the water, because what kept me walking all that time was my faith and hope.

I have this same faith that God will help us win our struggle. I have this faith. And I have hope.

When I started working with the mothers' clubs in the Catholic Church, it was the first time I realized that we women work even harder than the men do.

We get up before they do to grind the corn and make tortillas and coffee for their breakfast. Then we work all day—taking care of the kids, washing the clothes, ironing, mending our husband's old rags, cleaning the house. We hike to the mountains looking for wood to cook with. We walk to the stream or the well to get water. We make lunch and bring it to the men in the field. And we often grab a hoe and help in the fields. We never sit still one minute....

I don't think it's fair that the women do all the work. Maybe it's because I've been around more and I've seen other relationships. But I think that if two people get together to form a home, it should be because they love and respect each other. And that means that they should share everything....

Machismo is a historical problem. It goes back to the time of our great-grandfathers, or our great-great-grandfathers. In my mind, it's connected to the problem of drinking. Drinking is man's worst disease. When men drink, they fight with everyone. They hit their wives and children. They offend their neighbors. They lose all sense of dignity.

How are we going to stop campesinos from drinking? First of all, we know the government isn't interested in stopping it, because it's an important source of income. Every time you buy a bottle of liquor, part of that money goes to the government.

That's why the government doesn't let the campesinos make their own liquor, because the government doesn't make any money off homemade brew. So a campesino can go into town anytime, day or night, spend all his money, and drink himself sick. But if he gets caught making *choruco*—that's what we call homemade spirits made from corn and sugar—they throw him in jail. The government wants the campesinos to drink, but only the liquor that they make money off of.

If we're ever going to get campesinos to stop drinking, we first have to look at why so many campesinos drink. And for that we have to look at what kind of society we have. We've built up a society that treats people like trash, a society that doesn't give people jobs, a society that doesn't give people a reason to stay sober. I think that's where this vice comes from.

I've seen what happens when campesinos organize and have a plot of land to farm. They don't have time for drinking anymore, except on special occasions. They spend the day in the hot sun—plowing, planting, weeding, irrigating, cutting firewood for the house, carrying the produce to market. Most of them are very dedicated to their work and their families.

So I've noticed that once the campesinos have a purpose, once they have a way to make a living and take care of their families, they drink less. And they usually stop beating their wives, too. And I've seen that once the women get organized, they start to get their husbands in line.

I know that changing the way men and women treat each other is a long process. But if we really want to build a new society, we have to change the bad habits of the past. We can't build a new society if we are drunks, womanizers, or corrupt. No, those things have to change.

But people *can* change. I know there are many things I used to do that I don't do anymore, now that I'm more educated. For example, I used to gossip and criticize other women. I used to fight over men. But I learned that gossip only destroys, it doesn't build. Criticizing my neighbors doesn't create unity. Neither does fighting over men. So I stopped doing these things.

Before, whenever I'd see the slightest thing I'd go running to my friends, "Ay, did you see so-and-so with what's-his-face?" I'd go all over town telling everyone what I saw. Now I could see a woman screwing a man in the middle of the street and I wouldn't say anything. That's her business.

If someone is in danger, then, yes, we have to get involved. For example, I heard a rumor that a landowner was out to kill one of the campesino leaders I work with. I made sure to warn the campesino so he'd be careful. That kind of rumor we tell each other—but not idle gossip.

When you think about it, the campesino has the patience of a saint. He's deceived, cheated, and tricked, time and time again. But the campesino is patient....

But there comes a time when their patience wears thin. There comes a time when they get tired of being humiliated and they say, "We've been pushed around for too long. Enough is enough."

It's dangerous when the campesinos react, because their reaction is often violent. They say, "Now we'll see who's got balls. We're gonna solve this with our machetes." And when the campesinos fight, they really fight.

So one of our biggest problems is calming the campesinos when they get mad. We say, "Yes, it's true we've been cheated. It's true we've been suffering for too long. But we have to keep struggling peacefully, because if we take the violent route we'll lose everything."

Sometimes we have to calm them down, and other times we have to give them courage. When we go to recover the land, we have to keep their spirits up. The odds against us are so great that we constantly have to convince the campesinos that it's possible to win.

At the same time we have to prepare them for the worst. We tell them how the landowners pay thugs to kill the campesinos; we explain that others have died in recoveries. We make sure they understand that they have to be ready to be jailed, to be abused, to be persecuted, and if need be, to die.

And we have to be right there with them in the trenches. Otherwise they'll say, "Our leaders are worth shit." We have to show them that we're with them all the way. That's the only way we can gain their trust.

Because the land recoveries are no joke. And the only ones that get killed are the campesinos.

You never hear of a landowner getting killed. That's unheard of.

But look at how the campesinos die. There's the massacre at Talanquera in 1972, where the landowner found out the day and time the campesinos planned to recover the land. When this group entered at four in the morning, the landlord's thugs were waiting for them and opened fire. Six campesinos were killed.

Then there's the massacre at Los Horcones in 1975, when one of the unions, the UNC, was staging a march on the capital to pressure the government to pass the Agrarian Reform Law. The cattle ranchers paid the military to kill the campesinos. Five demonstrators were killed at a UNC training center. Nine others—including two priests—were tortured and killed at the ranch of José Manuel Zelaya, and their mutilated bodies were found stuffed in a well....

It makes me so mad. I just get furious when I see how we campesinos die, like dogs. Our lives aren't worth a penny. When a rich man dies, a fleet of fancy cars takes him to his grave. When a campesino dies, we're lucky if we can find a few pieces of wood to make a coffin. And that hurts. It hurts bad to see a campesino die in a land recovery. I've never in my life cried like I cried when I saw our *compañeros* killed.

I know that the life of the poor is one of suffering, and I don't cry over that. But when I see a campesino killed, then I cry. I cry to see them die with no way to defend themselves. Like a dog.

I don't even want to remember. I don't want to remember the time the four *compañeros* were shot in Talanguita. Four good friends. We all went to bury them. We all had to look at the four of them in those boxes, with their heads blown to bits by the landowner's bullets. It pains me to remember those moments.

That's why I struggle and why I'll never stop struggling. Never. Because with all these campesinos who have died fighting for a stinking piece of land, how can we stop now? No. We have to fight with more courage, more conviction, more strength.

Discussion Questions: **Elvia Alvarado**

1. Describe Alvarado's living conditions: where her family lives, what the children eat, how she relates to her mate Alberto, and so on. Does her description of campesina life match that of Carney?

2. Why does Alvarado write that the Church opened her eyes? Why does the Church begin to criticize her and her friends as communists and Marxists?

3. Alvarado writes that Christ was a great organizer. What does she mean? Why does she call herself an organizer? In what way does she compare herself to Christ?

4. What is machismo? How does Alvarado propose to change it?

5. Like Carney, Alvarado believes that owning land is very important for the campesinos. Why?

6. What strategies does Alvarado try in order to protect the campesinos' rights to landownership?

7. Which author do you think is more "religious," Carney or Alvarado? Why? Do you think Alvarado sees Jesus more as a divine figure to worship, or more as a political hero to imitate?

Chapter 9

African-American Protestantism

COURSE

Y the "course" of a religion we mean its history, the trajectory it has taken through the past. History has assumed a central place in the academic study of religion as religion scholars have become sensitive not only to the different ways in which men and women participate in their traditions but also to the profound influence of changing times on the identity of religious individuals and communities. For example, the influence of the United States's foreign policy on the lives and religious pieties of Honduran peasants has been extensive. As we saw in his autobiography, Padre Carney emphasizes the effect of U.S. "gunboat diplomacy" on the economic stability of large Honduran landowners and the profitability of large U.S. agribusiness interests. Without studying the political and economic history of Honduras we cannot really understand the particular kind of Catholicism followed by campesinas like Elvia Alvarado. To study the history of a religion is to try to trace the multitude of factors influencing a tradition from past to present.

There are at least two foci of religious history: the self and the community. The anthology of religious autobiographies you are reading provides an extensive introduction to the religious history of various individuals, because autobiographies focus primarily on the development of selves. Individual religious history proceeds in relatively small temporal units, such as years, days, hours, or even minutes. Communal religious history, on the other hand, proceeds in larger temporal units, such as years, decades, centuries, even millenia. But individual and communal histories are closely intertwined and we should not try to separate them; communal histories consist of the accumulated stories of individuals, and individual histories emerge only against the backdrop of communal history. Longer stories stand behind every individual's story, informing Padre Carney's Catholic imagery, shaping Judith Magyar Isaacson's will to live, and motivating Shudha Mazumdar's affection for Shaivite *puja*. The religious histories of individuals can no more be abstracted from communal religious histories than religious codes can be abstracted from religious creeds.

The religious autobiographies of the two authors in this chapter must be understood in the context of the communal development of African-American Protestantism, itself a tradition that must be understood in the light of the history of oppression of blacks in the United States. As early as the 1600s, Europeans were raiding Africa and forcing captives to the American colonies to work in bondage. The first author in this chapter, Benjamin Mays, writes that both of his parents were born into slavery in the nineteenth century and that his father was nine years old in 1865 at the end of the Civil War, the war allegedly fought to end slavery. So influential is the history of racism on the development of his character that Dr. Mays's earliest memory is of armed white men on horseback humiliating his father. So influential was the history of racism on the community and character of African Americans that it occupies a major role in Dr. Mays's autobiography.

Mays wrote his autobiography around 1969. At the time, the term then preferred by most African Americans to describe themselves was different from the term preferred today. In describing an important part of the course of African-American religion, Mays writes that "Negros" were

> emancipated from Southern slavery in 1865...[and] promptly deserted by the North. Had forty acres and a mule been given to each emancipated slave family, as had been proposed, the economic plight of the Negro would have been greatly ameliorated.

But freed black slaves were not given the assistance they had been promised, and discrimination against them soon became official policy of the nation, a policy endorsing the segregation of black and white educational facilities. As Mays explains, "As far back as 1896, the United

States Supreme Court had ruled that segregation was constitutional, provided that separate facilities were equal." The challenges of racism and segregation figure prominently in Mays's life and, in the longer book from which our selection is taken, *Born to Rebel*, he relates incident after incident of racial injustice. Mays devoted his life to education, seeing it as his way to fight segregation and racism.

Benjamin Mays was born in 1894 and raised in the Mount Zion Church, a Baptist church some four miles from his house in rural South Carolina. Baptists are one of the branches of Protestantism and believe that only adults should be baptized, and only when they have become convinced about the "Gospel." The Gospel teaches that humans are sinners and must be saved from this condition by the atoning work of Jesus Christ. The black church may well be the most important institution in the black community, for

> Negroes had nowhere to go but to church. They went there to worship, to hear the choir sing, to listen to the preacher, and to hear and see the people shout. The young people went to Mount Zion to socialize, or simply to stand around and talk.

There are important differences between the white and black churches in the South, and Mays comments on them frequently. Black churches are always open to whites, although few whites ever enter, but white churches are not analogously open to blacks. White Christians, Mays writes, do not

> live up to their professed Christianity, because Christian fellowship across racial barriers is so inherent in the very nature of the church that to deny fellowship in God's house, on the basis of race or color, is a profanation of all that the church stands for.

The church should stand for justice and peace and the brotherhood of all, but Mays does not find the white church standing for these ideals.

The course of Mays's life is interesting because, in an era when few African Americans attended college, he graduated from Bates College in Lewiston, Maine, in 1920, an honors student with a degree in philosophy. He became an excellent speaker while at Bates and was elected Class Day Orator by his classmates. In addition to his study of philosophy, Mays displayed a talent for mathematics and was hired to teach math at Morehouse College immediately after graduation. He served on the faculty at Morehouse for three years, then was admitted to the graduate program at the University of Chicago Divinity School, where he received his M.A. in 1925. He intended to go on immediately for his Ph.D. degree, but was offered a position teaching at South Carolina State College, and took the job. Later, he was awarded a Ph.D. from the University of Chicago, became the president of Morehouse College, and served as dean of the School of Religion at Howard University.

As a result of his religious experiences as a child and his advanced study at the University of Chicago, Mays found his calling in higher education and resolved to help change the racist culture that had resulted from centuries of slavery. Mays's exploration of the course of Christianity along with his study of mathematics, psychology, and other university subjects enabled him to fashion his own version of a liberal Baptist Christianity and a vision for an integrated America in which the contributions and value of African Americans would no longer be demeaned.

There are at least two approaches to the history of a community. We might call one the "sacred memory" approach and the other the "social scientific" approach. In the sacred memory approach, mythic events are enshrined in the oral literature and devotional history of a tradition in much the way that the Hebrew Bible and New Testament record sacred memories of the founding events of Judaism and Christianity. Sacred memory approaches events from inside the tradition, and preserves them for use in its devotional life. The social scientist, however, approaches events from outside the tradition and is concerned to use objective and impartial methods in reconstructing what happened. These critical methods might include the methods of archeologists, sociologists, and anthropologists.

Mays's autobiography uses sacred memory insofar as he represents himself as a Christian, because the memories of saints and Christian heros are important to him. But Mays was also skilled in the social sciences, as we learn early on in his story. In order to write his autobiography as accurately and objectively as possible, Mays checked his memories against those of other blacks his age, and found out what they remembered by conducting a survey of 118 of his contemporaries.

Mays could claim to be a professional sociologist because one of his positions was as executive secretary of the Tampa Urban League, a job that required him to collect data on the lives of blacks in Tampa, Florida, in 1926. Mays's autobiography, then, combines both the sacred memory and the social scientific approach.

Our second author leans more heavily on sacred memory. Bessie Jones tended to accept and develop the traditions with which she grew up, and she tended not to be critical of or rebellious against the beliefs she inherited. Jones told her story to a writer, and from that account we learn that oral traditions, and especially the folk songs and folktales of South Carolina she learned from her parents and grandparents, were crucial in forming her identity. The folk songs she had in mind generally were not written down but rather were circulated orally in her culture.

In the history of religion, we try to trace the multitude of factors influencing a tradition from past to present, a task made simpler if there are material artifacts to study: religious texts, objects, paintings, hieroglyphics. Of these artifacts, texts may be the most desirable because they can tell us directly what religious adherents are thinking. But many of the world's religions lack texts, and we call these religions "tribal" or "traditional" religions of "oral" cultures. Ethnographers who study such traditions often must create texts out of oral conversations.

Unlike most of the other autobiographies in this volume, Jones's was not composed initially as a text but rather was written by John Stewart after he interviewed Jones. Jones's autobiography is significant not only because it represents the oral tradition within African-American Protestantism, but also because it contains evidences of the influence of African religion on the black church. Mays's religious roots come primarily from the European Protestant tradition, but African-American Protestantism has also been shaped by the sights and sounds and memories of African religion brought to the United States by the slaves and passed down from generation to generation. As Bedell, Sandon, and Wellborn put it, "Today it is recognized that the slaves' proverbs, folk tales, sexual attitudes, material culture, and religious practices came directly from Africa. To be sure, these Africanisms have not been kept in static form. Albert J. Raboteau has observed: 'The fact is that they have continued to develop as living traditions putting down new roots in new soil, bearing new fruit as unique hybrids of American origin.'"[1]

These African roots display themselves in Bessie Jones's story. Like Mays, Jones was born around the turn of the century in the South and adhered to a form of Christianity that practiced adult baptism. Whereas Mays was born and raised in the church in South Carolina, however, Jones was born and raised in coastal Georgia, in what are called the Georgia Sea Islands. She converted to Christianity as a seventeen-year-old and was baptized, even though she was "born again" later, an experience causing her to want to be rebaptized.

Jones tells Stewart that she remembers singing from the earliest days of her life and that she began singing for money in Saint Simons, Georgia. In 1955, she met Alan Lomax, a well-known figure in the music industry who had come to Saint Simons to hear Jones sing with John Davis. Lomax helped Jones and Davis cut a record and, shortly thereafter, the Georgia Sea Island Singers were born. Led by Smith and Davis, they toured the country and cut a half dozen records including *Georgia Sea Islands,* Volume I and Volume II.

Jones describes growing up in a kind of magical world. People believed, for example, that Jones's Uncle Sam could make himself disappear at will, and Jones herself had visions, seeing the spirits of dead people return to earth. She tells Stewart her elders had "powers" and "knew signs." For example, if your ears burn, that means someone is talking about you; if you hear a screech owl hooting to your left it means someone is going to die. The wisdom of the elders also carries medical knowledge, such as the healing powers of different herbs and plants. Ethnographers and medical scientists alike are now recognizing the importance of traditional local knowledge such as the kind Jones relates here, and connecting it to ecological and spiritual wholeness.

Jones remembers that at her own baptism a lady named Mary was teased by her husband George about going down in a suck-hole in the millpond. The experience shows Jones as a jovial, fun-loving character for whom religion is not entirely solemn, spooky, or straight-

---

1. Albert J. Raboteau, *Slave Religion: The "Invisible Institution" in the Antebellum South* (New York, N.Y.: Oxford, 1978), p. 4. Quoted in George C. Bedell, Leo Sandon, Jr., and Charles T. Wellborn, *Religion in America*, 2nd ed. (New York, N.Y.: Macmillan Publishing Co., Inc., 1982), p. 389.

laced. As you read Jones's story you may sense a different tone and mood than that found in the other texts in this volume. For example, when talking about all of the songs passed down orally, Jones addresses Stewart directly:

> By them not having much understanding in reading, the part that God handed down to them [in these oral traditions], they sure used it. All those songs that were handed down to them without [written] notes, without any education—you think about it!

The final phrase of this quotation reminds us again that the text we have before us is a transcription of Jones's oral comments. As you read her "text," try to imagine yourself as John Stewart sitting with Bessie Jones and listening to her reminisce. See if you can identify the places not only where she directly addresses her audience, but where the ethnographer may have left traces of his own editorial hand.

Benjamin E. Mays

From Benjamin Mays, *Born to Rebel: An Autobiography*
(Athens, GA: University of Georgia Press).
Reprinted by permission of University of Georgia Press.

I remember a crowd of white men who rode up on horseback with rifles on their shoulders. I was with my father when they rode up, and I remember starting to cry. They cursed my father, drew their guns and made him salute, made him take off his hat and bow down to them several times. Then they rode away. I was not yet five years old, but I have never forgotten them.

I know now that they were one of the mobs associated with the infamous Phoenix Riot that began in Greenwood County, South Carolina, on 8 November 1898, and spread terror throughout the countryside for many days thereafter. My oldest sister, Susie, tells me, and newspaper reports of that period reveal, that several Negroes were lynched on the ninth and others on subsequent days.

That mob is my earliest memory.

Susie says I was born on 1 August 1895. The 1900 United States Census gives my birth date as 1 August 1894, and this date I accept. My birthplace is ten miles from the town of Ninety Six, South Carolina,[1] and fourteen miles from Greenwood, the county seat. The first post office I recall was named Rambo; later it was renamed "Epworth." Epworth is four miles from my birthplace, six miles from Ninety Six, and ten miles from Greenwood. The train ran through Ninety Six, which is seventy-five miles from Columbia. My birthplace is about midway between Greenwood and Saluda, not far from Edgefield.

Both my parents were born in slavery, my father, Hezekiah Mays, in 1856 and my mother,

---

1. According to local legend, the town of Ninety Six, South Carolina, got its name from an event during the Revolutionary War when a Cherokee Indian maiden rode from the Cherokee reservation to Old Star Fort, then occupied by the British, to warn the British that the Americans were approaching. The distance was ninety-six miles; the warning was not successful; the Americans overcame the British; but the name Ninety Six was born.

Louvenia Carter Mays, in 1862. My mother was too young to remember anything about slavery, but Father could, for he was nine years old when the Civil War came to an end in 1865.

I know virtually nothing about my ancestors. I have been told that my grandmother, Julia Mays, and her two children were sold as slaves by someone in Virginia to a buyer in South Carolina. Her daughter died early, and her son was shot to death in the field by a white man. After coming to South Carolina, she married my grandfather, James Mays. Six children were born to them, four girls and two boys: Frances, Roenia, Janette, Polly, Hezekiah (my father), and Isaiah.

I never knew my grandfather, James Mays, but I remember my grandmother, Julia, quite distinctly. She lived to be ninety or more years old. As I remember her features, I think she might have had a strain of Indian or white blood. However, I do not recall ever hearing her or my parents make any reference to white ancestry. I never knew my maternal grandparents. My mother had three brothers and two sisters: Abner, Harper, John, Sarah, and Susie.

My mother and father were very dark-skinned, and the color of their children ranged from black to dark brown. Color was never a problem in my family, nor did we ever feel any discrimination based on color among Negroes in my community, whose colors ranged from black to white. To protect the "purity" of the white race, South Carolina had decreed that any person with one-eighth of Negro blood in his veins belonged to the Negro race.[2] So there were a good many mulattos and white Negroes in my area. We never felt sorry for ourselves because we were dark, and we accepted Africa as the home of our ancestors. Although I can appreciate the current emphasis on blackness, I am mighty glad I didn't have to wait seventy years

for someone in the late 1960s to teach me to appreciate what I am—black! Many times my mother, unlettered and untutored though she was, said to us children, "You are as good as anybody!" This assurance was helpful to me even though the white world did not accept my mother's philosophy!

My heroes were black. Every once in a while, some Negro came along selling pictures of, or pamphlets about, a few Negro leaders. Pictures of Frederick Douglass, Booker T. Washington, and Paul Laurence Dunbar hung on our walls. In my high school days, Booker T. Washington meant more to me than George Washington; Frederick Douglass was more of a hero than William Lloyd Garrison; Dunbar inspired me more than Longfellow. I heard about Crispus Attucks and was thrilled. The Negro preachers and teachers in my county, I worshiped. I didn't know any of the white preachers and teachers. (I doubt that I would have worshiped them if I had!) The Negroes in the South Carolina Legislature during the Reconstruction and post-Reconstruction years were the men held up to us in high school history classes as being great men, and not the Negro-hating Benjamin Ryan Tillman and his kind, who strove so long and hard to deprive the black man of his vote. I had identity.

My mother could neither read nor write. She enjoyed having me read to her, especially sections of the Bible. Until this day, I regret that I didn't teach my mother to read, write, and figure. Father could read printing fairly well but not script. I often wondered how my father—a slave for the first nine years of his life—had learned to read as well as he did. My sister Susie, ninety years old now, told me much about our parents when I visited her in the summer of 1967 as I was beginning this book. She remembers well two of my father's stories. He frequently told how the slave children on his master's plantation were fed. While the slaves were working in the fields, the master's wife would feed the slave children. She would pour

---

2. South Carolina Constitution, 1895. *States' Laws on Race and Color,* compiled and edited by Pauli Murray (Cincinnati, Ohio, 1951), p. 407.

milk into a trough and then call the slave children—my father among them. The children would rush to the trough, scoop up the milk in their hands and slurp it into their mouths. The other story is delightful. The slave master's son liked my father very much. Though it was unlawful to teach a slave to read, this white boy would take my father down in the woods to a secluded spot and there teach him to read.

I am the youngest of eight—three girls and five boys: Susie, Sarah, Mary, James, Isaiah, John, Hezekiah, and Benjamin—me. I never knew Isaiah, who died early. Hezekiah was the only one of my siblings to finish high school. The others went hardly beyond the fifth grade in our ungraded one-room school. The maximum school term of the Negro school was four months—November through February. The white school usually ran six months. Discrimination and farm work accounted for the shorter term for Negroes. Most of the cotton was picked in September and October; and early in March work on the farm began. It would never have occurred to the white people in charge of the schools that they should allow school to interfere with the work on the farms. I was nineteen years old before I was able to remain in school for the full term.

Education was not considered essential in those days, not even by or for whites. By law, slaves were kept illiterate. Consequently, when four million Negroes were freed in 1865 most of them were unable to read or write. It is not surprising, therefore, that, according to the Census of 1900, 57 percent of the Negro males of voting age in my county were illiterate.[3] Even the 43 percent who could read and write could not vote. In the state as a whole 52.8 percent of Negroes ten years old and above were illiterate in 1900 as against 64.1 percent in 1890. I suppose that the literacy in my

-----

3. Negroes in the United States, U.S. Bureau of the Census, 1900.

family was slightly above the average of Negroes in my county.

Two of my brothers, James and John, tried farming. James stuck with it until he was killed at the age of forty-eight or fifty by a brother-in-law.

Earlier, however, John had left for the city. Another brother, Hezekiah, after an altercation with Father, pulled off his sack and left the cotton field and his home, never to return except on visits to the family. My three sisters all married farmers in the community.

It could hardly have been otherwise than that most of the Negroes in my county at the turn of the century were wage hands, sharecroppers, and renters. Only a very small minority owned farms or were buying them. How could it be different? Thirty-five years earlier, Negroes had been freed without being given a dime or a foot of land by the federal government. Emancipated from Southern slavery in 1865, the Negro was promptly deserted by the North. Had forty acres and a mule been given to each emancipated slave family, as had been proposed, the economic plight of the Negro would have been greatly ameliorated. Today the harvest might well have been of wheat and not tares.

In 1900, Greenwood County, in which I lived, had a population of 28,343, of which 18,906, or 66.7 percent, were Negroes. The fact that Negroes so far outnumbered the whites contributed to the whites' determination to exclude them from politics. The evil result of this determination was the infamous Phoenix Riot. Negroes in my county were heavily dependent upon the white people for land to till; the whites were equally dependent upon the Negroes to get their farms worked. In 1900, close to 20 percent of the Negro farmers in South Carolina owned their homes. However, in Greenwood County in 1910 only 112 Negroes owned their farms free of debt; 95 had farms but they were mortgaged; 68 were part-owners; 1,230 were cash tenants; 1,296 were share tenants; 43 share-cash tenants; and 89 were not specifically designated.[4] These figures add up to 2,933 farms run by Negroes. The free-of-debt owners, plus the owners with the mortgages, and the part-owners totaled 275, or 9.4 percent, who had some ownership in their farms. Roughly speaking, only one Negro farmer in ten owned his land, and only one in twenty-six owned a farm absolutely free of debt. Ninety percent of the Negro farmers in Greenwood County were renters, sharecroppers, and wage hands. Despite poverty, however, Negro life was very stable. As a rule, men did not desert their families. There were not many illegitimate children in my community. A girl who had an illegitimate child was usually looked down on as having brought disgrace to her family.

My father was a renter. As far back as I can remember, I think we owned our mules. Any man who owned his mules or horses, buggy, wagon, or other farm equipment occupied a little higher status than the one who worked for wages or was a sharecropper. The wage hand was one who worked by the month for ten, twelve, or fifteen dollars a month. The sharecropper, or the one who worked on "halves," had his house, mules, and other farm implements provided for him. The owner of the land received half of all the sharecropper made.

As I recall, Father usually rented forty acres of land for a two-mule farm, or sixty acres if we had three mules. The rent was two bales of cotton, weighing 500 pounds each, for every twenty acres rented. So the owner of the land got his two, four, or six bales out of the first cotton picked and ginned. Many Negroes rented as many as sixty acres of land, paying as rent six bales of cotton weighing 500 pounds each. From the first bales ginned, Father got only the money that came from selling the cottonseeds.

I was elated when that time came, for my father always celebrated by buying a big wheel of sharp yellow cheese out of the first cottonseed money. I still enjoy the taste of cheese. I have eaten the finest varieties in many parts of the world, but nothing has ever tasted as good to me as the cheese my father used to bring home from the sale of cottonseeds.

Although I do not recall that we were ever hungry and unable to get food, we did have very little to go on. To make sixteen bales of cotton on a two-mule farm was considered excellent farming. After four bales were used to pay rent, we would have twelve bales left. The price of cotton fluctuated. If we received ten cents a pound, we would have somewhere between five and six hundred dollars, depending upon whether the bales of cotton weighed an average of 450, 475, or 500 pounds. When all of us children were at home we, with our father and mother, were ten. We lived in a four-room house, with no indoor plumbing—no toilet facilities, no running water. When my oldest brother got his own farm, and after the death of Isaiah, there were eight of us; and things changed as my sisters got married and the oldest brothers, James and John, began to fend for themselves. If we were lucky enough to get twelve or fifteen cents a pound for cotton, things were a little better. But six or seven hundred dollars a year was not much when Father had to pay back, with interest, money borrowed to carry us from March to September, and when shoes, clothing, and food for all of us had to be bought out of this money. Then there were the mules, the buggies, wagons, and farm tools to be bought and paid for.

We were never able to clear enough from the crop to carry us from one September to the next. We could usually go on our own from September through February; but every March a lien had to be placed on the crop so that we could get money to buy food and other necessities from March through August, when we

---

4. Negro Population in the United States: 1780–1915, U.S. Bureau of the Census, p. 746.

would get some relief by selling cotton. Strange as it may seem, neither we nor our neighbors ever raised enough hogs to have meat the year round, enough corn and wheat to ensure having our daily bread, or cows in sufficient numbers to have enough milk. The curse was cotton. It was difficult to make farmers see that more corn, grain, hogs, and cows meant less cash but more profit in the end. Cotton sold instantly, and that was *cash* money. Negro farmers wanted to *feel* the cash—at least for that brief moment as it passed through their hands into the white man's hands!

Though never hungry, we were indeed poor. We supplemented our earnings by working at times as day hands, hoeing, chopping, and picking cotton for white farmers in the neighborhood. The price paid for this work usually was forty cents a day, sometimes only thirty-five, though when a man was desperate for help on his farm he would pay fifty cents a day. One made more money picking cotton, especially if he were a good cotton picker. The pay was forty or fifty cents per hundred pounds. All of us worked on the farm, including my sisters. Except in cases of dire necessity, Negro fathers preferred to have their daughters work on the farm rather than cook in the white man's kitchen. My sisters did not plow or cut wood, but they hoed and chopped and picked cotton. We usually got to the field about sunup and worked until sundown.

It was and still is a belief among Negroes that most white people who had Negro tenants cheated them. This belief had no lack of confirming evidence! Many Negroes did not know how to keep their own accounts, and even when they could, all too many of them were afraid to question a white man's figures. His word was not to be disputed, and if he said a Negro owed him so much, questions were not in order and no explanations were forthcoming. If he told John, "We broke even this year; neither of us owes the other," even if John knew

he had cleared a hundred dollars, he would ask no questions, register no protest.

To support my own recollections about a great deal of my past, I have either personally interviewed or had someone else interview 118 Negroes who were born about the same time I was.[5] The majority believed that Negroes who worked for white people in the South were grossly cheated by their white "bosses." Of the 118 interviewed for this study, 101 (85.6 percent) expressed the belief, from their own experiences and observations, that Negroes were cheated by white people. One was emphatic: "Whites didn't cheat Negroes—they robbed them!" Seven disagreed. Ninety-one (77.1 percent) were convinced that Negroes were also cheated in the courts. I share these majority opinions. In my county, whenever a white man was involved, the Negro was automatically guilty. As these interviews showed, it is difficult even now to get Negroes to believe otherwise. They know that Negroes were cheated in slavery, were worked and treated like animals. They know that Negroes are still cheated by whites on such things as rentals or contract buying, so they are certain that Negroes were taken advantage of on the plantations of the South after emancipation....

I cannot say that my home life was pleasant. Quarreling, wrangling, and sometimes fighting went on in our house. I got the impression early that Father was mean to our mother. He fussed at her; and when he drank too much he wanted to fight and sometimes did. All too many times we children had to hold him to keep him from hurting Mother. He would take out his knife

---

5. A team of interviewers composed of teachers and senior and graduate college students, using a carefully prepared schedule of questions, conducted in-depth personal interviews of 118 selected persons living in the Atlanta area and born in the South just before and after the turn of the century.

and threaten to cut her. Often at night, we were kept awake by Father's loud and abusive raging. I think if Mother had said nothing, there would have been fewer arguments. But Mother had to talk back. Our sympathy was with her.

Father did his trading and buying in Greenwood, and it was there that he bought his liquor. We knew when he was "high," as he would come roaring home in the wagon, beating the mules (normally he was very careful about keeping the mules in good condition) for no other reason than that he had been drinking too much. When we heard him coming at such times we knew that there would be fussing and feuding that night.

Father's drinking embarrassed me, especially so when he did it at church. Largely under the influence of my mother, I made a vow at twelve years of age that I would never drink liquor. I have kept that pledge, not because I felt this made me better than those who drink but because I never discovered any good reason for breaking it. My decision was not based on religious or moral grounds but on what I saw drinking do to my father and our family. I claim no virtue for keeping this pledge. For the same reason, I never developed the habit of smoking. Father smoked and chewed tobacco, and was not always careful where he spat. Here again I claim no special virtue; I was repelled and disgusted by my father's indulgence in these habits and I never found any reason to follow his example. At Christmastime, we used to share a little toddy, a mixture of whiskey, sugar, and water. After I was twelve, I didn't take any more of the toddy.

As I look back over the years, I am convinced that my father was not a heavy drinker. He simply could not hold his liquor. I believe that a little whiskey "did him up." When he was under the influence of drink, his eyes sparkled and became bloodshot. At most times he was a very kindly man, but when he was otherwise one would shiver in his presence and feel like running for safety. I was afraid of my father until I was past eighteen. I was then ready to defy him when he scolded me or said harsh things to me. But he was not really an alcoholic. He lived to be eighty-two years old, and in his older years he stopped drinking altogether. When he lived with me in Washington, D.C., during the time when I was dean of the School of Religion at Howard University, he never took a drink.

My mother was very religious. Every night she called the children together for evening prayer before going to bed. She always led in prayer. Occasionally all the children said short prayers, too. Father usually prayed with us. Any one of us who got sleepy and went to bed early would say prayers alone. Often I read the Bible before evening prayer, and when Father was in good humor he would read. Frequently I would read the Bible to my mother, especially certain consoling passages in the Psalms and sections of the Sermon on the Mount. How often I read to her the Thirty-seventh Psalm after one of Father's tirades!

There was no doubt in Mother's mind that God answered prayers. She believed this to her dying day. When I made a trip around the world in the latter part of 1936 and the early months of 1937, Mother "knew" that it was her prayers that brought me safe home. Shouting in church was common in my youth, and Mother did her share. The preaching was usually otherworldly, and the minister often stirred up and exploited the emotions of the people. This fact, along with her somewhat turbulent home life, accounted for Mother's emotional outbursts in church. The depth and sincerity of her religious faith had great influence on me.

In later years, my wife was shocked when she first saw the Brickhouse School, for she had expected to see a real brick building. It was named the Brickhouse School after a large brick house nearby owned by a white man. It was a frame, one-room building with a wood stove in the center of the room, with boys seated on one side and girls on the other. The school ran for four months, from the first of November through February. When we moved from the Childs' place to the Mays' place, the round trip to school was increased from about six to approximately seven miles.

It was a happy day for me when I entered the Brickhouse School at the age of six. I discovered on that eventful day that I knew more than any of the other children who were entering school for the first time. Susie, my oldest sister, had taught me to say the alphabet, to count to a hundred, and to read a little. Since I was the only one in the beginners' class who could do these things, I was praised and highly complimented by the surprised teacher. As we put it, she "bragged on me." The next church Sunday, the second Sunday in November, my teacher sought my parents and told them, with other people standing around, "Bennie is smart." From that moment on, I was the star of that one-room school. The experience made a tremendous impression on me, so much so that I felt I had to live up to my teacher's expectations. I became Exhibit A when visitors came around and I was called upon to recite, which I was always eager and ready to do....

Old Mount Zion was an important institution in my community. Negroes had nowhere to go but to church. They went there to worship, to hear the choir sing, to listen to the preacher, and to hear and see the people shout. The young people went to Mount Zion to socialize, or simply to stand around and talk. It was a place of worship and a social center as well. There was no other place to go.

This was my church, six miles from the town of Ninety Six and four miles from our house. Preaching was held every second Sunday, the pastor having other churches. If all of us were to go to church, we had to ride in a two-mule wagon, seated either on chairs or on wheat straw in the bottom of the wagon. As a rule, however, someone stayed home, and then two buggies were ample for the rest of us.

On the farm, we worked hard six days a week. Father wanted the mules to rest on the sabbath; but he never tried to keep them rested on the first and second Sundays when there were services at Mount Olive and at Mount Zion, our own church. Mount Olive, though not our church, was closer, and we usually worshipped there on the first Sunday in each month. Fairly often on the third and fourth Sundays, however, Father would insist that the mules needed rest, so if we wished to go to Sunday school at Mount Zion on those Sundays we had to walk—round trip, eight miles.

Although the members of Mount Zion were poor and most of them were renters, they were a proud lot, and many of them owned good-looking buggies and at least a couple of fine-looking horses or mules, although it is highly probable that most of them were in debt. As a youngster, I watched them driving up in beautiful rubber-tired buggies drawn by fine horses or mules. I think some of them came late to church just so they could be seen. This was the one place where the Negroes in my community could be free and relax from the toil and oppression of the week. Among themselves they were free to show off and feel important. My brother John was the sporty one in our family. He worked and saved until he could buy a white rubber-tired buggy and a beautiful white mule that he named Kate. John and Kate created quite a sensation in the community and at Mount Zion. When the boys came to church alone, they were expected to take their girlfriends home—a duty that they did not find at all burdensome.

Fighting and heavy drinking on church property were common practices in many churches, but not much of this went on at Mount Zion, thanks largely to the man who pastored Mount Zion for fifty years or more.

The Reverend James F. Marshall was hardly more than a fifth-grade scholar, but he knew the scriptures, at least so far as knowing where certain passages were to be found. He could quote almost any passage of scripture from memory. He accepted the Bible as it was printed and held it was "wicked" to doubt any part of it. We thought he was the best preacher in the world (our world was Greenwood County). He was eloquent. He could moan, and did. Almost invariably he made some of the people shout. If he did not moan a bit and make the people shout, his congregation felt he had not preached well. The intellectual content of his sermons was not nearly as important as the emotional appeal.

The Reverend Marshall set a good example for the people. I believe no one ever accused him of any dishonesty or immorality. Wives and daughters were safe in his presence. He did not touch liquor. The same could not be said of all the ministers who pastored in Greenwood County. The Reverend Marshall, who lived twenty-four miles away from the church, usually held Conference on the second Saturday afternoon and stayed overnight with a family of the church. It was a rare privilege to have the pastor spend the night in one's home. The house was spic and span when the preacher came, and the best food was served. He was the only hero we had around Zion to worship. So impeccable (or discreet) was the Reverend Marshall's conduct that the only story circulated about him was that once he got up in the middle of the night and left a certain woman's house because she had approached him in an immoral way. The young people heard all the gossip the old people talked, and if there had been any scandal about Marshall, the young people would have heard and no doubt circulated it. He was accused of loving money too well, but he was never accused of stealing it. Why shouldn't he have loved it? Why, indeed, should he not have lusted for it? He had ten

children or more; and from his four churches he received a total of only $800 a year.

The Reverend Marshall's preaching was highly otherworldly, emphasizing the joys of heaven and the damnation of hell. He preached funerals according to the life the deceased had lived. He didn't hesitate to preach the dead "smack into heaven" or into hell, according to the life he or she had lived. The church was usually full at funerals, especially if the deceased had been well known; and when a man of bad reputation died the church was jammed. The people wanted to hear what kind of funeral sermon Marshall would preach. I am sure that a burning hell and a golden-streeted heaven were as real as their farms to a majority of the people in Mount Zion and in the community at large. They believed the trials and tribulations of the world would all be over when one got to heaven. Beaten down at every turn by the white man, as they were, Negroes could perhaps not have survived without this kind of religion.

There was no doubt in the minds of some that Marshall had special power with God. Even when he prayed for rain and it didn't come, they still believed he had influence with God. If he prayed for rain on the second Sunday in the month and it came the next day, it was obviously in answer to Marshall's prayer.

Members who had done great wrongs were brought before the Church Conference on the second Saturday in the month. Frequently they were turned out of the church if the Conference proclaimed them guilty. But a person could repent, or make a pretense of repentance, and be taken right back into the fold. I was present at a Church Conference when a young couple appeared who had been sexually intimate; the young woman was pregnant. They admitted what they had done. Marshall advised the young man to marry the girl. With his right hand lifted toward heaven, Marshall told the young man that if he didn't marry the young woman and live with her, fulfilling the duties of a husband, something unspeakably bad would happen to him. The young man married the girl on the spot, but then went on his way, never assuming any responsibility for his wife or child. Not long afterward, he was killed one midnight, so viciously beaten to death with a club that his brains were spattered all over the ground. In the summer of 1968, my sister told me Negroes believed that this young man had been killed by a certain white man because he was hanging around a Negro woman with whom the white man was having relations. Neither whites nor Negroes did anything to apprehend the murderer. The apparent fulfillment of Marshall's prophecy in this case skyrocketed his prestige in the community. Thereafter nobody wanted Preacher Marshall to "put bad mouth" on them.

Although Marshall taught the people to be honest and upright, the Gospel he preached was primarily an opiate to enable them to endure and survive the oppressive conditions under which they lived at the hands of the white people in the community. I never heard him utter one word against lynching. If he had, he would probably have been run out of the community—or lynched. When a visiting minister attempted to condemn white people, Pastor Marshall stopped him. I was there. I saw it and I heard it. I am not necessarily condemning the use of religion as an opiate. Sometimes an opiate is good in medicine. Sometimes it may be good in religion. Certainly religious faith has helped me in my struggles.

As my pastor accepted the system and made no effort to change it, so it was in other churches—Negro and white—in my day. Of the 118 persons interviewed who could remember what kind of sermons were being preached around the turn of the century, fifty-nine (50 percent) said that their ministers taught them nothing about white people. Twenty (17 percent) reported that their ministers instructed them to obey white people, be submissive and humble, and get along with whites. Twenty-one said their ministers taught them to be respectful

to whites. Nineteen did not answer the question on the church and race. Only four said that their ministers taught them to demand their rights. One woman said that her pastor was bitter about the racial situation. The vast majority of them said the church was helpful to them.

Pastor Marshall "stayed in" with the local white Methodist preacher, although Marshall believed that all who were not Baptists were hellward bound. When certain elements in the church wanted to get rid of Marshall, he invited the Reverend Pierce Kinard, a white Methodist, to come to Zion and advise the Negroes to keep Marshall, which of course effectively ended the incipient move to have Preacher Marshall removed.

The Reverend Marshall baptized every member in my family, including Mother and Father. Father did not join the church until after the earthquake in 1886. My parents told me that, after the quake, the Reverend Marshall baptized a hundred men at one session. "God moves in mysterious ways!"

Mother believed, as Marshall did, that only Baptists could get to heaven—that is, she did until my brother, H. H., joined the Presbyterian Church! When I teased her about this, Mother replied, "All things are possible with God." As a small boy, I really felt sorry for the Methodists who passed our house going to the Methodist church. Not for long, however, could I believe that they were all bound for hell, for some of my best friends were non-Baptists; some of the girls I began to like were not Baptists; and indeed I ended up marrying a member of the CME Church.

Though the people of Mount Zion, for the most part, were poor and unlettered, nevertheless they did much for me. As I sat as a boy in Sunday School, discussing the Sunday School lessons with the adults, asking questions and making comments, they encouraged me and gave me their blessings. Each Sunday in June, we had what was called "Children's Day." I do not remember exactly how old I was—possibly nine—when I participated, having committed to memory a portion of the Sermon on the Mount. After my recitation, the house went wild: old women waved their handkerchiefs, old men stamped their feet, and the people generally applauded long and loud. It was a terrific ovation, let alone a tremendous experience, for a nine-year-old boy. There were predictions that I would "go places" in life. The minister said I would preach; and from that moment on the Reverend Marshall manifested a special interest in me. All of this was part of the motivation that had started with my oldest sister's teaching me how to count and read and write, thereby winning for me the encouragement and praise given me by my first teacher, Ellen Waller. The people in the church did not contribute one dime to help me with my education. But they gave me something far more valuable. They gave me encouragement, the thing I most needed. They expressed such confidence in me that I always felt that I could never betray their trust, never let them down....

At revival time in August, people could go from one church to another for a whole month if they chose because there were churches within an eight- or ten-mile radius of our house that held preaching one Sunday each month, and August was "Big Meeting" month. For the church that held worship on the first Sunday in August, the Big Meeting, or Revival, was held the first week in August, and so on through the month. Many buggies and wagons were on the road. There were no paved roads; when it was dry the roads were very dusty, and when it rained they were very muddy. As a rule, Negroes did not pass white people on either a dusty or a muddy road. If a Negro did pass a white person, throwing dust on him, the Negro was supposed to apologize for passing. I have been with my father when he apologized for passing a white driver by saying, "Excuse me, Boss, I'm in a hurry." Did this mean that my father mentally accepted or emotionally approved this cringing

behavior? I doubt it. It was a technique of survival. But I have always wondered how long one can do a thing without eventually accepting it. I believe my father rebelled against the system as best he knew how. Dozens of times, I heard him tell, in gleeful tones and with a sparkle in his eyes, how when he was young he had whipped two white men. He knocked one of them down and, while that one was getting up, he knocked the other man down. Every time he told the story, he would laugh, and laugh, and laugh. It was his prize story.

I never had a white playmate; but seventy-two (63.7 percent) of those interviewed for my study said that they had had white playmates. The vast majority of them admitted that such shared play ceased in the preteen or early teen years, usually at twelve or thirteen. When play stopped, so did friendship.

My parents advised us further, especially my mother. They admonished my brothers and me to stay clear of white women. My mother told us that white women were dangerous and would surely get us into trouble. Whenever we met them on the road, or on the street in town, we were to "give them space and the time of day." If there were white women in the community whom we knew, we tipped our hats to them and passed on. Although Negroes were lynched for minor offenses as well as for major ones, real or trumped up, the white press tended to give the impression that Negroes were lynched only when white women were involved. A careful review of the Southern newspapers published at the turn of the century reveals that scores of articles on lynching carried statements such as: "Lynched for the Usual Crime." However, all well-informed people knew that this was a cover-up, a false front to justify the lynching of Negroes. *Thirty Years of Lynching in the United States, 1889–1918* (NAACP: New York) discloses that of the 3,255 victims of lynching during this period only 19 percent of the cases involved rape or any alleged sex offense. The white press deliberately created the myth that lynching was necessary in order to protect white womanhood.

The false pretense of protecting white women expressed itself in ways other than lynching. Even a very young, innocent Negro boy could be beaten up—even killed—if by mere accident he touched a white girl. Not long ago, Arthur L. Johnson, deputy superintendent of the Detroit public school system, a graduate of Morehouse College during my presidency, told a representative of the Civil Rights Documentation Project what happened to him on a street in Birmingham, Alabama, when he was only thirteen years old. Through no fault of his, he accidentally put his hand on the shoulder of a white girl of about five or six, for which he was immediately almost murdered.

Mays is determined to get an education, even though his father is convinced that "education went to one's head and made him a fool and dishonest." He follows his mother's example and prays for God to move "every hindrance and cause" out of his way so that he can get away to school. An opportunity arises, and he attends high school at South Carolina State College in Orangeburg, then goes on to graduate from Bates College in Maine in 1920. From there he goes to the University of Chicago, and then to Tampa, Florida, as head of the Tampa Urban League. Mays's wife, Sadie, earns an M.A. from the University of Chicago in 1931, and Mays receives the Ph.D. in 1935, after he has already been hired as dean of the School of Religion at Howard University. He continues to think and write about the relationship of the Christian Church and racism in the United States.

I believe that throughout my lifetime, the local white church has been society's most conservative and hypocritical institution in the area of white-Negro relations. Nor has the local black church a record of which to be proud. The states, schools, business enterprises, industries, theaters, recreation centers, hotels, restaurants, hospitals, trains, boats, waiting rooms, and

> When the church maintains a segregated house, and simultaneously preaches the fatherhood of God and the brotherhood of man, then surely *hypocrisy* is the mildest term one can apply.

filling stations have all played their ignominious roles in the tragedy of segregating the black man and discriminating against him; but at least none of these enterprises claims to have a divine mission on earth. The church boasts of its unique origin, maintaining that God, not man is the source of its existence. The church alone calls itself the House of God, sharing this honor with no other American institution. The church is indeed sui generis.

The local white churches, the vast majority of them, have not lived up to their professed Christianity, because Christian fellowship across racial barriers is so inherent in the very nature of the church that to deny fellowship in God's House, on the basis of race or color, is a profanation of all that the church stands for. Secular organizations make no commitments, nor do they prate about brotherhood among men and a gospel of redemption and salvation. When the church maintains a segregated house, and simultaneously preaches the fatherhood of God and the brotherhood of man, then surely *hypocrisy* is the mildest term one can apply. *Whited sepulcher* comes to mind.

Although the local black church has never denied white people the privilege of entrance for worship in their churches, and has often inflated the white man's already bloated ego by giving him preferential seating, Negro church members would hardly welcome large numbers of white people to membership in their congregations. I believe this attitude is not based so much on race as it is on the desire of Negroes to maintain control of their churches. Then too, Negroes would hardly want to run the risk of being hurt or humiliated by whites who so often exhibit a superior air in their association with Negroes. The basic difference between the black and white churches is that the black church has never had a policy of racial exclusiveness. The white church has.

Leadership in the church is supposedly different from that in secular life. In earlier years, and even today, the minister was said to be specially "called of God" to do His work, to preach His truth. Early in my life I became aware of the dichotomy in the preaching and the practice of the church leadership. Now and then the Reverend James F. Marshall, my pastor, would invite white ministers to preach at Mount Zion, especially the Methodist minister, the Reverend Pierce Kinard. My father, though illiterate, was never impressed with the Reverend Kinard's message. He once remarked about the Reverend Kinard's emphasis on living right in order to be assured of God's blessings and of eternal salvation, while at the same time Negroes were being cheated, beaten, and lynched throughout South Carolina. As young as I was, I got the message. The few Negroes who attended the Reverend Kinard's tent meetings were thoroughly segregated. Members of my family never attended because they were

Methodist meetings for whites, and, frankly, we were actually afraid to attend a white church.

The gospel in Negro and white churches alike was definitely otherworld-oriented and never even hinted at bringing whites and blacks of the county closer together for the improvement of social and economic conditions. After all, if the "righteous" were to be rewarded in heaven, where there would be no more night, no sickness, no death, where the angels had wings and the streets were paved with gold, it mattered little that black people were exploited and mistreated here on earth! The Negro's song, "Take All the World and Give Me Jesus," was never considered seriously by the white man, even though he may have believed in heaven. He had as much of Jesus as the Negro—and the world besides!

My early unhappy racial experiences explain my cynicism about the sincerity of many white ministers. I have never cared to listen to any minister who would deny fellowship on a racial basis. More than once I have turned off the radio or the television rather than listen to the preaching of a man known to advocate a segregated church. I tuned out Billy Graham as long as he held revivals under segregated conditions. When he came to Atlanta early in his career, the Council of Presidents of the Atlanta University Center was asked to provide a segregated meeting for the students and faculties of the Center. Needless to say, we refused, and we felt it was an insult to us to be asked to do this. I listen to Billy Graham now with appreciation of what he says and the hope that he is a sincere convert of his own teaching. Segregation in the House of God has been a great strain on my religion.

In the process of writing this book, I read widely the most reputable newspapers of the South published between 1880 and 1910. I was anxious to find out what they had to say about lynching, the most vicious evil of my early years, and what their attitude was toward the

Negro. I do not recall ever having seen a single article by a minister, a group of ministers, or by anyone speaking in the name of the church and Christianity that condemned the horrible crime of lynching. During this time, the church was truly both in the world and of the world. Earlier in this book, I have related in detail examples of the horrifying lynchings which took place in Phoenix, South Carolina, in the county of my birth. The Phoenix Riot, with its accompanying lynchings, is one of the most hideous records in the history of this country. One would think that somewhere, in at least one of the South Carolina newspapers, the voice of the church would have been heard speaking out for justice and stamping its disapproval upon such savagery. I found no record of a church voice raised in protest. The church was so much a part of the system that lynching was accepted as part of the Southern way of life just as casually as was segregation. Ironically enough, when the Southern people did begin to cry out against lynching, it was not the voice of organized southern and northern ministers but of southern white women under the leadership of the Commission on Interracial Cooperation. The Southern Association of Women for the Prevention of Lynching was organized in Atlanta in 1930, under the leadership of Jessie Daniel Ames, and did much to denigrate lynching in the South. Time has not done much to change the silence of the local church in the midst of racial ills.

The local white church has always been conservative when it comes to taking a stand on social issues, especially so if the issue involves black people. Local black churches have been far more prophetic than the local white churches. So-called radical movements, such as the National Association for the Advancement of Colored People, have always had access to black churches. The Southern Christian Leadership Conference, under the leadership of Martin Luther King, Jr., and, since 1968, under Ralph David Abernathy, and the National Conference of Black Churchmen have involved the local Negro churches in programs designed to bring about social and economic justice for black people. But North and South, Negro and white churches remain highly segregated. A thoroughly desegregated church, embracing a representative number of blacks and whites, is a *rara avis* in the United States.

In the area of race, local churches have followed, not led. When segregation in the public schools was declared unconstitutional on 17 May 1954, one would have expected the local churches to urge compliance on moral and religious grounds. But for too long a time the local white ministers in Atlanta and in other Southern cities were silent, and when they did speak it was as a group. For the most part, the individual pastor was afraid to urge compliance, afraid to stand alone. He wanted protection from the group as well as the benefit of the impact that the group might make if he were to speak out.

The local Atlanta white ministers certainly did not lead in a program to abolish segregation in the public schools. Indeed, it can hardly be said that they even followed. It was three and a half years after the 17 May 1954 decision of the Supreme Court before some eighty white ministers in Atlanta broke their silence on the Court's decision. It is disgraceful that it took the Atlanta white ministers forty-two months to come out with a statement on segregation in the public schools, and it is even more shameful that when they did speak it was only as individuals, for they did not dare speak for their congregations. They felt that they had to say they were opposed to intermarriage and against the amalgamation of the races. They expressed belief in "preserving the integrity of both races through the free choice of both." It is utterly fantastic for white ministers to speak for white men against the amalgamation of the races. The white man's activities in this area of behavior are a matter of history the world around. The black race in America has been amalgamated for centuries. I suppose these men of the cloth felt compelled to say such things to please the white public.

Speaking three and a half years after the 1954 decision outlawing segregation in the public schools, the white ministers of Atlanta issued a statement both weak and inconclusive. They said, in part:

> As Americans and as Christians we have an obligation to obey the law. This does not mean that all loyal citizens need approve the 1954 decision of the Supreme Court with reference to segregation in the public schools. Those who feel that this decision was in error have every right to work for an alteration in the decree, either through a further change in the Supreme Court's interpretation of the law, or through an amendment to the Constitution of the United States. It does mean that we have no right to defy the constituted authority in the government of our nation. Assuredly also it means that resorts to violence and to economic reprisals as a means to avoid the granting of legal rights to other citizens are never justified.

If I had been a segregationist, I could have freely signed this document.

A year later 312 Atlanta ministers spoke somewhat more pointedly to the issue at hand. This group was speaking in the interest of preserving the public schools. These ministers were also cautious. They were against massive integration and sincerely opposed to the amalgamation of the races. They pleaded for time where desegregation of schools was most difficult and expressed the hope that state and local authorities would be allowed to do the job when good faith in compliance had been shown. This group, too, urged law and order, and said that those who were dissatisfied with the decision should seek legal ways to change it. They insisted, however, that closing the public schools would be a tragedy.

All in all, their November 1958 manifesto was a plea for gradualism. It called for intelligent discussion of the issues of integration, asked that creative thought be given to preserving the public schools, and advocated a citizens' committee to preserve harmony within the community. It was clearly not a manifesto for integration but rather one for law and Christian duty. And its sponsors did what "Christian" and "religious" people usually do when they lack the will to act: They called on God. They said, "Man cannot will himself to do this. The Christian, or Jew, can do this only with the help of God." They called for prayer and the strength to do it. It is indeed strange that when man does evil, he has the will, but when he faces a moral crisis and needs to do what is right, he calls on God to give him the strength to do it.

The one white minister who did speak on his own, Dr. Roy D. McClain, of Atlanta's First Baptist Church, preached a sermon that was absolutely safe, and this was two years after the 17 May decision. Any way one read his statement, it was clear that he was opposed to the decision of the Supreme Court outlawing segregation in the public schools. It was distinctly more pro-segregation than pro-integration.

Dr. McClain is an eloquent and convincing speaker. When in early summer, 1956, he spoke about the 17 May decision, his words were as usual carefully chosen and beautifully uttered. Both the Atlanta *Constitution* and the Atlanta *Journal,* in their issues of 25 June 1956, quoted heavily from Dr. McClain's pro-segregation sermon. The *Constitution* quoted Dr. McClain as follows: "the last twenty-four months have engendered more strife and hatred than the last decade of normal progress." The Atlanta *Journal* quoted Dr. McClain thus: "Righteousness cannot be legislated any more than education can be; one cannot be forced into the acquisition of facts; instead he can be encouraged, shown and nurtured." He said that coexistence is possible without cohabitation, but that "this does not mean, however, that there is a first and second class citizenry. Such could never be justified in democracy, Christianity, or anything." Evidently Dr. McClain had forgotten history. Negroes and whites had coexisted in this country for three and a half centuries, and a glance at any Negro audience testifies that there has been considerable cohabitation.

Organized church bodies, unlike the local churches, did support the Supreme Court's 1954 decision. Several denominations spoke out: for example, the Southern Baptist Convention, the Southern Presbyterians, the North Georgia Methodist Conference, and the Council of Church Women from fifteen Southern states.

However, even the pronouncements of these Southern church bodies made no real impact on the local churches. They continued their segregated ways. Dr. Martin Luther King, Sr., tells of his experience in a local Atlanta church:

> I had heard of Roy McClain's ability as a preacher, so, shortly after he came to First Baptist Church on Peachtree, I decided to go hear him preach. I asked Mrs. Crawford, one of the trustees of Ebenezer, since deceased, and Mrs. Hudson if they would like to ride out with me...for Sunday morning worship.
>
> We went early...and arrived before Sunday School was out. I parked and we went in the front door into the sanctuary. We were met at the door very cordially, and we went in and seated ourselves about two seats down on the right-hand side, with me taking the aisle seat. We had been given bulletins of the order of worship at the door. A white woman came in, bowed to us, smiled, and seated herself alongside the two ladies who were with me.
>
> We sat for about twenty minutes, and then I noticed two or three people near the podium deep in a discussion. Finally, one of them came back and said to me, "You folks can worship down in our chapel." I told him we were quite all right where we were, and

he went away muttering to himself. Another came, much rougher talking than the first, and said, "Now you folks know we have a place where you can worship down in our chapel. You will have to go down there and you will have to go *now*."

> I said to my companions, well, I guess we'll just go back. The man kept saying to me, in a very ugly mood, "Well, are you going? Are you going?" Mrs. Crawford said, "We didn't come here to cause any trouble." The man said, "Well, you are going away somewhere!" and grabbed me by the arm. "You are just here to make trouble, that's all." I told him he was mistaken and he shoved me, and we left....

Paradoxical as it is, churches that believe in and practice segregation have been sending missionaries to Africa and Asia for years to convert the "heathens" to Christianity.... I heard Africans talk about this dichotomy when I was in Liberia, Ghana, and Ethiopia. African students at Morehouse during my presidency remarked about the way missionaries from America segregated Negroes in the United States and sought to save the souls of black Africans in Africa. Many black people in this country believe that some white missionaries go to foreign lands to evangelize colored people in order to atone for the way in which black people are brutalized here in the United States.

Though persuaded to Christianity by Southern missionaries in Africa the converted Africans would hardly be welcomed to fellowship and membership in the very local Southern churches that helped to foster the foreign missionary enterprises....

In 1944 Mays is elected vice-president of the Federal Council of Churches of Christ in America. His election makes national news because he is the first black man chosen for that position since the Federal Council was formed in 1912.

Two experiences that happened during my two years as vice-president of the Federal Council are worth relating here.

First, the Council held a special meeting in Columbus, Ohio, 5–7 March 1946. President Truman was a guest speaker. Winston Churchill was traveling on the presidential train with Truman. Mr. Churchill chose to remain on the train while the President spoke to the delegates of the Federal Council. The officers of the Council thought it would be a good gesture if we went down to the train to greet Winston Churchill, and we did. He showed no particular enthusiasm for our visit, and I thought he received us rather coldly. Consequently, I felt no particular enthusiasm for nor was I impressed by this great man.

Though vice-president of the Council, I evidently posed a problem to some of the Council leadership. Where was I to sit—on the platform with the President of the United States or in a special seat up front in the audience? I have always wondered whether there would have been any debate if the vice-president of the Council had been white. As the second officer in the Council, I should have helped decide who would sit on the rostrum. The decision was made for me to sit in the front row in the audience. Several rows in front were being left for dignitaries and secret service men. I was advised to take my seat in the front row before the presidential party came in and before other guests had taken the reserved seats.

Several persons came to request me to move, saying that the place where I was sitting was reserved for special people. I didn't move. Finally Earl F. Adams, secretary of the Protestant Council of New York, came to me and said, "Why are you sitting here? As vice-president of the Council, you belong on the rostrum with the President of the United States." He said, "Wait, I'll fix it." Another chair was placed on the rostrum and, when the President came in, I was escorted to the rostrum. Evidently I had presented a problem that Earl Adams solved. People in the audience had wondered why I didn't move as requested. When I went to the rostrum, the mystery seemed solved. They thought it was planned from the beginning that I would sit on the rostrum. Not so.

Secondly, at the same conference, the Federal Council took a giant step. It issued an official document stating in forceful language that it was opposed to segregation in any form and that the Council from that moment on would work to eliminate it. This was, I believe, the first time the Federal Council had made such a declaration, and so was assuming national leadership among church bodies. It was significant, too, that Will W. Alexander, who had been head of the Commission on Interracial Cooperation until the new organization, the Southern Regional Council, was organized, was chairman of the seminar on race. The Commission on Interracial Cooperation never did declare itself against the segregated system. The seminar on race of the Federal Council, chaired by Alexander, raised its voice in opposition to segregation in every area of life. I think it important to quote one paragraph of a document from the seminar on church and race of which I was a member:

> The Federal Council of the Churches of Christ in America hereby renounces the pattern of segregation in race relations as unnecessary and undesirable and a violation of the gospel of love and human brotherhood. Having taken this action, the Federal Council requests its constituent communion to do likewise. As proof of their sincerity in this renunciation, they will work for a nonsegregated church and a nonsegregated society.

I was glad to see Will Alexander move to this position. He fought for this statement vigorously, and I am mighty glad that I was a member of the seminar that assisted in its formulation. The Federal Council, and now the National Council, never retreated from this position. The National Council has gone beyond mere pronouncements to participation in the arena where the action is. It has taken a leading role in such action projects as: The Delta Ministry; The Ghetto Investment Program; the Crisis in the Nation Program; and The Mississippi Summer Project on Voter Registration. It has also been active in the field of legislation, has participated in Project Equality, and given encouragement to the National Urban Coalition....

Sadie, her sister Emma C. W. Gray, and I drove from Toronto to Cleveland, Ohio, to attend the Eighth Baptist World Congress, which met in 1950. As we drove from Toronto to Cleveland, we did not expect to find any kind of discrimination. We were wholly unprepared for being refused accommodations at a motel in Niagara Falls, Canada. We had certainly not expected to encounter discrimination in Canada. Nothing we said moved the proprietor. We were black, and he didn't take our kind. We finally found a motel that housed us for the night.

This experience was grist for my mill. I was going to the Eighth Congress of the World Baptist Alliance, where representatives came from forty-eight nations and some fifty thousand people were in attendance. I had two important assignments in the Congress: I chaired the Commission on Social Justice; and was to give a major address on the subject "Christian Light on Human Relationships." The experience at the motel in Niagara apparently helped me in my seminar and in my address. My seminar got through a resolution calling upon all Baptists and affiliated organizations to use their influence to have discriminatory laws repealed and other laws enacted to safeguard the rights of oppressed racial groups. Our

resolution further asked each Baptist to examine his own soul with a view toward freeing himself of racial and cultural prejudices and embodying in his own person the mind and spirit of Christ in all human relations.

My seminar subject, "Social Justice," was closely related to my speech. I have always tried to take an objective view of responses to my speeches, knowing perfectly and sadly well that such responses may be largely emotional outbursts and nothing more lasting. When I finished my address in Cleveland, the people in the huge auditorium sprang to their feet and applauded long and loud. As good as this made me feel, I knew that nothing would really change as a result of that address. I knew that local churches would remain segregated, that discriminatory laws would remain on the statute books, that, as I drove from Cleveland home to Morehouse, I would meet the discrimination I had always met in hotels and restaurants, and that national and world bodies would go on passing resolutions, and that things would go on as before. But, like the Hebrew prophets, one must make his witness even though we do not repent....

Of the countless incidents I could relate about Martin Luther King, Jr., I have chosen three because it seems to me that they illustrate so perfectly the quality of the man's soul—his vision, his courage, his magnificent capacity for self-denying love.

The first of these concerns Rosa Parks, who was arrested 1 December 1955. Nobody knows just why, on this particular occasion, she didn't choose to obey the bus driver's order to get up so a white man might sit down. Perhaps she was tired after working all day; perhaps she was just tired of being pushed around all her life by white folks. At any rate, she sat—and the Boycott was on!

When the Montgomery officials discovered that violence could not stay the protest or stop the Boycott, they resorted to mass arrest, using an old state law against boycotts. Dr. King, who was in Nashville at the time, knew that if he returned to Montgomery he would be arrested too. En route to Montgomery, he stopped overnight in Atlanta. His father, frantic for his son's safety, assembled a group of friends to consult with them about the wisdom of Martin Luther Jr.'s immediate return to Montgomery. It was on 22 February 1956 that we met at the residence of Martin Luther King, Sr., and according to Martin Luther's own book, *Stride Toward Freedom,* the following persons were present: A. T. Walden, a distinguished attorney; C. R. Yates and T. M. Alexander, both prominent businessmen; C. A. Scott, editor of the Atlanta *Daily World;* Bishop Sherman L. Green of the AME Church; Rufus E. Clement, president of Atlanta University; and Benjamin E. Mays, president of Morehouse College. As I myself remember, Attorney Dan Duke was also present.

Reverend King, Sr., stated his reason for calling us together and expressed his conviction that his son should not return to Montgomery right away. In *Stride Toward Freedom,* Martin Luther King, Jr., writes that after his father's statement

there were murmurs of agreement in the room, and I listened as sympathetically and objectively as I could while two of the men gave their reasons for concurring. These were my elders, leaders among my people. Their words commanded respect. But soon I could not restrain myself any longer: "I must go back to Montgomery—my friends and associates are being arrested. It would be the height of cowardice for me to stay away. I would rather be in jail ten years than desert my people now. I have begun the struggle, and I can't turn back. I have reached the point of no return." In the moment of silence that followed, I heard my father break into tears. I looked at Doctor Mays, one of the great influences in my life. Perhaps he heard my unspoken plea. At any rate, he was soon defending my position strongly.

I had to defend Martin Luther's position. Here was a man of deep integrity and firm convictions. How could he have decided otherwise than to return to Montgomery? How could he hide while his comrades in nonviolent arms

> ## We were wholly unprepared for being refused accommodations at a motel in Niagara Falls, Canada. We had certainly not expected to encounter discrimination in Canada.
>
> ## Nothing we said moved the proprietor.
>
> ## We were black, and he didn't take our kind.

were being carried to jail? That, in essence, was what I said.

I am mighty glad that I had the wisdom to give him the moral support he needed at that time. I had admired him ever since he entered Morehouse as a freshman: now my respect for him mounted on wings. In the light of this definitive statement of Dr. King's, I shall always wonder why Louis E. Lomax, in his book *To Kill a Black Man,* stated that at this meeting I had been opposed to Dr. King's return to Montgomery.

As for the second event, the officials in Alabama, and particularly in Montgomery, took great delight in harassing Martin Luther King, Jr., even after the Montgomery Bus Boycott ended. In 1957, when Ralph Abernathy was being tried on some trumped-up charge, the Montgomery courtroom was almost full. When Dr. King wanted to get in, the officers refused him permission, and upon his insistence, he was arrested. Twisting his arms, they pushed and kicked him into a cell. Before Mrs. King and others could plan a strategy for getting Dr. King out, he was suddenly released. At the trial, he was convicted of *loitering,* and given the choice: He could serve time or pay a fine. Here came the great decision. Convinced that he had been unlawfully arrested and unjustly convicted, and therefore could not in good conscience pay the fine, Dr. King announced that he would serve his time in jail. This pronouncement shocked and stunned the court. I understand that the judge almost begged Dr. King to pay the fine. Some person—at the time unknown—paid it. Later it was learned that Clyde Sellers, the chief of police, had paid it, remarking that it would be cheaper to pay the fine than to have Martin Luther King, Jr., in jail at the city's expense.

Dr. King's decision not to pay went almost unnoticed at the time, but to me it was one of the most momentous decisions of his whole civil rights career. It made a tremendous impression on me. He would obey an unjust verdict. But by serving time rather than paying a fine for something he should never have been convicted of, he registered for the whole world his protest against injustice. His great decision has motivated and will continue to motivate the actions of others as we pursue this long journey up the precipitous hill toward racial justice, democracy, and Christian living in this country.

A third incident will dramatize Martin Luther King, Jr.'s high regard for the law, even for unjust laws. Those who have condemned him for admonishing people to break unjust laws have not realized that when he himself violated them he was not being irresponsible nor was he advising others to be irresponsible. It was his way of seeking to achieve social change without instigating physical violence. If he had violated the law and then cried for amnesty, his action in a sense would have been irresponsible and would have indicated disrespect for law. But when Martin Luther violated the law he did so consciously and deliberately and was always willing to pay the penalty exacted by law, even though the law was blatantly unjust. He was willing to suffer for a righteous cause in the firm belief that this kind of suffering was redemptive.

I saw him demonstrate this belief on 29 October 1967. President Glenn H. Leggett had invited a group of distinguished Americans to Grinnell College [in Iowa] to confer honorary degrees. Dr. King and I were among them—he to give the convocation address in the morning before the conferring of degrees in the after-noon, and I to introduce him. His schedule was so tight that he had warned Grinnell that he might not be able to get there, so an official of the college asked me to stand in if he couldn't make it. An emphatic "No" had to be my answer to this request—this huge crowd had come to hear Dr. King, not me. No substitute would have been adequate. To make his appearance, Dr. King had to come by a private plane provided by a friend. The crowd that had waited patiently for ninety minutes for his arrival gave him a standing ovation when he appeared, and applauded long and loud when he finished speaking.

This was the speech Martin Luther King, Jr., made just before he returned to Alabama once more to serve time for contempt of court. He had a heavy cold, and I was greatly concerned when he left me in Grinnell to go to Birmingham. He could have ducked another ordeal by staying out of Alabama, but true to his character he would not run and hide even though he knew he was being punished unjustly. Only one who has the highest respect for law is willing to serve time for violating laws whether just or unjust. This man never cried for mercy; he never asked for amnesty.

The Grinnell experience was five months and eight days before his assassination. My next public speech about Martin Luther was the eulogy I gave at his funeral on 9 April 1968.

Mays becomes one of the most recognized and respected leaders of the African-American church. His autobiography, Born to Rebel, *tells of his many accomplishments. Here is the way it ends.*

Despite my constant rebellion against a cruel and unjust system for almost seventy years, life has been kind to me in many ways. I have earned degrees from one of the best colleges and from one of the best universities in the nation. I have never had to ask for a job; offers—more than I could accept—have come unsolicited, and still do. I have traveled fairly extensively in North America, Europe, Asia, and Africa, on missions for my government, the church, the YMCA, and educational institutions. Twenty-eight distinguished colleges and universities have conferred honorary degrees upon me. Many people have helped me on my way, and Sadie and I in turn tried to help as many as we could. I have spoken and written what seemed to me to be the truth, even when there was the risk of being branded a Communist or a fellow traveler. I have always hated injustice and discrimination of every descrip-

tion, and I have fought them all of my life and shall continue to do so, but I am not bitter.

I have developed my friends across racial and religious lines, and I have never placed superior or inferior value on friendship on the basis of race or religion. I have never believed that the white man belongs to a race that is superior to other races of men. I believe that factors other than intellect and technical know-how must be taken into account when one is evaluating superiority. I believe that no race can claim superiority that has achieved its place by exploiting other peoples and conquering them through war. The criteria of superiority must include manifestations of justice, mercy, and social concern for the weak. If these are included in the criteria for superiority, the white man hardly qualifies as a superior race. He has exploited the weak, the ignorant, and the poor across the face of the earth.

I have not considered my social standing enhanced either by association with distinguished Negroes or by association with distinguished whites. I have enjoyed and appreciated my friends regardless of their stations in life. People are people. I have never sought "acceptance" as such, but I have wanted respect from all mankind. Love is wonderful; but if I could not have both, I would prefer respect. In the days when I was forbidden to ride Pullman, I insisted on doing so not because I wanted to be with white people but because I desired to ride comfortably and sleep well at night and because I had as much right to these accommodations as anyone else. It was fine when the passengers were friendly, but when they were not I was neither hurt nor embarrassed. When dining-car service and hotel accommodations were denied me, I kept hammering away at the problem because I wanted to be able to eat a decent meal and sleep comfortably—never just because I wanted to be with white people. When I ran into my black or white friends, and we visited together, I was delighted to be with them, but their color was incidental. Two and a half years ago, Sadie and I moved into a tokenly integrated neighborhood, now mostly black, in southwest Atlanta. We purchased our home in that vicinity because we wanted a pleasant location in which to spend our last years—that there were white people in the area neither attracted nor repulsed us. I have always felt that white people who defend segregation as if it were a very God must be shivering cold in their emotional insecurity.

I do not know whether there is a solution to the Negro-white problem. Whether racism in the United States can ever be abolished, I am not omniscient enough to say. To date, education and religion have not abolished racism, despite the fact that education is supposed to enable a man to find truth and follow it, while religion is designed to make men good. When I consider the Jew, I find no comfort in history for the Negro's plight. No other group in the annals of time has contributed so much, with so few in number, to the well-being of mankind. And yet anti-Semitism is centuries old and still shows its ugly face with alarming frequency throughout this and every other land.

It seems to me, however, that we have no choice but to continue our efforts to make this country a decent place for all Americans. As Henry van Dyke says, in *The Other Wise Man,* "It is better to follow even the shadow of the best than to remain content with the worst." I have the faith to believe that whites and blacks can improve their relationship to the extent that they can live together in peace, each respecting the other. Whether we like it or not, we can neither elude nor escape each other. I am convinced that any program designed to solve the black-white problem by providing a geographically segregated place for twenty million blacks is destined to failure. Moreover, believing as I do that offensive nonviolent actions of the

Gandhi–Martin Luther King, Jr., type are the best way by which to improve Negro-white relations, I am convinced that any offensive, violent programs instigated by Negroes will profit little. Nor do I believe that the black man's salvation lies in the total destruction of the present social, economic, and political systems, and that on the ruins a new order of justice, freedom, and equality for all Americans will spring, full-blown. The same tainted and distorted humanity that built the present systems will build the new. Whatever the future holds for the American people, it must be accepted that the United States belongs to the black man as much as to the white man. Most of us were born in this country and we will live here and die here.

Finally, if the governments, private businesses, schools, churches, individuals, and the American people have the will, they can contribute to the solution of this problem. We can, within a ten-year span, provide decent housing for every family, make adequate jobs available for every able-bodied person, provide the kind of education that each child is able to absorb, make accessible medical care for all, abolish poverty and malnutrition, and permit each man to advance on his merit without his being penalized because he is black.

President John F. Kennedy could predict that in ten years we would place a man on the moon, and his prophecy came true. President Nixon asserted that we could fly to Mars in ten years or more. If we can set a timetable to get to the moon and to Mars—and meet it— God knows we can set a timetable to build a more just society. It's a matter of national will and commitment. It is also a matter of individual responsibility. If these things are not done, I predict that there will be terrifying days ahead in the "land of the free and the home of the brave."

Discussion Questions: **Benjamin E. Mays**

1. What stories of discrimination does Mays relate? How have African Americans historically been treated? How does this story affect his spiritual development? How does the story affect your views about African Americans?

2. Would you say Mays's Baptist tradition is more "this-worldly" or "otherworldly"? Describe his experience at the Mount Zion Church. Would you say the preacher, Reverend Marshall, affirms this world in his sermons, or rejects it?

3. What is Mays's attitude toward the Southern white churches? How does he react to their statement published three and a half years after the 1954 decision outlawing segregation?

4. One of the country's leading scholars of black religion, C. Eric Lincoln, has written about the central role of the church in African-American society.

   > [The African American's] church was his school, his forum, his political arena, his social club, his art gallery, his conservatory of music…. His religion was his fellowship with man, his audience with God. It was the peculiar sustaining force that gave him strength to endure when endurance gave no promise, and the courage to be creative in the face of his own dehumanization (C. Eric Lincoln, preface in Gayraud S. Wilmore, *Black Religion and Black Nationalism* [Garden City, N.Y.: Doubleday, 1972], p. vi. Quoted in Bedell, Sandon, and Wellborn, p. 411).

   Do you think this description accurately characterizes Mays's experience in the black church? Are there other authors in this volume whose experience with religious institutions is analogous to Mays's experience?

5. What does Mays mean when he writes that white Christians treat Africans differently from the way they treat American blacks? Why do you think whites act that way?

6. Mays mentions Martin Luther King, Jr.'s distinction between just and unjust laws. What do you think King means by this distinction?

Bessie Jones

From Bessie Jones, *For the Ancestors*
(Urbana, IL: University of Illinois Press, 1983).
Reprinted by permission of University of Illinois Press.

I was born in Smithville, Georgia, on February 8, 1902. My mother never had any other children, and I grew up an only child. My mother was born in a place called Preston, Georgia, not far from Americus, and she was brought up in Buena Vista, Georgia. Her grandmother, which is her mother's mother, she stayed there. My mother had a long name—Abby Lou Frances. At home up around Buena Vista they called her Abby. But down here on the coast they called her Miss Frances. Now Abby, that's God's name. Like my own name. They call me Bessie but that ain't my name. Some people even call me Lizzie, and when they do I won't answer because I want to forget it. My momma always called me Bess which—that is my name. Folks put the Bess-ie to it after we came down to Fitzgerald. It started right down in there. I didn't never want to be called that, and I had a great reason why, but God fixed it like he wanted to and that's the whole name now everywhere—Bessie. But my name is Mary Elizabeth, and I'm named after Momma's mother and Momma's grandma. Momma's mother was named Elizabeth, and her grandmother Mary. I'm named after both of them....

Elizabeth, my grandmother, never was married. She never did marry, but she had her share of children. My momma say I took after her, 'cause I didn't never want to marry. Never wanted to marry. I didn't prefer marrying. My momma say that's the way her mother was. Say she didn't look for no marriage at all. She had her freedom. And then when she had it, she finished righteous. Told them, say, "You see where God don't care nothing about that little stuff you do?" Told them what time she was going, and she was leaving that evening at three o'clock, and just before she died she was singing a song about get on board li'l chillun [children].

Momma said they stayed around that bed trying to watch her, trying to keep her from going to doing something like that; and, say, then there was just a certain sound—I've seen that happen and I been to places where that happen—like something fall somewhere. And everybody looked around, looked back and she's gone. Ain't that something?

You see, the Lord don't care nothing about that stuff. What I'm saying is that all those things like that didn't send my grandmother to hell 'cause she didn't marry a man. She raised her chillun, she did them well. She brought them up well, sure thing. So I would've thought that too. I could raise my chillun, and I couldn't raise my man, see. I don't think I ever would have married if I hadn't wanted to go on and live for the Lord. That's the only way, because I wasn't ready to marry anybody. But I wanted to live for the Lord, and I knew since I was a singer, and being the way I am with people, friendly people, they would accuse me of every man that came by. I didn't want to be slurred all the time, so I thought I better go ahead and get my own husband. That's the only reason I married, and that's the truth. Course I liked him alright, but I wouldn't have married him. I would have just gone on. But after you've decided to live your life in the church, and you're a grown woman, you need your own husband.

My grandmother and all of them were farm workers. All of them were—my grandmother, and my great-grand too. And they worked in white people's houses too, you know, like when there wasn't no work out in the fields and things like that for them to do. But they mostly stayed near the cities from where they'd go out and work, rather than stay on the plantations. Momma say most all the black folks stayed in Buena Vista or in Smithville, or Americus. They stayed in the town—what they called inside the city limits—but they worked out in the country. People used to come or send wagons into town to get them. They hoed cotton, and were called hoe-hands. They went and came back every day.

I used to do that too, in Milan, when I stayed in the town part. I had to go out and come in. I reckon I got a whole lot of that and more from my grandmother. I don't like to stay too far away from town. I don't like living in the sticks. I love it for going out there, and think it's a glorious thing to go way out there in the sticks to see people. Way out in the country, oh, it's beautiful. Yards, and chickens walking, and they so free out there, but at night when I want to go to the store, then I don't want to be so far away from it. I may want to go to a drugstore if somebody get sick or something and I don't want to be so far away from it. And when I want to leave there, I don't want to be so far from the train or bus. See, that's just the way it is. I never want to be too far off from town that I can't walk there. And that's just why Momma said that I took all that after her momma. When they be living like that Momma and them wouldn't be living in their own house, they'd be renting....

Momma was brought up up there around Buena Vista. My grandmother Elizabeth had done passed, after which she went to stay with Lilla. Aunt Lil was married—her married name was Evans—and so Momma said when she inspired with me that was a scandal in Lil's home. That's why Momma say she didn't care whether she went to see Aunt Lilla or not after I was born. She didn't go back to see her until I was eight years old. Anyway, I was born down there in Smithville, out of wedlock but come into wedlock. My mother say she carried me down to Dawson when I was seven months. That's how I come to be in Dawson; because she remained there.

Uncle Gene—his name was Eugene Reese—he was my momma's granduncle. Her grandmother's brother. He was already down there in that part of the country around Dawson and Cuthbert, Georgia. There were a great family of us down there and Uncle Gene, I sing a lot of his songs. When he knew this baby was born, which was me, and it was in his momma's house, he knew his momma was old so he decided to let my momma come down and live with him. That's how come Momma went down to Dawson after I was born. She was there about three weeks when she run into James Sampson, who I call Daddy. She run into him and he married her there. Momma stayed with him a long, long time. So I was brought up with that and that's how Jet Sampson came to be my grandfather.

My real father was Ronnie Smith, but James Sampson was the man I call Poppa. That's right. I sure say it that way, and his people after a while considered me nothing but their own child. Some of them up to today don't know there's a difference. The older ones do, but the younger ones that come along, they don't know the difference. But I know the difference.

My real daddy's name was Ronnie Smith— Momma say his name was Joe Ronnie, but nobody quite call him that. His daddy's name was Tom and his momma's name was Molly. She was an Owens before she married. And he had two brothers—John Smith and Coot Smith—and one sister, Hattie, who we used to call Aunt Nen. We used to call Coot Uncle Tunk. They were farming people too. My grandfather, old man Tom Smith—I called him Uncle Tom, but he was my grandpa—I stayed with his family, in and out, and used to tend my auntie's little boy. The older Smiths, they know I'm theirs, but them that I was brought up with didn't know the difference—that Poppa Sampson wasn't my real poppa. It's like that story about the woman who said to her child, "Your daddy ain't your daddy, nohow." But they treat me so good, if they had never told me, I would have never known the difference. And I'm glad they told me....

Uncle Tom, my granddaddy, he didn't never in his life to my knowledge have to go out and buy meat. On the Sampson side they didn't have to go buy any meat either. If they wanted meat in July they went out and killed a hog. That's when they wanted fresh meat. They'd take and kill him in July—it wouldn't make any difference. They were smart. They always raised their own meat. They were very smart in keeping something or other, that's why I could tell folks I've never known what hungry is. A lot

of chilluns and a lot of persons can say they suffer. But Uncle Tom and Ma and Pa and them—they were always friends—they had the habit of going and helping a person if he was mistreating his chillun or couldn't feed his chillun or down sick, or something of the kind. There were some men in those days—a lot of men—who just wouldn't do right. They'd know they weren't making nothing, ain't got nothing, and the chillun suffering, yet they didn't want the chillun to ask nobody for nothing. A lot of that was around Dawson. We knew some women to be so low-down and hungry till they couldn't nurse the baby. Didn't have milk. We had to slip food to them and they had to slip and ask for it....

Poppa's family came into Georgia from Virginia right after slavery time. There was Uncle Sam—he was the oldest brother, I think —and Uncle Jesse. They were brothers to Poppa and his sister Aunt Mattie. Jet Sampson—he was the one who mostly brought me up—their daddy, he was married to Julia. Uncle Sam, after freedom, he never lived with anybody. He never did live on no farm or nothing; he just lived in the woods. He worked in the fields and like from time to time to make a little money, but he stayed on the side of the creeks in huts, and mostly made medicine and belts out of snake hides. He was a snake-catcher. When he got free he just meant it to be that way—free— and he never did hitch to nobody. That was Uncle Sam, and they called him a root man. I don't know whether it was or not, but he was very funny. Different.

I remember the last time being in his presence we were going fishing. He lived down on the creek in a hut. When I looked in that little hut there was a couch in there and fireplace—fireplace outside too—and he didn't bother nobody. He just stayed there and sold hides and brung hides to town. That day he cooked fried rattlesnakes and Pa ate some and didn't know it. When he told him, Pa tried to spit and spit and we knew then so we didn't eat none. But Pa had a plenty. I was little, about eight or nine years old right then when Uncle Sam was staying there. And they were talking 'bout how Uncle Sam could be walking just like from one side of the road to the next and they say we're gonna watch and see how he go. And you look off and watch, and look back and you don't see Uncle Sam. It was something to him. He was a little different or at least he made it look like it. But Pa say he believe Uncle Sam sold himself to the devil. I don't know. He never did hurt anybody, but back in those times didn't nobody mess with him either. That's the main thing. I really don't know how he died, but I heard that he died and they buried him in Calhoun, Georgia….

As a child people always used to say I was very musical, and most of my life has been taken up with music. My mother used to play the autoharp—they were different then from what they are now, the way you used to tune them up—and up in Dawson she bought me an accordion. Later on I bought me a guitar. I can fram a guitar now but I can't pick it. In those days we didn't have parties—so-called parties—we had frolics. And then we'd have different musicians with accordions and banjos and we'd have a big time. But I was scared of a banjo—big-belly man with a long neck. That's what they used to say he was—big-belly man with a long neck. When I was a little girl I didn't like getting around them things. I wasn't scared of the fiddle but they pitied him. Say the fiddle is like a little baby and they didn't want anybody meddling with him. And when he called his neighbors, poor li'l thing, he was just crying. But the banjo is different now; they so big and round. They're made up prettier, all fancy. Poppa and them used to make them, great big African banjo we called it. They made them out of wood, and I don't know where they got the string from, but they made them and then they put rattlesnake rattles in them. After they caught the rattlesnakes they'd make belts out

of the skins, and they'd take the rattles and let them dry out, then put them into the guitar or the banjo, either one. It gives a great tone. And you can do it now; it's the same thing. It makes a great tone. My grandfather made his own bam-bam, too, and chairs, and such. They made lots of things for themselves in those days.

Music has always been a big part in my life, but in those early days we had the church too, and I was brought up in a church, liked to go to church and go to meetings and everything, but I didn't like no preacher. You see, in those days when I was coming up little, if you were the pastor of a church, widows and such who had chillun getting unruly would tell you about it, and you were supposed to help make those chillun mind. I've known Reverend Perry to come out of church and bring that buggy whip with him to see about chillun getting sassy with their momma. Yes sir. Mary Jane was sassy. She was growing up right with me, same time, and old Mary Jane used to get behind the bed—they had a big old house—and he would whip her out from under that bed. He never would hurt her bad, just enough to make her mind, but that made me mad and I didn't want no preacher in my house. None at all. I understand now what I didn't understand then. If you ain't got no husband and you're a widow, then the preacher is supposed to come and help. His wife, too, is supposed to come and help get those chillun straight in that house. Help that woman if she needed help. But all I saw was there's that preacher; yon he walk. He gonna beat them chillun. Course he was doing right but I didn't want that. And God said, "I'm going to fix you. I'm going to let you birth one." See, my older son is a pastor. I'm telling you, you don't know what you're going to do!

In those days after you got a whipping or something like that we used to beat our mommas, stomp on them, and bury them—only they didn't know it. We'd get a long stick with knots in it or some piece of wood or some-thing and name it her. And we'd go down in the back and beat the devil out of it. Beat Grandma; call her all kinds of stuff. We'd just tear them up, then go back home looking nice. You better go in there looking nice. That's right. But we felt good, just like Pa and them would when they sung songs. We done beat you and we really felt good. They never knew that we tore them up, or that would've been a whipping.

But kids don't do that now; they cuss their real momma….

I didn't have to be baptized when I was little because my grandfather, my mother, and all of them didn't believe in baptizing children since children don't know anything about that water you pour on them. Ain't no need in sprinkling around like that and they just didn't do it. I wasn't baptized as a child but I had to go to church, Sunday School and church. I got converted when I was seventeen years old and that's when I got baptized. That was in Fitzgerald. You had to do something in those days—the crew that I came along with—to prove yourself. You couldn't just walk up to be baptized, and I'm glad of it. People prayed and cried over us and we had to pray too. Some of us came through and some didn't, quite naturally, but I often think of the vision I had when I was praying there.

A man came up to me in this vision and he was real tall. I was standing and he came up to me with a little book or something in his hand. He took this book and he brought some cards out of it—look like address cards—and the first one had a church on it. The next card he brought out had a church on it and the next one had a church on it. He brought out three cards, all with churches. Two of the churches had steeples and the other church didn't have a steeple. He passed that card to me—the one that didn't have a steeple. I didn't know what it meant for a long time, then it came to me and I knew. The two big churches had steeples, yet the little church without a steeple, basically that was great. The writing beneath the church on

that card said, "Holy." There was no writing on the other cards at all. So I figured that thing out and I joined the church then.

The day I got baptized—baptized in a millpond—in this little pond there was a suck-hole. A lot of folks teased us about that thing. They had a staff stuck down there for the preacher and you could feel that water pulling at you. They had to hold you; we were that close to the suck-hole. A man and his roadcart had gone down in that thing once, 'cause his ox wanted water and when a cow wants water he ain't joking; he's going to get it. And this ox stood his feet in the pond and ducked his head for the water. The man tried to pull the ox back and lost his own life. No man can pull an ox back. We used to take great big logs and shove them over there, and now a log would usually stay afloat but there that log would turn on end and it'd go down. That was a suck-hole!

The funniest thing: when we got baptized, there was a lady there that day named Mary. Mary came out there and they just had to hold her. She was hollering and oh she was hollering. She had a wicked husband named George and he was standing right there. George said—he got to mocking Mary—"Lord I'm so glad I didn't go down in that suck-hole! Lord I'm so glad I didn't go down in that suck-hole." And when Mary turned around like she wanted to go back, he said she was looking back as if to say, "I'm sure glad I didn't go down in that suck-hole. Thank you Jesus!" We had fun that day. And during the fellowship that night I was so tickled because George had teased her so bad Mary was angry. She was fit to be tied. And George was still teasing her. Lord, we had some fun in those days!

But the Lord blessed me. I never was all that good until I came to be born again; I wasn't born again when I got baptized, I was just converted, but I thank God for it. Later on I was born again when I was in Okeechobee, Florida, where I stayed a long time. To be born again you have to be baptized again and I was baptized again—quite naturally. When you're born again you join a membership but you are the church. That's where I'm at now. We join this membership and we go to the same building, but when Jesus says I'm coming to the church, He ain't coming to that thing out there; He's coming to you. You are the church. I am the church. Sometimes folks ask me, "What church do you belong to?" and I say, "I belong to myself." I am the church. If your body is the temple for the Holy Ghost to dwell in and if you believe, you might as well believe in that church.

My grandfather used to teach us all that, too. You never knew where some people had the Holy Ghost sometimes because so many of them had it and didn't even know. They used to sing the song about "The comforter has come / The Holy Ghost in heaven / That Father's promise given," and that's true. They had it. But they didn't know how to name it and they went under the name of some other church. But in themselves they were saved. I was brought up in that way. And they'd sing that song, "The comforter has come," and that comforter wasn't nothing but the Holy Ghost itself and that's it. And so anyhow, they had it. The true light was coming. By them not having much understanding in reading, the part that God handed down to them, they sure used it. All those songs that were handed down to them without notes, without any education—you think about it! That's why I like to keep it up. I keep up the slave songs that they learned in church, and the play songs too, and the stories, the riddles and things.

Yet people had fun times those days in Dawson too. Momma and them gave frolics or went to somebody else's frolic regularly. They wouldn't go to places that were too rough or where there wouldn't be any respect for the house, with people using all kinds of language. You know, it's natural, when you come in people's house you're supposed to respect them in their own house if they got any respect there. But if there ain't none there, you don't care.

And especially the places they called outlaw places, Momma and them wouldn't go there. My grandfather and them used to make their own whiskey out of corn, then let it stand for three, four, or five years before they drink it, and I ain't never seen any one of them drunk. Never seen any one of them act like they were drunk, although I have seen other people drunk and I didn' like it. But when Momma and them gave frolics at our house they didn't allow any cutting up and acting. And when we got older and people weren't giving frolics but were having candy-pullings and egg-crackings and parties like that, they still called themselves respectable, and never had any flirting or nothing like that.

There were many games they played back then. At an egg-cracking there would be tubs of boiled eggs, and each person would buy about three, and then see how many eggs they could crack with their own. You'd knock your egg against somebody else's—the sharp ends—and if my egg cracked your egg then I won it. That way a person could start with just a few eggs and leave with many. These were parties to help out somebody who was sick, or the church, and you'd pay for all your eggs that got cracked—sometimes a quarter for every one—and all the money was turned over to the cause, whatever it was. In those days a quarter was big money. If you had a boiled rotten egg it would crack them all and you'd go home with a big bucket of eggs. It was fun and I liked those parties....

Pa and them used to say that the spirits of the dead most always visit back to the places where they passed away, and I believe that they do come back sometimes. When I first moved into the house I'm in now, I used to sleep in the front room on account it was easy to get to the telephone there in case somebody called. I had a couch in there that used to open down into a bed. One night I was asleep there and in my sleep it appeared that somebody was sitting on my pillow. I don't like for anybody to sit on my pillow, period. So I pushed myself back. I pushed myself back so hard I woke myself. And he spoke so plain I could hear it all in the house, "You don't know who this is sitting here." It kind of scared me. It shook me so until I was scared to go to bed the next night. That voice spoke all over the whole room. But I prayed it off. I never tried to find out who he was, either.

After that happened, I was sitting in the bathroom one day and had the door opened. The door across the hallway to the dining room was opened too and my great-grand-son—a little bitty boy about two years old or better—he was playing out there and I could just see him playing and laughing like there was somebody in there with him. I looked at him; I looked in front of him. I didn't see anybody. Then he got up and started to the door going from the dining room to the front room. The door opened and when he got right up to it, it shut. He looked at the door; he looked up there and I called to him not to go out of the dining room. He looked at me, and then he went on back to playing. I walked the floor then and I talked to whoever it was. I didn't see anybody, but I told them I was there to stay, and I wanted to stay there. I didn't want to be scared, and besides, I said, "I wouldn't do you like that." I talked to whoever it was, and I ain't been worried that way since. But I wonder about things like that sometimes.

When someone died people used to sit up. They'd have a sitting-up all night praying and singing. I never heard my people say they were praying them in—you know what I mean. If they ain't got it, they won't get it. We didn't try to give it to them afterwards. They sang and prayed with one another, that's all. 'Cause God knows, if he ain't already got it, that's it. That's all of that. And you know, I remember in Miami—and also I heard of it in Milan, Georgia, a man was declared dead and he come back. You know now, if he had fell to that undertaker he would have killed him sure enough. Mr. Jim, one of my stepfathers, saw

that. He was real scared of dead peoples. I mean he was a good man; my mother married him and I know what I'm talking about. That man, he would wait on you; he would give you his last. But you die, you shut your eyes, and he was through with you. I ain't joking. Well anyway, he was at this sitting one night, and this boy came back. My stepfather had marks on his leg where he jumped and was running, 'cause he got scared when the boy raised up there and the barbed-wire cut him as he was flying to get home. They were all running. He was in front, and a lady named Miss Sue, she say when he jumped that fence, Miss Sadie grabbed his coat. She wasn't gonna let him leave her! She liked to broke his leg. But anyhow, a lot of people were running. That happened right in Milan, Georgia. It's true. It was really something. Now the boy didn't know what they were running for, didn't know what it was all about, what was the matter with the people. They just tore down and ran, folks hollering all outside. After a while, somebody went in there where he was and talked with him. So that's why I say a lot of them ain't dead now when they take them in, 'cause sometimes they just go in that way and folks say, ah, she dead, she dead. She might be in a trance sometimes, we don't know. When my momma died, Mr. Julius, he say they gonna wait sure enough a long time before the doctor carried her away from there. He say they gonna sure enough wait....

The old people used to know all kinds of signs, and they had powers, too. They knew signs, like what the itching of the palm meant—and it's not the same for everybody—or the itching of the nose. You got to watch these things about yourself and learn to tell what they mean for you. Some old people used to take a sign from their ears burning. When your ears burned, that meant somebody was talking about you and you're supposed to rub it and say, "If you're talking good, talk on; if you're talking bad, please stop." And if the burning stops immediately that means they must've been talking bad. If they keep on talking, they must be talking good. And they had the nose-itching sign too—and that one works for me. If my nose itches on the end, that means somebody is coming riding; if it's itching way up at the top, that means they're coming walking. Or if they aren't actually coming they're talking about it or got their mind on it.

When you're going somewhere and the screech owl quivers on the left-hand side of you, they said it was a sign of death. A woman's death. When the screech owl was on the right-hand side of you, then it was a man's death. And if the owl came into the house, you knew there was going to be a death there, or else you were going to move. Either way you were getting out of there. Some people say the fire or the light draws the owl inside, but he knows that ain't no tree when he comes in.

The old people had those signs and we learned about them. But there were other things they knew about living as well, that some was passed down and some weren't, like using herbs and plants, and just knowing the way of things around you. My grandfather used to be able to talk to a table. It had to be a diamond table with five legs. But he'd take his little finger and put it in the middle of that table and say something—I don't know what—and that table's leg would bump. He never did teach me how to do that.

And he could go about wherever he wanted. If he came up on a bad dog, I don't care how bad a dog it was, he could make that dog shut up. He'd look right at it and that dog wouldn't even bark. There's a passage in the Bible that says, "Not a dog shall rule this child." I know where the word is, but I don't know how to handle that one. Poppa could do it. All of them could do it. They understood how to hold the attention of the animals and things around them....

Then there's nettleweed—it keeps you built up, and it takes worms and stones out of you.

That's the same common little thing called stinger nettle or bull nettle. It'll sting if you walk and touch it any old way, but if you hold your breath and touch it, it won't sting you. Just don't breathe if you're gonna touch it. That's how folks used to do years back, my grandfather said, when they broke the chain gang. They'd just come right through the stinger nettle so the dogs couldn't trail them. God gave us wisdom for something and they had to study well, those people who got put on chain gangs for nothing. That ain't no joke. But that nettle is good for more than one thing—it'll build you up, it'll help you.

Passion weed is something I used to play with as a child, but that's the best stuff to use for your nerves. It used to be plentiful on Saint Simons, but now they've done built so many houses you can't find it. We used to play with the little fruit off it in my grandfather's time and we called it maypop. We'd chunk them when they were green, and you had to catch them right else they "may pop." We'd call, "Heel over, may pop!" to let you know you shouldn't grab it, cause if you grab it too hard, you may pop it. Some children used to eat the little melon when it got yellow ripe, but I never did because it smelled too high.

The way I know for people to learn to read the signs is simple. You have to watch them, pay attention, and see what happens. Like when your hand itches you, some folks pay it no mind but there's a sign in it. My left hand is letters, my right hand is money. You watch yours. Momma used to tell me one thing about it, she said, "Your right hand is money but don't think you're gonna have it all the time." You're gonna handle it but it may just pass through your hand; that's true. Sometimes when people are writing checks I can just tell that somebody's fixing to load up the wagon. Somebody's fixing to send me something. Money in my hand. And we had a way of doing, say, "Rub it on wood and make it good," if you got any wood, you know. But

I have other ways with mine. I kiss mine and say, "God the Father, Son, and Holy Ghost command it whatever we do...."

People sometimes want work; they need it and would work if they could get a job. I could help a lot of folks here in town that way—I mean streetwalkers and such, women or men—but they don't want it. And you're not supposed to give that which is holy unto a dog. Anything that you have good and really righteous, you don't give it to just anybody out there who cares nothing about it, ain't studying you, and don't have any appreciation. Don't give anything holy unto the dog; that's what the Bible says. But sometimes when it seems you can't hardly get a job, can't hardly stay on a job even after you've done the best work you can because the evil spirit or whatever is in your way, then read the Fourth Psalm. Read that psalm and if you're out of a job, you can get a good job. Not only that, after you get that job, then you continue to read it and you'll have more work then you'll be able to do. And that's the truth. God's got everything in there for us. It ain't hidden: it's true and it's not there just for certain ones but for the ones that need it.

I was helped with that in a church. This preacher was standing up in the pulpit telling the people, "If y'all want a job, those who want one, take this reader and read the Fourth Psalm. It's an old law—

> Answer me when I call, O God of
>   my righteousness;
> Thou hast set me at large when I was
>   in distress!

You're in distress when you ain't got no work to do and you can't do nothing. And it goes on to say,

> Son of man, how long will you turn
>   my glory into shame?

You have to be tried, and you're gonna be tried—it says so in the Bible.

But most times people bring hardship on theirselves by not paying attention to what they ought to be studying and following behind what they ain't supposed to.

It don't take much to know what's right and what ain't.

If you want to know, you can learn sure enough.

That's when somebody is trying to kick you down, you see, and don't want to see you climb. Say,

How long will you seek for less?

You see, seeking for the lesser things about me all the time, wanting to see me down all the time. Say,

Know ye that the Lord hath set apart
    for himself him that is godly.
The Lord will hear when I call upon him.
Stand in awe and sin not:
Commune with your own heart upon
    your bed and be still.
Offer the sacrifices of righteousness
And put your trust in the Lord.

And he goes on to say there will be many that will say, who will show us any good? and say

Lord, lift up the light of thy
    countenance upon us
For I have the gladness in my heart
From the time that thy corn and
    thy wine increased.

And you know that's God's corn when it has increased, when the wine has increased. And you want that gladness in your heart, all the time.

Sometimes you'll find folks who have all kinds of strange signs, but it ain't nothing but foolishness. Like, they used to spit in the fire and if your spit dried up fast they said that was a sign you were going to die. Nothing but foolishness. Old folks had all kinds of junk like that. But now, the nose itch, that's a sign with me. Different people do have all kinds of different signs. Some people say if you go to sit in a chair and miss, then you ain't gonna marry. You'll never marry. But that's not true. I don't

believe that. You just missed the chair, and maybe wanted to say something about it.

Yet people, no matter who you are, the spirits are around us all the time. Especially the old ones that know us and have gone on before—the ancestors. And we have the plants and animals that would do our bidding if we'd learn how to get through to them, plus the signs that tell us everything we need to know about what's going on around us. You have to be tried, and you're gonna be tried—it says so in the Bible. But most times people bring hardship on theirselves by not paying attention to what they ought to be studying and following behind what they ain't supposed to. It don't take much to know what's right and what ain't. If you want to know, you can learn sure enough.

See, the Lord warns some people. Fact is, I believe He warns everybody but they don't pay it any mind. I heard a woman once crying at her sister's grave. She said, "Lord, you showed me this but I didn't know what it was." God does show people things, but most of the time they just figure there's nothing to it. A lot of times the warning would be about you yourself. You know, when a woodpecker pecks on your house you're supposed to give it up, baby. Somebody close to you is going, or it may be you. That woodpecker, I know him. He done it to me. You got to look out for him because there's trees for him to peck on and he don't get no sap out of a house. He's a true sign. A lot of these things are natural truth. All the way down through the Bible it says, "These signs shall follow you." And some people can read signs so well until they can look at things and see beyond, and look at people and see things about them....

My baby son was born on G Street in Brunswick [Georgia] on the twenty-sixth day of December 1937, although I'd told myself I would wait until New Year's day to birth him after I didn't give birth on Christmas morning. Course I had walked all night Christmas Eve with a little girl who I had staying there with me—one of my first husband's cousin's child from the Island—and we had taken two or three turns downtown. I had a dime—it didn't cost but a dime to get a cab in those day—and I held that dime in my hand so if pain striked me I'd get a cab and go right on. That pain ain't struck all night. So Christmas morning came and they all had their big Christmases and I had mine too. I said, "Oh, well." Now in Brunswick, if you have a baby early New Year's morning, you get a prize. So I said, "I'm going to do that." I'm talking to myself: "I'm going to wait until New Year's morning and have the baby." But the twenty-sixth day was a Sunday and that's the day he came. Dr. Chapman came out to see me, and gave me some kind of medicine to hold me since he had to go and tend to another girl—a blind lady's daughter—who was in labor at the same time but she was closer. Then he came on back there with me. When the baby was born he came right away. The folks next door were still having Christmas right on; the doctor said, "What're you going to name him?" Now I had my mind fixed about that. I'd wanted a child named Cordell or one named K.C. I wanted that. So I wanted to name the baby K.C. in my mind. So I said to the doctor, "I'll have a name when you come back." He say, "Why don't you name him Joe, after his daddy's uncle?" And I said, "Okay," and went on. It wasn't until later, when I almost done signed his name at the courthouse—Joseph James—I thought, "Joseph! I don't want no Joseph in my house!" But it was written by then. And that's the way it be—you don't never know what you're going to do.

I was real young when my first baby was born, and I didn't have any more children for twenty-one years, but I was tending other people's children on and on, over and over. I used to go and get children out of the hospital and take care of them—friends I knew who didn't want to tend to their children, I would take them away from there, you know, 'cause

if somebody didn't, ain't no telling what would happen. I've kept children two and three years, and then gave them back to their owner. Just to keep them. I just love children, that's all. And some of them have children and they want to go to dances, want to go this way or that way, they let the children stay with me. Just like my child. Some of them would do something for me, some of them never did do anything for me after I kept the children. I love the ways I find out among all children. Any color. I've never found any disrespectfulness about children, no matter what their race. Old people and little children, I just love to spend my time with them. I love it—right on! You can hardly find people older than me now, but yet and still I spend my time on them because I just love them....

I had one daughter—she's dead and gone now—and she got eight whippings in her whole life to my knowing. Unless the schoolteacher whipped her otherwise and I don't think so. I gave her eight whippings to my knowing. When she was a little bitty thing playing around the house, if something fell or anything happened, I used to talk to myself before I would whip her. She talked to herself, too, 'cause she grew up by herself. And a many a day, that way, she'd say no, I didn't do such-and-such a thing 'cause I told myself if I do that then you're gonna whip me. That was something. I remember the first whipping I gave her, that was a spanking. I got a little switch right across the back of her hand and a little whelp came there. She said, "Look what you've done." You don't know how far that hurt me. That went a long ways with me. She never knew it, but it went a long ways. I patted the whelp and rubbed it, and talked to her and told her she should listen when I say not to do something. And as for talking back, she never talked back at me in her life, in no way, shape, or form. And I had never talked back to my momma in no way, shape, or form.

And I mean even when I was grown—of course I've never gotten that grown yet, even though I had children and grandchildren. My daughter was the same. She had children and grandchildren but she never talked back. She was just that same submissive way. And anything happened, then you know how to talk to them; you know how to speak to them.

But there are some who don't know from the beginning coming up: they're loose; they're slack. And I don't understand it sometimes. But you know, Jesus will fix that. Like when he had that woman with two nationalities in one womb—I forget her name but you'll find it in the Bible. She had two nationalities in one womb. God fixed it so they were twins, but they weren't alike—even in nationality. He can change anything. He knows how to make it and that's all there is to it. So I say this—whatsoever it is that you have, when you have children don't think because Jack can do such-and-such a thing so well that Tom can do the same thing all the time. They're different. Don't think that if Jack's got such a vim for getting up in the morning and helping or doing something around the house that Tom is going to have that same vim. He may have something else....

Now a lot of fuss has been made about children coming up in homes without fathers, and some people even claim that that makes them go wrong because they don't have any fathers in the house. I don't think that's necessarily true. If the father leaves the mother, or they're separated and he's not over them—or no other man—the mother has to be careful not to go astray herself. Sometimes she doesn't have to do nasty things to go astray. For instance, when she's trying to find work to take care of the children and not leaving them in good care, not being particular whether they go or come, and letting the children have their own way in every respect, and not taking care to see if the children bring something into the house where they got it from—the mother has to be careful against

these things. If the child brings something into the house, you find out where he got it from or who gave it to him, and if he got it in the wrong place you make him carry it right back, and go with him to see that he carries it back. Now a child who ain't got a father might try to get away with such kinds of things, especially when at mealtimes with meals to be fixed the momma ain't there. Or, either, she didn't leave it in such a way the child could fix for himself. My husband died when my boys were ten and twelve. Alright. I allowed my children to fix their own food, such as that they could fix. Like my great-grandson who stays with me now, he can fix his own eggs; he can fix mine. 'Cause you don't know what you may run into sometimes. If you have to go somewhere sometimes then they don't have to go hungry.

You almost make little girls out of them if they're little boys, but if they're boys and girls, you let them all be the same. You don't make the girl do all for the boy and then the boy runs out and do anything he want to do and come back. The first thing you know, he'll be gone astray. They got to be right there together, and if they ain't got no daddy, then you got to be momma and poppa with them and daily train them. You got to talk to them and teach them how they should treat theirselves. And just be as strict as you can be about how they treat people out there. And if somebody out there is saying something to the children that you don't like, you go to that person. Don't encourage the children in sassing them. Talk to the children, especially at nights when nobody's there. And if they have complaints about what certain people out there say or do, they should come home and tell you, because as children they don't know; they may have to go to that same door and knock for bread. They don't know what's likely to happen to them.

And another thing about it, if the children ain't got a daddy and the momma tries to give them everything they want—daddy could be there or not really—that leads to ruin. Because when the day comes that she can't do it, they're gonna get what they want somehow. She must let them know that they have to wait on some things; that they can't wear their best clothes all the time. Keep their mind right. Then you feel good about it....

In the next passage, Jones talks about her entourage and their traditional and spiritual songs.

My main concern with the music is that it should go right, and that we should do right with it. Because if I should go and get a good hold, I want everybody with me to have everything equal. Some say you shouldn't do that. They say leaders should do so-and-so. And I tell them that this is not a church thing, you know. We just go on and we help one another. And if one stayed off for sickness—like if we were traveling and one got sick—well he got the same amount of money because he couldn't help himself from getting sick, see. Sometimes Mabel wanted to kick against that, but I'd say, "Uh, uh." If she were sick she'd get the same thing. Some will miss a day or two; don't worry about that. Those other folks ain't gonna worry about it. They gonna give you the same amount of money, and they ain't gonna take none from you.

The Georgia Sea Island Singers made three records *Deep South, Georgia Sea Islands* Volume I, and *Georgia Sea Islands* Volume II. And somebody made a record of the Alabama Choir and put me on there. I've never sung with them in my life but I'm on their record. Then there's the *Step It Down* book that [Alan] Lomax started but was finished by his sister, Bess Hawes. And there's a Rounder record with just Doug Quimby and myself and some children.

You had to know how to live with that older crew, but I miss them. John Davis is dead. Willis Proctor is dead. Mr. Ben Foster's been dead for a long time. Emma Ramsey was the last one to die. She died from a stroke. Peter Davis and Jerome Davis are still living but they don't sing with the group anymore. Jerome, he went a time or two with us to Washington but he never went way off. They would come out and sing with the group, I guess, if I asked them. But they drink so hard I just ain't asked them. I was glad to get somebody with me where I wouldn't have to smell liquor on the stage all the time. They were really good singers but they couldn't sing without whiskey. They had that stuff going all out in the morning. And Mabel, she wanted to sing blues. Course we got rid of her on account of that and the drinking. Mabel was a blues singer and that's why they wanted to come in with the Saint Simons festival 1977 as the Georgia Sea Island Blues Singers. Couldn't do it. I told them they couldn't do that. However else they wanted to name the singing after Mabel would've been good, but I said, "You can't name it the Georgia Sea Island Blues Singers because I named it the Georgia Sea Islanders and I never had blues singing in it." I told them that was the reason Mabel had to leave us, on account of her wanting to keep up blues and we didn't. We couldn't hang two in one that way.

Henry Morrison is dead too and he was the best one we had. He's the one who used to sing "I ask Aunt Dinah / Do her dog run rabbit." Charlotte Reese never traveled with us; Alberta Ramsey, she's been gone a long time. She's in Florida. On the record *[Georgia Sea Island Songs]* Nat Rahmings plays the drums but he wasn't one of our group. He was from Nassau. We picked him up in Miami and he just settled and made that record. On that same record Herbert Smith, a white man, is playing the banjo and Ed Young from Mississippi is playing fife. He's one who would sing with us when we're on the same program. Herb Smith too.

But now that time has passed on up, we have my grandchildren and other friend's children in the group, and Doug Quimby, who's completely into it. Doug is husband to the mother of some of my grandchildren—Frankie. She and my son Joseph used to be married but they're divorced now, and Doug is her husband. He'd been singing a long time with other groups, singing mostly gospel, but he knew some of the old songs and games and I asked him one day to go with me when I had to go traveling. I wasn't feeling too well and I asked Frankie did she reckon I could get Doug to go. She said that he had often wished he could go singing with us, so I asked him. And he's been there ever since. He likes it and he's good at it. He's really good and that's why he's in there.

When we had the 1977 festival Mr. Alfred Jones, who owns Sea Island Hotel, just got completely stuck on Doug. He came up to me and said, "Now Bessie, when you come out to sing, I want you to bring that man with you." I said to myself, "You've already seen and heard this man," because I'd already carried Doug out there to Altama twice. You see, Mr. Jerry and George Cohen and them who've been going to Altama a long time, they usually step in front when we sing out there. Doug doesn't ever try to take over, and me, I'd rather lay right down beside them and go along. I know when it's wrong but I don't go over them, because I don't want them to be angry with me and get to saying that I'm trying to do this or that.

Here on the Island I'm a visitor. I'm a stranger. And it wouldn't make any difference whether I had been here twenty or forty years; I'm still a stranger. I'm talking about among the Negro people. They treat you well but you understand certain steps in there and you don't go too far. You go all around the pile but don't step in it, because the older heads that have been here a long time, they ain't going to have it. And so I just know how to get along with them and we're friends. I know I'm a stranger. Let me die and you'll see where I go. I ain't going to King's cemetery, no sir. I'm going to Strangers' cemetery, or out there at Rose Hill, wherever my children put me—but not in the others. We have a lot in Strangers' cemetery. And a number of people who we thought weren't strangers, when they died they went down there. They sure did. Cousin Clara's father when he died went there and I didn't know they were strangers. They came from Riceboro years and years ago when the mill was here. But they *came* here. Saint Simons is a spot. You stay here long enough, you'll find what you are. The very young—those under thirty-five or thirty—I don't believe they feel that way about outsiders because they can't understand any of this.

Course the white folks out there, if it suits them then it suits me because we're all singing for them, and I don't try to make anyone look little and don't want them to make me look little. So that's why Alfred Jones didn't recognize that Doug had been to his place. We just went along with what they were doing, that's all. But over at the festival when we were singing together, you had to know Doug was there.

I'm trying to get my grandchildren to carry it on out—the songs and the games and the way of singing—but if they don't then I'm going to get somebody else. I told Doug the other week when we were in California, I said, "Every time that clock ticks, I'm getting older." I said, "Now I want to get someone to help you, because you're the only one here who's grabbed ahold of the thing and know what to do." I said, "You get someone to help you and maybe they can hear you and they can go on and help us." But I want to settle this now. My granddaughter Vanessa is good, and when we go onstage or go to a singing, she goes with us but she doesn't take over anything. That's what I want her to do, take over something in the songs or play-leading. But instead of being that way, she stands there hitting on the tambourine. Now I just can't keep standing there talking to her after I know she knows what I'm trying to do and say I want to see her do it. I want to see her talent. Hitting the tambourine every once in a while and helping sing, that's not it. You got to know how to do it. That's what I'm asking, to get someone to just go on through with it and help Doug carry it on out, 'cause he can't just do it by himself....

You can make yourself happy; you can make yourself miserable, money or no money, because money does not enrich us. You may be rich with money but money is not riches. Riches is when you got something within you that you own right there. I'm proud because I know I belong to God. I'm proud because I depend on The Man that owns everything. Sometimes I tell people that I can stand up in my riches and turn around in it, 'cause every way I turn it's God's work; it's God's world. I don't care what I do, it's God's work. And when the way looks like it gets rugged with me, I have this to think about: Jesus had this before. Jesus went through this before. And God carried him through it. Why not me? See, I got to go through it too....

I was at a camp once when Pete Seeger came and asked me to sing at Carnegie Hall. That was the first big stage I'd ever been on in my life but it came naturally. I could see that Pete himself thought I was shy, or scared. And I heard one man say, "Ooh, I ain't going out there. Ooh, I'm nervous. I've been singing for five years and I still go out on that stage nervous." And I looked at him and thought, why should he be nervous? He was a white man who played a guitar by himself. I thought to myself, "He's got a guitar. If I could play a guitar it ain't nothing I'd be nervous about." I don't ever remember being nervous, and if I were I just wouldn't go. That's all there is to it. I wouldn't see the need in it. If you're afraid, then you better go and hide. That's the way I see it.

But whatsoever it is, do what you can. You may not do what you want to do but do what you can. And I've always had it this way with myself. I asked God for what I'm doing. I asked God long before Lomax called me, I asked the Lord for me to come out. I didn't know how I was coming out, when or where, or who I was coming out with, but I wanted to come out and do something because none of the people had left anything here. And I wanted to leave—

when the Lord takes me out of this body—I want to leave something here of me. Fact is, I told the Lord, and I meant it, I never want to die. I never, never want to die. When the world folds in, I want to be here, in my work, in my doings, and with the people, among the people. They don't see me but they can see of me. Now that's what I want to do. See, I just wish sometimes that I could see that handwriting or something from my grandfather and people of his time, something that they had done. So when I have anything that belonged to them back there now, I feel good about it. And I like to show them that I'm holding up their songs, holding up their doings that they told me about. That's great to me. They didn't write it down but I know they did it. And I didn't know whether it would get written down!

After I went to Carnegie Hall, I just continued on. People in the schools would call me, and that was fun. So I asked God to let me do it, and He sent somebody for me and the place where he knew it could be done. All I said was, "Lord I want to come out: I want to do something. I just don't want to die, I truly don't." And He knew how to do it.

I believe when it comes time to give that body back to the dirt, preparations must be made so that inward man would be clear. And when you get worried, troubled and scared like something's gonna bite you, or somebody's gonna shoot you in a minute—when you get so scared you can hardly go to the next room—that's that soul crying. That soul inside needs attention. And now the devil says, "You go get you a big drink and that will stop that," and then he just run it up so that worry can come again. But you've got to see the other man. Let him come in: let the spirit of God come in and that will clear it up completely. But you've got to hear what God says. I myself was tested with Him twice. Once when I was in the state of Maryland on the eastern shore, and which before I left home I was intending to help build a church for our group—the Church of God—that had started having meetings in my house.

In those days I'd been traveling with George, my second husband, who was an agricultural man before he took in sick and died. I had to work for the children, and the best work I saw then was right in the agriculture business so I stayed in it, and I was at a canning factory in Maryland and staying in their quarters. Those quarters were no place for me, particularly with my two boys. Nobody told me anything, but I knew those quarters weren't for me. I was working there but I wasn't quite like the rest of them. I just didn't agree, that's all. It was just a wrong place. But I worked, trying to get some money so when I came home I'd have something. And so I was nipping and grading beans, taking the ends off beans and sorting them at this time—though I had done every kind of work in there down to driving the line and everything—and we used to sing church songs. Different people from different places—I was the only one from Saint Simons—but we'd sing those good church songs. We'd start a song and crowds of people would join in. It sounded so good, you know, we just sang and sang while we were working—pretty sound—and white folks just listening to their factory ringing with nigger music and the machines running and it's going. But something said to me, "You ought to have a church just like this: you should have them singing in church just like this. You got to do it. God wants you to do it." So one day there were about eighteen of us on the line and I got a letter from Elder Hunter saying he'd be glad when I came home so we can try to build a church. That was on my mind, alright, but I was still pressing against it.

Then another day I was working on the line, making tomato puree, tomato paste, and tomato foods and stuff, and I could see some of the other workers talking to one another saying, "Not me child!" There were about twenty-five of us in that little bunch, and I could hear them hollering, "Not me!" and I

> ## The Lord told me, in a way of speaking, there's your money, go home; build your church.

wondered what was the matter. My two boys were on the top running cans. According to the government they weren't supposed to work, but when they came in from school the man would hire my boys and another lady called Butterfly—she had a birthmark like a butterfly—her boys and mine were the only children working at that time. She was a quiet, good woman, tended to her business, and she made her boys mind. But those four boys were up there and I thought maybe something happened to the children. People were still talking, "Child not me; shut my mouth," "Hush, don't say nothing," and I was still running the line watching what happened, until finally here comes the boss man with two white men. Those men had been trying to get to me all that time but nobody knew me. Everybody knew me but nobody knew me. They thought since I came from the South and they didn't know what had happened, they figured it might be something that would put me in jail so they wouldn't say that they knew me.

So anyway, here they come, the boss and these two white men, and he says, "These two men want to talk to you." I said, "Okay, I'm coming. I'll talk with them." And that was my money—eleven hundred dollars from the insurance people. The Lord told me, in a way of speaking, there's your money, go home; build your church. So I got my two boys ready—Joe the baby boy and George the older—and got them both tickets to travel on the bus so I could travel on the truck with the other workers and bring a lot of that stuff I had. I had peaches, apples, cucumbers, and all kinds of stuff—almost a half truckload myself. But Joe wouldn't ride with George on the bus by himself: "I ain't gonna ride; you got to go with us." George said, "Momma, I'll go." And so George left on the bus that would get him home to Saint Simons long before we would, and I got on that truck with Joe and the other men and women and all that crowd. It was a crowd of us on there! But we wagged it on in here, and they brought me all the way to Saint Simons 'cause they wanted to see the Island.

There were nine of us when we got there, and Momma fixed dinner and we had a nice time. Well I had to go to the outdoor toilet—that's all we had then—and while I was out there something said, "You ain't got enough money. Give that money you got to your momma, all but seventy-five dollars, and you go on down with them, 'cause where they're going there's lots of money and you can make enough to help build the church." Something said, "Don't do it." I came to the door of that outhouse and I stood there and looked. I couldn't get my mind right to ask God what to do. Something said "Do it" and something said "Don't." Finally, it whipped me out and I decided I'd go on and try two weeks anyhow down there and see if I could make some more money. Money's not all, baby! So I gave Momma all my money except seventy-five dollars, just like He said, and I boarded that truck. I went down there and let me tell you, I'd never been in such a bad place in all my life! It was a bad word for good morning!

The place up in Maryland was bad enough but it was nothing compared to that one in Florida. That was truly a testing place there. The water in the pump was pulled over a graveyard and everybody was getting sick off that water.

Bad weather, and foul cussing. All in the fields it was "kiss my so-and-so," "your mother." All day long Mr. So-and-so cussing with Miss So-and-so, even cussing at beans! It was sad. Not much fighting, but just an ignorant, dirty crew. I thought, "The devil has put me in it now; Lord have mercy!" I got acquainted with one good woman there named Frances. She and I did have some fun, and when I managed to save some money, I gave it to her to keep 'cause I was afraid to keep any money in the little room I was in, because those women were rough and you didn't know when they'd break in and search your place. That was a nasty crew around there: some women slept with women, and some men with men. I'd never seen such things. I wanted badly to get out of there. Anyway, after about two weeks and two days I went fishing with Frances and I fell in the water.

Sometimes I think about it and it just gives me the creeps. I had set my pole on a rock to bait my hook again—the fish had eaten off the bait—and I baited it and threw the line back out there. I was sticking the pole up underneath that rock when the rock went over. And I went over. Frances, who was there with me, she heard the splash, and when she came she had a pole drawn back to throw to me—she knew I had fallen in there—but I was already coming up on the side of the bank. When I got up on the side of the bank I was laughing. She said, "Woman! You fall in this canal and you come out here laughing?" I told her, "Just as well laugh as to cry." She said, "Let's go home," and we went on to the house. She didn't know my mind. You can walk along and talk with God and nobody hear you. And when I did, He said, "It will be worser next time if you don't go back and do what I told you."

The seven o'clock bus next morning couldn't get in too soon for me. I packed and wrestled all that night not to go to sleep so I could be on that bus. Nobody knew it. Next morning I called Frances and told her, "I'm going home. I'll write you when I get there."

Later I wrote and told her all about it: how come I had to fall in that canal and God brought me out. You don't play with God. That canal was so deep, the drag-line couldn't hardly touch the bottom. I fell head over heels in there and had never swam a lick in my life, but I'm here and I ain't no spirit. God brought me out. He's got a way of whipping you and He's got a way of bringing you out. "I ain't gonna let you drown; I will do you like I did Jonah: put you down there, and you're coming out." You've got to hear what God says. I asked Him a favor and He did it; then Satan comes in and he tried to show me another point, another thing. But if you let Satan override that good spirit, then you get messed up. I did it. He said, "It's going to be worser than that if you don't go and build that church." That's what He told me and I didn't ask anybody's advice. I told God, "I'm gone," and I did like Jonah when he got out of that whale. I took a beeline to the Island. That was on the eleventh of March; I got home on the twelfth. Elder Hunter came to see me and we talked over that church business and on the thirteenth of March we started right on there.

We had a meeting at my house again, then we bought a tent. The tent took up enough from time to time to buy that lot that we've got. After we got the lot, we had to get the lumber and all the other stuff, but we had enough members to help out with that. Now, who was going to build the church? And behold, we couldn't get anybody to sign a contract to put up that building. We didn't have the money, and nowhere to turn for the security. The preacher's word didn't go, the deacon's word didn't go, nothing. Then they tried going to a lawyer, and he came to me one day and said, "Mrs. Jones, you can build that church down there. If you get you two more trustees, then you can build that church." I said, "Me?" I said, "I ain't got no money." He said, "I know it, but with your word you can build a church." That got me. "Just get you two more trustees and write it down and bring it to me over to the

court and you can build that church. If you had a husband you couldn't do it." I was the mother of a church and I didn't even know it, and with a requisition I could build. See, he said that mother stands when that preacher's gone. You can turn the preacher off or he can get mad and leave, but with that mother, that church is gonna stand. I didn't know that. And that's how I came to build our church.

During the building once, I remember, we needed some more lumber. I had thirty-two dollars and that old dry wood cost thirty dollars and twelve cents. So we got the lumber and took it there that evening. Next morning we didn't have a piece; everything was gone. A little later on we could hear the hammering, and they built a little house. But God doesn't like ugly. That house burned down, they done died, and all little things like that just happened. We finished the church and it's still standing. You see, He doesn't like ugly. We got some more lumber and the lumberyard didn't charge us any more when I told them that somebody had stolen what we had bought. It was no use fussing, because many folks were building then and you couldn't walk up and say, "This is my lumber," because you ain't got no mark on it. But I knew where some of it went. You see, when I was borned again—and this goes until the Lord takes me out of this world—I told the Lord not to let anybody in this world give me nothing. Nothing. No way. And anything that they took from me, don't let me try to get it back from them.

Everything is owed to God. But whatsoever people may do for me, Jesus, you pay them, because you know more of what they need than I do; you know how to pay them. No matter how rich a person is, God can pay them. He did it. He done done it so widely that right now a very rich white woman is telling me that she wouldn't have had so-and-so if she hadn't helped me. She's a millionaire; she's the one who bought me the home I'm in. She has orchards and vineyards and all that kind of stuff in California, but her blessing came because of me. He'd never have blessed her if she hadn't needed it, and I didn't even know it was happening….

On TV and PTL [a Christian televangelism show] some of them are hitting these old songs we used to sing, but not in the same spirit. Ain't nothing to what they do, nothing extra to it. Ain't nothing much in it, no deep feelings. The Lord said he's gonna appoint a spirit upon all flesh and then all sons and daughters shall prophesy. And that's true. He's doing it. 'Cause He said, before He let the devil have more souls than Him, He'd make souls out of stone. He didn't mean rocks: that means stony-hearted people who wouldn't bow, stony-hearted people who wouldn't yield. I used to hear white folks praying, when they called themselves praying or talking to the Lord, and they didn't hardly ever say anything about Jesus. I told a white man that once at our house. I said, "You white people, you figure 'cause you're white and you're so high and have money and everything else in the United States and other places too in your hands, you figure that you don't talk to that little boy, you talk to God." Everything they say, they say "Oh God!" But Jesus said, "You got to come in by me," you see. And now you can hear them talking to Jesus. The son of the living God. Now you can hear them doing that, see. So they come in that way, and they're singing the same old songs and they're doing what the Lord said, "I will place into your mouth a new song." And so, even though there ain't much in the way they do, it sounds just as good to them as the old songs sound to us. And they sing about "Lift him up until he speaks from eternity," and they got so much stuff in there till I wouldn't hardly know it if I hadn't heard them say the words. But yet and still, God ain't gonna lie. "I will place into your mouth a new song." And so let it come that way. Then go right back and don't forget the old path.

And when you find it, walk therein. Don't forget the old path. I can sing all these new songs; can sing right along with them—those that I know—but I just don't forget the old path.

If the Lord hadn't let me have the knowledge and the understanding to bring in these yard games and songs like we did long years ago, and get them on record, they would have already run out somewhere. They would have, 'cause at some schools the teachers sing some of the same things we did but it's way off. It's different. And when she was in New York Mabel Hilary had them children playing my games— she knew the right way—but she had them in her way. In "Little Johnny Brown" she had them get down on their knees to fold the blanket. And I spoke about that onstage. I said I was glad to see the children come to know the games that Mabel had taught them, 'cause Lomax had already told them on the stage that they were my games. I said I was glad to see that she was keeping them up but that I didn't have any lazy Johnny Brown. I had never seen anyone get on their knees to play Johnny Brown before. And in the "Aunt Dinah" game there wasn't any skipping, no zest. The verses were given out like hymns:

> Way down yonder in an old cornfield
> Blacksnake popped me on my heel
> Pop my whip I run my best
> I run my head in a hornet's nest
> I'm goin' away to see Aunt Dinah
> I'm goin' away to see Aunt Dinah

and they walk away but no tune. Not that much tune. A funny tune. But see, it was just out of the way. It was what you call modern. The modern style. They're changing to stay up with the times but that just makes it go away. You wouldn't know where it went, wouldn't know where it came from.

I hear a lot of young people singing gospels—what they call gospel—and I don't feel

> **And I think to myself when I'm singing something that my old foreparents knew, that if their spirits came around me, I believe they would be rejoicing.**
>
> **They would know it; they would say, "That's the song that we used to sing."**

any particular way about that. I do like for the young people to sing spirituals. But I don't feel any particular way about gospel, not if they name it that, 'cause gospel ain't nothing but gospel—I don't care where it comes from and how it goes—and I think they should preach the gospel and sing spiritual songs and jubilee songs and do it that way. That's what I think. And when they're singing and putting all that stuff in it, like "...and you know what? I'll tell ya...," I don't like that. But I just take it. That's their way of doing it. And I just sit up there and listen at it and go on. But that's their way. I ain't never told them to stop it 'cause they ain't singing for me, but I don't think it fits; it's not natural. I sure don't think it fits. But everybody's got their own way, and you sure have to sing spirituals and jubilee songs and hymns and zions. Now zion songs are good. A lot of people don't realize it but zion songs are very slow. Jubilee songs are fast. Spirituals are either fast or slow. We sing spirituals. A lot of the gospel songs that are sung these days are fast, and they put all kinds of things in there I don't think they should, but God knows their heart. That's the main thing.

And a lady asked me one day, she said, "You don't sing blues?" I said, "Not with this. I been quit singing them things many years now." "And no love songs?" I said, "Oh yes sir." She drew up, "Oh, you sing love songs?" I said, "Yeah." And she asked, "What's the difference?" I said, "There's a lot of difference, because I sing love songs to Jesus." I said, "Every one of the songs I sing is a love song." I couldn't sing a love song years ago, because I wasn't singing love. I was just singing wishing songs, and good-time songs; backyard blues wishing you were this way or that way or this place or that place. And wishing you could be with somebody you ain't with and all that kind of stuff. Wasn't no love in it at all. And hatred songs, where you call people all sorts of names. You could make up any kind of a song you want to with that; I could. I used to could. But when you sing a love song you're going the straight way; it's going to be about the Lord; it's going to be about your soul. I said, "All I sing now is love. That's all I do...."

I went to a church not too long ago, and wasn't a Bible in there. The preacher, he brought me home, and he said he had over three hundred members but all they talked about in that church was themselves, about the nature of the earth, about the cows, and rocks, and mountains. But who put it there? Who put the breath in the cow, who grew the grass? They ain't got that background. Who blows the wind? They get nothing about that. To me that teaching ain't worth a dime. It's just a way to make money. The preacher said that if he went to telling them how they ought to live, he wouldn't have a church. I said, "But you will have a bunch of hell to get in, because the Lord wants you to tell the people the truth. If you don't tell them the truth, you and they are going to be buckled together, because they're going to try to beat the devil out of you for fooling them." And we've seen that in the prophecies: the men and women hanging, moaning and groaning, and when the meaning was told, it was these were the false prophets that were teaching the people the wrong way. That were them and their disciples.

Everybody is a disciple of something, and anything you're a member of, that's what you get paid for. You can turn your head, or get drunk, or kiss a bear if you want to; it doesn't matter. As long as you've not paid you're in debt. But Jesus said you must be born again, and if you're born in the spirit you're going to do right. That's all there is to it, that's why we don't have a preacher. We don't pay a preacher to preach, that's crazy. That's wrong all over the world; I don't care who does it. And I tell them that in their own churches—I don't go up in their pulpits because I don't have any business there—but I tell them it's wrong to pay a preacher. It says go without stripe, without coat, without anything, and I will pay your rewards. And you pay your tithes [10 percent of your income] and give your offerings. If you pay your tithes, God will make your job so good! If you pay your tithes God will make your health so good. God would open up doors and windows you never thought about….

And I've been to many places, schools and such, and wherever I go I teach it. I teach the word, because that's all they need—the word. It's all in me and it's all I'm going by—the word. The word was sent me. I asked God to give me something to do to come out of myself, that I could do something for somebody and do something good. All my people are dying and going, and nobody's leaving anything. Don't even have land to leave although the land doesn't do any good since the cracker will take it. Too many of us die and don't leave what we know. Mr. Julius, my stepdaddy, he could make tombstones, he could make fans and other beautiful things. I said, "Mr. Julius, teach it to me." He said, "No. The white folks might arrest me if I do." And he never did teach it.

Things have changed a whole lot so nowadays people don't have to sing songs at anybody. People sing now for their own benefit and joy, except maybe for blues singers and stage singers that sing against one another. I'm not talking about myself, because I sing the old-time songs and they can come if they want to or they can let it alone. I'm right there and I ain't moving, because that's all I want to do. But most of the songs now, they just make them up, just trying to make something new, something different. And we get some that ain't no song at all.

I get lots of satisfaction out of my music, quite naturally, and other folks' music too, 'cause I just love music. But for myself, it's great to me when I'm singing and can think to myself that I'm singing something I need to sing. And I think to myself when I'm singing something that my old foreparents and the other folks of that tribe along in those days knew, that if their spirits came around me, I believe they would be rejoicing. They would know it; they would say, "That's the song that we used to sing." What we have to understand is that they're here all the time. Not yesterday or tomorrow, but all the time. And as long as they're around me, I believe they'd be happy.

Discussion Questions: **Bessie Jones**

1. Read Jones's first paragraph, which tells about her mother, Abby Lou Frances, her grandmother, Elizabeth, and her great grandmother, Mary. Given what Jones writes in the rest of her autobiography about the role of women, why do you think she begins her narrative with these three women? Who were the people in her religious community during the first phase of her life? Did she think she needed a male preacher for her church in order to secure a loan from the bank?

2. Jones's biological father was Ronnie Smith, but her mother married another man before Bessie was born, James Sampson, and Bessie was "mostly brought up" by James's brother, Jet. Was there much birth out of wedlock in Jones's community? Did there seem to be much stigma attached to it? Were children often brought up by grandmothers or aunts and uncles? What is Jones's view of the men "who just wouldn't do right" by their wives?

3. Were there many interracial children in Jones's community? How does she explain their presence?

4. Describe Jones's relationship as a child to the authority figure, the preacher, in her religious community. Compare her attitude toward Reverend Perry to Dr. Mays's attitude toward Reverend Marshall.

5. Does Jones believe that spiritual phenomena can cause physical phenomena? Explain her belief in "signs, like what the itching of the palm meant...or the itching of the nose." Are there any comparable superstitions prevalent in contemporary mass American culture?

6. Does Jones think Christian churches should have preachers? Did she try to convince other Christians that they should not pay preachers?

7. Some students find Jones's autobiography less clear or interesting than others. Can you explain why they might have this reaction? What is your own view on the matter?

8. Jones writes that she was tested by God. Part of this experience was her falling into a canal, unable to swim. What was it God wanted her to do? Why does she compare herself to Jonah?

9. Does Jones approve of white people's attempts to sing some of the old songs, such as on television shows like "PTL"? What is her opinion of modern black gospel singers?

Chapter 10

Islam

C H A R A C T E R

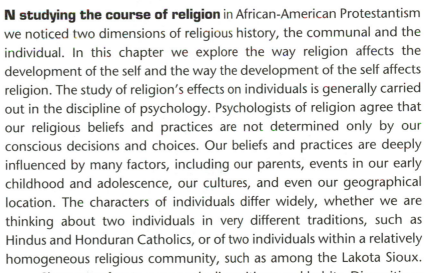

IN **studying the course of religion** in African-American Protestantism we noticed two dimensions of religious history, the communal and the individual. In this chapter we explore the way religion affects the development of the self and the way the development of the self affects religion. The study of religion's effects on individuals is generally carried out in the discipline of psychology. Psychologists of religion agree that our religious beliefs and practices are not determined only by our conscious decisions and choices. Our beliefs and practices are deeply influenced by many factors, including our parents, events in our early childhood and adolescence, our cultures, and even our geographical location. The characters of individuals differ widely, whether we are thinking about two individuals in very different traditions, such as Hindus and Honduran Catholics, or of two individuals within a relatively homogeneous religious community, such as among the Lakota Sioux.

Character refers to a person's dispositions and habits. Dispositions and habits are inclinations to act, and each of us has different inclinations: Some are inclined to act favorably toward religious authorities; others are inclined to act skeptically toward anyone who tells them what to do or think; some are inclined to seek strange religious experiences; others are wary of novel and unusual experiences. Whatever character you have is determined in part by molecular biology, including the genes your parents gave you, in part by environment, including the town and school district in which you were educated, and in part by you, including the choices and decisions you make. When we concentrate on religious character, we concentrate on a person's identity, its formative influences and future trajectories.

In this chapter we are presented with autobiographies giving insight into the character of two adherents of Islam, the youngest of the world's three monotheistic religions. Like Jews and Christians, Muslims worship one and only one God whom they call *Allah*. Allah revealed His will to the prophet Muhammad (570–652 C.E.) through the angel Gabriel in 610 when Muhammad lived in Mecca, a holy city in what is now Saudia Arabia. Gabriel showed Muhammad the holy book of Islam, the Qur'an, or Koran, which proclaims the singularity and power of Allah. Muslims believe that Muhammad was the last of a long line of prophets, including Adam, Abraham, Moses, and Jesus. Muslims accept the sacrality of the Hebrew Bible and the New Testament, but believe the Qur'an is the final revelation, completing the message found in the earlier works. As you might expect, there is significant overlap of Islamic, Jewish, and Christian beliefs and values.

What is Islam? The Five Pillars of Islam outline its ritual cultus. One of the pillars is the *hajj*, or pilgrimage to Mecca, of which we will learn more later. The other four pillars are the confession of faith, prayer, almsgiving, and the fast of Ramadan. The confession, the prayers offered five times a day, and the giving of money to the poor—all are practices intended to show submission to the will of Allah, and submission is the central religious value. Islam's moral code includes a proscription against the eating of pork and consumption of alcohol, and restrictions on the participation of women in legal and religious ceremonies.

A central determinant of Muslim character is the *hajj*, the Mecca journey required of all the faithful once in a lifetime. If Muslims have not yet been on their *hajj*, they may well spend some time in anticipation, wondering what the journey will be like and trying to live their lives to prepare for it. If they have already been to Mecca, they may spend some time in remembrance, reflecting on its images and sounds and the emotions it generated in them. Their *hajj* may continue to affect them, shaping the way they respond to new challenges. For example, after Malcolm X's *hajj*, the African-American leader underwent a dramatic conversion experience. Although he was once an angry man, bitter against all whites, he became a forgiving man who saw the humanity of all individuals. Malcolm X encountered Muslims from around the world on his pilgrimage, and was deeply impressed by the absence of racist attitudes among the whites he met:

> White, black, brown, red, and yellow people, blue eyes and blond hair, and my kinky red hair—all together, as brothers!... All ate as one, and slept as one. Everything about the pilgrimage atmosphere accented the Oneness of Man under One God.[1]

Malcolm X continued with a comment about the importance of Islam for those in the United States: "America needs to understand Islam, because this is the one religion that erases from its society the race problem." The *hajj* had a profound effect on Malcolm X's character.

Few activities are more clearly delineated as "religious" than a Muslim's holy pilgrimage to Mecca, and yet Muslims will participate in this part of the cultus of their religion with varying purposes and states of mind. Islam is as pluralistic a religion as any other, and Muslims display a wide range of beliefs from fundamentalist to liberal. Like adherents of other religions, Muslims may be complete devotees who think that being at the heart of the tradition requires them to believe literally every word of scripture, or they may be more skeptical followers who think their religion requires an open and critical attitude toward inherited customs. This chapter's first autobiography is that of Jalal Al-e Ahmad, an Iranian writer and well-known critic of the established Iranian political and religious order. His account of his *hajj* shows that he falls into the group of more liberal and skeptical Muslims. An intellectual with a restless mind, he finds himself questioning many Islamic beliefs and rituals even as he is joining a quarter million other *hajjis* on their way to Mecca.

Al-e Ahmad knows that Islam shares central beliefs and values with Christianity and Judaism, beliefs such as monotheism and values such as the sanctity of every individual. But he is not enthusiastic about Judaism and Christianity because he is concerned about the influence of the Western consumeristic mentality on Islamic culture and, consequently, devotes his life to writing imaginative stories and essays intended to hone the critical skills of his Muslim readers. In

---

1. See the chapter titled "Mecca" in Malcolm X, *The Autobiography of Malcolm X*, with Alex Haley (New York, N.Y.: Random House, 1965).

order to help his readers find an intellectual basis of their own, however, he finds that he himself must answer the central question of religious personal identity: Who am I? He poses this question in the very first paragraph of his story.

As a way of answering the question, Al-e Ahmad not only goes on his pilgrimage, but writes about his experiences as a way to observe and find himself. Al-e Ahmad was born in 1923, the son of an Islamic cleric in Tehran, the capital city of Iran. His father led noon prayers and preached sermons at the local mosque, making it clear to his son that he was to follow in his father's footsteps. Al-e Ahmad rebelled against this expectation and while he was in college stopped praying and observing Islamic law. He traveled outside of Iran and gained exposure to other cultures, then published his first book in 1946, a collection of stories that did not present his father's Shi'i Muslim tradition in a favorable light.

Shi'i Muslims constitute one of the two major groups of Islam. The second group, to whom the majority of Muslims belong, are the Sunnis, or orthodox Muslims. The Shi'i are a messianic sect who believe a leader will emerge from among them to bring justice and peace to the oppressed. As you might expect, Sunnis and Shi'is disagree about who should lead the Islamic world. Sunnis believe that the caliph, or leader, should be elected by each new generation. The Shi'is, on the other hand, believe that the leadership should be passed down along hereditary lines, descending from Ali, who was elected to the Caliphate in 656 C.E., twenty-two years after Muhammad's death. Al-e Ahmad criticized the Shi'is, and one commentator wrote of Al-e Ahmad that he was not "in his adult life...deeply religious, or, for that matter, [did he believe] in Allah, the Shi'i Imams, or heaven and hell."[2] Al-e Ahmad clearly was not a fundamentalist Muslim, but his autobiography is important as a religious document because it presents the critical and liberal side of Islam, a pluralistic tradition too often perceived by Westerners as monolithic, repressive, and unthinking.

In 1962 Al-e Ahmad published an essay titled *Weststruckness*. In his introduction to Al-e Ahmad's autobiography, Michael C. Hillmann describes *Weststruckness* as

---

2. Michael C. Hillmann, "Introduction," in Jalal Al-e Ahmad, *Lost in the Crowd* (Washington, D.C.: Three Continents Press, 1985), p. xxii.

a forceful, angry polemic secondarily attacking the hollowness and decadence of contemporary Western civilization and primarily warning Iranians not to succumb to the disease of adopting Western evils. Al-e Ahmad argues that although Iran and the West have been in conflict for millenia, only in recent centuries has it been an uneven, unequal contest with the dominant West forcing upon Iran treaties, products, educational ideas, and alien cultural values. The essay struck a chord in many Iranian readers.[3]

The Iranian authorities were not among Al-e Ahmad's fans, however, and his critical essays brought him suspensions from his teaching positions in the 1950s and 1960s. During these times his family survived off the income of Simin Daneshvar, the woman he married in 1950.

While Al-e Ahmad leveled deep criticisms against Shi'i Islam, he also saw it as a unifying force standing against both the external Western forces of imperialism and the internal threats of those who would assert authoritarian control over Iran. Although Al-e Ahmad might have sympathized with the anti-Western tendencies of the recent Khomeini regime in Iran, he would not have agreed with the theocratic impulse of Khomeini to impose a fundamentalist form of Islamic law on all of Iran.

Al-e Ahmad's journey to Saudi Arabia took two weeks, and his journal of the trip makes clear that he was not sure why he made the pilgrimage. He admits not having prayed for some twenty years, and yet he participates in the ritual prayers that mark the beginning of *hajj*. If Al-e Ahmad's view of the pilgrimage seems distant and ironic, there is no reason to think his account somehow deficient, because the most revealing religious autobiographies are often written by those on the margins of a tradition. We need not think that every religious "believer" must be a fundamentalist. As you read Al-e Ahmad's autobiography, be attentive to its mood and watch for indications of his type of character. Is he an optimist or pessimist? Is he beset with difficulties like Satomi Myodo, who was constantly battling depression and anxiety? Is he happy and upbeat, always looking on the bright side? Or is he sardonic and wry, finding irony in the ritual actions of hundreds of thousands of fellow pilgrims?

Our second author grew up in Egypt during the years Al-e Ahmad was growing up in Iran. Zaynab al-Ghazali was raised by a cotton

---

3. Ibid., pp. xii–xiii.

merchant and scholar, Sheikh al-Ghazali al-Jabili, *Sheikh* being the designation for spiritual teacher or master. Like Al-e Ahmad, al-Ghazali's father was a powerful person, and from him she learned of Nusayba, the daughter of Ka'b al-Mazini and a model Muslim woman. Al-Ghazali's father challenged his daughter to follow the path of submission and become a true Muslim woman like Nusayba al-Mazini, but the scholar's daughter struggled with her father during her teenage years and, like Al-e Ahmad, went through a rebellious period. She was attracted during this time to the secular path of Huda al-Sha'rawi, a famous Egyptian feminist who refused to wear the veil during the 1920s and who established the Egyptian Feminist Union. After flirting with secular feminism, however, al-Ghazali took a different path and chose to follow the Islamic way of submission. She donned the veil, believing she could work for the elevation of women's status from *within* traditional Islamic law, or *shari'ah*. When she was eighteen she established the Muslim Women's Association (1936–64).

Al-Ghazali married twice, divorcing her first husband because he did not support her in her religious leadership role. When asked about her two marriages by an interviewer, she called marriage "a sure Sunna," or a law binding on all Muslims. Just as many Jewish laws are found outside the Torah in the Talmud, many Islamic laws are found outside the Qur'an in the *hadith*, laws regarded by Islamic tradition as obligatory. Al-Ghazali explained that marriage is a *hadith* incumbent on all Muslim women and men. However, even marriage must serve the purpose of submission to God and, after her second husband died, al-Ghazali devoted all of her energies to serving Islam. She had done her duty in marriage, and felt no obligation to marry again.

One of the religious communities defining al-Ghazali's character was the Muslim Brotherhood, founded in 1928. At the time, Western influences were calling for a separation of religion and state in Egypt, moving Egypt away from its tradition as a country in which Islam played a major role. The Muslim Brotherhood was organized to combat this trend, but it met only with limited success.

The Brotherhood was established by Hasan al-Banna and held that Egypt should be ruled by the Qur'an, a very controversial position that threatened Egyptian President Abdel-Nasser's political establishment. Nasser cracked down on the Brotherhood during the 1950s, throwing many of its members into jail and banning the organization after an alleged attempt on Nasser's life by one of the Brothers in 1954. In the early 1960s, al-Ghazali helped to reorganize the group, but in 1965 she was imprisoned with a twenty-five-year sentence after an alleged attempt to overthrow Nasser's regime. In jail she was repeatedly beaten and terrorized and twice threatened with rape. She writes that she survived only on the strength of visions and miracles: her religious faith. She was released in 1971 when Anwar Sadat was president.

Al-Ghazali believed that the United States had told Nasser to single her out as a major threat. In her book, *Ayyam min hayati [Days of My Life],* she affirmed the view that one of Islam's missions is to destroy the power of America.

Al-Ghazali's text is composed of two parts. In the first, Valerie Hoffman interviews al-Ghazali about her religious and political views. In the second part, Hoffman translates part of al-Ghazali's book.[4] Fulfilling an ethnographic role such as John Stewart fulfilled for Bessie Jones, Hoffman provides us with helpful background material, writing that al-Ghazali's book "aims mainly to expose the Nasser regime's persecution [in the 1940s and 1950s] of the Muslim Brothers." Hoffman adds that al-Ghazali

> consciously depicts the Brotherhood as a peaceful and peace-loving association of pious Muslims, with no reference to its numerous internal conflicts or to the Brotherhood's violent tendencies. Zaynab al-Ghazali was editor of the section of *Al-da'wa* magazine entitled "Toward a Muslim Home." This section includes a mini-magazine for children with a feature entitled "Know the Enemies of Your Religion" that encourages children to hate and fear Zionists, imperialists, and evangelicals, who are accused of working to undermine Islamic religion and society. *Al-da'wa* was banned in September 1981 along with a number of other religious publications.[5]

As you read Hoffman's interview and al-Ghazali's story, ask yourself whether there are analogous women's movements within Christianity or Judaism. Be alert for clues about al-Ghazali's own personal

---

4. Zaynab al-Ghazali al-Jabili, *Ayyam min hayati* (Cairo and Beirut: Dar al-Shuruq, n.d.), as referenced in Valerie J. Hoffman, "An Islamic Activist: Zaynab al-Ghazali," in Elizabeth Warnock Fernea, ed., *Women and the Family in the Middle East: New Voices of Change* (Austin, Tex.: University of Texas Press, 1985), p. 233.

5. Hoffman, pp. 233–34.

development; her vision of the world; the forces that helped to form this vision; and the relationship between her religious convictions and her hopes for an Islamic Egyptian society. Try to develop a clear picture of her character, how it was shaped by religious and secular influences, and how it helped to shape Egyptian Islam.

Finally, you will notice in both articles a different system for numbering years. Different religions have different calendars, and different calendars reflect the different worldviews of traditions. Religions often date historical events from the central event of their tradition; the Christian calendar of B.C. and A.D. divides history into the times before and after the birth of Christ. Muslims believe the dividing line is Muhammad's *Hijra,* or migration from Mecca to the city of Medina, which happened, in the Christian calendar, in the year A.D. 622. Therefore, you can generally convert the Muslim dating system into the Christian dating system by adding 622 to the Muslim year. In the two texts reprinted here, the editors and translators have performed this task for us. Being attentive to the difference in the way time is measured is a good way to bear in mind the radically different historical perspectives of traditions like Christianity and Islam.

Jalal Al-e Ahmad

From *Lost in the Crowd* by Jalal Al-e Ahmad, translated by John Green (Washington, D.C.: Three Continents Press, 1985). Reprinted by permission of Three Continents Press.

The footnotes were written by John Green.

Friday 21 Farvardin 1343
[10 April 1964] Jedda

We started at 5:00 A.M. from Mehrabad airport. We got here [in Jedda] at 8:30 (7:30 local time), having had breakfast on the plane without tea or coffee. Bread, a piece of chicken, and an egg, in a box bearing the airline's logo. The "*hajjis*-to-be," however, were unsure at first. Was it edible or not? Had it been killed according to religious law? I missed whatever it was that removed their doubts. It may have been our *hamlehdar*,[1] who took such an interest in helping the flight attendants distribute the food that one would have thought he was paying for it himself. After the meal we each got an orange, again with the guide's help. Then one of the passengers asked for water. A Lebanese stewardess brought it. I heard a young man who was her colleague tell her *"Commeenc pas si tôt,"* exactly like that in French. I laughed, and they saw me. They spoke in Armenian after that. A Lebanese Armenian Arab flight attendant taking pilgrims from Tehran to Jedda! But who am I? I remember praying this morning in the pilgrim's assembly area at the Tehran airport, after who knows how many years. I probably quit praying during my first year at the university. Those were the days! I would do my ablutions and pray. Sometimes I even did *namaz-e shab!*[2] Of course, towards the end I didn't even put a *mohr*[3] under my forehead. This was the beginning of infidelity. Frankly, it isn't the same anymore. I feel like a hypocrite. It just isn't

1. A *hamlehdar* (hereafter referred to as guide) acts as a guide for a group of Muslims throughout the pilgrimage, providing them with details on ritual formalities at the shrines themselves as well as obtaining practical information on procedures and arranging for facilities and provisions. (tr)

2. *Namaz-e shab* is an extra, nonobligatory prayer that may be offered between the first light and sunrise. (tr)

3. A *mohr* is a small rectangle of packed clay from Mecca or Karbala that is placed on the ground by Shi'is when they pray. (tr)

right. If it isn't hypocrisy, neither is it faith. You just do it to blend in with the crowd. But does one go to Mecca without praying?

We were supposed to leave yesterday morning, but we did not. We had gone to the airport at four in the morning, but we went back home at seven with weary looks on our faces; the pilgrim assembly area had been full of people, with sleeping children littering the floor in various postures, curled, stretched, and contorted. There had been a group of Kurds praying, wearing *kalaghis* on their heads, hands on their chests; their *imam*[4] was wearing a white turban. One of the ones in the prayer line was so tall that he looked like a chess king standing in a row of pawns, while the *imam,* with his white turban, wasn't even the size of a pawn. Such is the *hajj!* There was consolation in the fact that we slept yesterday afternoon and from the early evening on. We were awakened by a telephone call at 2:00 A.M. telling us to hurry to the airport. Then farewells, kisses, and such joy for those seeing us off! They imagined the lost lamb returning to the flock. There were two friends with knowing smiles, thinking to themselves, "What is this character trying to pull?" They didn't know it was neither a trick nor a matter of a lamb and the flock. It was something entirely different. The lost sheep had now turned into a mangy goat that simply wished to hide himself in the crowd.

As we waited for the plane at the *hajj* assembly point, the young inspectors looked upon us with a mixture of amazement and contempt. All of us. Especially me (was I imagining things, thinking I stood out in the crowd?), thinking yes, "What fools!" No doubt. And themselves? They were topnotch consumers of razor blades, ties, and toothpaste. And the *hajjis*-to-be? Villagers, merchants, bossy old ladies, stuffy old men, and one or two people like me. And, wonder of wonders, all of them

had abandoned their razors and face paint; each was out to gain insight in his own way. One sought the insights of travel, another to discover the Kaaba,[5] another to discover self-discovery. A merchant had gotten out his Mecca compass and was busy discovering Mecca right there behind the door to the ablutions pool. The first experiences of the journey! You'd have thought we were lost in the African desert (now they're sounding the call to prayer over the loud speakers, right on the edge of the Hajj Village, for the evening prayer; it is exactly twenty minutes to five), even though the Mehrabad airport had a specially constructed area for pilgrims that even had a mosque where one could read the direction to Mecca written above the prayer niche…What was the real meaning of the *hajj* assembly area? It was there to separate the lambs from the goats. Those bound for Paris, London, or New York must not be allowed to see these *hajjis,* each one holding an *aftabeh,*[6] his thermos over his sack of dry bread, home-made yogurt, and other odds and ends. Anyway, these two groups must be separated! Of course the man or the made-up woman headed for Europe must be protected from the sight of these people who have answered the primal call of a desert religion.

We flew above the clouds for a time in the aircraft, a fluffy blanket of them beneath our feet, with the occasional hole. The clouds passed and were replaced by dust, and everything below turned red. Then we were over the desert and there were mountaintops rising up out of the sand, like islands protruding out of the sea. In other places there were bright ochre depressions, places where it had probably just rained. Black, rocky heights. No trace of civilization. Sand, sand, sand. I wearied of it.

---

4. The word *imam* as used here refers to the one who stands in front of the ranks of praying Muslims and leads the prayer. (tr)

5. An irregular cube-shaped structure located in the courtyard of the Grand Mosque at Mecca. (tr)

6. A long-spouted water can or ewer used by Muslims to comply with the Prophet Muhammad's injunction that one cleanse oneself with water after answering a call of nature. (tr)

Sitting next to me was a swarthy old man submerged in himself, somewhat frightened. It was his first flight. He was snapping at people. I helped him position the little tray so his food could be served. "Yes," he said, "thanks, but I know how this works." We talked a little then. A retired police major. His children had married and he and his wife were alone. Now he was going to go into the presence of God and offer thanks. He was frightened, however. "Is 'Arafat[7] as strenuous as they say?" I told him it was my first pilgrimage too….

When we changed locations in the morning—from the aircraft to the Hajj Village (and it took two hours to move that fifty steps!)—I dashed outside and grabbed the first taxi (what a lot of new Chevrolets!) and made a deal with him in my terrible Arabic to drive me around the city for fifteen Saudi rials. He drove me, but my driver and makeshift guide knew nothing but Arabic. This was enough to enable me to get information from him about prices, however. A liter of gasoline costs four of our qerans (an eighteen-liter can costs four Saudi rials), a taxi costs two rials, a bus four piastres—and so on. He provided firsthand information: Jedda has a population of 250–300 thousand, Saudi Arabia itself 7–8 million.[8] There are three newspapers in the whole country, *al-Bilad, al-Nadwah,* and a weekly called *Umm al-Qura.* All three are run by the state. The Arabs of the east drink coffee, in the aristocratic style of the Bedouins. The

westerners (the ones from the Hijaz[9]) drink tea, or *"shay,"* as the Arabs say…We passed Eve's grave at this point. High, thick walls, just like the walls of an old ice house, with a short, narrow door in one corner. It had fallen into disrepair and looked worse than the most obscure and forgotten shrine of an *imam*'s descendant in Abarqu. The grandmother of humanity! Then we passed the Foreign Ministry. Such splendor! Then the Bedouin bazaar, which was still bustling. Then we passed alongside "The Palace of the Great King," with its walls reaching to the sky and its gate guarded by soldiers shouldering machine guns. Then we passed beside a low, crumbling wall, which they had laid around a large tract of land. "The Place of Prayer." The place for Friday prayers. Too bad we got there late. In the middle of it were a number of assembly areas or pulpit-like structures for preachers (no doubt), or for the *mu'azzins.* The area is the size of Tupkhaneh Square. An old city shedding its skin, becoming modern, and laying down new streets, the same sort of surgery they're performing on Yazd, Tehran, and Kerman. There is dirt, dust, construction machinery, mud and sludge….

The air is miserably humid. The body stays wet all the time, and the bones will surely ache tonight. If you can sleep, that is, with legs exposed, and an even more exposed chest and neck area. No matter what, one must get used to it for the days of *ihram.*[10] And these ceiling fans

---

7. *'Arafat* is the name of a mountain and the plain surrounding it in the vicinity of Mecca. In order for a pilgrimage to be valid, each pilgrim must be standing on the plain of 'Arafat on the afternoon of 9 Dhu al-Hijjah, Standing Day. This is arduous because it necessitates a full day of walking and exposure to the hot sun. (tr)

8. Yet the population of Saudi Arabia is 3 to 4 million at most. I have to question the other information provided by this unsalaried guide of Jedda. In any case, as a patriot (though an Arab), he had the right to show off, put on airs, and so on for a foreign tourist. (Al-e Ahmad)

9. The Hijaz is the area of highlands and narrow sea coast in the northwestern Arabian peninsula that was the cradle of Islam. It is now a province of contemporary Saudi Arabia which includes Medina, Mecca, and Jedda. (tr)

10. The term *ihram* refers both to the ritual of purification that pilgrims perform prior to entering the shrine area and to the garments that are worn by one who has completed the rituals during his stay in the shrine area. For men, the garments are two seamless, usually white, pieces of toweling or sheeting, one covering the body from waist to ankle, the other thrown over the shoulder. For women it is usually a simple white gown with a headcovering. (tr)

go continuously. What would we do if they didn't? When the wind stopped at sunset, we ourselves turned on the fans. According to what they say, we will be traveling tonight. I went in the afternoon to visit the other corners and floors of the building. In front of the balconies around the building were clusters of flags of various nations and the names and emblems of this or that guide: Turkish, Persian, Iraqi, Syrian, and Moroccan. Guards continually walked the path going around the building. All of them young, wearing khakis, berets, revolvers, and carrying clubs, watching. A black stood to one side with a small bag of a hand's width and a combination lock over his shoulder, praying and holding his hand over his chest. He didn't curtail the prayer or leave out the *qonut*.[11] A trickle of water passed beneath his feet—that same ubiquitous water—and, interestingly, there were three diagonal scars on each of his cheeks. I have seen a lot of those scars this morning. The scars on all of their cheeks are just alike. Some of them have plus signs, some multiplication signs, some have vertical lines, and some have two horizontal lines, cut in the same manner....

Evening
Saturday 23 Farvardin 1343
[11 April 1964] Medina

Early evening in the Prophet's Mosque. I took a walk after the sunset prayer. The people were talking in groups or saying *zekr*[12] and reading the Qur'an individually. After the prayer rank had been formed two or three people passed back and forth and fanned the crowd. One of them didn't have a fan. He opened his head-cloth and waved that, in a whip-cracking motion. The ceremonial water distributors

began their work at the conclusion of the prayer. Each one carried a cup or a pitcher. And such pitchers! I took a gulp from each one, whether white or yellow. Most of them were made in India or Pakistan. So cool. At the mosque entryway there were small groups of people listening to preachers. A Pakistani was preaching in Urdu, which I didn't understand. Three were speaking in Arabic. I stood between the groups assembled around two of them. One spoke fluently and eloquently on the virtues of the Prophet, [quoting Surah 20, verses one and two of the Qur'an] saying "Taha. We have not sent down the Qur'an to thee to be (an occasion) for thy distress." As I left, I heard: "'A'ishah[13] awoke inthe night, saw her husband making a prostration, and thought him dead..." Another one, who looked like an Indian, speaking in relatively clear Arabic, surprised me by talking about the same nonsense that was in [my book] *Weststruckness!* The concept is so commonplace that even the preachers in Medina discuss it, probably every day! And in such epic language. His upper teeth were pushed forward and his lips were parted; yet he spoke of faith, of Islam, and of the great danger to the Western world in the event of Islamic unity. (The power has now been cut off. I'm scrawling by the light of Javad's flashlight. A moth that looks like a mature silkworm has flown up from the lamp base and is now flying around the face of the flashlight. He's fuzzy! The fuzz is short and shaggy, and it flies loose when you blow on it. Now he's landed on my notebook. I put him out through the window and return.) The guy understood the relationship between manufacturer and consumer and was explain-ing it tothe people. I don't know why, but there was something about it I didn't like. I remembered Sayyid Jamal al-Din

---

11. *Qonut* is the second standing phase of the Muslim prayer, done with the upturned palms resting on the chest while reciting a prayer formula. (tr)

12. *Zekr* is the repetitive utterance of Muslim litanies. (tr)

---

13. 'A'ishah (ca. 614–678) was the daughter of the first Muslim caliph Abu Bakr, and the child bride and "favorite wife" of the Prophet Muhammad. (tr)

Asadabadi[14]...And I left. The people gathered around the Prophet's grave, touching and kissing it. The Saudi police put a stop to that and dispersed them. There was no violence or bad language involved, however. On my way someone placed his *mohr* on the ground and did a prostration. Then when he lifted his head the *mohr* was clasped in his hand.

In the afternoon I went to the post office. The postal clerk gave me an eleven-piastre stamp for an envelope and a twelve-piastre stamp for a postcard. (I haven't yet determined whether a rial is twenty or twenty-one piastres.) As I was coming out of the post office they were giving the afternoon call to prayer and by the time I began to move [to get a place] the alley and the street were clogged with files of people praying. This happened in a flash. The shop keepers continued doing business, however. I stood barefoot next to a woman in the middle of the street. I touched my brow to my shoulder bag on the ground as I did my prostrations. The woman had a daughter who was playing in front of her. She herself wore a white mantle and didn't look Arab. When the prayer ended (no one left out anything, or at least I didn't see it), I went looking for a map. From this store to that store. There were five stores identified as hardware stores. I visited five stationery stores and bookstores before I finally found a map of *Madinat al-Salam,* printed God knows when, based on designs produced during the Ottoman occupation, about two palms wide. The "Zahra Date Tree" was shown planted just as it is now in a corner of the Prophet's Mosque. They've repaired the Prophet's Mosque two or three times since then. They had expanded it and knocked down the date trees and other odds

---

14. Better known as Afghani (1838–97), Sayyid Jamal al-Din was a controversial nineteenth-century thinker. An Iranian by birth, Afghani usually said he was from Afghanistan. He was an influential pioneer in the development of secular political thought in the Middle East, and helped organize the tobacco rebellion of 1892 in Iran. (tr)

and ends, but the map still depicted the situation as it was fifty or sixty years ago....

Sunday 23 Farvardin 1343 [12 April 1964]
Today I didn't set foot outside the house. I slept from eight to eleven in the morning, in order to compensate for the lack of sleep these two or three days. I was in such a state that at night I didn't hear what anyone said. I couldn't focus my attention. The day before that I couldn't focus my memory, that is I couldn't find words. I'm trying to drink less water. The heat is such, however, that you perspire away whatever you drink. It's such a pleasure, this perspiring after drinking one's fill, and the kidneys are amazingly comfortable! (Again I'm preoccupied with myself!) Last night I no sooner laid my head down when it was four in the morning and a new group of *hajjis* came in and made a commotion in the house. They turned on the lights and everyone got up. Then we cleansed ourselves and went to the Prophet's Mosque. The greatest damage from these years of not praying was the loss of the mornings, with their delicate coolness, and the energetic activity of the people. If you get up before sunrise it's like getting up before creation, every day witnessing anew this daily transformation from darkness to light, from sleep to wakefulness, from stillness to motion. I was feeling so good this morning that I said hello to everyone, didn't feel like a hypocrite when I prayed, nor that I was doing my ablutions out of imitation. Yesterday and the day before I still couldn't believe this was me performing a religious rite just like everyone else. I remember all the prayers and the short and long verses from the Qur'an I memorized as a child. Arabic words, however, weigh heavily on my mind and tongue excessively so. I can't pronounce them quickly. In those days I could read them off like a litany with no problems. I realized this morning, however, that Arabic has become a heavy burden on my conscience. In the morning when I said "peace

be upon you, O Prophet," I had a sudden start. I could see the Prophet's grave and the people circumambulating. They were climbing all over one another to kiss the shrine. The police were continually scrambling to prevent forbidden behavior...I started crying and abruptly fled the mosque....

There's no alternative but to international-ize these shrines, Mecca, Medina, 'Arafat, and Mina, to place them under the management of a joint council of Muslim nations, and to remove them from Saudi Arab control. The revenues must come from income generated by the *hajj*. Instead of Saudi Arabian police there must be guides from every nation. Legitimacy must be granted to the special customs of each sect. Road tolls must be lifted, and gardens, courtyards, houses, and dwelling places must be constructed for every group. Especially since most of the Medina businessmen are foreigners: Iraqis, Iranians, Pakistanis, and even Javanese, who have come and settled permanently. They pay exorbitant fees for key money and tolls, and they barely survive.

But this heat! It's so intense that I carefully poured three bowls of water over my head to-day—so it wouldn't seep under the walls of the shower stall and run under the belongings of my fellow travelers—and it felt like the best cold water shower I'd ever had. My God, what will it be like here in the summer? This itself could explain why my poor brother died in this city....

Tuesday 25 Farvardin 1343
[14 April 1964] Medina

Among those four or five preachers, *rowzeh 'khans,* and mullahs, there is a sayyid in our group from Borujerd; he's hot to find supporters for some mosque they're building in Tehran; I don't know the name of it. He has acquired a following of four or five merchants, and every day they pray together in their room. They have asked us indirectly two or three times why we don't join their prayer. Mohaddes, who

follows no one. Uncle, who is not up to it. And Javad, who's strung out all over the place. By process of elimination, I'm the last one left in our family. He is one of those who think that five extra minutes of prostrations will take him five kilometers closer to the throne of God. Worse than that, he insists that I go listen to his talk to the villagers following the *maqhreb* prayer. I finally went last night. Up on the roof. He did such a job of spoiling the delicate air with the same old nonsense about *shakkiyat* [uncertainties], *ghusl* [cleansing], *tathir* [purifica-tion], and *nejasat* [uncleanness] that it made me sick at my stomach. These things ought not to be said even to the dummies of Mazandaran. Anyway, how long must religion be tied to the handle of an *aftabeh,* and be confined to the realm of "cleansing uncleanness?" Or be a menace to an old fool like me? Do these people bear the highest responsibility of religion? The guy doesn't even have the decency to refrain from immediately raising the subject of the unallowability of a mustache the minute you come near him. Worse than him is the hired mourner in our group, who's evidently de-ranged. He is in the habit of asking, "Why don't you beat yourself about the head and shoul-ders?" That's like saying "Why don't you jump off the roof" when I talk about the tragedy. Praise be unto the preacher in our group, who speaks in terms of history and *hadith,*[15] and reasonably. He has begun a discussion of the historical period in which the Kaaba was built and the customs of the *hajj* were established. For the villagers. It is useful in any case, if his sermon finally gets around to the Karbala desert situation. He brings tears to the people's eyes, but not with images of tragedy and martyrdom. His words are warm. His own heart has broken. I have explained why....

---

15. Also called a "tradition," a *hadith* is an accepted account of something said or done by the Prophet Muhammad, his companions, or one of the *imams. Hadiths* have the status of scripture in the determination of precedent in Islamic law. (tr)

> There's no alternative but to internationalize these shrines, Mecca, Medina, 'Arafat, and Mina, to place them under the management of a joint council of Muslim nations, and to remove them from Saudi Arab control.
>
> Instead of Saudi Arabian police there must be guides from every nation.

Wednesday 26 Farvardin [15 April]

It is now clear that the Saudis have set Tuesday as the first day of the *hajj* month. Next Wednesday is therefore *'Ayd,* one day away from the Shi'i day. This very thing is the subject of unbelievable controversy. They all reinforce each other in the belief that one must follow a practice, that individualism has no meaning on the *hajj.* But can you be a Shi'i, after all, and stand aside without complaining among the Sunnis?[16] Our entire gathering last night was taken up with this matter. Our *akhonds* ascended the pulpit one after another to address it. Then our *maddah* [panegyrist] started in. He has a good voice, when he doesn't shout. He also recited a lovely poem. Our preacher discussed the *symbolique* [French for symbolic] quality of the *hajj* rituals (using that very European term. I must convince him that he has no business altering his language just because of a few educated

people) saying that the *sa'y*[17] between Safa and Marveh[18] represents Hagar's effort to find water for Isma'il, and that the *ihram,* the attire of submission, is an unadorned form of clothing, and the clothing of the next life. He did not know, however, that the construction of the Kaaba and its attribution to Ebrahim

---

16. Sunnis are followers of the majority "orthodox" sect of Islam, the sect of "the way and customs of Muhammad." They all subscribe to one of the four Sunni schools, the Maliki, the Shafi'i, the Hanbali, or the Hanafi. (tr)

17. *Sa'y* is the Arabic name for the ritual run performed by pilgrims in commemoration of Hagar's search for water. Hagar was one of the wives of Abraham [Ebrahim], and the mother of Isma'il. There is a story that Abraham's wife Sarah was jealous of Hagar and her son and persuaded Abraham to abandon them in the desert. He did so reluctantly, but only after determining that the place of abandonment was the site of the Kaaba, where no harm could come to them. After being abandoned, Hagar ran after a water mirage until she reached the top of Safa, then ran to the top of Marveh, chasing another one. After running back and forth several times, she returned to Isma'il and found the Zamzam well miraculously flowing in the place where she had left him. (tr)

18. Safa and Marveh are two small hills about 400 yards apart now enclosed within the Grand Mosque, between which Hagar is said to have run in search of water for her son. (tr)

Khalil represent the settlement of a tribe in an area, and is a mark of urbanization. I will tell him this also. He is a good man. Now how does this go? Ebrahim Khalil is an architect and the builder of the Kaaba. The prophet Noah is a carpenter and a ship builder. David is a player of pandean pipes and a poet. Our prophet is a merchant, or a liaison between cities. (Wasn't this why he ordered the trading practices at Ukaz to be aligned with the *hajj?*) Thus, each of them was engaged in an urban occupation. But why are Moses and Jesus shepherds? I think this can be explained by the fact that under the Pharaonic rule of Egypt and that of Caesar's Rome there was probably no alternative but to flee the city, to go out into the wilderness and get close to the soil and to nature. The others, who are connected with the early settlement of the Semitic tribes, all take up trades....

Al-e Ahmad leaves Medina on Friday night for Mecca.

> *Saturday 29 Farvardin [18 April] Mecca*
We got to Mecca at 4:30 in the morning. We left Medina last night at 8:30. Our vehicle was a bus—one of those red ones—whose top had been removed. The passengers took their places in the bus at five in the afternoon. Then there was a very long wait, until eight o'clock, when Javad came and called me. I got stuck with a bad seat, on the third row, next to my uncle. I was the third person in a two-person seat. The driver was a good man. His bus was in good condition, and our guide was claiming he had greased his palm. And so we came directly here, with only one stop in Rabigh, and another one at the beginning of the trip at the Haflah Mosque, where we made ourselves *muhrim*.[19] In the dark of the night, with no water and no privy.

We performed the ritual purifications in the light of the bus's headlights. We had already put on the *ihram* garments in Medina, followed by the mosque rituals, getting back on the bus, and riding on and on and on. The sky and stars overhead were very low, the sky was amazingly close, Scorpio was right in front of us, and the wind blew in our faces constantly (some 8,100 kilometers per hour). We were huddling all the time. Then there was the job of looking after my uncle, an old man who was continually nodding off and in danger of hitting his head on the back of the seat in front of him. Never have I spent a night so awake, and so mindful of nothingness. Under the cover of that sky and that infinity, I recited every poem I'd ever memorized—mumbling to myself—and looked into myself as carefully as I could until dawn. I saw that I was just a "piece of straw" that had come to the *Miqat*, not a "person" coming to a "rendezvous." I saw that "time" is an "infinity," an ocean of time, and that *Miqat* exists always and everywhere, and with the self alone. A "rendezvous" is a place where you meet someone, but the *Miqat* of time is just such a meeting with the "self." I realized how beautifully that other atheist, Mayhaneh'i, or Bastami, had put it when he told that *hajji* bound for the House of God at the gates of Nishapur, "put your sack of money down, circumambulate *me,* and go back home." I realized that traveling is another way of knowing the self, of evaluating it and coming to grips with its limitations and how narrow, insignificant, and empty it is, in the proving ground of changing climes by means of encounters and human assessments.

> *Same day. At Bayt al-Haram*[20]
It appears that even the Kaaba will have been rebuilt with steel reinforced concrete by

---

19. The term *muhrim* is applied to someone who is in the state of ritual purity required for entry into the Mecca shrine areas for the *hajj*. (tr)

20. *Bayt al Haram,* or "The Sacred House," is the Arabic term for the Grand Mosque in Mecca, the goal of the *hajj*. (tr)

next year, just like the Prophet's Mosque. Not only has the *mas'a*[21] between Safa and Marveh been transformed to a huge two-level cement passageway, they are already busy putting in a new rectangular two-story outer colonnade, thereby destroying the one built by the Ottomans. They've already taken out one side of the old outer colonnade, the one facing the *mas'a*, and will undoubtedly destroy its other parts within a year or two. It's true that the space available for circumambulation will be wider and that a larger crowd—three or four times the size of the current one—will be able to circumambulate the Kaaba, but the problem is that they will still be using these cement slabs attached to reinforced concrete pillars, and building upward with them...With beautiful hard rock close at hand, they still use this cement and these cement forms. Apparently, the only thing left of the old outer colonnade will be two or three minarets. They've covered the circumambulation track around the Kaaba with marble, and those in the covered colonnades as well. There were more people doing the run between Safa and Marveh than there were making the circumambulation. As soon as the sun gets hot the circumambulation virtually ceases. (I'm now sitting on the upper level of the outer colonnade, writing.) From up here the Kaaba is just half the size I had imagined. That individual who was architect of this new outer colonnade was evidently unaware that when you destroy proportion you change architecture. The Kaaba is still the same size, but they've made the outer corridor twice as wide, and twice as high. How about destroying the Kaaba itself and making it higher and larger? Out of reinforced concrete, no doubt? (A tall, fat, swarthy man carrying an umbrella just passed, saying "Hajji sir, mention me in your journal too—Qandahari of Mashhad."

---

21. The *mas'a* is the long covered runway where the *sa'y* is performed between Safa and Marveh. (tr)

"Sit down," I said, although there was a hint of mockery in his voice. It seems that this sort of activity is distastefully ostentatious in this setting, although so far I myself have seen two or three others writing on paper, note pads, or what-have-you. I must be more careful after this. Out in public and writing?)

Same day. Saturday. Mecca

This *sa'y* between Safa and Marveh stupefies a man. It takes you right back to 1,400 years ago, to 10,000 years ago (it isn't hopping, it's simply going fast) with its *harvaleh* [jogging], the loud mumbling, being jostled by the others, the self-abandon of the people, the lost slippers—that will get you trampled underfoot if you go back for one moment to recover them—the glazed stares of the crowd, chained together in little groups in a state not unlike a trance, the wheelchairs bearing the old people, the litters borne by two people, one in front and one behind, and this great engulfing of the individual in the crowd. Is this the final goal of this assembly? And this journey? Perhaps 10,000 people, perhaps 20,000 people, performing the same act in a single instant. Can you keep your wits in the midst of such vast self-abandon? And act as an individual? The pressure of the crowd drives you on. Have you ever been caught in the midst of a terrified crowd fleeing from something? Read "self-abandon" for terrified, and substitute "wandering aimlessly" and "seeking shelter" for fleeing. One is utterly helpless in the midst of such a multitude. Which one is really an "individual?" And what is the difference between 2,000 and 10,000?

Each of the Yemenis, filthy, with tangled hair, sunken eyes, and a rope tied around the waist, looks like another John the Baptist risen from the grave. The blacks, heavy, tall, and intense, froth on the lips, moving with all the muscles of their bodies. A woman with her shoes under her arm runs crying like someone lost in the desert. Whatever they are, they don't seem to be human beings to whom one may turn for help. A strong, smiling young man collides with someone and moves on, like a fool in a frenzied bazaar. An old man, panting, is unable to continue, but he is swept on by colliding bodies. I realized I could not watch him be trampled by the people. I took his hand and guided it to the rail in the middle of the runway that separates those coming from those going back. A group of women (there were twelve to fifteen of them) wearing the white *ihram* garments, had marked the backs of their necks with violet flower designs, and each held onto another's *ihram* by the waistband. They were moving in one line towards the circumambulation.

You see the ultimate extent of this self-abandon at the two ends of the *mas'a,* which are a bit elevated, and at which you must turn around and go back. The Yemenis jump and spin every time they get there, say *salam* to the Kaaba, then start again. I realized I couldn't do it. I began to cry and fled. I realized what a mistake that infidel Mayhaneh'i or Bastami made by not coming to throw himself at the feet of such a crowd, or at least his selfishness... Even the circumambulation fails to create such a state. In the circumambulation around the House, you go in one direction shoulder to shoulder with the others, and you go around one thing individually and collectively. That is, there's an objective and a system. You're a particle in a ray of being going around a center. You are thus integrated, not released. More importantly, there are no encounters. You're shoulder to shoulder with the others, not face to face. You see selflessness only in the rapid movement of the bodies of people, or in what you hear them saying. In the *sa'y,* however, you go and come, in Hagar's same wandering manner. There's no aim to what is being done. In this going and coming, what's really disturbing is the continual eye contact. A *hajji* performing the *sa'y* is a pair of legs running or walking rapidly, and two eyes without a "self," or that have leaped out of the "self," or been released

from it. These eyes aren't really eyes, but naked consciousnesses, or consciousnesses sitting at the edge of the eye sockets waiting for the order to flee. Can you look at these eyes for more than an instant? Before today, I thought it was only the sun that could not be regarded with the naked eye, but I realized today that neither can one look at this sea of eyes...and fled, after only two laps. You can easily see what an infinity you create in that multitude from such nothing-ness, and this is when you are optimistic, and have just begun. If not, in the presence of such infinity you see you are less than nothing. Like a particle of rubbish on the ocean, no, on an ocean of people, or perhaps a bit of dust in the air. To put it more clearly, I realized I was going crazy. I had an urge to break my head open against the first concrete pillar. Unless you do the *sa'y* blind.

When you leave the *mas'a* there is a bazaar, with people packed tightly together. I sat in a corner with my back against the wall of the *mas'a*. I was quenching my thirst with one of these "colas" and thinking of something I'd read by a European on the question of the "individual" and society, and that the greater the society that envelops the "self," the nearer the "self" comes to being nothing. I realized that the Eastern "ego" that forgets itself and its troubles in such a state of equality in the presence of the world of the unseen is the same one that, in the ultimate individualism of seclusion, claims to be divine. Just like that infidel, Mayhaneh'i, or Bastami, and others. The Joks of India as well. I realized that this "ego" is sacrificed in isolation just as much as it "sacri-fices itself" in society. At its highest levels of satisfaction, what is the ultimate attainment in yoga if not this? To give peace of mind over to asceticism, for if one is nothing in the manifest world of action outside the self, one can at least impose the design of one's will on one's body! Therefore, what is the difference between existentialism and socialism? In the *sa'y* we escape our confinement, and we do something

> **These eyes
> aren't really eyes, but
> naked consciousnesses, or
> consciousnesses sitting at
> the edge of the eye
> sockets waiting for the
> order to flee.**
>
> **To put it more clearly,
> I realized I was going crazy.**

that is to "our" benefit, whether in the mind or in reality. In yoga, we remain in "self" confinement, which is to say that since we have no power to act outside the body, we settle for the small, weak domain of our bodies. In the *sa'y,* we accept society's domination, but only in the presence of the world of the unseen. If you came and took the "world of the unseen" out of this multitude, what would be left? In our system, neither the individual nor society has priority. Priority goes to the world of the unseen, which is connected to the bazaar, and has come under the control of companies. The individual and society are two transient phenomena contrasted with something that signifies eternity: but they are two sides of the same coin. It is only in such a domain that "Sign of God"[22] and "Shadow of God"[23] have

meaning. Both individually and as a society, we have closed the door to the manifest world of action. When a meaning is found for the relationship between the individual and society, whether by the individual or by society, you move in the direction of manifestation and action, or society does. Just like that evangelist Qobadiyani.[24] Otherwise, we've been doing the *sa'y* for 1,400 years, and for 1,000 years we've had isolation, seclusion, and martyrdom, but not for the sake of manifesting anything. This is the opposite of self-sacrifice. This self, if it doesn't exist as a particle working to build a society, is not even a "self." It is absolutely nothing. It is a piece of rubbish or particle of dust, except (and 1,000 exceptions) when it exists in the context of a great faith, or a great fear. Then it becomes the builder of everything from pyramids to the Great Wall of China, and even China itself. This goes for the entire Orient, from the Fall of man until today....

It's quite a spectacle when the people are poising themselves outside the Kaaba or beneath a portico for the circumambulation. The *mutawwif* gives instructions and the others, who have already made arrangements among themselves, listen attentively. Holding onto one another's hands, chadors or *ihrams,* they start out, walking in place at first, then swarming ahead. I'm certain, however, that they become dispersed and scattered at the very outset. Each one in the multitude goes in a different direction, and each loses his way going home and spends half a day wandering around aimlessly. The women are really just spectators in these rites. They're not admitted to the graveyard, nor to the shrines of Uhud and Zamzam. Tonight, on the second floor above the *mas'a* between Safa and Marveh, there were a number of them in front—at the edge of the room—having taken places for the prayer. They were quite happy,

22. *Ayat Allah* (Ayatollah), the Arabic-Persian term the author has used here, can refer to verses from the Qur'an as well as to high-ranking Shi'i clergymen. (tr)

23. *Zell Allah,* or "Shadow of God," was originally applied to the Muslim caliphs, emphasizing the religious sanctity of their authority. It was later adopted by secular monarchs, such as the Shah of Iran. (tr)

24. Qobadiyani Marvazi, A.D. 1004–88, better known in the West as Nasir-i Khusraw, was a famous Iranian poet and writer. (tr)

watching the "House" and the circumambulation around it, when two or three Turks came up insisting that the women ought to be behind the men. And the women yielded.

Then there are these huge cloths they spread out underfoot! First they soak them with water from the Zamzam well, then they spread them out beneath the *hajjis'* feet, end to end, over the House of God's marble carpet and over the hot sand (the marble carpet over the mosque floor is not yet completed) both to prevent the *hajjis* from burning their feet and to bless the cloth as a commodity for the next life. Apart from the *ihram,* which each keeps, the *hajji*'s greatest souvenir is his burial shroud.

I then went up on the eastern roof and kneeled to pray in a place at the roof's edge overlooking the entire House and the surrounding area. The call to prayer came at 6:20, later than the usual Medina time. As the call arose, the crowd circumambulating the Kaaba, moving to the center from the edges, began to quiet down and form circular ranks. By the time the words *Allah u Akbar* [God is great] were heard the entire mosque population was in concentric files. The last circumambulators lined up instantly, but there was still a flurry of activity in that corner where the Black Stone[25] sits in one of the Kaaba's walls as I began my prostrations. By the time I raised my head again the entire mosque population was lined up, from one end of the porticos and rooftops to the other. The greatest number of human beings anywhere who are gathered in one place in response to a command. This assembly must have some meaning! A meaning higher than

---

25. The Black Stone is mounted about five feet above the ground in the eastern corner of the Kaaba, surrounded by a stone ring and held in place by a silver band. It has no direct relationship to Islam, but is kissed and touched by pilgrims in emulation of a similar gesture of respect made to the Stone by the Prophet Muhammad on his last pilgrimage to Mecca. (tr)

> **By the time I raised my head again the entire mosque population was lined up, from one end of the porticos and rooftops to the other.**
>
> **The greatest number of human beings anywhere who are gathered in one place in response to a command.**
>
> **This assembly must have some meaning!**

this dealing, marketing, tourism, discharge of obligation and ritual enactment, economy, government, and a thousand other inevitable things! When the prayer reached the second *salam,* from that corner in front of the Stone there was a sudden explosion of people rushing to kiss it. Then the prayer ranks broke and the circumambulating began anew. At first the ranks nearest the Kaaba arose and began circling, then those behind them followed in a stately rippling motion moving away from the center. The gentlemen who built these new arched porticos were aware of the grandeur of their task, but it's a pity. And God save us from all these molded reinforced concrete structures. Despite this, when finished it will be the largest uncovered temple on earth, with two new monstrous minarets competing for height.

As I descended the steps I suddenly realized my foot was burning painfully. I withdrew into a corner and bent over to find the cause of the burning, and saw that there were new blisters. Then I looked at my shins and saw that they were covered with strange red blemishes, which continued higher up. I hiked up my *ihram.* It was on my chest and belly too, as well as my arms. Because of my bad liver and this hot sun. As I straightened up to leave, I caught a woman lifting her eyes, looking me over.

It is Sunday, 19 April.

The local Arabic newspapers were full of boastful pride today because the Kaaba's shroud was made by the Saudis themselves this year, and they did not accept one from the Egyptians. They had washed the Kaaba in the morning in order to change the shroud. Each one of our fellow travelers returning from circumambulation was full of talk about having seen the changing of the Kaaba's shroud. There was an unspeakable uproar. One of their feet was black and blue from being stepped on so much. Another had lost his shoe. Another had stood guard with three others so a fourth one could pray at *Maqam-e Ebrahim.*[26] They had taken turns. As for myself, my side hurt. The run between Safa and Marveh is a long one, and tiresome, even though I was never able to do more than two laps without stopping. I get exhausted and stop. The circumambulation is easier. But why does my side hurt? Aha. These Yemenis are very rough. In order to clear a path for themselves they elbow the *hajjis* in the side,

pushing on both sides. I saw this two or three times. I can't recall if they did this to me or not. They surely must have, however. If they hadn't I'd be able to walk now.

Yesterday at sunset I cut my hair like the others, in order to remove the *ihram.* That is, I cut my mustache. At the two ends of the runway on the heights of Safa and Marveh, a group of people stood holding scissors and mirrors in order to cut the *hajjis'* hair. They were clipping hair from heads, beards, and mustaches, and taking money. The hilltops of Safa and Marveh were like the floor of a barbershop, just from the single finger's width of hair they cut from the *hajjis'* beards and fuzz. I took the scissors and mirror from a fellow and trimmed my own mustache. I gave him half a rial and went on....

Same day. Same place.

In the evening when it was cool I came out of the house to go for a walk. I had thrown an Arab head cloth over my head like a scarf, with Javad's mantle on my shoulders, like the others. There is no alternative. It was so dusty! And so sunny! I went to the north as far as *al-Mu'abidah* Square. The sunlight was reflected on the upper side of the mountain. There was beautiful landscaping in the middle of the square with benches amidst little flower gardens. The tropical trees are still young and without a shadow, except for one or two eucalyptus trees that cast shadows and were covered with a lot of dust. Here and there were zinnias and verberas around the garden, on a little patch of lawn. I made a circuit once or twice and sat down beside a tall young man who was reading some photocopied pages to prepare a lesson. I said "hello" in my limited Arabic and asked to sit down; he stopped reading to talk. It seems that he was an officer just returned from al-Khamis on leave. (The days of *'Ayd-e Qorban* are an annual, official holiday for the Saudi government, something on the order of our New

---

26. According to legend, when Ebrahim [Abraham] was rebuilding the Kaaba he had to stand on a large stone after the height of the building had risen above his reach; the stone now called *Maqam e Ebrahim* is said to be the one he used. It is enclosed in a kiosk near the Kaaba. (tr)

Year's.) Al-Khamis is at the border between Yemen and Saudi Arabia, and he was in charge of I don't know how many soldiers, protecting the border from Sallal and providing a kind of shield for al-Badr. His monthly salary was 750 rials, with one wife and a child. He was himself an Anizah Arab. I never thought an Anizah could be just like a human being, and so neat. He recited some of their poems in praise of Wahhabi power and their government. He really wanted to know if I was *muwatin salih* or not. I didn't understand what he meant. I resorted to English, which he knew a little. "Do you mean 'good citizen'?" I asked. He didn't understand. I had to explain to him that if he was talking about a world state, I was not in favor of such a thing.

"Why not?" he asked.

"Although a human being is not a stone to be laid on a foundation and held in place," I said, "everyone is subject to the limitations of his language, culture, and traditions," and this kind of thing. I had to hear something from him, however, so I cut it short and gave him my attention. The book he was reading was a history of World Wars I and II in Arabic, a translation of an American text. He said he was a communist, a "revolutionary." He mentioned Machiavelli, Marx, and Hegel, talked about "tempered steel," and *ra's maliyah* (which I realized was a literal translation of our word for capitalism). Some time ago he had gone to Egypt for three months for some kind of military training, and he had brought back all these books and names. From the names he mentioned and his reliance on Harold [Joseph] Laski [1893–1950], I realized that he was about where we were twenty years ago. He also knew a bit of Hebrew, which they had taught him in the military school, so they would not be at a loss to manage Israel after they captured it! We inevitably turned to the subject of Israel. I used the example of the hand and the heart (which I also remember explaining to the young men of 'Ur'ur at the ice cream stand), saying that one

must disable the heart in order to stop the hand, and the dangerous heart in the East is foreign capitalism, and Aramco [Oil Company] and the other oil companies are its hands. Israel is one of them also. He didn't accept this, however. I tried to find the word for "demagoguery" in Arabic (he didn't understand it in English) in order to describe [Egyptian President] Nasser's behavior towards Israel for him. The words didn't come to hand, however, or to my tongue. He was aware of the danger of capitalism, but didn't understand that the Arabs ought to be united against the oil companies instead of Israel.

He later became alarmed that I was taking notes, especially when I wrote down the command of the Great King of Saudi Arabia, who said "Don't teach your young or they will eat you." He said they would seize a man in a second and take him away (or something like that). I wanted to know where the Saudi prisons were located. He looked around and then quickly mentioned a name or perhaps two which I didn't understand. He knew I wanted to write it down, so he wouldn't repeat it.

"Where is it?" I asked.

"In the Empty Quarter," he said. Then he said he was not alone. There are many like him in the army. Then he leaned over and said into my ear, "Israel must first be killed in the palaces of the Arab kings, and afterwards in Palestine itself." Then he deplored such things as poverty and the lack of medical care…I forgot to ask his rank. Judging from his youth, however, he must have been a first or second lieutenant.

After I left him I was thinking that the West has really used Israel as a cover for its own misdeeds, or as a way of hiding them. They have planted Israel in the heart of the Arab lands so that the Arabs would forget the real troublemakers in the midst of Israel's troublemaking, and not realize that the water and the fertilizer for the tree of Israel comes from the Christian West, the French and American capitalists. Then there was the support that the

Pope of Rome gave them, in lifting the curse of Christ from them, I think by a decree from Pope John 22. Then I was thinking that if Nasser became famous overnight it was because he took a stand against the West—without having any underground oil reserves—and that channel of water, the Suez Canal, was not worth a lot of trouble. When we opposed them we had such oil deposits, and this is one of the reasons we failed /with Dr. Mosaddeq and the events of his time not because of outsiders, but because of internal problems. Of course the West penetrated, because something was rotten on the inside/.[27] If the West is pushing the wagon of Christianity with its neocolonialism, why have we in our area allowed the cart of Islam to become so rusty and abandoned it? I asked myself, wouldn't these *hajj* rituals themselves be a good launching pad for taking a stand against the West? (Oh ho! I'm back to *Weststruckness* again...)

It is Wednesday 22 April. After Al-e Ahmad has eaten diluted yogurt and cucumbers for lunch, it is "time to go make animal sacrifices."

A word about this slaughterhouse. It's a huge area surrounded by a wall with two entrances. There are large pits dug and prepared in groups, with mounds of earth scooped out of the pits and piled up higher than the walls, visible from the outside. All the ground is covered with carcasses, goats, sheep, and camels; there are no cattle to be seen. The muscles quiver on freshly killed carcasses. Children, knives in hand, play with their remains. One's feet are constantly stepping in blood and entrails, and I held up the hem of my *ihram* as I walked. One individual wearing the *ihram* was making a film with a sixteen millimeter camera. Two or three employees of the "Office of Health and Security" were with him. Everyone was standing

around holding dull knives. They decapitated a goat and threw the head to one side. A young boy came and drove the point of a knife into the goat's throat, and the goat went into violent convulsions as the blood spurted out of its throat. It was clear that the boy was experienced and knew what to do to make the carcass dance. I don't know where he thrust the knife to make the convulsions greater. In any case he knew something that I did not know. A camel lying on the ground jerked twice—from one end to the other—by the time I got to him, and that was all. The blood coming out of a hand's-width gash in its neck was frothy, looking like fluffy light purple soapsuds on the ground. Such a huge carcass! A man had thrust a dagger into its neck above the sternum right where it stood, in the tuft of hair at the base of the neck. He made a hand's-width slash downward, and when the animal tried to turn its head he struck it in the nose with his fist. The animal roared and tried to run, but its legs were hobbled. It fell on the ground. It tried to get up, but the blood spurted out, it couldn't, and it slowly, slowly collapsed. It lowered its neck gradually until its head touched the ground. When I got there it was gasping; this stopped a moment later. Then two jerks, and that was the end. This is the most terrifying facet of this motorized primitivity. I almost passed out two or three times. I remembered the first time I visited the anatomy hall at the medical school. I had stopped to look with blind, adolescent courage. I rationalized to myself that this day of killing—and of animals—was perhaps originally a way to prevent the killing of people. If we go back to Abraham's sacrifice of his son...this is true. It can be rationalized, in any case, but a slaughterhouse of this type is a scandal. Seeing it once is the best possible advertisement for vegetarianism. If they had had just one scene from this slaughterhouse in the film *Mondo Cane,* they would have made a fortune.

All the streets end at a slaughterhouse, covered with mutilated carcasses. They quickly

---

27. The section between slashes was censored in earlier editions of the book. (tr)

cut away the choice pieces of meat and abandon the rest, especially the goat and sheep heads, which have been crushed under cars. Then comes the grave digger for this entire huge wasted sacrifice, a red bulldozer, which is continually digging pits in the corners and sides of the slaughterhouse, filling this one and going on to another. This huge wasted sacrifice! In any case, what would happen if they got ten refrigerator trucks and took all these carcasses to Jedda in an hour (it's less than 100 kilometers from Mina to Jedda), put them all in a two- or three-thousand-ton ship for cooking and preserving, freezing and salting, and sent them as gifts to the poor people of the world? Why doesn't the Red Cross see this barbaric waste, when two-thirds of the people don't even eat meat once a year? Why don't they pack this meat in containers identifying it as sacrificial meat from the slaughterhouses of Mina, to be used as a spiritually powerful gift for all the afflicted Muslims of the world, or for all those who are dying of malnutrition? Enough of this. The Saudis are too busy to think about these things. These things can only be resolved through Islamic internationalization, and if you want to take the narrow, calculated point of view of the Europeans, let me tell you that all the administrative expenses of Medina and Mecca could be met just through the proceeds from the sale of this meat. During these rites, a million pilgrims have made animal sacrifices, each one at least once. Let's suppose that each one of them kills a skinny sheep or goat. Every carcass would have twenty to thirty kilograms of meat. Let's forget about the camels. This would be about 20,000 tons of meat, apart from the skin and entrails...such wealth! And thrown on the ground! Such a stench! So sickening! Who provides these corpses? According to what I have heard, most of the animals come from Sudan and Ethiopia, and a few from Yemen, Syria, and Iraq. Is it possible to develop a system for breeding special sacrificial stock according to the number of pilgrims in each nation and also

with a view to their easy shipment and thereby return the wealth of the Muslim nations back to them? You see there are many questions. Enough of this.

The slaughterhouse ground and the surrounding streets are covered with blood, entrails, skin, bowels, meat, bones, and finally, black and muddy earth. Everyone is carrying a knife. They are either paid butchers, trimming carcasses to get next year's meat supply, or carrying entire carcasses on their shoulders. They don't even skin the carcasses. I had heard that the Saudi government takes the skin and intestines, but I saw that they were cutting off the heads and those making the sacrifices took whatever meat they wanted, even with the skin. The rest they laid aside and left. People were bringing a white-haired sheep out of the slaughterhouse where they were stopped by the police. They were told to remove the skin and keep the meat. Was the government going to take these hides?

I saw three blacks—a woman, a man, and a child—who had claimed a camel. They were cutting the red flesh away from the bones piece by piece. The animal's large white ribs were just like long stalks of rhubarb.

In another place a young man holding a knife stood up from inside the rib cage of a fallen, half-stripped camel so suddenly that I was stopped in my tracks. It startled me. Groups of live sheep and goats stood waiting in the midst of this filth, with the occasional huge camel. The goats were chewing their cuds, the sheep napping. Only the goats sensed what was happening; they were very upset and kept bleating. The police at the slaughterhouse entrance would not allow new groups to enter before the others already inside had been killed.

As I see it, they satisfy two or three primitive human urges with this huge sacrifice. One was mentioned previously: sacrificing animals instead of human beings. Sheep instead of Isma'il. Kill animals, in order to refrain from killing human beings. It is also the best possible practice in the use of knives, in shedding blood, seeing blood. Women, men, and children, knives in hand, take such delight in carcasses, for procuring provisions, or simply for the thrill of it. Several times I saw people cutting up carcasses just for fun, and such a gleam of delight in their eyes. You'd think they were all studying anatomy, or exulting in victory after some heroic deed. Finally, this is itself a form of exercise. Standing and bending, skinning the carcasses, dallying with them, and so on. We get no other exercise on the *hajj* except walking and pelting the pillars. This primeval picnic needs two or three vigorous activities in any case, and this is the third and last of them.

In all of Mina there are perhaps twenty or thirty trees. The rest of it is the valley itself, surrounded by rocky mountains. Under the eternal blackness of the scorched rocks is the body and flesh of a white mountain that looks green, or bluish. Zubaydah's water is truly a blessing here. For years now they've been moving oil from Dhahran to Syria by pipeline, but after 1,000 years they still haven't been able to install a proper water pipe for the *hajj* rites. Of course, during the Saudi period they have made some improvements on these same ancient water wells, with plaques above every faucet that say *"al-sabil al-malik* [for the King's sake]," and *"Zubaydat al-'azizat al-Sa'udiyah* [dear Zubaydah the Saudi]."

As for electricity, Mina has it. They've even wired the tents. They brought a long cable in the afternoon with a socket and bulb and hung it on the tent post. It is now well lit. Tents have been pitched the whole way from east to west, usually in pairs, with the sun constantly circling above them. I heard that the United Nations assumed the task of providing water and power for the *hajj*, but can this be true, and in the kingdom of Saudi Arabia yet! Never!

The poor people that thrive parasitically on the *hajj* and its pilgrims, and serve as its porters, are so beneficial to the antiquated Saudi system, and such a well-established institution, that I don't think they'll take steps to eliminate their poverty so soon.

It's clear for years and years to come the *hajj* rites will continue, because they provide visits to shrines, tourism, business, entertainment, and experience for every villager who leaves his farm and has no other opportunity to see the world and have the experiences of a journey. If, however, we were able to make this pilgrimage suitable, not for a man of the twentieth century, but for a man of the fourteenth century, one could hope that the *hajj* would be a stage of development and an experience in the lives of the people of the Muslim nations. If not, as it stands now the *hajj* is mechanized barbarism. That's all. My hand is aching.

Thursday 3 Ordibehesht 1343 [23 April] Mina
I forgot to write that on *'Ayd-e Qorban* (yesterday) they fired cannons in Mina (which we heard in *Mash'ar al-Haram*) both in the morning and at noon instead of the call to prayer. Three shots. That is, *'Ayd-e Azha*. The Saudi government has placed a sword on the green field of its flag and written above it "There is no God but God," and now to announce *'Ayd-e Qorban* they fire cannons. I am unable to say what this means. By putting a sword beneath "There is no God but God," do you want to say that Islam conquered the world with the sword? The Europeans put these words in your mouth. Anyway, when Islam conquered the world with the sword, you were nothing, sir! A Wahhabi tribe owning lands rich with oil, and now keepers of the Kaaba! You drove the Hashemites out with help from the Aramco company. Now you're just a keeper of pipes. Nothing else....

The only bird I saw in Mina and 'Arafat was there on top of the mountain, a little sparrow with black wings and a grey body, hopping among the thorns. It seems that what I have been calling heather up until now is actually camel's thorn. I looked at it closely. Later when I was sitting on a high point resting and smoking a cigarette, three Arabs came up and said hello. They were Yemenis. As the sun set behind us and lights were coming on one by one on the valley floor at the foot of the mountain, we talked politics. They were supporters of Imam [Muhammad] al-Badr, opponents of Nasser and Sallal, and in agreement with the Saudis. One of them, who spoke for all three, claimed that they were secure from armed attack. No matter how I tried to learn from them where the "Imam" and his front line were, they couldn't comprehend maps and weren't even literate. I drew maps on rocks hoping they could give me an idea of their location, but it was useless. Or were they hiding things from me? They said they would be returning to Ta'izz in three days. It turned out they weren't Zaydis, but Shafi'is.[28] It appears that these Yemenis are the poorest of all the pilgrims in the world. They're all ragged and excessively thin from poor nutrition. These people are the ones who've been having a real feast the last two or three days in the vicinity of the slaughter-house. As I came down from the mountain I passed among the belongings of the pilgrims, each of whom had spent the entire day hiding from the sun behind a rock and was now coming out into the open. In the moonlight and in the dim light that came up from the valley I saw a wristwatch on a rock along my way. I involuntarily bent over and picked it up. I went two steps, and remembered where I was and who I am. I went back and replaced the watch.

Tonight I realized why the lunar calendar is the official one here instead of the solar calen-

> # If we were able to make this pilgrimage suitable, not for a man of the twentieth century, but for a man of the fourteenth century, one could hope that the *hajj* would be a stage of development and an experience in the lives of the people of the Muslim nations.

dar, throughout this region, from ancient Babylon to Egypt. The solar calendar can have no meaning in these parts. The winter here is like the fall, and both of them are like summer. They have had to rely on the moon to light the cold nights. For this reason religious rites are usually held during the first half of the month: 10 Dhu al-Hijjah, 15 Sha'ban, 3 Rajab, 10 [Muharram] *'Ashura,* and so on. Religious rites, celebrations, and days of mourning usually take place on days when the moon is full and high, or is on the rise, so that the desert, with its cool nights, will be well lit for religious ceremony.

Mina's electric power is weak and insufficient, despite the lavish illumination of the

---

28. Shafi'is are followers of the Sunni school of Islamic jurisprudence founded by Muhammad ibn Idris al-Shafi'i (d. 820). The movement arose from the Maliki school, and introduced the notion that local traditions and authorities could be appealed to for resolution of religious and legal questions, without referring to the theologians in Medina. (tr)

official buildings and their rooftops, but it is evident that year after year the facilities, electricity, and water are improving. It is also evident that after the conclusion of the *hajj* rites, life also goes on here in Mina; it's just a little village the rest of the year.

Our *rowzeh khwans* and preacher—and every Iranian group I've visited is the same—are very insistent everywhere that the Imam of the Age is present at the *hajj*, and that he comes on the pilgrimage every year. They seem to want to convince all the pilgrims that every ordinary man at the *hajj* could be the Imam of the Age, lest you show disrespect to others, and so on... and this, of course, is very good.

You see, however, how simply these pilgrims can live, even though they aren't wealthy, meaning they aren't slaves to consumerism, but they're so eager for Western industrial products! Everything they use during the ceremonies is either Western or Japanese. The only thing used during the rites that is not machine-made by companies is the sacrificial animals, which they waste the way they do. If you look at things through Western eyes, "civilization" means "consuming" (and greater need). Thus, all these pilgrims are "backward," and in the process of developing. When will they be "developed"? No doubt when they "consume" as many "Western products" as possible. The point is precisely that this closed cycle (the export of raw materials, the importation of finished products, then consumption and the need of money or credit for this consumption so you can buy Western products. Where does this money and credit come from? From the export of raw materials, and it starts anew) must be opened somewhere. Gandhi gave the Indians the spinning wheel in order to break this cycle, and Mosaddeq cut off the flow of oil...I will leave this.

After a week in Mecca, Al-e Ahmad returns to Jedda on Wednesday 30 April. On Thursday night he waits to board an aircraft to return to Tehran.

10:15 P.M.

We're now next to the aircraft, and the same abusive quarreling has begun anew. Airport officials continually make the pilgrims line up in some semblance of order, but as soon as they turn their heads the passengers jumble like a flock of sheep; it's something to see. In any case, the boarding process is taking so long that it's possible to write.

11:00 P.M.—aboard the aircraft

Now that we've boarded, it's a four-engine propeller-driven craft. They claimed we'd return by "jet." There was no place for myself and three or four other people who came aboard last. They had to bring us into a little compartment behind the cockpit used as a resting place for the crew. There is a table in the middle with two long benches on each side. It was hard to get in. Its disadvantage is the sound of the motor right in your ear. You can't sleep, neither can you do anything while awake. I must again take refuge in this notebook. What would have happened on this trip if I hadn't had the companionship of this notebook? We will be airborne three hours and thirty-five minutes, they announced. The aircraft vibrates a lot. The nuts and bolts of the seats were loose. I tightened two of them with the screwdriver in my pocketknife. They tore my clothes. An *Engrish* woman in her forties is the crew chief, and two Armenian Lebanese women are her assistants. The tall young Lebanese man who came with us and rebuked his assistants for giving the passengers so much water is also here. I think he must hold a high position in this Lebanese company, which is collaborating with Iran Air in its monopoly over the *hajj* season. He's a handsome young man who gives orders easily. He engaged one of the passengers to help distribute water, and another to distribute bread. He also got one to tell passengers over the aircraft's public address system not to smoke, to fasten their seat belts, how long we would be en route, and this sort of thing. He knows a little Persian. The evening meal consisted of a piece of Holland cheese—which again aroused doubt as to its religious admissibility or inadmissibility—a banana, a pear, two small pieces of white bread, egg, and four biscuits. I don't know what they did in the main cabin, but here they watched each other constantly to see if they would eat the cheese or not, including me, but I wasn't hungry and settled for just the banana and the pear. Now I've turned to my notebook, to see whether I can write something worth reading.

The way I see it, I've come on this trip mostly out of curiosity, the same way I poke my nose into everything, to look without expectations. Now I've seen it, and this notebook is the result. This was an experience too, in any case—or perhaps a very simple event. Every one of these experiences and events was simple and "uneventful." Although it was quite ordinary, it was the basis of a kind of awakening, and if not an awakening—at least a skepticism. In this way I am smashing the steps of the world of certainty one by one with the pressure of experience, beneath my feet. And what is the result of a lifetime? That you come to doubt the truth, solidity, and reality of the primary axioms that bring certainty, give cause for reflection, or incite action, give them up one by one, and change each of them to a question mark. At onetime I thought my eyes saw through all the world's illusions. Now that I belong to one corner of the world, if I fill my eyes with images from all other corners of the world, I will become a man of the entire world. I think it was Paul Nizan who wrote in *Aden-Arabie* that "Aman is not merely a pair of eyes. If, in your travels, you cannot change your position in history just as you change your geographical position, what you have done is futile."[29] Along the same lines I realized that a man is an aggregation of life and culture mixed together, with certain capabilities and circumscribed ties.

In any case, a man is not merely a mirror, but a mirror in which specific things are reflected, even that Hamadani pilgrim who's still wearing his sheepskin vest. But then, a mirror has no language, and you want to have only a language. Is this not what separates the eye in the head from the eye of the heart? When I assess the matter I can see that with the eye of my heart I don't even know myself and the familiar life of Tehran, Shemiran, and Pachinar.[30] So what image have I given in the mirror of this notebook? Wouldn't it have been better if I had done the same thing a million other people did this year who came on the *hajj?* And those millions of millions of other people who've visited the Kaaba during these 1,400 or so years and had things to say about it, but said nothing and took the results of the experience with them selfishly to the grave? Or simply discussed it with their sisters, mothers, children, and families for four days and then nothing? Isn't it really better if we let the experience of every event rot like a seed in the center of its fruit? Instead of eating the fruit and planting the seed? Obviously, with this notebook I have given a negative answer to this sincere question. And why? Because Iranian intellectuals spurn these events, and walk among them gingerly and with distaste. "The *hajj?*" they say. "Don't you have anywhere else to go?" Ignoring the fact that this is a tradition that calls a million people to a single place every year and prevails upon them to engage in a single ritual. Anyway, it was necessary to see, to be there, to go, and to witness, to see what changes there have or have not been since the time of Nasir-i Khusraw.

In any event, whether it be a confession, a protest, heresy, or whatever, I mainly came on this trip looking for my brother—and all those other brothers—rather than to search for God. And God is everywhere for those who believe in him.

---

29. Paris: F. Maspero, 1960. (tr)

30. Shemiran is an upper-class district in north Tehran. Pachinar is an old district in south Tehran. (tr)

Discussion Questions: **Jalal Al-e Ahmad**

1. Al-e Ahmad was the son of a Shi'i cleric and renounced his father's tradition. Why, then, would Al-e Ahmad go on the *hajj?* Can you tell from our author's autobiography what he dislikes about his father's tradition?

2. Al-e Ahmad writes that even though he does not believe in Allah, he prays nonetheless "in the pilgrim's assembly area at the Tehran airport" at the very beginning of his pilgrimage. Why would a nonbeliever pray? Is there anything in Islam that attracts him?

3. Al-e Ahmad writes that "The greatest damage from these years of not praying was the loss of the mornings, with their delicate coolness, and the energetic activity of the people." What do you think he means? In the same paragraph he writes that he began crying upon seeing all the people circumambulating the Prophet Muhammad's grave. What do you think caused him to cry?

4. Al-e Ahmad gives ironic descriptions of his fellow *hajjis.* One of them is a sayyid, or descendant of the Prophet Muhammad, from Borujerd. When Al-e Ahmad goes up to the roof to listen to the man's sermon, he writes that the cleric "did such a job of spoiling the delicate air with the same old nonsense about *shakkiyat* [uncertainties], *ghusl* [cleansing], *tathir* [purification], and *nejasat* [uncleanness] that it made me sick at my stomach." What was it about this cleric and his form of Islam that turned Al-e Ahmad off? What do you learn about Al-e Ahmad from his commentary about his fellow travelers?

5. When the party with which he is traveling gets to Mecca, Al-e Ahmad goes through the ritual purifications to make himself *muhrim,* or pure. But then he writes that "that other atheist," Mayhaneh'i, once told the *hajji* to "put your sack of money down, circumambulate *me,* and go back home." What do you think Mayhaneh'i means? Why does Al-e Ahmad cite Mayhaneh'i at this point? And what does Al-e Ahmad mean by the next sentence: "I realized that traveling is another way of knowing the self, of evaluating it and coming to grips with its limitations and how narrow, insignificant, and empty it is..."? Do you think this insight, coming from an atheist, has religious implications?

6. What influence does the geography and climate of Saudi Arabia have on Al-e Ahmad? What attracts him to its deserts, bazaars, and people? Does he object to anything about the weather?

7. The title selected by the English translators for Al-e Ahmad's autobiography was *Lost in the Crowd*. Discuss the following passage in light of their choice of title, and comment on its significance for understanding Al-e Ahmad's character:

   > It's quite a spectacle when the people are poising themselves out the Kaaba or beneath a portico for the circumambulation... Holding onto one another's hands,...they start out, walking in place at first, then swarming ahead. I'm certain, however, that they become dispersed and scattered at the very outset.

8. In light of the fact that Al-e Ahmad regards himself as an atheist, his final paragraph seems enigmatic:

   > I mainly came on this trip looking for my brother—and all those other brothers—rather than to search for God. And God is everywhere for those who believe in him.

   What do you think Al-e Ahmad means by saying he went on the *hajj* to look for his brother? What do you think his last sentence means?

Zaynab al-Ghazali

From *Women and the Family in the Middle East: New Voices of Change,* edited by Elizabeth Warnock Fernea. © 1985 by University of Texas Press. Reprinted by permission.

The following interview was conducted by Valerie J. Hoffman, who also selected and translated the passages reprinted here from al-Ghazali's book. Professor Hoffman, now Professor Hoffman-Ladd, also wrote the footnotes, which are used with her permission.

QUESTION: How did your contact with the Muslim Brotherhood begin?

ANSWER: The Muslim Brotherhood is the association of all Muslims in the world, so it is natural and imperative for every Muslim to be in contact with it. If I did not have contact with the Muslim Brotherhood, that would be strange and incomprehensible according to sound Islamic understanding, but the fact that I have had contact with it is natural. My contact with it began at the beginning of 1939. It was a direct contact with the martyred *imam* and renewer of the faith,[1] Hasan al-Banna.

Q: How did you come to know him?

A: I came to know him because he is an *imam* and a renewer of the faith, calling people to God. At that time I was actively propagating Islam, calling people to God.... I was working in the general headquarters of the Muslim Women's Association, which I founded in A.H. 1356/A.D. 1936.

Q: How did you come to assume this role?

A: At the time I was eighteen years old. I was working with Mrs. Huda al-Sha'rawi in the women's movement, which calls for the liberation of women. But I, with my Islamic upbringing, found that this was not the right way for Muslim women. Women had to be called to Islam, so I founded the Muslim Women's Association after I resigned from the Feminist Union.

---

1.   The *imam,* from the beginning of the Islamic community, is the one who leads the prayer in the mosque. Originally it was the Prophet [Muhammad] himself, and after him his successors, the four caliphs, who filled this office; thus, *imam* came to be a title for the ruler of the Muslim community and in theory claims to the title should not be multiple. In the passage from her book translated here, the title *imam* is applied to Hasan al-Banna, Hasan al-Hudaybi, Banna's successor, and Sayyid Qutb, who became the intellectual leader of the Muslim Brotherhood. (tr)

Q: At first you were with Mrs. Huda al-Sha'rawi, and then you discovered—

A: That this was a mistake.

Q: Why? How did you discover that this was wrong?

A: Islam has provided everything for both men and women. It gave women every-thing—freedom, economic rights, political rights, social rights, public and private rights. Islam gave women rights in the family granted by no other society. Women may talk of liberation in Christian society, Jewish society, or pagan society, but in Islamic society it is a grave error to speak of the lib-eration of women. The Muslim woman must study Islam so she will know that it is Islam that has given her all her rights....

Q: But why were you convinced at first of the validity of Huda al-Sha'rawi's movement, but later changed your mind? What brought about this change of mind?

A: Studying, reading, and attending lectures and Islamic meetings.

Q: So you established the Muslim Women's Association when you were eighteen, by yourself.

A: Yes. I called women together for Islam.

Q: Was it successful?

A: Very.

Q: What were its activities?

A: Our goal was to acquaint the Muslim woman with her religion so she would be convinced by means of study that the women's liberation movement is a deviant innovation that occurred due to the Muslims' backward-ness. We consider the Muslims to be backward; they must remove this backwardness from their shoulders and rise up as their religion com-mands, as it should be in Islamic lands.

Q: So there were lessons for women?

A: There were lessons for the women. The association also maintained an orphanage, offered assistance to poor families, and helped reconcile families. It attempted to give useful work to young Muslim men and women who were unemployed; that is, they helped in religious activities. The association also has a political opinion, that Egypt must be ruled by the Qur'an, not positivistic constitutions.

Q: You say that your contact with the Muslim Brotherhood was natural. Do you think that the Muslim who is not in the Brotherhood is not a true Muslim?

A: He is a deficient Muslim, and the remedy for this deficiency is for him to join the Muslim Brotherhood.

Q: What is the goal of the Brotherhood?

A: The return of the Islamic state, which rules by the Qur'an and Sunna.[2]

Q: Would there be states other than the Islamic state?

A: The Islamic nation possesses one-third of the world. Geographically, we are richer than the rest of the world, in oil we are richer than the rest of the world. So why are we backward? Because we are not following our religion, we are not living in accordance with our constitu-tion and laws. If we return to our Qur'an and to the Sunna of our Prophet, we will live Islam in reality, and we will control the whole world.

Q: Do you think it is wrong for there to be something called Egypt, Saudi Arabia, or Pakistan?

---

2. The Sunna is the exemplary behavior of Muhammad, the Prophet of Islam, as depicted in the Hadith literature. Although the Hadith is not a revelation from God, it is considered, along with the Qur'an, as one of the foundations of Islamic law. (tr)

A: They remain. But there would be a federation, like the United States.

Q: What methods does the Brotherhood use to attain its goal?

A: Very simple methods. We teach the child his religion, and that he should be governed by nothing but the Qur'an and should govern by nothing but the Qur'an. That is all. The day is coming when we will see the whole nation upholding the Qur'an. When all the people say, "Our religion is Islam," no ruler will be able to say, "I don't want Islam."

Q: Have you seen changes in the Brotherhood in the many years you have been with it?

A: Of course. Whenever one goes deeper, one becomes more refined, stronger. Of course, the Muslim Brotherhood passed through martyrdoms, imprisonments. Brothers were taken to prison, exiled from their country. All these trials gave them power, experience, wisdom, and an ability to patiently endure, so they will not be content unless they are following this path.

Q: Do you think the Brotherhood is stronger now than it was before?

A: Much stronger. Because it learned from the experience of persecution from such people as Gamal Abdel Nasser. It has become wiser, more knowledgeable, in better contact with God, knowing more about human nature.

Q: What is the role of women in the Muslim Brotherhood? Are there many women like you?

A: The Brotherhood considers women a fundamental part of the Islamic call. They are the ones who are most active because men have to work. They are the ones who build the kind of men that we need to fill the ranks of the Islamic call. So women must be well educated, cultured, knowing the precepts of the Qur'an and Sunna, knowing world politics, why we

are backward, why we don't have technology. The Muslim woman must study all these things, and then raise her son in the conviction that he must possess the scientific tools of the age, and at the same time he must understand Islam, politics, geography, and current events. He must rebuild the Islamic nation. We Muslims only carry arms in order to spread peace. We want to purify the world of unbelief, atheism, oppression, and persecution…. Islam does not forbid women to actively participate in public life. It does not prevent her from working, entering into politics, and expressing her opinion, or from being anything, as long as that does not interfere with her first duty as a mother, the one who first trains her children in the Islamic call. So her first, holy, and most important mission is to be a mother and wife. She cannot ignore this priority. If she then finds she has free time, she may participate in public activities. Islam does not forbid her.

Q: Must all women marry in Islamic society? Is there no place for the single woman?

A: Marriage is a sure Sunna in Islam. There is no monasticism in Islam. Men must marry unless they have an excuse, that is, an illness. Women are also excused if they have an illness. But marriage was instituted to reproduce children and to establish the family, which is the fundamental unit in building the Islamic state. Marriage is a mission and a trust in Islam. Sexual life in Islam is a necessity for both men and women, but it is not the first and last goal of marriage. It is to preserve the human race, establish the family, build the man and the woman, to build the ruler, to bring about righteous government…. Any sexual relations outside marriage are totally prohibited. When a man has relations with his wife, it is Sunna that they both wash themselves. And it is Sunna that before he approaches her he says, "In the name of God, the Compassionate, the Merciful. God, protect us from Satan." He begins in this way, because it is a human duty, a duty imposed by God, a divine duty.

Q: You were married?

A: I married twice. I found that [my first] marriage took up all my time and kept me from my mission, and my husband did not agree with my work. I had made a condition that if we had any major disagreements we would separate, and the Islamic cause was the essential. My second husband knew that I left my first husband because of the cause. He gave me written agreements that he would not come between me and my mission, but that he would help me and be my assistant. And in fact we had an enjoyable married life in which there was cooperation, love, faithfulness to God, and purity of soul and conscience. We separated only when I was sent to prison, and he died twenty-one days after I was sentenced. After that, since I had done my duty in marriage, I was free to give all my time to the cause.

Q: You said it was your father who had the greatest influence on you in your Islamic upbringing. Who was he, and how did he influence you?

A: He was Sheikh al-Ghazali al-Jabili, a scholar who completed his education in al-Azhar [University]. He refused to accept a government job, but he was a big cotton merchant. When it was not the cotton season, he devoted himself to preaching Islam. He went around the country, exhorting the people, preaching in the mosques on Fridays, teaching the Islamic call and religion. He always used to say to me that, God willing, I would be an Islamic leader. That's what he used to say to me. He would say, "Huda al-Sha'rawi does this, and Malak Hifni Nasif does that, but among the Companions of the Prophet Muhammad, may God bless him and grant him peace, there was a woman named Nusayba, the daughter of Ka'b al-Mazini. He would tell me of how she struggled in the path

of Islam, and then he would ask me, "Whom do you choose? Do you choose Huda al-Sha'rawi, or will you become Nusayba, daughter of Ka'b al-Mazini?" And I would say to him, "I will be Nusayba, daughter of Ka'b al-Mazini." So I decided to be a Muslim woman.

From Days of My Life, *chapter 2, pages 26–41.*

My connections with the Muslim Brotherhood were not new, as the foolish would have people believe, for its history goes back to the year A.H. 1357/A.D. 1937.

On that blessed day, long ago, in about A.H. 1358, approximately six months after the founding of the Muslim Women's Association, I first met the martyred *imam,* Hasan al-Banna. This was after a lecture I gave to the Muslim sisters in the Brotherhood headquarters, which at that time was in 'Ataba Square.

The guiding *imam* was preparing to create a division for the Muslim Sisters. After first stressing that the ranks of all Muslims must be unified and there must be no differences of opinion, he asked me to head the Muslim Sisters' division. That would mean incorporating the newborn of which I was so proud, the Muslim Women's Association, and considering it a part of the Muslim Brotherhood movement. I no more than discussed the matter with the general assembly of the Muslim Women's Association, which rejected the proposal, though it approved of a first cooperation between the two organizations.

We continued to meet together, though each of us held to his own opinion. The Muslim Sisters' division was founded without changing our Islamic relationship at all. I tried, in our last meeting in the headquarters of the Muslim Women's Association, to appease his anger by promising to take it upon myself that the Muslim Women's Association be one of the supports of the Muslim Brotherhood on condition that it retain its name and independence, which would be more beneficial to the cause.

But this too did not please him as a substitute for incorporation. Then events happened quickly, and the incidents of 1948 occurred.[3] A resolution was issued dissolving the Brotherhood and confiscating its possessions, locking up its people and throwing thousands into prison camps. The Muslim Sisters did things for which they received much gratitude. One of them was Mrs. Tahiya al-Jabili, my brother's wife and my cousin; from her I learned many of the details, and for the first time I found myself longing to reconsider all of al-Banna's opinions and his insistence on complete incorporation. On the morning following the dissolution of the Muslim Brotherhood I was in my office in the headquarters of the Muslim Women's Association, in the same room in which I had had my last meeting with the guiding *imam*. I found myself sitting at my desk with my head in my hands, weeping bitterly. I felt that Hasan al-Banna was right, and that he was the leader to whom allegiance is due from all Muslims, to strive in the path of God to restore the Muslims to their responsibilities and their true and rightful existence, the apex of the world, which they will lead as God wills, and which they will judge by what God has revealed. I felt that Hasan al-Banna was stronger than I, and more sincere in unambiguously spreading and proclaiming the truth.

Such courage and boldness are the c that should be worn by every Muslim. Al-r had worn it and called us to it.

Then I found myself calling my secretary and telling her to get me in touch with Brothe 'Abd al-Hafiz al-Sayfi, whom I commissioned to carry a verbal message to Imam al-Banna, reminding him of my promise in our last meeting. When he returned to me with his greeting and appeal, I summoned my brother, Muhammad al-Ghazali al-Jabili, and asked him to deliver a slip of paper either by himself or via his wife to the guiding *imam*. On the paper was written:

"My lord, Imam Hasan al-Banna:

"Zaynab al-Ghazali al-Jabili approaches you today as a slave who has nothing but her worship of God and her total devotion to the service of God's call. You are the only one today who can sell this slave at the price he wishes for the cause of God the Exalted.

"Waiting for your orders and instructions, my lord the *imam*...."

My brother returned to arrange a hasty meeting in the headquarters of the YMMA.[4] It was to happen as if it were a coincidence. I had no lack of justification for being there, for I was on my way to the YMMA hall to give a lecture. I met Mr. al-Banna and said to him as we went up the stairs, "By God I pledge allegiance to you, to work to establish the state of Islam. The least I can offer you to achieve it is my blood, and the Muslim Women's Association with its name." He said, "I accept your pledge of allegiance. The Muslim Women's Association may remain as it is." We separated on the agreement that we would be in touch by means of my brother's family. The first charge I received from the martyred *imam* was a commission to mediate between al-Nahhas and the

---

3. In 1948 the government believed the Muslim Brotherhood was planning imminent revolution: a cache of arms was found in the Muqattam hills in January and another in Isma'iliyya in October, the Brothers were believed to be involved in the coup d'etat in Yemen, a respected judge was assassinated by a Brother, the confiscation of Society papers brought to light the existence of the Brotherhood's Secret Apparatus, and the Brothers were accused of inciting riots at the university in which the Cairo police chief was killed. The Society was dissolved by government order on 6 December. For details, see Richard P. Mitchell, *The Society of the Muslim Brothers* (London: Oxford University Press, 1969), pp. 58–67. (tr)

---

4. The Association of Muslim Youth (Jam'iyyat shubban al-Muslimin), commonly called the YMMA and thought of as the Muslim answer to the YMCA, was founded in 1927.

hood. At that time Mustafa Pasha al-
~~as~~ was outside the government; the late
~~ahhas~~ appointed Amin Khalil to try to
~~.ng~~ an end to the misunderstanding, and the
martyred *imam* was pleased with this choice;
I was the contact.[5] One night in February 1949
Amin Khalil came to me and told me, "Immediate steps must be taken for al-Banna to leave
Cairo. The criminals are conspiring to kill
him." I found no way to contact him directly,
because my brother had been imprisoned.
I tried to contact the martyred *imam* in person.
While I was on my way to get in touch with
him, I got word of the assassination attempt
and that he was taken to the hospital. Then the
news of his bad condition quickly got worse.
He departed as a martyr to his Lord, with the
prophets, the truthful, the martyrs, and the
upright, and they are the best companions.

My grief was intense and my desire for
revenge against the criminals was bitter; I made
no attempt to hide it. The government of the
coalition of parties came into power and issued
an order dissolving the Muslim Women's
Association. I opposed the order in court, which
ordered us to resume our activities during the
government of Husayn Sirri Pasha in 1950. The
lawyer was Mr. 'Abd al-Fattah Hasan "Pasha."
Then came the Wafd government, and the
Brotherhood resumed its activities. At that time
its allegiance was to the guiding *imam*, Hasan
al-Hudaybi. On the first day of the opening of
the general headquarters of the Muslim Brotherhood, I wanted to announce my faithfulness to
the cause in an indirect way, and may God

ordain whatever He wills in the matter. So I
contributed the most expensive and precious
piece of furniture in my house, an arabesque
parlor set inlaid with mother of pearl, to furnish
the office of the General Guide.

All was calm and peaceful. The martyr
'Abd al-Qadir 'Awda[6] visited me and thanked
me for the donation, and said, "I am happy
that Zaynab al-Ghazali al-Jabili has become a
member of the Muslim Brotherhood." I said,
"May it be so, with God's permission." He said,
"It is so, praise be to God."

Events passed in a calm and friendly
atmosphere between me and many members of
the Brotherhood. Then the revolutionary
military government came under the leadership
of Major General Muhammad Neguib, who had
visited me only a few days before the revolution
accompanied by Prince 'Abdallah al-Faisal, Yas
Sirag al-Din, Sheikh al-Baquri,[7] and my brother
'Ali al-Ghazali on the occasion of Prince
'Abdallah al-Faisal's visit to Egypt. The Brotherhood was sympathetic to the revolution, and so
was the Muslim Women's Association, for a
while. Then I began to feel that things were not
going as we had hoped, and this was not the
revolution we had anticipated, a crowning of
previous efforts at the hands of those who were
working to save this country. I began to express
my opinion to other members of the Brotherhood. When ministerial positions were offered
to some Brotherhood members, I expressed my
opinion in the magazine of the Muslim

---

5. Mustafa al-Nahhas was leader of the Wafd party,
    which rivaled the Muslim Brotherhood as
    champion of the anti-British nationalist move-
    ment prior to the revolution of 1952.... Relations
    between the Wafd and the Brotherhood were
    usually antagonistic, with periods of cooperation
    and mutual support when their interests coin-
    cided. As al-Ghazali explains later, she had a
    personal friendship with Nahhas, but did not
    agree with the Wafd platform. (tr)

6. 'Awda was a lawyer and al-Hudaybi's deputy, but
    he quickly became part of the leadership clique
    antagonistic to al-Hudaybi (Mitchell, *Society of the
    Muslim Brothers*, footnote p. 108).... In the after-
    math of a Brother's attempt on the life of Nasser,
    'Awda was among the six Brothers who were
    publicly executed (ibid., pp. 160–61).

7. Sheikh Hasan al-Baquri was a member of the
    Muslim Brotherhood's Guidance Council. Later he
    became minister of Awqaf under the revolutionary
    government, for which he was expelled from the
    Brotherhood.

Women's Association that none of the Brotherhood should pledge loyalty to a government that does not rule by what God has revealed, and whoever does so must separate from the Brotherhood, and that the Brotherhood must define its position, now that the government's intentions had become clear.

The martyr 'Abd al-Qadir 'Awda visited me, asking me to postpone writing on this subject. So I withdrew two issues of the magazine. Then I resumed writing until the martyr 'Abd al-Qadir 'Awda visited me for the second time, this time bearing a command from the General Guide ordering me not to write on this subject. I recalled my pledge to al-Banna, may God have mercy on him, and I believed that loyalty was transferred to al-Hudaybi, so I obeyed the order.

From that time on my pledge of allegiance governed my behavior, even in such matters as the peace conference in Vienna. I did not travel until I had obtained permission from the guiding *imam,* al-Hudaybi.

Time passed, and then came the events of 1954 with its infamies and calamities, which revealed Gamal Abdel Nasser for what he really is: an enemy of Islam, fighting it in the persons of its propagators and the leadership of its movement. Heinous death sentences were passed on the top Islamic leaders: the martyr and councillor 'Abd al-Qadir 'Awda, a man of virtue, a scholar of al-Azhar, a pious man, for whom the British leadership in the canal zone in 1951 offered a reward of 10,000 pounds to whomever brought him in dead or alive; Sheikh Muhammad Farghali, who was given to the imperialists dead without any loss to the British treasury; and the other noble martyrs.

Even the great struggler for God, Imam Hasan al-Hudaybi, was sentenced to death, though the sentence was not carried out because he was suddenly struck with a severe angina in the heart and was taken to the hospital. The doctors said he had only a few hours to live, so at that point Abdel Nasser issued a pardon for him, expecting to read his obituary in the papers the next morning. But God's power foiled his stratagem. The *imam* lived. Every life term is fixed by God. Yes, he lived, to again render services—and what services!—to the Muslims and to lead the Islamic call in its darkest hour. He demonstrated an ability to steadfastly cling to the truth while he was ill with a number of diseases. This baffled his torturers and caused them to take him to the war prison once more and torture him in the most hideous manner. But he continued to cling to the truth, taking the road of those who follow the call until he came to see the end of Abdel Nasser and his clique, while he survived, raising the banner of truth and the unity of God in which he believed, involved with every kernel of his being. He was steadfast, and allowed himself no weakness or languishing in the religion of God. He refused to be lenient with himself and remain in his home, disapproving only in his heart, as some religious scholars allow and practice.[8]

Indeed, I remember how brave and noble he was when some of those who felt things had gone on too long and who suffered from some weakness wanted him to be lenient and write to the tyrant expressing support for him and asking his pardon. They asked Imam Hasan al-Hudaybi for permission to do that. At this he uttered his famous words: "I will not force anyone to be determined and stand with us, but I tell you, the Islamic call never stood a single day with those who were soft."

---

8. Al-Ghazali's unambiguous praise for Hudaybi's resolve and leadership was not unanimously felt, as Mitchell's account of the history of the Brotherhood makes clear (ibid., pp. 111–26, 139, 142–50), and opposition even took the form of one attempted "coup," though Hudaybi apparently had the support of the rank and file. Hudaybi's distaste for violence, emotionalism, and the separate leadership of the Secret Apparatus brought him into conflict with the leaders of the latter group.

> # I saw that it was not enough for us to grieve while people who struggled in the path of God cruelly suffered from hunger, whip lashes, and nakedness; our grief was not enough to make the word of God paramount.

He said that when he was an old man of eighty years. He remained in the Mazra'at Tarra prison until the last group of prisoners was released after the death of Abdel Nasser....

In 1955 I found myself drafted into the service of the Islamic call without an invitation from anyone. It was the cries of the orphans who lost their fathers to torture, and the tears of the women who were widowed and whose husbands were behind prison bars, and the old fathers and mothers who lost their heart's delight. These cries and tears penetrated my innermost being. I found myself feeling as if I were one of those responsible for the loss of the starving and the wounds of the tortured. I began to offer a little help.

But the numbers of the starving increased day by day, as well as the number of those who were naked, and the news of the martyrs who died under the whips of the debauched apostates, the cruel infidels. Schools and universities needed money, supplies, and clothes, and landlords were demanding rent. The problem grew more difficult, the burden grew heavier, and the hole in the garment grew larger, especially after a year and a half. It was precisely the middle of the year in 1956 when some of those who had been in prison but not sentenced were released. Some were in direst need of someone to provide them with money, food,

clothes, and shelter. All of this was happening while the Muslims were in the good country, in Egypt, which veered with those who led the revolution; no one was aware of his duty. On the contrary, we found many religious scholars and sheikhs who washed their hands of those who struggled in the cause of Islam.

All those who were released, even those who wept at the tragedy and were in pain, hid their pain and their tears out of fear, lest the tyrant accuse them of being Muslims. When my grief at what had happened became overwhelming and I found no way out of it, I went to visit my honorable teacher, Sheikh Muhammad al-Awdan. He was one of the very few men of al-Azhar who were sincerely pious, and I used to ask his advice on everything pertaining to the Islamic cause and the religious sciences. He believed, as I did, that the fact that the Muslim Women's Association had not merged with the Brotherhood could prove useful to the Brotherhood at a later time. He knew of my pledge of allegiance to al-Banna, and he blessed it and supported it. Likewise he knew of my loyalty to the cause after al-Banna's martyrdom, and he accepted it.

I sat with him and told him of the tragedy of the families, and he listened to me in profound grief. I finished what I had to say by explaining what I thought of doing within the limits of my capabilities. I saw that it was not enough for us to grieve while people in the circles of those involved in the Islamic cause, those who were obedient, those who struggled in the path of God, cruelly suffered from hunger, whip lashes, and nakedness and women and children were homeless; our grief was not enough to make the word of God paramount. I saw that as president of the Muslim Women's Association, God willing, I could help the families of the Brotherhood as God enabled me.

The sheikh kissed my head and wept, saying to me, "Don't hesitate to offer any assistance. God is the one who blesses our plans." I again explained to him my position in the association and my complete confidence in the women who were its members. The sheikh said to me, "It has become your irrevocable duty to not hold back any effort in this path and the work you are doing. Place it between you and God the Blessed and Exalted." Then he added, "The only salvation for Islam by God's commandment is these tortured Muslim Brothers. We hope only in God and in their devotion and efforts in the path of the call. Do all you can, Zaynab." So I did in fact all I could. I spent my efforts to offer something, though no one knew that I was doing anything. I gave one or two individuals what I could, saying these things were sent to me and I was only charged with seeing that they were delivered to them.

Then I learned that the virtuous mother, the great struggler in the path of God, the wife of Mr. al-Hudaybi, also took great pains, along with some other noble and virtuous women in the Muslim Sisters, including Amal al-'Ashmawi, wife of the councillor Munir al-Dilla (she was head of the Muslim Sisters), Khalida Hasan al-Hudaybi, Amina Qutb, Hamida Qutb, Fathiyya Bakr, Amina al-Jawhari, 'Aliya al-Hudaybi, and Tahiya Sulayman al-Jabili.

My contacts gradually widened. I contacted Khalida al-Hudaybi in extreme secret, then Hamida Qutb and Amina Qutb. All of this was for the sake of the tortured, the children, and the orphans.

My first meeting with 'Abd al-Fattah Isma'il[9] was in 1957 in the season of the pilgrimage. I was in the port of Suez at the head of a delegation from the Muslim Women's Association going on the pilgrimage. Among those bidding us farewell was my brother, Muhammad al-Ghazali al-Jabili. I saw him coming toward me, accompanied by a man whose face was clothed with light and reverence, averting his eyes. My brother introduced him to me, saying, "Brother 'Abd al-Fattah Isma'il, one of the young men who was best loved by the martyred *imam,* Hasan al-Banna. The honored Guide loved him and had absolute confidence in him. He asked me to introduce him to you in this way, so you would know him." The Brother greeted me and said, "God willing, I will be with you on the ship." I welcomed him, and he left.

We climbed up into the steamship and it moved far from the shore. I busied myself with the needs of the delegation of the Muslim Women's Association. When I went to my room to rest after lunch, I heard a knock on the door. I told the person to come in, but the knock came a second time, and the person who knocked had moved away from the door. When he heard my voice permitting him to enter for the third time, he came in. It was the Brother whom my brother had introduced to me at the pier. He said humbly with his head bowed, after greeting me, "I know, with praise to God, that there was a vow of allegiance between you and the martyred *imam,* Hasan al-Banna, after a long dispute." When I asked him how he knew this, he answered, "From the martyred *imam* himself, may God rest him in peace." I asked him what he wanted, and he answered, "That we meet in Mecca for the sake of God, to speak of what al-Banna wanted of you, God willing."

These words were simply expressed and well intentioned, soft in their simplicity, strong and truthful, with heavy responsibilities, carrying

---

9. 'Abd al-Fattah Isma'il, al-Ghazali's chief collaborator, was also arrested in 1965 and was executed along with Sayyid Qutb in 1966.

the implication of a command that leaves no room for thought.

I said, "God willing, in the house of the Muslim Women's Association delegation in Mecca or in Jedda." When he asked for the addresses, I told him of two Brothers in Jedda whom he said he knew, Sheikh al-'Ashmawi and Mustafa al-'Alim, either of whom could guide him to where I was staying in Mecca and Jedda.

The Brother bid farewell and left.

One night in the month of the pilgrimage I had an appointment after the evening prayer with the late sheikh, Imam Muhammad ibn Ibrahim, Grand Mufti of the Kingdom of Saudi Arabia at that time. We were studying a memorandum I had given to His Highness the King in which I explained the necessity of educating the girls in the kingdom. I asked him to hasten the implementation of this plan, explaining that this was in the kingdom's best interests. The memorandum was transferred to the mufti, who asked to see me.

I spent two hours studying the plan with him. When I left him, I went my way to the Gate of Peace, intending to go around the Kaaba, when I was stopped by a voice calling my name and greeting me in the Islamic fashion. I turned, and there was 'Abd al-Fattah Isma'il. He asked me where I was going. When he heard I was going to go around the Kaaba and then to the house where the delegation was staying, he accompanied me to the mosque, and we went around it together. After performing the prayer that accompanies the circumambulation, we sat facing the proper direction and he began to talk about what was on his mind.

He asked me my opinion of the resolution to dissolve the Brotherhood. I answered that it was a legally invalid resolution. He said, "That is the matter I wished to study with you." When I asked him to visit me in the house where the delegation was staying, he thought it an inappropriate place to discuss such matters for fear of Nasser's spy networks. We agreed to

meet in the construction office of the sacred places of Mecca, the office of a righteous man, Sheikh Salih al-Qazzaz. We met there, but he whispered to me that it would be better for us to meet in the sacred place. So he left on agreement that we meet behind Abraham's abode.

After two prostrations of the circumambulation, we sat behind the Zamzam building near the place where Abraham stood, and he began to talk about the invalidity of the resolution to dissolve the Muslim Brotherhood and the necessity of organizing the ranks of the Brotherhood and resuming its activities. We agreed to get in touch after returning from the holy land with Imam Hasan al-Hudaybi, the General Guide, to ask his permission to work.

When we turned to go, he said, "We must be linked here by a vow with God to struggle in His path, and not to waver until we gather the ranks of the Brotherhood and separate out those who do not want to work, whatever their circumstances and status." We made a vow to God to struggle even to the point of death in the path of His call.

And I returned to Egypt.

In the first months of 1958, my meetings with 'Abd al-Fattah Isma'il became more frequent, both in my home and in the headquarters of the Muslim Women's Association.

We studied the affairs of the Muslims, attempting with all our might to do something for Islam, to restore to this nation its glory and its creed, beginning with the life of the Prophet, blessing and peace be upon him, and the pious ancestors, and those who came after them, deriving our program from the Book of God and the Sunna of His Messenger, may God bless him and grant him peace.

Our plan of action aimed at bringing together everyone who wanted to work for Islam to join with us. All this was only studies and setting up rough outlines, so we would know the way to go. When we wanted to start working, we had to ask permission from Mr. Hudaybi, as General Guide of the Brotherhood, because our legal studies on the resolution to dissolve the society ended in the conclusion that it was null and void, because Abdel Nasser has no claim to allegiance, and cannot command obedience from the Muslims, since he is fighting against Islam and does not rule by the Book of God.

I met with Mr. Hudaybi to ask his permission in my name and in the name of 'Abd al-Fattah Isma'il, and he granted us permission to work after several meetings, in which I explained to him the purpose and details of the studies 'Abd al-Fattah and I had done.

We decided to begin the work by having Brother 'Abd al-Fattah 'Abduh Isma'il conduct a survey throughout the length of Egypt at the level of the province, the administrative center, and the village with the aim of finding out which Muslims wanted to work and were suitable to work with us. We would begin with the Muslim Brothers, to make them the first nucleus of this coming together.

Brother 'Abd al-Fattah Isma'il began his tour, starting with those Brothers who were released from the prisons and who had not been sentenced, to test their mettle: did the persecution affect their determination, and did imprisonment make them withdraw from what might expose them to imprisonment once again? Or were they still loyal to the cause, ready to sacrifice everything, great and small, in the path of God and the support of His religion?

The survey was necessary so we might begin to work on firm ground, so we might know who was really suitable. Together we studied the reports 'Abd al-Fattah Isma'il brought from each region, and I would visit the General Guide and inform him of what we had agreed upon and the conclusions to which we had come. If we presented him with descriptions of the difficulties we would encounter, he would say, "Keep going, and do not look back. Do not be misled by the titles or reputations of men. You are building a new structure from its foundation."

Sometimes he would support what we presented to him, and sometimes he would give some instructions. One of his instructions was

that we add to our sources of study the *Muhalla* of Ibn Hazm.[10]

In 1959 our studies ended, and we drew up a program of Islamic education. I call God as my witness that our program consisted of nothing but the education of the Muslim individual so he would know his duty toward his Lord, and the creation of the Muslim society, which will of necessity be separate from pagan society.

Since the activities of the Society of the Muslim Brotherhood were halted due to the pagan resolution of dissolution of 1954, it was necessary for these activities to be secret.

My work in these activities did not prevent me from fulfilling the duties of my mission in the general headquarters of the Muslim Women's Association or cause me to neglect my family duties, though my noble husband, the late Muhammad Salim Salim, noticed the frequent visits of Brother 'Abd al-Fattah and some of the pure Muslim youth to our house. My husband asked me, "Are the Muslim Brothers having activities?" I said, "Yes." He asked me about the extent and type of these activities. I said, "They are to restore the organization of the Society of the Brotherhood." When he began to ask me probing questions, I said to him, "Do you remember, dear husband, what I said to you when we agreed to marry?"

He said, "Yes. You stipulated certain conditions. But now I'm afraid for you, that you will expose yourself to the tyrants."

Then he was silent, his head bowed. I said to him, "I remember well what I said to you. I told you that day, 'There is one thing about my life that you must know, because you will become my husband; if you still agree to marry

10. Abu Muhammad 'Ali ibn Hazm (A.D. 994–1064) was a famous theologian and legist of Muslim Spain. He belonged to a school known for its rigorously literal interpretation of the Qur'an and Hadith and is therefore called *al-Zahiriyya*, "those who adhere to the apparent meaning" (*al-zahir*). (tr) (*Shorter Encyclopaedia of Islam*, ed. H. A. R. Gibb and J. H. Kramers [Ithaca, N.Y.: Cornell University Press, 1953], p. 148).

me, then I must tell you, on condition that you not ask me about it later. I will not go back on my conditions with regard to this matter. I am the president of the general headquarters of the Muslim Women's Association. This is true, but most people think I adhere to the political principles of the Wafd party. That is not true. What I believe in is the mission of the Muslim Brotherhood. I am linked with Mustafa al-Nahhas by personal friendship; but I have given my oath of loyalty to Hasan al-Banna to die in the path of God, though I am not planning a single step toward entering the circle of that divine honor. But I believe I will take this step someday—in fact, I dream of it and hope for it. On that day, if your personal welfare and economic work conflict with my Islamic work, and I find that my married life interferes with the way of the call and the establishment of the Islamic state, then we will separate.'

"On that day you lowered your eyes to the ground. Then you lifted your head, and your eyes were filled with tears. You said, 'I asked you what material goods you wanted, and you asked for no dowry or wedding gifts. You stipulated that I not keep you from the path of God. I didn't know that you had any ties with Mr. al-Banna. What I knew was that you had a disagreement with him over his request that the Muslim Women's Association be incorporated into the Muslim Brotherhood.'

"I said, 'Praise be to God; we came to an agreement during the persecution of the Brothers in 1948, before al-Banna's martyrdom. I had decided to banish marriage from my life, and to devote myself entirely to the call. I cannot ask you today that you join me in this struggle, but it is my right to stipulate that you not interfere with my struggle in the path of God, and that the day that responsibility places me in the ranks of the strugglers, that you not ask me what I am doing. Let the trust between us be complete, between [me and] a man who wants to marry a woman who gave herself to the struggle in the path of God to establish the Islamic state when she was eighteen years old.

If there is a conflict of interests between marriage and the call to God, then the marriage will come to an end and the call will remain in my whole being.'"

Then I stopped speaking for a moment. I looked at him and said, "Do you remember?"

He said, "Yes."

I said, "Today I ask you to keep your promise. Don't ask with whom I am meeting. I ask God to give you a portion of the reward of my struggle as a grace from Him if He accepts my work. I know that you have the right to give me orders, and it is my duty to obey you. But God is greater in our souls than ourselves, and His call is dearer to us than our own selves. We are in an important phase in the life of the cause."

He said, "Forgive me. Do your work, with God's blessing. May I live to see the day that the Brothers achieve their goal and the Islamic state is established."

The work and activities increased, and the young men crowded into my house night and day. My believing husband would hear the knocks on the door in the middle of the night and get up to open the door. He would escort the visitors to the office, then he would go to the maid's room and wake her, asking her to prepare some food and tea for the visitors. Then he would come to me and wake me gently, saying, "Some of your sons are in the office. They look like they have been traveling or working hard." I would dress and go to them, while he went back to sleep, saying to me, "Wake me if you pray the morning prayer together so I can pray with you, if that's no bother." I would say, "God willing."

And if we prayed the morning prayer together, I would wake him so he could pray with us. Then he would leave, greeting those who were present in a fatherly way, full of warmth, love, and compassion.

In 1962 I met with the two sisters of the martyred *imam*, the legist and great struggler in the path of God, Sayyid Qutb, with the agreement of Brother 'Abd al-Fattah 'Abduh Isma'il and permission from Mr. Hasan al-Hudaybi, the General Guide of the Muslim Brotherhood. The purpose of this meeting was to contact Imam Sayyid Qutb in prison to solicit his opinion on some of our studies and to ask for his guidance.

I asked Hamida Qutb[11] to convey our greetings to Brother Sayyid Qutb and to inform him of the assembled society's desire to study an Islamic course under the guidance of his views. I gave her a list of references that we were studying. This included the *Tafsir* of Ibn Kathir, the *Muhalla* of Ibn Hazm, *al-Umm* by al-Shafi'i, books on the unitarian religion by Ibn 'Abd al-Wahhab, and *In the Shadow of the Qur'an* by Sayyid Qutb. After a short time Hamida returned to me with instructions to study the introduction to *Surat al-an'am,* second edition. She gave me a section of a book, saying, "Sayyid is preparing it for publication. It is called *Ma'alim fi al-tariq* (Signposts on the way)."[12] Sayyid Qutb had written it in prison. His sister said to me, "When you finish reading these pages I will bring you more."

I learned that the General Guide had read portions of this book and had given the martyr Sayyid Qutb permission to publish it. When I asked him about it, he said to me, "With God's blessing. This book has fulfilled my hopes in Sayyid, may God preserve him. I read it and re-read it. Sayyid Qutb is the great hope for the call now, God willing." The General Guide gave me portions of the book and I read them. He had them so he could give permission for them to be

> "If there is a conflict of interests between marriage and the call to God, then the marriage will come to an end and the call will remain in my whole being."

published. I confined myself to a room in the home of the General Guide until I had finished reading *Ma'alim fi al-tariq.*

We recommended our studies in the form of short pamphlets distributed to the young men for them to study. Then they would be extensively studied in group discussions. Our ideas and goals were in agreement, so the plan of study incorporated the instructions and pages brought to us from the martyred *imam,* Sayyid Qutb, may God have mercy on him, while he was in prison. Those were good nights and unforgettable days, holy moments with God. Five or ten young men would gather and read ten Qur'anic verses, reviewing their precepts and ordinances and all their implications for the life of the Muslim servant. After we had fully understood them, we would decide to go on to ten other verses, following the example of the Companions of the Prophet, peace and blessing be upon him.

Those days were sweet and good. A blessing from God surrounded us as we studied and studied, training ourselves and preparing men for the cause, with youth who were convinced of the necessity of preparing to establish the call of truth and justice. We believed in the absolute

---

11. Hamida Qutb and Zaynab al-Ghazali were the only women brought to trial in 1966 along with the Brothers, including Sayyid Qutb. They spent five years together as cellmates. At the end of her book, al-Ghazali describes her grief at being released while her "daughter" remained in jail. (tr)

12. Jane I. Smith notes that this book, critical of the regime, made Qutb so dangerous in the eyes of the government that he was executed, along with six other Brothers, in 1966 (*An Historical and Semantic Study of the Term "Islam" as Seen in a Sequence of Qur'an Commentaries* [Missoula, Mont.: Scholars Press, 1975], p. 205). (tr)

necessity of preparing future generations in the persons of these young men, whom we hope will be the teachers who will guide and prepare the coming generations.

Among the decisions we made, with the instructions of Imam Sayyid Qutb and the permission of Hudaybi, was that the period of training, formation, preparation, and planting belief in the unity of God in hearts would continue. This was accompanied by the conviction that there is no Islam without the implementation of Islamic law and government by the Book of God and the Sunna of His Prophet, so that the precepts of the Qur'an would be supreme in the life of the Muslims. We decided that our training program would last thirteen years, the duration of the call in Mecca, with the understanding that the foundation of the Islamic nation now is the Brothers who adhere to the law and precepts of God.

We insisted on performing all the commands and prohibitions revealed in the Book and Sunna within our Islamic circle, and that obedience to our *imam,* to whom we had given our oath of loyalty, was necessary, since the establishment of the punishments of Islamic law was not imminent—although we believed in them and defended them—until the Islamic state was established. We were also convinced that the world today does not have a foundation that would supply the necessary attributes of the Islamic nation in a complete way, as had been the case in the days of the prophethood and the rightly guided caliphs.[13] Therefore it is incumbent on all Muslims who want to see God's rule and the consolidation of His religion on earth to join in the struggle until all Muslims return to Islam and the true

religion is established—not slogans, but an actual, practical reality.

We also studied the condition of the entire Islamic world, searching for examples of what had existed before in the caliphate of the rightly guided caliphs and of what we wanted in God's society now. We decided, after a broad study of the existing painful reality, that there is no single state corresponding to that ideal. We excepted the Kingdom of Saudi Arabia, with some reservations and observations that the kingdom must rectify and correct. All the studies confirmed that the nation of Islam does not exist, although some states have raised slogans claiming they established God's law.

After this broad study, we decided that after thirteen years of Islamic training for young men, old men, women, and girls, we would conduct a comprehensive survey of the country. If we found that the harvest of those who followed the Islamic call, believing that Islam is both religion and state and convinced of the necessity of establishing Islamic rule, reached 75 percent of all the individuals of the nation, men and women, then we would call for the establishment of the Islamic state and demand that the state establish Islamic law. If we found that the harvest was 25 percent, we would renew the teaching and study for thirteen more years, and more if necessary, until we found that the nation was ripe to accept Islamic government.

It does not matter if generations come and go; what matters is that the preparation be continuous, that we keep working until our term of life ends. Then we will give the banner of "There is no god but God, and Muhammad is the Messenger of God" to the noble sons who come after us.

---

13. The "rightly guided caliphs" are the first four successors to leadership of the Islamic community after Muhammad's death: Abu Bakr, 'Umar ibn al-Khattab, 'Uthman ibn 'Affan, and 'Ali ibn Abi Talib. Al-Ghazali's comments reflect a common perception of the pristine condition of early Islamic society,

which has suffered a steady disintegration in morality and religious integrity ever since. This view ignores the fact that 'Umar and 'Uthman were both murdered, the latter for corruption, and 'Ali was never universally recognized as caliph. He was even suspected of approving of 'Uthman's murder. (tr)

Discussion Questions: **Zaynab al-Ghazali**

1. During her teenage years, al-Ghazali was active in the secular feminist movement in her country. What happened to cause her to renounce that movement and devote her energies to the cause of women within Islam?

2. Al-Ghazali claims that Muslims are "backward." However, Muslims in the Middle East control the world's largest reservoirs of oil, and consequently have immense riches. What was it about Islamic culture that al-Ghazali thought was not advanced, progressive?

3. What was al-Ghazali's answer to the question about the role of women in the Muslim Brotherhood? What does she believe should be a Muslim woman's highest priority?

4. Submission to Allah is central to the practice of Islam. In what ways did al-Ghazali demonstrate submission? In what ways did she submit to the men in her life? In what ways did she refuse to submit? Why did she write to Imam Hasan al-Banna that she would be his "slave" whom he "can sell...at the price he wishes"?

5. Why did al-Ghazali not want the Muslim Women's Association to merge with the Muslim Brotherhood?

6. Did al-Ghazali's submission to Allah overrule her submission to any men in her life? How does she defend her relationship to her last husband, Muhammad Salim Salim, whom she said she would not allow "to come between me and my mission"?

7. What effect did al-Ghazali's father have on the development of her personal identity?

8. What caused al-Ghazali to join the Islamic call again in 1955? Of what did her work consist? What does she mean in writing that "many religious scholars and sheikhs...washed their hands of those who struggled in the cause of Islam"? What does this opinion reveal about her character?